INDUSTRIAL ECONOMICS
Economic Analysis and Public Policy

INDUSTRIAL ECONOMICS

Economic Analysis and Public Policy

Stephen Martin

Michigan State University

Macmillan Publishing Company
New York

Collier Macmillan Publishers
London

Copyright © 1988, Macmillan Publishing Company, a division of Macmillan, Inc.

Printed in the United States of America

Macmillan Publishing Company
866 Third Avenue, New York, New York 10022

Collier Macmillan Canada, Inc.

Library of Congress Cataloging-in-Publication Data

Martin, Stephen.
  Industrial economics.

  Includes index.
  1. Industrial organization (Economic theory)
2. Industry and state. I. Title.
HD2326.M35   1988   338.9   87-24031
ISBN 0-02-376780-4

Printing: 4 5 6 7 8   Year: 0 1 2 3 4 5 6 7

Idées non point neuves, mais renouvelées.
Charles de Gaulle

Preface

This is a book about firm behavior and market performance. The central topic of the book is the exercise of market power—the control of price and exclusion of competitors. Roughly equal attention is given to the economic analysis of market power and to the policy treatment of market power under the antitrust laws of the United States of America.

The book is written to serve as the primary text in undergraduate courses in industrial economics. It may also be useful as a reference book for graduate courses in the same field, and in business-oriented microeconomics classes, particularly those taught in connection with MBA programs.

My intention has been to peg the exposition at a level comparable to that found in intermediate macroeconomics texts. To this end, I have relied on models which can be formulated in simple algebraic terms, and which can be illustrated graphically. End-of-chapter problems hint at some of the details of the models treated in the text. I have found term papers to be an invaluable element of the undergraduate course in industrial economics, and paper topics are suggested at the end of most chapters. A floppy disk, available to instructors, contains data sets reported in the text. Some of these data sets may be useful for term papers. An Instructor's Manual is also available.

It is impossible to understand the fitful progress of the contentious field of industrial economics without an appreciation for the fundamental dichotomy between the analytical and policy positions of the Chicago and structure-conduct-performance schools. Rather than gloss over these differences, I have tried to present the full range of opinions held by industrial economists on major topics. The result is a "history of thought" aspect of the text which, although perhaps unusual, will give the student an appreciation for the background of the disparate policy positions taken by economists in this field.

Chapters 1, 2, and 3 introduce the field of industrial economics, basic microeconomic tools, and the American antitrust laws, respectively. Chapters 4 through 6 elaborate the analysis of dominant firm markets and oligopoly. Chapter 7 reviews empirical tests of the hypotheses developed in Chapters 4 through 6. Chapters 8, 9, and 10 treat the economics of market structure, firm structure, and public policy toward mergers.

Chapters 1 through 10 will form the kernel of most courses. A one-quarter course which focuses on economic analysis will continue with Chapters 11 through 14 and, time permitting, Chapter 18. A one-quarter course which emphasizes policy applications will cover any two of Chapters 15, 16, and 17, and conclude with Chapter 18. Those fortunate enough to operate on a semester basis will be able to cover most of the final eight chapters.

Acknowledgments

My debt to those who have commented on various portions of the manuscript is enormous. I have appreciated the various advice of Walter Adams, Michigan State University; Morris Adelman, Massachusetts Institute of Technology; Bruce Allen, Michigan State University; Mark Bagnoli, University of Michigan; Sanford V. Berg, University of Florida; Kenneth Boyer, Michigan State University; Elizabeth deGhellinck, Universite Catholique de Louvain; Elias Dinopoulos, Michigan State University; Catherine C. Eckel, Virginia Polytechnic Institute & State University; Daniel O. Fletcher, Denison University; Gary M. Fournier, Florida State University; Gary Galles, Pepperdine University; Alexis Jacquemin, Universite Catholique de Louvain; Albert N. Link, University of North Carolina, Greensboro; John Lunn, Louisiana State University; Craig R. MacPhee, University of California, at Los Angeles; Ellen M. Miller, University of North Carolina, Charlotte; David E. Mills, University of Virginia; Edward L. Sattler, Bradley University; Peter M. Schwarz, University of North Carolina, Charlotte; John T. Scott, Dartmouth College; Wade L. Thomas, Ithaca College; Michael Waldman, University of North Carolina, Charlotte; Lawrence J. White, New York University; Glenn A. Woroch, GTE Laboratories, Inc.; Bruce Yandle, Clemson University. Special thanks are due to Frederick H. deB. Harris and Diana L. Strassmann, who classroom-tested the manuscript, and to students in successive classes at Michigan State University, who endured and contributed to the development of the text.

I am further grateful to the Centre de Recherches Interdisciplinaires Droit & Economie Industrielle at the Universite Catholique de Louvain, Louvain-La-Neuve, for providing a unique vantage point for the contemplation of antitrust economics. I am grateful to the College of Business, Michigan State University, for subsidizing the purchase of a Zenith Z-170 portable computer, and to Matthieu Wirtz, Zenith Data Systems, Brussels, for providing me with an AC power source conformable with European power outlets.

Despite these debts, responsibility for errors is entirely my own. Readers are invited to bring sins of omission and of commission to my attention.

The process of writing a textbook can be compared to the process of having a child. It is rather great fun at the beginning, involves a long gestation, a delivery which even at its best is not much to write home about, and finally is followed by many a sleepless night. Like having a child, writing a textbook disrupts the entire family. For putting up with it all, this book is dedicated to my family, and especially to Linda.

S. M.

Contents

INDUSTRIAL ECONOMICS
Economic Analysis and Public Policy

1

Introduction

*All the world over and at all times there have been practical
men, absorbed in irreducible and stubborn facts; all the world
over and at all times there have been men of philosophic
temperament, who have been absorbed in the weaving of
general principles.*

Alfred North Whitehead, Science and the Modern World

The subject matter of *industrial economics* is the behavior of firms in industries. Industrial economists study the policies of firms toward rivals and toward customers (which includes at least prices, advertising, and research and development). Industrial economists study firms in industries that are competitive, and they study firms in industries that are less than competitive. But this is nothing more or less than the subject matter of *microeconomics*—specifically, the theory of the firm. At a fundamental level, there is no difference between industrial economics and what is sometimes called *price theory*.[1]

Beyond this basic level, however, there are differences between microeconomics and industrial economics. Especially at the introductory level, the focus of micro courses is usually on simple market structures—competition and monopoly. Here the arguments are straightforward and results come easily. In contrast, the most interesting and important applications of industrial economics concern *oligopoly:* the type of market in which firms are neither monopolists nor perfect competitors, but something in between. By and large, these are the kinds of firms and markets that we find in the real world.

There is another factor that distinguishes industrial economics from microeconomics. Industrial economics, in contrast to microeconomic theory, is profoundly and fundamentally concerned with policy questions. These questions concern government policy toward business. Government policy toward business includes antitrust policy, regulation, and public ownership of business, but industrial economics has special relevance for antitrust policy. In what sorts of markets, if any, will firms be able to exercise monopoly power—control over price? In what sorts of markets will cartels work, and in what sorts of

---

[1]Stigler, George J. *The Organization of Industry.* Homewood, Illinois: Richard D. Irwin, Inc., 1968, p. 1.

markets will cartels break down? Can firms act in such a way as to make their environment less competitive? If the answer is yes, *can* the government do anything about it? *Should* the government do anything about it? Is there a way for government to set the rules for competition that will improve the way markets work?

Anyone who doubts the importance of public policy toward business should contemplate the impact of the Organization of Petroleum Exporting Countries (OPEC) on economies around the world after October 1973. Price theory lays the foundation for the analysis of public policy, business behavior, and market performance, but it is in industrial economics that these questions occupy center stage.

Two schools of thought have long contested the analysis of industrial economics. One group of economists feels that the private exercise of monopoly power is a persistent feature of many markets. In this view, the most serious impediment to the effective functioning of markets is strategic behavior by some firms, which prevents other firms from competing on the basis of merit. By using such strategic behavior, it is argued, firms can acquire and maintain the power to control the price of their products.

Another group takes a quite different position. They argue that anything one firm can do can be done by any other equally efficient firm, unless some higher power intervenes. In this view, the main source of monopoly power is government interference in the marketplace. Government, by intent or ineptitude, can prevent some firms from competing, to the advantage of other firms.

The debate over these two approaches to industrial analysis has shaped current industrial economics and has had a fundamental influence on the development of public policy toward business.[2] An understanding of the differences between these two approaches to the analysis of market power is essential if one is to follow the current debate over public policy toward business.

Structure-Conduct-Performance

Economists' concern with the private exercise of market power goes back at least to Adam Smith, who wrote:[3]

> People of the same trade seldom meet together, even for merriment and diversion, but the conversation ends in a conspiracy against the public, or in some contrivance to raise prices.

[2]This is perhaps more so for the United States than for other countries, but the difference is only one of degree.

[3]Smith, Adam. *An Inquiry Into the Nature and Causes of the Wealth of Nations.* Edwin Cannan, editor. New York: The Modern Library, 1937, p. 128.

Structure ———————▶ Conduct ———————▶ Performance

Figure 1-1 The linear structure-conduct-performance framework.

Economists who shared this concern developed what has come to be known as the *structure-conduct-performance* framework of industrial analysis. The simplest version of this framework is illustrated in Figure 1-1. In this basic view, market structure determines the behavior of the firms in the market, and the behavior of firms determines the various aspects of market performance. There is a sense in which the study of industrial economics amounts to fleshing out the relationships outlined in Figure 1-1.[4]

Structure

You will perhaps recall that the economist's model of perfect competition assumes many small buyers and sellers, dealing in a standardized product, under conditions of free and easy entry and complete and perfect knowledge. The major elements of market structure describe ways in which markets depart from the conditions that describe perfect competition.

Number and Size Distribution of Sellers

A classroom competitive market consists of many small buyers and sellers, no one of whom is able to influence the price. From a social point of view, a competitive industry is efficient under conditions and in a sense that will be made precise in Chapter 2. Among other things, a competitive industry will in the long run supply a product at a price equal to its *opportunity cost*—the value of the resources needed to produce it.

In contrast, a monopolized market is supplied by but a single seller, who is able to restrict output and hold the price above the opportunity cost of production. Some consumers who would be willing to pay the cost of producing the product are unable to obtain it. It is this output restriction that is central to economists' belief that monopoly is an inefficient way to organize production.

Concern with the number of sellers reflects the intuitive notion that the fewer the number of sellers in a market, the more likely is the market to perform as a monopoly. Concern with the size distribution of sellers reflects the belief that a market with one very large firm and several small ones is more likely to perform as a monopoly than a market with a few firms of roughly equal size. Like many intuitive notions, these (as we shall see) are sometimes correct and sometimes not.

---

[4]A referee has suggested that this sentence would read better if the word *fleshing* were replaced by the word *flushing*. You should reserve judgment on this until the end of the course.

Number and Size Distribution of Buyers

Interest in the number and size distribution of firms on the buying side of the market has a long tradition in economics, although it generates less publicity than conditions related to market power on the supply side. An important influence here is the theory of *countervailing power*.[5] The gist of this theory is that concentrations of power in one part of a market will evoke balancing concentrations of power in other parts of the market. When a few large buyers bargain with a few large sellers (as when automobile manufacturers purchase steel or rubber tires), it will be more difficult for sellers to hold the price above the cost, all else equal. Thus the number and size distribution of buyers is an element of market structure that affects firm conduct and market performance.

Product Differentiation

In simple models of competition, rival firms sell a standardized product. This is never the case in the real world. Products are always differentiated in some way, if only by the location of the supplying firm. As differentiation increases, the products of different producers become poorer substitutes for one another. As differentiation increases, each producer becomes more and more like a monopolist. This makes competitive industry performance less likely.

But the overall implications of product differentiation are complex. One expects, for example, that an increase in differentiation in the cheese market would increase the power of individual producers to control the price of their brands of cheese. This is not a particularly convincing argument for compelling all cheese manufacturers to produce cheese spread. There is, in other words, a tradeoff between *market power*—the power to control price—and *variety*. Society will usually be willing to put up with some market power in order to get some product variety.

Entry Conditions

The economic analysis of entry conditions focuses on the various factors that influence the decision of a firm to enter a market. How large must a firm be to produce efficiently? How large an investment must a firm make to begin operations? If a firm enters a market and fails, how much of its investment can be recovered by selling off assets and how much will be sunk in the market? What sorts of sales efforts, if any, will be needed for a successful operation? How will established firms react to the prospect of new competition?

On a basic level, entry conditions help explain the number and size distribution of firms that operate in a market. Because entry conditions determine

---

[5]Galbraith, John K. *American Capitalism: The Concept of Countervailing Power*. Boston: Houghton-Mifflin, 1952. For a summary treatment, see Galbraith, John Kenneth. "Countervailing Power," *American Economic Review* Volume 44, Number 2, May 1954, pp. 7–14. For a critical appraisal, see Stigler, George J. "The Economist Plays with Blocs," *American Economic Review* Volume 44, Number 2, May 1954, pp. 7–14.

the nature of potential competition between established firms and firms that can enter a market, entry conditions affect market performance in their own right, as well as through their effect on market structure.

Conduct

Firm conduct is a subject that becomes interesting only when competition is imperfect. Under competition, a firm can sell all it wishes at the market price, but only at the market price. In such circumstances, a firm has no incentive to advertise, to react to what rivals do, or to attempt to discourage entry. Firms in a competitive market with free and easy entry have an incentive to collude, but any such attempt is doomed to failure. Even if all of the many small firms in a competitive industry could coordinate a cartel, new firms would come into the market. This situation is different when competition is imperfect.

Collusion

In the era of OPEC, there is no need to justify the interest of industrial economists in collusion. If nominally independent firms can coordinate their actions, they may be able to restrict group output and raise the price of their product above the marginal cost of production. By so doing, each firm will increase its own profit.

But by raising the price above the marginal cost, a cartel creates a situation in which each member has an incentive to increase its own output, and new firms have an incentive to enter the market. If cartel members cheat and increase their output, the price will fall and the attempt to restrict output will fail. If new firms enter the market, the cartel will have to cut back its own output, or total output will increase and the attempt to control the price will fail. In either case, whether collusion can be maintained will depend, in ways that will be specified in Chapter 6, on the elements of market structure: number and size distribution of firms, product differentiation, entry conditions.

Strategic Behavior

In some kinds of markets, established producers may be able to discourage the entry of new firms. They can do so by holding down the price, so that entry is less attractive. This works to the disadvantage only of less efficient firms and gives society the benefit of lower prices. This sort of rivalry is socially beneficial.

On the other hand, there are a variety of ways in which established firms can raise the costs of actual or potential rivals.[6] This sort of strategic behavior is not socially beneficial, especially when (as is usually the case) it involves a costly investment.

---

[6]Examples may include vertical integration, advertising, R&D, and predatory pricing, all of which will be discussed in the chapters that follow.

Advertising/Research and Development

Advertising and research and development (R&D) are multifaceted phenomena. They contribute to product differentiation and (as noted previously) may allow existing firms to manipulate the entry decision of potential competitors. But advertising also conveys information, and by so doing may make a market more competitive. Indeed, a new firm can advertise to let potential customers know that it has arrived on the scene. Advertising may thus be a tool by which new firms compete.

Similarly, society often benefits from R&D. R&D may result in completely new products (*product innovation*) or in more efficient ways of producing existing products (*process innovation*). New products and new production techniques are essential to technological progress, a desirable element of market performance.

Performance

In a competitive market (and in long-run equilibrium), the quantity demanded equals the quantity supplied at a price equal to the marginal cost of production. Production is efficient: all firms have access to the same technology, and firms unable to use the available technology effectively lose money in the short run and disappear in the long run. The issue of technological progress does not fit comfortably in the model of perfect competition, which assumes complete and perfect knowledge of the available technology. This situation, too, is different when competition is imperfect.

Profitability

Under competition, firms are able to earn only a normal rate of return on their investment. *Monopoly profit*—profit above the normal rate of return—is the reason why firms seek to acquire and maintain market power. The closer is profit to the normal rate of return, the less is output restricted below the competitive level, the closer is price to marginal cost, and the better is market performance.

Efficiency

A widely quoted observation holds that "The best of all monopoly profits is a quiet life."[7] A firm that is insulated from the throes of competition may be a little slower to reorganize production, when that needs to be done, because there are no competitors nipping at its heels. The suspicion that market power will sometimes show up as a waste of resources—higher cost as well as higher price—causes us to single out efficiency as an element of market performance.

---

[7]Hicks, John R. "Annual Survey of Economic Theory: The Theory of Monopoly," *Econometrica* Volume 3, January 1935, p. 8.

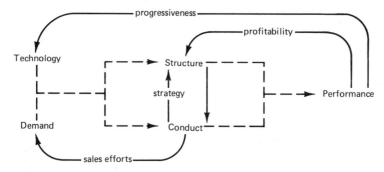

Figure 1-2   The interactive structure-conduct-performance framework.

Progressiveness

What is meant by *efficiency* in the preceding discussion is in a strict sense *static efficiency*—the extent to which production occurs at minimum cost (whether or not output is being restricted to keep the price up). *Progressiveness,* or *dynamic efficiency,* refers to the rate of technological progress. A debate of respectable vintage among economists[8] concerns the tradeoff, if any, between market power and technological progress. Must we grant firms monopolies to encourage innovation? If we must, should we? Slide rule manufacturers and Swiss watchmakers take note.

Interactions

The linear structure-conduct-performance model depicted in Figure 1-1 presumes very simple causal relationships. Structure determines conduct, conduct determines performance, and it's time to go home. But it is evident from our brief discussion of the structure-conduct-performance model that industrial relationships are not so simple. The linear structure-conduct-performance model has been augmented to reflect the interactions among structure, conduct, and performance that occur in real-world markets (Figure 1-2).

The relationships among structure, conduct, and performance are complex and interactive.[9] Structure and conduct are both determined, in part, by underlying demand conditions and technology. Structure affects conduct, as shown in Figure 1-1, but conduct—strategic behavior—also affects structure. Structure and conduct interact to determine performance. Sales efforts—an element of conduct—also feed back and affect demand.

[8]Some of whom are also of respectable vintage. But I digress.

[9]See Phillips, Almarin. "Commentary," in Goldschmid, Harvey J., Mann, H. Michael, and Weston, J. Fred, editors. *Industrial Concentration: The New Learning.* Boston: Little, Brown and Company, 1974, pp. 409–413.

Performance, in turn, feeds back on technology and structure. Progressiveness molds the available technology. Profitability, which determines how attractive it is to enter the market, has a dynamic (intertemporal) effect on market structure.

Methodology

Research in the structure-conduct-performance tradition has always had a strongly empirical flavor. In the early post–World War II period, research was dominated by studies of single industries.[10] Later work employed statistical techniques to determine the average relationship between various structural and conduct elements and performance (especially profitability) over many industries.

This empirical approach was not accidental. It reflected a belief that a more abstract approach, although useful in defining important questions, would not be of much help in generating answers to those questions:[11]

> It would no doubt be extremely convenient if economists knew the shape of individual demand and cost curves and could proceed forthwith, by comparisons of price and marginal cost, to conclusions regarding the existing degree of monopoly power. The extent to which monopoly theorists, however, refrain from an empirical application of their formulae is rather striking. The alternative, if more pedestrian, route follows the direction of ascertainable facts and makes use only of empirically applicable concepts.

Historically, the methodology of the structure-conduct-performance approach has consisted of drawing general propositions from empirical observations. This practice contrasts sharply with the methodological approach of the second major school of industrial economics, which has emphasized theory as the foundation of industrial analysis.

The Chicago School

The structure-conduct-performance school has emphasized the private exercise of market power as a source of poor market performance. Other economists have concluded that the main source of monopoly or anticompetitive

---

[10]See, for example, Wallace, Donald H. *Market Control in the Aluminum Industry*. Cambridge, Mass.: Harvard University Press, 1937; Kaysen, Carl. *United States v. United States Shoe Machinery Corporation: An Economic Analysis of an Antitrust Case*. Cambridge, Mass.: Harvard University Press, 1956; Adelman, Morris A. *A & P: A Study in Price–Cost Behavior and Public Policy*. Cambridge, Mass.: Harvard University Press, 1966.

[11]Mason, Edward S. "Price and Production Policies of Large-Scale Enterprise," *American Economic Review* Volume 29, Number 1, March 1939, p. 62.

behavior is likely to be government interference in the marketplace. Adam Smith shared this concern as well:[12]

> A monopoly granted either to an individual or a trading company has the same effect as a secret in trade or manufactures. The monopolists, by keeping the market constantly understocked . . . sell their commodities much above the natural price. . . .

Indeed, in large measure, *The Wealth of Nations* was written to discredit the mercantilist system of government-sponsored monopoly current in eighteenth-century Great Britain.

The position that the best thing a government can do to bring about desirable market performance is to stand back and let market forces work has been pursued by what has come to be known as the *Chicago school* of industrial economics. *Chicago,* in this context, denotes a school of thought rather than a geographic location. Important recent work in the Chicago tradition of industrial economics has occurred in Los Angeles and Cambridge, Massachusetts,[13] as well as in Chicago.

The approach of the Chicago school to industrial economics has always been fundamentally theoretical, with emphasis on a particular kind of theory. While the structure-conduct-performance school has viewed *imperfect* competition as the most appropriate lens through which to view industrial behavior, the Chicago school has taken the position that the model of *perfect* competition has substantial explanatory power:[14]

> in applied work, adherents of [the Chicago view] have a strong tendency to assume that, in the absence of sufficient evidence to the contrary, one may treat observed prices and quantities as good approximations to their long-run competitive equilibrium values.

What this approach involves is not quite the assumption that monopoly power does not exist. Rather, it reflects the view that private monopoly power—not supported by the government—is temporary:[15]

> Chicago concedes that monopoly is possible but contends that its presence is much more often alleged than confirmed, and receives reports of its appearance

[12]Smith, p. 61.

[13]Near Kendall Square, not Harvard Square. It is also true that the work of Henry Simons, at the University of Chicago, has what seems today a distinctly un-Chicagoish flavor. See Simons, Henry C. *Economic Policy for a Free Society.* Chicago: University of Chicago Press, 1948. In academics, as in war, alliances shift but the battle goes on.

[14]Reder, Melvin W. "Chicago Economics: Permanence and Change," *Journal of Economic Literature* Volume 20, Number 1, March 1982, p. 12.

[15]Ibid., p. 15.

Figure 1-3 The Chicago framework.

with considerable skepticism. When alleged monopolies are genuine, they are usually transitory, with freedom of entry working to eliminate their influence on prices and quantities within a fairly short time period.

The Chicago approach generally denies the possibility of successful strategic behavior by established firms, either toward other established firms or toward potential entrants. A schematic version of the Chicago framework, as shown in Figure 1-3, would have technology and freedom of entry determining market structure, with freedom of entry guaranteeing optimal conduct and performance.

There is no assumption of complete and perfect knowledge,[16] but otherwise the assumptions and results are those of the basic competitive model. It is admitted that relationships might be more complicated in the short run, but such departures from the competitive model are not expected to persist unless the government somehow blockades entry.

With this strongly held belief that departures from competition are at most temporary, it is not surprising that the Chicago school has been critical of research in the structure-conduct-performance framework:[17]

> Casual observation of business behavior, colorful characterizations (. . .), eclectic forays into sociology and psychology, descriptive statistics, and verification by plausibility took the place of the careful definitions and parsimonious logical structure of economic theory. The result was that industrial organization regularly advanced propositions that contradicted economic theory.

The Chicago approach is to view business behavior through a very different set of lenses, explaining[18]

---

[16]Thus firms may advertise to inform consumers. But in the Chicago view, firms advertise only to the extent that this is socially beneficial; if they advertise too much, new firms would come into the market, advertise a little less, and undersell them. See Chapter 11.

[17]Posner, Richard A. "The Chicago School of Economic Analysis," *University of Pennsylvania Law Review* Volume 127, Number 4, April 1979, p. 929.

[18]Ibid., p. 931. We will discuss tie-ins in Chapter 15 and resale price maintenance in Chapter 17.

tie-ins, resale price maintenance, and other business behavior described by antitrust cases not by studying the practices but by looking for an explanation for them that squared with basic economic theory.

If there is an explanation for observed behavior that is consistent with basic competitive theory, that explanation is taken to be correct (even if there are other explanations that involve the private exercise of market power). Empirical work is judged by the consistency of its results with basic economic theory:[19]

> Chicago economists tend strongly to appraise their own research and that of others by a standard which requires (inter alia) that the findings of empirical research be consistent with the implications of standard price theory. . . .

There has been little primary empirical Chicago research into the kinds of market structure and firm conduct that create or sustain market power (which undoubtedly reflects the belief that market power is temporary at worst). Empirical research from the Chicago school has been devoted mainly to criticizing research in the structure-conduct-performance tradition.

Synthesis: The "New" Industrial Economics[20]

Industrial economics through much of its development was a dialogue between groups of researchers with very different world views. The structure-conduct-performance school believed that elementary price theory was often inadequate to explain real-world events and that observation should guide the development of models sophisticated enough to explain the real world. The Chicago school believed that contradictions between the predictions of elementary price theory and observations of the real world should be explained by assuming that the observations were in error.[21]

Those of you who reach the end of this book will learn that research in industrial economics has been rather contentious.[22] This history is largely a

---

[19]Reder, p. 13.

[20]See Jacquemin, Alexis. *The New Industrial Organization*. Cambridge, Mass.: MIT Press, 1987, Chapter 1.

[21]In Chapter 2 we will review empirical estimates of welfare losses due to market power, which have generally turned out to be smaller than expected. Rader predicts the reaction of the Chicago school if the estimates had turned out to be large: "the measurement would have been attacked, both substantively and methodologically, and research would have proceeded on the assumption that the measurements were incorrect" (op. cit., pp. 12–13, fn. 28).

[22]This may be responsible for the following observation: "Lawyers were never like economists. If you disagreed with someone, you didn't call him a fool" (Trillin, Calvin. "Harvard Law," *The New Yorker* March 26, 1984, p. 54). But I digress.

result of the fact that research in industrial economics has been a long conversation in which participants talked past each other rather than to each other.

This failure to communicate is less today than was once the case. By and large, the two schools of industrial economics maintain policy positions that are as distinct as ever. But there has been a convergence of methodology, creating to some extent a synthesis between the two schools.

Much current research, which clearly has its roots in the structure-conduct-performance framework, has assumed a distinctly theoretical tone. There are two main reasons for this development.

First (as noted previously), empirical research in industrial economics has come to employ statistical techniques that allow the analysis of large collections of data. These techniques require the researcher to write down general versions of equations describing structure-conduct-performance relationships. Specific versions of the general equations are then estimated from real-world data to obtain average relationships for the sample. Once researchers started to formalize the structure–conduct–performance relationship in terms of equations, it was only a matter of time until attention turned from estimation to the theoretical underpinnings of the models that produced the equations in the first place.[23]

Second, strictly theoretical research in the structure-conduct-performance tradition has responded to the theoretical criticisms of the Chicago school. Since the arguments of the Chicago school are often made on a strictly theoretical basis, attention has been given to the ways the conclusions of arguments change as the underlying assumptions are changed.[24]

One can argue that if policy recommendations are based on theoretical models, they should receive little weight if the models omit important aspects of the problem with which they are supposed to deal and if the results of analysis depend on these omissions.[25] This is especially the case if the models are advanced to discredit empirical observations without themselves being tested.

---

[23]For examples, see Cowling, Keith. "On the Theoretical Specification of Industrial Structure–Performance Relationships," *European Economic Review* Volume 8, 1976, pp. 1–14, and Cowling, Keith and Waterson, Michael, "Price–Cost Margins and Market Structure," *Economica* Volume 43, August 1976, pp. 267–274.

[24]For examples, see Caves, Richard E. and Porter, Michael E. "From Entry Barriers to Mobility Barriers," *Quarterly Journal of Economics* Volume 91, 1977, pp. 241–261; Krebs, David M. and Spence, A. Michael. "Modeling the Role of History in Industrial Organization and Competition," in George R. Feiwel editor. *Issues in Contemporary Microeconomics and Welfare*. London: Macmillan, 1985, pp. 340–378. Comanor, William S. "Vertical Price-Fixing, Vertical Market Restrictions, and the New Antitrust Policy," *Harvard Law Review* Volume 98, Number 5, March 1985, pp. 983–1002.

[25]This view touches on a large literature treating the methodology of economic research. For an introduction, see Boland, Lawrence A. "A Critique of Friedman's Critics," *Journal of Economic Literature* Volume 17, Number 2, June 1979, pp. 503–522 and Boland, *The Foundations of Economic Method*. Boston: Allen & Unwin, 1982.

The Chicago school does not directly test the assumption that the competitive model can be used to make predictions for the real world, but maintains it as an a priori belief.[26]

A result of the increasingly theoretical nature of structure-conduct-performance research has been a convergence at least in the methodologies of the two schools of thought that debate industrial economics. There is a partial synthesis of results as well. Economists in the structure-conduct-performance school are less likely than they once were to assume that the search for or exercise of market power explains observed market conduct. But they remain unwilling to assume, as does the Chicago school, that efficiency is the dominant explanation for firm conduct and that government is the primary source of market power.

Outline of the Book

Study of the theoretical foundations of industrial economics is essential to the understanding of modern industrial economics. We will review the basic models used in industrial economics and the empirical work that tests those models. We will trace the implications of this research for public policy toward business.

Chapters 2 and 3 lay the foundation for the work that follows. Most of the material in Chapter 2 is usually covered in introductory and intermediate courses in price theory. We emphasize the portions of price theory that will be used later in the book. Chapter 2 also reviews estimates of welfare losses caused by market power in the United States. Chapter 3 introduces American antitrust laws.

Chapters 4 through 7 are fundamental. They outline theory and evidence on markets that are neither competitive nor monopolized, but somewhere in between. By and large, these are the kinds of markets found in the real world.

Chapter 4 examines the consequences of modifying the classroom model of monopoly to allow for a fringe of actual or potential small competitors that confront a dominant firm. Public policy toward dominant firms is also reviewed.

Chapters 5 and 6 analyze markets in which there are only a few competitors, no one of which enjoys a dominant position (oligopoly). Here we ask what it means for a firm with rivals to have power over price, how one might recognize such market power, and what sorts of structure and conduct sustain market

---

[26]Reder, pp. 12–13: "Hard use of the good [competitive] approximation assumption is a hallmark of Chicago applied research; but the assumption is not tested directly. Instead of investigating the descriptive accuracy of this assumption, or the precise extent of the resource misallocation caused by its failure to hold exactly the Chicago style is to treat it as a maintained hypothesis and apply it, using the resulting research findings as a test of [the Chicago position]."

power. We also cover the treatment of oligopoly under the antitrust laws. Chapter 7 reports on empirical tests of the models developed in Chapters 4, 5, and 6 and discusses the Chicago school's criticisms of those tests.

Chapters 8 and 9 examine the determinants of market and firm structure. When is it efficient to organize production in large firms? When is it efficient to organize production in diversified firms? What are the motives behind mergers? Chapter 10 deals with public policy toward mergers.

Chapters 11 and 12 deal with advertising and R&D, respectively. The advertising of products and the development of new products occur particularly when products are differentiated. They are important aspects of nonprice competition. R&D is also essential to technological progress.

Chapter 13 traces the implications of industrial economics for international trade. How does market structure affect imports and exports? When do firms trade, and when do they engage in foreign direct investment?

Chapter 14 is a digression from the basically microeconomic orientation of the rest of the book. It deals with the implications of market power for the macroeconomic problems of inflation and unemployment.

Chapters 15 through 18 focus on public policy toward private enterprise. They emphasize the controversial areas of antitrust policy, including exclusionary practices, predation, and vertical restraints. Chapter 18 is a summary chapter that ties together the main strands of the policy analysis touched on earlier.

Suggested Reading

Fuchs, Victor R., editor. *Policy Issues and Research Opportunities in Industrial Organization.* New York: National Bureau of Economic Research, 1972.

Grether, E. T. "Industrial Organization: Past History and Future Problems," *American Economic Review* Volume 50, Number 2, May 1970, pp. 83–89.

Kitch, Edmund W., editor. "The Fire of Truth: A Remembrance of Law and Economics at Chicago, 1932–1970," *Journal of Law and Economics* Volume 26, Number 1, April 1983, pp. 163–234.

Martin, David Dale. "Industrial Organization and Reorganization," Chapter 13 in Warren J. Samuels, editor, *The Chicago School of Political Economy.* Association for Evolutionary Economics and Division of Research, Graduate School of Business Administration, Michigan State University, 1976.

Phillips, Almarin and Stevenson, Rodney E. "The Historical Development of Industrial Organization," *History of Political Economy* Volume 6, Number 3, Fall 1974, pp. 324–342.

Posner, Richard A. "The Chicago School of Antitrust Analysis," *University of Pennsylvania Law Review* Volume 127, Number 4, April 1979, pp. 925–948.

Reder, Melvin W. "Chicago Economics: Permanence and Change," *Journal of Economic Literature* Volume 20, Number 1, March 1982, pp. 1–38.

Schmidt, Ingo and Rittaler, Jan B. Das wettbewerbstheoretische und-politische Credo der sog. Chicago School, Diskussionsbeitrage aus dem Institut fur Volkswirtschaftlehre, Universitat Hohenheim, Number 23, 1985.

Sullivan, Lawrence A. "Book Review," *Columbia Law Review* Volume 75, Number 5, June 1975, pp. 1214–1229.

2 The Welfare Consequences of Market Power

Begin at the beginning . . . and go on till you come to the end: then stop.

Alice's Adventures in Wonderland

Much of industrial economics concerns the consequences of market power—the ability of firms to influence the price of the product or products they sell. Here we review the basic economic theory of market power. To establish a reference point, we begin with an outline of the economics of competitive markets. We proceed to a discussion of monopoly. Part of this discussion will be familiar to most of you. We emphasize, however, certain concepts (the degree of market power and consumers' surplus, among others) that are used repeatedly in industrial economics. Some of this material will be new for most of you. Even if it is a review, however, you are likely to find a new emphasis in our discussion.

After covering the basic theory of monopoly, we focus on the welfare consequences of market power. The chapter concludes with a discussion of economists' efforts to measure these welfare consequences empirically.

Competition

Adam Smith's notion of an *invisible hand* as the guiding mechanism of an economy is essential to the economist's idea of a competitive market. The formal model of competition abstracts from many aspects of real-world competition to highlight the essential elements of resource allocation under competition. The pattern of resource allocation under competition is optimal in a way that we will explain subsequently. In this sense, competition is a Shangra-La up to which no real-world market can measure. Perhaps the most interesting parts of industrial economics involve modeling more realistic markets and comparing the results with those of the competitive model. Much antitrust policy involves the development of rules for real-world rivalry that, it is hoped, will move markets toward the competitive ideal. It follows that to address economic and policy questions, we need to understand the basic competitive model.

Formal Assumptions of the Competitive Model

When economists speak of a competitive market, they have in mind a market with four characteristics:

1. There are many small buyers and sellers.

We are usually as vague as our students will let us be[1] about what *small* means. What is important is that no single buyer or seller should be large enough to influence the market price.

2. The product is standardized.

Physically identical goods sold in the same place but at different times are different products from an economic point of view. The same is true of physically identical goods sold in different places at the same time. The assumption that an industry's product is completely standardized is thus unlikely to be satisfied, in the strictest sense, in any real-world market. Often the assumption of standardization is an acceptable approximation. Often it is not. When we study oligopoly in Chapters 5 and 6, we will deal with both cases.

3. There is free and easy entry and exit.

In a competitive market, at least in the long run, producers must be able to start up or shut down operations if they find it in their interest to do so. If a firm wants to set up shop, it must be able to buy the necessary physical assets and hire the necessary workers, and it must be able to do so at the same cost as that of firms already in the market.

Similarly, the assets (tangible and intangible) needed to operate in a competitive market must not be *sunk*. In other words, if a firm wants to close down, it must be able to dispose of its assets without suffering extraordinary capital losses. The prospect of such capital losses might well make a firm think twice about coming into a market.

4. There is complete and perfect knowledge.

All firms know the available technology. Buyers and sellers know the market price.

---

[1]This is, of course, true in general. But that is (was) a trade secret.

Fixed and Variable Inputs, Fixed and Variable Costs

For short time periods, it is often useful to think of the inputs employed by a firm as being of two types. The firm employs a given amount of *fixed inputs*, determined by its past investment decisions. These cannot be changed in the short run and are used in the fixed available amount regardless of the short-term level of output. In contrast, the firm can increase or decrease the use of *variable inputs* at will, even in the short run. The use of variable inputs will rise and fall with the level of output.

Costs fall into two corresponding categories. *Fixed cost* is the cost of the services of fixed factors. *Variable cost* is the cost of variable factors of production. Fixed cost is constant, no matter how much the firm produces, because the available supply of fixed factors is constant. Variable cost increases as the firm's output increases, because the firm will have to hire more variable factors as its output increases.

For concreteness, we will call the variable factors *labor* and the fixed factors *capital*. Since firms employ many kinds of variable and fixed inputs, these labels are chosen mainly for convenience.

Variable cost, then, is simply the wages of labor. Fixed cost is somewhat more complicated and involves one of the fundamental ideas of economics: *opportunity cost*.

What we need is a measure of the cost of the *services* of capital assets. Imagine a building erected at a cost of $5 million and with a useful life of 50 years. It would clearly make no sense to treat the cost of the building as $5 million in the year the building goes up and as zero every year thereafter. What we need is a year-by-year measure of the cost to the firm of *using* the building.

The correct notion of cost is that of the *rental cost* of capital services. Even if a firm owns its plant and equipment, from an economic point of view the cost to the firm of using them is the amount the firm could earn by renting them to some other firm.[2] This is the opportunity cost to the firm of using its own plant and equipment. If it did not use the plant and equipment itself, the firm could rent them to some other firm and earn the market rental rate. By using the plant and equipment itself, the firm gives up the opportunity to earn this rental income. That decision transforms the foregone rental income into a cost, as far as the firm is concerned.

If the firm does rent its plant and equipment in a competitive rental market, the rent includes a normal profit to the owner of the capital assets. For this reason, economists include an allowance for the normal rate of return on investment as part of the rental cost of capital services.

---

[2]Equivalently, the opportunity cost to a firm of using a wholly owned plant and equipment is what the firm would have had to pay to rent them. Provided the rental markets for plants and equipment are competitive—a strong assumption—these two definitions of rental cost are equivalent.

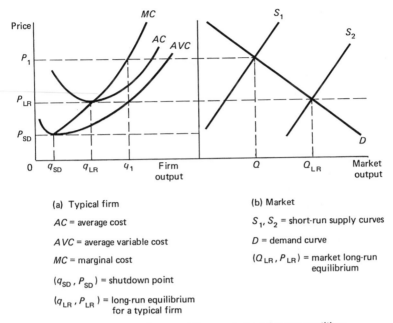

(a) Typical firm

AC = average cost

AVC = average variable cost

MC = marginal cost

(q_{SD}, P_{SD}) = shutdown point

(q_{LR}, P_{LR}) = long-run equilibrium
for a typical firm

(b) Market

S_1, S_2 = short-run supply curves

D = demand curve

(Q_{LR}, P_{LR}) = market long-run
equilibrium

Figure 2-1 The firm and the market under competition.

Accountants treat the normal rate of return as a profit. From an economic point of view, the normal return on an investment is part of the opportunity cost of production—a return that is necessary to get the owners of the capital assets to commit them to production in the market. *Economic profit* is any accounting profit over and above the normal rate of return on an investment.[3]

Cost Curves

Figure 2-1 illustrates the elements of the basic competitive model. Figure 2-1(a) refers to a typical firm; Figure 2-1(b) describes the entire market. We

[3]Suppose a firm could earn an interest rate r^* by investing in a risk-free asset, like a Treasury bond. Then r^* is the basic element of the rental or opportunity cost. If, in addition, the plant and equipment wear out at a rate of δ per period, the rental cost of capital is $r^* + \delta$. Finally, if the price of capital goods increases at a rate π^K per period, the firm enjoys a capital gain on the fraction $(1 - \delta)$ of its capital stock that remains at the end of the period. This capital gain must be subtracted from the rental cost of capital. The cost of the services of the amount of capital that could be purchased for $1 is

$$\lambda = r^* + \delta - (1 - \delta)\pi^K.$$

In intermediate-level courses, it is common to ignore capital gains, leaving $\lambda = r^* + \delta$. In introductory courses, it is common to ignore depreciation, leaving the basic $\lambda = r^*$.

first deal with the firm's cost curves—the average cost curve, the average variable cost curve, and the marginal cost curve—illustrated in Figure 2-1(a).

Using rental cost for the cost of the services of fixed capital, *average cost* is total cost—fixed cost plus variable cost—per unit of output. *Average variable cost* is variable cost per unit of output.

The short-run average cost and average variable cost curves are usually drawn with the parabolic shapes of Figure 2-1(a). These illustrate *the law of diminishing marginal productivity:* as more and more variable inputs are combined with a given amount of fixed inputs, a point is reached after which output per unit of variable input begins to decline.

In the short run, the capital stock is fixed. It does not vary with output or with the number of workers hired. When output is low, the firm will hire only a few workers. There will not be enough workers to handle the available capital stock efficiently; that is, workers will not be terribly productive. Output per worker will be relatively low, so that the variable cost per unit of output will be high.

Output can be increased, in the short run, only by hiring additional workers. As output rises and more employees are added, the work force approaches the size that can most effectively manage the available capital stock. Workers become more productive, and variable cost per unit of output declines. There is therefore an intermediate range of output over which the average variable cost curve falls toward its lowest level.

As output increases even more, additional workers are hired. But a point is reached at which labor starts to "crowd" the available capital stock. Congestion develops, labor productivity begins to decline again, and average variable cost begins to rise. When the output per unit of variable input falls, the variable cost per unit of output rises. The change in output per worker as the size of the work force changes explains the shape of the average variable cost curve in Figure 2-1(a).

Average cost is the sum of average fixed cost and average variable cost. At low output levels, average fixed cost is quite large because the rental cost of capital assets is spread over only a few units of output. Hence, at low output levels, average cost is substantially greater than average variable cost.

On the other hand, when output is large, average fixed cost is relatively small. When output is large, average cost and average variable cost are nearly the same because fixed cost is spread over many units of output and fixed cost per unit is very small. This gives average cost the shape shown in Figure 2-1(a).

Marginal cost is the change in cost per unit change in output. The preceding story, which analyzes the shape of the average variable cost curve, also explains the shape of the marginal cost curve drawn in Figure 2-1(a). At low output levels, additional workers are very productive and the cost of an additional unit of output is relatively small. The marginal cost curve declines when output rises from low levels and the work force approaches the most efficient size for the capital stock. When the point of diminishing marginal productivity is reached, the marginal cost curve begins to rise.[4]

The Firm's Supply Decision—Competition

The logic behind the supply decision of an individual firm in a competitive market is straightforward. The first two characteristics of a competitive market—many small firms producing a standardized product—mean that each firm is a price taker. In a competitive market, a firm can sell as much or as little as it wishes without having any appreciable effect on the market price.

To earn as large a profit as possible, a firm in a competitive market will choose the output that makes marginal cost equal to the market price. To see this, refer to Figure 2-1(a) and suppose that the market price is P_1. If the firm were to produce q_{SD}, marginal cost would be less than price. By increasing its output, the firm would increase its profit because the marginal cost of the additional output would fall short of the marginal revenue that the sale of the additional output would bring in. But by increasing its output, the firm would increase marginal cost, moving marginal cost closer to price. As long as marginal cost is less than the market price, the firm will gain by increasing its output. When the firm reaches the output that makes its marginal cost equal to the market price, it will not profit by further increases in output. In Figure 2-1(a), the output level q_1 makes marginal cost equal to the market price P_1. q_1 is the firm's profit-maximizing output.

A similar argument—which you should work through for yourself to make sure that you understand the logic involved—shows that if the price was P_1 and the firm was producing more than q_1, the firm would maximize its profit by reducing its output until marginal cost was equal to price.

In any event, when the price is P_1, the quantity supplied by the firm to maximize its profit is q_1. Thus (q_1, P_1) is one point on the *firm supply curve,* which shows the output that the firm will bring to the market at different prices. For prices like P_1, the firm supply curve coincides with the firm's marginal cost curve.

Sometimes, however, the firm will maximize its profit (actually, minimize its losses) in the short run by shutting down. If the firm shuts down, its losses equal the rental cost of the fixed factors of production, a cost that must be covered no matter how much output is produced. If the price falls below its

---

[4]The description of the cost curves in Figure 2-1(a) is valid only for the short run. In the long run, at least in principle, all inputs become variable (management may be an exception). The long-run average cost curve of the firm is derived, by a limiting process, as the "lower envelope" of short-run cost curves. The shape of the long-run average cost curve of the firm depends on the underlying technology. The long-run marginal cost curve is derived from the long-run average cost curve. We gloss over the distinction between long-run and short-run cost curves but note that the long-run price is the minimum value of the long-run average cost curve.

average variable cost, the firm would lose even more than its fixed cost if it put output on the market. Not only would the firm lose its fixed cost, but it would have an additional loss on every unit sold: the shortfall of the price from the firm's average variable cost. To avoid such a loss, the profit-maximizing firm will shut down if the market price falls below the minimum average variable cost. This price is labeled P_{SD} in Figure 2-1(a).

Combining the arguments of the preceding two paragraphs, we see that the supply curve of a single firm in a competitive industry is its marginal cost curve above the shutdown point.

Short-Run and Long-Run Equilibrium—Competition

Short-Run Competitive Equilibrium

We now move from Figure 2-1(a) to Figure 2-1(b). The market supply curve is obtained by adding up the supply curves of the individual firms in the market. In Figure 2-1(b), the initial short-run market supply curve is S_1.

The market demand curve shows the quantity that consumers will purchase at different prices. Short-run market equilibrium occurs at the intersection of the market demand and supply curves. In Figure 2-1(b), the initial short-run equilibrium price is P_1, and the short-run equilibrium industry output is Q_1. Taking the price P_1 back to Figure 2-1(a), the typical firm will produce an output q_1 in short-run equilibrium.

Long-Run Competitive Equilibrium

But this situation cannot persist. At the equilibrium E_1 in Figure 2-1, firms are earning an economic profit on every unit sold. This can be seen in Figure 2-1(a), where price P_1 is greater than the average cost for q_1 units. Remember that average cost includes a normal rate of return on the firm's investment as part of the opportunity cost of production. The difference between price and average cost is a pure economic profit on every unit sold.

In the long run, new firms will be able to come into the market. Firms already in the market will be able to set up new plants if they find it profitable to do so. The equilibrium at E_1 offers an opportunity to earn an economic profit, and this will attract new capital to the market. As additional plants are built, the output they produce at different prices is added to the short-run market supply curve. The short-run supply curve shifts to the right, and market equilibrium slides down the demand curve. The short-run equilibrium price falls, and the quantity supplied increases.

This process of entry, increased supply, and reduction in price will continue so long as there is a profit to be made by entering—so long as the price exceeds the firm's average cost. Eventually the price will fall until it equals the minimum average cost. This is P_{LR} in Figure 2-1. The long-run equilibrium for the single-plant firm is q_{LR}. Industry output in long-run equilibrium is Q_{LR}.[5]

In long-run equilibrium, each firm's marginal cost equals the market price, so each firm is maximizing its profit. The market price also equals average cost, so firms are earning only a normal rate of return on investment. Resources invested in the industry are earning only their opportunity cost. Because individual firm profit is maximized, no firm has any incentive to change its behavior. Because economic profit is zero, there is no incentive for new firms to come into the industry (and no incentive for firms in the industry to exit). This is an equilibrium because it will persist unless some external force shifts firm cost curves or the market demand curve.

Economies and Diseconomies of Scale

As we will see (in Chapter 7 when we examine empirical tests of structure–performance relationships and in Chapter 8 when we examine the determinants of market structure), important policy questions turn on whether or not firms must be large to be efficient. The question of size and efficiency hinges on whether or not the cost per unit rises or falls as output increases. This, in turn, depends on whether average cost is greater or less than marginal cost. This can be explained using Figure 2-1(a).

Consider the output q_{SD}. Here the marginal cost curve is below the average cost curve, which means that the cost of the factors needed to produce an additional unit of output is less than the average cost per unit of output. Inputs become more productive as output increases: there are *economies of large-scale* production. As the firm's output increases from q_{SD}, the average cost curve falls, because the marginal units produced cost less than average. As less expensive marginal units are added to output, average cost is pulled down.

Contrast this situation with output at q_1, where the marginal cost curve is above the average cost curve. At q_1, the cost of the inputs needed to produce the marginal unit is greater than the average cost. Producing additional output pulls the average cost curve up because the marginal units of output cost more than average: there are *diseconomies of large-scale* production.

Based on this reasoning, economists say that there are economies of scale if average cost is greater than marginal cost, and diseconomies of scale if average cost is less than marginal cost. The borderline case—between increasing returns to scale and decreasing returns to scale—is called *constant returns to scale*. Here average cost is just equal to marginal cost. In Figure 2-1 this is

[5]By a corresponding argument, if the price in the short-run is less than P_{LR}, some firms will leave the industry, some plants will be shut down, and the short-run industry supply curve will shift back up the demand curve. This process will continue until the market reaches (Q_{LR}, P_{LR}).

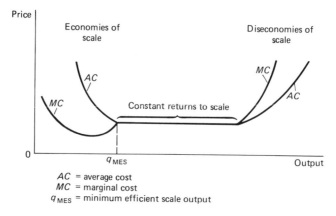

Figure 2-2   Economies and diseconomies of scale.

a single point, q_{LR}, which is termed *minimum efficient scale* output, the output at which the average cost curve reaches its lowest point.[6]

Statistical studies of costs for real-world firms and industries typically[7] find cost curves of the kind shown in Figure 2-2. There is an initial region of economies of scale as output rises from very low levels.

After a point of minimum efficient scale is reached, there begins a range of output over which average cost and marginal cost are the same and constant. At greater output levels, the cost per unit begins to rise. This increase in unit cost may reflect managerial loss of control in very large firms (a topic to which we will return in Chapter 9), or it may simply be a characteristic of the technology. The result is a region of diseconomies of scale at large output levels.

There is some theoretical basis for expecting this result. Multiplant firms can always open a new plant if average cost in existing plants begins to rise.

[6]As a convenient way of summarizing the nature of returns to scale, economists use the *function coefficient* (*FC*) the ratio of average cost (*AC*) to marginal cost (*MC*):

$$FC = \frac{AC}{MC}.$$

If the function coefficient is greater than 1, average cost is greater than marginal cost and there are economies of scale: The average cost curve falls as output increases. If the function coefficient is less than 1, average cost is less than marginal cost and there are diseconomies of scale: the average cost curve rises as output increases. If the function coefficient equals 1, average cost equals marginal cost and returns to scale are constant: the average cost curve neither rises nor falls as output rises.

[7]For a lucid discussion, see Scherer, F. M., Beckenstein, Alan, Kaufer, Erich, and Murphy, R. D. *The Economics of Multi-Plant Operation: An International Comparisons Study.* Cambridge, Mass.: Harvard University Press, 1975, Chapter 2. Johnston, J. *Statistical Cost Analysis,* New York: McGraw-Hill, 1960, summarizes his survey of estimated cost functions as showing a predominantly constant marginal cost or a declining marginal cost in the short run, with *L*-shaped average cost curves (average cost declines from low levels of output, then remains constant, resembling an *L* laid on its side) over the long run. See also Walters, A. A. "Production and Cost Functions: An Econometric Survey," *Econometrica* Volume 31, January–April 1963, pp. 39–51.

Thus cost curves for the firm should exhibit economies of scale when output is so low that the firm operates only one plant and roughly constant returns to scale thereafter. The cost per unit will rise when the firm operates so many plants that corporate management starts to lose track of local operations.[8]

Monopoly

In this section, we describe the monopolist's output decision. This discussion allows us to develop a measure of the degree of market power and to discuss alternative conceptions of the welfare loss imposed on society by monopoly. Finally, we discuss economists' attempts to measure the economic effects of market power.

Monopoly Defined

Two things distinguish a monopoly from a competitive market: There is only one supplier, and entry is blockaded. The first condition ensures that the monopolist faces no actual competition. The second ensures that the monopolist faces no potential competition. Life should always be so simple.

Marginal Revenue

The competitive firm is a price taker. The monopolist is a price maker. The competitive firm takes the market price as a given and adjusts its output until its marginal cost equals price, because the competitive firm is so small in the market that it can sell all it wants at the market price. When the monopolist produces and sells an extra unit of output, it must move down the market demand curve. In so moving, it suffers a price reduction on outputs it previously sold at a higher price. This price reduction as output increases leads us to the concept of *marginal revenue*.

Marginal revenue is the change in total revenue per unit change in the quantity demanded. As shown in the notes to Figure 2-3,

$$MR = P + Q\frac{\Delta P}{\Delta Q} < P. \qquad (2.1)$$

(where the Greek letter Δ denotes a change in the corresponding variable). Marginal revenue is less than price because the sale of an additional unit of output requires a move down the demand curve, and hence a reduction in price and a loss in revenue on units that might have been sold at a higher price.

---

[8]See, for example, Dewey, Donald. *The Theory of Imperfect Competition*. New York: Columbia University Press, or Baumol, William J. "Contestable Markets: An Uprising in the Theory of Industry Structure," *American Economic Review* Volume 72, Number 1, March 1982, pp. 1–15.

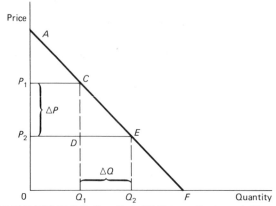

Notes: Let the price fall from P_1 to $P_2 = P_1 + \Delta P$. The quantity demanded increases from Q_1 to $Q_2 = Q_1 + \Delta Q$. The change in price, ΔP, is negative, and the change in quantity, ΔQ, is positive. The change in total revenue, ΔTR, is area $OP_2EQ_2 -$ area OP_1CQ_1, which also equals area $Q_1DEQ_2 -$ area P_2P_1CD (since the revenue represented by the area OP_2DQ_1 is part of total revenue both before and after the price reduction). Then $\Delta TR = P_2\Delta Q + Q_1\Delta P$, and

$$\text{Marginal revenue} = MR = \frac{\Delta TR}{\Delta Q} = P_2 + Q_1\frac{\Delta P}{\Delta Q} < P_2.$$

Since the demand curve slopes downward, $\Delta P/\Delta Q < 0$; in order for the monopolist to increase its sales, it must lower its price.

Figure 2-3 Marginal revenue.

The Firm's Supply Decision—Monopoly

To earn as large a profit as possible, a monopolist will choose the output that makes its marginal cost equal to its marginal revenue. To see this, refer to Figure 2-4.[9]

If the monopolist were producing the output q_1, its marginal revenue would exceed its marginal cost. If the monopolist increased the output from q_1, its revenue would increase more than its cost, meaning that its profit would increase. The monopolist will have an incentive to increase output as long as marginal revenue exceeds marginal cost. When marginal revenue equals marginal cost, the profit will be a maximum. This is output Q_m in Figure 2-4.

The logic leading to the conclusion that a monopolist will maximize its profit by picking an output that makes its marginal revenue equal to its marginal cost is the same as that used to show that a competitive firm will maximize its profit by picking the output that makes its marginal cost equal to the market price.

[9]As shown in Figure 2-4, the marginal revenue curve for a linear demand curve is also linear. It turns out that for a linear demand curve, the marginal revenue curve is not only linear but also has the same price-axis intercept and a slope exactly twice as large (in absolute value) as the slope of the demand curve. This means that the marginal revenue curve for a linear demand curve can be easily drawn by connecting the point where the demand curve cuts the price axis and the midpoint of the base of the demand curve. You are given the opportunity to prove these relationships in Problem 2-1.

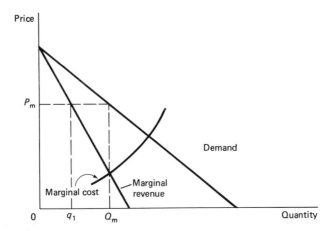

Figure 2-4 Demand, marginal revenue, and monopoly output.

The difference in the result occurs because a competitive firm can sell all it wishes at the market price, while a monopolist must lower the price to increase sales.[10]

Having determined the profit-maximizing output, the monopoly price is found by going up to the demand curve. In Figure 2-4, the price at which Q_m units of output will be the quantity demanded is P_m.

The Degree of Market Power

Adam Smith wrote: "The price of monopoly is upon every occasion the highest which can be got."[11] That sounds pretty bad, but it leaves unanswered the question of just how high the monopoly price will be.

We make precise the answer to this question[12] by making use of the fact that a monopolist will select the output level that makes its marginal cost equal to its marginal revenue. Recall from equation (2-1) that marginal revenue is the price at which the monopolist can sell the marginal unit of output, reduced by the loss of revenue on output that could have been sold at a higher price:

$$ MR = P + Q\frac{\Delta P}{\Delta Q} = P\left(1 + \frac{Q}{P}\frac{\Delta P}{\Delta Q}\right) = P\left(1 - \frac{1}{\epsilon_{QP}}\right). \qquad (2.2) $$

[10]It is not being claimed that firms will analyze their own output decisions in terms of the relationship between marginal revenue and marginal cost; these are analytical devices that economists use to analyze firms' decisions. We return to this topic in Chapter 14, where we discuss markup pricing and target rate-of-return pricing.

[11]*The Wealth of Nations.* New York: The Modern Library, 1937, Book I, Chapter VII, p. 61.

[12]Following Lerner, Abba P. "The Concept of Monopoly and the Measurement of Monopoly Power," *Review of Economic Studies* Volume 1, June 1934, pp. 157–175.

Something new appears in Equation (2-2): ϵ_{QP}, the *price elasticity of demand*. This is the percentage change in the quantity demanded of a good per percentage change in the good's price. Formally, this is defined as follows:

$$\epsilon_{QP} = -\frac{\Delta Q/Q}{\Delta P/P} = -\frac{P}{Q}\frac{\Delta Q}{\Delta P}. \tag{2.3}$$

The negative sign in Equation (2-3) appears mostly as a matter of convenience. Price and quantity demanded move in opposite directions, so $\Delta Q/\Delta P$ will always be negative. Putting the negative sign in Equation (2-3) makes the price elasticity of demand a positive number, which simplifies discussions.

The price elasticity of demand tells us how sensitive the quantity demanded is to price. If the price elasticity of demand is 1, a 1 per cent increase in price will result in a 1 per cent decrease in the quantity demanded.

When the price elasticity of demand is large, the quantity demanded is very sensitive to price. A small percentage reduction in price causes a large increase in the quantity demanded. If the price elasticity of demand were 5, a reduction in price of only $\frac{1}{5}$th of 1 per cent would be needed to bring about a 1 per cent increase in the quantity demanded.

In the same way, when the price elasticity of demand is small, the quantity demanded is insensitive to price. If the price elasticity of demand is $\frac{1}{5}$, it will take a 5 per cent reduction in price to produce a 1 per cent increase in the quantity demanded.

Using this notion of sensitivity of demand to price, we obtain the *Lerner index of the degree of market power* from Equation (2-2). A monopolist will maximize its profit by picking the output that makes its marginal cost equal to its marginal revenue. Using Equation (2-2), this becomes the following:

$$MR = P\left(1 - \frac{1}{\epsilon_{QP}}\right) = MC. \tag{2.4}$$

Recall that the source of the welfare loss under monopoly is the restriction of output, which raises the price above marginal cost. It seems natural to measure the degree of market power by the extent to which the monopolist can hold the price above marginal cost. From Equation (2-4), the proportional excess of price over marginal cost under monopoly is as follows:

$$\frac{P - MC}{P} = \frac{1}{\epsilon_{QP}}. \tag{2.5}$$

Even for a monopolist, there is a limitation on control over price: the extent to which customers leave when the price is increased. If the quantity demanded is very sensitive to price, the price elasticity of demand will be large. The right-hand side of Equation (2-5) will be small, and the profit-maximizing price will be close to marginal cost. In such a market, the profit-maximizing monopolist will restrict output only slightly below the competitive level.

On the other hand, if the price elasticity of demand is small, the monopolist has more leeway to raise the price. When the quantity demanded does not decline very much as the price rises, the profit-maximizing monopolist will be able to raise the price above marginal cost without suffering substantial losses in patronage.

Welfare Consequences of Market Power

Much of public policy toward business is based on the notion that monopoly, in contrast to competition, is an inefficient way to organize production. In this section, we will examine the sense in which this belief is correct.

Consumers' Surplus[13]

Monopoly is undesirable because a monopolist will restrict output and charge more for the product than the opportunity cost of the resources used. To measure the size of the inefficiency due to monopoly, we need to measure the social value of a given quantity of a product. This brings us to the concept of *consumers' surplus*.

In the preceding discussion of the difference between marginal revenue and marginal cost, we used the fact that all consumers in the market pay the same price for a unit of output. In a market situation, consumers are usually indistinguishable from one another. It is through market demand that individual demands influence the market price. But market demand merely summarizes the demands of individual consumers. Different individual consumers are willing to pay different amounts for the product. If consumers wore labels describing their individual demand curves, a monopolist could charge different prices to different consumers. If this price discrimination were possible, consumers could be lined up along the demand curve according to the maximum amount they would be willing to pay, as in Figure 2-5.

In Figure 2-5, the consumer taking the first unit of output would be willing to pay P_1, the consumer taking the second unit of output would be willing to pay P_2, and so on. If a monopolist supplier could force each customer to pay

---

[13]See Willig, Robert D. "Consumer's Surplus without Apology," *American Economic Review* Volume 66, Number 4, September 1976, pp. 589–597.

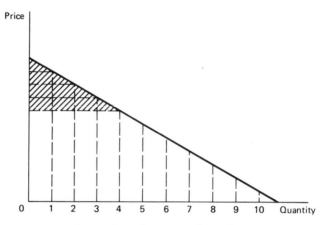

Figure 2-5 Consumers' surplus.

his or her personal maximum, the total revenue would be $P_1 + P_2 + P_3 + P_4$. This is the social value of four units of output—the most that consumers would be willing to pay for four units. Since all consumers in fact pay the same price, if four units of output are sold, the total revenue will be $4P_4$. The excess of social value over purchase price—which consumers would pay if forced, but need not pay because all consumers purchase at one price—is consumers' surplus for 4 units of output. In Figure 2-5, this is roughly the area of the triangle above P_4 and below the demand curve.[14]

The Economic Effects of Market Power—Theory

Allocation and Redistribution

To facilitate the comparison of competition and monopoly, we assume constant returns to scale. Marginal cost and average cost are then the same, as shown in Figure 2-6. The same general results hold when returns to scale are not constant.

The economic effects of market power are to misallocate resources, to redistribute income from consumers to producers, and to reduce aggregate economic welfare. If the industry is competitive (and in long-run equilibrium), the price (P_c) will equal the marginal cost (c). The quantity demanded (and supplied) will be Q_c. A profit-maximizing monopolist will equate marginal revenue and marginal cost, restricting output to $Q_m < Q_c$. For this demand curve, the quantity Q_m will clear the market at price $P_m > P_c$. The monopoly price is higher by $\Delta P = P_m - P_c$.

---

[14]The combined area of the small triangles carved out by the "stair steps" just below the demand curve in Figure 2-5 is small enough so that we can safely ignore it when we measure consumers' surplus.

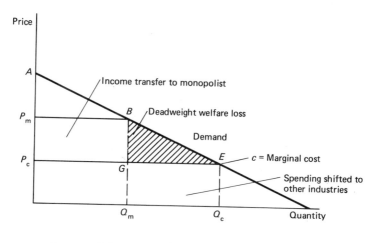

Resource misallocation = $(1/2)\Delta P \Delta Q$ = area GBE

Income transfer = $\Delta P Q_m$ = area $P_c P_m BG$

Spending shifted to other industries = $c\Delta Q$ = area $Q_m GEQ_c$

Figure 2-6 Allocative and redistributive effects of market power.

The cost to society—the opportunity cost—of a unit of output in this industry is c. Under monopoly, output is restricted by $\Delta Q = Q_c - Q_m$ units. Consumers who would be willing to pay at least the cost of production of these units are unwilling to pay the monopoly price. They withdraw from the monopolized market and spend their income (in amount $c\Delta Q$) on other products. As far as the individual consumer is concerned, these other products yield more utility per dollar than the monopolized product. Other products become more attractive precisely because the price of the product is artificially inflated by the monopolist. The quantity demanded of the monopolized product falls, and the quantity demanded of other goods increases. Correspondingly, inputs are allocated away from the monopolized product and toward other industries.

But the utility per dollar of cost—opportunity cost—is greater for the monopolized product than for other products. By restricting its output and raising the price, the monopolist sends a false signal about relative value to the consumer. The consumer reacts optimally, from a private point of view, to this false signal and reduces consumption of the monopolized good. This reduction creates a misallocation of resources among industries. Not enough of the monopolized good is produced, from a social point of view, and too much of other goods is produced. It is this resource misallocation that produces the welfare-reducing and income-redistributing effects of market power.

Under competition, consumers' surplus would be $P_c AE$. Under monopoly, consumers' surplus would be $P_m AB$. The loss of consumers' surplus is $P_c P_m BE$. This loss of consumers' surplus can be divided into two parts.

The area P_cP_mBG—ΔPQ_m—represents a transfer of income from the remaining consumers to the monopolist. The reduction in consumers' surplus makes consumers worse off, but producers are better off to the extent that they earn a monopoly profit. The triangle GBE—$(\frac{1}{2})\Delta P\Delta Q$—represents the remaining loss of consumers' surplus, a loss that is not balanced by the transfer of income to the monopolist.

This net loss of consumers' surplus is the *deadweight* loss resulting from market power. Deadweight loss measures the aggregate welfare loss to producers and consumers due to monopolistic output restriction. In this analysis, the cost of monopoly is the social value of the output the monopolist does *not* produce.[15]

The deadweight loss measure of the social cost of monopoly places producers and consumers on the same plane. Under the deadweight loss standard, the income transfer from consumers to producers is not considered a social welfare loss, because it is offset by the monopoly profits that go to the owners of the firm exercising market power.

Using deadweight loss as the welfare cost of monopoly depends on the political judgment that the transfer of income from consumers to the monopolist is socially acceptable. This is the kind of value judgment that economists have traditionally refrained from making on the ground that it lies beyond their professional competence:[16]

> any program or project that is subjected to applied welfare-economic analysis is likely to have characteristics upon which the economist as such is not professionally qualified to pronounce, and about which one economist is not professionally qualified to check the opinion of another. These caveats—which surely include the income-distributional and national defense aspects of any project or program, and probably its natural-beauty aspects as well—may be exceedingly important, perhaps even the dominant factors governing any policy decision, but they are not a part of that package of expertise that distinguishes the professional economist from the rest of humanity.

In other words, society may well make the judgment—through its policymakers—that the transfer of income from consumers to producers is socially acceptable. Or society may decide that it is not socially acceptable. That judgment cannot be made, on a scientific basis, by economists (or anyone else). As we will see in Chapter 3, whether or not Congress intended the antitrust

---

[15]The phrase is from Posner, Richard A. *Antitrust Law: An Economic Perspective* Chicago: The University of Chicago Press, 1976, p. 11.

[16]Harberger, Arnold C. "Three Basic Postulates for Applied Welfare Economics: An Interpretive Essay," *Journal of Economic Literature,* Volume 9, Number 3, September 1971, p. 785.

laws to treat both deadweight loss and income transfer as costs of market power remains a subject of lively controversy.[17]

Cost of Monopolization

In any event, deadweight loss ignores the cost of strategic efforts to obtain a position of market power.[18] The monopoly profit (ΔPQ_m) is, after all, a prize worth having. A firm that spends anything less than this monopoly profit (per period) to acquire or maintain a position of market power will still be ahead of the game; it will still earn more than a normal rate of return on its investment.

As we shall see in Chapter 4, a firm may pursue a variety of strategies to gain market power. The costs of such strategies reduce social welfare; they are a cost of monopoly not captured in the deadweight loss measure.

How large will *monopolization costs* be? At a maximum,[19] competition among potential monopolists will persist until monopolization costs consume *all* monopoly profits. In this extreme case, the costs of monopoly rise from deadweight loss alone (($\frac{1}{2}$)$\Delta P\Delta Q$) to deadweight loss plus what appears in Figure 2-6 as monopoly profit (($\frac{1}{2}$)$\Delta P\Delta Q + \Delta PQ_m$).[20] Uncertainty, risk aversion, and strategic behavior will in practice prevent this full transformation of monopoly profit into social cost, but we can take deadweight loss plus monopoly profit as an upper limit of the welfare cost of monopoly. Deadweight loss alone is a lower limit. The welfare cost of monopoly power lies between deadweight loss and deadweight loss plus monopoly profit (measured with reference to the level of cost excluding monopolization expenditures).

[17]Economists have often opted for deadweight loss as a measure of the welfare cost of market power on grounds of neutrality: if the decision to treat producers and consumers differently is to be made, in this view, it should not be made by economists. This is the position of Harberger, op. cit. See also Bork, Robert H. *The Antitrust Paradox: A Policy at War with Itself*. New York: Basic Books, 1978, p. 111.

[18]Tullock, Gordon. "The Welfare Costs of Tariffs, Monopolies, and Theft," *Western Economic Journal* Volume 5, June 1967, pp. 224–232; Posner, Richard A. "The Social Costs of Monopoly and Regulation," *Journal of Political Economy* Volume 83, Number 4, August 1975, pp. 807–827 and *Antitrust Law: An Economic Perspective*. Chicago: The University of Chicago Press, 1976, Chapter 2.

[19]For monopolization costs to arise, there must be barriers to entry, which permit incumbent firms to compete for market power without attracting new firms: see Posner, Richard A. *Antitrust Law: An Economic Perspective*. Chicago: The University of Chicago Press, 1976, p. 11; Williamson, Oliver E. "Economies as an Antitrust Defense Revisited," *University of Pennsylvania Law Review* Volume 125, Number 4, April 1977, pp. 714–715. There must also be an absence of transaction costs; see Williamson, op. cit., pp. 714–723. Other necessary assumptions are given by Posner, Richard A. "The Social Costs of Monopoly and Regulation," *Journal of Political Economy* Volume 83, Number 4, August 1975, p. 809: Firms compete to acquire a position of market power under conditions of constant cost, and the strategies employed have no social benefits; it is clear that this last condition will sometimes not occur (advertising, R&D).

[20]Another implication—to be pursued shortly—is that estimates of average cost for firms with market power will be inflated above the competitive level.

The Economic Effects of Market Power—Measurement

A Lower Bound

The first attempt to measure the welfare cost of market power was made by Harberger.[21] He estimated the deadweight loss due to market power for 73 U.S. manufacturing industries,[22] using data averaged over the period 1924–1928. Harberger confronted the perennial problem of empirical researchers in economics: the real world is rarely kind enough to furnish data as they appear in economists' models. The models generally must be transformed to accommodate available data.

It is easy enough to measure deadweight loss if one knows the price and output under both competition and monopoly (P_c, Q_c, P_m, Q_m). However, one is never so lucky. What is observed is sales revenue—$P_m Q_m$—and a measure of accounting profit. As we pointed out in our discussion of the rental cost of capital services, accounting measures of profit do not allow for the opportunity cost of investment—the normal rate of return on capital. To use the accounting measure of profit as a basis for an estimate of economic profit, $(P_m - c)Q_m$, it must be adjusted to allow for a normal rate of return on capital. Supposing this can be done, how does one get from sales revenue and economic profit data to a measure of deadweight loss? As you probably suspect, by a combination of algebraic sleight-of-hand and assumption of the kind that so endears economics to undergraduates.[23]

Since we compare the price under market power with the price under competition, $\Delta P = P_m - P_c = P_m - c$. Then

$$
\begin{aligned}
\mathrm{DWL} &= \tfrac{1}{2}\Delta P \Delta Q = \tfrac{1}{2}(\Delta P)^2\left(\frac{\Delta Q}{\Delta P}\right) \\[2mm]
&= \tfrac{1}{2}\left[\frac{P_m - c}{P_m}\right]^2 \frac{P_m}{Q_m}\frac{\Delta Q}{\Delta P} P_m Q_m \\[2mm]
&= \tfrac{1}{2}\left[\frac{P_m Q_m - cQ_m}{P_m Q_m}\right]^2 P_m Q_m \epsilon_{QP} \\[2mm]
&= \tfrac{1}{2}r^2 P_m Q_m \, \epsilon_{QP}.
\end{aligned}
\tag{2.6}
$$

---

[21]Harberger, Arnold C. "Monopoly and Resource Allocation," *American Economic Review* Volume 44, Number 2, May 1954, pp. 77–87.

[22]We defer discussion of the Bureau of the Census' scheme for classifying industries until Chapter 4.

[23]And lawyers.

The final expression for deadweight loss in Equation (2-6) depends on three things, two of which can be measured. The first,

$$\frac{P_m - c}{P_m} = \frac{P_m Q_m - c Q_m}{P_m Q_m} \tag{2.7}$$

is just the rate of return on sales. It can be computed by dividing accounting profit—adjusted for the normal rate of return on capital—by revenue (this is the final expression on the right). Harberger took the average rate of return on capital as an estimate of the normal rate of return, subtracted it from accounting profit, and divided the resulting estimate of economic profit by revenue to get a measure of r.

The second term in the final expression for DWL is revenue, $P_m Q_m$, which can be measured directly. The last term, ϵ_{QP}, is the price elasticity of demand. Harberger made the judgment[24] that elasticities were probably low for the industries in his sample and assumed that $\epsilon_{QP} = 1$.

On this basis, Harberger estimated the deadweight loss due to market power for the 73 industries in his sample. Assuming the same proportion of deadweight loss to output in all manufacturing industries, Harberger estimated the deadweight loss due to market power in the manufacturing sector at just under $\frac{1}{10}$th of 1 per cent of U.S. national income.

An Upper Bound

Harberger's seminal work spawned a large literature, which suggests that his estimate of the welfare cost of market power is best regarded as a lower bound. A study by Cowling and Mueller[25] summarizes much of this discussion.[26] We now review the changes they made in Harberger's methodology to obtain an upper-bound estimate of the welfare cost of market power in the United States. These changes involved the way elasticity of demand was estimated, the estimate used for a normal rate of return on capital, the use of company rather than industry data, and an estimate of the costs of monopolization.

---

[24]Op. cit., p. 79.

[25]Cowling, Keith and Mueller, Dennis C. "The Social Costs of Monopoly Power," *Economic Journal* Volume 88, December 1978, pp. 727–748. See also Sawyer, Malcolm C. "Monopoly Welfare Loss in the United Kingdom," *Manchester School of Economic and Social Studies* Volume 48, Number 4, December 1980, pp. 331–354.

[26]Reference should also be made to the general equilibrium approach of Bergson, Abram. "On Monopoly Welfare Losses," *American Economic Review* Volume 63, Number 5, December 1973, pp. 853–870 (plus two comments and a reply in the December 1975 issue of the *American Economic Review*). References to partial equilibrium studies will be found in Cowling and Waterson.

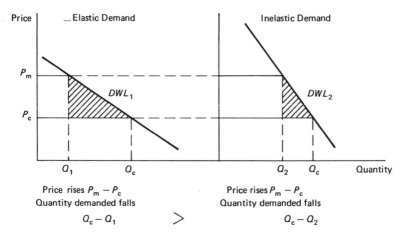

Figure 2-7 Elasticity and estimates of deadweight loss.

Elasticity

Harberger's assumption that the price elasticity of demand is 1 is essential to his conclusion that the deadweight loss due to market power is small. This is evident from the final expression in Equation (2-6): the larger is ϵ_{QP}, the greater will be deadweight loss. This may also be shown graphically.

Figure 2-7 shows two markets with different price elasticities of demand subjected to identical price increases. In the high-elasticity market, the quantity demanded falls substantially as the price rises. Because deadweight welfare loss is the consumers' surplus lost when socially desirable output is not produced, the deadweight loss in the high-elasticity market is relatively large.

In the low-elasticity market, the quantity demanded falls relatively little as the price rises. This, after all, is what is meant when one asserts that demand is inelastic: the quantity demanded is insensitive to changes in price. Just as the reduction in output is less when elasticity is low than when it is high, the deadweight loss is less in the low-elasticity market.

By assuming that firms maximize their profit, we can derive an alternative expression for deadweight loss, an expression that does not depend on an arbitrary assumption about elasticity.

We know from Equation (2-5) that a profit-maximizing monopolist will pick an output that makes the rate of return on sales equal to the inverse of the price elasticity of demand:

$$\frac{P_m - c}{P_m} = \frac{1}{\epsilon_{QP}}. \tag{2.8}$$

By substituting this value for the price–cost margin into Equation (2-6), we get an estimate of deadweight loss that does not involve the price elasticity of demand:

$$
\begin{aligned}
DWL &= \tfrac{1}{2} \left[\frac{P_m - c}{P_m} \right]^2 P_m Q_m \epsilon_{QP} \\[2mm]
&= \tfrac{1}{2} \left[\frac{P_m - c}{P_m} \right] (P_m Q_m) \\[2mm]
&= \tfrac{1}{2} \left[\frac{P_m Q_m - c Q_m}{P_m Q_m} \right] (P_m Q_m) \\[2mm]
&= \tfrac{1}{2} (P_m Q_m - c Q_m).
\end{aligned}
\tag{2.9}
$$

This last expression simply estimates the deadweight loss as one-half of the monopoly profit (see Problem 2-3).

As we will see in Chapters 5 and 6, oligopolists are ordinarily not so successful in coordinating their actions so that they maximize their joint profit. Actual output reduction and deadweight loss can be expected to be less than those implied by Equation (2-8).[27] For this reason, estimates based on Equation (2-9) should be regarded as an upper bound for deadweight loss.

Normal Rate of Return

Studies in the Harberger tradition estimated the normal rate of return on capital by the average rate of return on capital. Such an estimate is likely to be too high, since monopoly profits throughout the economy are included in the average rate of return. An overestimate of the normal rate of return on capital results in an underestimate of the rate of economic profit on sales, and therefore an underestimate of deadweight loss due to monopoly power.

Use of a stock market measure of the normal rate of return avoids the problem caused by including monopoly profits in the average rate of return on capital. Investors will pay more for shares of a firm with market power than they will for an otherwise identical firm without market power. Hence, the

---

[27]Yet another approach would be to explicitly model oligopolistic interactions, as in (5-6) and (5-8). This is discussed, without empirical tests, by Cowling, Keith and Mueller, Dennis C. "The Social Costs of Monopoly Power Revisited," *Economic Journal* Volume 91, September 1981, pp. 721–725. A step in this direction is taken by the simulation study of Gisser, Micha. "Price Leadership and Welfare Losses in U.S. Manufacturing," *American Economic Review* Volume 76, Number 4, September 1986, pp. 756–767, who models oligopoly as price leadership by a dominant core facing a competitive fringe. Gisser's results—simulated deadweight losses close to the Harberger estimates— are guaranteed by his assumptions, as the fringe supply minimizes the reduction in output following monopolistic price increases.

entrepreneurs who first sell shares of stock in a firm with market power will be able to capture the value[28] of the firm's monopoly. But these investors, having paid a price for stock that was inflated to allow for market power, will earn only a normal rate of return on their investment. For the period of the Cowling-Mueller study, the average stock market rate of return was 12 per cent, while the rate of return on capital for the firms in the Cowling-Mueller study was 14 per cent. Cowling and Mueller used 12 per cent as an estimate of the normal rate of return on capital.

Industry vs. Firm Data

Use of industry data results in an underestimate of economic profit in an industry and therefore of the rate of return on sales. This, in turn, means an underestimate of the deadweight welfare loss due to market power.

When industry data are used, the profits of firms exercising market power are offset by the losses of firms operating with inefficiently high costs. Firms making economic losses impose a cost on society: they are in a short-run disequilibrium in which the costs are inefficiently high. Such firms may reorganize production to bring costs down to competitive levels, or they may leave the market. These losses represent a welfare loss to society but not a loss due to market power.

With firm-level data, this offsetting of profits by losses does not take place. Welfare losses can be estimated for firms making economic profits. For firms making economic losses, the deadweight welfare loss due to market power is zero.[29]

Cost of Monopolization

Harberger's estimates of deadweight loss did not allow for the costs of monopolization.[30] Nonetheless, Harberger acknowledged that it might be appropriate to treat advertising expenses as a social cost.[31] Following up on this suggestion, Cowling and Mueller measured the monopoly profit before the cost of monopolization as $\pi + A$, where π is an estimate of economic profit and A is expenditures on advertising. From Equation (2-9), deadweight loss is then estimated as $(\frac{1}{2})(\pi + A)$.

Monopoly profit, after taxes but before the cost of monopolization, is then $\pi + A - T$, where T is taxes. If this profit is transformed entirely into social costs, the total welfare cost of market power (cost of monopolization plus deadweight loss) is [32]

[28]Actually, the present discounted value, a concept we return to in Chapter 3.

[29]Cowling, Keith and Mueller, Dennis C. "The Social Costs of Monopoly Power," p. 731.

[30]See footnote 18 and the accompanying text.

[31]Op. cit., p. 85.

[32]Littlechild, S. C. "Misleading Calculations of the Social Costs of Monopoly Power," *Economic Journal* Volume 91, June 1981, p. 351.

Table 2-1 Alternative Estimates of the Welfare Cost of Market Power

	DWL		DWL + Monopolization	
	Har*	C&M†	Har*	C&M†
General Motors	123.4	1,060.5	770.2	1,780.3
AT&T	0	0	781.1	1,025.0
All firms	448.2	4,527.1	8,440.1	14,997.6
As a percentage of corporate output	0.40	3.96	7.39	13.14

Figures are millions of dollars per year, averaged over 1963–1969. DWL is based on profit only; *DWL* + monopolization includes profit and advertising.

*Estimates following the Harberger methodology assume that $\epsilon_{QP} = 1$.
†Estimates following the Cowling-Mueller methodology assume that the rate of return on sales maximizes profit.

Source: Cowling, Keith and Mueller, Dennis C. "The Social Costs of Monopoly Power," *Economic Journal* Volume 88, December 1978, Table 2.

$$\pi + A - T + \tfrac{1}{2}(\pi + A) = \tfrac{3}{2}(\pi + A) - T. \qquad (2.10)$$

Of course, the transformation of economic profit into monopolization expenses is likely to be incomplete. This is another reason to treat estimates based on Equation (2-10) as an upper bound on the welfare cost of market power.[33]

Revised Estimates

Cowling and Mueller estimated the welfare loss due to market power for 734 U.S. firms for the period 1963–1966 and for 103 U.K. firms for 1968–1969. They presented a variety of estimates, which facilitates comparison of their results with those of Harberger and others. Representative results for the U.S. sample are reported in Table 2-1.

Considering estimates of deadweight loss alone, the Cowling and Mueller estimates, which assume profit maximization (Equation 2-9), are nearly 10 times as large as estimates that assume that the price elasticity of demand is 1 (equation (2-6)). The Harberger-type estimate of deadweight loss, although small (0.4 per cent of the value of corporate product), is roughly four times as large as Harberger's own estimate (0.1 per cent of national income). Cowling and Mueller attribute this to the use of firm rather than industry data.

When advertising expenses are used to approximate the social costs of monopolization, the Cowling-Mueller estimates of the welfare cost are roughly

---

[33]To some extent, advertising conveys information and therefore provides some social benefit. On the other hand, firms may engage in nonadvertising sales efforts to support product differentiation or may invest in lobbying efforts to obtain preferential treatment from the government. These qualifications to the use of $\pi + A$ as a measure of the cost of monopolization work in opposite directions.

twice as great as Harberger-type estimates. The results for AT&T indicate the importance of monopolization expenses.

AT&T's average rate of return was less than the 12 per cent normal rate of return on capital assumed by Cowling and Mueller, so its economic profit (and therefore its estimated deadweight loss) is zero for estimates that ignore the cost of establishing market power (the first two columns in Table 2-1). But AT&T's large advertising expenditures—which Cowling and Mueller report as $750 million per year during their sample period—give it one of the top two welfare losses according to the estimates that treat advertising expense as a cost of monopolization (the final two columns in Table 2-1).

As indicated previously, the Cowling and Mueller estimates represent an upper bound on monopoly welfare losses. Even so, these estimates suggest that the costs of market power are substantially higher than the Harberger estimates indicate. In particular, the resources devoted to the creation and preservation of market power are an important part of the social cost of market power.[34,35]

The Income Transfer Effects of Market Power

The transformation of monopoly profit into social cost is likely to be incomplete. The transfer of income from consumers to the monopolist is not a welfare loss if the transfer of income from consumers to producers is socially acceptable.[36] It is nonetheless an effect of market power. Cumulated over many years, this income transfer may substantially alter the distribution of wealth in society.

Comanor and Smiley[37] estimated the impact of market power over the period 1890–1962 on the distribution of wealth in the United States. They made strong assumptions—in particular, that the rate of monopoly profit is fixed at 3 per cent of Gross National Product for the entire period—but the results are much the same under reasonable alternatives.

In the Comanor-Smiley study, the most wealthy households were those with

---

[34]Op. cit., p. 744.

[35]For a criticism of this entire literature, see Littlechild, op. cit. Littlechild argues that the comparison between monopoly and competition is irrelevant and that monopoly should be compared with a situation in which the monopolized product is not provided at all. In this reasoning, monopoly profit and consumers' surplus under monopoly should be treated as social gains from monopoly, since they measure the benefits that would be lost if the monopolist did not provide the product. This position is not generally accepted by economists. Littlechild also provides a detailed criticism of Cowling and Mueller, although many of his points are acknowledged by these authors in their original paper; see also Cowling and Mueller, "The Social Costs of Monopoly Power Revisited," pp. 721–725.

[36]Presumably, wealth transfers to OPEC would be a loss as far as the U.S. economy is concerned. Recycling of petrodollars might qualify this conclusion.

[37]Comanor, William S. and Smiley, Robert H. "Monopoly and the Distribution of Wealth," *Quarterly Journal of Economics* Volume 89, Number 2, May 1975, pp. 177–194. For a simulation study of the same issues, see Powell, Irene. "The Effect of Reductions in Concentration on Income Redistribution," *Review of Economics and Statistics* Volume 69, Number 1, February 1987, pp. 75–82.

a net worth (in 1962) of at least $500,000. Only 0.27 per cent of all households fell into this category, but they controlled 18.5 per cent of all household wealth. The Comanor-Smiley estimates suggest that without monopoly profits such households would control at most 10 per cent of household wealth, and perhaps as little as 3 per cent.

On the other hand, the poorest 28.25 per cent of households in the Comanor-Smiley sample had a negative net worth. Their debts exceeded the value of their assets. In the absence of income transfers due to market power, the net worth of these poor households would be at least 1.39 per cent, and perhaps as much as 2.00 per cent, of all household wealth.

The primary distributional effect of market power appears to be an increase in the wealth of the very wealthy. Market power appears to increase the inequality of the distribution of wealth. Whether this is to be considered bad from a social point of view is, of course, a political and not an economic decision.

Summary

Competitive markets allocate resources efficiently, from a social point of view, because they provide goods and services to all consumers willing to pay the opportunity cost of production. Under monopoly, some consumers willing to pay the opportunity cost of production are turned away. Resources are misallocated among industries. Income is transferred from consumers to producers. Some of this income may be dissipated as producers compete to acquire or keep positions of market power.

Available estimates of the social cost of monopoly power are imprecise. They suggest that monopoly power costs the U.S. economy something between $\frac{1}{10}$th of 1 per cent and 13 per cent of national income per year. The first estimate is certainly too low and the second estimate is certainly too high; the truth, as is usually the case, is somewhere in between.

Even if the social cost of market power falls toward the lower end of this range, it is high enough to merit policy attention. The policy concerns raised by the exercise of market power are even more serious if market power affects income distribution in a way that is regarded as socially undesirable.

Problems

2-1 (Marginal revenue curve for a linear demand curve) Write the equation of a linear demand curve as

$$P = a - bQ,$$

where a is the intercept of the demand curve and $-b$ is the slope.

a. What is the change in price (ΔP) per unit change in quantity (ΔQ)?

b. Substitute the answer to (a) and the equation of the demand curve into Equation (2-1) to show that the equation of the marginal revenue curve is

$$MR = a - 2bQ.$$

2-2 The cost function for a single plant is

$$C(q) = 5q.$$

The market demand curve is

$$P = 1005 - Q.$$

a. Find the long-run competitive equilibrium price and output. Illustrate graphically. What is consumers' surplus in competitive equilibrium?
b. Find the price and output if the industry is monopolized. Illustrate graphically. How much profit does the monopolist make? What is the welfare loss under monopoly?
c. What is the Lerner index of market power at the monopoly price?

2-3 Suppose a linear demand curve and a constant marginal cost.
a. Show that for a linear demand curve and a constant marginal and average cost, the deadweight loss is always one-half of the monopoly profit.
b. Suppose that oligopolists coordinate the price imperfectly and are able to raise the price to, say, one-half as much above marginal cost as would a monopolist. How large is the deadweight loss in relation to the economic profit taken by the oligopolists?

2-4 In this problem, we explore the notions of fixed and variable costs. This example will be continued in Chapter 4 to examine the notion of contestable markets.

Production requires minimum amounts of labor and capital, after which they are employed in fixed proportions to output:

$$q = \text{minimum } [(K - \overline{K})/a_K, (L - \overline{L})/a_L],$$

where K is capital input, L is labor input, $\overline{K}$ is the minimum amount of capital needed if the firm is to operate at all, $\overline{L}$ is the amount of labor needed if the firm is to operate at all, and a_K and a_L are fixed constants determined by the technology.
a. Assuming the inputs are chosen to minimize the cost of production, write expressions for labor and capital inputs as functions of output q.
b. If w is the cost per unit of labor and λp^k is the rental cost per unit of capital services, what is the cost function for output q? Identify the fixed and variable elements of cost.

Paper Topic

2-1 Consult Pagoulatos, Emilio and Sorensen, Robert. "What Determines the Elasticity of Industry Demand?," *International Journal of Industrial Organization* Volume 4, Number 3, September 1986, pp. 237–250, for estimates of the price elasticity of demand for 46 (basically) four-digit Standard Industry Classification industries. Use the 1972 Census of Manufactures to get comparable industry sales data. Use the 1972 Input-Output Tables of the United States to obtain the industry-average advertising–sales ratio (an alternative source is Ornstein, Stanley I. *Industrial Concentration and Advertising Intensity*. Washington, D.C.: American Enterprise Institute for Public Policy Research, 1977). Use the Federal Trade Commission's 1974 "Annual Line of Business Report" to obtain an industry-average figure for nonadvertising sales efforts per dollar of sales. Using this information, replicate the Cowling-Mueller estimates of the welfare cost of market power for the 46 Pagoulatos and Sorensen industries. Evaluate economists' efforts to measure the welfare effects of market power.

3

Public Policy Toward Private Enterprise— Introduction

The goals of antitrust . . . are wonderful in their variety.

Donald Dewey[1]

Government influences the course of business in many ways. Examples are tax and tariff policy, laws that aim to prevent fraud or misrepresentation, and price controls. But our interest is in government policies that concern market performance.

Such policies fall into three broad categories: public ownership, regulation of private enterprise, and what in the United States is called *antitrust policy*, by which the government sets the rules according to which independent firms compete. As we will see, much of industrial economics has direct policy implications for antitrust policy.

Although antitrust laws now exist in many Western nations, they received their earliest and fullest development in the United States during a period covering the end of the nineteenth century and the early decades of the twentieth century. The U.S. antitrust laws have been amended from time to time since then, sometimes in important ways. But they still reflect the character of the economy and society of the United States at that time. In this chapter, we introduce the antitrust laws of the United States and discuss the concerns that led to their passage.

The Framework of Antitrust Policy

Basic Legislation

The Sherman Act

The Sherman Antitrust Act was passed in 1890. It has two substantive provisions, which are deceptively simple:

[1]"Antitrust and Economic Theory: An Uneasy Friendship," *Yale Law Journal* Volume 87, Number 7, June 1978, p. 1525.

Section 1. Every contract, combination in the form of trust or otherwise, in restraint of trade or commerce among the several States, or with foreign nations, is declared to be illegal. Every person who shall make any contract or engage in any combination or conspiracy hereby declared to be illegal shall be deemed guilty of a felony. . . .

Section 2: Every person who shall monopolize, or attempt to monopolize, or combine or conspire with any other person or persons, to monopolize any part of the trade or commerce among the several States, or with foreign nations, shall be deemed guilty of a felony. . . .

The Clayton Act

Two pieces of legislation, enacted in 1914, largely complete the structure of American antitrust law. The first of these is the Clayton Act.

The Clayton Act prohibits a number of specific business practices. Section 2 of this act[2] prohibits price discrimination:

Section 2(a). It shall be unlawful for any person engaged in commerce, in the course of such commerce, either directly or indirectly, to discriminate in price between different purchasers of commodities of like grade and quality . . . where the effect of such discrimination may be substantially to lessen competition or tend to create a monopoly in any line of commerce, or to injure, destroy, or prevent competition. . . .

Price discrimination arises when different customers are charged different prices for the same product. Note that the Clayton Act prohibits price discrimination only when it is likely to be anticompetitive: "where the effect . . . may be . . . to lessen competition." No guidelines are given for deciding whether or not this condition has been met. In Chapter 15, we will discuss the interpretation courts have given to this qualification.

In language that is omitted here, this section of the Clayton Act allows price differences if they can be shown to reflect differences in cost. The burden of proof is on the firm accused of discrimination to prove that the price difference in question reflects a cost difference.

Section 3 of the Clayton Act prohibits marketing goods "on the condition, agreement, or understanding that the lessee or purchaser . . . shall not use or deal in the goods . . . of a competitor . . . where the effect . . . may be to substantially lessen competition or tend to create a monopoly in any line of commerce." It has been applied mainly to three types of marketing practices.

First, it prohibits exclusive dealing contracts, under which a sale is made on the condition that the customer agrees not to purchase from rival suppliers. Second, it prohibits requirements contracts, under which a sale is made on the condition that the customer agrees to take all of the required product from the

---

[2]As amended by the Robinson-Patman Act of 1936.

same source. Exclusive dealing contracts and requirements contracts have the same effect: They bind a customer to a particular supplier. (However, such contracts may also allow long-term planning, which reduces the costs of one or both parties.) Third, it prohibits tying contracts, under which one good is sold only if the customer agrees to purchase some other good.

Section 7 of the Clayton Act, which was subject to important amendment[3] in 1950, has a different target. It aims to prevent anticompetitive mergers:

> Section 7. No corporation engaged in commerce shall acquire, directly or indirectly, the whole or the part of the stock or other share capital and no corporation subject to the jurisdiction of the Federal Trade Commission shall acquire the whole or any part of the assets of another corporation engaged in commerce, where in any line of commerce in any section of the country, the effect of such acquisition may be substantially to lessen competition, or to tend to create a monopoly.

The Federal Trade Commission Act

The remaining basic piece of U.S. antitrust legislation is the Federal Trade Commission (FTC) Act. Section 1 of this act established the independent Federal Trade Commission, with five members. They are appointed by the President and confirmed by the Senate for a term of 7 years. The important part of the FTC Act, from the point of view of antitrust policy, is the following:

> Section 5(a)(1). Unfair methods of competition in or affecting commerce, and unfair or deceptive acts or practices in or affecting commerce, are declared unlawful.

Enforcement

The Federal Trade Commission Act introduces our next topic: the methods by which the antitrust laws are enforced.

The Department of Justice is charged with the enforcement of the Sherman Act and the Clayton Act. Fines of up to $1 million are allowed for corporations that violate the Sherman Act. Fines of up to $100,000 and jail terms of up to 3 years are allowed for individuals who violate the Sherman Act.[4] Even more important, the Department of Justice may ask federal courts to issue injunctions to constrain business behavior that violates either of these acts.

---

[3] By the Celler-Kefauver Act.

[4] These penalties date from 1974 amendments.

Section 5 of the FTC Act gives the Federal Trade Commission the authority to control ''unfair methods of competition.'' In a landmark antitrust case,[5] the Supreme Court held that violations of the Sherman Act are unfair methods of competition within the meaning of Section 5 of the FTC Act. Anything that violates the Sherman Act also violates Section 5 of the FTC Act.

At the same time, the FTC Act and the Clayton Act are companion pieces of legislation. Section 11 of the Clayton Act gives the FTC authority to enforce the Clayton Act.

This arrangement effectively establishes a two-track system for public enforcement of the antitrust laws. Both the Department of Justice and the Federal Trade Commission are empowered to enforce antitrust legislation.

This two-track system reflects congressional recognition that the enthusiasm with which the Justice Department enforces the antitrust laws has varied with the political philosophy of the administration occupying the White House. The Federal Trade Commission is less susceptible to such changes of regime, because Federal Trade Commissioners are appointed for staggered 7 year terms.

Congress has provided still another avenue for enforcement of the antitrust laws. Section 4 of the Clayton Act provides for private enforcement:

> Section 4. Any person who shall be injured in his business or property by reason of anything forbidden in the antitrust laws may sue therefore in any district court of the United States in the district in which the defendant resides or is found or has an agent, without respect to the amount in controversy, and shall recover threefold the damages by him sustained, and the cost of suit, including a reasonable attorney's fee.

The original version of the Sherman Act contained a similar provision for treble damages under private antitrust litigation. This was superseded by Section 4 of the Clayton Act. Treble damages, therefore, have always been part of the U.S. antitrust laws.

The treble damage provision provides individuals and firms with a powerful incentive to enforce the antitrust laws privately. It is for this reason that many of the antitrust cases we discuss in later chapters are private antitrust suits, not suits begun by either the Justice Department or the Federal Trade Commission. But the issue of private enforcement of the antitrust laws is complex, and is the focus of much current controversy. Does the treble damage provision provide a way for firms to use private antitrust suits to harass large, efficient rivals, with a net effect of worsening market performance? This is an important policy question to which we will return in Chapter 18.

---

[5]*Federal Trade Commission v. Cement Institute*, 333 U.S. 683 (1948).

The Goals of Antitrust Policy

The Times[6]

The latter half of the nineteenth century saw the creation of a national economy in the United States. The railroad, telephone, and telegraph linked together what had been regional or local markets. A reorganization of production and distribution followed the establishment of this industrial infrastructure. Many of the large manufacturers and retailers of the present day trace their lineage to this time.

These large firms were often formed by consolidation through the merger of much smaller, previously independent, firms. Frequently, these consolidations were carried out by holding companies or trusts. More often than not, they dominated the markets in which they operated.

For this reason, small firms provided a natural constituency in support of antitrust legislation. But they were not alone. The rise of railroads and large manufacturing firms was simultaneous with a period of agricultural depression. In a period of low farm prices, the pattern of rail rates, which had to be paid to move farm products to market, seemed discriminatory to many in agriculture. Industrial prices were protected by tariffs that limited foreign competition. They remained high in relation to farm prices. When depression hit manufacturing, large firms combined to form cartels, an option not open to farmers.

In response to mergers and the formation of cartels, several states passed their own antitrust legislation toward the end of the nineteenth century. This action demonstrated a broad base of public support for such regulations. But the state laws were ineffective: trusts operated nationally, and could freely relocate to states that took a more permissive view of their activities. To set the ground rules in a national marketplace, federal legislation was required. The result was the Sherman Act, followed by later legislation as previously described.

Congressional Intent

What purpose(s) did Congress intend the antitrust laws to serve? Only if we answer this question can we understand the courts' interpretations of the antitrust laws, which we will discuss in the following chapters. Only then can be consider the fundamental question of Chapter 18: what purpose *should* the antitrust laws serve?

---

[6]For a discussion, see Stigler, George J. "The Origin of the Sherman Act," *Journal of Legal Studies* Volume 14, Number 1, January 1985, pp. 1–12, and the references cited therein.

The Sherman Act—Economic Goals

Interpreting the debates and reports that preceded the passage of the Sherman Act is rather like reading the Bible: the words seem to be clear, but (otherwise) reasonable people have profoundly different views about what they mean. Given the religious ferocity that sometimes accompanies debates about antitrust policy, this is not an inappropriate analogy.

For example, the author of a seminal analysis of congressional intent for the Sherman Act writes:[7]

> Sherman's views on the policy to be served by antitrust legislation are clear. They appear on the face of the bill he drafted and reported from the Committee on Finance, S.1. Section 1 of that bill declared illegal two classes of "arrangements, contracts, agreements, trusts, or combinations": (1) those "made with a view, or which tend, to *prevent full and free competition,*" and (2) those "designed, or which tend, *to advance the cost to consumer*" of articles of commerce. Sherman employed these two criteria of illegality in every measure he presented to the Senate.

There is no doubt what the words say. But what do they mean? For those who (like the author just quoted) work in the tradition of the Chicago school of industrial economics, they mean that Sherman was concerned with the restriction of output:[8]

> Though an economist of our day would describe the problem of concern to Sherman differently, as a misallocation of resources brought about by a restriction of output rather than one of high prices, there is no doubt that Sherman and he would be talking about the same thing. Indeed, Sherman demonstrated more than once that he understood that higher prices were brought about by a restriction of output.

The argument being made here is as follows:

1. Sherman expressed concern for increased costs to the consumer—a higher price.
2. A higher price is caused by restricting output.[9]
3. We know that the welfare loss due to output restriction is the deadweight loss due to output restriction.

[7]Bork, Robert H. "Legislative Intent and the Policy of the Sherman Act," *Journal of Law and Economics* Volume 9, October 1966, p. 15; footnotes omitted.

[8]Ibid., p. 16.

[9]The argument that a higher price results from restricted output involves the "Which came first?" question. One might just as well say that restricted output is caused by raising the price or that a price increase and output reduction simultaneously result from a move up the demand curve. But I digress.

Therefore, the original goal of the Sherman Act was to minimize the dead-weight loss due to market power, that is, the welfare loss due to misallocation of resources among industries. Equivalently, the goal is to maximize social welfare: monopoly profit plus consumers' surplus.[10]

One can give a similar interpretation to the expressions of concern about monopolistic prices that appear throughout the congressional debates. Such comments indicate concern with output restriction; hence they support the view that the purpose of the Sherman Act was to minimize allocative inefficiency.

Other students of the legislative history of the Sherman Act find this inter-pretation forced. Is it reasonable to give words uttered by lawyers in 1890 the meaning they would convey if used by an economist nearly a century later? The notion of deadweight loss was poorly understood by economists in 1890, and in any event, economists had precious little influence on the passage of the Sherman Act.[11] The words are, after all, subject to another interpretation. The discussion of high prices could just as well reflect concern with the transfer of income from consumers to producers.

Income transfer is a tangible and obvious effect of monopolistic pricing. Resource misallocation is an intangible and subtle effect. It is clear from the congressional debates that Senators knew that monopolistic pricing transferred income from consumers to producers. Speaking in support of his bill, Senator Sherman said:[12]

> This bill does not seek to cripple combinations of capital and labor, the for-mation of partnerships or of corporations, but only to prevent and control combinations made with a view to prevent competition, or for the restraint of trade, or *to increase the profits of the producer at the cost of the consumer* (emphasis added).

---

[10]Bork describes this as a *consumer welfare* goal, which by ordinary usage might be taken to mean the maximization of consumer surplus or, equivalently, the minimization of profit plus deadweight loss. It is by now reasonably well understood in the literature that what Bork means by consumer welfare would be more descriptively referred to as *producer plus consumer welfare;* in the phrase of the March 1987 National Association of Attorneys General Horizontal Merger Guidelines (p. 6, footnote 15): "For the unwary Judge or practitioner stumbling upon this term it is important to understand . . . that 'consumer welfare', when used in this manner, has nothing to do with the welfare of consumers." On pedagogical grounds, it seems best to avoid Bork's misleading terminology in a textbook.

[11]See Lande, Robert H. "Wealth Transfers as the Original and Primary Concern of Antitrust: The Efficiency Interpretation Challenged," *Hastings Law Journal* Volume 34, September 1982, pp. 88–89, and the references cited therein; and Scherer, F. M. "The Posnerian Harvest: Separating Wheat from Chaff," *Yale Law Journal* Volume 86, Number 5, April 1977, pp. 977–978.

[12]21 Congressional Record 2457 (1890), quoted by Bork, op. cit., p. 16, and Lande, op. cit., fn. 111.

Further:[13]

> It is sometimes said of these combinations [the monopolistic trusts] that they reduce prices to the consumer by better methods of production, but all *experience shows that this saving of cost goes to the pockets of the producer.* The price to the consumer depends upon the supply, which can be reduced at pleasure by the combination (emphasis added).

These are clear expressions of concern for the distributional effects of market power.[14] The second statement, in fact, suggests approval of efficiency only insofar as its benefits are passed on to consumers in the form of lower prices.

It is unlikely that income distribution was the sole concern of Congress when it passed the Sherman Act. But it seems clear that the redistribution of income from consumers to producers was an effect of market power that Congress hoped to prevent by passing the act. A modern economist would describe consumer welfare—the maximization of consumers' surplus or, equivalently, the minimization of monopoly profit plus deadweight welfare loss—as a likely goal of Congress in passing the Sherman Act.[15]

Debate over the intentions of the Congress that passed the Sherman Act will no doubt continue. The mainstream view is that the Sherman Act had multiple goals, both economic and noneconomic. Even scholars who defend efficiency as the preferred goal of the antitrust laws concede that efficiency was not the only thing Congress had in mind when it passed the Sherman Act.[16]

The Sherman Act—Noneconomic Goals

Protection of Small Business

There is no doubt that hostility toward big business—at that time an unfamiliar form of enterprise—motivated the passage of the Sherman Act. From this point of departure, critics of the antitrust laws sometimes assert that the antitrust laws have served to protect small business from the competition of

---

[13]21 Congressional Record 2460 (1890), quoted by Bork, op. cit., p. 27, and Lande, op. cit., fn. 84 (quoting Bork) and p. 91.

[14]Note that in his study Bork points out that the prohibition of monopolistic mergers in the Sherman Act (op. cit., p. 11) "derived in large measure from a desire to protect consumers from monopoly extortion."

[15]For similar conclusions, see Scherer, op. cit., p. 979, and Fox, Eleanor M. "The Modernization of Antitrust: A New Equilibrium," *Cornell Law Review* Volume 66, August 1981, fn. 12.

[16]Elzinga, Kenneth G. "The Goals of Antitrust: Other Than Competition and Efficiency, What Else Counts?," *University of Pennsylvania Law Review* Volume 125, Number 6, June 1977, pp. 1191–1213.

rivals.[17] Despite a few statements in debate that indicate concern for the fate of the individual competitor,[18] the consensus is that the protection of small firms was not among the original goals of the Sherman Act.

Recall that Section 2 of the Sherman Act prohibits monopolization, not monopoly. It seems clear that this section reflects the intent of Congress to permit market power acquired by competition on the merits. In a revealing exchange,[19] the Senator from West Virginia asked:[20]

> Suppose a citizen of Kentucky is dealing in shorthorn cattle and by virtue of his superior skill in that product it turns out that he is the only one in the United States to whom an order comes from Mexico for cattle of that stock for a considerable period, so that he is conceded to have a monopoly of that trade with Mexico; is it intended by the committee that the bill shall make that man a culprit?

Members of the committee that offered the Sherman Act for consideration responded[21]

> in the case stated the gentlemen has not any monopoly at all. He has not got the possession of all the horned cattle in the United States. . . . He has not done anything but compete with his adversaries in trade, if he had any, to furnish the commodity for the lowest price. So I assure my friend he need not be disturbed upon that subject.

Further:[22]

> a man who merely by superior skill and intelligence, a breeder of horses or raiser of cattle, or manufacturer or artisan of any kind, got the whole business because nobody could do it as well as he could was not a monopolist, [unless] it involved something like the use . . . [of unfair] competition, like the engrossing, the buying up of all other persons engaged in the same business.

---

[17]Posner, Richard A. *Antitrust Law: An Economic Perspective*. Chicago: The University of Chicago Press, 1976, p. 4, states that the protection of small business is the only goal of antitrust policy, other than efficiency, suggested with any frequency or conviction. This is certainly incorrect.

[18]For example, Representative Mason: "Some say that the trusts have made products cheaper, have reduced prices; but if the price of oil, for instance, were reduced to 1 cent a barrel, it would not right the wrong done to the people of this country by the "trusts" which have destroyed legitimate competition and driven honest men from legitimate business enterprises." 21 Congressional Record 4100 (1890) (quoted in Lande, op. cit., fn. 145).

[19]Which is cited by Bork (op. cit., pp. 29–30) and Lande (op. cit., fn. 105). Lande's quotation is more complete and reveals the ambiguity (inevitably) present in the dialogue.

[20]21 Congressional Record 3151 (1890).

[21]Senator George Edmunds, 21 Congressional Record 3151–3152 (1890).

[22]Senator George Hoar, 21 Congressional Record 3152 (1890).

If protection of small enterprises were a goal of the Sherman Act, the act would condemn all monopoly, however gained.[23] But the Sherman Act does not prohibit monopoly: it prohibits restraint of trade (Section 1) and monopolization (Section 2). As the exchange just quoted suggests, and as we will see in Chapter 4, monopoly gained by competition on the merits is not prohibited by the Sherman Act.

It seems likely that the Sherman Act was passed in the belief that maintaining *opportunities* for all competitors would serve an important purpose. This purpose was not in the first instance economic but rather[24]

> psychological and moral. It sprang from the conviction that competition has a disciplinary value for character, quite aside from its strictly economic uses. . . . For this process to take place it was important that business be carried on fairly . . . and that newcomers be able to enter the game as entrepreneurs on reasonably open terms.

Maintaining opportunities for new enterprises to take their chances, whatever noneconomic purposes it serves, also helps to ensure efficiency and to minimize income transfers from consumers to producers.[25] But there is little support for the notion that Congress wished to protect firms that could not take advantage of their opportunities.

Dispersal of Power

When it passed the Sherman Act, Congress viewed "the diffusion and decentralization of power as an end in itself."[26] Senator Sherman defended his bill partly on this ground:[27]

> If we will not endure a king as a political power we should not endure a king over the production, transportation, and sale of any of the necessities of life. If we would not submit to an emperor we should not submit to an autocrat of trade, with power to prevent competition and fix the price of any commodity.

[23]Bork, op. cit., p. 30.

[24]Hofstadter, Richard. "What Happened to the Antitrust Movement?" in *The Paranoid Style in American Politics and Other Essays.* New York: Alfred A. Knopf, 1965, p. 209.

[25]Letwin, William L. "Congress and the Sherman Antitrust Law: 1887–1890," *University of Chicago Law Review* Volume 23, 1955–1956, p. 226; Lande, op. cit., pp. 103–104.

[26]Scherer, op. cit., p. 980.

[27]21 Congressional Record 2457 (1890) (quoted by Scherer, op. cit.; Lande, op. cit., footnote 136.; Blake, Harlan M. and Jones, William K. "Toward a Three-Dimensional Antitrust Policy," *Columbia Law Review* Volume 65, Number 3, March 1965, p. 422).

In a similar spirit, Senator George Hoar argued:[28]

> The complaint which has come from all parts and all classes of the country of these great monopolies, which are becoming not only in some cases an actual injury to the comfort of life, but are a menace to republican institutions themselves, has induced Congress to take the matter up.

This statement lends credence to the idea that one of the advantages that Congress hoped to achieve through the Sherman Act was a system of self-regulating markets in which success and failure would be determined by competition on the merits. In the words of one analyst:[29]

> The competition process is the preferred governor of markets. If the impersonal forces of competition, rather than public or private power, determine market behavior and outcomes, power is by definition dispersed, opportunities and incentives for firms without market power are increased, and the results are acceptable and fair.

Fairness is, perhaps, beyond the realm of economics. But if society, through the laws it passes, selects fairness as a goal, economics teaches that some economic goals should be sacrificed to obtain fairness:[30]

> It is not clear, however, why a distaste for power (for example) does not merit some weight even at the cost of some sacrifice of efficiency. One of the major teachings of economics is that whenever marginal benefits would be provided by a change, it is worth incurring some marginal costs to secure those benefits.

If increasing fairness yields social utility, it is worthwhile to sacrifice some productive efficiency in order to increase fairness. Of course, if one can increase fairness by reducing the exercise of market power, one may be able to increase fairness without having to sacrifice efficiency. Reducing monopolistic price distortions reduces deadweight welfare loss, reduces income transfers due to market power, and, presumably, increases the perception that resources are allocated fairly. Thus fairness seems consistent with the economic goals usually attributed to the antitrust laws.

---

[28]21 Congressional Record 3146 (1890) (quoted by Bork, op. cit., footnote 105). Bork's conclusion that "The supposed threat of some trusts to 'republican institutions' gives no reason to suppose that Hoar wanted courts to weigh such an imponderable in the decision of specific cases" seems forced.

[29]Fox, op. cit., p. 1154; see also Blake and Jones, op. cit.

[30]Steiner, Peter O. "Book Review," *University of Chicago Law Review* Volume 44, Spring 1977, p. 875, fn. 11.

The Sherman Act—Reprise

Although some argue that the Sherman Act was intended exclusively to promote a specific economic notion of efficiency, it seems clear that the aims of the act were much broader. The Sherman Act was intended to promote not only efficient production and low prices, but also dispersal of political and economic power and a public belief in the fairness of the economic system. Nor were these multiple goals thought to be inconsistent. In short:[31]

> Perhaps we are even justified in saying that the Sherman Act is not to be viewed exclusively as an expression of economic policy. In safeguarding rights of the "common man" in business "equal" to those of the evolving more "ruthless" and impersonal forms of enterprise the Sherman Act embodies what is to be characterized as an eminently "social" purpose. *A moderate limitation of the freedom of contract was expected to yield a maximization of the freedom of enterprise* (emphasis added).

The FTC Act and the Clayton Act

The FTC Act and the Clayton Act were passed in 1914 to supplement the policy embodied in the Sherman Act. The Federal Trade Commission was intended to become a repository of economic expertise within the federal government. The substantive policy element of the FTC Act, from the point of view of antitrust policy,[32] is Section 5, which prohibits "unfair methods of competition."

On its face, this terminology suggests concern with equity. Debate in the Senate and the House of Representatives reveals concern for productive efficiency, maintenance of opportunities to compete, the desire that the benefits of efficiency be passed along to the consumer, and the intent to promote public satisfaction with existing political institutions. Thus[33]

> Fair competition is competition which is successful through superior efficiency. Competition is unfair when it resorts to methods which shut out competitors who, by reason of their efficiency, might otherwise be able to continue in business and prosper. Without the use of unfair methods no corporation can grow beyond the limits imposed upon it by the necessity of being as efficient as any competitor. The mere size of a corporation which maintains its position solely through superior efficiency is ordinarily no menace to the public interest.

---

[31]Thorelli, Hans B. *The Federal Antitrust Policy.* Baltimore, The Johns Hopkins University Press, 1955, p. 227.

[32]The Federal Trade Commission is also responsible for information dissemination and consumer protection.

[33]Senator Hollis, 51 Congressional Record 12,146 (1914); quoted by Lande, op. cit., p. 109, fn. 171.

Further:[34]

> This measure—by regulating efficiency of organizations and institutions so that
> the people can get the benefit of that efficiency, can maintain a prosperity for
> the masses of our people, can assure them that their Government continues for
> their benefit, can assure stability and harmony and in such way conduce to the
> general satisfaction with our institutions.

The coverage of Section 5 of the FTC Act is very broad. In contrast, Sections 2 and 3 of the Clayton Act deal with specific practices. Section 2 prohibits price discrimination. Section 3 prohibits various practices (tying, requirements contracts, exclusive dealing contracts) that have the effect of binding a consumer to a particular supplier. In each case, the prohibitions apply ''where the effect'' of the practice ''may be substantially to lessen competition.''

Congress prohibited these practices because they were thought to interfere with the opportunity for equally efficient rivals to compete.[35] Exclusive dealing contracts, for example, were condemned in part because they denied rivals ''opportunities to build up trade.''[36]

The 1936 Robinson-Patman Act amendment to Section 2 of the Clayton Act, which prohibits price discrimination, was an explicit reaction to the spread of chain stores and the declining share of independents in wholesale and retail trade, especially in food distribution. The Robinson-Patman Act aimed at[37]

> the preservation of equal opportunity to all usefully employed in the service of
> distribution comportably with their ability and equipment to serve the producing
> and consuming public with real efficiency, and the preservation to that public
> of its freedom from threat of monopoly or oppression in obtaining its needs
> and disposing of its products.

As we will see in Chapter 15, economists continue to argue over whether or not the practices condemned as exclusionary by the Clayton Act are in fact exclusionary. But there is little doubt that these practices were condemned because Congress believed them to be exclusionary and wished to condemn behavior perceived as interfering with opportunities to compete on the merits.

There is no reason to think that the Congresses that passed these sections of the antitrust laws wished to protect firms that could not take advantage of their

[34]Representative Frederick C. Stevens, 51 Congressional Record 8852 (1914), quoted by Lande, op. cit., p. 110, footnote 172.

[35]Fox, op. cit., p. 1149.

[36]H.R. Rep No. 627, 63rd Congress, 2d Session (1914); Senate Report No. 698, 63rd Congress, 2d Session 8 (1914); quoted in Blake and Jones, op. cit., p. 441.

[37]Senate Judiciary Committee, quoted by Bork, Robert H. *The Antitrust Paradox.* New York: Basic Books, Inc. 1978, p. 64.

opportunities.[38] The concern with maintenance of opportunities to compete, however, is consistent with the view that the antitrust laws aim to establish a system of self-regulating markets within which the invisible hand of competition rather than (public or private) administrators allocate resources.

The Celler-Kefauver Act[39]

The original Section 7 of the Clayton Act prohibited anticompetitive mergers carried out by the acquisition of stock. It proved to be ineffective in regulating mergers under a Supreme Court interpretation that held that it did not apply to mergers carried out by the transfer of physical assets.[40] By the Celler-Kefauver Act of 1950, Congress amended Section 7 of the Clayton Act to prohibit mergers carried out by stock or asset acquisition, where the effect of the merger "may be substantially to lessen competition."

An important motive for the passage of the amendment was congressional fear of increasing concentration of sales among fewer and fewer firms.[41] This fear was fueled by a 1948 Federal Trade Commission study that depicted a merger movement, over the period 1940–1947, as the cause of a trend to greater levels of market concentration.

It is by now generally accepted that this report was incorrect.[42] But congressional intent should be judged in terms of the problems Congress thought it faced, even if subsequent study has shown that the problems were not as great as feared.[43]

The problems that were of concern to Congress—and it must be remembered that this debate took place in the immediate aftermath of a war against totalitarian states—revolved around the political implications of concentrations of economic power. In the words of Senator Kefauver:[44]

[38]Ibid.

[39]For a comprehensive discussion, see Bok, Derek C. "Section 7 of the Clayton Act and the Merging of Law and Economics," *Harvard Law Review* Volume 74, 1960, pp. 226–355. See also Pitofsky, pp. 1060–1065; Fox, op. cit., pp. 1150–1151; and Lande, op. cit., pp. 130–142.

[40]In other words, the original Section 7 of the Clayton Act might, under some circumstances, prohibit firm A from purchasing the stock in firm B. It would not prevent firm B from selling all of its assets to firm A.

[41]We introduce economists' measures of concentration in Chapter 5. Stay tuned!

[42]Bok, pp. 232–233. Lintner, John and Butters, J. Keith. "Effect of Mergers on Industrial Concentration, 1940–47," *Review of Economics and Statistics* Volume 32, February 1950, pp. 30–48; Blair, John and Houghton, Harrison, "The Lintner-Butters Analysis of the Effect of Mergers on Industrial Concentration, 1940–47," *Review of Economics and Statistics* Volume 33, 1951, pp. 63–64.

[43]Bok, op. cit., p. 234: "even in the foggy world of antitrust, it is no simple thing for a court to overrule a major premise of Congress by appeal to the supervening authority of the *Review of Economics and Statistics*."

[44]96 Congressional Record 16,452 (1950); quoted in Pitofsky, op. cit., p. 1063, and in part by Lande, op. cit., p. 138.

The control of American business is steadily being transferred, I am sorry to say, from local communities to a few large cities in which central managers decide the policies and the fate of the far-flung enterprises they control. Millions of people depend helplessly on their judgment. Through monopolistic mergers the people are losing power to direct their own economic welfare. When they lose the power to direct their economic welfare they also lose the means to direct their political future. I am not an alarmist, but the history of what has taken place in other nations where mergers and concentrations have placed economic control in the hands of a very few people is too clear to pass over easily. A point is eventually reached, and we are rapidly reaching that point in this country, where the public steps in to take over when concentration and monopoly gain too much power. The taking over by the public through its government always follows one or two methods and has one or two political results. It either results in a Fascist state or the nationalization of industries and thereafter a Socialist or Communist state.

By no stretch of the imagination can these concerns be confined to economics alone:[45]

To anyone used to the preoccupation of professors and administrators with the economic consequences of monopoly power, the curious aspect of the debates is the paucity of remarks having to do with the effects of concentration on prices, innovation, distribution, and efficiency. To be sure, there were allusions to the need for preserving competition. But competition appeared to possess a strong scoio-political connotation which centered on the virtues of the small entrepreneur to an extent seldom duplicated in economic literature.

It is clear that Congress intended to attack these political problems by maintaining opportunities for rivals to compete:[46]

The bill is intended to permit intervention in . . . [a process of mergers] when the effect of an acquisition may be a significant reduction in the vigor of competition, even though this effect may not be so far-reaching as to amount to a combination in restraint of trade, create a monopoly, or constitute an attempt to monopolize. Such an effect may arise in various ways: such as elimination in whole or in material part of the competitive activity of an enterprise which has been a substantial factor in competition, increase in the relative size of the enterprise making the acquisition to such a point that its advantage over its competitors threatens to be decisive, undue reduction in the number of competing enterprises, or establishment of relationships between buyers and sellers which deprive rivals of a fair opportunity to compete.

[45]Bok, op. cit., pp. 236–237.

[46]H.R. Report No. 1191, 81st Congress, 1st Session 8 (1949); quoted by Bok, op. cit., p. 237, and Bork, *The Antitrust Paradox*, p. 65.

Interpretation of the Antitrust Laws

The thoughtful reader realizes that the debates previously quoted (and the legislation in which those debates resulted) are delightfully vague. That is no accident. In enacting the antitrust laws, Congress recognized that business behavior was too complex and too flexible to be regulated by detailed legislation. The very general wording of the antitrust laws is deliberate, embodying basic principles so that their interpretation can change with the situation to which they are applied.

The interpretation of the antitrust laws is the province of the federal courts and ultimately of the Supreme Court.

There is a story of three baseball umpires discussing their job. The youngest began by saying, "I call them the way I see them." The second, more experienced, countered, "I call them the way they are." The senior umpire thought a while and said, "They're nothing until I call them."

This story aptly describes the place of the courts, including the Supreme Court, in the development of antitrust law. In a real sense, federal laws mean nothing until the courts, specifically the Supreme Court, interpret them.[47] This is especially the case when the legislation is phrased, as are the antitrust laws, in deliberately general terms.

For this reason, when we discuss the application of the antitrust laws to different kinds of markets, we will do so by reviewing major decisions by which the courts have given content to the general principles contained in the legislation. This practice serves the dual purpose of explaining the development of the antitrust laws and giving real-world examples of the kind of behavior analyzed in models of industrial structure, conduct, and performance.

Conclusion

The antitrust laws were intended to advance multiple goals, both economic and noneconomic. Congress was certainly concerned with encouraging and preserving productive efficiency—least-cost production—so long as its benefits were passed along to consumers in the form of lower prices. Congress was equally concerned with minimizing the transfer of income from consumers to producers. To achieve these goals with as little direct government intervention as possible, Congress wished to preserve opportunities for efficient rivals to compete.

Major noneconomic goals included the desire to disperse power and promote a system of self-regulating markets. These political goals were based on a desire to promote the appearance of fairness of market outcomes and avoid the alter-

---

[47]Notwithstanding the contrary opinion of Attorney General Edwin Meese.

native evils of fascism and socialism, which were thought to result from failure to cultivate public support for a system of market competition.

In short:[48]

> the goals of antitrust were of three kinds. The first were economic; the classical model of competition confirmed the belief that the maximum of economic efficiency would be produced by competition, and at least some members of Congress must have been under the spell of this intellectually elegant model, insofar as they were able to formulate their economic intentions in abstract terms. The second class of goals was political; the antitrust principle was intended to block private accumulations of power and protect democratic government. The third was social and moral; the competitive process was believed to be a kind of disciplinary machinery for the development of character, and the competitiveness of the people—the fundamental stimulus to national morale—was believed to need protection.

Paper Topic

3-1 Analyze the original goals of the Sherman Act. How were these goals modified by later antitrust legislation?

---

[48]Hofstadter, Richard. *The Paranoid Style in American Politics and Other Essays.* op. cit., pp. 199–200.

4

The Dominant Firm

God gives it to me. Beware those who would take it.

Napoleon Bonaparte

Introduction

In Chapter 2, we reviewed the basic models of competition and monopoly. We saw that a monopolist will restrict output and raise price, compared with the price of a competitive industry. The result is a misallocation of resources, causing a deadweight welfare loss and a transfer of income from consumers to the monopolist. But monopoly in the strict sense—one and only one supplier— is extremely rare. There are, however, many industries supplied by a large firm and a fringe of smaller rivals. Many of these *dominant firms* have maintained their leadership positions for generations. Their names are among the most familiar in American (and world) industry. Campbell Soup, General Electric, IBM, and Kodak are examples.

A dominant firm differs from a monopolist in one important respect. The only constraint on the monopolist's behavior is the market demand curve: if the monopolist raises the market price, some customers will leave the market. Like the monopolist, the dominant firm is large enough to recognize that a price increase will drive some customers from the market. But the dominant firm faces a problem that the monopolist does not: the possibility that a price increase will induce some customers to begin to buy from firms in the fringe of small competitors. The dominant firm, in other words, must take into account the reaction of its fringe competitors.

We include among fringe reactions the possibility that new firms will enter the fringe, an eventuality excluded by assumption from models of monopoly. Dominant-firm markets include the case of a monopolist who faces the prospect of entry.

Because dominant firms face fringe competition, we ask questions about dominant-firm markets that we do not ask about monopoly. When we study monopoly, we basically ask how much a monopolist will produce, what it will charge, and how monopoly compares with competition. We explore the im-

61

plications of a position of market power but never inquire too closely about its origin. When we study a dominant-firm market, we ask not only what a dominant firm does with its position, but also how it acquires that position and how it keeps it.

Conceptually, dominant-firm markets provide a bridge between the pure monopoly market described in Chapter 2 and oligopolistic markets—markets with a few roughly equal-sized firms—which are the topic of Chapters 5 and 6. Because dominant-firm markets are as close as we get in the real world to monopoly, they raise important policy questions as well. Is a dominant market position enough to violate the antitrust laws? Should it be? What limits do the antitrust laws place on the strategies a firm might use to develop a dominant position? If a firm has a dominant position, what limits do the antitrust laws place on the tactics it might use to keep that position? These questions were confronted by courts in the earliest landmark antitrust cases, and the answers courts gave to them are fundamental to the development of the antitrust laws.

In this chapter, we begin by examining the behavior of a dominant firm: how will the presence of a competitive fringe alter market performance, compared with monopoly? We then study strategies firms use to acquire and maintain dominant positions. Finally, we consider the treatment of dominant firms under the antitrust laws.

Behavior of the Dominant Firm

Recall the story we told in Chapter 2 about the way a competitive industry adjusts to long-run equilibrium (in the discussion of Figure 2-1). Suppose, we said, a competitive industry is in short-run equilibrium, and firms in the market are making an economic profit. Since there is free and easy entry into a competitive market, profits will attract new suppliers or encourage old suppliers to open new plants. The market supply curve will shift outward as additional capacity is installed. The quantity supplied at any price will increase, and the price will fall as the supply curve moves down the market demand curve. When price equals the minimum value of average cost, firms in the industry will just break even—earning the opportunity cost of the funds invested in the industry, but no economic profit. Since there is no economic profit, no new suppliers will be attracted to the industry, and existing suppliers will have no reason to change capacity. The market will be in long-run competitive equilibrium, with the price equal to the opportunity cost of the resources needed to bring the product to the market.

If this adjustment process took place whenever a dominant firm attempted to restrict its output and raise the market price, the exercise of market power by dominant firms would not be a long-run problem. A dominant firm that used its position to control price would set in motion a process of expansion and entry that would topple it from its dominant position. But this adjustment process is not automatic if there are costs of entry or expansion. What we ask in this section is how the possibility of expansion by existing fringe firms, or entry of new rivals, affects dominant-firm behavior when there are some costs of entry or expansion.

A Static Limit Price Model[1]

The *static limit price model* focuses on the most obvious way a dominant firm can maintain its position: it can keep the price so low that entry by new firms or expansion by existing fringe firms is not profitable. The model is called *static* because the analysis does not deal with time in any formal sense. We will bring time into the discussion after we work through the static model.

The Entrant

The basic factor affecting the entry decision—we will consider others in due course—is profit. If there is a profit—an economic profit, more than the normal rate of return—to be made *after entry,* a potential entrant will come into the market. Otherwise, it will not. Whether or not a there is a profit to be made after entry will depend on the postentry price and on costs, including entry as well as operating costs.

The postentry price will depend on the combined output of the dominant firm and the entrant. Assume for the present that the potential entrant expects the dominant firm to maintain output at its current level if entry occurs (we will presently discuss less unrealistic assumptions). If the potential entrant believes this, it can maximize its profit by acting like the monopolist of Chapter 2 *in the portion of the market left for it* by the dominant firm.

Residual Demand

As shown in Figure 4-1, a *residual demand curve* shows what remains of the market demand curve after the dominant firm—the former monopolist—has disposed of its output. The residual demand curve is obtained from the market demand curve by subtracting the dominant firm's output from the quantity demanded at every price (equivalently, sliding market demand curve horizontally to the left by a distance equal to the dominant firm's output). The residual demand curve shows the quantity demanded *from the entrant* at any price, after the dominant firm has sold its output.

From the residual demand curve comes a residual marginal revenue curve. The residual marginal revenue curve shows the additional revenue received by the entrant if it increases its output (see Figure 2.3). Since the entrant is trying

---

[1]Bain, Joe S. *Barriers to New Competition.* Cambridge, Mass: Harvard University Press, 1956. The model described in this section has the dominant firm act as a Stackelberg quantity leader; this approach is generalized in the models of quantity-setting oligopoly presented in Chapter 5.

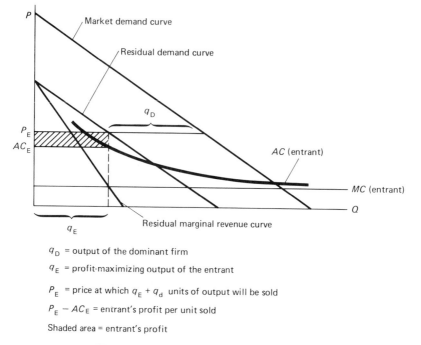

q_D = output of the dominant firm

q_E = profit-maximizing output of the entrant

P_E = price at which $q_E + q_d$ units of output will be sold

$P_E - AC_E$ = entrant's profit per unit sold

Shaded area = entrant's profit

Figure 4-1   The entrant's output decision.

to make as large a profit as possible, the entrant will decide what to produce—
if it produces at all—by picking an output that makes its marginal cost equal
to its marginal revenue—marginal revenue for movements along the residual
demand curve. For the marginal cost and residual marginal revenue curves
shown in Figure 4-1, the entrant will produce an output q_E, if it produces at
all. The total output supplied to the market is $q_D + q_E$. The price at which
this output will be willingly demanded is P_E.

Whether or not the potential entrant will chose to come into the market
depends on whether it can make a profit by selling q_E units at price P_E. Whether
the entrant can make a profit depends, in turn, on its average cost, not its
marginal cost.

Suppose entry costs give the entrant a downward-sloping average cost curve,
as shown in Figure 4-1.[2] If the entrant produces q_E units, its average cost will
be AC_E per unit. In Figure 4-1, the entrant's average cost at this profit-maximizing output is less than the market price, so the entrant will make a profit
on every unit sold if it actually comes into the market. The entrant's total profit,

---

[2]This will be the case if there are economies of scale; in particular, the average cost curve will
decline for the cost function of footnote 6: $C(q_e) = c_e q + F_e$.

which is profit per unit times the number of units sold, is shown as the shaded area in Figure 4-1.

Sunk Cost[3]

A firm's investment in capital assets is said to be *sunk* if its assets would have to be sold at a substantial loss, compared to the purchase price, if it decided to leave the market. Investments in tangible assets are likely be sunk if the assets are specific to a single industry.[4] Investments in intangible assets— like an advertising campaign to create recognition of a brand name, or an R & D program aimed at bringing a new kind of product to market—are especially likely to be sunk. It is hard to sell goodwill for anything like the cost of creating it, especially if business is so bad that the seller is leaving the industry.

Entry always involves some sunk costs. The expenses associated with making the entry decision—the costs of gathering and evaluating information about the target market—are sunk. Such spending creates an asset—information— but the firm will not be able to recover what it has invested in information if it decides to leave the market.

The extent to which costs are sunk determines the cost of capital—the rental cost of capital services—to an entrant. When a corporation borrows funds (for example, by the sale of bonds), the loan is secured by the promise that if the debt cannot be paid, lenders will be able to sell off the assets of the firm to recover a portion of their capital. The more a firm's assets are sunk in its market, the less valuable that promise is; when assets are sunk, their resale value is only a fraction of their purchase price. Therefore, the greater the sunk costs, the higher the rate of interest charged by lenders. Since the rental cost of capital services depends on the opportunity cost of invested funds, the greater

---

[3]The notion of sunk costs should be kept distinct from that of fixed costs. Whether or not costs are sunk depends on the resale market for capital assets. Whether or not costs are fixed depends on the extent to which they vary with output.

Suppose capital assets can be purchased at price p^k, but must be sold at price αp^k, where $0 \leq \alpha \leq 1$. Then if $\alpha = 0$, capital costs are completely sunk; if $\alpha = 1$, capital costs are not sunk at all. Now consider the production function of Problem 2-4:

$$q = \text{minimum } [(K - \overline{K})/a_K, (L - \overline{L})/a_L].$$

If $\overline{K} > 0$ or $\overline{L} > 0$ and $\alpha = 1$, there are fixed costs (independent of output) but no sunk costs (capital assets can be resold for their purchase price). If $\overline{K} = 0$ and $\overline{L} = 0$ but $\alpha = 0$, there are no fixed costs (all inputs vary with the output level) but capital costs are completely sunk (once purchased, capital assets cannot be resold).

[4]An entrant into the pharmaceutical industry, for example, will have to invest in special refrigerated storage facilities for some drugs. Such facilities could be used only by other firms in the same industry. If the entrant wanted to leave the industry because operations were not as profitable as expected, it would have to take a capital loss on its investment in the storage facilities. Holding resale prices constant, sunk costs of entry will be larger, the larger the capital investment required to enter an industry.

the sunk costs, the higher an entrant's rental cost of capital services will be.[5] Sunk costs place an entrant at a fixed and marginal cost disadvantage compared with an incumbent firm.[6]

The Dominant Firm

We now transfer our attention from the potential entrant to the dominant firm. Sunk costs raise the rental cost of capital for the entrant. In so doing, sunk costs place the entrant at a fixed and marginal cost disadvantage compared with an incumbent firm. A dominant firm can exploit this disadvantage to maintain its position.

The more output the dominant firm puts on the market, the closer will the residual demand curve be to the origin. If the dominant firm puts enough output on the market, it can push the residual demand curve *below* the entrant's average cost curve. In Figure 4-2, if the monopolist puts q_L units of output on the market, the best price the entrant could get after entry, P_L, will just equal the entrant's average cost. The entrant would make only a normal rate of return on its investment if it came into the market. A dominant firm's output only slightly greater than the *limit output*, q_L, would push the best price the potential entrant could get below the *limit price*, P_L, producing losses for the entrant. In such circumstances, a profit-maximizing potential entrant will stay out of the market.

The size of the limit output is determined by two factors: the size of the market and the entrant's average cost curve. In Figure 4-2, an increase in the size of the market would show up as a rightward shift in the market demand curve. Such a change would mean a greater quantity demanded at any price. An increase in the size of the market would increase the output a dominant firm would have to put on the market to keep an entrant out. The larger the

---

[5]Let λ_i be the rental cost of capital if entry is successful, which for simplicity we take to be the same as the rental cost of capital to an incumbent firm. Let λ_f be the rental cost of capital if the entry is unsuccessful, and the entrant must sell capital goods at a loss. Because of this capital loss, $\lambda_f > \lambda_i$. Then if π_f is the probability an entrant attaches to the prospect that it will fail, its expected rental cost of capital is

$$\lambda_e = (1 - \pi_f)\lambda_i + \pi_f\lambda_f > \lambda_i$$

The entrant faces a greater expected rental cost of capital than the incumbent firm.

[6]For the production function of footnote 3, and using the notation of Problem 2-4, we can compare the fixed costs

$$F_e = w\overline{L} + \lambda_e p^k\overline{K} > w\overline{L} + \lambda_i p^k\overline{K} = F_i$$

of the entrant (F_e) and the incumbent firm (F_i). Note, in particular, that the costs of gathering information about the market will be both sunk and fixed, and will have to be paid by the entrant but not by the incumbent firm.

Similarly, a comparison of marginal cost gives

$$c_e = wa_L + \lambda_e p^k a_K > wa_L + \lambda_i p^k a_K = c_i$$

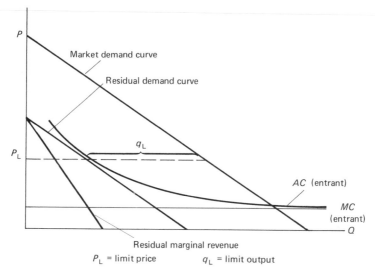

Figure 4-2 Limit output and limit price.

market, the greater the limit output a dominant firm will have to produce to preclude entry at the limit price.

On the other hand, the more costs are sunk, the greater the entrant's average cost at any output level.[7] In Figure 4-2, an increase in cost sunkenness would shift the entrant's average cost curve upward and reduce the limit output. If the entrant has higher costs, it will need a higher price to survive after entry. Correspondingly, the dominant firm will need to put less on the market to push the price below the entrant's average cost.

The fact that a dominant firm *can* keep entrants out does not mean that it will choose to do so. A dominant firm will pursue the strategy that yields the largest profit. If it will reap a greater profit by letting a rival into the market than by keeping it out, it will prefer to let the rival in.

If the market is large and sunk entry costs are small, a dominant firm will have to produce far more than a monopolist, and charge a price only slightly above the entrant's marginal cost, to preclude entry. In large markets with easy entry, a dominant firm will make a greater profit by charging a higher price and sharing the market with a competitive fringe than it will by setting a low price and keeping the fringe out. Thus the same factors that determine the limit quantity determine whether or not a dominant firm will want to preclude entry (in a static model).

---

[7]Continuing footnotes 5 and 6, an increase in the sunkenness of costs means a greater capital loss in the event of exit, and hence an increase in λ_f and λ_e. This will increase the entrant's fixed and marginal costs, raising the average cost curve.

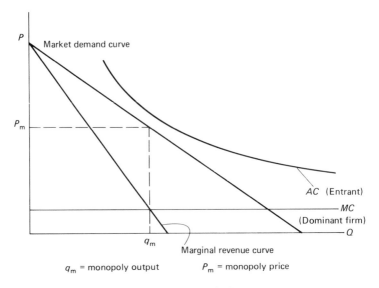

Figure 4-3 Blockaded entry.

Blockaded Entry

It is instructive to consider two special cases. If the market is very small and entry costs are very high, it will not be profitable for an entrant to come in even if the existing firm charges the monopoly price. This is the case of *blockaded entry*, which is shown in Figure 4-3. If entry is blockaded, the monopoly model of Chapter 2 applies. Such a market is said to be a *natural monopoly*, a candidate for public regulation.

The Contestable Market

If costs are not sunk at all, the entrant has exactly the same costs as the dominant firm. Any price that generates an economic profit for the dominant firm will generate an economic profit for the entrant. The only way the dominant firm can keep an entrant out is to set a price that yields zero economic profit.

Such a market is called *contestable*,[8] and in it the force of potential competition alone is sufficient to produce the same performance as a competitive market. The recent formal mathematical version of the theory of contestable

[8]Baumol, W. J., Panzar, J. C., and Willig, Robert D. *Contestable Markets and the Theory of Industry Structure*. New York: Harcourt Brace Jovanovich, Inc. 1982. The theory of contestable markets requires other implausible assumptions, including the assumption that an existing firm will not lower its price if an entrant comes in, undersells it slightly, and captures the entire market. See Spence, Michael A. "*Contestable Markets and the Theory of Industry Structure:* A Review," *Journal of Economic Literature* Volume 21, Number 3, September 1983, pp. 981–990, and Shepherd, William G. " 'Contestability' vs. Competition," *American Economic Review* Volume 74, Number 4, September 1984, pp. 572–587, and the references cited therein.

markets was announced[9] with great fanfare as a new "unifying framework" for industrial economics.[10] This formal theory, however, embodies arguments that were made a century ago, in literary form, by economists who challenged the need for anything like the antitrust laws.[11]

As we will see in Chapter 7, the theory of contestable markets has received little support in empirical tests. Its authors now concede that unless markets are *perfectly* contestable—no such costs at all—its predictions are consistent with those of the structure-conduct-performance analysis of industrial economics.[12] The theory of contestable markets is best viewed as a generalization of the model of perfect competition, which provides a standard against which the performance of real-world markets can be measured.[13]

Case Study: Limit Pricing (I)

Evaporative cooler pads are commonly used in air conditioning equipment throughout the western and southwestern United States. The pads are made of wood shavings bound in cloth. They were traditionally made by hand, but around 1960 a Texas firm, AMXCO, developed a method of producing them by machine. Handmade and machine-made pads are perfectly substitutable, but the latter are cheaper to produce. Based on this technical advance, AMXCO became the leading firm in the cooler pad market.

Another firm, Vebco, Inc., operated a heating and air conditioning business in Arizona, New Mexico, and West Texas. Vebco distributed pads for AMXCO to retail establishments from 1953 on.

---

[9]By its authors.

[10]Baumol et al., op. cit., p. 3; see also Baumol, William J. "Contestable Markets: An Uprising in the Theory of Industry Structure," *American Economic Review* Volume 72, Number 1, March 1982, pp. 1–15.

[11]Giddings, Franklin H. "The Persistence of Competition," *Political Science Quarterly* Volume 2, Number 1, March 1887, pp. 62–78; Gunton, George. "The Economic and Social Aspect of Trusts," *Political Science Quarterly* Volume 3, Number 3, September 1888, pp. 385–408.

[12]Baumol, William J., Panzar, John C., and Willig, Robert D. "Contestable Markets: An Uprising in the Theory of Industry Structure: Reply," *American Economic Review* Volume 73, Number 3, June 1983, p. 494: "models which support the robustness of contestability analysis follow a relatively long tradition going back at least to the work of Joe S. Bain." The reader must judge whether this statement is consistent with the claim that the theory of contestable markets is "an uprising in the theory of industry structure" (Baumol, op. cit.).

[13]The fundamental contributions of the theory of contestable markets seem likely to lie in the analysis of multiproduct firms, rather than the analysis of the determinants of market performance.

In 1969, Vebco began to distribute its own cooler pads, which were hand-made. When AMXCO discovered this, it terminated Vebco as a distributor. AMXCO did not change its prices, and Vebco gradually gained market share.

Distributors' prices in this market are usually expressed as discounts from list price; the purchasers then mark the prices up for resale. January 1971 began with Vebco and AMXCO charging the same price to discount houses: 9.5 percent below list price. The following sequence of changes in the price then took place (dates are given when available):

January 1971	Vebco cut its price to a 14.5 percent discount below list
	AMXCO cut its price to a 25 percent discount below list
	Vebco matched the AMXCO price cut
	AMXCO cut its price to 32.5 percent below list
March 1971	Vebco matched the AMXCO price cut
March 29, 1971	Vebco raised its price to 25 percent discount below list
1972	AMXCO offered discounts of 19–25 percent below list

Discussion: AMXCO was a dominant firm with a cost advantage over fringe firms. The fringe firms had to use a less efficient technology. AMXCO set its price so close to list that it was profitable for Vebco, a fringe firm, to expand its output, even though Vebco had higher costs. A price war followed; AMXCO located the limit price by cutting its price until Vebco "sued for peace" by raising its price on March 29, 1971. AMXCO remained a dominant firm in 1972, but competition from fringe firms forced it to set lower prices (19–25 per cent below list, rather than the 9.5 percent that had prevailed at the start of 1971).

This episode is rich in examples for students of industrial economics. It involves a market in which firms compete by setting a price and selling whatever is demanded at that price. We will study price-setting oligopoly in Chapter 4, and we will see that price-setting oligopolies that produce a standardized product are susceptible to price wars of the kind involved here.

Vebco filed a private antitrust suit against AMXCO, alleging price discrimination in violation of the Robinson-Patman Act (Section 2(a) of the Clayton Act) and attempted monopolization in violation of Section 2 of the Sherman Act. A trial court found in favor of AMXCO, and Vebco appealed the decision. The Circuit Court of Appeals upheld the lower court's decision. The critical *economic* issue for both charges, in the view of the Circuit Court, was whether or not an *injury to a competitor*—Vebco—constituted an *injury to competition* in violation of the antitrust laws. The Circuit Court ruled that in order to prove an injury to competition, it was not enough for Vebco to prove that it had been injured. As the Circuit Court interpreted the antitrust laws, to prove that AMXCO had injured competition, Vebco would have had to show that AMXCO had set its price below AMXCO's average variable cost. So long as a price is above the firm's average variable cost, the court ruled, only less efficient firms are injured, and that is not an injury to competition. The Circuit Court reviewed the decision of the lower court and found that Vebco had not proved an injury to competition. The distinction between injury to competitors and injury to competition recurs repeatedly in courts' interpretations of the antitrust laws. We will return to this subject in Chapter 16 when we deal with antitrust treatment of predatory behavior.

For more information, see: *International Air Industries, Inc. and Vebco, Inc. v. American Excelsior Company*, 517 F. 2d 714 (1975).

Dynamic Limit Pricing[14]

The static model of limit pricing ignores the fact that entry is a process that takes time. When we take account of the time needed to bring new capacity to the marketplace, we highlight an important element in the dominant firm's decision making: the tradeoff between current and future profit.

If a dominant firm sets a limit price, it can maintain its dominant position and earn a corresponding profit year after year. Alternatively, a dominant firm can set a higher price and earn a larger profit in the short run. A higher price will induce fringe firms to expand, but the expansion will not take place immediately or all at once. As in the Vebco case study, only gradually will the dominant firm lose market share to the fringe. With the loss of market share will come a loss of profit. The dominant firm faces a choice: it can earn a high profit in the short run, with eventual loss of its dominant position, or it can earn a somewhat lower profit indefinitely.

As a profit-maximizing firm, the dominant firm will choose the alternative that yields the income stream with the greatest present discounted value,[15] using

[14]For formal treatments, see Gaskins, D. W., Jr. "Dynamic Limit Pricing: Optimal Limit Pricing Under Threat of Entry," *Journal of Economic Theory* Volume 3, September 1971, pp. 306–322;, Ireland, N.J. "Concentration and the Growth of Market Demand," *Journal of Economic Theory* Volume 5, October 1972, pp. 303–305; Flaherty, M. T. "Dynamic Limit Pricing, Barriers to Entry, and Rational Firms," *Journal of Economic Theory*, 1980, pp. 160–182; Milgrom, P. and Roberts, J. "Limit Pricing and Entry Under Incomplete Information," *Econometrica* 1982, p. 443–460, and Judd, K. L. and Peterson, B. C. "Dynamic Limit Pricing and Internal Finance," *Journal of Economic Theory*.

[15]If r is the interest rate used to discount future income, the present value of $1 1 year in the future is $1/(1 + r)$; the present value of $1 2 years in the future is $1/(1 + r)^2$, and so on. The present value of an income stream that consists of $1 a year forever is thus

$$1 + 1/(1 + r) + 1/(1 + r)^2 + \cdots = (1 + r)/r.$$

as a discount rate the opportunity cost of funds to the firm. This is the rate of return the firm could earn if it invested in a risk-free asset (such as Treasury bills). The greater the discount rate, the more weight the firm gives to income received in the near future and the less weight it gives to income received in the distant future.

Three factors determine which alternative will yield a dominant firm the greatest present discounted value. The first factor is the difference between the limit profit the firm will earn if it sets a low price and the larger short-run profit it will earn if it sets a high price. The second factor is the rate at which the dominant firm loses market share (and therefore profit) to the fringe if the fringe begins to expand. The third factor is the discount rate.

Profit Difference

Here we can draw on the conclusions of the static limit price model. If the market is large and entry costs are small, the limit price will be near marginal cost and the limit profit will be small. The smaller the per-period limit profit, the more likely it is that the dominant firm will achieve a greater present-discounted value income stream by taking a larger short-run profit and giving up market share over the long run. If the market is large enough and entry costs are small enough, the dominant firm will prefer to take such short-run profits as it can get, even at the expense of market share. Dominant firms are most likely to take the money and run in large markets with easy entry.

Fringe Expansion Rate

In many cases, the maximum rate at which fringe firms *can* increase their output will depend on technological factors. The rate at which fringe firms *do* increase their output will be affected by the profit to be gained after entry, which is what motivates expanding firms. If the dominant firm sets a price far above the limit price, it can expect entry to be more rapid than if it sets a price only slightly above the limit price.

If fringe firms can increase their output rapidly and take market share away from the dominant firm quickly, the dominant firm will gain little by setting a high price. High short-run profits will evaporate quickly, as will market share. When fringe firms can expand rapidly, a dominant firm is more likely to hold the price down and retain market share.

Discount Rate

The third factor that determines the dominant firm's choice is the discount rate. When the discount rate is high, current income can be invested at relatively high rates of return. The opportunity cost of postponing current income for future income is high. If the discount rate is high enough, the dominant firm will prefer to take a greater profit in the short run and give up market share.

On the other hand, if the discount rate is low, the rate of return at which the extra short-run profit could be invested is small. The dominant firm will attach almost as much importance to profit to be earned in the distant future as to current profit. If the discount rate is low enough, the dominant firm will prefer to take a lower profit in the short run and hold on to market share.

Tradeoff

Of course, the dominant firm does not face an either-or decision. It can initially set a high price and then lower it toward the limit price. It would give up some market share to the fringe but maintain a dominant position over the long haul. The three factors just discussed—the profit to be gained in the short run, the rate of fringe expansion, and the discount rate—will determine how rapidly a dominant firm will bring the price down to the limit level. The case of OPEC from 1973 through 1985 (which we will discuss in detail in Chapter 5) seems to fit this scenario.

Case Study: Limit Pricing (II)

Historically, there have been substantial costs of entry into the steel industry. The technology favors vertical integration at least from the extraction of iron through smelting, refining, rolling, and the production of finished steel products (such as steel plate and bars). Fully integrated entry requires a substantial investment. Because such entry is risky, the cost of financial capital will be higher for an entrant than for a going concern. This will place entrants at a cost disadvantage compared with operating firms. Further, entry into the steel industry involves large sunk costs: there is not much one can do with a steel mill except produce steel. If a firm decided to leave the industry, it could not easily transfer its investment in the assets to another market. It would have to be content with the best price it could get for the assets in the steel industry. This increases the risk of deciding to enter the steel industry.

Toward the end of the nineteenth century, cartels were unsuccessful in controlling frequent price wars and intense rivalry in the U.S. steel industry. This induced a series of mergers that concentrated steel sales in the hands of a few large firms. The culmination of this movement came in 1901, when U.S. Steel was formed by the merger of a dozen companies. Each of these companies was itself the survivor of previously independent firms. U.S. Steel combined the assets of some 180 previously independent firms. At the time of its formation, U.S. Steel controlled roughly 65 per cent of the nation's steel capacity. The merger prompted one of the early landmark antitrust cases under the Sherman Act, a case which we will later discuss.

As shown in Figure 4-4, U.S. Steel's market share has declined throughout the twentieth century. There have been many changes in the steel industry over this long period. In particular, new technology now enables steel "minimills" to

Figure 4-4 U.S. Steel's market share. Sources: American Iron and Steel Institute, *Annual Statistical Report; Moody's Industrial Manual,* 1976; United States Steel, Annual Reports, various issues.

compete on a cost-effective basis with large integrated firms. It seems likely that entry into the steel industry is substantially easier today than it was at the turn of the century. But the gradual decline in market share depicted in Figure 4-4 is just what the dynamic limit price model predicts: a high price set to gain short-run profits, with a gradual loss of market share to rivals.

For additional information, see:

Adams, Walter. "The Steel Industry," in Adams, Walter, editor, *The Structure of American Industry,* 7th ed. New York: The Macmillan Co., 1986.

Miller, Jack Robert. "Steel Minimills," *Scientific American* Volume 250, Number 5, May 1984, pp. 32–39.

Parsons, Donald O. and Ray, Edward John. "The United States Steel Consolidation: The Creation of Market Control," *Journal of Law and Economics* Volume 18, Number 1, April 1975, pp. 181–219.

Szekely, Julian. "Can Advanced Technology Save the U.S. Steel Industry?," *Scientific American* Volume 257, Number 1, July 1987, pp. 34–41.

United States v. United States Steel Corporation, 251 U.S. 417 (1920).

Market Performance Under Entry-Limiting Behavior

How does the presence (actual or potential) of a competitive fringe affect market performance? How much control over price is a dominant firm able to exercise, compared with competition and monopoly?

The answer, of course, is, "It depends" (as it is to almost all questions in economics). In most of the classes that use this textbook, however, you will not get much credit for that answer unless you are able to explain what market performance depends on. It is to that topic that we now turn.

Market Performance Under Static Limit Pricing

First, consider the static limit price model. If entry is blockaded—if the dominant firm can charge the monopoly price and if it is still not profitable for new firms to come into the market—we are back to the basic monopoly model of Chapter 2. The only limit on the exercise of market power is the price elasticity of demand: if the monopolist raises the market price, some consumers will go away.

If there are some entry costs but entry is not blockaded, two possibilities arise. If entry costs are sufficiently great, a dominant firm will be able to preclude entry with only a moderate expansion of output above the monopoly level and only a moderate reduction in price below the monopoly level. The dominant firm will exercise some market power, but not as much as a monopolist. It will charge the highest price it can, without inducing entry. This possibility of entry will improve market performance, but the dominant firm will continue to exercise some market power.

If entry costs are sufficiently small, the monopolist would have to expand output greatly to prevent entry. In this case, the most profitable thing for the dominant firm to do is to set a higher price and give up market share. Eventually, the market will be supplied by several firms of roughly equal size. Such markets—oligopolies—are important, because they are the most common form of real-world market. We study them in the next two chapters. Here we simply note that firms in such markets will, in general, be able to exercise some market power.

At the other extreme, if there are no entry costs at all, the market is contestable. If average cost is the same for the entrant and the dominant firm, the dominant firm will be unable to exercise any market power without losing the entire market to the entrant. The market will perform as a competitive industry, even though it is supplied by a single dominant firm.

Although perfectly contestable markets are no doubt rare, the theory of contestable markets serves to remind us of one thing: having a monopoly or a large market share is no guarantee of having monopoly power—the power to hold price above marginal cost. A large firm can only get away with what its rivals will permit. As we will see, the same is true in oligopoly.

Market Performance Under Dynamic Limit Pricing

How are these conclusions altered when we take a dynamic view of limit pricing? If entry takes time, a dominant firm will face a tradeoff between short-term profit and longer-term loss of dominance. Formal models show that a dominant firm in such circumstances will set a high price and gradually lower it, as entry occurs, down to the average cost of fringe firms. At this point, entry will cease. The dominant firm will exercise some market power, but the degree of market power—the excess of price over marginal cost—will fall over time. If average cost is constant and is the same for the fringe and the dominant firm, the dominant firm will eventually lower price to marginal cost. It will not be able to exercise market power in the long run.

The Entry Decision—A Closer Look[16]

Reactions

One assumption of the static limit price model is that the potential entrant/fringe firm expects the dominant firm to maintain output in the face of entry. We used this assumption to draw a residual demand curve for the potential entrant (Figure 4-1). The entrant may very well expect different behavior from the dominant firm. It may expect the dominant firm to expand its output and lower its price in the face of entry in order to preserve market share (this was AMXCO's reaction to entry by Vebco, in the first case study). If the entrant expects the dominant firm to expand output on the entry of a rival, it will figure on a residual demand curve closer to the origin than suggested by Figure 4-1. All else equal, a smaller residual demand will make entry less likely.

In other circumstances, the entrant may expect the dominant firm to restrict output after entry and cooperate to maintain a high price and profit (this is not a bad description of Saudi Arabia's behavior in the first few years of OPEC control of the world oil market). Then the entrant will figure on a residual demand curve further away from the origin than Figure 4-1 suggests. All else equal, a greater residual demand will make entry more likely.

The general point is that whether or not an entrant will come into a market, and whether or not a fringe firm will try to expand, will depend as much on how it expects a dominant firm to react as on how much it sees a dominant firm producing. This is an important factor in the analysis of oligopoly, and we will return to it in Chapter 5.

If there are several potential entrants or fringe firms, each will have to consider the likely actions and reactions of all of the others, not just those of the dominant firm. Potential entrants may hesitate to come in if they think they will have to share the residual demand curve with other potential entrants.[17]

---

[16]For additional discussion, see Caves, R. E. and Porter, M. E. "From Entry Barriers to Mobility Barriers," *Quarterly Journal of Economics* Volume 91, Number 2, May 1977, pp. 241–261.

[17]See Sherman, Roger and Willett, Thomas D. "Potential Entrants Discourage Entry," *Journal of Political Economy,* Volume 75, August 1967, Part 1, pp. 400–403.

Other Considerations

Other factors will complicate the entry/expansion decision. We have talked about a situation where one firm is thinking about entry or expansion. In practice, there are likely to be several such firms, and costs of entry or expansion may well differ from one to another. There will be costs of making the entry decision, and these costs will be lower for some firms than others. A firm that distributes a number of consumer products through retail outlets will be able to make a fairly accurate assessment of the costs it will incur if it adds an additional product to its line. A manufacturing firm that has not done its own distribution will have less information about the cost of entry at the retail level. Firms in related product or geographic markets will have better information and lower costs of decision making than new firms.

The Entry Process

A firm seeking profitable investments is likely to have more information about some target industries than others. This being the case, the entry decision is likely to break down into a two-stage process. In the first stage, a firm considering expansion will identify industries that are likely prospects and about which it has enough information so that the decision-making costs are not prohibitive. In the second stage, the firm will study each target industry in detail and decide whether or not to enter.

Reprise

Limit price models emphasize the size of the market and the entrant's costs, especially sunk costs of entry, as determinants of market performance. The greater the investment needed to enter the market, and the more specific to the industry are the assets necessary for entry, the greater the entry costs are likely to be. Vertical integration and product differentiation will raise sunk entry costs. In any event, the costs of making the entry decision will be sunk, and these costs will vary from entrant to entrant. An entrant will also need to consider the possible reaction of the dominant firm and of other rivals.

Case Study: Entry

Sodium chlorate is a standardized chemical used in the pulp and paper industry to bleach the pulp and improve the quality of the final product, paper.

In 1959 the Pennsalt Chemicals Corporation operated a sodium chlorate plant in Portland, Oregon, with a capacity of 15,000 tons per year. Pennsalt's market share west of the Rocky Mountains was 57.8 per cent. It also sold sodium chlorate in the southeastern United States, using the Olin Mathieson Chemical Corporation as its main distributor. Olin Mathieson did not produce sodium chlorate, although it did produce a wide variety of other chemicals. Some of these chemicals required production methods similar to those used in making sodium chlorate, and Olin's marketing organization had contacts with pulp and paper mills in the Southeast.

Early in the 1950s, Olin Mathieson developed a process for bleaching pulp, using sodium chlorate, and it made the process generally available to the pulp and paper industry. The result was a general increase in the demand for sodium chlorate, particularly in the Southeast.

Between 1951 and 1957, Pennsalt conducted cost and market studies concerning a possible sodium chlorate plant in the Southeast, but it never built one. In December 1956, the largest producer of sodium chlorate, the Hooker Chemical Corporation, announced that it was going to expand the capacity of its Columbus, Mississippi, plant (the original capacity of this plant was 16,000 tons per year; this was doubled in 1962). In response, Pennsalt conducted additional market studies on the prospects for entry into the market.

During the same period, Olin considered entry into the sodium chlorate market. Its chemical division wrote a report that described such entry as "an unparalleled opportunity." Olin's management disagreed, and no entry took place.

In December 1957, Pennsalt's management decided against entry, apparently in the belief that the return on investment would not be sufficiently great.

In 1960, Olin and Pennsalt formed a joint venture, the Penn-Olin Chemical Company, for the production of sodium chlorate. Each parent firm owned 50 per cent of the offspring's stock. In 1961, Penn-Olin began operating a new plant in Calvert City, Kentucky. The plant had a capacity of 26,500 tons per year.

Discussion: As this incident shows, a decision on entry or expansion involves a careful consideration of market conditions, including the likely reactions of firms already in that market and of other potential entrants. It is often the case—as here—that the most likely entrants are firms that already operate in related product or geographic markets.

A special feature of this case study is the actual entry of a *joint venture* formed as a wholly owned subsidiary of two independent parent firms. The joint venture resulted in the actual entry of a new firm but eliminated the possibility of competition between the two parent firms. If the joint venture had been prohibited, at least two potential entrants would have remained poised on the edge of the market. Conceivably, one of the two parent firms might have come into the market on its own, with the other remaining as a potential competitor. The policy question is whether or not the actual competition offered by the joint venture is worth the loss of potential competition it engenders.

The government challenged the formation of the joint venture, Penn-Olin, as a violation of Section 7 of the Clayton Act (which prohibits mergers that have the effect of lessening competition). The District Court ruled that Section 7 did not apply to joint ventures, and the government appealed this ruling to the Supreme Court. The Supreme Court reversed the District Court and indicated that Section 7 of the Clayton Act did apply to joint ventures. It sent the case back to the District Court with instructions to decide if either of the parent firms would have entered alone, with the other remaining as a potential competitor. In a dissenting opinion, Justice William O. Douglas sharply disagreed with the majority's action. He read the record as showing an agreement among the parent firms to divide the market, and he thought this enough of a lessening of competition to violate Section 7 of the Clayton Act. Subsequently, the District Court found no reasonable probability that either parent firm would have entered on its own and allowed the joint venture.

For more information, see: *United States v. Penn-Olin Chemical Co.,* 378 U. S. 158 (1964); 246 F. Supp. 917 (D. Del. 1965); 389 U. S. 308 (1967).

Strategy

As noted in a recent survey,[18] "Dominance is a power relation between two agents in which the dominator restricts the actions of the dominated." But the dominant firm of limit price models is quite restricted in its actions toward actual or potential fringe rivals. The dominant firm has one weapon with which it can affect their decisions: its output level, which influences the price that rivals think will hold after entry or expansion. From the point of view of the dominant firm, this is not particularly satisfactory. The dominant firm is able to maintain its position, but it does so only by giving up profit, so that fringe firms do not seek a bigger slice of the pie.

There are tactics a dominant firm can employ to influence fringe firms' costs and beliefs about the way the dominant firm will react to fringe behavior. In this way, a dominant firm can maintain market share *and* earn a high profit. By studying such tactics, we can understand not only how some dominant firms have been able to maintain their dominant positions over time, but also how they achieved those positions in the first place.

[18]Geroski, P. A. and Jacquemin, A. "Dominant Firms and Their Alleged Decline," *International Journal of Industrial Organization* Volume 2, Number 1, March 1984, pp. 1–29. See also Encaoua, D., Geroski, P., and Jacquemin, A. "Strategic Competition and the Persistence of Dominant Firms: A Survey," in Stiglitz, J. and Mathewson, G. F., editors, *New Developments in the Analysis of Market Structure.* Cambridge, Mass. The MIT Press, 1986, pp. 55–86.

Strategies to Achieve and Maintain Dominance

The notion of strategy as a *source* of dominance extends the concept of rivalry backward in time to a period during which the structure of the industry is established. During this initial period, firms compete in an attempt to acquire a dominant position. Strategies aimed at achieving a dominant position involve investing resources that secure assets for the firm that cannot be duplicated, at least not without some passage of time and some sunk expenditure by a rival. This commitment of resources places later arrivals at a cost disadvantage vis-à-vis the dominant firm. Once a firm achieves a dominant position, it can employ strategic behavior to maintain that position.

Merger

Merger is an obvious method used to obtain a dominant market position. The formation of dominant firms by merger was an important motive for the passage of the Sherman Act, which is after all an anti*trust* act. As we will see in Chapter 10, the antitrust laws now place restrictions on such mergers. But there are strategies that a firm can employ to reach a dominant position through internal growth. Such strategies fall into three broad categories: strategies that act directly to raise rivals' cost, and strategies that act indirectly to raise rivals' costs through some aspect of the technology or marketing.

Direct Cost-Based Strategies[19]

As a strategy for dominance, increasing rivals' costs is superior to lowering the market price. Expanding output and lowering the price requires the dominator to bear the burden of lost profit. Raising rivals' costs places the burden on the entrant and allows the dominator to act as a monopolist under blockaded entry.

A dominant firm gains by accepting higher costs for itself if that strategy protects it from entry and allows it to exercise greater control over the market price and recoup the higher costs. Thus a dominant firm might accede to union demands for a higher wage rates as a way of raising the wage costs of later entrants.[20] More generally, a dominant firm may bid up the price of necessary inputs or acquire control of low-cost supplies as a way of raising rivals' costs.[21]

Other strategies act indirectly to raise rivals' costs by increasing the investment needed for successful entry.

---

[19]See Salop, Steven C. and Scheffman, David T. "Raising Rivals' Cost," *American Economic Review* Volume 73, Number 2, May 1983, pp. 267–271 and "Cost-Raising Strategies," Working Paper No. 146, Bureau of Economics, Federal Trade Commission, Washington, D.C., July 1986.

[20]Williamson, Oliver E. "Wage Rates as a Barrier to Entry: The Pennington Case," *Quarterly Journal of Economics* Volume 82, Number 1, February 1968, pp. 85–116.

[21]Such behavior was alleged in the 1946 *American Tobacco* case, which we discuss in Chapter 5.

Technology-Based Strategies

Capacity Expansion[22]

Excess capacity may be dictated by the technology. If the only efficient way to increase capacity is in plants of relatively large size, a firm will have to maintain some excess capacity or risk being caught short by an unexpected increase in demand.

Excess capacity may also be dictated by marketing considerations. Where distributors' services are essential to commercial success and manufacturers do not integrate forward into distribution, a manufacturer will have to convince distributors to support his product. Excess capacity will demonstrate a commitment to distributors that the firm that has invested in the capacity is in the market to stay.

But by the same token, an investment in excess capacity will demonstrate this same intent to potential entrants. It will signal to such firms and to existing fringe firms a willingness to defend a dominant market position.

For such a signal to be convincing, the capacity must be sunk. If an investment could be liquidated with relatively small capital losses, it does not demonstrate a commitment to the industry. If excess capacity is sunk, then it, like vertical integration, can help a dominant firm maintain its position without suffering the reduction in profit or of market share predicted by limit price models.

Vertical Integration[23]

If a dominant firm manufactures consumer goods, it may integrate forward into wholesale and retail distribution. By integrating forward, the dominant firm can guarantee itself secure access to the final consumer and control efforts to differentiate its product.

Backward integration into the production of the input ensures supplies and reduces the cost of coordinating activities at different stages of production (undoubtedly a factor in the vertical integration of steel firms and iron mines). But a decision to integrate, even if made for reasons of efficiency, will have implications for the entry decision of rivals. A decision by a dominant firm to integrate vertically can place an entrant at a cost disadvantage and increase its sunk entry costs. U.S. Steel's control of iron supplies, for example, is thought to have played a pivotal role in maintaining its position during its long dominance of the steel industry.[24]

---

[22]See Spence, Michael. "Entry, Capacity, Investment and Oligopolistic Pricing," *Bell Journal of Economics* Volume 8, Autumn 1977, pp. 534–544; Dixit, Avinash. "The Role of Investment in Entry Deterrence," *Economic Journal* Volume 90, March 1980, pp. 95–106; Bulow, Jeremy, Geanakoplos, John and Klemperer, Paul. "Holding Idle Capacity to Deter Entry," *Economic Journal* Volume 95, March 1985, pp. 178–182.

[23]See Porter, Michael E. *Competitive Strategy.* New York: The Free Press, 1980, chapter 14.

[24]Parsons, Donald O. and Ray, Edward John "The United States Steel Consolidation: The Creation of Market Control," *Journal of Law and Economics* Volume 18, Number 1, April 1975, p. 201.

Consider the plight of a firm considering entry into a manufacturing industry dominated by a vertically integrated firm. If the entrant comes in at the manufacturing level only, it will have to distribute its product through independent wholesalers and retailers. It will have to pay for their support, either directly or by offering the product to the distributor at a lower price (recall the Vebco case study).

If the entrant does not want to bargain with distributors, it may try to develop a favorable brand image by advertising directly to the final consumer, counting on the consumer to demand the product from distributors. The cost of cultivating a positive brand image will be largely sunk: if unsuccessful, the entrant could hardly expect to sell its goodwill, recover its investment in differentiation, and leave the market.

If the entrant comes in on a vertically integrated basis, most of the investment in distribution facilities will be a fixed cost (the rental cost of the distribution facilities will have to be paid no matter how much output moves through them). If the product requires specialized distribution facilities, the investment in these facilities will be sunk as well as fixed.

The dominant firm can achieve these effects by making its own investment in the sunk assets that make up a distribution system. But any potential entrant that makes serious inquiries into market conditions will know that the dominant firm has made this commitment of sunk assets. Such entrants are unlikely to expect the dominant firm to yield market share passively in the face of entry. They are much more likely to expect it to lower its price and defend its position if entry occurs.

This discussion shows that vertical integration will serve not only to raise entrants' costs but also to increase the chances that entrants will expect a hostile reaction. On all counts, vertical integration discourages entry without reducing output or revenue.

Marketing-Based Strategies

Product Differentiation

Product differentiation is another strategy for market dominance. R&D may aim at the development of distinctive product varieties. Advertising and other sales efforts can be used to cultivate a favorable brand image among final consumers and distributors. The resulting brand loyalty can create a dominant position because it raises entry costs for rivals who will have to either overcome or duplicate the brand loyalty in order to compete successfully.[25]

For consumer goods industries, vertical integration from manufacturing to wholesale and retail distribution facilitates product differentiation, if only because it promotes the flow of information from consumers to producers. A firm

---

[25]As we will see in Chapter 11, entrants may well have to spend more to overcome the incumbent's brand image advantage than the incumbent had to spend in the first place to establish the brand image.

that controls access to final consumers is in a strong position with respect to rivals, especially if that access cannot be duplicated without some sunk investment and some passage of time.

The policy questions raised by product differentiation as a competitive strategy are complex. R&D can create new and more satisfactory products, and advertising can give consumers information that will improve market performance. But these strategies will require costly expenditures and will have the additional effect of increasing market power for the firm that uses them successfully. As we will see in Chapter 8, firms with market power are likely to invest too much, from a social point of view, in product differentiation.

Access to Consumers

A firm with an established market position can employ various tactics to make it harder for new firms to obtain a trial for their product. It may employ tying and exclusive dealing contracts (which we discuss in Chapter 15). It may also offer products only for lease, rather than sale, especially if the leases are for a long term (a marketing technique commonly employed in the photocopying industry). A new firm can also offer products on a rental basis, but this involves a substantial investment in inventory.

By offering a variety of brands (as in the breakfast cereal industry), a dominant firm can preempt opportunities for a new firm to come in on a small scale and serve a narrowly focused segment of the market.[26] If learning by doing is important, small-scale entry may be the only practical way a firm can enter a market.

Discounts for volume purchases can encourage customers to patronize only a single supplier.[27] By tying volume discounts to purchases of many different products, a multiproduct firm can disadvantage rivals that compete against it in a single market. To offer similar discounts, entrants or fringe firms would have to market an equally wide range of products, with the corresponding increase in entry/expansion costs. By raising rivals' distribution costs, the dominant firm may be able to raise the price of the products to which the discounts are applied, so that customers end up paying more even with the discounts.

A similar effect can be achieved by offering the product and postsale service at a single price. Rivals would then have to set up their own service department to come into the market (increasing the cost of entry/expansion).[28]

A dominant firm can invest in training customers' purchasing agents to use specially designed software to order from it by computer. Anyone who has

---

[26]See Schmalensee, Richard. "Entry Deterrence in the Ready-to-Eat Breakfast Cereal Industry," *Bell Journal of Economics* Volume 9, Autumn 1978, pp. 305–327.

[27]Brooks, Robert C., Jr. "Volume Discounts as Barriers to Entry and Access," *Journal of Political Economy* Volume 69, Number 1, February 1961, pp. 63–69.

[28]If there is an independent service industry, the entrant can rely on firms in that market to supply postsale service. But if the dominant firm in the product market combines the sale of the product and postsales service, this strategy will impede the development of an independent service industry.

ever learned to use one word processing system and then had to switch to another will believe that this practice tends to lock in purchases with the firm that designed the software.

Implications of Strategic Behavior for Market Performance

Limit price models suggest a relatively sanguine attitude toward the exercise of market power by dominant firms. In a world of limit price behavior, dominant firms that wish to preserve their position can charge a price no higher than the average cost expected by a new firm after entry. Dynamic limit price models predict that dominant firms will yield market share over time and gradually give up the ability to control the market price.

Consideration of possible strategic behavior by dominant firms suggests a much less optimistic view. A dominant firm can employ a number of tactics to discourage entry or expansion by rivals and to preserve its market position while continuing to exercise market power. In markets where such strategies are used, policymakers will have to cope with the prospect of long-term exercise of market power by dominant firms.

Case Studies: Strategic Behavior

I: Alcoa

Before World War II, the Aluminum Company of America (Alcoa) was the only domestic U.S. producer of aluminum ingot from ore. It faced some competition from recyclers, who produced aluminum ingot from scrap aluminum. Alcoa owed its dominant position to licenses that allowed it to use a low-cost production technique under patent protection, but it maintained its position after the basic patent expired in 1909. In a suit alleging monopolization of the aluminum ingot market, the government accused Alcoa of purchasing bauxite deposits beyond its own needs to deny potential competitors access to material necessary for the production of aluminum ingot. The government also alleged that Alcoa had signed contracts with public utilities designed to prevent competitors from purchasing low-cost electric power (production of aluminum ingot requires a great deal of electric power). In the view of the courts, the government did not succeed in proving that Alcoa had acted to preserve its monopoly.

But the courts did find that Alcoa had monopolized the aluminum ingot industry

*United States v. Aluminum Company of America, 148 F.2d 416 (2d Cir. 1945), at 431.

in violation of Section 2 of the Sherman Act. The critical factor was Alcoa's continual expansion of capacity:*

> It was not inevitable that it should always anticipate increases in demand for ingot and be prepared to supply them. Nothing compelled it to keep doubling and redoubling its capacity before others entered the field. It insists that it never excluded competitors; but we can think of no more effective exclusion than progressively to embrace each new opportunity as it opened, and to face every newcomer with new capacity already geared into a great organization, having the advantage of experience, trade connections and the elite of personnel.

Discussion: This case began before the United States entered World War II. The U.S. government constructed a number of ingot plants during the war, and at the end of the war it sold the plants to various producers to promote competition.

This case shows the use of capacity expansion to maintain market position. But it raises disturbing policy questions. Throughout this period, aluminum faced competition from other metals. There was no demonstration that Alcoa had earned more than a normal rate of return on its investment. What would Alcoa have had to do to avoid being found guilty of monopolization? Should it have restricted output, raised its price, and attracted new firms to the market? What sorts of signals does this decision send to business?

II: American Hospital Supply

The American Hospital Supply Corporation (AHSC) is a vertically integrated manufacturer and distributor of supplies to hospitals. It markets a wide variety of products, including surgical equipment, pharmaceuticals, intravenous fluid, furniture, uniforms, and linens.

In 1979, AHSC signed a purchasing agreement with a loosely associated group of 29 hospitals, the Voluntary Hospitals of America, located throughout the country. Part of the agreement, which was to run for 3.5 years with an option for renewal, provided for individual hospitals to receive rebates or "volume discounts" from AHSC, based on purchases by all hospitals of all products. Rebates were calculated and distributed retroactively on a year-by-year basis.

In 1979, four regional distributors of hospital supplies filed a private antitrust suit against AHSC, challenging the purchasing agreement as a restraint of trade and an attempt to monopolize in violation of the Sherman Act. The District Court that heard the case found that AHSC was guilty of these offenses. AHSC appealed to the Circuit Court of Appeals, which overturned the District Court's decision. The Circuit Court ruled that the District Court had employed too narrow a definition of geographic markets (standard metropolitan statistical areas) and that there had been no proof that AHSC possessed the power to control price in more broadly defined markets.

Apparently, however, the purchasing agreement did not prove entirely satisfactory. Within a few years, the Voluntary Hospitals of America was distributing its own private-label brands of hospitals supplies, which were produced by independent manufacturers and distributed in cooperation with regional distributors. In an independent development, AHSC merged, in 1985, with the number two firm in the hospital supply market, Baxter-Travenol.

For additional information, see:

White and White, Inc., et al. v. American Hospital Supply Corporation, 540 F. Supp. 951 (1982), and Martin, S. and Goddeeris, J. "Policy Change and Structural Change in the Health Care Industry" *Antitrust Bulletin* Volume 30, Number 4, Winter 1985, pp. 949–974.

Public Policy Toward Dominant Firms

The passage of the Sherman Act was motivated by public concern over trusts—dominant firms formed by merger in the great consolidation wave of 1895–1904. Many of the earliest landmark antitrust cases, in which courts gave content to Section II of the Sherman Act, involved dominant firms.

Courts were bound by the language of Section 2, which as we have seen condemns

> Every person·who shall monopolize, or attempt to monopolize, or combine or conspire with any other person or persons, to monopolize any part of the trade or commerce among the several States, or with foreign nations. . . .

This does *not* condemn monopoly. Nor could it. Our study of strategies that create dominance shows that monopoly, within the meaning of the antitrust laws, can arise as the result of the normal process of competitive rivalry. A firm may achieve a dominant position by developing a low-cost method of production. Alternatively, it may become dominant by developing a new product, which drives rivals from the market because it better satisfies consumer needs (the government might even grant the firm a legal monopoly on the new product in the form of a patent). It would make no sense to condemn monopoly, under laws designed to promote competition, if monopoly can sometimes result from competition. What Section II prohibits is *monopolization,* the act of acquiring a monopoly. We now trace the cases in which courts made the distinction between legal and illegal acquisition of monopoly.

Standard Oil[29]

The Standard Oil Company of Ohio was organized in 1870, combining the oil refining and distribution operations of the Rockefeller brothers and others. Within 2 years, they had acquired control of most of the oil refineries in and around Cleveland. By 1882, Standard controlled some 90 per cent of the production, refining, and distribution of oil in the United States.

In one of the earliest monopolization cases to reach the Supreme Court, the government alleged (and the Supreme Court accepted) that Standard Oil had employed the following techniques on its way to achieving this market position:

1. Local price wars to drive rivals out of business (or to reduce the price paid by Standard Oil for a merger agreement).[30]
2. Purchase of rivals for the purpose of dismantling their refineries and taking them out of production.
3. Negotiation of preferential rebates, not available to competitors, from railroad companies.
4. Control of pipelines needed to ship oil from oilfields to refineries.
5. Operation of bogus independent companies, actually controlled by Standard Oil, to maintain an appearance of competition.

The Supreme Court recognized that Section II of the Sherman Act does not prohibit monopoly as such:[31]

> although the statute by the comprehensiveness of the enumerations embodied in both the first and second sections makes it certain that its purpose was to prevent undue restraints of every kind or nature, nevertheless by the omission of any direct prohibition against monopoly in the concrete it indicates a consciousness that the freedom of the individual right to contract when not unduly or improperly exercised was the most efficient means for the prevention of monopoly, since the operation of the centrifugal and centripetal forces resulting from the right to freely contract was the means by which monopoly would be inevitably prevented if no extraneous or sovereign power imposed it and no right to make unlawful contracts having a monopolistic tendency were permitted.

[29]*Standard Oil v. United States,* 221 U.S. 1 (1911). See the discussion in Chapter 16.

[30]As noted in Chapter 16, John S. McGee. "Predatory Pricing: The Standard Oil (N.J.) Case," *Journal of Law and Economics* Volume 1, October 1958, pp. 137–169, makes a convincing case that Standard Oil in fact did not engage in local price cutting. What is important for the interpretation of Section 2, however, is that the Court thought this strategy had been employed.

[31]*Standard Oil v. United States,* 221 U.S. 1 (1911), at 62.

In other words, Section 2 of the Sherman Act does not prohibit all monopoly, since monopoly can result from legal competition (freedom to contract). Section 2 does prohibit monopoly that results from certain types of competition. Drawing on a review of both the common law concerning monopoly and the legislative history of the Sherman Act, Chief Justice Edward D. White indicated the general standard used to decide whether or not a monopoly position had resulted from improper competition and thus violated Section 2 of the Sherman Act:[32]

> the criteria to be resorted to in any given case for the purpose of ascertaining whether violations of the section have been committed, is the rule of reason guided by the established law and by the plain duty to enforce the prohibitions of the act and thus the public policy which its restrictions were obviously enacted to subserve.

To elaborate this general standard of the *rule of reason,* White outlined the tests to be applied by lower courts in monopolization cases. A monopoly violates Section 2

1. if obtained by contracts in restraint of trade that violate Section 1 of the Sherman Act.
2. if obtained "not as a result of normal industrial development."
3. if obtained by actions showing "an intent and purpose to exclude others."

The Supreme Court's reading of Section 2 in this decision is that a firm violates Section 2 if it has a monopoly position and if it acquired that position in a way that did not reflect competition on the merits. As we will see in Chapter 10, courts have considered mainly market share in deciding whether or not a firm has a monopoly within the meaning of the antitrust laws. To decide whether or not a firm's conduct represents normal industrial development, courts have carried out a detailed review of the development of the industry.

The Supreme Court had no trouble finding Standard Oil in violation of Section 2 of the Sherman Act, in view of its market share and in view of the techniques employed by the company as it grew to dominance in the oil industry. As a result of this decision, Standard Oil was broken up into 33 "survivor" companies. This remedy did not bring about competitive structure or behavior in the U.S. oil industry, however, since ownership of the survivor companies remained in the hands of the owners of the parent firm.

---

[32]Ibid.

U.S. Steel[33]

As indicated earlier, the U.S. Steel Corporation was formed in 1901 by a merger that combined the assets of 180 companies. U.S. Steel's market share began to decline almost immediately after its formation.

From 1907 to 1911, the president of U.S. Steel, Judge Elbert Gary, sponsored the industry get-togethers known as the *Gary dinners*. The purpose of these dinners, as Gary frankly admitted, was to promote industry solidarity and prevent outbreaks of price competition:[34]

> These meetings were calculated to influence people to maintain their prices. There is no doubt of that but as I understand the vice of the law is in obligating to maintain prices. . . . It was intended to influence people so far as we legitimately could maintain fair prices, each one for himself using his best judgment, after full knowledge of the business of all.

In 1911, the government challenged the merger that led to the formation of U.S. Steel as a monopolization in restraint of trade, a violation of Section 2 of the Sherman Act, and asked for the dissolution of the company. Under the *Standard Oil* rules, the government had to prove that U.S. Steel had a monopoly position and that it had obtained that position by methods that were not normal industrial development.

The majority of the Supreme Court felt, however, that the government had failed to show that U.S. Steel had ever attained a monopoly. Its market share had declined. It had had to meet with rivals to control prices, suggesting an inability to control prices on its own.[35] The majority of the Court noted the absence, on the part of U.S. Steel, of the exclusionary behavior that had been laid to Standard Oil. By a vote of 4 to 3, the merger that had created U.S. Steel was legitimized, and the stage was set for the long decline illustrated in Figure 4-4. Section 2 of the Sherman Act lay dormant for a generation.

---

[33]*United States v. United States Steel Corporation*, 251 U.S. 417 (1920).

[34]Testimony before the Staley Commission, quoted in Parsons and Ray, op. cit., p. 209.

[35]At one point, 251 U.S. 417 (1920), at 449, the majority points out that the government failed to charge the firms that attended the Gary dinners as confederates of U.S. Steel. This suggests that a charge of conspiracy to monopolize in violation of Section 2 of the Sherman Act might have been acceptable to the Court. But under the U.S. judicial system, courts are like oracles; they answer only the questions put to them. The government did not ask the courts to decide if U.S. Steel was guilty of conspiracy to monopolize.

Alcoa[36]

The facts and the outcome of the *Alcoa* case have already been given. Against the charge of monopolization in violation of Section 2 of the Sherman Act, Alcoa offered the defense that it had earned no more than a fair profit— a rate of return of about 10 percent on its investment. Judge Learned Hand disposed of this contention with logic focusing on the purpose of the antitrust laws and the faith of these laws in competition as the guarantee of effective market performance:[37]

> it is no excuse for "monopolizing" a market that the monopoly has not been used to extract from the consumer more than a "fair" profit. The Act has wider purposes. Indeed, even though we disregard all but economic considerations, it would by no means follow that such concentration of producing power is to be desired, when it has not been used extortionately. *Many people believe that possession of unchallenged economic power deadens initiative, discourages thrift and depresses energy; that immunity from competition is a narcotic, and rivalry is a stimulant, to industrial progress; that the spur of constant stress is necessary to counteract an inevitable disposition to let well enough alone.* Such people believe that competitors, versed in the craft as no consumer can be, will be quick to detect opportunities for saving and new shifts in production, and be eager to profit by them. In any event the mere fact that a producer, having command of the domestic market, has not been able to make more than a "fair" profit, is no evidence that a "fair" profit could not have been made at lower prices (emphasis added).

The immediate point of this comment is the recognition that a firm that is insulated from the pressure of competition may, through inefficiency, exercise its market power by incurring higher costs, leaving the worst of all possible worlds as far as market performance is concerned: higher prices without monopoly profit because of wastefully high costs.[38]

The deeper point is the view of the antitrust laws as a device for the maintenance of competitive rivalry as a method of market regulation. The antitrust laws prohibit exclusionary behavior by dominant firms as the best way to ensure efficient market performance.

---

[36]*United States v. Aluminum Company of America,* 148 F.2d 416 (2d Cir. 1945).

[37]*United States v. Aluminum Company of America,* 148 F.2d 416, at 427.

[38]This way lies the theory of X-efficiency. For an introduction to this literature, see Leibenstein, Harvey. "Allocative Efficiency vs. 'X-Efficiency,' " *American Economic Review* Volume 56, Number 3, June 1966, pp. 392–415; Stigler, George J. "The Xistence of X-Efficiency," *American Economic Review* Volume 66, Number 1, March 1976, pp. 213–216; Leibenstein, Harvey. "X-Inefficiency Xists—Reply to an Xorcist," *American Economic Review* Volume 68, Number 1, March 1978, pp. 203–211.

The "competitive process" rationale for the preservation of competitive opportunities is entirely consistent with the models of dominant firm behavior presented earlier in this chapter. The presence of a competitive fringe tempers the ability of a dominant firm to control price. Antitrust emphasis on maintaining the opportunity to compete is also consistent with the interpretation of congressional intent for the antitrust laws given in Chapter 3: the antitrust laws promote competition as a regulatory process, as a device for obtaining efficient market performance without direct government intervention in the workings of the market.

Judge Hand followed the rule of *Standard Oil:* monopoly obtained or maintained by normal methods of industrial development does not constitute a violation of the Sherman Act. But the evidence upon which Judge Hand relied for a showing of intent to monopolize—Alcoa's continual expansion of capacity in anticipation of demand—raises more questions than it settles. If such conduct is evidence of an intent to exclude, few firms with a position of market power can avoid being found guilty under the antitrust laws. This standard—which was later endorsed by the Supreme Court[39]—seems to reverse the lenient attitude toward dominant firms taken in *U.S. Steel.*

United Shoe[40]

The *United Shoe* decision is worth noting for at least two reasons. It provides an example of the kind of behavior that courts have taken as sufficient to condemn a monopoly position of under the Sherman Act. Further, in giving his opinion, Judge Charles E. Wyzanski, Jr. provided a succinct summary of the development of the law under Section 2.

The United Shoe Machinery Corporation was formed in 1899 by a merger that combined seven previously independent firms. The government challenged this merger under the Sherman Act, but in a 1918 decision the Supreme Court declined to find a violation.[41] From that point on, United Shoe Machinery dominated the U.S. market for machines used to manufacture shoes.

At the time of the 1953 case, shoe manufacture involved 18 separate processes. Although United Shoe Machinery faced some competition in the manufacture of machines for individual processes, it was the only company in the United States that marketed a complete line of machines. Many of the machines were protected by patents. United Shoe Machinery had 75 to 85 per cent of the U.S. shoe machinery market.

The major machines were leased to customers but not sold. The leases ran

[39]In the second American Tobacco case, *American Tobacco Co. et al. v. United States,* 328 U.S. 781 (1946), discussed in Chapter 4 in connection with the application of the Sherman Act to oligopoly.

[40]*United States v. United Shoe Machinery Corporation,* 110 F. Supp. 295 (1953).

[41]*United States v. United Shoe Machinery Company of New Jersey et al.,* 247 U.S. 32 (1918).

for 10 years. They included a penalty if the user returned the machine before the lease expired, if it was returned was so that it could be replaced by a competing product. There was no such penalty if one United Shoe machine was replaced by another from the same company.

The leases contained what was called a *full capacity* clause. This clause provided that the United Shoe machine could not be idle if work was available in the shop. If business was insufficient to use all machines at capacity, the machines of rival manufacturers had to be idle.

In addition, United Shoe Machinery provided service for its machines at no additional charge. This prevented the development of independent service companies, which increased the costs of rival companies. They would have to establish their own service departments to compete with the integrated United Shoe operation. The effect of this collection of marketing techniques was to make it difficult for rival manufacturers to compete for business on the merits.[42]

Against this pattern of behavior, Judge Wyzanski distinguished three judicial interpretations of Section 2 of the Sherman Act:

1. Pre-*Alcoa:* Section 2 is violated if a firm has acquired or maintained the power to exclude by techniques that are a restraint of trade in violations of Section 1 of the Sherman Act.
2. *Alcoa:* a firm with an overwhelming share of the market is in violation of Section 2 when it does business unless its position is due solely to skill.
3. *Griffith:*[43] there is a violation of Section 2 of the Sherman Act if a firm has the power to exclude competition and either has exercised it or has the purpose to exercise it.

Judge Wyzanski found that United Shoe Machinery's leasing practices were sufficient to established a violation under either the *Alcoa* or the *Griffith* standards. The leasing practices seem to fall most clearly within the original "rule of reason" prohibition of practices that are not normal industrial development, and may thus signal a retreat from *Alcoa* to *Standard Oil.*

The remedy that followed was dictated by the nature of the offense. The District Court required United Shoe to shorten its leases, to eliminate the full capacity clause, to offer machines for sale, and to charge separately for repair services. Without restrictive practices, United Shoe was free to compete on the merits (as were its rivals).

---

[42]For a contrary conclusion, see Posner, Richard A. *Antitrust Law: An Economic Perspective.* Chicago: The University of Chicago Press, 1976, pp. 202–206, who argues that no one of the practices employed by United Shoe could have an exclusionary effect. For a critique of Posner's arguments, see Scherer, F. M. "The Posnerian Harvest: Separating Wheat from Chaff," *Yale Law Journal* Volume 86, Number 5, April 1977, pp. 992–993. Scherer argues that Posner fails to confront the combined effect of the jointly employed exclusionary practices.

[43]*United States v. Griffith,* 334 U.S. 100 (1948).

Law and Economics of Monopolization

Section 2 of the Sherman Act condemns monopoly acquired or maintained by exclusionary behavior. The theory of dominant firms emphasizes strategic behavior to acquire or maintain positions of market power. If a dominant firm does *not* engage in strategic entry-deterring behavior, over the long run it will be able to exercise only as much market power as entry conditions permit. Any greater short-run use of market power will induce entry and erode the firm's dominant position.

Thus the received interpretation of Section 2 of the Sherman Act is broadly consistent with the economic analysis of dominant firm behavior. Beneath this broad consistency, however, two questions remain.

First, how are courts to judge whether or not a firm has market power? Second, what practices should be condemned by courts as showing ''an intent and purpose to exclude others?''

These questions are fundamental to much of antitrust economics, going beyond Section 2 of the Sherman Act. The problem of assessing market power arises in particular in the context of Section 7 of the Clayton Act (as amended in 1950 by the Celler-Kefauver Act), which has largely superseded Section 2 of the Sherman Act as far as the regulation of mergers is concerned. We will discuss the treatment of mergers under Section 7 of the Clayton Act in Chapter 10.

In different circumstances, a variety of exclusionary practices and strategies have been used to justify a finding of monopolization. These include the practices condemned in Sections 2 and 3 of the Clayton Act,[44] predatory pricing, and various contractual restraints agreed upon by manufacturers and distributors. We analyze these practices in Chapters 15, 16, and 17, respectively.

Summary

Firms may achieve a dominant position by superior competitive performance, by merger, or by strategic behavior designed to exclude competitors and prevent competition on the merits.

If a firm acquires a dominant position, its ability to control the market price will be tempered by the presence of a competitive fringe. A dominant firm can employ strategies to increase the sunk expenses associated with entry, to make it more likely that rivals will expect a hostile reaction to entry, or to slow the rate at which rivals can expand. Such strategies will increase the extent to which a dominant firm can raise price without losing market share to the fringe.

Section 2 of the Sherman Act, which condemns monopolization, does not condemn monopoly that results from competition on the merits. It does con-

---

[44]Price discrimination, tying, exclusive dealing, and requirements contracts; see Chapter 3.

demn monopoly that is achieved "not as a result of normal industrial development." There are a few cases that come close to condemning size for its own sake, but most applications have required some evidence of exclusionary or anticompetitive practices. This is consistent with the economic analysis of dominant firm behavior.

Problems

4-1 Suppose the market demand curve is

$$P = a - b(Q + q),$$

where P is the market price, Q is the output of a dominant firm, and q is the output of the single fringe firm. The dominant firm's cost function is

$$C(Q) = cQ,$$

and the cost function of the fringe firm is

$$C(q) = e + cq,$$

where $e > 0$ is sunk costs of entry or expansion.
  a. What output would the dominant firm produce if it were a monopolist? What price would it charge?
  b. If the fringe firm observes the dominant firm producing Q units of output and expects this output level to be maintained, what is the equation of the residual demand curve that the fringe firm expects?
  c. If the fringe firm maximizes its profit on the residual demand curve, what output will it produce?
  d. How much output will the monopolist have to produce to keep the fringe firm out of the market (i.e., to make $q = 0$)? What price will this amount of output bring? What is the degree of market power exercised by the monopolist if it chooses to keep the fringe firm out of the market?

4-2 Answer the same questions if

$$P = 4000 - (\tfrac{1}{20})(Q + q)$$
$$C(Q) = Q \qquad C(q) = 80 + q.$$

4-3 Using the same notation as Problems 4-1 and 4-2, suppose the market demand curve is

$$P = 1000 - (\tfrac{1}{10})(Q + q)$$

and the cost functions of the two firms are

$$C(Q) = 5Q \qquad C(q) = 10q.$$

What price will the dominant firm have to charge to keep the fringe firm out of the market? What degree of market power would it exercise at this price?

Hint: One way to answer this question is to write the equation of the residual demand curve and do the algebra. Another is to graph the demand curve and the average/marginal cost curves and think about the question. The latter is advised.

4-4 In September 1984, as part of the settlement of a private antitrust suit, major oil companies agreed to allow franchised retail gasoline dealers to sell gasoline and other products from any manufacturer, even if that meant that a dealer would sell a brand of gasoline other than that of the oil company that franchised the station.

    a. Why would an oil producer wish to require its franchised dealers to sell only its brand of gasoline?

    b. What will the effect of this settlement be on the ability of fringe gasoline refiners to expand? Why?

Paper Topics

4-1 In May 1986, the trial began of a private antitrust suit filed by the United States Football League (USFL) against the National Football League (NFL). The USFL alleged that NFL contracts with all three major television networks, which kept the USFL off the television airwaves, were part of a campaign by the NFL to maintain its dominant position. Review news stories about this case and learn the USFL's economic theories. How did the NFL defend itself? What role was played by Professor Michael Porter of Harvard University? Finally, as an element of competitive strategy, why would an editorial writer for the *Wall Street Journal* (June 13, 1986) describe the USFL's motto as "If you can't beat 'em or join 'em, sue 'em"?

4-2 Review the following cases and analyze the treatment of the Aluminum Company of Americal under the antitrust laws:

United States v. Aluminum Co., 19 F. Supp. 374 (W.D. Pa. 1937), 20 F. Supp. 608 (W.D. Pa. 1937), 302 U.S. 230 (1937); 20 F. Supp. 13 (S.D.N.Y. 1937); 1 F.R.D. 1 (S.D.N.Y. 1941); 2 F.R.D. 224 (S.D.N.Y. 1941); 44 F. Supp. 97 (S.D.N.Y. 1941); 320 U.S. 708 (1944); 322 U.S. 716 (1943); 148 F.2d 416 (2d Cir 1945); 91 F. Supp. 333 (S.D.N.Y. 1950); 1954 Trade Cases Paragraph 67745 (S.D.N.Y.); 1957 Trade Cases Paragraph 68755 (S.D.N.Y.)

4-3 Trace the market shares of major firms in the U.S. oil industry from the breakup of Standard Oil following the 1911 antitrust case. Was the breakup effective in achieving competitive market performance? Why or why not? Suggest and defend an alternative remedy.

4-4 How did the Supreme Court apply and elaborate the criteria of the *Standard Oil* case when it decided *United States v. American Tobacco Co.*, 221 U.S. 106 (1911)?

4-5 Discuss the place of the following cases in the interpretation of Section 2 of the Sherman Act:

  a. *United States v. American Can Company et al.*, 230 Fed 859 (1916).
  b. *United States v. United Shoe Machinery Co. of New Jersey et al.*, 247 U.S. 32 (1918).
  c. *United States v. International Harvester Co.*, 274 U.S. 693 (1927).

4-6 What evidence of exclusionary intent was presented in *United States v. the New York Great Atlantic and Pacific Tea Co. et al.*, 67 F. Supp. 626 (1946)? Is this evidence credible? See Adelman, M. A. *A&P: A Study in Price-Cost Behavior and Public Policy.* Cambridge, Mass.: Harvard University Press, 1959.

4-7 Trace the history of the United Shoe Machinery Corporation after the 1953 decision. How did this decision affect market performance?

5

Oligopoly—The Recognition of Interdependence[1]

No man is an island, entire of itself.

John Donne

In a competitive market, each firm is so small that it can put as much or as little output as it wishes on the market without affecting the price. For this reason, a firm in a competitive market has no reason to worry about what other firms will do when it makes its own plans. No farmer adjusts the number of acres he plans to sow based on the acreage he believes his neighbor will plant.

At the other extreme, the monopolist has no rivals to worry about. The dominant firm—as close as we get to monopoly in the real world—does consider the reaction of fringe firms, but the recognition of interdependence is one-sided because the dominant firm is typically much larger than its rivals. In many markets, however, this one-sided recognition of interdependence does not persist. If entry costs are sufficiently low, a dominant firm will chose to exercise some market power and gradually give up market share, rather than pursue a limit price strategy and preserve a dominant position. At some point, fringe firms will become as large as the once dominant firm, and the market will become an oligopoly—supplied by a few firms, which recognize their mutual interdependence.

In this chapter, we investigate the consequences of that recognition of interdependence when firms independently pursue what they believe to be their own self-interest. We do this by generalizing the static limit price model presented in Chapter 4.

The static limit price model includes a dominant firm and a potential entrant. The potential entrant makes its output decisions to maximize its profit, given what it believes the dominant firm will do. The dominant firm knows how the

[1]For a survey of the oligopoly literature, see Shapiro, Carl, "Theories of Oligopoly Behavior," in Schmalensee, Richard and Willig, Robert D., editors, *Handbook on Industrial Organization*. Amsterdam: North Holland Publishing Company, forthcoming.

entrant makes decisions and uses this information when it makes its own decisions.

The models of noncooperative oligopoly that we discuss in this chapter explore what happens when all firms behave the way the potential entrant behaved in the static limit price model: maximizing their profit, given the output of other firms. The first model is a simple one in which firms expect no reaction to their decisions from rivals. We use this model to ask how the degree of market power is related to the number and size distribution of firms.

We then move beyond this basic model and see how market performance changes when firms expect rivals to react to what they do. We also examine the impact of product differentiation on market performance under oligopoly.

These models are the building blocks for the models of collusion and strategic behavior that follow in Chapter 6. They set the stage for the discussion of empirical research in Chapter 7. As the final topic of this chapter, we cover the application of the antitrust laws to firms that recognize their interdependence but do not explicitly collude.

The Place of Oligopoly in the U.S. Economy

What makes oligopoly important is its ubiquity. Oligopoly exists everywhere in the American economy (and in the economies of industrialized countries generally). To make this clear, we need to see how economists measure the number and size distribution of firms in an industry.

The Standard Industrial Classification

The Bureau of the Census, which conducts a Census of Population every 10 years, periodically conducts censuses of various sectors of the U.S. economy.[2] These censuses classify firms in industries according to what is called the *Standard Industrial Classification*[3] and report information by Standard Industrial Classification industry.

The Standard Industrial Classification divides the economy into a hierarchy of industries ranging from very broadly defined groups to narrowly defined product classes. The larger the number of digits in the industry or product code, the more finely divided the category.

Table 5-1 shows the breakdown of the two-digit Standard Industrial Clas-

---

[2]Industrial censuses have been carried out roughly every 5 years. Recent Censuses of Manufactures appeared for 1963, 1967, 1972, 1977, and 1982. In the noncensus years, the Census of Manufactures is supplemented by the Annual Survey of Manufactures.

[3]The Standard Industrial Classification is revised periodically; for details of the most recent revision, see U.S. Department of Commerce, Bureau of the Census. *Standard Industrial Classification Manual 1987.* Washington, D.C.: U.S. Government Printing Office, 1987.

Table 5-1 Standard Industrial Classification Industry 38: Instruments and Related Products

3811	Engineering, Laboratory, Scientific, and Research Instruments and Associated Equipment
3822	Automatic Controls for Regulating Residential and Commercial Environments and Appliances
3823	Industrial Instruments for Measurement, Display, and Control of Process Variables; Related Products
3824	Totalizing Fluid Meters and Counting Devices
3825	Instruments for Measuring and Testing of Electricity and Electrical Signals
3829	Measuring and Controlling Devices Not Elsewhere Classified
3832	Optical Instruments and Lenses
3841	Surgical and Medical Instruments and Apparatus
3842	Orthopedic, Prosthetic, and Surgical Appliances and Supplies
3843	Dental Equipment and Supplies
3851	Ophthalmic Goods
3861	Photographic Equipment and Supplies
3873	Watches, Clocks, Clockwork Operated Devices, and Parts

sification group 38, "Instruments and Related Products," into 13 four-digit industries. Each such industry combines firms that manufacture a variety of related products. For example, Standard Industrial Classification industry 3842 includes[4]

> Establishments primarily engaged in manufacturing orthopedic, prosthetic, and surgical appliances and supplies, arch supports, and other foot appliances; fracture appliances; elastic hosiery, abdominal supporters, braces, and trusses; bandages; surgical gauze and dressings; sutures; adhesive tapes and medicated plasters; and personal safety appliances and equipment.

The Standard Industrial Classification continues down to the very finely divided seven-digit level. Economists have most often used information reported for four-digit industries. This is partly because four-digit industries seem to come closest, among publicly available data sources, to markets in an economic sense.[5] It is also because the government provides more information at the four-digit level than it does for less aggregated industries or product classes.

[4]U.S. Department of Commerce, Bureau of the Census. *Standard Industrial Classification Manual 1987*. Washington, D.C.: U.S. Government Printing Office, 1987, p. 250.

[5]This is not to say that four-digit Standard Industrial Classification data do not have shortcomings. The information is reported on a national basis, which is fine for industries like steel or motor vehicles but not for fluid milk or bread. Further, Census publications report only information for manufacturers located in the United States, which can be misleading for industries in which imports are important. Economists recognize these shortcomings, but most feel that Census data are of satisfactory quality. For a contrary view, see Liebowitz, S. "What Do Census Price–Cost Margins Measure?" *Journal of Law and Economics* Volume 25, Number 2, October 1982, pp. 231–246.

Measuring Fewness—Concentration Ratios

The Bureau of the Census conducts a Census of Agriculture, a Census of Manufactures, a Census of Transportation, a Census of Wholesale Trade, and a Census of Retail Trade. The greatest detail appears in the Census of Manufactures, which covers what has been the largest sector of the economy, at least since the Industrial Revolution.[6]

The Census of Manufactures reports (among many other things) information about the number of firms operating in each four-digit industry and the relative size of those firms. The Bureau of the Census is bound to maintain the confidentiality of the data submitted by individual firms, so it does not publish the market shares of individual firms. Instead, it reports the percentage of industry sales accounted for by the largest 4 firms, the largest 8 firms, the largest 20 firms, and the largest 50 firms. These *concentration ratios* are widely used as a measure of the fewness of suppliers in a market.

The average four-firm concentration ratio for all four-digit U.S. manufacturing industries was 40 per cent in both 1972 and 1977.[7] In 1982, as shown in Table 5-2, 193 of 442 four-digit manufacturing industries had four-firm concentration ratios of 40 per cent or more.

When the four largest firms in an industry together supply 40 per cent or more of industry sales, each *must* be aware of the others. Such industries are oligopolies, and their importance in the economy justifies the attention industrial economists give to oligopoly.

Measuring Fewness—the Herfindahl Index

Concentration ratios are commonly used as a summary index of fewness because the government publishes them on a comparable basis for a wide range of industries. But concentration ratios contain information only about the shares of the largest few firms—usually four or eight—in an industry. They therefore discard a considerable amount of information about the relative size of smaller firms in the market and provide only a limited picture of the size distribution of firms in the market.

---

[6]This is changing as the nature of the U.S. economy changes and services increase in importance at the expense of manufactures. In view of this change, economists have begun to test the models of industrial economics against nonmanufacturing sectors of the economy. See White, L. J. "What Has Been Happening to Aggregate Concentration in the United States?," *Journal of Industrial Economics* Volume 29, Number 3, March 1981, pp. 223–230; and Martin, S. "Structure and Performance of U.S. Wholesale Trade," *Managerial and Decision Economics* Volume 5, Number 3, September 1984, pp. 160–167.

[7]Shepherd, W. G. "Causes of Increased Competition in the U.S. Economy, 1939–1980," *Review of Economics and Statistics* Volume 64, Number 4, November 1982, pp. 613–626. The average is weighted by the value of shipments, so the concentration ratios of larger industries are given greater weight in computing it.

Table 5-2 Distribution of Four-Firm
Sales Concentration Ratios by
Four-Digit Standard Industrial
Classification Industry, U.S.
Manufacturing, 1982

CR4	Number of Industries
90–100	7
80–89	11
70–79	20
60–69	34
50–59	49
40–49	72
30–39	77
20–29	86
10–19	65
0–9	21
	442

Notes: CR4 is the percentage of industry
sales supplied by the four largest firms in the
industry. Four-firm concentration ratios for sev-
en industries were suppressed by the Bureau
of the Census for reasons of confidentiality.

Source: U.S. Department of Commerce, Bureau of the Census, *Concentration Ratios in
Manufacturing, 1982 Census of Manufactures.*

A four-firm concentration ratio of 60 per cent could mean that the largest firm in the market had a market share of 54 per cent, sharing the market with 23 firms, each with a 2 per cent share. It could also mean that the four largest firms each had 15 per cent of the market, which they shared with four smaller firms, each with a 10 per cent share. The two cases would require very different analysis: the first case would be a dominant-firm market, the second an oligopoly. The four-firm concentration ratio provides little guidance here.

For these reasons, economists sometimes employ an alternative measure of sales concentration, the Herfindahl index.[8] This index often emerges in theoretical models of oligopoly. It has the merit of combining information about the market shares of all firms in the market, not just the largest four or the largest eight firms.

The Herfindahl index is also used for policy purposes. The 1984 Department of Justice Merger Guidelines employ it to explain to businessmen which mergers the government will consider challenging.[9] The government has published

[8]For a recent survey, see Kwoka, John E., Jr. "The Herfindahl Index in Theory and Practice," *The Antitrust Bulletin* Volume 30, Number 4, Winter 1985, pp. 915–947.

[9]We review the Justice Department Merger Guidelines in Chapter 10.

101

Table 5-3 Sample Herfindahl Indices

Market Shares	Herfindahl Index
1. $s_1 = 1$	$H = (1)^2 = 1$
2. $s_1 = \frac{1}{2}$; $\quad s_2 = \frac{1}{2}$	$H = (\frac{1}{2})^2 + (\frac{1}{2})^2 = \frac{1}{2}$
3. $s_1 = \frac{1}{3}$; $\quad s_2 = \frac{1}{3}$; $\quad s_3 = \frac{1}{3}$;	$H = (\frac{1}{3})^2 + (\frac{1}{3})^2 + (\frac{1}{3})^2 = \frac{1}{3}$
4. $s_1 = \frac{1}{2}$; $\quad s_2 = \frac{1}{4}$; $\quad s_3 = \frac{1}{4}$;	$H = (\frac{1}{2})^2 + (\frac{1}{4})^2 + (\frac{1}{4})^2 = \frac{3}{8}$

Herfindahl indices at the 4-digit SIC level beginning with the 1982 Census of Manufactures. It can also be computed on an industry-by-industry basis, from trade sources (as in Table 5-4).

Suppose there are N firms in an industry, and s_i is the market share of firm i. The Herfindahl index is the sum of squares of the market shares of the firms in the industry:

$$H = s_1^2 + s_2^2 + s_3^2 + \cdots + s_N^2. \tag{5.1}$$

In what sense is the Herfindahl index a measure of fewness? Sample values of the H-index for different distributions of firms are shown in Table 5-3. To begin with, if an industry is supplied by a monopolist, the monopolist's market share is 1, and the value of the Herfindahl index is 1. If there are two firms, each with half the market, then the value of the index is $\frac{1}{2}$. If there are three firms, each with one third of the market, the value of the index is $\frac{1}{3}$. It is generally true[10] that if there are N equal-sized firms, the value of the Herfindahl index is $1/N$.

Considering for the moment the case of equal-sized firms, as the number of firms increases, the value of the Herfindahl index falls from 1 toward 0. This makes it a useful indicator of fewness: the larger the Herfindahl index, the fewer the number of firms supplying the industry.

What if firms are not of equal size? The last line of Table 5-3 shows the Herfindahl index for an industry with three firms, one with half of the market and two each with one-quarter of the market. The value of the index is $\frac{3}{8}$. This is less than one half (the value of the Herfindahl index for two equal-sized firms) but more than one third (the value of the index for three equal-sized firms). That is exactly the way we would want a concentration index to behave: three firms, one larger than the other two, represent a greater concentration of sales than three equal-sized firms but a smaller concentration of sales than two equal-sized firms.

[10]Proof: suppose there are N firms, each with a market share of $1/N$. Then the Herfindahl index is

$$H = \left(\frac{1}{N}\right)^2 + \left(\frac{1}{N}\right)^2 + \cdots + \left(\frac{1}{N}\right)^2 = N\left(\frac{1}{N}\right)^2 = \frac{1}{N}.$$

In fact, we can ask the following question:[11] how many equal-sized firms would an industry need to produce a Herfindahl index of $\frac{3}{8}$? For N equal-sized firms, the value of the index is $1/N$, so if there were

$$\frac{8}{3} = 2\frac{2}{3}$$

equal-sized firms in an industry, the industry would have the same Herfindahl index as the industry in line 4 of Table 5-3. We recognize that there is no such thing as two thirds of a firm, but describing the market concentration as equivalent to that which would be produced by $2\frac{2}{3}$ equal-sized firms is a convenient way of making clear that the industry in line 4 of Table 5-3 is less concentrated than the industry in line 2 (two equal-sized firms) but more concentrated than the industry in line 3 (three equal-sized firms).

Table 5-4 illustrates the computation of the Herfindahl index for the U.S.

Table 5-4 Herfindahl Index for the U.S. Auto Industry, 1984

Firm	Car Sales	Market Share
1. General Motors	4,600,512	0.4432
2. Ford	1,979,317	0.1907
3. Chrysler	1,078,716	0.1039
4. Toyota	557,982	0.0538
5. Honda	508,420	0.0490
6. Nissan (Datsun)	485,298	0.0468
7. American Motors	202,570	0.0195
8. Volkswagen	177,322	0.0171
9. Mazda	169,666	0.0163
10. Subaru	157,383	0.0152
11. Volvo	97,915	0.0094
12. Mercedes Benz	76,051	0.0073
13. Audi	70,220	0.0068
14. BMW	68,650	0.0066
15. Mitsubishi	39,104	0.0038
16. Saab	32,768	0.0032
17. Peugeot	19,406	0.0019
18. Porsche	18,550	0.0018
19. Jaguar	18,044	0.0017
20. Isuzu	17,233	0.0017
21. Alfa Romeo	3,702	0.0004
22. Ferrari	568	0.00005
23. Fiat	391	0.00004
24. Lancia	21	0.000002

Herfindahl index = 0.2525 Numbers equivalent = $1/H$ = 3.96

Source: 1985 Ward's Automotive Yearbook

[11]Adelman, M. A. "Comment on the 'H' Concentration Measure as a Numbers Equivalent," *Review of Economics and Statistics* Volume 51, February 1969, pp. 99–101.

automobile industry for 1984. In Problem 5-1, you are asked to perform similar calculations for the world automobile industry.

Although there are 24 firms that sell automobiles in the United States, the numbers equivalent derived from the Herfindahl index shows that the industry is about as concentrated as an industry with four equal-sized firms. That is, the U.S. automobile industry is a highly concentrated oligopoly.

Table 5-4 can be used to illustrate one property of the Herfindahl index. The index is computed by squaring and adding the market shares of individual firms. The smallest 14 firms in the U.S. automobile market have market shares of less than 1 per cent each. When these very small market shares are squared, the contribution each makes to the Herfindahl index is less than 1/1000th—they will affect the Herfindahl index at most in the fourth decimal place. In practice, such firms can be safely ignored without affecting the picture the Herfindahl index gives about industry concentration. It is not necessary to measure the market share of every firm in the market to compute a Herfindahl index that will give an accurate indication of sales concentration. It is only necessary to measure the market shares of the larger firms.

Quantity-Setting Oligopoly

The models economists use to analyze oligopoly fall into two broad categories. In the first, which we examine in this section, firms decide how much to produce and let the market determine the price at which output is sold. Models in this class describe industries in which firms must set production schedules in advance and cannot alter them without incurring some sunk cost. The automobile industry is an example: once cars are on the dealers' lots, discount programs are used, if necessary, to find a price at which they will sell.

In the second class of models firms set their price and sell whatever quantity is demanded at that price. This sort of model is appropriate for industries in which the technology allows rapid changes in the rate of output. The insurance industry is an example. Insurance companies typically set rates for (say) automobile insurance, and will sell insurance to as many people with reasonable driving records as are willing to buy it.[12]

We begin with models of quantity-setting oligopoly, which are a natural extension of the dominant-firm model of Chapter 4. Price-setting oligopoly is dealt with in the following section.

---

[12]We usually think of the distinction between quantity-setting and price-setting behavior as determined by the technology: how quickly can a firm alter the rate of output? Dixon, Huw, "The Cournot and Bertrand Outcomes as Equilibria in a Strategic Metagame," *Economic Journal* Volume 96, Supplement, 1986, pp. 59–70, takes a different approach and examines what happens when firms choose whether to set the quantity or the price as part of strategic rivalry.

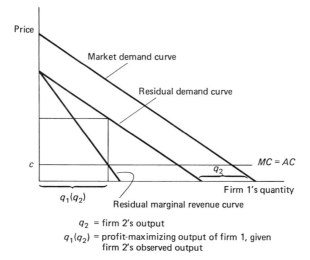

Figure 5-1 Firm 1's output decision in a quantity-setting oligopoly.

Cournot Duopoly

The seminal model of oligopoly[13] makes the smallest possible departure from monopoly and examines a market supplied by two identical firms. As we will see, the results of this duopoly model generalize in a natural way to markets with more than two firms and to markets in which the firms are not identical. But we begin at the beginning.

Figure 5-1 (which nearly duplicates Figure 4-1) illustrates the output decision of the first firm. For the moment, we assume that the first firm behaves as the potential entrant did in the static limit price model of Chapter 4. To keep the diagram as simple as possible, assume also that there are no fixed costs and that marginal cost per unit is constant at some level c. Then the marginal cost curve and the average cost curve coincide, as in Figure 5-1.[14]

What output level will firm 1 pick to maximize its profit? Firm 1, like the potential entrant of Chapter 4, acts in the belief that firm 2 will maintain a constant output level. This is the assumption Cournot made about the way firms expect rivals to behave, and for the moment we will make it as well. In due

---

[13]Due to Cournot, A. A. *Researches Into the Mathematical Principles of the Theory of Wealth.* New York: The Macmillan Co., 1927 (originally published in 1838).

[14]Fixed costs raise problems with the existence of equilibrium. With fixed costs, if firm 2 produces a large enough output, firm 1 will shut down, and vice versa. The reaction curves will be discontinuous: at some positive output of firm 2, firm 1's output will drop suddenly to zero. For large enough fixed costs, the reaction curves of the two firms may not intersect, and there will not be an equilibrium. See Friedman, James. *Oligopoly Theory.* Cambridge: Cambridge University Press, 1983.

course, we will see what happens when firms make more realistic assumptions about the way rivals will behave.

Firm 1 will then maximize its profit along a residual demand curve obtained by subtracting firm 2's output from the market demand curve. Firm 1's profit-maximizing output will make its marginal cost equal to marginal revenue along the residual demand curve. This output is designated $q_1(q_2)$ in Figure 5-1 because the output firm 1 decides to put on the market depends on the output of firm 2.

By going through firm 1's profit-maximization exercise for different values of q_2, we can derive firm 1's *reaction curve*. This reaction curve shows the output firm 1 will produce to maximize its profit, depending on the output of firm 2.

What should the reaction curve look like? We can at least pin down the endpoints. First, suppose that firm 2 produces nothing at all. Then firm 1 is a monopolist, and it will maximize its profits along the market demand curve, as shown in Figure 5-2(a). If $q_2 = 0$, $q_1 = q_m$ (the output of a profit-maximizing monopolist). $(q_m, 0)$ is one point on firm 1's reaction curve. We can use the results of the static limit price model to determine how much firm 2 would have to put on the market to keep firm 1 out. Firm 1 and firm 2 have the same cost function: the cost per unit is c. If firm 2 restricts output at all, holding the price above c, it will be possible for firm 1 to put some output on the market and make a profit. To keep firm 1 out of the market, firm 2 would have to produce so much that the price would be forced down to marginal cost. But this is the price that would occur in long-run equilibrium in a competitive market (see Chapter 2). It follows that in order to make firm 1 choose to stay out of the market (to shut down), firm 2 would have to produce the output that would be produced, in long-run equilibrium, in a competitive industry (as shown in Figure 5-2b). $(0, q_c)$ is another point on firm 1's reaction curve.

It turns out (and you are asked to verify this in Problem 5-2) that if the

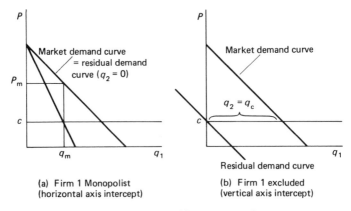

Figure 5-2 Endpoints of firm 1's reaction curve.

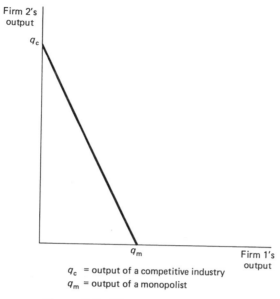

Figure 5-3 Firm 1's reaction curve.

market demand curve is a straight line, the reaction curve will also be a straight line. In this case, as shown in Figure 5-3, we obtain firm 1's reaction curve by connecting the point labeled q_m on the horizontal axis with the point labeled q_c on the vertical axis.

Firm 1's reaction curve shows the output it will choose to maximize its own profit, given what it believes firm 2 will produce. By going through the same analysis of firm 2's output decision, we can obtain a reaction curve for firm 2. This shows the output firm 2 will choose to maximize its own profit, given what it believes firm 1 will produce. Firm 2's reaction curve joins the points $(q_c,0)$ and $(0,q_m)$. The two reaction curves are drawn together in Figure 5-4.

The output each firm will choose depends on what it thinks the other firm will do. In general, these beliefs are inconsistent. Consider point A in Figure 5-4. If firm 1 believes that firm 2 will produce $q_{2,A}$, firm 1 will put $q_{1,A}$ on the market. But if firm 2 believes that firm 1 will produce $q_{1,A}$, firm 2 will produce $q_{2,B}$, not $q_{2,A}$. A little experimentation with the reaction curves will convince you that there is only one point on the diagram at which the beliefs of each firm about the actions of the other will be correct—the point at which the reaction curves cross. For this reason, we describe the intersection of the reaction curves as the *equilibrium of the Cournot market.*

If (as shown in Figure 5-5), firm 2 believes that firm 1 will bring q_1^* units to market, firm 2 will bring q_2^* units to market. If firm 1 believes that firm 2 will bring q_2^* units to market, firm 1 will bring q_1^* to market. At the output pair (q_1^*,q_2^*), each firm's actions will confirm and be consistent with the beliefs of

107

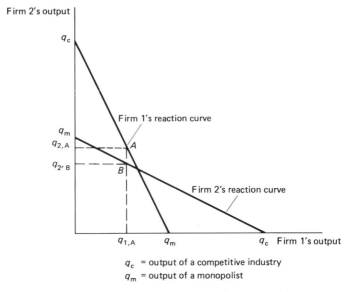

q_c = output of a competitive industry
q_m = output of a monopolist

Figure 5-4   Reaction curves for firms 1 and 2.

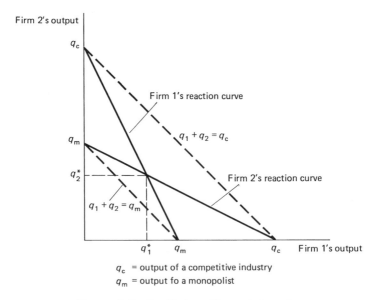

q_c = output of a competitive industry
q_m = output fo a monopolist

Figure 5-5   Equilibrium, Cournot duopoly.

the other. Each firm will be maximizing its profit, given what it believes the other will do. Neither firm will have any incentive to change its output. This makes (q_1^*, q_2^*) an equilibrium.[15]

How will the Cournot market equilibrium compare with the equilibrium of a competitive market? Refer to Figure 5-5. The dashed line connecting the point $(q_c, 0)$ on the horizontal axis and the point $(0, q_c)$ on the vertical axis shows all combinations of output, by the two firms, that add up to competitive market output. The reaction curves intersect below this line. This shows that the combined output of the duopolists in equilibrium will be less than the output of a competitive industry. If the Cournot market equilibrium output is less than the output of a competitive industry, the Cournot market equilibrium price will exceed the competitive equilibrium price (as the equilibrium moves up the demand curve).

How will the Cournot market equilibrium compare with monopoly? Refer again to Figure 5-5. The dashed line connecting the point $(q_m, 0)$ on the horizontal axis and the point $(0, q_m)$ on the vertical axis shows all combinations of output by the two firms that add up to monopoly output. The reaction curves intersect above this line. This shows that the combined output of the duopolists exceeds the monopoly level. The result is that Cournot market equilibrium price will fall short of the monopoly price.

Discussion

Each Cournot duopolist restricts output, trying to maximize its own profit. In so doing, each misunderstands the way the other makes decisions. Individual output decisions are imperfectly coordinated, and total output exceeds the monopoly level. The Cournot equilibrium price falls short of monopoly price.

Cournot duopolists succeed in exercising some market power, some control over price. But because they act independently, they do not maximize their joint profit.

The *particular* misunderstanding that is built into the Cournot model—the assumption that each firm believes that its rivals hold output constant—is im-

---

[15]The nature of equilibrium is one question. The stability of equilibrium—the circumstances, if any, under which the market will move to the equilibrium—is another. A story is often told in intermediate microeconomics classes about the stability of Cournot duopoly. The story involves a back-and-forth movement in which firm 1 observes firm 2's output and adjusts q_1; then firm 2 observes firm 1's adjusted output and adjusts q_2; and the process repeats. If you try this story in Figure 5-4, you will see that it does move the market to (q_1^*, q_2^*). Friedman observes that there are two principal problems with this story. First, it requires the firms to behave stupidly: each firm is supposed to make its own plans on the assumption that the other firm will hold its output constant, even though it sees the firm change its output, cycle after cycle. Second, this story supposes that each firm maximizes its profit period by period, when it would make more sense to examine the behavior of firms that maximize the present discounted value of profits. As Friedman notes, the Cournot equilibrium of Figure 5-5, period by period, is an equilibrium in a multiperiod model. See Friedman, op. cit., chapter 2, for further discussion.

plausible. But the general prospect that in oligopoly firms will misunderstand the way rivals behave is quite plausible. Output under oligopoly will fall short of the competitive level but exceed the monopoly level. The implied prediction for price is that oligopoly price will fall short of the monopoly price but exceed the competitive price.[16]

Beyond Duopoly

How does Cournot market equilibrium change if there are more than two firms? Cournot duopoly output exceeds monopoly output because the duopolists act independently and because each misunderstands the way the other is making decisions. As more and more oligopolists are added to the market, Cournot market equilibrium output moves closer and closer to competitive market equilibrium output. Correspondingly, as more and more oligopolists operate in the market, the equilibrium price falls from the monopoly level toward the competitive level. You are asked to verify this in Problem 5-3.

This progression from monopoly to competition as the number of firms increases is perhaps one of the most appealing aspects of the Cournot model. Despite the unreality of its assumptions, the Cournot model smoothly bridges the whole range of market structures from monopoly to competition. It does so with the intuitively appealing result that the more firms there are in the market, the closer performance approaches the competitive standard.[17] Equivalently, the more concentrated the market, the more nearly will market performance approach the monopoly outcome.

Unequally Sized Firms—Firm Market Power

The intuitive result that increased market concentration moves Cournot market performance toward monopoly generalizes in a straightforward way to the more realistic case in which firms are of different size. This extension produces the Herfindahl index as a measure of market concentration. It also suggests empirical tests of market performance, which we will explore in Chapter 7.

We know from Chapter 2 that for a monopolist the Lerner index of market power is the inverse of the price elasticity of demand:

---

[16]It follows that oligopolists will have an incentive to collude, because if they collude successfully they will increase their profit. We pursue this idea in Chapter 6.

[17]As you are asked to show in Problem 5-4, the equilibrium output in N-firm Cournot oligopoly is

$$q_N = \left(1 - \frac{1}{N + 1}\right)q_c.$$

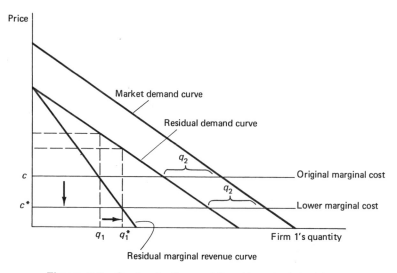

Figure 5-6 Cost reduction and firm 1's output decision.

$$\frac{P - c}{P} = \frac{1}{\epsilon_{QP}}. \tag{5.2}$$

Recall the economic logic behind this algebraic relationship: if a monopolist raises price, the quantity demanded falls. When the price elasticity of demand is large, a small increase in price will cause a large decline in sales. In such circumstances, the monopolist will not find it profitable to raise price far above marginal cost.

How will this situation change in oligopoly? Examine Figure 5-6 and ask how firm 1's output will change, given firm 2's output, as firm 1's unit cost falls. If firm 1 discovers a new production technique, so that its marginal cost falls to $c^* < c$, firm 1's marginal cost curve shifts down. Firm 1's profit-maximizing output will increase, for any output from firm 2, as the marginal cost curve moves down the residual marginal revenue curve.

Given firm 2's output, firm 1's output will increase. As shown in Figure 5-6, firm 1's reaction curve shifts outward. If the lower-cost technology is unavailable to firm 2 (the new technique may be patented; it may be kept secret; it may depend on particular inputs that are unavailable to firm 2), there is no change in firm 2's reaction curve.

As firm 1's marginal cost falls, the Cournot equilibrium point—the intersection of the two reaction curves—slides down firm 2's reaction curve (from E to E^*). Firm 2's output falls and firm 1's output rises (Figure 5-7). It is a general result—whatever the number of oligopolists—that in quantity-setting

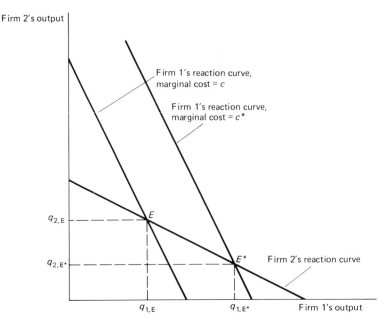

Figure 5-7 Equilibrium, Cournot duopoly, unequal-sized firms.

models, firms with lower marginal costs have greater market shares (see Problem 5-3).

If costs differ across firms, market power will differ from firm to firm. The Lerner index of market power for firm i is

$$\frac{P - c_i}{P} = \frac{s_i}{\epsilon_{QP}}, \qquad (5\text{-}3)$$

where s_i is firm i's market share (see Problem 5-5).

The greater a firm's market share, the greater its market power. In Cournot-type models, each firm acts independently, and each fails to understand what the others are doing. Hence total output exceeds the monopoly level, and the price falls short of the monopoly level. But if firm i has a very large market share—if s_i is near 1—the fact that firm i misunderstands what its small rivals are doing is of little consequence for the market price. When firm i is large in the market, price will depend mostly on its own actions, and firm i will exercise almost as much market power as would a monopolist. The result is that even though firms act independently, larger firms will have more market power than smaller firms.

Unequal-Sized Firms—Industry Performance

What does Equation (5.3) imply for industry performance? Multiply both sides of this equation by s_i and add the resulting expressions for all firms to obtain

$$\frac{P - \bar{c}}{P} = \frac{H}{\epsilon_{QP}}, \tag{5.4}$$

where $\bar{c}$ is the industry-average value of marginal cost,[18] and H is the Herfindahl index of market concentration.

What is the economic interpretation of Equation (5-4)? There is a recognition of interdependence in this market, but no cooperation. Each firm restricts its own output, given what it thinks other firms will do. No firm considers the fact that when *it* puts output on the market, the revenue that its rivals receive will go down. As a result, combined output exceeds the monopoly level. The more sales are concentrated in the hands of a few large firms, the greater the effect of output restrictions, which push the price up, and the smaller the effect of independent decision making, which pushes the price down. The more concentrated the market in quantity-setting oligopoly, the greater the industry-average degree of market power.

Expected Reactions

Cournot's original model, and the models we have developed from it, have each oligopolist believe that its rivals hold their output constant. This belief seems especially implausible, given that the defining characteristic of oligopoly is that firms recognize their mutual interdependence.

We can get around this implausibility by adding to the Cournot model a new variable that describes the way each firm expects others to react to what it does. The new variable is the elasticity of rivals' output with respect to firm i's output,

$$\alpha_i = \frac{\Delta q_{-i}/q_{-i}}{\Delta q_i/q_i} = \frac{q_i}{q_{-i}} \frac{\Delta q_{-i}}{\Delta q_i}, \tag{5.5}$$

where in an oligopoly of N firms, we write q_{-i} for the output of all firms except firm i.[19]

---

[18]The average is weighted by market shares, that is,

$$\bar{c} = s_1 c_1 + s_2 c_2 + \cdots + s_N c_N.$$

[19]That is, $q_{-1} = Q - q_1 = q_2 + q_3 + \cdots + q_N$. This is done simply for notational simplicity.

This is the percentage change in all other firms' output that firm i expects in response to a 1 per cent change in its own output. It is usually called a *conjectural variation* for firm i because it describes the way firm i thinks competitors will react to what it does.[20]

If $\alpha_i = 0$, this means that firm i thinks that other firms will not change their output in response to its own output decisions. This is merely the basic Cournot assumption about behavior.

Suppose instead that $\alpha_i = 1$. Then firm i makes its plans in the belief that if it restricts output by 1 per cent, other firms will do the same. Firm i, in other words, expects rivals to cooperate in pulling output off the market.

Suppose $\alpha_i = -1$. Then firm i makes its plans in the belief that if it restricts output by 1 percent, its rivals will expand their output by the same percentage. Firm i believes that if it tries to pull output off the market, rivals will act to neutralize its attempt.

Table 5-5 shows estimates of conjectural variations for firms in the U.S. steel industry.[21] The estimates are derived from data covering a long period, so they should be considered average values over that period. The firms in Table 5-5 are listed in order of declining market share.

The conjectural variation estimated for U.S. Steel is virtually the same as that assumed for the basic Cournot model: zero. Smaller firms apparently expected greater matching of output restrictions by rivals, with the exception of Inland Steel. The conjectural variation estimated for Inland is still greater than those estimated for the four largest firms. None of the estimated conjectural variations are negative: rivalry has not been a hallmark of the U.S. steel industry.

---

[20]For early discussions of conjectural variations, see Frisch, R. "Monopole—Polypole—La Notion de Force dans l'economie," *Nationalokonomisk Tidsskrift,* 1933; and Hicks, J. R. "Annual Survey of Economic Theory: The Theory of Monopoly," *Econometrica* Volume 3, Number 1, January 1935, pp. 1–20. Recent contributions include Cowling, Keith. "On the Theoretical Specification of Industrial Structure–Performance Relationships," *European Economic Review* Volume 8, June 1976, pp. 1–14; Cowling, Keith, and Waterson, Michael. "Price–Cost Margins and Market Structure," *Economica* Volume 43, August 1976, pp. 267–274; Bresnahan, Timothy F. "Duopoly Models with Consistent Conjectures," *American Economic Review* Volume 71, December 1981, pp. 934–945; and Ulph, David. "Rational Conjectures in the Theory of Oligopoly," *International Journal of Industrial Organization* Volume 1, Number 2, June 1983, pp. 131–154.

[21]Iwata, Gyoichi. "Measurement of Conjectural Variations in Oligopoly," *Econometrica* Volume 42, Number 5, September 1974, pp. 947–966, reports estimates of conjectural variations for the Japanese flat glass industry; Gollop, Frank M. and Roberts, Mark J. "Firm Interdependence in Oligopolistic Markets," *Journal of Econometrics* Volume 10, Number 3, August 1979, pp. 313–331, report estimates of conjectural variations for the U.S. coffee roasting industry; Geroski, Paul A. "Some Reflections on the Theory and Application of Concentration Indices," *International Journal of Industrial Organization* Volume 1, Number 1, March 1983, pp. 79–94, reports estimates of conjectural variations for the U.S. cigarette industry.

Table 5-5 Conjectural Variations—
U.S. Steel Industry (Average,
1920–1940 and 1946–1972)

Firm	
U.S. Steel	0.004
Bethlehem	0.212
Republic	0.245
National	0.381
Jones & Laughlin (LTV)	0.559
Armco	0.730
Inland	0.385

Source: Rogers, Robert P. "The Measurement of Conjectural Variations in Oligopoly Industry," Federal Trade Commission Working Paper No. 102, November 1983, Table II (transformed into the specification used here). The estimated conjectural variations are the values that make the firms' output decisions consistent with profit maximization.

Expected Reactions—Firm Market Power

For duopoly we can work through the way conjectural variations change the Cournot market equilibrium by looking at the way conjectural variations move the reaction curves of the two firms. This exercise is contained in Problem 5-6. In the general case of N firms with unequal costs, the individual oligopolist's degree of market power becomes

$$\frac{P - c_i}{P} = \frac{\alpha_i + (1 - \alpha_i)s_i}{\epsilon_{QP}} \qquad (5.6)$$

where, as for Equation (5.3), s_i is firm i's market share.

If firm 1 expects a one-for-one matching of output restrictions, $\alpha_i = 1$ and Equation (5.6) reduces to the monopoly case. If $\alpha_i = 1$, firm i's degree of market power is the inverse of the price elasticity of demand. If all firms restrict output whenever one firm restricts output, they are in effect acting as one firm, even though they make their decisions independently.

If $\alpha_i = 0$, we are back to the basic Cournot model, and Equation (5.6) reduces to Equation (5.3). Market power at the firm level is directly proportional to market share and inversely proportional to the price elasticity of demand.

If α_i is negative, the reaction of other firms *reduces* firm i's market power. This is what we ought to expect: market power is the power to raise the price by holding output off the market, and a negative conjectural variation means that other firms act to neutralize attempts to keep output off the market.

The extent to which rivals' output changes can reduce firm i's market power depends critically on firm i's market share. From Eq. (5.6), firm i will have market power so long as

$$\alpha_i + (1 - \alpha_i)s_i > 0. \tag{5.7}$$

If $s_i = 0.9$, the left-hand side of Eq. (5.7) will be positive unless α_i falls below -9. If firm i's rivals are small in the market, they must be extremely aggressive to prevent firm i from exercising some control over the price: a 1 per cent reduction in firm i's output would have to be met by a 9 per cent increase in the output of rivals. It is precisely when rivals are small that they are unlikely to be able to expand output to such an extent that the market power of large firms would be eliminated.

Suppose, on the other hand, that firm i is small in the market: $s_i = 0.1$. Then if $\alpha_i = -\frac{1}{9}$, firm i will be unable to hold the price above its marginal cost. A firm with only 10 per cent of the market will be unable to exercise market power if a 1 per cent reduction in its output will be met with an increase of as little as a $\frac{1}{9}$th of 1 per cent in rivals' output.

Aggressive rivals will temper the ability of oligopolists to hold the price above the marginal cost. But rivals will have to be very aggressive to prevent large firms from exercising some control over the price.

Expected Reactions—Industry Performance

Suppose all of the oligopolists have the same conjectural variation—which can be thought of as an average for all firms in the industry. Then Equation (5.6) implies a relationship between market concentration and the industry-average degree of market power.

Multiply both sides of Equation (5.6) by s_i and add the resulting expressions for all firms to obtain

$$\frac{P - \bar{c}}{P} = \frac{\alpha + (1 - \alpha)H}{\epsilon_{QP}}. \tag{5.8}$$

The relationship between market concentration and the average degree of market power depends on the expected rivalry in the market, as summarized by the conjectural variation parameter α.

If $\alpha = 1$, the industry-average degree of market power is the inverse of the price elasticity of demand, as for monopoly. If all firms cooperate perfectly to match output restrictions, changes in concentration (H) have no effect on the degree of market power.

If firms match output changes, but imperfectly (α between 0 and 1), the market power index rises as the Herfindahl index rises. The same effect occurs if firms work at cross purposes, with rivals expanding their output if one firm restricts its output (α negative).

Recapitulation—Quantity-Setting Oligopoly

Models in the Cournot tradition examine quantity-setting firms. Such firms decide how much output to produce and let the market determine the price at which the output is sold.

The simplest model describes Cournot duopoly with equal-sized firms. Cournot's behavioral assumption, embodied in this model, is that each firm makes its decisions in the belief that the other will hold its output constant. The model predicts a market performance intermediate between competition and monopoly. As the number of firms increases, price and output approach the competitive outcome.

When the model is changed to allow for firms of unequal size, the predictions are that the market power of the firm will rise with its market share and the industry-average market power will rise with the Herfindahl index. This prediction is modified somewhat when we abandon the Cournot behavioral assumption and recognize that oligopolists will anticipate rivals' reactions as they make their own plans. Unless firms match their output changes perfectly, however, economic theory continues to predict an increase in market power as the firm's market share rises and an increase in industry-average market power as market concentration (as measured by the Herfindahl index) increases.

Case Study: Concentration, Rivalry, and Performance

Commercial jet manufacturing is a concentrated industry. Firms that manufacture commercial aircraft are included in Standard Industrial Classification industry 3721, which in 1982 had a four-firm seller concentration ratio of 64 percent. This industry, however, includes many firms that do not compete with the manufacturers of commercial aircraft (for example, firms that produce gliders), so the manufacture of commercial jets is even more concentrated than this figure would suggest. The Boeing Company is the dominant firm in this market. It competes with Lockheed, McDonnell Douglas, and the European firm Airbus Industrie in what is increasingly a world market.

Despite this concentration of sales among a few suppliers, rivalry is intense. The reason is the need to commit resources of immense value to airplane designs years before the planes can be brought to market; failure to achieve commercial success can spell disaster for even the largest supplier.

An example is the 1984 sale by McDonnell Douglas of 67 planes to American Airlines. The sales followed from a strategy implemented in 1982, when McDonnell decided that it[22]

> would push sales of Douglas's new MD-80 airliner, a 150-seat aircraft . . . , by leasing the plane to airlines. The deal could save the commercial airliner division, if the five-year leases led to sales. Or it could sink the division and saddle the parent company with big losses if the airlines returned the planes at the end of the lease period.
>
> Some analysts have argued that the risks . . . were not all that high, considering the company's only other option during the 1982 recession. That option was to close the huge factory here and leave the business of manufacturing airliners. . . .
>
> [McDonnell decided] to build 35 MD-80s at a cost of more than $500 million, even though the company had no buyers for those 35 planes. Once the decision was made to take the gamble . . . McDonnell Douglas selected two airlines, American and Trans World, and offered them a deal they couldn't refuse: An offer to lease the planes, returnable after five years with no questions asked, at low "loss leader" rates in the hope that it would create an appetite for the MD-80 among other airlines and keep its production line running. . . .
>
> After American leased 20 MD-80's on favorable terms and TWA leased 15, [McDonnell Douglas] began to bear down hard on efforts to pull off a pump-priming big sale of the aircraft. . . .
>
> . . . indications are that Douglas made it so attractive to American that its own profits on the sale will be relatively small. . . . McDonnell Douglas plainly is hoping that the production experience will generate higher profits from future sales.

Discussion: The Cournot model is applicable to this industry, in which firms set production schedules far in advance of putting goods on the market. Sales are so concentrated that producers must recognize their mutual interdependence. But the consequences of missing out on a single big sale are so great—the survival of the enterprise—that firms must engage in intense rivalry. The result is that performance is much closer to the competitive mark than examination of concentration ratios or Herfindahl indices alone would suggest.

[22]Lindsey, Robert. "A New Lift for McDonnell Douglas," *New York Times*, March 18, 1984, Section 3, p. 1.

Two further lessons can be drawn from this example. First, it is difficult for firms to collude in markets in which sales are infrequent and large; we will discuss this topic in Chapter 6.

Second, the final sentence of the preceding extract refers to the hope "that the production experience will generate higher profits from future sales." This sort of learning by doing—lower cost per unit because of production experience—is one reason firms in a market can have a cost advantage over potential entrants. Such cost differentials, even though they reflect efficiency and save scarce resources, allow limit price behavior by firms in the market.

Price-Setting Oligopoly

Bertrand,[23] in a critical review of Cournot's work, sketched a model of oligopoly in which firms set prices rather than quantities. Models in the Cournot tradition highlight market concentration and firms' market shares as determinants of market performance. In contrast, models in the Bertrand tradition emphasize product differentiation.

Price-Setting Oligopoly—Homogeneous Product

The basic price-setting model, however, follows the quantity-setting model and assumes that the product is standardized. In such a market, the product of one producer is a perfect substitute for the product of any other producer.

Begin with duopoly, and make the same kind of behavioral assumption as in the quantity-setting model. Each firm assumes that the other will hold its price constant as it makes its own pricing decisions.[24] We use Figure 5-8 to work out the difference that this seemingly minor change—having firms set prices instead of quantities—makes in market performance.

Firm 1 observes P_2 and believes it will be maintained. Given this belief, and the fact that the product is absolutely standardized, what does the demand curve look like from firm 1's point of view?

Since the product is standardized, if firm 1 charges a price even slightly higher than that of firm 2, the quantity demanded from firm 1 will be zero. All customers will patronize firm 2, the lower-priced firm. On the other hand, if

---

[23]Bertrand, J. Book review, *Journal des Savants*, Volume 67 1883, pp. 499–508; see also Edgeworth, F. Y. "The Pure Theory of Monopoly," in *Papers Relating to Political Economy*. London: Royal Econometric Society, 1925, pp. 111–142.

[24]For an analysis and estimation of price conjectural variations, see Liang, J. Nellie. "An Empirical Conjectural Variation Model of Oligopoly," Working Paper No. 151, Bureau of Economics, Federal Trade Commission, Washington, D.C., February 1987.

firm 1 sets a price even slightly lower than that of firm 2, firm 1 will capture the entire market. As far as firm 1 is concerned, its demand curve is the market demand curve for prices less than P_2 and zero—the vertical axis—for prices above P_2.[25]

In the usual case, firm 1's profit-maximizing strategy would be to pick an output that makes its marginal revenue equal to its marginal cost. In Figure 5-8, the price (p) at which this output (q) sells is above P_2, and all sales go to the rival firm. In these circumstances, the best firm 1 can do is to set a price slightly below P_2. If this is done, firm 1's price will still be above its marginal cost. Firm 1 will make a profit on every unit it sells. Because the product is standardized, it will also capture the entire market. No one will buy from firm 2 if P_2 is slightly greater than P_1.[26]

Whatever price firm 2 charges, it will be optimal for firm 1 to undercut, and capture the entire market, as long as P_1 remains above its marginal cost. But this is only firm 1's side of the story. The same argument shows that firm 2's optimal strategy will be to undercut firm 1's price slightly and capture the entire market.

There is only one equilibrium at which this undercutting stops. It occurs when the price equals marginal cost. Neither firm will reduce price below marginal cost, since that would mean a loss on every unit sold.

When products are standardized, equilibrium in the Bertrand model—price-setting oligopoly—has all the properties of competitive equilibrium. The apparently modest respecification—having firms pick prices instead of quantities—of oligopoly behavior completely reverses the predictions of the quantity-setting model.

In this most basic version of the price-setting model, a firm's market share has no impact on its market power. Market concentration has no impact on industry average market power. Regardless of firm size or market concentration, in equilibrium the price-setting market yields the same performance as a competitive market.

This result is implausible, and it behooves us to understand upon what it depends. It is *not* implausible to investigate markets in which firms set prices and sell whatever is demanded at those prices. Insurance is sold in one such market. Airlines are another example; so, for that matter, are universities.

---

[25]The way the two firms divide up the market if they charge the same price is not clear. This ambiguity is another consequence of the unreasonable assumption that products are absolutely standardized. Since that assumption is to be abandoned, there seems no need to dwell on this topic.

[26]Technically, firm 1's demand curve is discontinuous at P_2. This induces a discontinuity in firm 1's marginal revenue curve, which can be thought of as a horizontal line at (or just below) P_2 running from the vertical axis to the market demand curve, then jumping discontinuously down to the market marginal revenue curve. The usual profit-maximizing condition that the firm pick an output that makes its marginal revenue equal to its marginal cost is then replaced by the condition that the firm pick an output that places its marginal cost between the two values of marginal revenue at the point of discontinuity. This occurs where P_1 is slightly less than P_2 at the market demand curve.

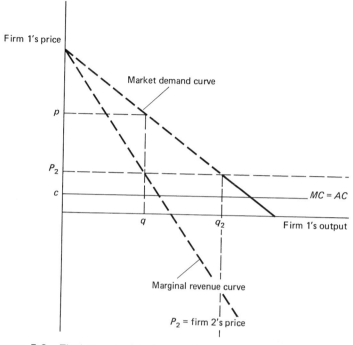

Figure 5-8 Firm 1's price decision, price-setting model, standardized product.

The implausible assumption in the basic Bertrand model is not the assumption that firms set prices. The implausible assumption—and the one that drives the results—is the assumption that products are completely standardized.

The products of different producers are almost always differentiated to some extent. Even if products are physically identical—which is rare—they are differentiated by the location of the distributor, by the terms of credit offered with the sale, by the service offered after the sale, and so on. The day when one could say—with Henry Ford—''Any customer can have a car painted any color that he wants, so long as it is black'' are long gone.

Price-Setting Oligopoly—Differentiated Products

How does the standardization assumption affect the analysis of the price-setting model? Previously, we assumed that if firm 1 undercut firm 2's price even slightly, the entire market would shift to firm 1. It is this implication of product standardization that is implausible. If firm 1 cuts its price, we expect it to attract some customers from firm 2, but never all of them. I will not buy limburger if it happens to cost $0.25 less per pound than caraway gouda. Others might. Without wishing to comment on the utility functions of such individuals,

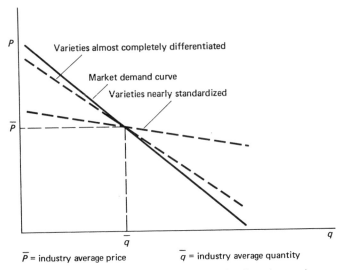

Figure 5-9 Product differentiation and the firm demand curve.

the point to be drawn is that the entire market will not move from one supplier to another for relatively small price differentials.

The simplest way to describe this imperfect substitutability[27] is to suppose that if a firm raises its price above that of its rivals, it loses *some* sales, but not *all* sales.

Suppose that each firm operates on a demand curve that is specific to the variety of the product it produces. If a firm raises its price above the industry average, it loses sales to rivals. The rate at which sales will be lost as the price rises above the industry average depends on the extent to which products are differentiated.

As shown in Figure 5-9, if products are almost completely standardized, each firm will operate on a demand curve that is very elastic around the industry average price and quantity $(\bar{q}, \bar{P})$. Even a slight increase in $\bar{P}_1$ above $\bar{P}$ will cause firm 1 to lose sales rapidly to rivals. But because there is some product differentiation, firm 1's sales will not drop to zero if firm 1 raises its price. On the other hand, even a slight reduction in price below $\bar{P}$ will cause firm 1 to gain sales rapidly from rivals.

At the other extreme, if different varieties of the product are almost completely differentiated, each variety has a demand curve very much like the

[27]Due to Shubik, M. *Market Structure and Behavior.* Cambridge, Mass.: Harvard University Press, 1980. The model illustrated here (and in Problem 5-8) has each product inheriting a market as large as the original market if the products are completely differentiated. This specification is consistent with Spence's quantity-setting model of product differentiation ("Product Differentiation and Welfare," *American Economic Review* Volume 6, Number 2, May 1976, pp. 407–414). An alternative specification would have oligopolists dividing a market of fixed size as product differentiation increases.

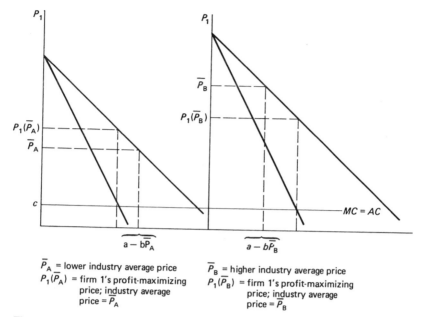

$\overline{P}_A$ = lower industry average price
$P_1(\overline{P}_A)$ = firm 1's profit-maximizing
price; industry average
price = $\overline{P}_A$

$\overline{P}_B$ = higher industry average price
$P_1(\overline{P}_B)$ = firm 1's profit-maximizing
price; industry average
price = $\overline{P}_B$

Figure 5-10 Firm 1's pricing decision, price-setting oligopoly, differentiated products.

market demand curve. If firm 1 raises its price above the industry average, it loses relatively few customers to other firms. When products are highly differentiated, each firm is almost a monopolist of its own variety.

Given firm 1's demand curve, there is nothing unusual about firm 1's price decision. As shown in Figure 5-10, firm 1's profit-maximizing price, $\overline{P}_1(\overline{P})$, is chosen so that its marginal cost equals its marginal revenue.

Firm 1's profit-maximizing price will depend on the average price charged in the market, P. The higher the industry average price, the higher firm 1's profit-maximizing price.

In duopoly, this is equivalent to saying that firm 1's profit-maximizing price will depend on the price charged by firm 2. The higher is P_2, the higher will be the industry average price and the more will consumers turn to firm 1. The higher is P_2, the higher the price firm 1 will be able to set without causing customers to switch to firm 2.

By computing firm 1's profit-maximizing price for different values of P_2, we obtain firm 1's price reaction curve. In a model of price-setting duopoly, firm 1's reaction curve shows the profit-maximizing price charged by firm 1 for each price charged by firm 2. Because firm 1's profit-maximizing price rises as P_2 rises, firm 1's price reaction curve slopes upward (in contrast to the quantity reaction curves of the previous section, which sloped downward).

By going through a similar profit-maximization process, we obtain firm 2's

123

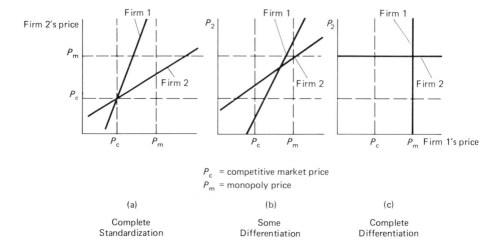

P_c = competitive market price
P_m = monopoly price

(a)
Complete
Standardization

(b)
Some
Differentiation

(c)
Complete
Differentiation

Figure 5-11   Reaction curves, price-setting duopoly with product differentiation.

price reaction curve, which shows the profit-maximizing price of firm 2, given the price charged by firm 1. The two price reaction curves are shown, for different degrees of differentiation, in Figure 5-11.

As in the quantity-setting model, market equilibrium occurs at the intersection of the two reaction curves. Each firm makes its plans to maximize its profit in the belief that the other firm will charge a certain price. At the intersection of the reaction curves, each firm will find its beliefs confirmed.

The location of the reaction curves depends on the extent of product differentiation, which in turn means that the location of the intersection of the reaction curves—and equilibrium prices—depends on the extent of product differentiation. At one extreme (Figure 5-11a), the products of the two firms are completely standardized. Here we have the result of the basic Bertrand model. In equilibrium, at the intersection of the two reactive curves, each firm charges the competitive price.

As differentiation increases (Figure 5-11b), firm 1 is able to charge a price above the competitive level for any price set by firm 2. The price charged by each firm becomes less sensitive to the price charged by the other, and the reaction curves move away from the origin. Firm 1's reaction curve becomes steeper, while firm 2's becomes flatter. The equilibrium prices increase from the competitive level.

At the other extreme (Figure 5-11c), products are completely differentiated. Each firm will charge the monopoly price, no matter what price is charged by the other firm. With complete differentiation, each firm is a monopolist of its own product.

Recapitulation—Price-Setting Oligopoly

When firms set their prices and sell whatever is demanded at those prices, the critical factor that determines market performance is the extent of product differentiation.

If there are only a few firms, but they all sell a nearly standardized product, market performance will approach the competitive ideal. In such a market, small price changes will induce a large number of customers to switch suppliers, and price competition will force the price to approach marginal cost.

If products are highly differentiated, each firm will be able to exercise near-monopoly market power over its own brand. If customers have strong preferences for specific brands, the force of price competition will be relatively weak, and the equilibrium price will be near the monopoly level.

Public Policy Toward Oligopoly—Recognition of Interdependence

Section 2 of the Sherman Act forbids not only monopolization but also attempts and conspiracies to monopolize. There is a group of antitrust cases in which the courts seemed to come close to applying these prohibitions to non-collusive oligopoly behavior, only to retreat.

Interstate Circuit[28]

Interstate Circuit and an affiliated firm managed over 100 movie theaters in Texas and New Mexico. Interstate Circuit had a dominant market position in the markets in which it operated. In 1934, Interstate's manager sent a letter to eight major distributors of motion pictures. The address block of the letter made it clear that the same letter was being sent to all eight distributors. The manager asked the distributors to agree to two proposals.

The first proposal was that if the Interstate theaters took a film on its first release to the public (a so-called first-run film), there would be a minimum admission price on any showings of the film in later releases. The second proposal was that if Interstate took a first-run film for its theaters, that film would not be shown, in later releases, as part of a double feature.

The effect of both of these proposals is to raise the price, directly or indirectly, at second-run theaters. By preventing these theaters from showing films at a low price or from showing two for the price of one, these proposals made it harder for second-run theaters to compete with first-run theaters. This reduction in competition directly benefited the first-run theaters, which faced less pressure to compete in terms of price. It indirectly benefited the motion picture distributors, who could use their cooperation to bargain for a share of the higher price at the first-run theaters. By cooperating, the vertically related firms—

---

[28]*Interstate Circuit, Inc. et al. v. United States,* 306 U.S. 208 (1938).

producers and exhibitors—were able to reinforce their ability to hold the price above marginal cost.[29] After some negotiations, the distributors agreed to the demands contained in Interstate's letter.

The trial court found evidence of conspiracy in the fact that each distributor knew that the same demands had been made of the others. In the trial court, this evidence was sufficient to sustain a finding that the distributors were guilty of a conspiracy in restraint of trade. The distributors appealed to the Supreme Court, which was not sympathetic:[30]

> While the District Court's finding of an agreement of the distributors among themselves is supported by the evidence, we think that in the circumstances of this case such *agreement for the imposition of the restrictions* upon subsequent-run exhibitors *was not a prerequisite to an unlawful conspiracy.* It was enough that, knowing that concerted action was contemplated and invited, the distributors gave their adherence to the scheme and participated in it. Each distributor was advised that the others were asked to participate; each knew that cooperation was essential to the successful operation of the plan. They knew that the plan, if carried out, would result in a restraint of commerce, which . . . was unreasonable within the meaning of the Sherman Act. . . . (emphasis added).

On this interpretation, it is not necessary for courts to find evidence of agreement among firms in order to conclude that the firms had conspired within the meaning of the Sherman Act. A recognition of interdependence seems to be enough to prove a violation. If firms tacitly cooperate in a way that has the effect of exercising market power, that is considered conspiracy within the meaning of the Sherman Act.

American Tobacco[31]

The original American Tobacco Company was broken up as a result of an antitrust case that elaborated the rules laid down by the Supreme Court in the *Standard Oil* case.[32] Twenty-five years later, the survivor companies appealed to the Supreme Court to reverse their conviction, in yet another landmark antitrust case, of conspiracy to monopolize.[33]

The basis of the appeal was the instructions that the trial court judge had given the jury on the meaning of Section 2 of the Sherman Act. Those instructions in part, were as follows:

[29]The notion that vertically related firms—manufacturers and distributors—can cooperate to exercise market power is an important and controverisal one, to which we return in Chapter 17.

[30]*Interstate Circuit, Inc. et al. v. United States,* 306 U.S. 208 (1938), at 226–227.

[31]*American Tobacco Co. et al. v. United States,* 328 U.S. 781 (1946).

[32]*United States v. American Tobacco Company,* 221 U.S. 106 (1911).

[33]They were also convicted of conspiracy in restraint of trade, monopolization, and an attempt to monopolize; it is the conspiracy to monopolize charge that is of most interest here.

> Now, the term *monopolize* as used in Section 2 of the Sherman act . . . means the joint acquisition or maintenance by the members of the conspiracy . . . of the *power to control and dominate interstate trade and commerce in a commodity to such an extent that they are able, as a group, to exclude actual or potential competitors from the field, accompanied with the intention and purpose to exercise such power* . . . *an indispensable ingredient of each of the offenses charged* . . . *is a combination or conspiracy* (emphasis added by the Supreme Court).

The tobacco companies asked the Supreme Court to rule that these instructions were incorrect.

In this case, the existence of a conspiracy was inferred from a pattern of parallel conduct on the part of the tobacco companies. The major tobacco companies advertised heavily (advertising that might be expected to create the kind of product differentiation analyzed in the previous section).

Tobacco company agents at tobacco leaf auctions bid in ways that had the effect of controlling the price of this essential ingredient in the manufacture of cigarettes. The major companies purchased the lower-grade tobacco leaf used by fringe firms, even though they did not use the lower-grade leaf themselves.[34] In addition, the major tobacco companies engaged in parallel pricing behavior:[35]

> On June 23, 1931, Reynolds, without previous notification or warning to the trade or public, raised the list price of Camel cigarettes, constituting its leading cigarette brand, from $6.40 to $6.85 a thousand. On the same day, American increased the list price for Lucky Strike cigarettes, its leading brand, and Liggett the price for Chesterfield cigarettes, its leading brand, to the identical price of $6.85 a thousand.

Despite this pattern of similar behavior, there was no evidence of formal agreement by the tobacco companies. But the Supreme Court did not think such evidence essential to the finding of the lower court:[36]

> It is not the form of the combination or the particular means used but the result to be achieved that the statute condemns. . . . No formal agreement is necessary to constitute an unlawful conspiracy. Often crimes are a matter of inference deduced from the acts of the person accused and done in pursuance of a criminal purpose. . . . The essential combination or conspiracy in violation of the Sherman Act may be found in a course of dealing or other circumstances as well as in an exchange of words.

---

[34]This had the effect of raising the price, to fringe firms, of an essential input. This is an example of strategic behavior, discussed in Chapter 4, employed by a dominant group to raise entry/expansion costs for small rivals.

[35]*American Tobacco Co. et al. v. United States,* 328 U.S. 781 (1946), at 805.

[36]*American Tobacco Co. et al. v. United States,* 328 U.S. 781 (1946), at 809–810.

The result condemned as a conspiracy to monopolize is the joint exercise of market power. As in the *Interstate Circuit* case, the Supreme Court seemed to say that the existence of a conspiracy can be inferred from acts performed in the exercise of market power. If this is the law, it would seem that Section 2 of the Sherman Act can be applied to oligopolies in which firms jointly, but independently, exercise market power.

Theatre Enterprises[37]

The final case we consider as we trace the application of the antitrust laws to consciously parallel behavior by oligopolists also involves the motion picture industry. It stems, however, from a private action under the Sherman Act.

Theatre Enterprises managed the Crest Theatre, which was located in a shopping center in suburban Baltimore. It solicited first-run films from major film distributors, which independently refused the request.

Theatre Enterprises sued the film distributors, alleging a conspiracy in restraint of trade in violation of the Sherman Act. The company did not come to court with evidence of an agreement, but relied on the parallel behavior of the distributors to prove a conspiracy. The film distributors responded that they had independently exercised their best business judgment. Downtown theaters were more accessible than the Crest, they argued, and would provide a better forum for film exhibition. A jury found against Theatre Enterprises, which appealed to the Supreme Court.

The Court's decision marked a retreat from the frontier reached in *Interstate Circuit* and *American Tobacco:*[38]

> The crucial question is whether [the film distributors'] conduct . . . stemmed from independent decision or from an agreement, tacit or express. To be sure, business behavior is admissible circumstantial evidence from which the fact finder may infer agreement. . . . But this Court has never held that proof of parallel business behavior conclusively establishes agreement or, phrased differently, that such behavior itself constitutes a Sherman Act offense . . . "conscious parallelism" has not yet read conspiracy out of the Sherman Act entirely.

Law and Economics of Parallel Behavior

Building on this decision, later rulings have established that if oligopolists are to be convicted of conspiracy in violation of the Sherman Act, there must be evidence from which the existence of an agreement can be inferred. The agreement need not be explicit; it need not be written down or manifested through meetings. But it must exist.

[37]*Theatre Enterprises, Inc. v. Paramount Film Distributing Corp. et al.*, 346 U.S. 537 (1953).

[38]*Theatre Enterprises, Inc. v. Paramount Film Distributing Corp et al.*, 346 U.S. 537, at 540–541.

This interpretation of the "conspiracy to monopolize" charge under Section 2 of the Sherman Act is entirely consistent with the (dare we say it?: parallel) development of the Sherman Act treatment of monopolization. As we saw in Chapter 4, Section 2 of the Sherman Act does not condemn a dominant firm for monopolization unless it has acquired or maintained its dominant position through predatory or exclusionary behavior.

Single-firm exercise of market power is not condemned under the Sherman Act unless it is accompanied by anticompetitive strategic behavior. Joint exercise of market power is not condemned unless it is accompanied by an agreement. Independent behavior is not condemned by the antitrust laws even if it results in the exercise of market power.

Section 2's policy with respect to dominant firms and to parallel but independent action by nondominant firms demonstrates a concern for competition as a regulatory process. If a dominant firm exercises market power but does nothing to exclude equally efficient rivals, its market power will eventually be eroded by entry. If a small number of firms independently restrict output,[39] their market power will eventually be eroded by the entry of independent rivals.

Although the antitrust laws forbid anticompetitive behavior, they do not compel rivalous behavior. They rely on market forces to produce such behavior. In the words of Mr. Justice Holmes,[40] in *Swift and Co. v. United States,* "The defendants cannot be ordered to compete, but they properly can be forbidden to give directions or make arrangements not to compete."

Summary

Models of oligopoly behavior predict that oligopolists, acting independently, will be able to exercise market power under some circumstances.

Oligopolists will be better able to exercise market power if sales are concentrated in the hands of a few firms and if those firms are not too rivalous, but instead match restrictions of output.

Oligopolists will be better able to exercise market power when products are differentiated, so that a firm can raise its price without losing the bulk of its sales to rivals.

Antitrust laws do not effectively control truly independent exercise of market power. Courts are willing to infer the existence of a conspiracy, but if the facts show that firms have acted independently, the fact that they exercise market power, in and of itself, does not constitute a violation of the antitrust laws. The premise of the antitrust laws is that market forces will erode market power that is not supported by joint or independent action to exclude rivals.

[39]If a small number of firms make decisions using conjectural variations close to 1.

[40]*Swift and Co. v. United States,* 196 U.S. 375 (1905).

Problems

5-1 The following table gives world auto sales, by firm, for 1984 (excluding sales of Lada in the USSR):

General Motors	5,323,765	BMW	412,447
Ford	3,563,212	Audi	344,733
Toyota	2,413,133	SEAT	255,324
Nissan	1,846,407	Subaru	242,680
Volkswagen	1,507,723	FASA Renault	214,780
Renault	1,429,138	Alfa Romeo	200,103
Peugeot SA	1,284,151	American Motors	192,196
Chrysler	1,247,820	Volvo	191,400
Fiat Group	1,208,065	Suzuki	164,058
Honda	982,379	Diahatsu	162,405
Opel	776,486	Vauxhall	117,114
Mazda	764,309	Citroen Hispana	98,506
Mitsubishi	547,838	Talbot/Dodge	95,122
Daimler-Benz	469,385	Isuzu	88,536
British Leland	416,666	Saab	73,151

Source: 1985 Ward's Automotive Yearbook.

a. Compute the market share of each firm.
b. Compute the 4-, 8-, and 20-firm concentration ratios.
c. Compute the 1984 Herfindahl index for the world auto market. How many firms of equal size would produce the same Herfindahl index?
d. How would the Herfindahl index and the numbers equivalent change if you computed them using only sales figures for firms with as much as 1 per cent of world sales? Five percent?

5-2 (Cournot duopoly) A market is supplied by two firms. The equation of the demand curve is

$$P = a - bQ = a - b(q_1 + q_2),$$

where q_1 is the output of firm 1 and q_2 is the output of firm 2. The firms have identical cost functions,

$$C(q_i) = f + cq_i, \quad i = 1, 2,$$

where f is the fixed cost and c is the marginal (and average variable) cost per unit.
a. What is the equation of the residual demand curve for firm 1? Firm 2?
b. Use the fact that for a linear demand curve the residual marginal revenue curve has the same intercept as the residual demand curve and exactly twice the slope to derive the equation of the residual marginal revenue curve for each firm.
c. Set marginal revenue equal to marginal cost for each firm in order to obtain the equations of the reaction curves.

d. Graph the reaction curves. Solve the equations and find the equilibrium output of each firm. What is the price in equilibrium?

5-3 For the demand curve of Problem 5-2, find the equilibrium output and price if the cost function for firm i is

$$C(q_i) = c_i q_i, \qquad i = 1,2.$$

5-4 For the demand curve and cost function of Problem 5-2, find the equilibrium output and price if there are N firms ($Q = q_1 + q_2 + \cdots q_N$) instead of two firms. (*Hint:* derive the reaction curve for firm 1; then use the fact that in equilibrium, each firm will produce the same output, since all firms are identical.)

5-5 Continuing Problem 5-4, suppose that the marginal cost of firm i is c_i. Show that firm 1's reaction curve can be written

$$P = c_1 + bq_1,$$

where (as in Problem 4-2) $-b$ is the slope of the demand curve. From this, write firm 1's degree of market power as

$$\frac{P - c_1}{P} = \frac{bq_1}{P} = \left(\frac{bQ}{P}\right)\left(\frac{q_1}{Q}\right).$$

Use the fact that the price-elasticity of demand is P/bQ to obtain Eq. (5-3).

5-6 (Cournot duopoly with conjectural variations) For the demand curve of Problem 5-2, if firm 1 and firm 2 have the same conjectural variations, show that the marginal revenue curves are

$$MR_1 = a - (1 + \alpha)bq_2 - 2bq_1$$
$$MR_2 = a - (1 + \alpha)bq_1 - 2bq_2.$$

a. Find the reaction curves for the two firms.
b. Graph the reaction curves for the special cases $\alpha = -1, 0$, and $+1$, respectively.
c. Find equilibrium output and price for each value of α; compare with competition, with Problem 5-2, and with monopoly.

5-7 In the same way that Problem 5-4 generalizes Problem 5-2 to the case of N firms, generalize Problem 5-6 to the case of N firms.

5-8 (Price-setting duopoly with product differentiation) There are two firms in a market. Each has a constant marginal and average cost c per unit. Products are differentiated, so each firm has its own demand curve:

$$q_i = a - p - \left(\frac{1}{\gamma}\right)(p_i - \bar{p}),$$

where $\bar{p}$ is the average price (i.e., $\bar{p} = (\tfrac{1}{2})(p_1 + p_2)$ and γ is a parameter that measures the extent of product differentiation. If the products are perfect substitutes, $\gamma = 0$; if the products are completely differentiated, $\gamma = \infty$. Make a version of the Cournot assumption for a price-setting model: each firm assumes that the other will hold the price constant.

a. Set firm 1's marginal revenue $p_1 + q_1(\Delta p_1 / \Delta q_1)$ equal to marginal cost to obtain firm 1's reaction curve:

$$p_1 - c = \left(\frac{1}{2 + (\frac{1}{\gamma})}\right)(a - c) + \frac{1}{2}\frac{1}{1 + 2\gamma}(p_2 - c).$$

Similarly, obtain firm 2's reaction curve.

b. Graph the reaction curves. How do they shift position as γ changes from 0 to ∞?

c. Obtain the equilibrium price by solving the equations of the reaction curves:

$$p_e = c + \left(\frac{1}{2 + \frac{1}{2\gamma}}\right)(a - c).$$

How does the equilibrium price change as γ changes from 0 to ∞?

Paper Topics

5-1 a. Read Joskow, P. L. "Cartels, Competition and Regulation in the Property-Liability Insurance Industry," *Bell Journal of Economics* Volume 4, Number 2, Autumn 1973, pp. 375–427.

b. Consult *Best's Executive Data Service.* Identify the firms that market automobile insurance in your state. Compute a Herfindahl index for this market. How is such insurance regulated in your state? Find out what you can about the profitability of the firms that sell automobile insurance in your state. How does investment income affect automobile insurance rates? Relate performance in this market to the model of price-setting oligopoly discussed in the text.

5-2 Consult the index to the *New York Times* and the *Wall Street Journal* from 1983 to the present, and write a paper analyzing structure, conduct, and performance in the manufacture of jet engines. What is the role of the Pentagon in this market?

5-3 What was the "breakfast cereal" case? What role did product differentiation play in the economic theory of the case? How did this case seek to extend public policy toward the exercise of market power by oligopolists?

5-4 Analyze the following cases, and trace the application of the antitrust laws to consciously parallel behavior:

a. *United States v. Chas. Pfizer & Co., Inc.,* 367 F. Supp. 91 (S.D.N.Y. 1973).

b. *du Pont v. Federal Trade Commission; Ethyl Corp. v. Federal Trade Commission,* 729 F.2d 128 (1984).

6

Oligopoly—Collusion

All for one, one for all, that is our motto, is it not?

d'Artagnan to Athos, Porthos, and Aramis,
The Three Musketeers

Introduction

In this chapter, as in the previous one, our topic is oligopoly—the market with few enough suppliers so that there is recognition of mutual interdependence. Here we consider the economics of explicit cooperation or collusion among oligopolists.

We know from Chapter 5 that even when oligopolists independently pursue their own self-interest, they are usually able to exercise some control over price. Exactly how much control they have depends on market concentration, on the degree of rivalry,[1] and on product differentiation.

Independent oligopolists will not ordinarily succeed in maximizing their joint profit: their combined earnings will fall short of the profit a monopolist would take. It follows that oligopolists will usually be able to increase their joint profit by explicitly coordinating their actions and acting as if they were a single monopolist or dominant firm.

A single firm has the problem of deciding what is in its own best interest. As Chapter 4 shows, this problem is far from trivial. It involves not only finding the profit-maximizing price but also deciding how to confront the possibility of entry. But a single firm at least knows that it will be able to carry out whatever decisions it reaches.

Life is less simple for colluding oligopolists. They must first reach *agreement* on the profit-maximizing strategy. All of the strategic alternatives discussed in Chapter 4 (vertical integration, branding, excess capacity, exclusionary behavior) are available. In addition, oligopolists often serve different product and geographic submarkets, and employ different production and distribution tech-

---

[1]The degree of rivalry can be described in terms of conjectural variations.

niques. For this reason, different members of a cartel can be expected to have different views about the best strategy for the group. Some common ground will have to be found.

Assuming agreement is reached, oligopolists will have to secure *adherence* to the agreement. A successful cartel, by raising price, creates an incentive for entry; we know this from Chapter 4. As we will see in this chapter, a successful cartel also creates an incentive for individual members to cheat and produce more than their allotment. If one firm cheats, its profit goes up. If all firms cheat, the cartel breaks down and loses control of the market.

Agreement and *adherence* are the two problems that are unique to collusive oligopoly, and it is on these problems that we focus in this chapter. Entry is another major problem, but the issues it raises for oligopoly are much the same as those discussed in Chapter 4.

The Organization of Petroleum Exporting Countries (OPEC) successfully—for a time—forged a cartel that controlled the world market for a vital natural resource. Because the nation-firms that form OPEC are sovereign states, they are not subject to national antitrust laws. As such, OPEC is a choice example of cartel dynamics in the laissez-faire economy that existed before the development of antitrust laws. We use OPEC and the world oil market to illustrate the way market structure and firm conduct affect collusion.[2]

In the first section of this chapter, we examine the implications of market structure and firm conduct for the likelihood that oligopolists will reach a collusive agreement. In the following section, we analyze adherence. The analysis is primarily structural, since the decision to adhere to or break an agreement is itself a form of conduct. Finally, we examine public policy toward collusion.

Agreement

Structure and Agreement

Market Concentration

Economists were long put off by the implausibility of the behavioral assumption built into the basic Cournot and Bertrand models. This assumption, you will recall, is that oligopolists, recognizing their mutual interdependence, nonetheless act on the belief that rivals will not react to changes in output (Cournot) or price (Bertrand).

The device of conjectural variations is one way to generalize this restrictive assumption. But in a simpler, less formal, and no doubt happier age, one of the great students of industrial economics offered a model of oligopoly behavior

---

[2]This discussion draws on Measday, Walter S. and Martin, Stephen. "The Petroleum Industry," in Walter Adams, editor, *The Structure of American Industry,* 7th edition. New York: The Macmillan Co., 1986, pp. 38–73.

that was a direct reaction to the basic Cournot model. Chamberlin[3] based his analysis of oligopoly on the presumption that oligopolists would not behave stupidly. He argued that once concentration passed a critical level, oligopolists would recognize their mutual interdependence and put only the monopoly output on the market. This would not require overt collusion but simply a recognition of the direct (on price) and indirect (on the behavior of rivals) consequences of the firm's decisions.

Chamberlin therefore expected to find the monopoly price in oligopoly markets where concentration exceeded some critical level:[4] "the break towards purely competitive levels comes when the number of sellers is so large that each is led to neglect his influence upon the price." Chamberlin's model of oligopoly predicts a discontinuous, one-time jump in profitability as concentration rises past the critical level.

This theory of recognition of interdependence can be rephrased in terms of the conjectural variations model of Chapter 5. The recognition of interdependence theory of oligopoly basically predicts that when concentration exceeds some critical level, the conjectural variation parameter α jumps from -1 to $+1$. Below the critical concentration level, market performance is competitive. Above the critical concentration level, the market performs as a monopoly.

How high is the critical level of concentration? The theory makes no universal prediction, and the recognition of interdependence will differ from industry to industry, depending on factors we will discuss: product differentiation, cost differences, and others. Early empirical tests of the Chamberlin model suggested that recognition of interdependence takes place when the largest eight firms in the market have 70 per cent or more of market sales. Recent studies suggest that the critical concentration ratio may be much lower and may involve many fewer firms. One study finds that industry performance moves from competition toward monopoly when the largest two firms reach a combined market share of 25 to 35 per cent.[5]

Product Differentiation

When a product is differentiated, members of a cartel must fix a whole schedule of relative prices, not just a single price. The need to determine relative prices makes the task of securing an agreement all the more difficult. The difficulty is even greater if the demand for different varieties changes over time. Changes in demand alter profit-maximizing relative prices. Every time relative prices must be adjusted, the whole bargaining process begins anew.

[3]Chamberlin, Edward H. *The Theory of Monopolistic Competition.* Cambridge, Mass.: Harvard University Press, 1933. See especially chapter 3.

[4]Op. cit., p. 48.

[5]Kwoka, John E., Jr. "The Effect of Market Share Distribution on Market Performance," *Review of Economics and Statistics* Volume 61, Number 1, February 1979, pp. 101–109.

The world oil market provides an example. Oil is not homogeneous. Some OPEC members produce mainly light (low specific gravity), low-sulfur oil. Others produce heavy (high specific gravity), high-sulfur oil. High-sulfur oil is more expensive to refine than low-sulfur oil, and it yields a less valuable mix of refined products. All else equal, light, low-sulfur oil is more attractive to refiners than heavy, high-sulfur oil.

In addition, at the time of the first oil crisis (1973), most U.S. refineries were designed to handle low-sulfur oil. Low-sulfur oil causes less wear and tear on a refinery than high-sulfur oil, and at the time the refineries were designed, there was no shortage of low-sulfur oil.

For these reasons, "sweet" (low-sulfur) light oil traditionally sold at a higher price on world markets than "sour" (high-sulfur) oil. OPEC built such price differentials into its price schedules when it first took control of the world oil market.

But OPEC soon discovered that the market presents a moving target. OPEC had created an artificial shortage in the supply of oil, and oil refiners wanted to have access to as wide a range of supplies as possible. After OPEC forced an increase in the price of oil, refineries throughout the industrialized world were upgraded, at considerable expense, so that they could refine high-sulfur as well as low-sulfur oil.

The result was a gradual increase in the demand for heavy oil and a reduction in the premium that light oil could command on world markets. These changes in relative demand put continuing pressure on OPEC to reduce the official price spread between the two varieties of oil. OPEC members who produced light, low-sulfur oil were reluctant to give up their traditional price advantage. Demands to revise price differentials were a source of disagreement among OPEC oil ministers that continued throughout the OPEC era.

Cost Differences

Cost differences make it difficult for a cartel to secure an agreement that will maximize joint profit. Joint-profit maximization requires that output be distributed among firms so that marginal cost is the same for all firms. If marginal cost is not the same for all firms, the cartel can always increase its joint profit by shifting output away from higher marginal cost producers toward lower marginal cost producers.

An implication of the fact that joint profit maximization requires marginal cost to be the same for all cartel members is illustrated, for a duopolists' cartel, in Figure 6-1. Because marginal cost rises more rapidly, as output increases, for the high-cost firm than for the low-cost firm, joint-profit maximization requires the high-cost firm to accept a lower output, and therefore a lower market share, than the low-cost firm.

At the very least, this requirement complicates the life of the cartel: the low-cost firm will have to make some concession to the high-cost firm in order to secure its cooperation. But the high-cost firm may be unwilling to accept a

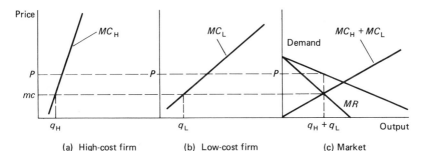

(a) High-cost firm   (b) Low-cost firm   (c) Market

Notes: at the market level, the cartel maximizes its joint profit by picking the cartel output that makes marginal cost equal to marginal revenue. Cartel output is allocated among the two members so that the marginal cost is the same for each firm. The high-cost firm receives the lower output quota.

Figure 6-1   Joint-profit maximization with cost differences.

lower market share on *any* terms. The high-cost firm may well judge that over the long run its bargaining power within the cartel will be tied to its market share. If this is the case, accepting a lower market share to maximize joint profit will amount to cutting its own throat within the cartel.[6]

The world oil market is plagued by substantial cost differentials. The nation-firms that have been the core of OPEC benefit from the richest oil deposits in the world. As shown in Table 6-1, the cost of extracting such oil is less than

Table 6-1 Cost and Capacity in the World Oil Market

Production Costs ($/Barrel)	Production Capacity (Million Barrels/Day)	Production Early 1986 (Million Barrels/Day)	Locations
Under $2	15	8	Middle East
$2–4	15	12	Middle East, Africa, Mexico, Indonesia, some North Sea
$4–12	22	22	Most U.S., North Sea, Canada
$12–24	4	3	U.S. stripper wells, Canadian oil sands, Arctic, offshore areas

Source: New York Times, February 9, 1986, Section 3, p. 3.

[6]The extreme form of this dilemma occurs when joint-profit maximization requires high-cost firms to shut down. For an example, see Adams, Henry C. "Relation of the State to Industrial Action," *Publications of the American Economic Association* Volume 1, Number 6, January 1887, p. 19, discussing an 1880 report of the Assembly of New York: "there were at Buffalo thirty-four [grain] elevators, of which twelve only were needed to do the work of elevating. 'It makes no difference . . . what elevator does the work, all get their respective shares of the money earned. One of these has not been used in twenty years, and many of them, according to the testimony, were built for the sole purpose of coming into and receiving a share in the pool.' "

$2 a barrel. It seems likely that the best deposits cost less than $0.50 a barrel to work.[7] Other OPEC members have costs as much as eight times greater. Yet it has often been the highest-cost producers who have had the largest share of OPEC output. One reason for this, to be discussed, is the likelihood that the producers with the richest deposits take the longest planning horizon when they decide their strategies for the world oil market. For whatever reason, the fact is that OPEC has not allocated output among members in a way that would maximize its joint profit. Despite the immense economic profit earned by OPEC from 1973 through (say) 1986, a monopolist could have done better.

Discount Rate

We encountered the discount rate in Chapter 4's discussion of dynamic limit pricing. The discount rate is a measure of the rate of time preference. A firm with a high discount rate places great weight on profits earned in the near future and little weight on profits earned in the distant future. Such a firm will prefer to set a high short-run price, even though a high price induces entry and reduces profit over the long run.

In contrast, a firm with a low discount rate will value profits in the distant future almost as much as near-term profits. Such a firm is more likely to prefer a limit price strategy, preserving market power—and economic profit—into the distant future.

When cartel members place roughly the same weight on current and future profits, it will be easier to reach an agreement: cartel members will want to set roughly the same price. If some firms want a high short-run price, because they are indifferent to the price of oil in the distant future, and other firms want a low price, because they take the long view, common ground will be difficult to find. This is true in the extreme for OPEC.

Some OPEC members (including Saudi Arabia, Kuwait, and the United Arab Emirates) have immense reserves of oil, small populations, and a political infrastructure that is well served by modernization at a slow pace. These countries know that they will be major factors in the world oil market well into the twenty-first century.

Other oil-producing countries (Indonesia, Nigeria, Algeria) have limited oil reserves, large populations, and an urgent need to develop their economies. The only hope such countries have to lift themselves out of the ranks of less developed countries is to earn as much as possible, as soon as possible, from the sale of oil and use the earnings to finance industrial development.

---

[7]M. A. Adelman (*The World Petroleum Market*. Baltimore: The Johns Hopkins University Press, 1972, pp. 76–77) estimates the average cost of Persian Gulf to be $0.10 to $0.20 per barrel. Allowing for inflation to the mid-1980s, this translates into a cost of $0.30 to $0.60 cents a barrel. More recent estimates by the same author place the per-barrel cost of the cheapest OPEC oil at $0.60 to $0.70; Adelman, M. A. "The Competitive Floor to World Oil Prices," Working Paper No. MIT-EL 86-011WP, April 1986, Table III.

More than one government in such countries has changed over the management of oil resources. The departing leaders often face a retirement more permanent than a move to San Clemente. The governments of such countries will press for the short-run monopoly price of oil, even if it costs the cartel control of the market in 10 years. For the leaders of such countries, 10 years is over the event horizon.

Recapitulation

Differences create disagreements. Firms in a moderately concentrated market are likely to recognize their mutual interdependence. But these firms are unlikely to achieve joint profit maximization *tacitly* unless they produce a standardized product, have the same costs, and share a common discount rate. If these conditions are met, the more concentrated the market, the more likely they are to reach an agreement.

One policy implication[8] is that it is not a waste of time to break up dominant firms.[9] Oligopolists may succeed in exercising some control over price, but problems of oligopolistic coordination suggest that oligopolists will ordinarily fall short of joint profit maximization. It follows that a merger policy that aims to prevent the formation of dominant firms is likely to improve market performance, all else equal.

Conduct and Agreement

Overt collusion is messy. In the age of the photocopying machine and the floppy disk, it invariably leaves behind records that come to lead lives of their own. Overt collusion has the disadvantage of (as we will see) being illegal, at least when committed by firms in the United States (and in most other industrialized countries).

To avoid such sticky wickets, oligopolists often use *facilitating devices* that allow effective collusion while falling short of formal cartelization. It is useful to think of such devices as a way of communicating an intent to cooperate in the restriction of output. Facilitating devices contribute to the formation of conjectural variations that allow oligopolists to exercise market power (see Chapter 5), and to the recognition of interdependence that is central to Chamberlin's model of oligopoly.

Signaling

It is not always necessary to *meet* in order to convey intentions about prices. Price changes, after all, must be announced. They can be announced in ad-

---

[8]Williamson, Oliver E. "The Economics of Antitrust: Transaction Cost Considerations," *University of Pennsylvania Law Review* Volume 122, Number 6, June 1974, pp. 1476–1479.

[9]Although, as noted in Chapter 4, with the exception of a few early cases, dominant firms have not often been broken up under the antitrust laws.

vance. If others in the industry don't go along, the changes can always be rescinded.

In its extreme form, this practice becomes *price leadership*. One firm is recognized, by general consent, as the arbiter of industry prices.[10] This solves one of the two critical cartel problems: agreement. However, it does not guarantee adherence.

We saw two examples of signaling in Chapter 3. One—a matching of price changes—arose in the 1946 *American Tobacco* case.[11] Another—an identically worded letter with a common letterhead—was essential to the finding of conspiracy in *Interstate Circuit*.[12] Price signaling has been common in the U.S. steel industry in recent years; an example appears in the following case study.

Case Study: Signaling

(September 21, 1985)* Although there was cheering yesterday in the steel industry for the United States Steel Corporation's move to lift the price of sheet steel, no other mills immediately followed suit. . . . Spokesmen at the LTV Corporation, Bethlehem, the Inland Steel Corporation and Armco Inc. said officials were still reviewing the U.S. Steel move. "What's clear to LTV Steel," said . . . a spokesman, "is that with the transaction prices being generally at the same level now as they were five years ago, improved price realization is required." To make a price increase on sheet products stick, some of the other major producers . . . would have to join in. . . . Other mills seeing a chance to pick up market share might continue deep discounting.

(September 26, 1985)† Major steelmakers, following U.S. Steel Corp.'s pricing action last week, said they will raise selling prices . . . on sheet-steel products. . . . The pricing moves, announced yesterday by LTV Corp.'s steel unit, Bethlehem Steel Corp. and Inland Steel Co., are designed to bolster the severely depressed prices in the sheet-steel segment, which accounts for about 40% of domestic steel sales. . . . In explaining its decision to follow U.S. Steel, a Bethlehem Steel spokesman said, "this action makes us competitive with U.S. Steel. . .".

*New York Times, September 21, 1985, p. 23.
†Wall Street Journal, September 26, 1985, p. 16.

[10]Donsimoni, Marie-Paule, "Stable Heterogeneous Cartels," *International Journal of Industrial Organization* Volume 3, Number 4, December 1985, pp. 451–467, outlines a model in which the most efficient firms in an industry comprise a price-leading cartel.

[11]*American Tobacco Co. et al. v. United States,* 328 U.S. 781 (1946).

[12]*Interstate Circuit, Inc. et al. v. United States,* 306 U.S. 208 (1938).

(November 7, 1985)[‡] The United States Steel Corporation today expanded its efforts to raise prices on key products, saying it intends to charge $40 a ton more for hot-rolled bar and semifinished steel. . . . In announcing today's moves, U.S. Steel, the nation's No. 1 steelmaker, is again taking the lead in trying to firm up pricing in an industry that has been battered by severe discounting, sluggish demand and strong competition from imported steel. In the last two months, U.S. Steel has announced adjustments in steel price formulas, generally leading to price increases, on three other product lines—steel sheet, plate, and tubular products. The Inland Steel Company and the Bethlehem Steel Corporation followed U.S. Steel's recent price adjustments on steel sheet and plate with similar moves of their own. Inland, Bethlehem and the LTV Corporation all said today that they were studying U.S. Steel's latest pricing actions.

[‡]*New York Times*, November 7, 1985, p. 29.

Pricing Rules

There is no need to collude overtly if there is some generally accepted rule by which prices are determined. Everyone can simply follow the rule. This greatly facilitates the achievement of consensus and the appearance of legality.

Perhaps the most prominent example of a pricing rule is the *basing point system,* which has been used in industries producing a bulky product, of low value per unit volume, and for which the transportation cost is a large part of the total cost to the consumer. The basing point system has been used at various times in the steel, cement, and plywood industries, among others.

We explain the basing point system by contrasting it with the alternative freight on board (FOB) mill pricing. FOB mill pricing is illustrated in Figure 6-2 for a market with three suppliers. To keep things as simple as possible, we

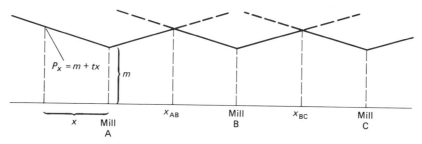

m = mill A's base price t = transportation cost/mile
The price at any point equals the price at the nearest mill plus transport cost from the nearest mill.

Figure 6-2 Freight-on-board pricing

compress three dimensions into two and suppose that the suppliers are located at different points along a straight line.

Under the FOB system, suppliers quote a price *at the mill gate*. The cost of transportation is added to the mill-gate price. In Figure 6-2, each supplier posts the price, m, at the mill gate. The cost of transportation increases in proportion to the distance from the mill. At a distance x miles away from mill A, the overall or *delivered* price to the consumer is $m + tx$, where t is transportation cost per mile.

Because it is the closest mill, B will have a natural market stretching from x_{AB} to x_{BC}. Mill B will compete with other suppliers only at the borders of its natural market. Within the natural market, the transportation cost advantage allows mill B to undersell its rivals. Under an FOB mill price system, if the mill price equals marginal cost, firms will sell only in their natural market. The temptation will be great—as always—to work out ways to avoid pricing at marginal cost.

The basing point system is such a method. Figure 6-3 illustrates a multiple basing point system for a three-mill market. Mills A and C are basing points. Under a multiple basing point system, the price at any location is the mill price plus the cost of transportation from the nearest basing point.

If mill B sells at x_1, the quoted price is the mill price plus the cost of transportation *from mill A*, because mill A is the nearest basing point. The customer at x_1 pays phantom freight to mill B. The customer at x_1 pays for shipment from A. But shipment occurs from B, which is closer to x_1 than A, so the customer at x_1 pays for some transportation services that are never rendered.

In contrast, if mill B makes a sale at x_2, the quoted price is the mill price

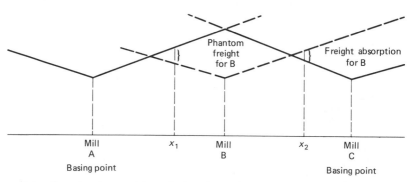

Notes: The price at any point equals the price at the nearest basing point plus the cost of transportation from the nearest basing point.

If mill B sells at x_1, the sale involves *phantom freight:* payment for transportation services that are never rendered. If mill B sells at x_2, the sale involves *freight absorption:* transportation services that are rendered are not explicitly paid for.

Figure 6-3 Multiple basing point system.

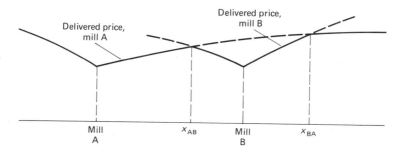

Figure 6-4 Efficient cross-hauling with nonlinear transportation costs.

plus the cost of transportation from mill C: mill C is the nearest basing point. Because mill C is closer to x_2 than mill B, mill B absorbs a portion of transportation cost for a sale at x_2.

Natural markets lose their relevance under a basing point system. Mills A and C may very well sell at points that can be supplied at a lower transportation cost from mill B. Mill B may well make sales at locations closer to either mill A or mill C. This supply pattern is called *cross-hauling*.

Cross-hauling will be inefficient if transportation costs are proportional to distance. If it costs twice as much to ship twice as far, it will never pay to buy from an unnecessarily distant supplier.

As Haddock[13] points out, efficient cross-hauling may arise if transport costs are not proportional to the distance shipped. This will often be the case: it will be cheaper to ship longer distances when the origin and the destination are connected by a major highway if shorter distances require the use of rural roads.

Figure 6-4 illustrates a situation in which one mill (A) is a low mill-cost and transportation-cost source, while mill B is a high mill-cost and transportation-cost source. Mill B has a natural market from x_{AB} to x_{BA}. Mill A will undersell mill B on *both* sides of mill B's natural market. Under an FOB mill system, mill A will haul across mill B's natural market.

The advantage of a basing point system, from the point of view of cartel members, is that it provides an easy way to compute the price to any customer and to detect departures from the agreed-upon price. All one needs is a (say, railroad) rate book and a map showing the distance to the nearest basing point. Any customer will be quoted the same delivered price by all suppliers. Any variation in price will be immediately recognized by cartel members as a departure from the collusive agreement, inviting retaliation.

The weakness of the basing point system as a mechanism for collusion is

[13]Haddock, David D. "Basing-Point Pricing: Competitive vs. Collusive Theories," *American Economic Review* Volume 72, Number 3, June 1982, pp. 289–307.

that it does nothing to allocate markets among producers.[14] Stigler[15] suggests that this is a way for oligopolists who benefit from increases in demand to accommodate firms that suffer from decreases in demand in their natural markets. The disadvantaged firms are allowed to "poach" in the natural markets of other firms. The freight absorption and cross-hauling that are characteristic of basing point systems is bound to aggravate relationships among "cooperating" firms. This will not facilitate the maintenance of oligopolistic agreements.

However—and here we jump ahead to our next topic—the basing point system provides a natural way to discipline cheaters. The cement industry provides an example. Under this industry's version of the basing point system, if a firm cut its price to get a particular order, its mill was made an involuntary basing point at a very low mill-net price:[16]

> The penalty of such a generalized ("open") price reduction affected mainly the offending mill. The mill which imposed the punitive base suffered comparatively little since the majority of its sales were presumably being made in that portion of its natural market unaffected by the base price reduction at the rival mill.

On the other hand, all the sales of the offending mill were made at the punitively low mill price. The usual result of an imposition of a punitive base was to bring the offending mill back into the fold. And the awareness that certain mills were being thus disciplined served to deter other competitors from selective cutting of prices.

Adherence

The Static Cartel Instability Problem

The argument that a successful cartel sows the seeds of its own destruction is illustrated in Figure 6-5. To focus on cartel behavior, suppose entry is not a problem. Oligopolists collude to maximize joint profits under the market demand curve. Each firm is assigned a quota output. Quota outputs for all firms add up to the monopoly (joint profit-maximizing) output.

If one firm believes that the others will produce their quota outputs no matter what it does, it could maximize its profit along the remaining residual demand curve. The basic Cournot model of quantity-setting oligopoly can be applied

[14]Carlton, Dennis W. "A Reexamination of Delivered Price Systems," *Journal of Law and Economics* Volume 26, Number 1, April 1983, pp. 51–70.

[15]Stigler, George J. "A Theory of Delivered Price Systems," *American Economic Review* Volume 39, December 1949, pp. 1143–1159, reprinted in Stigler, George J. *The Organization of Industry.* Homewood, Ill.: Richard D. Irwin, Inc., 1968, pp. 147–164.

[16]Loescher, Samuel M. *Imperfect Collusion in the Cement Industry.* Cambridge, Mass.: Harvard University Press, 1959.

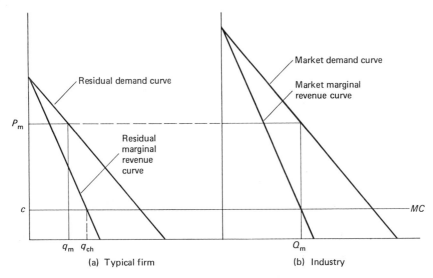

Figure 6-5 The static cartel instability problem.

to determine the firm's *individual* profit-maximizing output (as distinguished from its quota output).

In a static model, it will *always* pay the individual firm to produce more than its quota. Observe, in Figure 6-5, that if a firm produces its quota output, marginal revenue along the residual marginal revenue curve exceeds marginal cost.[17] If a single firm in a cartel increases its output, its revenue will rise more than its cost.

This is the cartel instability problem. If a cartel is successful in restricting its joint output and raising price, it creates an incentive for individual member firms to cheat, expand their output, and undermine the cartel. A *single* firm will always profit by cheating on the cartel. But *all* firms will have this same incentive, and if all firms expand their output, the cartel breaks down. On this reasoning, cartels are inherently unstable.[18]

---

[17]If q_m is the firm's quota output, (q_m, P_m) must be on the firm's residual demand curve. If the firm produces q_m and all other firms produce their quota outputs, the total output will be Q_m and the price will be P_m. To show that the individual firm's marginal revenue under Cournot assumptions at output q_m exceeds marginal cost, see Problem 6-1.

[18]The conclusion that cartels are inherently unstable depends on the assumption that a potential cheater believes that other members of the cartel will continue to produce their quota outputs after cheating. If the cheater expects cartel members to renegotiate the terms of the cartel agreement after his departure, the consequences of this renegotiation may make it unprofitable to cheat. An emerging literature suggests that when potential cheaters behave this way, it will be possible to form a stable cartel. See D'Aspremont, C., Jacquemin, A., Jaskold-Gabszewicz, and Weymark, J. "On the Stability of Collusive Price-Leadership," *Canadian Journal of Economics* Volume 16, February 1983, pp. 17–25; Donsimoni, M.-P., Economides, N. S., and Polemarchakis, H. M. "Stable Cartels," *International Economic Review* Volume 27, Number 2, June 1986, pp. 317–327; and Donsimoni, op. cit. This analysis is akin in spirit to the dynamic models to be discussed.

Structure and Adherence

Concentration

The Dynamic Cartel Instability Problem

The idea of intertemporal tradeoffs is central to the analysis of firms' incentive to cheat on a cartel agreement. A firm will cheat if it can gain enough by cheating to outweigh the profit it loses after the cartel breaks down. If the cheating is detected quickly enough, the gains from cheating will be small, the losses will come quickly, and cheating will not occur.

The essentially static—timeless—analysis depicted in Figure 6-5 misses an essential element of this tradeoff—the rate of time preference. If a firm cheats, it gains profit only until the cheating is detected. From that point on, the cartel will break down. Rival firms have no reason to restrict their output and hold up the price to the benefit of the firm that has broken the cartel agreement.

Cheating may be optimal—profit-maximizing—for a single firm, because the extra profits due to cheating come before the lost profits after detection. Whether or not cheating is profitable will depend on the discount rate—the rate of time preference. If the rate of time preference is low, a firm gives almost as much weight to the profits lost after cheating is detected as it gives to the short-run increase in profit before cheating is detected. If the rate of time preference is low enough, a firm will not wish to cheat.

If the cartel maximizes its joint profit, each firm will reap its share of monopoly profit. It follows (Problem 6-2) that a larger firm will have a stronger incentive to keep the cartel agreement; its share of the monopoly profit is larger. Because firms with larger shares are more likely to keep a cartel agreement, cartels are more likely to survive in concentrated markets.

The static model of cartel behavior simply predicts that each cartel member will have an incentive to cheat. A dynamic analysis replaces this conclusion with a more complicated prediction: a firm will have a greater incentive to cheat, the greater its rate of time preference and the smaller its market share. A cartel composed of a few firms, with large market shares, that take the long view, may well be stable.

Detection of Cheating

The preceding analysis ignores the impact of uncertainty on oligopolists' incentives to undercut a cartel price. Stigler[19] points out that a firm is more likely to cheat if the cheating will go undetected. If cheating is detected

---

[19]Stigler, George J. "A Theory of Oligopoly," *Journal of Political Economy* Volume 72, Number 1, February 1964, pp. 44–61; reprinted in Stigler, *Organization of Industry*, pp. 39–63.

promptly, it will invite swift retaliation. This, in turn, will reduce the extra profit earned by cheating, which will reduce the incentive to cheat.[20]

Even if oligopolists agree on price and output quotas, they will often resist revealing details about their operations to the cartel. In the past, cartels have gotten around this problem by making monitoring devices part of the cartel agreement, but such devices are now forbidden by the antitrust laws.[21]

Because members of a cartel will conceal details of their operations, it will not be immediately obvious if cheating takes place. An oligopolist will have to infer that cheating is taking place if it notices that its own sales are smaller than they should be under the cartel agreement. The problem is that an oligopolist's sales will fluctuate in the ordinary course of business. How is a firm to know if its sales have fallen because someone is cheating on the cartel, and not because of the normal practice of customers occasionally moving from one supplier to another?

It follows that collusion is more likely to be successful if customers do not switch suppliers very often. If customers usually purchase repeatedly from their previous supplier, a loss of sales will be a more reliable indicator of cheating somewhere in the industry.

Stigler is also able to show that fluctuations in sales[22] as customers change suppliers go down as the Herfindahl index of market concentration goes up. The fewer the numbers of suppliers, the less often will one firm lose customers to other firms. When the Herfindahl index is large, sales are concentrated in the hands of a few firms. In this case, an unusually large decline in sales will be a reliable signal that cheating is taking place.

Stigler's oligopoly model yields the prediction that the greater the concentration of sales, as measured by the Herfindahl index, the less likely is cheating to occur. This is consistent with the dynamic model of cartel stability previously outlined.

[20]For models that include agreements on retaliation as part of cartel agreements, see Porter, R. H. "A Study of Cartel Stability: The Joint Executive Committee, 1880–1886," *Bell Journal of Economics* Volume 14, Number 2, Autumn 1983, pp. 301–314; Porter Robert H. "On the Incidence and Duration of Price Wars," *Journal of Industrial Economics* Volume 33, Number 4, June 1985, pp. 415–426; Green E. J. and Porter, R. H. "Noncooperative Collusion Under Imperfect Price Information," *Econometrica* Volume 52, January 1984, pp. 87–100; Segerstrom, Paul S. "Demons and Repentance," Journal of Economic Theory, forthcoming.

[21]See, for example, *American Column & Lumber Co. v. United States,* 257 U.S. 377 (1921); *Maple Flooring Manufacturers Association v. United States,* 268 U.S. 563 (1925); *Sugar Institute, Inc. v. United States,* 297 U.S. 553 (1936); *Tag Manufacturers Institute v. Federal Trade Commission,* 174 F.2d 452 (1st Cir. 1949).

[22]Strictly, the variance of sales from customers of other firms.

Case Study: Oil Import Quota Auctions

In 1976, M. A. Adelman proposed a scheme designed to encourage cheating by OPEC member nations. He suggested that the U.S. government sell permits to import oil into the United States. The permits were to be sold fairly frequently, at sealed bid auctions. Revenue from the auctions would go to the government. Once purchased, import permits could be freely resold. The system was designed to produce secret price cutting:*

> Once the quota auction system was running smoothly, we would have created a market where the cartelist governments could cheat to gain incremental revenues by selling behind each other's backs, each knowing that others might be selling it out.
>
> The secrecy would be achieved by letting *anybody* bid, with no requirement except a certified check for the deposit. Then cartel governments could use front men. A lawyer or broker deposits a check for several million dollars, without revealing his sponsor. But the identity of nominal bidders could be kept secret. . . .
>
> There is a second barrier to knowing the real bidders: since tickets could be transferred, a given shipload of oil arriving here could be covered by tickets issued to various people at various times. A third barrier: transshipment terminals are fed by sources from all over the world. Oil would be arriving in the United States from the Bahamas, Japan, Rotterdam, France, etc. The cost of diversion, reloading, and even mixing would be very small relative to the price.

Discussion: The Adelman plan was never tried, and the world waited for a decade before the entry of non-OPEC suppliers so reduced OPEC's share of the world oil market that oligopolistic consensus broke down. It remains a fascinating application of Stigler's analysis of the relationship between the ease with which cheating can be detected and cartel stability.

*Adelman, M. A. "Oil Import Quota Auctions," *Challenge,* January–February 1976, pp. 17–22.

Size and Frequency of Sales

If a business involves frequent small sales, cutting the oligopoly price on a single sale will yield only a small incremental profit from cheating. But if the oligopoly price is cut on many small sales, rivals are more likely to find out about it. Customers, disloyal things, will often report low prices to rivals in an attempt to solicit even lower counteroffers. This will invite quick retaliation.

It ought, therefore, to be easier to maintain a collusive agreement in an industry characterized by frequent small sales. It ought to be harder to maintain an oligopolistic agreement if sales are large and infrequent. The commercial aircraft industry, described in Chapter 5, is an example.

Open Bidding

By the same logic, government agencies, which purchase goods at sealed-bid auctions and then publicly reveal all bids, are unlikely to benefit from secret price cutting. By revealing the delinquent bid, the government would bring down immediate retribution upon the guilty party.

Vertical Integration

OPEC provides a classic example of the way a vertically integrated producer can indirectly shade the cartel price if it operates in downstream industries. By integrating forward into refining and distribution, many OPEC nations have acquired the ability to cut the price of crude oil discreetly.

Official OPEC prices are for crude oil. If an independent refiner—any company not associated with an OPEC member nation—purchases crude oil at the official price, that official price is a cost to the independent firm that puts a floor under the price the refiner can charge for his products without losing money.

No such floor exists for the vertically integrated refiner-producer. If a producing nation extracts crude oil at a cost of \$0.50 a barrel and sells it an an official price of (say) \$15 a barrel, the cost of that oil to the producer's refineries is still \$0.50 a barrel. The vertically integrated producer-refiner can effectively cheat on the cartel price for crude oil by selling refined products at a price far below that of independent refiners.

Selling a refined product at a price below that at which any independent can survive has the same effect as cutting the price of crude oil to independents. Because the price cut occurs further along the distribution chain, it will be easier to conceal than a price cut at the crude oil level.

Excess Capacity

Economists have a schizophrenic view of the impact of excess capacity on the success of collusion.[23] The traditional view is based on elementary price theory. Specifically, the traditional view of excess capacity is based on the result that in the short run a profit-maximizing firm will produce unless the price falls below minimum average variable cost.

The cost of the capital assets that determine capacity will be a fixed cost, independent of the rate of output. If firms carry a great deal of excess capacity, average fixed cost will be a large part of average cost, and average variable cost will be a small part of average cost. Firms with such a cost structure will be willing to produce at quite low prices, relative to average cost, in the short run. For this reason, economists have argued that substantial excess capacity

---

[23]Among many other things.

increases the likelihood of price wars and a breakdown in oligopolistic control of prices.

As shown in Table 6-1, there is excess capacity in the world oil market. In early 1986, world oil production was about 45 million barrels a day, while the capacity was 56 million barrels a day. Roughly 20 per cent of the total capacity was unused. The excess capacity is in the hands of the Persian Gulf states, which are the core of OPEC. Middle East producers are estimated to have 55 per cent of world oil reserves; Saudi Arabia alone has nearly 25 per cent.

But this concentration of excess capacity in the hands of the OPEC members with the least incentive to cheat leads us to the other effect that excess capacity is sometimes alleged to have on the ability of oligopolists to maintain an agreement. Excess capacity *under the control of loyal cartel members* is a potential "big stick" that can be used to discipline a firm that has strayed from the path of righteousness.

After threatening throughout the early 1980s to initiate price wars if OPEC members did not adhere to production quotas, Saudi Arabia did just that toward the end of 1985:[24]

> Meanwhile, Saudi Arabia is pressing its campaign to restore its dominance as the premier world oil power.
>
> The Saudis want other oil producers, particularly those outside OPEC, to join an international oil-production sharing pact that the Saudis hope will return control of prices to producers. Endowed with the world's largest oil reserves— at least 170 billion barrels—Saudi Arabia began last October to flood world oil markets, determined to drive prices down until it prevails.

Does excess capacity serve to stabilize or destabilize cartels? Recent analysis[25] highlights trends in demand as the critical factor. If demand declines, some firms will have to leave the market in the long run. Firms with excess capacity will be tempted to use it to try and preserve their place. There are a number of examples[26] of industries carrying substantial excess capacity in which collusive agreements broke down following a general reduction in demand.

There is, no doubt, some truth to both views of excess capacity and collusion. Individual producers will have an incentive to shade the cartel price if they can do so without detection. Excess capacity will allow them to expand

---

[24]Ibrahim, Youssef M. "Global Oil Price War Is Expected to Affect the Industry for Years," *Wall Street Journal,* February 11, 1986, p. 1. Saudi Arabia abandoned its disciplinary strategy after less than a year. Paper Topic 6.2 invites you to follow up on this subject.

[25]Davidson, C. and Deneckere, R. "Excess Capacity and Collusion," manuscript, revised February 1985.

[26]Including rayon, cement, and heavy electrical equipment, as well as petroleum.

output. Excess capacity is at least necessary for cheating to occur, and in that sense makes cartel stability less likely. Larger firms may also use excess capacity to discipline cheaters. But the presence of excess capacity should not be taken as proof that it is held for disciplinary purposes. There is bound to be excess capacity in the period immediately after a successful cartel is formed, since a successful cartel will restrict output to hold up the price.

Demand Growth Rate[27]

A decline in demand may induce a cartel breakdown if cartel members carry excess capacity. By cutting the cartel price during a period of slack demand, a firm loses fewer sales than would otherwise be the case. By the same token, however, if a firm cuts prices during periods of rapidly growing demand, it will gain more sales than would otherwise be the case.

The most sensible prediction to make may therefore be that changes in demand, especially if unexpected, induce cartel instability. As noted previously, differences provoke disagreements. When the market changes in unforeseen ways, it may well be every firm for itself. A new agreement can be negotiated next week; the trick is to make sure that one is around to participate in the negotiations.

Case Study: the Mechanics of Collusion

The electrical equipment conspiracies show the lengths to which oligopolists will go to shackle competitive tendencies. More than 30 companies conspired to raise the price of a wide range of electrical equipment, including circuit breakers, generators, insulators, and switchgear. Government antitrust attention was drawn to the industry when the Tennessee Valley Authority complained about the bids it received in what were supposed to be competitive auctions. Ultimately, 29 companies were fined for conspiracy in violation of Section 1 of the Sherman Act. Seven corporate executives went to jail.

The switchgear conspiracy is fascinating both for its methods and for the way those methods were detected. Although there was no apparent pattern to the bids turned in by different companies for various contracts, the Antitrust Division was certain that the bids were being coordinated. A Justice Department attorney

[27]Rotemberg, Julio J. and Saloner, Garth. "A Supergame Theoretic Model of Price Wars during Booms," *American Economic Review* Volume 76, Number 3, June 1986, pp. 390–407. Rotemberg and Saloner present empirical tests using the Portland cement industry. It appears that the results of their empirical tests are reversed if this industry is modeled as consisting of regional geographic markets, with allowance made for capacity constraints. See Rosenbaum, David I. " A Further Test of a Supergame-Theoretic Model of Price Wars During Booms," Working Paper 86-9, Department of Economics, University of Nebraska, October 1986.

got enough information from an acquaintance to bring subpoenas to sales managers of I-T-E Circuit Breaker:*

> When the subpoenas did come, a pink-cheeked blond young man named Nye Spencer, the company's sales manager for switchgear, was resolutely waiting—his arms loaded with data. He had decided he wasn't about to commit another crime by destroying the records so carefully laid away in his cellar.
>
> There were pages on pages of notes taken during sessions of the switchgear conspiracy—incriminating entries like "Potomac Light & Power O.K. for G.E." and "Before bidding on this, check with G.E."; neat copies of the ground rules for meetings of the conspirators: no breakfasting together, no registering at the hotel with company names, no calls to the office, no papers to be left in hotel-room wastebaskets. Spencer, it seems, had been instructed to handle some of the secretarial work of the cartel and believed in doing it right; he'd hung onto the documents to help in training an assistant. But the most valuable windfall from the meticulous record keeper was a pile of copies of the "phases of the moon" pricing formula for as far back as May, 1958.
>
> . . . they immediately resolved the enigma of switchgear prices in commercial contracts. One group of columns established the bidding order of the seven switchgear manufacturers—a different company, each with its own code number, phasing into the priority position every two weeks (hence "phases of the moon"). A second group of columns, keyed into the company code numbers, established how much each company was to knock off the agreed-upon book price. For example, if it were No. 1's (G.E.'s) turn to be low bidder . . . then all Westinghouse (No. 2), or Allis-Chalmers (No. 3) had to do was look for their code number in the second group of columns to find how many dollars they were to bid above No. 1. These bids would then be fuzzed up by having a little added to them or taken away by companies 2, 3, etc. Thus there was not even a hint that the winning bid had been collusively arrived at.

*Smith, Richard A. "The Incredible Electrical Conspiracy," *Fortune* Volume 63, Number 5, May 1961, pp. 164–210.

Public Policy Toward Collusion

The Supreme Court enunciated and developed the "rule of reason" in cases applying Section 2 of the Sherman Act. Such cases are ordinarily complex and involve full-blown economic analyses of the markets involved. To prove a violation of Section 2, one must show not only that a firm has market power, but also that the firm acquired or maintained market power in some way that is not ''normal industrial development.''

The law under Section 1 of the Sherman Act, which forbids conspiracies in restraint of trade, is much more clear-cut: all conspiracies in restraint of trade violate the Sherman Act. This rule goes back to *Addyston Pipe and Steel,*[28] and a cartel formed by manufacturers of iron pipe in the Southern and Midwestern United States in the 1890s. The cartel faced potential competition from Eastern producers, and tried to raise the price as high as possible without making it profitable for Eastern producers to ship to the South and Midwest. This is limit pricing; the limit price differential was created by transportation costs.

The cartel practiced geographic market division. Some cities were assigned to specific firms. For the sake of appearances, other firms submitted bids for contracts in these cities. These bids were made high enough so that they would not obtain the business.

For contracts in areas that had not been reserved, the cartel conducted its own private ''auction'' in advance of the public bidding for the contract. At the private auction, cartel members bid ''bonus payments'' to the cartel for the right to win the contract. The cartel member that pledged the highest bonus to the cartel won the right to submit the low bid at the public auction. Periodically, the accumulated bonus payments were divided up among cartel members.

Addyston Pipe and its fellow conspirators were convicted of violating Section 1 of the Sherman Act (conspiracy in restraint of trade). They appealed to the Supreme Court to reverse their conviction. They proposed that the Supreme Court apply a ''rule of reason'' to Section 1 of the Sherman Act and exonerate them on the ground that the prices set by the cartel had been reasonable.

The Supreme Court rejected this argument, quoting Judge William Howard Taft's Circuit Court opinion:[29]

> It has been earnestly pressed upon us that the prices at which the cast-iron pipe was sold . . . were reasonable. . . . We do not think the issue an important one, because . . . we do not think that at common law there is any question of reasonableness open to the courts with reference to such a contract. Its tendency was certainly to give defendants the power to charge unreasonable prices, had they chosen to do so. But if it were important we should unhesitatingly find that the prices charged in the instances which were in evidence were unreasonable.

[28]175 U.S. 211 (1899). See Bittlingmayer, George. ''Decreasing Average Cost and Competition: A New Look at the Addyston Pipe Case,'' *Journal of Law and Economics* Volume 25, Number 2, October 1982, pp. 201–229.

[29]175 U.S. 211 at 237-8, quoting 85 Fed. 271 at 293.

In a later decision,[30] the Supreme Court clarified the relationship between the rule of reason and the rule that attempts to fix prices are illegal without regard to the reasonableness of the prices fixed:

> That only those restraints upon interstate commerce which are unreasonable are prohibited by the Sherman Law was the rule laid down by the opinions of this Court in the *Standard Oil* and *Tobacco* cases. But it does not follow that agreements to fix or maintain prices are reasonable restraints and therefore permitted by the statute, merely because the prices themselves are reasonable. . . . Whether this type of restraint is reasonable or not must be judged in part at least in the light of its effect on competition, for whatever difference of opinion there may be among economists as to the social and economic desirability of an unrestrained competitive system, it cannot be doubted that the Sherman Law and the judicial decisions interpreting it are based upon the assumption that the public interest is best protected from the evils of monopoly and price control by the maintenance of competition (citations omitted).
>
> The aim and result of every price-fixing agreement, if effective, is the elimination of one form of competition. The power to fix prices, whether reasonably exercised or not, involves power to control the market and to fix arbitrary and unreasonable prices. The reasonable price fixed today may through economic and business changes become the unreasonable price of tomorrow. Once established, it may be maintained unchanged because of the absence of competition secured by the agreement for a price reasonable when fixed.

From these decisions stems the *per se rule* against price fixing. To prove a violation of Section 1 of the Sherman Act, the government need only prove that firms conspired to fix price. It need not prove that the conspiracy obtained absolute control over price. It need not prove that the conspirators abused such control as they had. It need not prove that specific anticompetitive effects flowed from the act of fixing price. The policy of the antitrust laws is that the economy is best served when markets determine prices. Any conspiracy to interfere with this market mechanism is unreasonable within the meaning of the antitrust laws.

The per se rule against price fixing has two advantages compared with the rule of reason. Because the per se rule avoids the necessity for a detailed industry study, it economizes on the costs of enforcing the antitrust laws:[31]

> there are certain agreements or practices which because of their pernicious effect on competition and lack of any redeeming virtue are conclusively presumed to be unreasonable and therefore illegal without elaborate inquiry as to the precise harm they have caused or the business excuse for their use. This

[30]*United States v. Trenton Potteries Company et al.,* 273 U.S. 392 (1926), at 396.

[31]*Northern Pacific Railway Co. v. United States,* 356 U.S. 1 (1958), at 5.

principle of per se unreasonableness not only makes the type of restraints which are proscribed by the Sherman Act more certain but it also avoids the necessity for an incredibly complicated and prolonged economic investigation. . . .

Further, the per se rule provides a clear statement of *what the law is*. The business community is well served if it is given clear signals about public policy.

A critical feature of the per se rule, from an economic point of view, is that it is to be applied only to practices that have a "pernicious effect on competition and lack of any redeeming virtue." If the per se rule is applied to practices that sometimes (or often) are not anticompetitive, its effect is to deny to the business community a defense that would be available under the rule of reason. But there is, as always in economics, a tradeoff: if the scope of the rule of reason is expanded, antitrust enforcement costs rise. We return to this topic in Chapter 18, where we will see that the advice of the Chicago school is to limit the applicability of the per se rule.

Summary

"Gentlemen's agreements" usually involve neither gentlemen nor agreements. Oligopolists as a group will always have an incentive to collude; oligopolists as individuals will always have an incentive to cheat on a collusive agreement. The incentive in each case is the same: profit.

Oligopolists may collude overtly, or they may employ facilitating devices to collude tacitly and maximize their joint profit. The basing point system is one such device. It allows firms to compute the agreed-upon price without meeting, and it provides a way to punish recalcitrant firms (by making them a punitive basing point).

The more concentrated the market, the more standardized the product, the more comparable the costs and rates of time preference across firms, the more likely oligopolists are to reach an agreement.

The larger its market share, the lower its rate of time preference, and the more rapidly cheating will be detected, the more likely a firm is to adhere to an agreement. Firms that are vertically integrated forward will be able to cut the cartel price indirectly by shading the price on upstream products. If demand is declining, excess capacity can encourage price wars. If demand is stable, excess capacity can be used to threaten punishment of price cutters. The threat may be sufficient to maintain loyalty to the cartel.

The U.S. antitrust laws take a hard line against agreements among competitors on price. Such agreements are illegal per se. Defenses of reasonableness are not entertained. The per se rule economizes on enforcement costs and makes clear the nature of public policy. Because the per se rule does not permit defenses based on reasonableness, it may sometimes condemn socially desirable behavior.

Problems

6-1 (Static cartel stability) N firms form a cartel in a market with demand curve

$$P = a - bQ.$$

There are no fixed costs; the marginal and average cost per unit is c.
a. What output would a profit-maximizing monopolist produce?
b. If the cartel agrees to produce this output and divides it equally among the N firms, what is the residual demand curve faced by firm 1 if it expects other firms to produce their quota outputs? What is the residual marginal revenue curve faced by firm 1?
c. What is the marginal revenue for firm 1 if it produces the quota output? How does it compare with marginal cost? What output will maximize firm 1's profit if other firms produce their quota outputs? How does firm 1's profit-maximizing output compare with its quota output?

6-2 (Dynamic cartel stability)
a. If a firm adheres to a cartel agreement, it will earn its share of monopoly profit in each period:

$$s_i \pi_m,$$

where s_i is firm i's market share. What is the present discounted value of the income received by the firm if it adheres to the cartel agreement? (Call the discount rate "$r*$".)
b. If the firm cheats, it earns

$$s_i \pi_m + (1 - s_i) \pi_{ch}$$

in the period in which it cheats (where π_{ch} is the profit a new firm would earn by coming into the market and cutting the cartel price) and zero profits thereafter. Compare the present discounted value of the profit from cheating with the profit from adhering to the cartel and infer that the firm will earn more profit by adhering to the cartel if

$$s_i \pi_m / r* > (1 - s_i) \pi_{ch}.$$

c. Multiply this by s_i and add over all i to obtain

$$H \pi_m / r* > (1 - H) \pi_{ch}.$$

How does an increase in market share affect the stability condition in (b)? How does an increase in the Herfindahl index affect the stability condition in (c)?

Paper Topics

6-1 Beginning with the cases listed in footnote 21, analyze the role of trade associations in maintaining a cartel agreement and the treatment of trade associations under the antitrust laws.

6-2 Analyze the sharp decline in the price of crude oil that took place at the end of 1985 and early 1986. Discuss OPEC's attempts to control the price of crude oil from that time to the present.

6-3 Consult *Boise Cascade Corporation et al. v. Federal Trade Commission,* 637 F.2d 573 (1980), *In re Plywood,* 655 F.2d 627 (1981), and the references cited therein. Analyze the treatment of basing point systems under the antitrust laws.

6-4 Analyze the electrical equipment conspiraces of the 1950s. What structural characteristics induced firms in this industry to engage in an overt conspiracy to fix prices? Why didn't tacit collusion work?

6-5 Discuss the public policy and economic implications of the Supreme Court's holding in *Kiefer-Stewart Co. v. Joseph E. Seagram & Sons,* 340 U.S. 211 (1951).

6-6 Discuss the role of *United States v. Socony Vacuum Oil Company* 310 U.S. 150 (1940) in the development of the per se rule. Consult Comment, "Fixing the Price Fixing Confusion: A Rule of Reason Approach," *Yale Law Journal* Volume 92, 1983, pp. 702–730. Is the contention of the author of this comment generally accepted? Should it be?

7

Structure, Conduct, Market Power—The Evidence

Supposing is good, but finding out is better.

Mark Twain

We have generalized the most basic model of firm behavior under market power—monopoly—to cover structure-conduct-performance relationships in dominant-firm markets and in oligopoly.

These models suggest that market performance will be closer to monopoly the more difficult is entry, the more concentrated is the market, and the greater is product differentiation. In this chapter, we examine economists' empirical tests of these predictions.

Because of the large number of empirical studies of structure–performance relationships,[1] it is not feasible to present a comprehensive survey. Instead, we will hit the high points[2] of the literature. We review a few studies from the structure-conduct-performance school, whose findings are fairly typical. Then we discuss the Chicago school's criticisms of these studies. Finally, we cover some recent empirical work that seems to take off in new directions.

In the Beginning—Bain

Joe S. Bain's work is the foundation of modern empirical work in industrial economics. Bain contributed to the development of the static limit price model

[1]Weiss, Leonard, "The Concentration–Profits Relationship and Antitrust," in Goldschmid, H. J., Mann, H. M., and Weston, J. F., editors, *Industrial Concentration: The New Learning*. Boston: Little, Brown and Company, 1974, pp. 184–233, surveys more than 50 empirical tests of structure–performance relationships. It would not be surprising to find that at least that many such studies have been published since that time. Scherer, F. M., *Industrial Market Structure and Economic Performance*, 2nd edition, Chicago: Rand McNally, 1980, Chapter 9, gives a survey of the literature up to 1980.

[2]If that is the appropriate term.

(reviewed in Chapter 4) as a way of explaining his observation of real-world profits that persisted over time without being eroded by entry. Here we cover one of his most influential empirical studies.

Hypotheses

Bain sought to test the simultaneous influence of entry conditions *and* market concentration on market power. He did not elaborate the formal oligopoly models of the kind that were discussed in Chapters 5 and 6,[3] but the hypotheses he sought to test were broadly consistent with those models. Oligopoly models predict that market power increases with increasing market concentration and with the difficulty of entering a market. Bain set out to test these hypotheses:[4]

> This predicted influence of the condition of entry on the size of price-cost margins and profits is clearly subject to the concomitant influence of the degree of seller concentration within the industry. Specifically, it is expected to be evidenced in a verifiable simple association of the condition of entry on profits mainly as far as seller concentration throughout is high enough to support effective collusion in industries with both high and medium entry barriers.

Bain also expected entry barriers and concentration to benefit primarily the largest firms in an industry:[5]

> In regard to the appearance of the predicted association of the condition of entry to profit rates, it would be expected to be evident most definitely for the largest or dominant established firms in an industry, which will in general have the maximum aggregate advantage over potential entrants, and are most likely to be operating with minimal or close to minimal average costs. The profit rates of small firms, with inefficiently small plants or firm scales or with smaller product-differentiation advantages over entrants, might be expected to show a less certain or distinct relationship to a condition of entry calculated primarily with reference to the positions of the dominant firms.

Recall from Chapter 5 that in models of quantity-setting oligopoly, firms with larger market shares will exercise more market power, in equilibrium,

---

[3]The formal oligopoly models of Chapter 5, and those discussed in Chapter 6, have a long ancestry, going back the nineteenth-century work of Cournot and Bertrand. It is nonetheless true that many recent models in the Cournot-Bertrand tradition were motivated in part by a desire to formalize the literary arguments presented by Bain.

[4]Bain, Joe S. *Barriers to New Competition*. Cambridge, Mass.: Harvard University Press, 1956, p. 191.

[5]Ibid.

than firms with smaller market shares.[6] The second part of Bain's prediction is, therefore, broadly consistent with received oligopoly models.

In summary, Bain tested a threefold concentration-profits hypothesis:

1. Concentration will allow collusion.
2. Collusion will allow profit if entry is difficult.
3. These effects will be observed mainly for large firms.

Bain's Sample

Bain studied 20 manufacturing industries. He confined himself to the manufacturing sector because he thought that the impact of entry conditions on the exercise of market power might be different for manufacturing than for other sectors, such as mineral extraction or retail distribution. In other words, Bain did not want to mix apples and oranges.

Bain deliberately picked large industries with relatively high concentration levels. He described the use of 20 industries as a "practical limitation"[7] imposed by the amount of work needed to collect information about each industry.

Measurement Problems

Bain used the four-firm seller concentration ratio as a measure of market concentration because it was available from the 1947 Census of Manufactures. Later theoretical work—like Stigler's model of collusion and the oligopoly models reviewed in Chapters 5 and 6—usually produces the Herfindahl index as the measure of market concentration to be related to market power. The Herfindahl index was not available to Bain, but it is not thought that the use of the four-firm concentration ratio affected his results.[8]

Bain also confronted one of the perennial problems in testing structure-conduct-performance models: the measurement of profitability for tests of market power. Bain[9] recognized the theoretical superiority of the Lerner index—

---

[6]See Equations (5.3) and (5.6). In these models, firms with lower costs enjoy larger market shares in equilibrium, and the output decisions of firms with larger market shares have a greater impact on equilibrium price. For the model that produces equation (5.6), the nature of conjectural variations needs to be taken into account.

[7]Bain, p. 44.

[8]Studies that compare the Herfindahl index and Census concentration ratios against a common model usually find that they yield similar results; see Martin, Stephen. "Market, Firm, and Economic Performance," Salomon Brothers Center for the Study of Financial Institutions Monograph Series in Finance and Economics, Monograph 1983-1, for an example.

[9]Following his earlier work, Bain Joe S. "The Profit Rate as a Measure of Monopoly Power," *Quarterly Journal of Economics* Volume 55, February 1941, pp. 271–293.

the price-marginal cost margin—as a measure of market power. But he also recognized that it would usually be impossible to measure marginal cost. For this reason, he used the accounting rate of return on stockholders' equity as a measure of profitability. Because Bain expected the market power–concentration relationship to hold primarily for large firms, he identified up to four dominant firms for each industry in his sample and used the average of these large-firm profit rates as the market power variable in his study.

Entry Conditions

Bain made a detailed analysis of entry conditions for the 20 industries in his sample. For each industry, he considered the contribution to entry barriers of economies of scale, of product differentiation, and of capital requirements.

Returns to Scale

Bain looked mainly at two aspects of the nature of returns to scale in each industry. First, how large was *minimum efficient scale (MES)* as a fraction of industry output (see Figure 2-2)? In Bain's view, MES was large enough to impede entry if a firm that entered with an MES plant would cause the price to decline so much that existing firms would be bound to realize that entry had taken place.[10] Bain argued that in most industries entry at an MES capacity of 5 per cent or more of industry output would attract rivals' attention.

The second aspect of returns to scale considered by Bain was the extent to which average cost increased as the scale of entry slipped below the MES level. If a firm could not or would not come into an industry at MES capacity, it might nonetheless choose to come in at a smaller scale. But this would not be feasible if coming in at less than the MES involved average costs substantially higher than those of established firms. Established firms would then be in a position to engage in limit pricing.

Bain evaluated other factors that affect entry conditions, including the possibility of economies of multiplant operation and economies of scale in distribution. If there are economies of multiplant operation, an entrant may have to come in on a horizontally integrated basis—in several geographic markets at once.[11] If there are economies of scale in distribution, an entrant may have to come in on a vertically integrated basis—in several vertically related markets.[12]

---

[10]Bain also assumed that existing firms held output constant in the face of entry. Thus the question he asked was: if a new firm comes in at MES and other firms hold output constant, will the price fall so much that incumbent firms realize there is a new kid on the block?

[11]See Scherer, F. M., Beckenstein, A., Kaufer, E., and Murphy, R. D. *The Economics of Multiplant Operation*. Cambridge, Mass.: Harvard University Press, 1975.

[12]See Chandler, A. D., *The Visible Hand*. Cambridge Mass.: Harvard University Press, 1977, Part IV, for a discussion of vertical integration and its effect on competition.

Either factor will make entry more difficult, if only because it increases the investment needed for entry on a competitive basis.[13]

Product Differentiation

Bain singled out three ways in which product differentiation could impede entry. First, in markets with differentiated products, buyers can be expected to prefer the familiar brands of established firms over the unfamilar brands of an entering firm.

To overcome such a preference, an entrant would have to spend more on sales efforts, per dollar of sales, than established firms. If the entrant simply matched the advertising of established firms, the entrant would have to accept a lower price in order to attract consumers. In either case, a limit price differential is created: established firms have some room to raise the price without making entry profitable.

Recall from Chapter 4 that product differentiation is one of the strategies a firm may employ to acquire or maintain a dominant position.[14] Firms advertise to cultivate brand preference precisely *because* this will make entry more difficult.

Second, if there are economies of large scale in sales efforts, the need to advertise may increase the MES, where MES is defined in terms of the minimum average cost of production *and* of promotion.

Third, since the success of a promotional campaign is always in doubt, financial markets will impose a higher cost of capital—a risk premium—on new firms in industries where branding is important.[15]

Absolute Cost Advantages of Established Firms

New firms may face higher costs than established firms at *any* output level, not just when they enter at less than minimum efficient scale. Established firms may control the supply of vital inputs.[16] Financial markets, as noted previously, can be expected to impose a risk premium on new firms in order to compensate for the possibility of bankruptcy and failure to repay loans. The impact of such a risk premium will be greater, the greater the capital investment that a firm needs to finance in order to operate a minimum efficient scale plant.

For this reason, Bain evaluated absolute cost disadvantages by estimating the investment needed to set up an MES plant. When the available data permitted it, he also looked at capital requirements imposed by economies of multiplant or vertically integrated operation.

[13]We return to this topic in Chapters 8 and 9, where we examine the determinants of market and firm structure.

[14]Porter, Michael E. *Competitive Strategy*. New York: The Free Press, 1980.

[15]Here too we anticipate an argument we will pursue in Chapters 8 and 9.

[16]See the discussion of *Alcoa* in Chapter 4 and the 1946 *American Tobacco* case in Chapter 5.

Entry Conditions—Overall

Bain's evaluation of entry conditions was subjective. He made a detailed study of each industry, using publicly available material and information from a survey that he carried out. He devoted one chapter of his book to each of the three sources of entry barriers—scale economies, product differentiation, and absolute cost disadvantages. Then he divided the industries in his sample into three groups, according to the nature of entry barriers:[17]

1. that in the "very high" category, established firms might be able to elevate price 10 per cent or more above minimal costs while forestalling entry;
2. that with "substantial" barriers, the corresponding percentage might range a bit above 7 per cent.
3. that in the "moderate to low" category the same percentage will probably not exceed 4, and will range down to around 1 per cent in the extreme entries in this group.

The amount of work involved in carrying out such a study is incredible. An unavoidable side effect is that the results of the study depend heavily on Bain's subjective judgment. Other researchers faced with the same evidence might reach different conclusions about the nature of entry conditions. Table 7-1 summarizes Bain's conclusions about entry conditions and gives the profit and concentration ratio data for the industries in his sample.

Bain's Results

Figure 7-1 depicts the relationship between concentration and profitability for Bain's sample of 20 industries. Two major results are apparent.

Large firms in industries with very high barriers to entry generally earn higher rates of return than large firms in industries with either substantial or moderate to low entry barriers. In the Bain sample, higher barriers to entry are associated with greater large-firm profitability.

There is a general positive effect of market concentration on profitability. Especially among industries in the substantial entry barrier group, the greater the concentration, the greater the large-firm profit.rate.

Bain interpreted his findings as confirming the hypotheses that he sought to test: that concentration would allow collusion, tacit or otherwise, and that collusion would generate excess profit for large firms if entry barriers were sufficiently high.

The study reviewed here is just one of several influential studies by Bain.

---

[17]Bain, op. cit., p. 170.

Table 7-1 Entry Barriers, Concentration, and Profit—Bain Study
(1947–1951)

Industry	Profit Rate (%)	Four-firm Concentration Ratio
Very High Entry Barriers		
Automobiles	23.9	90
Cigarettes	12.6	90
Liquor	18.6	75
Typewriters	18.0	79
Fountain pens	21.8	57
Average	19.0	78
Substantial Entry Barriers		
Copper	14.6	92
Steel	11.2	45
Farm machines and tractors	13.4	36
Petroleum refining	12.9	37
Soap	15.8	79
Shoes[a]	13.4	28
Gypsum products	15.4	85
Metal containers	10.7	78
Average	13.4	60
Moderate to Low Entry Barriers		
Canned fruit and vegetables	9.8	27
Cement	14.3	30
Flour	10.1	29
Meat packing	5.1	41
Rayon	18.0	78
Shoes[b]	11.0	28
Tires and Tubes	12.7	77
Average	11.6	44

[a]high-priced men's and specialties
[b]women's and low-priced men's
Source: Bain, Joe S. *Barriers to New Competition.* Cambridge Mass.: Harvard University Press, 1956, Table I, p. 45; Table XVI, pp. 192–193, 195. Average values are unweighted.

These studies were replicated by other authors for later time periods. The results of these later studies were generally the same as Bain's original results.[18]

Criticism by those associated with the Chicago school focused on the possibility that Bain's industries were not representative of manufacturing generally

[18]See, for example, Mann, H. Michael. "Seller Concentration, Barriers to Entry, and Rates of Return in Thirty Industries, 1950–1960," *Review of Economics and Statistics* Volume 48, August 1966, pp. 296–307.

164

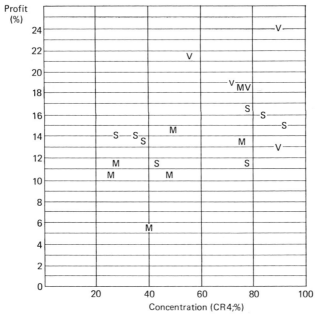

Notes: "Profit" is profit, after taxes, as a percentage of stockholders' equity, for the largest firms in the 20 industries studied by Bain, for the period 1947–1951. The four-firm seller concentration ratios are, for the most part, taken from the 1947 Census of Manufactures.

V, very high entry barriers; S, substantial entry barriers; M, moderate entry barriers.

Figure 7-1   Entry barriers, concentration, and profit, Bain study (1947–1951). Source: See Table 7-1.

and that Bain's work covered disequilibrium periods, so that the relationships he had uncovered would not persist.[19] We need not pursue these criticisms in detail here, because in time the methodology employed in empirical studies of structure–conduct–performance relationships changed. Later research employed different techniques to deal with the same questions addressed by Bain. We now turn to typical econometric studies of structure–performance relationships.

Econometric Studies

Industry-Level Studies

The use of specialized statistical techniques in empirical economic research became common in the 1960s. From that time on, industrial economists have employed econometric techniques to estimate the average relationship between profitability, used as a measure of market power, and various industry structural characteristics. Most econometric studies of structure–performance relation-

[19]Paper Topic 7-1 deals with the Chicago school's criticisms of Bain's work.

ships have used data on industries; a substantial minority of studies have used firm-level data. We consider each type of study in turn.

Collins and Preston

An early and influential econometric industry study by Collins and Preston appeared in 1969.[20] Their work was based on a sample of 417 four-digit Standard Industrial Classification manufacturing industries, virtually all such industries, for 1963.

Measurement Problems

Like Bain, Collins and Preston had to deal with the fact that the available data did not allow them to measure directly the Lerner index of market power. They argued that under some circumstances a gross rate of profit on sales could be used instead of the price-marginal cost margin to measure the degree of market power.

We know from Chapter 2 [Equation (2.5)] that the degree of market power for a monopolist is

$$\frac{P - MC}{P} = \frac{1}{\epsilon_{QP}}. \tag{7.1}$$

We also know (Figure 2-2) that if there are constant returns to scale, average cost and marginal cost are the same. Assume that returns to scale are constant on the ground that constant returns to scale are the most common finding in manufacturing industries.[21] Then

$$MC = AC = \frac{wL + \lambda p^k K}{Q}. \tag{7.2}$$

Average cost is the total cost divided by the number of units of output. Total cost, the numerator on the right-hand side, consists of labor cost (wL) and the rental cost of capital ($\lambda p^k K$).[22] Substitute Equation (7.2) into Equation (7.1) and rearrange slightly to obtain

[20]Collins, N. R. and Preston, L. E. "Price-Cost Margins and Industry Structure," *Review of Economics and Statistics* Volume 51, August 1969, pp. 271–286. For related work, see Collins, N. R. and Preston, L. E. "Concentration and Price-Cost Margins in Food Manufacturing Industries," *Journal of Industrial Economics* Volume 14, Number 3, June 1966, pp. 226–242, and *Concentration and Price-Cost Margins in Manufacturing Industries.* Berkeley: University of California Press, 1968.

[21]For empirical evidence, see Scherer, et al., op. cit. There are sound theoretical reasons for expecting constant returns to scale, rooted in the economics of multiplant operation; see Figure 2-2 and the accompanying text.

[22]λ is the rental cost per dollar's worth of capital assets, which includes a normal rate of return on investment. See Chapter 2, footnote 3. p^k is the purchase price of capital.

166

$$\frac{PQ - wL}{PQ} = \frac{1}{\epsilon_{QP}} + \lambda \frac{p^k K}{PQ}. \tag{7.3}$$

This is almost the relationship estimated by Collins and Preston for their sample of manufacturing industries. The profitability measure, on the left, is the gross rate of return on sales. Since the Census of Manufactures reports the value of shipments (PQ) and the wage bill (wL) for each industry, this price-cost margin can be computed on an industry-by-industry basis.

The final term on the right in Equation (7.3), $p^k K/PQ$, is the value of capital assets per dollar of sales, the capital-sales ratio (KSR). Because capital will earn a normal profit under competition, rates of return on sales (like the price-cost margin) will be larger, the more capital intensive the production techniques, even in the absence of market power. KSR controls for differences in price-cost margins across industries that are due to differences in capital intensity. The asset figures needed to compute the KSR are reported by the Bureau of the Census in the Annual Survey of Manufactures.

The first term on the right in Equation (7.3), the inverse of the price elasticity of demand, is the upper limit on market power for an industry—the degree of market power that would be exercised by a monopolist. The oligopoly theories reviewed in Chapters 5 and 6 suggest that the more concentrated its sales, the closer an industry will come to this maximum level. This can reflect tacit collusion (conjectural variations closer to 1); ease of detecting cheating under actual collusion; or a reduced likelihood of cheating as concentration rises. If we take the relationship between market concentration and market power to be linear, a version of Equation (7.3) that can be estimated with industry data is

$$\text{PCM} = a_0 + a_1 \text{CR4} + a_2 \text{KSR}. \tag{7.4}$$

Collins and Preston actually estimated a slightly more general version of Equation (7.4). They included an additional variable in their study, a measure of the geographic dispersion of producers. They did this to adjust for the fact that the Bureau of the Census computes concentration ratios on a national basis, when in fact some industries are regional or local. For such industries, national concentration ratios will understate the average level of market concentration in smaller markets. For simplicity, this portion of their results is not reported here.

There are two limitations to the test of Equation (7.4) carried out by Collins and Preston. Both were acknowledged by the authors.

When Collins and Preston estimated the average effect of market concentration on price-cost margins for their sample, they made no direct allowance for differences in entry conditions from industry to industry. The major conclusion of Bain's work was that *both* concentration and entry conditions appeared to affect the exercise of market power, so the failure to take account of differences in entry conditions across industries is a potentially serious omission.

Collins and Preston argued, first, that low concentration levels would, "at least implicitly," suggest low entry barriers. Thus concentration ratios would partially reflect differences in entry conditions.

Furthermore, Collins and Preston estimated Equation (7.4) separately for producer-good and consumer-good industries. They expected product differentiation, a major source of entry barriers, to be less important for producer-good industries than for consumer-good industries. Industrial purchasers are fairly knowledgeable about product characteristics and less likely than individuals to be swayed by advertising.

If product differentiation is less a barrier to entry in producer good industries, then splitting the sample of industries into consumer and producer good industries is a "rough" way to take account of differences across industries in entry conditions. Bain's work suggests that concentration will have a smaller effect on profitability in producer-good than in consumer-good industries because entry into producer-good industries will be easier.

The second weakness in the Collins and Preston study is their inability to measure the price elasticity of demand on an industry-by-industry basis. Since the price elasticity of demand places an upper limit on the degree of market power, a highly concentrated industry with a high price elasticity of demand will show a smaller price-cost margin than an equally concentrated industry with a low price elasticity of demand. This will make it harder to get an accurate estimate of the impact of concentration on market power.[23]

Collins and Preston's Results

Typical results from the Collins-Preston study are reported in Table 7-2. The coefficient of the capital-sales ratio is an estimate of the rental cost of capital, which is about 13 percent for producer-good industries and 10 per cent for consumer-good industries. These are generally thought to be reasonable estimates.

As far as structure–performance relationships are concerned, the coefficients of the four-firm seller concentration ratio are of primary interest. It is these coefficients that test the hypothesis that market concentration has a positive effect on market power.

For consumer-good industries, the coefficient of the concentration ratio is

---

[23]For a recent attempt to explain differences in the price elasticity of demand across industries, see Pagoulatos, Emilio and Sorenson, Robert. "What Determines the Elasticity of Industry Demand?," *International Journal of Industrial Organization* Volume 4, Number 3, September 1986, pp. 237–250; for an indirect attempt to incorporate demand variations in structure–performance tests, see Martin, Stephen. "Industry Demand Characteristics and the Structure–Performance Relationship," *Journal of Economics and Business* Volume 34, Number 1, January 1982, pp. 59–65.

Table 7-2 Collins and Preston's Results—Overall Sample

Producer	PCM $= 19.48 + 0.033^{c}$CR4 $+ 0.133^{c}$KSR	$R^2 = 0.26$	(1)
Consumer	PCM $= 17.36 + 0.199^{a}$CR4 $+ 0.103$ KSR	$R^2 = 0.38$	(2)

Notes:

[a] indicates statistical significance at the 1 per cent level; such an estimate would occur by chance only once in 100 times, on average.

[c] indicates statistical significance at the 10 per cent level; such an estimate would occur by chance only once in 10 times, on average.

PCM = price-cost margin; CR4 = four-firm seller concentration ratio; KSR = capital-sales ratio.

Source: Collins, N. R. and Preston, L. E. "Price-Cost Margins and Industry Structure," *Review of Economics and Statistics* Volume 51, August 1969, pp. 271–286, Table 3.

large and statistically significant—unlikely to occur by chance. An increase of 10 percentage points in the four-firm seller concentration ratio—say, from 40 to 50 per cent—has an average effect, for Collins and Preston's consumer-good industries, of increasing the price-cost margin by 1.99 percentage points. To put this result in perspective, the average value of the price-cost margin for the 417 Collins and Preston industries was about 25 per cent. Considering the range of concentration ratios in the economy (from near zero to virtually 100 per cent; see Table 5-2), differences in concentration among consumer-good industries account for a significant portion of the differences in profitability among such industries.

For producer-good industries, the estimated average effect of concentration on price-cost margins is smaller and much less significant (in a statistical sense). For these industries, an increase of 10 percentage points in the four-firm seller concentration ratio brings with it, on average, an increase of only about $\frac{3}{10}$th of 1 percentage point in the price-cost margin.

This is exactly what Collins and Preston predicted when they estimated Equation (7.4) separately for consumer-good and producer-good industries. They expected barriers to entry to be lower for producer-good industries, since product differentiation is likely to be less important there than in consumer-good industries. Following Bain's argument, concentration should allow the exercise of market power only to the extent permitted by barriers to entry.

Large Firms vs. Small Firms

The results reported in Table 7-2 show the average impact of concentration on price-cost margins when the average is over all firms in the industry. Like Bain, Collins and Preston expected the concentration–market power relationship to show up mainly for the largest firms in an industry. Their argument is worth quoting at length for two reasons. First, whether market power should be expected to benefit all firms in an industry or only large firms is an issue that has come to occupy center stage in the debate over the interpretation of results in empirical tests of structure–performance relationships. Second, the position on this issue that was *actually* taken by Collins and Preston (and, for that matter, Bain) has been largely lost in the shuffle:[24]

> We test here the hypothesis that the association between concentration and market power is stronger in those industries in which the largest firms had price-cost margin advantages over their smaller rivals. Theory would suggest that when the largest firms possess distinct advantages, the potential competitive impact of the smaller firms would be reduced and the ability of leaders to pursue a shared-monopoly behavior pattern would therefore be enhanced.
>
> Advantages of the largest firms, that would be reflected in wider price-cost margins, might arise from differences in either their cost or their demand conditions, as compared to those of smaller firms within their industries. If the smaller firms have higher costs, their ability to pursue aggressively competitive policies against the largest firms is substantially reduced. The largest firms will be able to gain higher profits from any given price common to both groups of firms; and they will also be able to use additional expenditures (out of those profits) and the threat of price reductions as a means of disciplining the industry and expanding their market control. Cost advantages of large firms may be due to many factors—longer operating histories, access to scarce resources, genuine scale economies—and these, in turn, may also be associated with entry barriers, which further strengthen the market positions and widen the range of discretion of the largest firms. On the demand side, advantages of the largest firms may arise from longer periods of buyer acceptance, more extensive distribution systems, or successful product differentiation. To the extent that such demand factors are operative, the largest firms may face different and less elastic demand schedules than their smaller rivals, and therefore be able to obtain higher prices and margins for their products.

Collins and Preston thus reasoned that the (tacit or overt) collusion allowed by concentration of sales would benefit only the largest firms, especially where larger firms have cost or product-differentiation advantages over smaller firms.

Collins and Preston also pointed out that the industry-average value of the price-cost margin will tend to be dominated by the price-cost margins of the largest firms.[25] If large firms are more efficient than small firms, this will tend to create a relationship between price-cost margins and concentration that has nothing to do with market power.

On the other hand, if concentration tends to raise the average price-cost margin of large firms, that result should reflect market power and not a differential efficiency effect. This is another reason to test Equation (7.4) separately for large and small firms.

---

[24]Collins, N. R. and Preston, L. E. "Price-Cost Margins and Industry Structure," *Review of Economics and Statistics* Volume 51, August 1969, p. 280.

[25]This is because this industry-average price-cost margin is a weighted average of firm price-cost margins, with weights equal to market shares. Larger firms' price-cost margins are given greater weight in computing the industry average.

Table 7-3 Effect of Concentration on Margins of the Largest Firms and Margins of Smaller Firms

	Large Firms' Margins Greater	Small Firms' Margins Greater
Producer-Good Industries		
Largest four firms	0.017	−0.021
All other firms	0.002	−0.009
Consumer-Good Industries		
Largest four firms	0.190[a]	0.091[c]
All other firms	0.061	0.047

Notes:

[a] indicates statistical significance at the 1 per cent level; such an estimate would occur by chance only once in 100 times, on average.

[c] indicates statistical significance at the 10 per cent level; such an estimate would occur by chance only once in 10 times, on average.

The table shows the estimated coefficient of the four-firm seller concentration ratio, in estimates of Equation (7.4), for large-firm and other firm price-cost margins and for two subsamples of the entire data set: industries for which large firms had greater margins than other firms, and industries for which large firms had smaller margins than other firms.

Source: Collins, N. R. and Preston, L. E. "Price-Cost Margins and Industry Structure," *Review of Economics and Statistics* Volume 51, August 1969, pp. 271–286, Table 7.

Collins and Preston estimated Equation (7.4) for the four largest firms in each industry and for other, smaller firms. The estimated coefficients of the four-firm seller concentration ratio are shown in Table 7-3.

For producer-good industries, the estimated impact of concentration on price-cost margins is never as large as in Table 7-2 (indeed, it is negative for small firms) and is never precise in a statistical sense.

For consumer-good industries, the story is different. Among 94 consumer good industries in which large firms had greater margins than small firms, the coefficient of CR4 in the estimate of Equation (7.4) was 0.190—almost as large as the 0.199 reported in line 2 of Table 7-2. For 48 consumer-good industries in which larger firms had smaller price-cost margins than small firms, the estimated coefficient of concentration in the estimate of Equation (7.4) was 0.091. The estimated effect of concentration on the price-cost margins of smaller firms was positive for consumer good industries, but never precise in a statistical sense.

In other words, for consumer-good industries, Collins and Preston found— as they had expected—that market concentration increased the price-cost margins of large firms, where large firms had greater margins than small firms.

They also found that market concentration in such industries did not mean greater margins for small firms.

Collins and Preston's results show that concentration raises price-cost margins only where small firms are at some competitive disadvantage. The fact that the most significant impact of concentration on price-cost margins occurred in consumer-good industries suggests that product differentiation is an important source of such competitive disadvantages. This result is entirely consistent with the oligopoly models of Chapter 5. When small firms are at no cost or differentiation disadvantage vis-à-vis large firms, small firms will be able to expand output if large firms achieve a collusive understanding and restrict output. Even if such markets are concentrated, the leading firms will not have much leeway to exercise market power.

Strickland and Weiss

As noted previously, the Collins and Preston study did not explictly control for differences in entry conditions across industries. An important question is whether or not their results hold up when such differences are taken into account.

To test this, a number of researchers have extended Collins and Preston's work. Typical results—those of Strickland and Weiss—are reported in Table

Table 7-4 Strickland and Weiss's Results

Producer-Good Industries
$PCM = 17.23 + 0.060^c CR4 + 0.119^a KSR + 1.778^a ASR - 0.142\ MES \qquad (1)$

Consumer-Good Industries
$PCM = 17.83 + 0.095^c CR4 - 0.004\ KSR + 1.396^a ASR + 0.520^b MES \qquad (2)$

Notes:
[a] indicates statistical significance at the 1 per cent level; such an estimate would occur by chance only once in 100 times, on average.
[b] indicates statistical significance at the 5 per cent level; such an estimate would occur by chance only once in 20 times, on average.
[c] indicates statistical significance at the 10 per cent level; such an estimate would occur by chance only once in 10 times, on average.
PCM = price-cost margin; CR4 = four-firm seller concentration ratio; KSR = capital-sales ratio; ASR = advertising-sales ratio; MES = minimum efficient scale as a fraction of industry output.
For compactness, coefficients of certain variables are not reported. The R-squared statistic is not available for these estimates, which were obtained using instrumental variables.

Source: Strickland, A. D. and Weiss, L. W. "Advertising, Concentration, and Price-Cost Margins," *Journal of Political Economy* Volume 84, Number 5, October 1976, pp. 1109–1121, Tables 3 and 4.

7-4. Like Collins and Preston, Strickland and Weiss studied manufacturing industries for 1963. Roughly the same number of industries were used in both studies.

Measurement

Strickland and Weiss were able to estimate the MES plant size from information on the distribution of plant size, as reported for each industry in the Census of Manufactures. They took the average plant size among plants in the middle of the size distribution (roughly: half of the plants in the industry are larger, half are smaller) and used that figure as an estimate of MES.

To control for differences in product differentiation from industry to industry, Strickland and Weiss used the industry-average ratio of expenditures on advertising per dollar of sales.[26]

Note that in contrast to Bain's subjective judgments about entry conditions, MES and ASR are objective. Any researcher who used the Strickland-Weiss methodology would obtain the same values for MES and ASR, industry by industry.

Strickland and Weiss's Results

The Strickland-Weiss results show the importance of product differentiation in determining price-cost margins. For consumer-good industries, the average ASR in their sample was probably[27] a little less than 4 per cent, with a range from nearly 0 to 29 per cent. An increase of 1 percentage point in ASR—say, from 4 to 5 per cent—would be relatively small for consumer-good industries. According to the Strickland-Weiss estimates, such a change would bring, on average, an increase of nearly 1.396 percentage points in the price-cost margin. This is nearly as large a change in the price-cost margin as Collins and Preston attributed to a 10 percentage point increase in CR4.

Strickland and Weiss found an impact of concentration on price-cost margins only about half the size of the effect estimated by Collins and Preston. By the estimates of Strickland and Weiss, a 10 percentage point increase in CR4 would result in an increase in consumer-good industry price-cost margins of 0.95 percentage points, versus 1.99 by Collins and Preston's estimates.

---

[26]The source for spending on advertising is the 1963 Input-Output Tables for the United States. Input-output tables, using a detailed industry classification that is comparable to, but not identical to, the standard industrial classification, are produced for the same years as the Census of Manufactures.

[27]Strickland and Weiss do not report average values for the data in their sample. The average values for ASR given in the text are from a similar sample, used by Martin, Stephen. "Advertising, Concentration, and Profitability: the Simultaneity Problem," *Bell Journal of Economics* Volume 10, Number 2, Autumn 1979, pp. 639–647.

For producer-good industries, the average value of the ASR was probably about 1 per cent, with a range from nearly 0 to 4 per cent. An increase of 1 percentage in the ASR would therefore be very large for producer-good industries. The Strickland-Weiss estimates suggest that the average effect of such an increase for producer-good industries would be an increase of 1.778 percentage points in the price-cost margin. Product differentiation is less important for producer-good than consumer-good industries, or at least there is less advertising for producer-good industries. But where advertising occurs in producer-good industries, it acts to raise price-cost margins.

For producer-good industries, including ASR as a right-hand-side variable roughly doubles the estimated effect of concentration on margins (0.060 for Strickland-Weiss vs. 0.033 for Collins-Preston).[28]

Strickland and Weiss' results for MES are weaker, in a statistical sense, than their results for ASR. For producer-good industries, Strickland and Weiss find no significant effect of MES on price-cost margins. There is a modestly significant effect of MES on price-cost margins for consumer-good industries. The average value of MES for consumer-good industries in the Strickland-Weiss study was probably around 4 per cent, with a range from nearly 0 to about 18 per cent. Doubling MES, from 4 to 8 per cent, would raise the price-cost margin by 2.08 percentage points. This is about the same change in the price-cost margin that would come from a 20 percentage-point increase in concentration ($20 \times 0.095 = 1.9$) or an increase in ASR of 1.5 percentage points ($1.5 \times 1.396 = 2.094$). For consumer-good industries, therefore, the Strickland-Weiss estimates suggest an important effect of MES on price-cost margins.

---

[28]Studies of the effect of advertising on rates of return on capital generally show results similar to those of Strickland and Weiss. For a seminal study, see Comanor, William S. and Wilson, Thomas A. "Advertising Market Structure and Performance," *Review of Economics and Statistics* Volume 49, Number 4, November 1967, pp. 423–440. Chicago school criticisms of this sort of study argue that the goodwill generated by advertising should be treated as a capital good, so that expenditures on advertising should be treated as an investment rather than a current expense. Other studies suggest that this treatment does not make much difference in the results, although this appears to depend on how rapidly one assumes advertising depreciates. See Bloch, Harry. "Advertising and Profitability: a Reappraisal," *Journal of Political Economy*, Volume 82, Number 2, Part 1, March–April 1974, pp. 267–286; Weiss, Leonard. "Advertising, Profits, and Corporate Taxes," *Review of Economics and Statistics* Volume 54, Number 4, November 1969, pp. 421–430; Siegfried, John J. and Weiss, Leonard W. "Advertising, Concentration, and Corporate Taxes Revisited," *Review of Economics and Statistics* Volume 56, May 1974, pp. 195–200. This entire literature seems misplaced, however: basic models show that for tests of market power, profitability should be measured gross of expenditures on product-differentiating activities, and the "capital" included in measures of capital intensity should be the value of capital assets that appear in the production function, not assets that affect the position of the demand curve. So far as I know, this point was first made by Sawyer, Malcolm W. "On the Specification of Structure–Performance Relationships," *European Economic Review* Volume 17, March 1982, pp. 295–306.

Industry-Level Studies—Summary[29]

The Strickland-Weiss results are generally characteristic of industry-level studies of structure–performance relationships. Such studies usually show a strong positive effect of advertising on price-cost margins, with weaker positive effects for market concentration and economies of scale. As Bain expected, the market most congenial to the exercise of market power is a concentrated market, where firms must operate at large scale and cultivate a brand image with consumers to survive.

Firm-Level Studies

Most empirical tests of structure–performance relationships have used industry-level data. The main reason is that industry-level data are easily available, being publicly reported in the Census of Manufactures. A smaller group of studies has used data for individual firms.

The advantage of using firm-level data is that one can examine the effect of changes in market share, rather then market concentration, on market performance. The oligopoly models of Chapters 5 and 6 suggest that market share will be one of the critical structural determinants of the degree of market power.

An early and influential study using firm-level data was carried out by Shepherd.[30] Shepherd's study included 231 large firms, almost all of them among the 500 largest industrial firms in the United States, for the period 1960–1969.

Measurement

Like Bain, Shepherd used profit after taxes as a percentage of stockholders' equity as a measure of profitability. By working with data on individual firms,

---

[29]A large literature examines the robustness of these basic results to controlling for various aspects of industry structure. Special mention should be made of the literature examining the effect of foreign competition on domestic market performance, reviewed in Chapter 13; and Lustgarten, S. R., "The Impact of Buyer Concentration in Manufacturing Industries," *Review of Economics and Statistics* Volume 57, Number 2, May 1975, pp. 125–132, who finds that concentrated industries that sell to concentrated industries have lower price-cost margins than would otherwise be the case. A related literature, which we do not cover here, suggests that monopoly profits may translate into higher wages for employees of firms that exercise market power; see Weiss, Leonard W. "Concentration and Labor Earnings," *American Economic Review* Volume 56, Number 1, March 1966, pp. 96–117; Martin, Stephen and Rence, Cynthia. "Vertical Spillovers, Market Concentration, Union Coverage, and Wages," *Journal of Labor Research,* Volume 5, Number 2, Spring 1984, pp. 177–189; Salinger, Michael A. "Tobin's q, Unionization, and the Concentration–Profits Relationship," *Rand Journal of Economics* Volume 15, Number 2, Summer 1984, pp. 159–170; and Karier, Thomas. "Unions and Monopoly Profits," *Review of Economics and Statistics* Volume 67, Number 1, February 1985, pp. 34–42.

[30]Shepherd, W. G. "The Elements of Market Structure," *Review of Economics and Statistics* Volume 54, Number 1, February 1972, pp. 25–37.

Shepherd was able to separate the influence of market share and market concentration on market power.

Shepherd used two variables to control for differences in entry conditions. The firm's ASR should give an indication of the product-differentiation advantages it enjoys. The firm's size, as measured by the value of its capital assets,[31] measures the absolute capital requirements for entry into the firm's industry, another element of entry barriers.

Shepherd's Results

As shown in Table 7-5, Shepherd found a large positive effect of market share on the after-tax rate of return. The average market share in the Shepherd study was about 21 per cent, and the average rate of return was a little less than 12 per cent. An increase in market share from 21 to 25 per cent would, on average, raise the rate of return by a full percentage point ($4 \times 0.24 = 0.96$).

In contrast, for Shepherd's sample, an increase of 35.5 percentage points in the four-firm seller concentration ratio would be required to get the same increase in the rate of return ($35.5 \times 0.027 = 0.96$). The average value of the concentration ratio for the Shepherd study is fairly high—63 per cent—but an increase of 35.5 percentage points would still be a major increase. Shepherd's results indicate that market share has a much more important effect on the rate of return than market concentration.

The result for ASR confirms Bain's entry barrier theory. The average ASR

Table 7-5 Shepherd's Results

$$(P - T)/SE = 6.67^a + 0.240^a MS + 0.027^c CR4 + 0.250^a ASR - 0.300^c(\text{asset size}) \qquad R^2 = 0.504$$

Notes:
^{a} indicates statistical significance at the 1 per cent level; such an estimate would occur by chance only once in 100 times, on average.
^{c} indicates statistical significance at the 10 per cent level; such an estimate would occur by chance only once in 10 times, on average.
$(P - T)/SE$ = profit after taxes over stockholders' equity; MS = market share; CR4 = four-firm seller concentration ratio; ASR = advertising-sales ratio.

For compactness, coefficients of certain variables are not reported. The coefficients, as estimated by Shepherd, have been adjusted for comparability with previously reported results.

Source: Shepherd, W. G. "The Elements of Market Structure," Review of Economics and Statistics Volume 54, Number 1, February 1972, pp. 25–37, Table 2.

[31]The precise variable used by Shepherd was the natural logarithm of the value of assets.

in the Shepherd sample is only about 2.5 per cent, but some firms spent much more than average. Firms that advertised twice as much as the average had, by the Shepherd estimates, a rate of return about $\frac{6}{10}$ths of 1 percentage point ($2.5 \times 0.25 = 0.625$) greater on that account. That is as large a change as a 2.6 percentage point increase in market share or a 23 percentage point increase in CR4.

Shepherd's results for firm size are less plausible than his other findings. His estimates indicate that large firms are less profitable than small firms after taking account of the effect of market share, market concentration, and advertising intensity. This is not the result that Shepherd expected. He interprets it as reflecting diseconomies of scale: higher costs for large firms as management loses control of operations at large scale.[32] Other studies on the effect of firm size on rates of return[33] find effects that are the opposite of Shepherd's, so his results on this point cannot be considered definitive.

Firm-Level Studies—Summary

The main result of the Shepherd study is that market share has a large positive effect on the firm's rate of return. This result is generally confirmed by other studies that use firm-level data to study the impact of firm and market characteristics on firm profitability.[34] It is consistent with the predictions of the oligopoly models of Chapters 5 and 6.

Shepherd's finding that the effect of concentration on firm profitability is relatively small is confirmed by other studies, which use firm-level data to study the impact of firm and market characteristics on various stock market–based measures of firm value.[35] What this finding suggests is that the positive effect of market concentration on market profitability, found in industry-level studies, reflects the firm-level effect of market share on firm profitability.

---

[32]For an introduction to this X-inefficiency hypothesis, see Leibenstein, H. "Allocational Efficiency and 'X-Efficiency,' " *American Economic Review* Volume 56, June 1966, pp. 392–416.

[33]For example, Hall, M. and Weiss, L. W. "Firm Size and Profitability," *Review of Economics and Statistics* Volume 49, August 1967, pp. 319–331.

[34]See Gale, Bradley T. "Market Share and Rate of Return," *Review of Economics and Statistics* Volume 54, Number 4, November 1972, pp. 412–423; Martin, Stephen, "Market, Firm, and Economic Performance," Salomon Brothers Center for the Study of Financial Institutions Monograph Series in Finance and Economics, Monograph 1983-1; and Ravenscraft, David J. "Structure–Profit Relationships at the Line of Business and Industry Level," *Review of Economics and Statistics* Volume 65, Number 1, February 1983, pp. 22–31.

[35]See, for example, Lindenberg, Eric and Ross, Stephen. "Tobin's q Ratio and Industrial Organization," *Journal of Business* Volume 54, January 1981, pp. 1–32; Harris, Frederick H. deB. "Growth Expectations, Excess Value, and the Risk-Adjusted Return to Market Power," *Southern Economic Journal* Volume 51, July 1984, pp. 166–179.

Econometric Studies—Recapitulation

Leaving out much detail, the results of empirical tests of structure on performance can be summarized as follows. At the industry level, the most important single factor explaining differences in performance is product differentiation, as measured by the ASR. There is evidence of an independent effect of scale economies (MES) and market concentration (CR4) on market power, especially for consumer-good industries. These results confirm the attention Bain gave to entry barriers as a determinant of market performance.

At the firm level, market share and market concentration appear to be the most important factors in explaining market power. Market concentration, although still a factor, seems less important than market share (and we will subsequently see that recent work raises additional questions about the effect of market concentration on performance).

Criticism

The empirical results just reported—a small positive effect of market concentration on profitability, generally larger positive effects for market share and product differentiation—are generally accepted. The proper interpretation of these results, however, has been and remains a matter of intense controversy.

This controversy stems from the kinds of policy standards that have been motivated by the research previously described. In interpreting the antitrust laws, courts have looked at a firm's market share to decide whether or not the firm possesses market power. Justice Department Merger Guidelines[36]—intended to give information to the business community about the kinds of mergers that will be challenged by antitrust authorities—are expressed partly in terms of the market shares of the merging firms and the Herfindahl indices of the markets involved. Research like the work we have studied justifies the belief that it is appropriate to express public policy standards in terms of market structural characteristics.

A high-water mark of sorts was reached in the early 1970s, when Senator Philip A. Hart of Michigan proposed an Industrial Reorganization Act. Under this proposal, a firm would have been found to have market power either if it earned a high after-tax rate of return on stockholders' equity[37] or if the industry's four-firm seller concentration ratio exceeded 50 per cent. In some cases, forced breakup of a company would follow a finding of market power.[38]

[36]Which we will examine in detail in Chapter 10.

[37]More than 15 per cent for 5 years in a row.

[38]For the text of the Hart proposal, see Appendix B of Goldschmid, H. J., Mann, H. M., and Weston, J. F., editors, *Industrial Concentration: The New Learning*. Boston: Little, Brown and Company, 1974.

The prospect of such severe regulation of market behavior prompted a close examination of the foundations of the relevant research. The most important criticism that emerged from this examination focused on the proper interpretation of the studies previously reported.[39]

Market Power vs. Efficiency

The most important criticism to emerge from the debates of the 1970s is associated with the work of Demsetz.[40] He argued that the commonly observed impact of market share and market concentration on rates of return reflected greater efficiency of large-scale operation, not market power:[41]

> A phenomenon that is likely to generate fairly persistent differences in accounting rates of return is the fact that some products are more efficiently produced by firms possessing a large share of the market, while in other industries large market shares are not necessary for efficiency. Those firms that first act on the belief that large scale is an advantage, and that invest in the marketing and production techniques prerequisite to executing the move to large scale, will possess a competitively secured advantage in timing and in obtaining early consumer acceptance that will be difficult to overcome in a short period. The market may not have grown large enough to accommodate more than a handful of such firms. These firms can produce at lower unit cost than smaller firms. They are superior in this respect, and they command an economic rent for achieving primacy. This rent will be measured as profit by accountants.

Taken literally, this argument seems little more than a description of the acquisition of a dominant market position through strategic competition. But Demsetz uses it to give an efficiency-based interpretation to the positive average relationship found between market concentration and rates of return.

[39]Other criticisms involved the quality of the data employed in structure–performance studies and statistical methodology. On the former, see Leibowitz, op. cit.; Fisher, F. M. and McGowan, J. J., "On the Misuse of Accounting Rates of Return to Infer Monopoly Profits," *American Economic Review* Volume 73, Number 1, March 1983, pp. 82–97, as well as comments and a reply in the June 1984 issue of the *American Economic Review,* and Kay, J. A. and Mayer, C. P. "On the Application of Accounting Rates of Return," *Economic Journal* Volume 96, Number 381, March 1986, pp. 199–207. On the latter, see Mancke, R. B. "Causes of Interfirm Profitability Differences: A New Interpretation of the Evidence," *Quarterly Journal of Economics* Volume 88, Number 2, May 1974, pp. 181–193, and Caves, R. E., Gale, B. T., and Porter, M. E. "Interfirm Profitability Differences: Comment," *Quarterly Journal of Economics* Volume 91, Number 4, November 1977, pp. 667–675.

[40]Demsetz, H. "Two Systems of Belief About Monopoly," in Goldschmid et al., op. cit.; "Industry Structure, Market Rivalry, and Public Policy," *Journal of Law and Economics* Volume 16, Number 1, April 1973, pp. 1–9; "More on Collusion and Advertising: A Reply," *Journal of Law and Economics* Volume 19, Number 1, April 1976, pp. 205–209. See also Brozen, Y. "Bain's Concentration and Rates of Return Revisited," *Journal of Law and Economics* Volume 14, October, 1971, pp. 351–369.

[41]Demsetz, H. "Two Systems," pp. 176–177.

Which industries will be concentrated? Industries in which large firms have a competitive advantage:[42]

> In a world in which information and resource mobility can be secured only at a cost, an industry will become concentrated under competitive conditions only if a differential advantage in expanding output develops in some firms. Such expansion will increase the degree of concentration at the same time that it increases the rate of return that these firms earn. The cost advantage that gives rise to increased concentration may be reflected in scale economies or in downward shifts in positively sloped marginal cost curves, or it may be reflected in better products which satisfy demand at lower cost.

Large firms with such cost advantages will have higher rates of return than small firms, but because their costs are lower, not because they are able to hold the price above the level needed to cover the cost of smaller, less efficient firms. Industry-average rates of return will be dominated by the rates of return of the largest firms. This means that the industry-average rate of return will be greater, the greater the degree of concentration. Empirical studies will find a positive relationship between market share or market concentration and industry-average rates of return.[43] Market concentration *and* high rates of return both result from greater efficiency of large-scale operation in some industries. The positive relationship between market concentration and rates of return does not (need not, in more careful statements) indicate tacit or overt collusion.

Efficiency and Market Power—Theory

The logic behind the ''efficiency'' hypothesis is that more efficient firms will have larger rates of return because of their efficiency. As economists usually model firm behavior, however, a firm will choose to exercise less market power as it becomes more efficient. A firm that can lower unit costs by expanding output will take a lower price, in order to sell more, so it can get the benefit of lower costs per unit.

To see this, return to Equation (7.1), which shows the relationship between price, marginal cost, and elasticity for a profit-maximizing monopolist. Taking (for simplicity) the case of constant marginal cost, we easily obtain from Equation (7.1)

$$\frac{c}{P} = 1 - \frac{1}{\epsilon_{QP}}. \tag{7.5}$$

[42]Demsetz, H. ''Industry Structure, Market Rivalry, and Public Policy,'' p. 1.

[43]This argument was anticipated by Collins and Preston, and motivated their examination of the structural determinants of large-firm profitability.

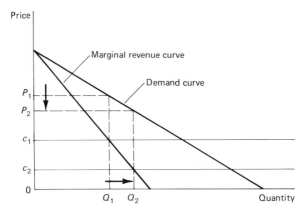

Figure 7-2 Efficiency and monopoly price.

For a profit-maximizing monopolist, price is proportional to marginal cost. Price is a markup over marginal cost, with the size of the markup depending on the price elasticity of demand. It follows immediately that if one compares two firms, one with a lower marginal cost than the other, the firm with the lower marginal cost will have a *lower* price.

The same point may be made graphically. Figure 7-2 shows the effect on monopoly price of a reduction in marginal cost. Suppose a monopolist's marginal cost falls from c_1 to c_2, because (say) a new technology has been discovered or the firm has been taken over by a superior management team. As marginal cost falls, the intersection of the marginal cost curve and the marginal revenue curve moves down the marginal revenue curve. The monopolist increases output and lowers price as costs fall. More efficient firms will charge a lower price, all else equal, if they seek to maximize their profit.[44]

The efficiency interpretation of the positive relationship between market concentration and rate of return is that firms with scale advantages will be able to take a higher return per unit than other firms, because their costs are lower. But a firm with scale advantages will want to take a lower profit per unit sold, because increases in output reduce its average cost and increase its total profit. It is not all clear that the efficiency hypothesis can explain an observed positive impact of market share (or market concentration) on price-cost margins.

Market Power vs. Efficiency—Empirical Evidence

Demsetz carried out an empirical test to support his interpretation of the concentration–rate of return relationship. He reasoned as follows: collusion will

---

[44]The point that a monopolist will lower its price as its costs fall is made by Robert Bork. *The Antitrust Paradox*. New York: Basic Books, 1978, p. 307. The same results hold for oligopoly and for cases in which the marginal cost is not constant. See Martin, Stephen. ''The Measurement of Profitability and the Diagnosis of Market Power,'' forthcoming, *International Journal of Industrial Organization*.

Table 7-6 Rates of Return by Firm
Size and Market Concentration

CR4	Number of Industries	R_1	R_4
10–20%	14	7.3%	8.0%
20–30	22	4.4	10.6
30–40	24	5.1	11.7
40–50	21	4.8	9.4
50–60	11	0.9	12.2
Over 60	3	5.0	21.6

Notes: Data are for 1963. The rate of return is profit plus interest payments as a percentage of the value of total assets, computed from Internal Revenue Service sources. R_1 is the smallest firm size class, firms with assets less than $500,000. R_4 is the largest firm size class, firms with assets over $50,000,000. Demsetz reports rates of return for intermediate size classes, but these are omitted for compactness.

Source: Demsetz, Harold. "Industry Structure, Market Rivalry, and Public Policy," *Journal of Law and Economics* Volume 16, Number 1, 1973, Table 2, p. 6.

benefit all firms in an industry. If concentration represents collusion, small firms as well as large firms should earn higher rates of return in concentrated industries. But if concentration represents the greater efficiency of large firms, only the rates of return of large firms will be higher in concentrated industries.[45]

Demsetz presented evidence reported in Table 7-6, which shows how the average rate of return changes for small and large firms as concentration increases.

There is a general tendency for the rate of return to rise with concentration for large firms, but no evidence at all that this happens for small firms. Demsetz interprets this result as supporting the efficiency hypothesis and as contrary to the market power explanation for a positive relationship between concentration and rates of return.

But this test depends on an artificially limited version of the concentration–market power hypothesis. Both Bain and Collins and Preston, in arguments previously presented, fully expected that the market power allowed by market concentration would benefit mainly the large firms in an industry.

The general position of the structure-conduct-performance school has been that small firms will suffer cost disadvantages compared with large firms, and that small firms will benefit less from product differentiation advantages than large firms. The conclusion that follows is that small firms in a concentrated industry are *not* expected to benefit from tacit or overt collusion in the same way as large firms.

[45]Demsetz, H. "Two Systems," p. 177.

Table 7-7 Market Concentration, Efficiency, and Market Power

$$PCM14 = -0.3160^a + 0.2241^a RP14 + 0.1933^a CR4 - 0.2071^b CR58 - 0.0138 CR9P \quad (1)$$
$$PCM58 = -0.3239^a + 0.2724^a RP58 + 0.1062^b CR4 - 0.1561^c CR58 - 0.0498 CR9P \quad (2)$$
$$PCM9P = -0.2453^a + 0.3507^a RP9P + 0.0664^c CR4 - 0.0257 CR58 - 0.0408^c CR9P \quad (3)$$

Notes: PCM14 = price-cost margin of largest four firms
　　　 PCM58 = price-cost margin of fifth—eighth largest firms
　　　 PCM9P = price-cost margin of remaining firms
　　　 CR4　 = combined market share of largest four firms
　　　 CR58　= combined market share of fifth—eighth largest firms
　　　 CR9P　= combined market share of remaining firms
　　　 RP14　= value-added/worker of largest four firms, divided
　　　　　　　　by industry-average value-added per worker
　　　 RP58　= value-added/worker of fifth—eighth largest firms,
　　　　　　　　divided by industry-average value-added per
　　　　　　　　worker
　　　 RP9P　= value-added/worker of remaining firms, divided
　　　　　　　　by industry-average value-added per worker

[a] indicates statistical significance at the 1 per cent level; such an estimate would occur by chance only once in 100 times, on average.

[b] indicates statistical significance at the 5 per cent level; such an estimate would occur by chance only once in 20 times, on average.

[c] indicates statistical significance at the 10 per cent level; such an estimate would occur by chance only once in 10 times, on average.

For a sample of 185 four-digit Standard Industrial Classification industries, 1972.

Source: Martin, Stephen "Market Power and/or Efficiency?," forthcoming, *Review of Economics and Statistics.*

The Chicago school has argued against the hypothesis that concentration raises the profit rates of all firms in an industry. They have not confronted the hypothesis that concentration will support market power that benefits large firms but not small firms.

Table 7-7 reports the results of an econometric test of the effects of concentration and efficiency explanations on the price-cost margins of the four largest firms in an industry, the fifth through eighth largest firms, and the remaining smaller firms.

Labor productivity is used to measure the way efficiency varies with firm size. In Table 7-7, RP14 is value-added per worker among the largest four firms, divided by industry-average value-added per worker. RP58 is value-added per worker for the fifth through eighth largest firms, divided by industry-average value-added per worker. RP9P is value-added per worker for the ninth and smaller firms, divided by industry-average value-added per worker. The larger each RP variable, the greater the productivity of the corresponding group of firms.

Concentration is measured, as usual, by the combined market shares of each group of firms. CR4 is the four-firm seller concentration ratio. CR58 is the combined market share of the fifth through eighth largest firms. CR9P is the combined market share of the ninth and smaller firms.

The results reported in Table 7-7 support *both* the market power and efficiency explanations for market power. The price-cost margins of each group rise with its own productivity. This finding is consistent with the efficiency explanation of market power. But the price-cost margins of each group also rise as the market share of the largest four firms increases. This finding is consistent with the strong Chicago school characterization of the concentration–market power hypothesis.

Price-cost margins of each group fall as the market shares of intermediate-sized (fifth through eighth) and smaller firms rise. Competition from smaller firms limits the ability of the largest firms to exercise market power.

Demsetz's Policy Conclusions

After making tests like those described in Table 7-6, Demsetz offered a "compromise explanation" for the results of empirical tests of structure–performance relationships:[46]

> Larger firms in concentrated industries have lower cost because there are scale economies in these industries or because of some inherent superiority of the larger firms in these industries. Nonetheless they succeed in colluding so that *their* profit rates are relatively high. The prices they set in this collusion are not so high as to yield high profits for less efficient, more moderately sized firms. Hence we observe a stronger positive correlation between profit rates and market concentration for the largest firms than for other firms.
>
> In this rationalization of the data, the cost of production to moderate-sized firms in concentrated markets apparently sets the upper limit to the prices that are (can be?) set through the collusion of large firms. . . .
>
> This compromise explanation hardly can justify a call for deconcentration, because considerable economies of large-scale production or other advantages of existing large firms would then be lost with no compensation in the form of lower prices.

This too is very much a limit price story: it is the presence of small firms that places a limit on the degree of market power exercised by large firms. It is also consistent with the results reported in Table 7-7. This compromise explanation of the observed positive relationship between market share, market concentration, and market power is probably acceptable to most economists.

Market concentration can reflect elements of efficiency *and* market power, and policymakers need to take both into account. Blanket deconcentration policies of the kind embodied in the Hart Industrial Reorganization bill are not appropriate, because they ignore possible efficiencies of large-scale operation.

[46]Demsetz, H. "Two Systems," pp. 178–179.

But by the same token, a permissive attitude toward strategies designed to maintain dominant positions is not appropriate, because such an attitude ignores the fact that large firms will exercise market power to the extent that they enjoy cost advantages vis-à-vis small firms.

Recent Work[47]

One result of the criticism of empirical studies in the Bain tradition has been a change in the kind of empirical research carried out by students of industrial economics.

The Bain tradition involves trying to explain differences in performance across fairly large groups of industries. The compromise explanation offered by Demsetz for the results of such studies is that the concentration–profitability relationship will reflect *both* market power and efficiency in an uncertain combination. In any industry, there will be a tradeoff between market power losses and efficiency gains. In some industries, the tradeoff will balance out in favor of efficiency; in other industries, in favor of market power. What this conclusion suggests is that it will be useful to study structure–conduct–performance relationships on an industry-by-industry basis.

Industrial economists continue to study the determinants of performance for groups of industries. But more and more empirical research involves studying structure–conduct–performance relationships for single firms or industries, which avoids the criticisms leveled at industry cross-sectional studies. Here we review a few studies that are typical of this new line of research.

Collusion

Chapter 6 gives some background on the electrical equipment conspiracies of the 1950s. Lean, Ogur, and Rogers[48] use survey data collected under the authority of the Federal Trade Commission to examine the impact of this collusion on the gross rate of return on sales (a variable similar to Collins and Preston's price-cost margin). The sample includes 70 firms, which were in-

---

[47]With some reluctance, I have omitted from this section a discussion of a line of research that employs stock market data to test structure–performance relationships. Lindenberg and Ross, op. cit., is one example; Harris, Frederick H. deB., "Market Structure and Price-Cost Performance Under Endogenous Risk," *Journal of Industrial Economics* Volume 35, Number 1, September 1986, pp. 35–59, is another. The decision to omit a discussion of this line of research is made on pedagogical grounds: to discuss it properly would require an excursion into the theory of financial markets, which is relatively unrelated to other material treated in the text.

[48]Lean, David F., Ogur, Jonathan D., and Rogers, Robert P. *Competition and Collusion in Electrical Equipment Markets: An Economic Assessment.* Washington, D.C.: Bureau of Economics, Federal Trade Commission, July 1982; "Does Collusion Pay . . . Does Antitrust Work?", *Southern Economic Journal* Volume 51, Number 3, January 1985, pp. 828–841.

Table 7-8 Collusion in Electrical Equipment Markets

$$\text{PCM} = -12.09^a + 13.09^a\text{CR2} + 127.99^a\text{MS3} + 32.59^a\text{MSOWN}$$
$$- 8.74^a\text{CUSTOM} + 2.02^b\text{CON5759} + 7.00^a\text{SIG6470}$$

Notes:
PCM	= firm's gross rate of return on sales
CR2	= two-firm concentration ratio (combined market share of the two largest firms)
MS3	= market share of the third largest firm
MSOWN	= firm's own market share in the product
CUSTOM	= 1 if the product is made to order, 0 otherwise
CON5759	= 1 if the year is 1957, 1958, or 1959, 0 otherwise
SIG6470	= 1 for turbine generators, 1964–1970; 0 otherwise

a indicates statistical significance at the 1 per cent level; such an estimate would occur by chance only once in 100 times, on average.

b indicates statistical significance at the 5 per cent level; such an estimate would occur by chance only once in 20 times, on average.

For compactness, coefficients of certain variables are not reported.

Source: Lean, David F., Ogur, Jonathan D., and Rogers, Robert P. *Competition and Collusion in Electrical Equipment Markets: An Economic Assessment.* Washington, D.C.: Bureau of Economics, Federal Trade Commission, July 1982, Table III-1, p. 46.

volved in the production of eight products that were covered by conspiracies. The portion of their results that is of interest here is shown in Table 7-8.

According to these estimates, a firm's gross rate of return on sales was larger the larger the combined market share of the two largest firms in the market (CR2), the larger the market share of the third-largest firm (MS3), and the larger the firm's own market share (MSOWN). These are exactly the results that the standard oligopoly models of Chapter 5 and Chapter 6 would lead one to expect.

As indicated in Chapter 6, we expect collusion to be more difficult when goods are differentiated, because firms will have to agree on the relative prices of different types of goods, as well as on the price level and the allocation of output among producers. The extreme form of product differentiation occurs when goods are made to order; then every unit is different from every other unit. Many electrical equipment products are custom built to the specification of individual public utilities. In the Lean et al. study, the variable CUSTOM takes the value 1 if the product is made to order and 0 otherwise.[49] The coefficient estimated for CUSTOM shows the average change in margins if a product is made to order, compared with an otherwise identical firm and market where the product is not made to order.

If product differentiation makes effective collusion harder, CUSTOM will have a negative coefficient. That is exactly what Lean et al. found. The gross

---

[49]Among econometricians, this sort of variable—taking one of two values—is called a *dummy variable.* Who says economists don't have a sense of humor?

rate of return on sales was nearly 9 percentage points lower if the product was made to order.

The electrical equipment conspiracies were at their height during 1957, 1958, and 1959. CON5759 takes the value 1 for these 3 years and 0 for other years. The gross rate of return on sales was 2 percentage points higher during those years than at other times.

The signaling variable, SIG6470, takes the value 1 for turbine generators for the years 1964 through 1970 and 0 otherwise. The Justice Department claimed that during this period General Electric engaged in behavior designed to signal its prices on turbine generators to Westinghouse. General Electric used a simplified rate book for turbine generators, which Westinghouse was able to obtain and copy. General Electric allowed customers to audit transaction prices in order to verify that no secret discounts were being given. This had the effect of communicating the same information to Westinghouse. General Electric published outstanding orders and prices whenever its prices changed.

The coefficient of SIG6470 is an estimate of the average effect of this signaling activity on margins, keeping everything else the same. Lean et al. found that signaling increased the gross rate of return on sales by 7 percentage points. This confirms that facilitating practices can help companies to reach tacit agreements without physical contact.

Lean, Ogur, and Rogers' work provides powerful support for the oligopoly theories reviewed in Chapters 5 and 6. For electrical equipment products, market concentration increased a profitability measure defined in the spirit of the Lerner index of market power. So did market share. Profitability was higher during the peak years of conspiracy and lower if goods were made to order. It is hard to see how these results could be interpreted as reflecting efficiency differences across firms.

Contestable Markets

The theory of contestable markets[50] argues that even in very concentrated markets, firms will not be able to hold the price above marginal cost—will not have the power to control price—if entry and exit are costless and can occur very rapidly. If these conditions are met, the force of potential competition alone will be sufficient to yield optimal market performance. This is, of course, essentially the same prediction that emerges from the static limit price model.

The commercial airline industry has long been touted as one of the markets most likely to meet the assumptions of the theory of contestable markets. Airplanes can easily be shifted from one route to another if profits make it attractive to do so. There are some problems with obtaining gates at major

[50]Baumol, W., Panzar, J., and Willig, R. *Contestable Markets and the Theory of Industry Structure*. San Diego: Harcourt Brace Jovanovich 1982.

airports, but the point that assets are not sunk in particular routes seems valid enough.

Strassmann[51] tested the contestable markets theory for commercial airlines. Her study analyzed average profitability for 92 heavily traveled routes, using quarterly data for 1981 and the first half of 1982. To explain differences in profit rates, she used a large number of variables designed to control for differences in market structure, but the portion of her results that is of interest here is

$$\text{Profit rate} = -1.2289 + 0.5800\text{HERF} + \cdots$$

(where HERF if the Herfindahl index of market concentration; both coefficients are highly significant, in a statistical sense). As Strassmann interprets her results:[52]

> The numbers equivalency property of Herfindahl indices helps provide some intuition regarding the effect of concentration on profits. The mean Herfindahl index of 0.37 in the sample would give 2.7 equal sized carriers. Adding another carrier to this market (and maintaining the assumption of equal shares) would reduce the Herfindahl index from 0.37 to 0.27, a decrease of 0.1. The effect on [the profit rate] would be approximately 0.5 (-0.1) or a decrease in profits of approximately five percentage points. This result indicates that barriers to entry exist and that the airline city-pair markets in the sample were not perfectly contestable markets during the sample time period.

The jury is still out on the real-world importance of the theory of contestable markets. Additional evidence will no doubt be assembled on an industry-by-industry basis. Strassmann's work does not suggest that the theory of contestable markets will be broadly applicable.

Firm Market Power

Martin

We know from Chapter 5 that when firms in an oligopoly have different costs, the index of market power of an individual firm is [this repeats equation (5.6)]

$$\frac{P - c_i}{P} = \frac{\alpha_i + (1 - \alpha_i)s_i}{\epsilon_{QP}}. \tag{7.6}$$

[51]Strassmann, D. L. "Contestable Markets and Dynamic Limit Pricing in the Deregulated Airline Industry: An Empirical Test," Rice University, February 1986. For similar results, see Morrison, Steven A. and Winston, Clifford. "Empirical Implications and Tests of the Contestability Hypothesis," *Journal of Law and Economics* Volume 30, Number 1, April 1987, pp. 53–66.

[52]Op. cit., p. 30.

Table 7-9 Firm-level Market Power Estimates

Firm	Average Market Share	Market Power Statistic
Hospital Supplies		
American Hospital Supply	0.2824	0.1144[a]
Baxter-Travenol	0.1511	0.3947[a]
Becton-Dickinson	0.1161	0.2261[a]
C. R. Bard	0.0320	0.1019[a]
Motor Vehicles		
American Motors	0.0193	0.1653[a]
Chrysler	0.0974	0.1492[a]
Ford	0.2592	0.2521[a]
General Motors	0.3946	0.3286[a]

Notes: For quarterly data from the first quarter of 1973 through the last quarter of 1982.

[a] indicates statistical significance at the 1 per cent level; such an estimate would occur by chance only once in 100 times, on average.

Source: Martin, Stephen, "The Measurement of Profitability and the Diagnosis of Market Power," forthcoming, *International Journal of Industrial Organization.*

This equation relates the firm's ability to hold the price above marginal cost to three variables, which describe market structure and rivals' conduct. For an oligopolist, market power depends on the following:

1. Its market share, which indicates how many customers it has.
2. The conjectural variation, which indicates whether rivals will cooperate in restricting output or compete for customers.
3. The price elasticity of demand, which indicates how quickly customers will leave the market as the price increases.

Martin[53] reports estimates of Equation (7.6) for firms in the hospital supply and motor vehicle industries. Typical results are reported in Table 7-9.

These industries are highly concentrated oligopolies. They are also characterized by extensive product differentiation. From the models in Chapters 5 and 6, it might be expected that such firms will have some power to control price.

---

[53]Martin, "Market Power," op. cit. The estimates are obtained from a model that includes financial costs as well as factor markets, using a specification that is a generalization of that used by Collins and Preston (Equation 7.3). For an earlier, similar approach, see Appelbaum, Elie. "The Estimation of the Degree of Oligopoly Power," *Journal of Econometrics,* Volume 19, 1982, pp. 287–299; for an extension that explicitly considers foreign trade, see Ilmakunnas, Pekka. "Identification and Estimation of the Degree of Oligopoly Power in Industries Facing Domestic and Import Competition," in Joachim Schwalbach, editor, *Industry Structure and Performance*. Berlin: Edition Sigma Rainer Bohn Verlag, 1985, pp. 287–308.

According to the estimates in Table 7-9, this is the case: the leading firms in these industries all exercise some degree of market power.[54]

Mueller

Mueller[55] models oligopolistic cooperation directly, rather than using the conjectural variations approach outlined in Chapter 5. He supposes that each oligopolist acts to maximize a weighted sum of its own profit and the profits of rival firms.[56]

The weight each firm gives to the profits of its rivals is a cooperation parameter, which plays a role in the Mueller model similar to that of α in the conjectural variations model. Mueller's model is general enough to include joint profit maximization, Cournot behavior, and rivalry.

In an ambitious study, Mueller used data for 551 major corporations to estimate the way the degree of cooperation varies with market concentration. An important result is that cooperation rises with seller concentration for four-firm concentration ratios below 24 percent, but that above this level, increases in market concentration reduce the degree of cooperation.[57] At fairly low levels of concentration, in other words, rivalry overcomes the recognition of interdependence.

Mueller's study joins the short but growing list of studies that find evidence of a *negative* impact of market concentration and a positive impact of market share on the rate of return.[58] His results support not only the criticism of the market concentration doctrine that emerged in the 1970s, but also the shift in emphasis from the industry to the firm as the focal point for the analysis of structure–performance relationships. As Mueller points out,[59] this portion of his results is consistent with the firm-level studies of Shepherd.[60]

---

[54]This interpretation of the results depends on the assumption of constant returns to scale, although there are extensions in the original that allow nonconstant returns to scale.

[55]Mueller, Dennis C. *Profits in the Long Run*. Cambridge: Cambridge University Press, 1986. Mueller uses a nonlinear functional form for his empirical tests, and we do not report his coefficient estimates.

[56]Specifically, Mueller supposes that firm i maximizes

$$\pi_i + \theta \sum_{j \neq i}^{N} \pi_j,$$

where π_i is firm i's profit, π_j is firm j's profit, and θ is a parameter that gauges oligopolistic cooperation. See Mueller, op. cit., p. 52, and footnote 1 for antecedents in the literature.

[57]Ibid, pp. 78–79.

[58]Among which, Martin, "Market, Firm, and Economic Performance," and Ravenscraft, "Structure-Profit Relationships," both of which employ disaggregated data collected by the Federal Trade Commission's Line of Business Program.

[59]Mueller, op. cit., p. 103.

[60]See Table 6-4.

Summary

We have covered a lot of hard ground. But we have gained a good perspective on what economists know, and the extent to which they know it, as far as structure–conduct–performance relationships are concerned.

Bain's early work was motivated by a desire to explain the persistence of high profits in some markets, profits that were not eroded by entry. That work spawned a large literature, using mainly industry-level data, that supported the belief that entry barriers (product differentiation, economies of large-scale operation) and market concentration increased market power. A few studies in the same tradition suggested that market share was an important factor in explaining *firm* market power.

From the 1970s on, the Chicago school mounted a frontal assault on these studies, the main theme of which interpreted the concentration–profit relationship as a reflection of the efficiency of large firms, not collusion.

The most extreme forms of the efficiency hypothesis—that high profits reflect efficiency and only efficiency, because actual or potential entry will prevent the exercise of market power—are not supported by the evidence. But most students of industrial organization accept the view that concentration in an industry will carry with it some elements of market power and some elements of efficiency, and that the breakdown between the two should be evaluated on an industry-by-industry basis.

As a result, empirical tests have turned from the industry level to the firm level. This line of research is by no means complete, but certain results seem evident.

Market share seems to carry with it market power. This finding is consistent both with generally accepted oligopoly models and with the firm-level work in the structure-performance framework.

Entry conditions remain an important factor in determining whether or not firms can exercise market power. At least, market power in a market thought likely to be contestable (commercial airlines) seems to be positively affected by market concentration.

It is possible to test market power, using specific oligopoly models, on a firm-by-firm basis. The results of such tests suggest the importance of market share and product differentiation as a source of market power. On the other hand, rivalry among firms may well increase as market concentration increases.

Paper Topics

7-1 (Requires access to a personal computer and econometric software) For the data in Table 7-1, the data reported in Table 1 of Brozen, Y. "Bain's Concentration and Rates of Return Revisited," *Journal of Law and Economics* Volume 14, October 1971, pp. 351–369:

    a. Estimate linear equations relating the rate of return on net worth to the four-firm seller concentration ratio. How do Brozen's results change if industries labeled "n.e.c." (not elsewhere classified) are excluded from the sample?

b. Now consult Schwartzman, David and Bodoff, Jean. "Concentration in Regional and Local Industries," *Southern Economic Journal* Volume 37, Number 3, January 1971, pp. 343–348. How do Brozen's results change if all industries identified by Schwartzman and Bodoff as "regional" or "local" are excluded from the estimation?

c. How do the results for the Bain sample change if you include an additional explanatory variable that takes the value 1 for industries classified by Bain as having very high barriers to entry and 0 otherwise? Interpret.

d. Evaluate Brozen's critique of Bain's work.

7-2 (Requires access to a personal computer and econometric software) Several two-digit Standard Industrial Classification industries are composed of 20 or more four-digit Standard Industrial Classification industries. For example, Standard Industrial Classification industry 20 contains 49 four-digit Standard Industrial Classification industries. Using the most recent Census of Manufactures, duplicate the Strickland-Weiss estimates for one such two-digit industry. You will have to use the Detailed Industry Input-Output Tables for the United States for the advertising data. How do the results change if you exclude industries labeled "not elsewhere classified"? If you are truly ambitious, create two such samples, one for a consumer-good industry and one for a producer-good industry, and compare the results.

8

The Determinants of Market Structure

I lose money on every suit I sell, but I make it up on volume.
Garment district saying.

We have explored the implications of market structure and firm conduct for market performance, in particular for the power to control price. But market structure is itself the product of economic forces, and it is these forces that we now examine.

Economists differ fundamentally over the nature of the forces that determine market concentration. The interactive structure-conduct-performance framework[1] holds that market concentration reflects the underlying technology (economies of scale) and strategic behavior by incumbent firms (which may create product differentiation and create absolute cost disadvantages for entrants). With this foundation for the explanation of the level of concentration in a market, the structure-conduct-performance school has gone on to models of the kind reviewed in Chapters 5 and 6 for an understanding of the circumstances under which firms in oligopoly will be able to exercise market power.

Economists working in the Chicago tradition have criticized this foundation as inadequate:[2]

> The essence of monopoly power is the ability to prevent an expansion of capacity when price exceeds unit cost; yet not one of the oligopoly theories . . . deals with the problem posed for colluding oligopolists by potential and actual entry. . . .
>
> . . . no good theoretical link has been forged between the structure of industry and the degree to which competitive pricing prevails, because no good

---

[1]See Figure 1-2.

[2]Demsetz, Harold. "Two Systems of Belief About Monopoly," in Goldschmid, Harvey J., Mann, H. Michael, and Weston, J. Fred., editors, *Industrial Concentration: The New Learning.* Boston: Little, Brown and Company, 1974, pp. 166–167.

explanation has been provided for how present and potential rivals are kept from competing without some governmentally provided restrictions on competitive activities.

It is much more in the spirit of the Chicago school to suggest that market structure reflects efficiency alone.[3] In the Chicago view, if the market is concentrated, it is because it is efficient to organize production in units that are large relative to the market.[4]

As we know from Chapter 6, Bain identified three elements of market structure as the main determinants of the nature of entry conditions: economies of scale, product differentiation, and absolute cost advantages of existing firms. We explore the implications of each of these factors for market structure. At the close of the chapter, we review empirical evidence on the determinants of market structure.

Economies of Scale

Cost Curves

If there are economies of scale, average cost falls as output increases. The simplest way to include economies of scale in a model is to assume fixed costs F and constant marginal costs c per unit for each plant:

$$C(q) = F + cq. \qquad (8.1)$$

Average cost is then

$$AC(q) = c + \left(\frac{F}{q}\right), \qquad (8.2)$$

which falls as output increases. Producing at large scale spreads the fixed cost over many units of output and pulls the average cost down toward marginal cost.

If fixed cost is small, average cost is close to marginal cost in any event, and the reduction in average cost as output increases is relatively small. But when fixed cost is large, average cost will fall rapidly as output increases. With

---

[3]See Figure 1-3.

[4]See the discussion in Chapter 7 of the Demsetz efficiency hypothesis.

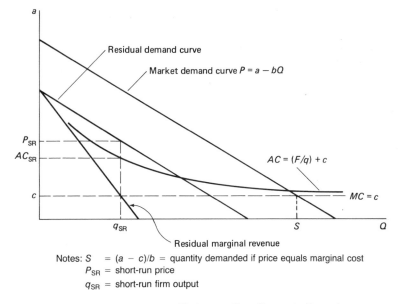

Notes: S = $(a - c)/b$ = quantity demanded if price equals marginal cost
P_{SR} = short-run price
q_{SR} = short-run firm output

Figure 8-1 Short-run equilibrium, n-firm Cournot oligopoly.

this sort of cost function, economies of scale become more important as fixed cost increases.[5]

Short-Run Equilibrium

Suppose that in the short run n firms supply the market, each able to produce with the cost function (8.1). Return to the basic Cournot model of quantity-setting oligopoly (Chapter 5).

Assuming independent behavior by each firm, we can describe the typical oligopolist (firm i) as maximizing its profits along a residual demand curve. This curve is obtained by subtracting the output of all other firms from the market demand curve. Graphically (Figure 8-1), we obtain the residual demand curve by shifting the market curve to the left a distance equal to the output of

---

[5]The usual microeconomic measure of economies of scale is the function coefficient, the ratio of average to marginal cost. If average cost is greater than marginal cost, average cost falls as output increases, and there are economies of large scale production. For the cost function (Equation 8.1), the function coefficient is

$$FC = \frac{AC}{MC} = \frac{c + (F/q)}{c} = 1 + \left(\frac{F}{cq}\right).$$

Thus, for this cost function, economies of scale increase as fixed cost F becomes larger relative to marginal cost c.

all other firms from the market demand curve. With this residual demand curve comes a residual marginal revenue curve, which shows how firm i's revenue will change as it changes its output. Firm i will maximize its own profit by picking the output level (shown as q_{SR} in Figure 8-1) that makes its marginal revenue equal to its marginal cost.

Firm i's marginal revenue is

$$MR_i = P + q_i \frac{\Delta P}{\Delta q_i} = P - bq_i = a - bQ - bq_i. \tag{8.3}$$

If marginal revenue is set equal to marginal cost, we obtain

$$a - bQ - bq_i = c \quad \text{or} \quad Q + q_i = \frac{(a - c)}{b}. \tag{8.4}$$

Equation (8.4) includes a natural measure of market size:

$$S = \frac{(a - c)}{b}. \tag{8.5}$$

This is the quantity that would be demanded, along the market demand curve, if the price were equal to marginal cost.

Since all firms have access to the same cost function, it is natural (and in any event simpler) to suppose that in equilibrium all firms produce the same output. If we write q for this common level of firm output, we have $Q = nq$ and Equation (8.4) gives us an expression for short-run equilibrium firm output:

$$q_{SR} = \frac{S}{(n + 1)}. \tag{8.6}$$

If n firms each produce this output, the price (from the market demand curve) is

$$P_{SR} = c + \frac{bS}{n + 1}. \tag{8.7}$$

Equations (8.6) and (8.7) illustrate results from Chapter 5: holding market size constant, the equilibrium price under Cournot oligopoly is closer to marginal cost, the greater the number of firms in the market.

Long-Run

Price exceeds average cost in the equilibrium shown in Figure 8-1. Each oligopolist earns a pure economic profit. In the absence of strategic behavior,

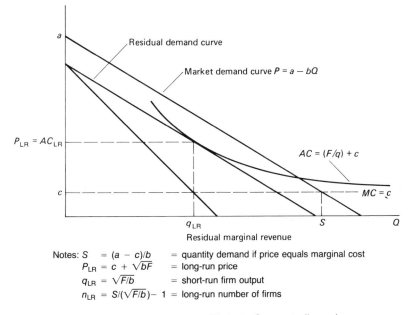

Notes: $S = (a - c)/b$ = quantity demand if price equals marginal cost
$P_{LR} = c + \sqrt{bF}$ = long-run price
$q_{LR} = \sqrt{F/b}$ = short-run firm output
$n_{LR} = S/(\sqrt{F/b}) - 1$ = long-run number of firms

Figure 8-2 Long-run equilibrium, Cournot oligopoly.

new firms will come into the industry[6] so long as there is a profit to be made by doing so.

As the number of firms in a Cournot market increases, the equilibrium price falls toward the competitive level. Long-run equilibrium is reached, as shown in Figure 8-2, when the firm's residual demand curve is just tangent to its average cost curve. At this point, each firm is maximizing its profit ($MR = MC$), so no firm has any incentive to change its own output. At the same time, each firm is just breaking even ($P = AC$), so there is no incentive for entry or exit.

Number of Firms

In the short-run equilibrium of Figure 8-1, each firm is earning a profit:

$$\pi_{SR} = b\left(\frac{S}{n + 1}\right)^2 - F. \tag{8.8}$$

As the number of firms in the market increases, output per firm falls (which increases average cost for each firm), price falls, and the profit per firm falls.

---

[6]Alternatively, existing firms may open additional plants. The critical point, in passing from short-run to long-run equilibrium, is that short-run economic profit creates an incentive to increase output.

197

The long-run equilibrium number of firms will make the short-run firm profit zero:[7]

$$n_{\text{LR}} = \frac{S}{\sqrt{F/b}} - 1. \qquad \qquad \textbf{(8.9)}$$

Thus the long-run number of firms falls—market concentration increases—as fixed costs increase. The more important are economies of scale, the greater will be the long-run market concentration. As Bain expected, a market ought to be more concentrated in the long run, the greater the economies of large scale production.

Scale Economies and Market Performance[8]

We now ask how market performance changes as fixed cost increases and economies of scale become more important. The lower the fixed cost, the greater the number of firms in long-run equilibrium. The greater the number of firms, the closer is the equilibrium price to marginal cost and the less the degree of market power exercised by individual firms.

It would seem, then, that a reduction in fixed cost, which increases the equilibrium number of plants, would always improve market performance. But each additional plant means another set of fixed costs, a social cost.

In the general case, there will be a tradeoff between fixed costs and market performance as minimum efficient scale rises. An increase in MES will reduce the number of plants in long-run oligopoly equilibrium. This will consolidate production in a smaller number of plants and may reduce total resources devoted to fixed costs. Or it may not—there are fewer plants, but the fixed cost per plant is larger. In any event, as the fixed cost per plant rises, the equilibrium number of firms falls. As this happens, the ability of these firms to hold the price above marginal cost increases. The tradeoff, as fixed costs increase, is between savings that come from consolidating production in fewer plants and losses that come from monopolistic output restriction.

How this tradeoff will balance out depends on the details of the cost function. In the model considered here, social welfare is given by consumers' surplus,[9] which is

---

[7]In general, Equation (8.9) will not be an integer; the number of firms can be expected to increase until the entry of one additional firm would induce losses for all firms.

[8]See von Weizsäcker, C. C. "A Welfare Analysis of Barriers to Entry," *Bell Journal of Economics* Volume 11, Number 2, Autumn 1980, pp. 399–420; and Martin, Stephen. "A Bainsian Interpretation of Von Weizsäcker's Model of Scale Economies," *Southern Economic Journal* Volume 50, Number 4, April 1984, pp. 1192–1195.

[9]Recall that in long-run equilibrium there are zero economic profits. Gross social value is consumers' surplus plus PQ, but the cost of production just equals PQ. Net social value is therefore simply consumers' surplus, which from is $(\frac{1}{2})(a - P_{\text{LR}})Q_{\text{LR}}$.

$$CS = \left(\frac{b}{2}\right)\left(S - \sqrt{\frac{F}{b}}\right)^2 \qquad \textbf{(8.10)}$$

Consumers' surplus increases as fixed cost falls and economies of scale become less important. Even though a reduction in fixed cost means more plants, each with its own set of fixed costs, the increase in output and the reduction in price that follows a reduction in fixed cost improves market performance.[10] Not only can we say that market concentration is expected to increase as economies of scale increase, but also that market performance is expected to worsen as economies of scale increase.

Policy Implications

If market concentration tends to reach the level dictated by available economies of scale, there would seem to be very little for policymakers to do about market concentration. In the long run, market concentration will approach the level dictated by the cost function.

Economists have from time to time estimated minimum efficient scale, and compared the estimates with observed levels of market concentration. Typical results from such a study[11] are reported in Table 8-1. In the United States, four-firm industry concentration ratios are much larger than the operation of efficient-scale plants would dictate.

This conclusion is qualified somewhat if one makes an allowance for the regional nature of some markets and for economies of multiplant operation. After taking such considerations into account, the senior researcher in the study reported in Table 8-1 concluded that[12] "national market concentration in most industries appears to be much higher than it needs to be for leading firms to take advantage of all but slight residual scale economies."

In terms of the interactive structure-conduct-performance framework, this result is not surprising. Strategic entry-deterring behavior will often allow leading firms to maintain positions of market power, even if large market shares are not necessary for efficient operation. It is for this reason that the structure-

---

[10]Since the cost function given by Equation (8.1) never exhibits diseconomies of scale, the socially optimal production arrangement would be to consolidate all production in one plant (minimizing the fixed cost per unit) and produce an output $Q = S$. Social welfare is then $(b/2)S^2$. Thus the Cournot oligopoly always has too many plants, but approaches optimal performance as fixed costs fall.

[11]The original source for the information reported in Table 8-1 is Scherer, F. M., Beckenstein, Alan, Kaufer, Erich, and Murphy, R. D. *The Economics of Multi-Plant Operation: An International Comparisons Study*. Cambridge, Mass.: Harvard University Press, 1975.

[12]Scherer, F. M. "Economies of Scale and Industrial Concentration," in Goldschmid et al., op. cit., p. 54.

Table 8-1 MES Plant Size vs. Market Concentration

Industry	MES/S	4 × MES/S	CR4
Beer brewing	3.4%	13.6%	40%
Cigarettes	6.6	26.4	81
Broad-woven cotton and synthetic fabrics	0.2	0.8	36
Paints, varnishes, and lacquers	1.4	5.6	22
Petroleum refining	1.9	7.6	33
Shoes (other than rubber)	0.2	0.8	26
Glass containers	1.5	6.0	60
Cement	1.7	6.8	29
Integrated wide-strip steel works	2.6	10.4	48
Ball and roller bearings	1.4	5.6	54
Household refrigerators and freezers	14.1	56.4	73
Storage batteries	1.9	7.6	61

Note: Engineering estimates of MES; figures are for 1967 and assume that markets are national.

Source: Scherer, F. M. "Economies of Scale and Industrial Concentration," in Goldschmid, Harvey J., Mann, H. Michael, and Weston, J. Fred, editors, *Industrial Concentration: The New Learning.* Boston: Little, Brown and Company, 1974, p. 26.

conduct-performance school includes conduct, as well as technology, among the determinants of market concentration.

The position of the Chicago school has been that economists' estimates of efficiency and MES are fatally flawed.[13] If such studies use accounting data, there are problems with the valuation of capital assets and with the allocation of overhead costs. Engineering studies concentrate on technical aspects of production, ignoring matters of management and marketing that ought to be included in any realistic assessment of efficiency. In any event, engineering studies tend to look backward—they are based on the experience of the engineers involved—which means that they are out of date even before they are published.

The inability of economists to estimate MES, however, is not (in the view of the Chicago school) very important. The market structure observed in the real world is efficient:[14]

> I see little reason to spend much more time estimating optimum plant or firm sizes except, perhaps, in a completely centralized and governmentally controlled economy in which the State tries hard to keep markets from working and consumers from expressing preferences. When property and markets are at work, and consumers are permitted to choose what and from whom to buy, it is, as far as I am concerned, a trivial matter what the facts of technical

[13]See McGee, John S. "Efficiency and Economies of Size," in Goldschmid et al., op. cit., pp. 55–96; see also Bork, Robert H. *The Antitrust Paradox: A Policy at War with Itself.* New York: Basic Books, Inc., 1978, pp. 124–129.

[14]McGee, John S. "Commentary," in Goldschmid et al., op. cit., p. 104.

economies are, or what economists and engineers have to say about them. Consumers will choose products and firms that offer what is, to their tastes, the best deal. Consumers will make the trade-off between prices and product qualities. The prices they pay for the qualities they buy are signals to anyone who would do better by them. Such economies as there are will assert themselves, and no one need be concerned how large or small they are.

Product Differentiation

Firms can attempt to differentiate their product by advertising, by the efforts of their sales forces, and by design changes (which might include a warranty or service package offered as part of the product). To simplify the discussion, we will call the firm's product-differentiating activity *advertising,* although it should be understood that we mean this to include all types of sales-promoting activity.

Advertising Policy

Advertising differs from other inputs purchased by the firm in that it moves the demand curve, while other inputs go into the production function.[15] When the firm can differentiate its product by advertising, the quantity demanded at any price depends not only on the price charged but also on the advertising, past and present, that the firm has invested in to develop a brand name.

In general, the quantity demanded at any price will increase, the greater the past (A_p) or current (A) advertising. Take the simplest case, in which past and current advertising have the same effect on the quantity demanded. To focus on advertising, suppose for the moment that the firm is a monopolist.

When a firm advertises, its profit is[16]

$$\pi = PQ(A_p + A, P) - cQ(A_p + A, P) - F - p^A A. \qquad (8.11)$$

There are now three elements of cost: fixed cost F, variable cost cQ, and the cost of current advertising, $p^A A$.

---

[15]See Spence, A. Michael, "Notes on Advertising, Economies of Scale, and Entry Barriers," *Quarterly Journal of Economics* Volume 95, Number 3, November 1980, pp. 493–507, for a clever reformulation of the firm's problem in which factors of production and advertising combine to produce revenue.

[16]In the strict sense, it is inconsistent to talk about "past advertising" but have the firm maximize its profit in a single period. A complete dynamic model would have the firm pick advertising for this period to maximize the present discounted value of profit over all future time. Such a model would show the firm advertising a little more, in the current period, than a static model predicts, because of the future brand image cultivated by current advertising. Qualitatively, however, the results are the same, and the inconsistency seems worth the simplicity it buys.

A profit-maximizing firm will adjust both its price and its advertising so that marginal revenue equals marginal cost.[17] For price, the "marginal revenue equals marginal cost" condition is

$$Q \, \Delta P + P \, \Delta Q = c \, \Delta Q. \qquad (8.12)$$

The marginal revenue from a reduction in price ($\Delta P < 0$) has two components. The first is lost revenue on units that could have been sold at a higher price (the first term on the left in Equation 8.12). The second is incremental revenue generated by the sale of additional units at a lower price (the second term on the left in Equation 8.12). Marginal cost is simply the variable cost of bringing the additional output to market (the right-hand side of Equation 8.12).

With a little rearrangement, Equation (8.12) becomes the (hopefully) familiar

$$\frac{P - c}{P} = \frac{1}{\epsilon_{QP}}. \qquad (8.13)$$

Even with advertising, a profit-maximizing firm will pick an output level that makes the price-cost margin equal to the inverse of the price elasticity of demand. When the firm can advertise, however, it can influence the price elasticity of demand.

For advertising, the "marginal revenue equals marginal cost" condition becomes

$$P \, \Delta Q = c \, \Delta Q + p^A \, \Delta A. \qquad (8.14)$$

Marginal revenue from an increase in advertising is the revenue generated by additional sales (the left-hand side of Equation 8.14). Marginal cost from an increase in advertising has two components. The first is the cost of producing the additional output sold because of the advertising (the first term on the right Equation in 8.14). The second is the cost of the additional advertising (the second term on the right in Equation 8.14).

---

[17]Since marginal profit equals marginal revenue minus marginal cost, another way to describe a firm's advertising decision is to say that the firm will advertise until the change in profit per unit change in advertising is zero. We return to this topic when we analyze the welfare consequences of advertising.

THE DETERMINANTS OF MARKET STRUCTURE

Less familiarly, Equation (8.14) can be rearranged and written as the *Dorfman-Steiner*[18] condition for optimal advertising intensity:

$$\frac{p^A A}{PQ} = \frac{P - c}{P} \, \epsilon_{QA}.$$

(8.15)

For a profit-maximizing firm, the advertising-sales ratio (the left-hand side of Equation (8.15) will be the product of two terms: the price-cost margin and the elasticity of demand with respect to advertising. Firms will advertise more, the more they make on the sale of the marginal unit. Firms will advertise more, the more sensitive is the quantity demanded to advertising.

Advertising and Absolute Cost Advantages

Time Lags

Now move on to oligopoly. The implications of advertising for strategic behavior depend in part on the way past advertising, A_p, affects current demand. If past advertising has no effect on current demand, a new firm can come into a market, advertise as much as established firms, and differentiate its product as successfully as established firms. If past advertising does not affect current demand, advertising is not a barrier. It is a tool used by the entrant as it competes with established firms.

If the effect of advertising lasts over time, the situation is entirely different. Established firms inherit a positive brand image because of their past sales efforts. A new firm will have to spend more on advertising per dollar of sales, than an established firm to reach a comparable demand curve, because it has no such inheritance. In this case, advertising can create an absolute cost advantage for incumbent firms.

The rate at which the effect of advertising on demand depreciates varies from industry to industry. A survey article that reviewed many industry-level estimates of the duration of advertising effects concluded:[19]

> the published econometric literature indicates that 90% of the cumulative effect of advertising on sales of mature, frequently purchased, low-priced products occurs within 3 to 9 months of the advertisement.

[18]Dorfman, R. and Steiner, P. O. "Optimal Advertising and Optimal Quality," *American Economic Review* Volume 44, December 1954, pp. 826–836; first written in this form, so far as I know, by Schmalensee, R., *The Economics of Advertising*. Amsterdam: North-Holland, 1972, and Cable, John, "Market Structure, Advertising Policy and Intermarket Differences in Advertising Intensity," in Cowling, Keith, editor, *Market Structure and Corporate Behavior: Theory and Empirical Analysis of the Firm*. London: Gray-Mills Publishing Ltd., 1972, pp. 105–124.

[19]Clarke, D. G. "Econometric Measurement of the Duration of Advertising Effect on Sales," *Journal of Marketing Research,* Volume 13, Number 4, November 1976, p. 355.

Brand loyalty that endures over such a short period will provide only a modest barrier to entry. For some products, however, the estimated effects of advertising last much longer than 9 months. For some brands of gasoline, it was estimated that 2 to 3 years were required for 90 percent of the cumulative effect of advertising to take place. For products like this, the entry barrier effect of advertising will be more enduring.

Noise

Even if the effect of past advertising on current demand depreciates quickly, advertising can create an absolute cost differential between established and new firms if the advertising of established firms interferes with that of new firms. Advertising messages of different firms compete for the consumer's attention. When this is so, entrants will be forced to advertise more, per dollar of sales, than established firms needed to spend when they first developed a brand image. A firm that comes late to a market will have to advertise more than early arrivals, precisely because the early arrivals are already in the market and are putting advertising messages in front of the consumer. In the phrase of Comanor and Wilson,[20] when there is " 'noise' in the market, one must 'shout' louder to be heard . . .".

Recapitulation

If the effect of advertising on demand lasts over time, or if the advertising of established firms interferes with the advertising of newcomers, the average cost of production and distribution will be higher for a new firm than for an established firm. This *market penetration cost,* as shown in Figure 8-3, will create the kind of limit price cost difference between new and established firms upon which Bain based his analysis of product differentiation as a barrier to entry. Product differentiation will enable established firms to maintain and exercise market power.

Product Differentiation and Economies of Scale

There will be economies of scale in advertising if some minimum amount of public exposure is needed before a sales campaign makes any impression at all on the public. The cost of this minimum amount of advertising will be a fixed cost—the same, no matter how much the firm sells. Like any fixed cost, it will create a region of economies of scale as the fixed advertising cost is spread over more and more units of output. Such a *threshold effect* can arise

---

[20]Comanor, William S. and Wilson, Thomas A. *Advertising and Market Power.* Cambridge, Mass.: Harvard University Press, 1974, p. 47. Cubbin, John, "Advertising and the Theory of Entry Barriers," *Economica* Volume 48, August 1981, pp. 289–298, shows formally that in the presence of this "noise effect" there is an advantage to established firms, even if they and the entrant have demand and cost functions of the same form.

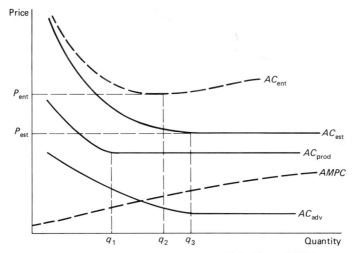

Notes: AC_{adv} is advertising cost per unit of output for established firms. $AMPC$ (average market penetration cost) is the additional advertising expense per unit of output required of an entrant to establish a brand image. It will rise with output if the entrant has to attract customers with stronger attachments to the brands of established firms as it expands output. AC_{prod} is average production cost, assumed to be the same for new and established firms. AC_{est}, the sum of AC_{adv} and AC_{prod}, is the average cost curve for established firms. AC_{ent}, the sum of AC_{adv}, $AMPC$, and AC_{prod}, is the average cost curve for an entrant. q_1 is the MES for production alone. q_2 is the MES of production and distribution, for an entrant. q_3 is the MES of production and distribution for an established firm. $P_{ent} - P_{est}$ is a limit price differential within which established firms can hold the price above the average cost without inducing entry.

Figure 8-3 Advertising and entry conditions. Source: Comanor, W. S. and Wilson, T. A. "Advertising Market Structure and Performance," *Review of Economics and Statistics* Volume 49, Number 4, November 1967, p. 427.

because it is the size of the audience that must be reached that determines necessary advertising expenditures, not firm sales.[21]

For example, entry into the U.S. automobile market[22] requires national advertising expenditures even in the early stages of market penetration. If an entrant and an established firm spend roughly the same amount to advertise to an audience of the same size, and the entrant's sales are smaller, the entrant's advertising cost per dollar of sales will be larger than that of the established firm.

[21]Porter, Michael E. *Interbrand Choice, Strategy, and Bilateral Market Power.* Cambridge, Mass.: Harvard University Press, 1976, p. 131.

[22]At this writing, the Yugo is the most recent example, although several foreign-based suppliers have come into the U.S. market in the last few years.

In industries composed of regional submarkets, a firm may be able to enter and advertise in a regional market, establish a solid foothold, and then expand to other regional markets.[23] In such cases, advertising expense and sales will be in roughly the same proportion for new and established firms. The threshold effect of advertising will not pose a barrier to entry if advertising can be carried out through local media.

There will also be economies of large scale in advertising if repetition makes advertising more effective. Repetition will make advertising more effective if the advertising affects demand simply by making the consumer aware of the function of the advertised product. It is precisely this role that advertising plays for *experience* goods, which must be purchased and used before their qualities can be fully appreciated. For such goods, advertising puts the name of the product in front of the consumer in order to increase the odds of a first purchase. Only if the product performs satisfactorily will the purchase be repeated. For such experience goods, an entrant will have to target the audience with repeated advertising messages in order to gain a competitive market position.[24]

Economies of scale in advertising may be induced by the rate structures of advertising media. There is some evidence that the average cost of advertising falls as its volume increases. This is a matter of rate structures, that is, it depends on the market for advertising services. A recent survey[25] concludes that after one adjusts television advertising rate schedules for the size of the audience and the value of advertising at different times of the day, "The available evidence indicates that discounts remain on certain types of purchases on network television, but it is still unclear whether they pervade the entire rate structure."

There are economies of national over local media:[26]

> Neglected in the discussion of the quantity discounts issue, however, is the presence of great economies of scale in national over local TV advertising. There appears to be a distinct cost advantage to advertising via the network versus utilizing spot advertising. Network rates range from approximately 10 to 70 percent of the sum of individual station rates, with the discount varying by time of day and season. This means that a potential entrant cannot effectively utilize spot advertising in a limited area to counter network advertising.

[23]Consider the case of Domino's Pizza, which began in the Midwest and gradually expanded into other areas. Retail fast food, of course, need only be advertised through local media.

[24]Nelson, Philip. "Advertising as Information," *Journal of Political Economy* Volume 82, Number 4, July–August 1974, pp. 729–754. We return to this topic in Chapter 11.

[25]Comanor and Wilson, op. cit., p. 468. For a negative assessment of the existence of scale economies in rate structures, see Peterman, John L. and Carney, Michael. "A Comment on Television Network Price Discrimination," *Journal of Business* Volume 51, Number 2, 1978, pp. 343–352.

[26]Porter, Michael E. "Interbrand Choice, Media Mix and Market Performance," *American Economic Review* Volume 66, Number 2, May 1976, p. 403.

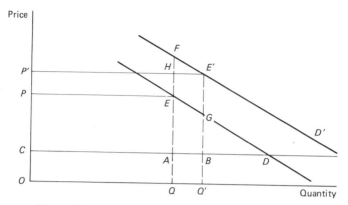

Figure 8-4 Welfare consequences of advertising.

Whether or not there are important economies of scale in advertising is a question that will have different answers for different industries. There are likely to be economies of scale for experience goods (repetition effect) that must be advertised nationally (threshold effect). For example, one study[27] finds that advertising poses "a considerable cost disadvantage" to new entrants in the cigarette industry. Advertising can make a consumer conscious of the brand name, but only experience will indicate whether or not the consumer finds the brand satisfactory. Cigarettes must be advertised nationally.[28]

Where such economies exist, they will increase minimum efficient scale for established firms (Figure 8-3) and contribute to a limit price differential of the kind envisaged by Bain. This effect is independent of any limit price gap created by market penetration costs.

Product Differentiation and Welfare

Dixit and Norman[29] offer a neat graphic analysis of the welfare effects of advertising by a monopolist. They show formally that similar results hold for oligopoly, but this part of their results does not lend itself to graphic exposition and will be omitted here.

Dixit and Norman's analysis is illustrated in Figure 8-4. Suppose advertising moves the demand curve from D to D'. The postadvertising position (E') will

[27]Brown, R. S. "Estimating Advantages to Large-Scale Advertising," *Review of Economics and Statistics* Volume 60, Number 3, August 1978, pp. 428–437.

[28]Fortunately, not on television. But as Porter, "Interbrand Choice," indicates, there are some economies of scale to the use of national magazines as opposed to local print media.

[29]Dixit, A. and Norman, V. "Advertising and Welfare," *Bell Journal of Economics* Volume 9, Spring 1978, pp. 1–17. See also Fisher, F. M. and McGowan, J. J. "Advertising and Welfare: Comment," *Bell Journal of Economics* Volume 10, Autumn 1979, pp. 726–727, and Dixit, A. and Norman V. "Advertising and Welfare: Reply," *Bell Journal of Economics* Volume 10, Autumn 1979, pp. 728–729.

involve some combination of higher price and higher output, compared with the preadvertising position (E).[30] How is social welfare changed by the move from E to E'?

The monopolist must make more profit by advertising. Otherwise, he would not advertise. Consider this monopoly profit as a welfare gain.[31] But consumers pay a higher price $(\Delta P = P' - P)$ for the Q units that they formerly obtained at price P. This is a welfare loss. The net change in social welfare is therefore

$$\Delta W = \Delta \pi - Q \, \Delta P. \qquad (8.16)$$

The monopolist's profit after advertising shows up, in Figure 8-4, as the rectangle $CP'E'B$. The monopolist's profit before advertising was the rectangle $CPEA$. The increase in profit (before allowing for the cost of the additional advertising), the first term on the right in Equation (8.16), is therefore the area $PP'E'BAE$.

The increase in cost imposed on consumers after advertising is the rectangle $PP'HE$. After subtracting this increase in cost from the change in the monopolist's profit, the change in welfare before allowing for the cost of advertising (the first two terms on the right in Equation 8.16) is the rectangle $AHE'B$.

The change in welfare can be given a consumers' surplus interpretation. The area $EHE'G$ is a small part of $AHE'B$, small enough so that we can take the area under the original demand curve and above the marginal cost line, as output increases from Q to Q', as a measure of the change in welfare before allowing for the cost of advertising. This is the area $AEGB$, and it is the consumers' surplus from the increase in output, measured with reference to the original demand curve.

But the triangle HFE' is also relatively small compared to the welfare changes involved. The first two parts of the change in welfare can be approximated equally well as the area $AFE'B$, which is the area under the new demand curve over the range of increased output. This is the change in consumers' surplus from the increase in output, measured with reference to the new demand curve.

Under either interpretation, the gross change in welfare—before allowing for the cost of advertising—appears approximately as the increase in consumers' surplus.

Suppose that the market for advertising services is competitive and advertising can be purchased at a constant cost per unit. Then we can simply subtract the cost of additional advertising from both sides of Equation (8.16)—from ΔW on the left and from $\Delta \pi$ on the right—to get a similar expression for the

---

[30]Of course, these positions are determined by having the monopolist equate marginal revenue and marginal cost. To keep the graph as uncluttered as possible, these curves are omitted.

[31]See the discussion in Chapter 2 of the welfare cost of market power.

change in welfare, where both change in welfare and change in profit are measured net of the cost of advertising.

To evaluate the net change in social welfare from advertising, divide through both sides of Equation (8.16) by ΔA, the change in advertising, to obtain

$$\frac{\Delta W}{\Delta A} = \frac{\Delta \pi}{\Delta A} - Q \frac{\Delta P}{\Delta A}. \tag{8.17}$$

To interpret Equation (8.17), recall that a profit-maximizing firm will pick the advertising level that makes the change in profit from a small change in advertising—which is the first term on the right in Equation (8.17)—equal to zero.[32] Then Equation (8.17) simplifies to

$$\frac{\Delta W}{\Delta A} = -Q \frac{\Delta P}{\Delta A}. \tag{8.18}$$

For the level of advertising chosen by a profit-maximizing monopolist, a decrease in advertising ($\Delta A < 0$) would increase social welfare ($\Delta W > 0$). Monopolists advertise too much, from a social point of view, because when they make their decisions, they equate their private marginal revenue with their private marginal cost. They do not consider the additional cost, in the form of higher prices, imposed on consumers who would have purchased without advertising.[33]

Oligopoly may result in even more excessive advertising. If oligopolists succeed in controlling price competition, they may well divert their rivalry into marketing efforts. In this case, some advertising under oligopoly would be internecine, aimed solely at neutralizing the advertising of rivals.

Capital Requirements

Bain considered several reasons (besides advertising) why established firms might have a cost advantage over potential entrants at all levels of output, independent of scale differences. Some of these reasons—patents, control of high-quality inputs—will be important for certain industries and not for others.

---

[32]If additional advertising would increase the firm's profit, it would advertise more. This is really just another way of saying that the firm will make the marginal revenue from advertising equal to the marginal cost of advertising, which leads to the Dorfman-Steiner condition (Equation 8.15).

[33]A similar argument appears in Chapter 17, where we analyze the welfare effects of resale price maintenance. Manufacturers will sometimes support higher retail prices as a way of inducing retailers to engage in costly sales-promoting efforts. Consumers who would have purchased without these efforts are hurt by resale price maintenance.

The *general* source that Bain cited for absolute cost advantages of established firms was the workings of the market for financial capital:[34]

> The market for investible [sic] funds may be such as to impose higher effective interest costs on entrants than on established firms, or alternatively to impose a more severe rationing of funds on potential entrants.

In a world of perfect certainty, this could happen only if financial markets were imperfect. In the words of Bork:[35]

> If there are greater-than-competitive profits being made in the industry, however, there seems no reason why the increased capital necessary for entry would not be forthcoming, unless there are impediments in the capital market that prevent capital from flowing to areas where it can most profitably be employed. Until such impediments have been shown to exist, the fact that increased capital is required . . . must be assumed to have no adverse effect upon entry into monopolized markets.

In a world of uncertainty, however, an *efficient* capital market will impose higher finance costs on the entrant.[36]

Borrowers and lenders have different information about the prospects of success for any particular enterprise. When established firms seek to borrow funds, lenders will be able to rely on the reputation of the borrowing firm as they make decisions on the amounts to be loaned at different interest rates.

But entrants have no reputation. *Some* potential entrants will be able to come into a market successfully; others will not. Lenders will not have enough information to distinguish the two groups.

Potential entrants seeking funds will have the information lenders need. But they will not be able to convey this information with certainty to lenders. The information needed to assess the chance for success of an investment project by a new firm will be trapped or *impacted* on the borrowers' side of the market, with no way of being reliably transmitted to lenders.

Poorly qualified borrowers have an incentive to mislead lenders. If such a borrower convinces lenders that he is a good risk, he will have a lower cost of capital. The combination of this *opportunism* with impacted information translates into a higher cost of capital for all potential entrants:[37]

---

[34]Bain, Joe S. *Barriers to New Competition.* Cambridge, Mass. Harvard University Press, 1956, p. 145.

[35]Bork, Robert. "Vertical Integration and the Sherman Act: The Legal History of an Economic Misconception," *University of Chicago Law Review* Volume 22, Autumn 1954, p. 195.

[36]Williamson, Oliver E. "The Economics of Antitrust: Transaction Cost Considerations," *University of Pennsylvania Law Review* Volume 122, Number 6, June 1974, pp. 1439–1496.

[37]Ibid., p. 1458.

Unable to distinguish between those unknown candidates who have the capacity and the will to execute the project successfully from opportunists who assert that they are similarly qualified, when objectively (omnisciently) they are not, the terms of finance are adjusted against the entire group.

Given the state of information in financial markets, it is not inefficient to charge a risk premium to entrants:[38]

There is no "imperfection" in a market possessing incomplete knowledge if it would not be remunerative to acquire (produce) complete knowledge: information costs are the costs of transportation from ignorance to omniscience, and seldom can a trader afford to take the entire trip.

Even though it is efficient, as far as the functioning of capital markets is concerned, to charge a risk premium to entrants, the premium will put potential entrants at a cost disadvantage vis-à-vis established firms. It will create a limit price differential within which established firms will be able to exercise market power without inducing entry.

The Determinants of Market Concentration

To what extent do differences in entry conditions across industries explain differences in market concentration across industries? This is the topic of a large empirical literature, the recent portions of which have adopted a common analytical framework. This framework takes the view that concentration adjusts slowly to a long-term level that is determined by scale economies, by advertising, and by other factors that establish the nature of entry conditions. In general, such a model can be written

$$CR4_t = \theta CR4^* + (1 - \theta)CR4_{t-1}. \qquad \textbf{(8.19)}$$

Subscripts denote time periods, and CR4* is the long-run level of concentration. The parameter θ measures the speed of adjustment, and indicates how quickly market concentration approaches the long-run level. If θ is small, current concentration depends largely on past concentration and very little on the long-run level of concentration. When θ is small, concentration adjusts slowly to the long-run equilibrium level. The value θ can be transformed to yield an estimate of the average time it will take for market concentration to reach the long-run level.

[38]Stigler, George J. "Imperfections in the Capital Market," *Journal of Political Economy* Volume 75, Number 3, June 1967, p. 291 reprinted in Stigler, George J. *The Organization of Industry*, Homewood, Ill.: Richard D. Irvin, Inc., 1962.

Table 8-2 Determinants of Market Concentration

Martin
CR467 = 7.15 + 0.31^{b}MES + 0.06ASR + 0.87^{a}CR463; LAG^a = 28 years   (1)
CR472 = −4.06 + 1.04^{a}MES + 5.44^a(PLANTS/FIRM) + 0.02ASR   + 0.73^{a}CR467; LAG^a = 14 years   (2)

Mueller and Rogers
CR472 = 23.48^a − 1.55^{b}SIZE + 1.06^{a}ASR + 0.77^{a}CR447; LAG = 84 years   (3)
CR467 = 22.93^a − 1.48^{b}SIZE + 1.82^{a}TVASR − 0.970OTHASR   + 0.77^{a}CR447; LAG = 84 years   (4)

Notes:
MES = minimum efficient scale as a fraction of industry output
ASR = industry-average advertising-sales ratio
TVASR = ratio of spending on television advertising to sales
OTHASR = ratio of spending on newspaper, outdoor, and magazine advertising to dollar value of sales
SIZE = a measure of industry size

a indicates statistical significance at the 1 per cent level; such an estimate would occur by chance only once in 100 times, on average.

b indicates statistical significance at the 5 per cent level; such an estimate would occur by chance only once in 20 times, on average.

In each case, certain explanatory variables have been omitted from the results reported here for compactness. Where necessary, coefficients have been transformed for comparability.

Sources: Martin, S. "Advertising, Concentration, and Profitability: The Simultaneity Problem," *Bell Journal of Economics* Volume 10, Number 2, Autumn 1979, pp. 639–647 and "Causes and Effects of Vertical Integration," *Applied Economics* Volume 18, Number 7, July 1986, pp. 737–755; Mueller, W. F. and Rogers, R. T. "The Role of Advertising in Changing Concentration of Manufacturing Industries," *Review of Economics and Statistics* Volume 52, Number 1, February 1980, pp. 89–96.

Typically, versions of Equation (8.19) have been estimated for 2 years in which the Bureau of the Census conducted a Census of Manufactures. Different studies have tested different variables as determinants of the long-run level of concentration, CR4*. Representative results are reproduced in Table 8-2.

The two studies by Martin suggest that minimum efficient scale is a significant factor in determining market concentration. According to Equation (1), which covers the period 1963 to 1967, an increase of 10 percentage points in MES would, on average, result in an increase of 3 percentage points in the four-firm seller concentration ratio.

The estimate of the same coefficient over the period 1967 to 1972 (Equation 2) is over three times as large, and is more precise in a statistical sense. Equation (2) may give a better picture of the strength of the effect of MES, because it controls for differences across industries in the average number of plants per firm. It is to be expected that the concentration of sales will be larger, for any level of minimum efficient scale, the more plants the average firm operates. This expectation is confirmed by Equation (2). Comparing two otherwise identical industries, an industry in which the average number of plants per firm was two would have a concentration ratio nearly 5.5 percentage points higher than an industry in which the average number of plants per firm was one.

Absolute capital requirements will have their greatest effect on entry conditions when the MES is large. In the Martin equations, the coefficients of MES and PLANTS/FIRM should be thought of as reflecting in part, the effect on entry conditions of differences across industries in capital requirements.

Mueller and Rogers found market concentration to be less, all else equal, in larger industries. That is exactly what is predicted by our discussion of scale economies.

Mueller and Rogers found a fairly large and significant effect of all advertising on concentration (Equation 3). They were also able to split advertising expenses into two components, one for television and the other for other media. The significant impact of advertising on concentration is seen to be entirely due to television advertising. This is what one would expect if volume discounts for advertising on television favor large advertisers, and if network television advertising is "indivisible," so that a small entrant competing with national firms has to advertise nationally in order to market its product effectively.

The studies described in Table 8-2 show an extremely slow adjustment of concentration to its long-run level. The lags implied by the Mueller-Rogers estimates are unrealistically large and may result from their failure to control for differences across industries in MES. The Martin estimates suggest that the speed of adjustment has increased in recent years.[39]

A recent study by Kessides[40] makes a careful attempt to distinguish procompetitive and anticompetitive effects of advertising. Kessides studied the impact of advertising on the entry of new firms, rather than the level of market concentration.

Kessides noted that advertising will discourage entry because its cost is sunk. A firm that builds a retail outlet in a new market knows that if its attempt at entry is unsuccessful, it will be able to recover most of the capital invested in the building (by selling the building to another firm). But if a firm invests in a marketing campaign in an attempt to cultivate goodwill, the cost of that campaign cannot be recovered upon exit. If the firm leaves the industry, its investment in goodwill will be entirely lost.

The larger the advertising campaign necessary for entry, the greater the sunk

---

[39]This is confirmed by Geroski, P. A., Masson, R. T. and Shaanan, J. "The Dynamics of Market Structure," *International Journal of Industrial Organization,* Volume 5, Number 1, March 1987, pp. 93–100, who estimate a model within which the speed of adjustment parameter is allowed to vary from industry to industry as a function of industry structural characteristics. They find adjustment to be slower where MES is large.

[40]Kessides, Ionannis S. "Advertising, Sunk Costs, and Barriers to Entry," *Review of Economics and Statistics* Volume 68, Number 1, February 1986, pp. 84–94.

investment that is risked by a decision to enter. In this sense, advertising will discourage entry.

But advertising can also alter the probability that entry will be successful. The structure-conduct-performance school[41] believes that entry is less likely to be successful in industries where advertising is important. According to this analysis, advertising encourages brand loyalty, increases minimum efficient scale, and reduces the odds of successful entry.

In contrast, the Chicago school[42] holds that advertising is a way for new firms to make their way in the market. By advertising, new firms can inform the public of their presence and induce consumers to take a chance on the new product. If this is its effect, advertising will reduce brand loyalty and make the odds of successful entry greater, not less, all else equal.

Kessides developed a model of entry, allowing for these different possibilities, which he tested for a sample of 266 four-digit Standard Industrial Classification industries over the period 1972 to 1977. His results confirm that an investment in advertising is a sunk cost, and to that extent acts to discourage entry. He also found, however, that the odds of successful entry increase as the advertising per dollar of sales grows. The net effect of advertising, considering both effects, is to make entry easier.

Kessides' empirical implementation of his theoretical model is open to criticism on a number of grounds.[43] Nonetheless, his work represents the best attempt to date to analyze the impact of advertising on market performance.

Finally, a number of recent studies[44] suggest that the importance of the factors that determine market concentration differ in different segments of the economy. As with the studies of profitability discussed in Chapter 6, this result indicates that it may be sensible to study the determinants of market concentration on an industry-by-industry basis.

---

[41]Represented by the work of Comanor and Wilson, and Porter, cited previously.

[42]See, for example, Nelson, op. cit., and Telser, Lester G. "Advertising and Competition," *Journal of Political Economy* Volume 72, Number 6, December 1964, pp. 537–562.

[43]Although these criticisms are technical, completeness requires that they be mentioned. Kessides' theoretical model focuses on the number of new firms that enter over a period, but it does not deal with the fact that different firms will enter at different sizes. He measures profitability by a price-cost margin that is net of advertising cost, while models in the Dorfman-Steiner tradition suggest that profitability should be measured gross of advertising (a point due to Sawyer, Malcolm. "On the Specification of Structure–Performance Relationships," *European Economic Review* Volume 17, March 1982, pp. 295–306). To compute the price-cost margin, he uses tax rates of depreciation on buildings and machinery, when it is the actual rates that are called for (Martin, Stephen. "The Measurement of Profitability and the Diagnosis of Market Power," forthcoming, *International Journal of Industrial Organization*). He uses a novel measure of MES that seems likely to result in underestimates.

[44]Among which, Martin, Stephen. "Causes and Effects of Vertical Integration," *Applied Economics* Volume 18, Number 7, July 1986, pp. 737–755, and Levy, D. "Specifying the Dynamics of Industry Concentration," *Journal of Industrial Economics* Volume 34, Number 1, September 1985, pp. 55–68.

Summary

The Chicago school has challenged the view that any sort of behavior by oligopolists will allow the exercise of market power, at least over the long run. In this view, if output is restricted and price is raised above marginal cost, rivals will come in, expand capacity, and force the price down to a competitive level.

As a general rule, this position is unduly optimistic. Entrants will not come in unless they believe they can make a profit after entry, which may not be the case even if firms in the market are earning a profit. If MES is sufficiently large relative to the market, a new firm will not be able to open an efficiently sized plant without substantially increasing industry output. The postentry price would then be lower than the preentry price. A firm that enters a market with less than the MES plant will have higher unit cost than incumbents and will leave itself vulnerable to strategic behavior. When MES is large and plants of less than MES are very inefficient, incumbent firms will be able to exercise some market power without inducing entry.

Product differentiation can also discourage entry. This will occur if the effects of sales efforts endure over time (there is evidence that they do, although not for an extremely long period), if there are economies of scale in advertising (it is apparently less expensive to advertise through national media than in several regional markets through local media), and if the expense of advertising is a sunk cost. On the other hand, advertising will also inform the public that a new product is available, and may make successful entry more likely.

The combination of impacted information and opportunism, under the uncertainty that characterizes real-world capital markets, means that established firms will enjoy an absolute cost advantage over potential entrants. This advantage will be larger, the larger the investment needed to set up an efficiently sized plant.

Empirical tests support the claim that entry conditions, as described by MES and expenditures on advertising, determine market concentration. Market concentration thus reflects a combination of technical factors and factors (such as cost fixity and product differentiation) that are under the control of established firms.

Provided oligopolists can overcome the problems of agreement and adherence (Chapter 6), there will be a range of prices within which they will be able to exercise market power without inducing entry. The dominant-firm models of Chapter 4, reinterpreted now as dominant-group models, suggest that such oligopolists may choose to induce some entry, take a greater profit, and slowly give up control of the market. OPEC may be an example of such behavior. But the speed of entry will not, in general, be so rapid and so automatic that policymakers can count on entry to eliminate market power wherever it develops.

Problems

8-1 (Cournot oligopoly, quadratic cost function) Let the cost function for each firm be

$$C(q) = F + cq + dq^2;$$

marginal cost and average cost are then

$$MC = c + 2dq \qquad AC = \frac{F}{q} + c + dq.$$

a. Show that the average cost curve reaches its minimum at output level $MES = \sqrt{F/d}$.

If the market demand curve is

$$P = a - bQ,$$

b. Find the short-run equilibrium price and firm output if there are n firms in the market, each making the Cournot assumption.

c. What is the equilibrium number of firms if entry occurs until equilibrium firm profit is zero?

d. How does market performance change as MES increases?

8-2 (Capital markets and entry conditions) Modern corporations borrow on bond markets. Bondholders receive an agreed-upon interest rate if the firm is solvent when the bonds are due; if the firm is bankrupt, its assets are sold and the proceeds (if any) are divided among the bondholders in proportion to the number of bonds held. Call π_B bondholders' estimate of the probability that the firm will be bankrupt when the bonds are due. Each bond represents a loan of $1 to the firm and entitles the holder to $1 + r$ unless the firm is bankrupt. B bonds are sold, and the firm has assets K, which can be sold for price $p^k K$.

a. Suppose bondholders have the option of investing in a safe asset, such as a U.S. government Treasury bill, which offers a return of $1 + r^*$ per dollar without any risk of bankruptcy. If bondholders insist that an investment in private bonds yield the same expected return as an investment in government bonds, what is the bond market equilibrium condition that defines r as a function of π_B (and B, $p^k K$)?

b. Considerations of impacted information and opportunism suggest that π_B will be larger for a potential entrant than for an established firm. How will this affect the cost of borrowed capital for a potential entrant? What are the implications for strategic behavior by established firms?

Paper Topics

8-1 Compare Scherer, F. M. "Economies of Scale and Industrial Concentration," pp. 16–54 and McGee, John S., "Efficiency and Economies of

THE DETERMINANTS OF MARKET STRUCTURE

Size," pp. 55–104, in Goldschmid, Harvey J., Mann, H. Michael, and Weston, J. Fred, editors, *Industrial Concentration: The New Learning.* Boston: Little, Brown and Company, 1974, and the references cited therein. Evaluate economists' ability to assess the efficiency of real-world firms.

8-2 How has modern technology changed what we mean by productive efficiency? Consult Nag, Amal. "Auto Makers Discover 'Factory of the Future' Is Headache Just Now," *Wall Street Journal* May 13, 1987, p. 1 and "Factory of the Future: A Survey," *The Economist,* insert, May 30, 1987.

9 The Determinants of Firm Structure[1]

For God and profits.

Motto of the Alberti family of Florence.

In the models of elementary microeconomics, the firm is essentially a "black box" that houses a production function. Factors of production flow into the box, and goods and services flow out. These flows occur in such a way as to maximize the firm's profit. The production function summarizes the technological relationships between inflow and outflow. Any differences in performance are due to the environment surrounding the black box—to the structure of its market—not to anything that goes on within the black box.

But in the real world, firms have an internal structure. Modern corporations typically operate in many markets. Sometimes these markets are at the same horizontal level, as when a single-product firm operates plants in distinct geographic markets (cement) or when a firm produces several varieties of a differentiated product (breakfast cereal). Sometimes the markets are related vertically (petroleum). Conglomerate firms operate in unrelated industries. Within the black box of the modern firm are multiple divisions and levels at which productive activity takes place and decisions are made. The real-world firm can be thought of as a *collection* of production functions, some producing inputs for others and some operating more or less on their own.

The internal organization of firms raises (at least) three interesting questions. First, why are certain collections of production functions assembled under a single corporate umbrella? Why, for example, does production in some indus-

[1]For recent surveys of the literature discussed in this chapter, see Marris, R. and Mueller, D. C. "The Corporation, Competition, and the Invisible Hand," *Journal of Economic Literature* Volume 18, Number 1, March 1980, pp. 32–63; Caves, R. E. "Industrial Organization, Corporate Strategy and Structure," *Journal of Economic Literature* Volume 18, Number 1, March 1980, pp. 64–92; and Williamson, O. E. "The Modern Corporation: Origins, Evolution, Attributes," *Journal of Economic Literature* Volume 19, Number 4, December 1981, pp. 1537–1568.

tries typically involve vertical integration, while in other parts of the economy vertically related markets are occupied by independent firms?

Second, how do firms organize the relationships among the productive activities of which they are comprised? What, in other words, is the internal structure of the firm? Are some forms of internal organization more efficient than others?

Third, how do all of these factors affect performance in the markets in which the firm operates? Is efficiency enhanced in any market if firms that operate in unrelated markets combine to form a conglomerate? Is market power at any level enhanced if a firm expands vertically?

In what follows, we first address a question that makes sense only if one recognizes that firms are *not* black boxes. What do firms do? Do they maximize their profit, as economists are wont to assume? What else might firms do, and why? Are there economic forces that limit the ability of firms to do anything other than maximize their profit?

We then turn to the questions of horizontal, vertical, and conglomerate structure. Horizontal and conglomerate structure are discussed in terms of mergers, the context in which they usually arise. In large measure, however, this discussion applies to internal growth as well.

Finally, we consider the internal organization of the firm, reviewing its major forms and their implications for market performance.

Firms' Goals

What Firms Do

The microeconomic theory of the firm is based on the work of economists who dealt with the entrepreneurial firms of the Industrial Revolution. In this world, the firm was largely an extension of its owner. Profit maximization, in this case, is a natural assumption to make: profit maximization for the firm is much the same as utility maximization for the individual who owns the firm. The more profit the firm makes, the greater the income of the owner/manager.[2]

But with large modern corporations, ownership and control are separate.[3] Individual stockholders "own" minuscule portions of the firm. Their proxies are signed over to management as a matter of routine, and it is usually difficult for a discontented stockholder to do anything other than sell the stock.

---

[2]For an accessible discussion in the context of American economic history, see Chandler, Alfred D., Jr. *The Visible Hand: The Managerial Revolution in American Business.* Cambridge, Mass.: Harvard University Press, 1977, chapters 1 and 2.

[3]Berle, A. A. and Means, G. *The Modern Corporation and Private Property.* New York: The Macmillan Co., 1932.

Managers may be interested in maximizing the flow of income to stockholders. But they may have other concerns as well. They may wish, for example, to maximize their own salaries. Managers' salaries may depend as much on the size of the firm—in terms of sales or assets—as on the firm's profit. Even if making a larger profit does not translate directly into a higher salary, a larger profit will mean more discretionary power for top management.

There is every reason to think that firms will be managed to maximize some combination of profit, growth, and size. The weights attached to the different goals are likely to be those of top management, not stockholders.[4]

The possibility of stockholder revolt will place a weak constraint on the ability of management to pursue its own interests. Financial markets present a more serious threat.[5,6]

Maximizing profit, over time, is the same as maximizing the present discounted value (Chapter 4) of the income earned by the firm. The present discounted value is what stockholders will pay, in the aggregate, for the shares of the firm. It is what the firm is worth on the open market.

If management is not maximizing the firm's worth, the stock of the firm will sell for less than it would under a different management. The firm will be vulnerable to takeover attempts. A different management—either independent or on behalf of some other firm—could purchase the firm's stock, throw the incumbent management out, and profit from the increase in the value of the firm under a new management. If financial markets work at all well, this sort of takeover should occur whenever the potential gain in income exceeds the costs of making a takeover bid.[7]

Takeover costs include the cost of planning the takeover and legal expenses to overcome attempts to resist it. Once the takeover attempt becomes known, speculators will purchase the stock of the target company in the hope of making a short-run profit. Such speculative purchases will drive up the price of the stock, and this price increase will be part of the cost of the takeover. If the takeover is successful, there will be costs of transforming the operations of the target firm. These management costs also have to be set against the potential gain from a takeover.

The transactions costs of a takeover attempt will interfere with the limits the

---

[4]See Donaldson, Gordon. *Managing Corporate Wealth*. New York: Praeger Publishing Co., 1984.

[5]Marris, R. "A Model of the 'Managerial' Enterprise," *Quarterly Journal of Economics* Volume 77, May 1963, pp. 185–209.

[6]See Demsetz, Harold and Lehn, Kenneth. "The Structure of Corporate Ownership: Causes and Consequences," *Journal of Political Economy,* Volume 93, December 1985, pp. 1155–1177, for an argument that the pattern of controlling interests in corporations serves as a mechanism for monitoring managements.

[7]A successful takeover will not require acquisition of *all* outstanding shares, just enough to acquire effective control.

capital market places on discretionary management behavior.[8] In part, this limitation reflects impacted information. The firm's management knows best whether or not profit is being maximized. It will be difficult for persons outside the firm to acquire the relevant information, and those in the firm have little incentive to reveal it.[9]

Further, takeover attempts involve appeals to stockholders. But stockholders will have to make their own decisions under conditions of imperfect and impacted information. How are they to know whether the claims of the takeover group are valid? Such a group will want to put only its best foot forward. Stockholders will know this, and will accordingly discount the claims of groups attempting a takeover. This is the same sort of *opportunistic* behavior that puts potential entrants at a disadvantage, compared to established firms, in capital markets.[10]

The threat of a takeover will discipline firms' managements *if* the costs associated with a takeover attempt are small in proportion to the gains. A study[11] of the effect of takeover offers on stock prices for 95 firms showed that the market value of a firm can fall to 87 per cent of its profit-maximizing value without inducing a takeover attempt. Managers clearly have some discretion to pursue goals other than profit maximization, although the threat of loss of control will encourage them to maximize the worth of a firm.

It appears (and we will later see) that growth maximization was a factor in the conglomerate merger movement of the 1970s. In contrast, the merger movement of the 1980s includes a significant number of divestitures and restructurings, which have the effect of undoing some of the conglomerate mergers of the past. This is evidence that financial markets will ultimately drive firms to maximize their profit. Over the long run, profit maximization is the best single explanation of firm behavior. However, it is not the only explanation, especially in the short run.

What Firms Don't Do

Firms may not have goals at all, in any meaningful sense. A firm is not, after all, a single individual, but rather a team. The largest firms have more

---

[8]Williamson, Oliver E. "The Economics of Antitrust: Transaction Cost Considerations," *University of Pennsylvania Law Review* Volume 122, Number 6, June 1975, pp. 1439–1496; see especially pp. 1481–1482.

[9]This explains the frequency of takeovers by current or former members of a firm's management; they will have an information advantage over true outsiders. An example is the June 1987 sale by Hospital Corporation of America of 104 acute-care hospitals to a group of managers and employees.

[10]See Chapter 8.

[11]Smiley, R. "Tender Offers, Transaction Costs, and the Theory of the Firm," *Review of Economics and Statistics* Volume 58, Number 1, February 1976, pp. 22–32.

221

employees than small nations have citizens. A bureaucratic management may simply want to avoid trouble—it may aim to "satisfice," not maximize. Earn enough profit to keep the stockholders happy. Pay high enough wages so that the unions don't walk. Squirrel away extra inventories to avoid shortages. Avoid doing anything that will attract the attention of those above you in the management pyramid. Don't make waves.

A result of the inability of management to impose meaningful goals on the firm is *X-inefficiency*,[12] the failure of a firm to minimize costs. The general question raised is how a firm can structure its internal organization so that the goals of management, whatever they are, are implemented as the goals of the organization. We return to this question when we discuss alternative forms of firm organization.

Horizontal Mergers

Four great merger waves have shaped the landscape of American industry. Two of them involved primarily horizontal mergers.

The first merger wave began at the end of one depression, in 1883, was fueled by the depression of 1893, and ended with the start of another depression in 1904. It was a natural response to a dramatic restructuring of the economy that followed the Civil War. During this period, national railway lines linked regional markets into a single national market. This national market supported substantially larger firms, in many industries, than had the earlier regional markets.[13]

These larger firms employed capital-intensive production techniques and carried a high proportion of fixed to variable costs. In periods of slack demand, such firms are susceptible to price wars.[14] Price wars were common following the depression of 1893. Collusion was unsuccessful in controlling them (and, in any event, was outlawed by the Sherman Act). Consolidation via merger was the result[15] and the product of the merger was typically a dominant firm in its industry. The 1901 combination of 180 independent firms to create U.S. Steel is an example.

The second great U.S. merger wave began after World War I and ended with the Great Depression of 1929. By this time, the antitrust laws had changed

---

[12]Leibenstein, H. "Allocative Efficiency vs. 'X-Efficiency,' " *American Economic Review* Volume 56, June 1966, pp. 392–415.

[13]As we have seen in Chapter 3, popular hostility toward these large firms was an important factor in the passage of the Sherman Antitrust Act.

[14]See chapter 6's discussion of cartel stability.

[15]Lamoreaux, Naomi R. *The Great Merger Movement in American Business, 1895–1904*. Cambridge: Cambridge University Press, 1985.

the nature of merger activity. Mergers were no longer combinations of dozens of firms, which together dominated their industries. They now combined fewer firms and often formed the second or third largest firm in the market. In Stigler's phrase,[16] the second merger wave consisted of mergers for oligopoly, while the first consisted of mergers for monopoly.

These early U.S. merger waves involved mainly horizontal mergers: mergers of firms that operated in the same market. It is the consequences of such horizontal mergers that we now examine.

This discussion will lead us to revisit familiar territory. In a broad sense, horizontal (and other) mergers can have two sorts of effects: they may increase market power or they may increase efficiency. The net impact of a merger on market performance will depend on the tradeoff between these two results. This is precisely the tradeoff that emerged from the debate over the concentration–profits relationship (Chapter 7).

Horizontal Mergers and Market Power

The search for market power is an obvious incentive for horizontal merger. If a merger combines all of the firms in an industry, the survivor becomes a dominant firm and the analysis of Chapter 4 comes into play. The survivor firm will be able to exercise some control over price; exactly how much will depend on entry costs. It may limit the price and maintain its position, or it may gradually give up market share to new producers.

The impact of mergers on market power when the merger combines some but not all firms in the market is more complex. To analyze mergers for oligopoly, we turn to the oligopoly models of Chapter 5.

Mergers in Quantity-Setting Markets

We consider an oligopoly of three firms, each with the same cost function. The firms produce a standardized product, and each maximizes its profit along a residual demand curve obtained from the market demand curve by subtracting the output of the other two firms. In other words, we consider a Cournot triopoly. How will a merger between firms 1 and 2 change market performance?

Firm 3's behavior will be described by a reaction curve obtained by setting the marginal revenue along firm 3's residual demand curve equal to its marginal cost. This will give us a reaction surface showing firm 3's output in response to the outputs of firms 1 and 2.

Since firms 1 and 2 have the same cost function, they will produce the same output in equilibrium. Keeping their output the same at nonequilibrium levels does not change the final result, and it allows us to draw the reaction curves

---

[16]Stigler, George J. "Monopoly and Oligopoly by Merger," *American Economic Review* Volume 40, Number 2, May 1950 pp. 23–34; reprinted in *The Organization of Industry*. Homewood, Ill.: Richard D. Irwin, Inc., 1968, pp. 95–107.

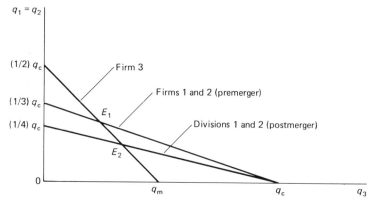

Notes: Firm 3's reaction curve shows its profit-maximizing output, given the outputs of firm 1 and firm 2, when firms 1 and 2 produce the same output. The other reaction curves show the common profit-maximizing output of firms 1 and 2, given the output of firm 3, when firms 1 and 2 produce the same output.

Figure 9-1   Merger and reaction curves in a quantity-setting market.

on a two-dimensional graph. Hence the reaction curve for firm 3 drawn in Figure 9-1 shows firm 3's output, given the outputs of firms 1 and 2, when firms 1 and 2 produce the same output.

Similarly, the premerger reaction curve for firms 1 and 2 shows the output each firm will produce, given firm 3's output and the output of the other firms, when firms 1 and 2 produce the same output.

It is worth asking why a merger changes market performance at all. In fact, nothing happens to change firm 3's reaction curve. After the merger, as before, firm 3 observes the outputs of firms 1 and 2 and maximizes its own profit along its residual demand curve.

But consider the corporate decision, after the merger, to determine the output of what was formerly firm 1 and is now division 1 of the mergered firm.[17] Profit maximization requires corporate management to pick an output level for division 1 that makes the marginal revenue of the corporation equal to its marginal cost. This is

$$MR_1 = P + q_1 \frac{\Delta P}{\Delta q_1} + q_2 \frac{\Delta P}{\Delta q_1} = MC, \qquad (9.1)$$

where $\Delta P/\Delta q_1 < 0$ is the reduction in price that follows a marginal increase in output by division 1.

Before the merger, marginal revenue for division 1 was simply the price less the marginal loss of revenue on division 1's output as the price fell (the first two terms in Equation (9.1)'s expression for marginal revenue). For the amalgamated firm, the merger adds a new element to marginal revenue. When

[17]For a graphic approach, see Martin J. Bailey. "Price and Output Determination by a Firm Selling Related Products," *American Economic Review* Volume 44, Number 1, March 1954, pp. 82–93.

division 1's output increases, the price received by division 2 for what it sells goes down. The resulting loss of revenue to the conglomerate is the third term in the expression for marginal revenue in Equation (9.1).

Before the merger, the management of firm 1 was indifferent to the loss of revenue that its output expansion would inflict on firm 2. After the merger, the management for both divisions will look at revenue changes in both divisions when it sets output levels.

Because a restriction in output by division 1 will raise revenue in division 2 (and vice versa), a corporate management will restrict division output, compared with premerger independent firms. In terms of Figure 9-1, the reaction curve for divisions 1 and 2 rotates in a counterclockwise direction. Whatever the output of firm 3, divisions 1 and 2 produce less after the merger than before (see Problem 9-1).

Oligopoly equilibrium shifts from E_1 to E_2. The restriction of output by firms 1 and 2 tends to raise the price. But the remaining independent firm takes advantage of the output restriction by firms 1 and 2 to expand its output. The net reduction in output supplied to the market is less than the reduction in output by firms 1 and 2 because of the expansion of output by firm 3.

Because the amalgamated firm cannot control the decisions of the remaining independent, it may earn *less* profit after the merger than before it. It turns out that if demand curves are linear and marginal cost is constant, a merger must include at least 80 per cent of the firms in the market before it will be profitable.[18]

In a way, this result is a natural extension of the main conclusion of Chapter 4: a dominant firm cannot exercise market power unless there are entry or expansion costs that prevent fringe firms from expanding their output. The same is true of a mergered firm. But it is worth examining whether or not the possibility of unprofitable mergers occurs in other kinds of markets.

Mergers in Price-Setting Markets

Return to the model of price-setting oligopoly presented in Chapter 5. Recall that in this model the demand for a firm's product depends not only on its price but also on the difference between its price and the average price in the market. When products are differentiated, a firm can raise its price somewhat above the average price level without losing all sales. The greater the degree of product differentiation, the less rapidly will sales fall as a firm's price rises above the industry average.

In such markets, price-reaction curves slope upward (Figure 5-11). The higher the prices of other firms, the higher the price a firm will find it profitable to charge.

---

[18]Salant, S. W., Switzer, S., and Reynolds, R. J. "Losses from Horizontal Merger: The Effects of an Exogenous Change in Industry Structure on Cournot-Nash Equilibrium," *Quarterly Journal of Economics* Volume 98, Number 2, May 1983, pp. 185–213.

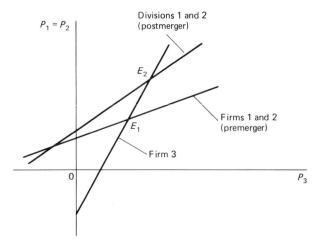

Notes: Firm 3's reaction curve shows its profit-maximizing price, given the prices of firms 1 and 2, when firms 1 and 2 charge the same price. The other reaction curves show the common profit-maximizing price of firms 1 and 2, given the price of firm 3, when firms 1 and 2 charge the same price.

Figure 9-2 Merger and reaction curves in a price-setting market.

The impact of a merger in a price-setting market can be illustrated using reaction curves, as in Figure 9-2. We again consider an oligopoly of three firms and a merger of firms 1 and 2. Figure 9-2 shows the reaction curve of firm 3, and the reaction curve for firms 1 and 2, when they set the same price.

A merger of firms 1 and 2 does not shift firm 3's reaction curve. But it does alter the composition of marginal revenue for the firms involved in the merger (as in Equation 9.1). After the merger, the management of the amalgamated firm will take account of the fact that a price increase by division 1 increases the demand for the variety of the product produced by division 2 (and vice versa). After the merger, divisions 1 and 2 will charge a higher price, whatever the price set by firm 3, than before the merger. The reaction curve for firms 1 and 2 rotates in a counterclockwise direction.

Firms 1 and 2 raise their price after the merger. This increases the demand for firm 3's product. The profit-maximizing response by firm 3, as shown in Figure 9-2, is to raise its own price.

The fringe firm reacts to the merger by changing its price in the same direction as the larger firm. This contrasts with the reaction in the quantity-setting market, in which the fringe firm expands its output as the dominant firm restricts its output. In each case, the independent firm acts to maximize its own profit. In the price-setting market, the independent works with the mergered firm. In the quantity-setting market, the independent works against it.

This difference is enough to reverse the results of the merger analysis in quantity-setting markets. In price-setting markets, firms that merge always enjoy an increase in profit and market power after the merger.[19]

Recapitulation

Mergers increase market power for the postmerger firm in price-setting markets. This may or may not happen in quantity-setting markets, depending on the market share of the postmerger firm. If there are expansion costs that prevent fringe firms from expanding their output in the postmerger world, mergers will increase the market power of the postmerger firm in quantity-setting models. The search for market power remains an important motive for merger.[20]

Mergers and Efficiency

Management

The search for efficiency may also motivate mergers. We previously discussed the possibility that the threat of takeover will discipline management and induce maximization of profit as a goal of the firm. Merger is a mechanism by which the threat of takeover may become reality. Some mergers will have the effect of transferring control of the firm from less efficient to more efficient administrative teams.

Multiplant Economies

Merger is a way for a firm to acquire additional plants. By so doing, a firm will be able to take advantage of any available economies of multiplant operation.

By operating more than one plant, a firm can spread the fixed costs of administration over a larger output. The result is a multiplant economy of scale that will encourage multiplant operation, at least to the point where the firm becomes so large that management loses administrative control.

If transportation costs are sufficiently high, relative to the value of the product, a firm may choose to operate several plants, each in a different geographic market. High transportation costs relative to price will encourage multiplant operation.

There will often be *product-specific* economies of multiplant operation.[21] If a firm produces different products in a single plant, production time will inev-

---

[19]Denercke, R. and Davidson, C. "Incentives to Form Coalitions with Bertrand Competition," *Rand Journal of Economics* Volume 16, Number 4, Winter 1985, pp. 473–486.

[20]Chandler, op. cit., documents the fact that the search for market power was an important motive in the first merger movement in the United States. But he concludes (chapter 10) that horizontal integration was not often a successful long-run strategy. It was, he indicates, vertical integration that ensured a dominant long-run market position.

[21]Scherer, F. M., Beckenstein, A., Kaufer, E., and Murphy, R. D. *The Economics of Multi-Plant Operation*. Cambridge, Mass.: Harvard University Press, 1975.

itably be lost as assembly lines are switched from one product to another. By operating more than one plant, a firm can specialize the production of high-volume products in single plants. This will reduce down time due to shifting production, resulting in *run-length economies*. A comprehensive study[22] indicates that run-length economies are as important as economies of scale in several industries, including fabric weaving and finishing, shoe making, bottle blowing, and bearing manufacturing.

Excess Capacity

Recall from Chapter 6 that cost differences are one of the industry characteristics that impede successful collusion. Joint-profit maximization will require inefficient plants to accept lower market shares. Extremely inefficient plants may have to shut down if an oligopoly is to maximize joint profits.

Mergers are an effective way to eliminate excess capacity.[23] A firm that assumes control of many plants will be able to close the oldest and least efficient ones, which independent owners would be loath to do. This is especially important in industries that face declining demand.[24]

Life Cycle Effects

A firm's propensity to engage in mergers will vary with its age.[25] When a firm is young, it is less likely to engage in mergers, all else equal.

Since young firms lack an established reputation, financial markets will impose a risk premium on any funds they borrow, including those needed to finance a merger. A young firm is less likely to generate enough cash flow to finance mergers internally, at least large mergers. It is less likely to merger, therefore, because its cost of capital will be greater than that for a mature firm.

Further, any expansion or development activity represents a claim on scarce management resources. A young firm will have plenty of opportunities for expansion without turning to mergers. Its management will have every incentive to devote all of its resources to internal expansion as the firm establishes a secure market position.

Once a firm has matured and has developed a market position that fully exploits its growth opportunities, it will have a substantial cash flow. It will be able to borrow funds at the lowest available commercial interest rate. By

---

[22]Ibid., p. 51.

[23]Williamson, O. E. "Economies as an Antitrust Defense: The Welfare Tradeoffs," *American Economic Review* Volume 58, Number 1, March 1968, pp. 18–36.

[24]The analysis of excess capacity as an incentive for merger is consistent with Lamoreaux's (op. cit.) analysis of the depression of 1893 as a factor motivating the first great American merger wave.

[25]Mueller, D. C. "A Life-Cycle Theory of the Firm," *Journal of Industrial Economics* Volume 21, July 1972, pp. 199–219.

definition, it will have exploited its best opportunities for internal expansion. At this point in its development, the firm is likely to turn to mergers as an avenue for expansion.[26]

Horizontal Mergers and Market Performance

Direct tests of the causes of merger activity indicate that there is some merit in all of the merger theories previously outlined. Merger is, in other words, a multifaceted phenomenon reflecting a number of underlying economic motives.[27] Here we examine evidence on the effects of mergers.

A recent case study[28] examines the impact of two mergers on price in the market for microfilm. The Xidex Corporation is a dominant firm in the market for duplicating microfilm. The mergers in question involved two types of microfilm: diazo and vesicular. Each is used to make microfilm copies of government records.

In 1976, Xidex acquired the diazo operations of Scott Graphics. This increased Xidex's share of the U.S. diazo microfilm market from 40 to 55 per cent. If (as the oligopoly models of Chapter 5 predict) increased market share brings increased market power, one would expect the price of diazo microfilm to rise, relative to the price of vesicular microfilm, after the acquisition of Scott Graphics.

In 1979, Xidex acquired the assets of Kalvar Corporation, which had been active in the vesicular microfilm market. This increased Xidex's share of the U.S. vesicular microfilm market from 67 to 93 per cent. If mergers to large market shares are a source of market power, such a merger to a near-monopoly market share would be expected to result in an increase in the price of vesicular microfilm relative to the price of diazo microfilm.

Figure 9-3 shows the effects of the two mergers on the relative price of products made from the two kinds of microfilm. After the diazo acquisition, the price of diazo microfilm products rose, relative to the price of vesicular microfilm products. After the vesicular merger, which increased Xidex's market

---

[26]A related argument is that firms will find merger more attractive when it is profitable to make investments that expand capacity. Thus mergers should be more common in rapidly growing industries, regardless of firm age. See Bittlingmayer, George. "Merger as a Form of Investment." Manuscript, Berlin: Science Center Berlin, January 1987.

[27]See Schwartz, Steven. "An Empirical Test of a Managerial, Life-Cycle, and Cost of Capital Model of Merger Activity," *Journal of Industrial Economics* Volume 32, Number 3, March 1984, pp. 265–276; and Stewart, John F., Harris, Robert F., and Carleton, Willard T. "The Role of Market Structure in Merger Behavior," *Journal of Industrial Economics* Volume 32, Number 3, March 1984, pp. 293–312.

[28]Barton, David M. and Sherman, Roger "The Price and Profit Effects of Horizontal Merger," *Journal of Industrial Economics* Volume 33, Number 2, December 1984, pp. 165–177.

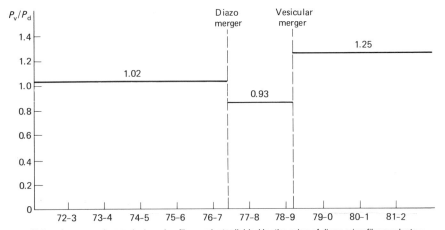

Notes: Average price vesicular microfilm products divided by the price of diazo microfilm products before and after acquisitions.

Figure 9-3 Price effects of mergers in microfilm industries. Source: Barton, David M. and Sherman, Roger "The Price and Profit Effects of Horizontal Merger," *Journal of Industrial Economics* Volume 33, Number 2, December 1984, p. 171.

share to a near-monopoly level, the relative price of diazo microfilm products rose above the initial premerger level.

These are exactly the price movements—increases in relative price following increases in market share—that one would expect if the mergers contributed to market power. The authors of the case study show that these price changes are statistically significant. The price changes would occur by chance less than once in 100 times.

In 1981, the Federal Trade Commission challenged the Xidex mergers. The case was settled in March 1982. Under the terms of the settlement, Xidex agreed to divest its acquisitions in the vesicular film market and to license the use of its vesicular and diazo technology to other firms.

Vertical Integration

Incentives

Why should a firm ever integrate vertically? If the invisible hand works, a firm should always be able to buy inputs on the open market. In fact, if markets are always an efficient way to organize production, a firm should be able to buy inputs at their marginal cost of production. Similarly, a firm should be able to purchase wholesale and retail distribution services, for use in marketing its product, at the marginal cost of distribution.

The incentive to integrate vertically stems from transaction costs involved in negotiating contracts among firms at different vertical levels.[29] These transaction costs reflect the impact of human nature and uncertainty on interfirm relationships.

Bounded Rationality

One such aspect of human nature is *bounded rationality*.[30] Human beings have a limited ability to process information and make decisions. Yet the world is complex and uncertain, and not all contingencies can be anticipated in advance. If a firm depends on the market for essential inputs and marketing outlets, any number of circumstances might arise under which the firm is unable to complete transactions upon which it had based its plans. By integrating vertically and bringing critical input–output relationships within the firm, the firm can acquire a flexibility that is unavailable in the marketplace.

Opportunism

Opportunism[31] will also raise the cost of interfirm transactions in an uncertain world. A firm's suppliers may find it in their own interest to mislead the firm, or to present the firm with correct but incomplete information. By integrating vertically and turning suppliers into employees, the firm can ensure their loyalty and straightforwardness with a certainty that is not possible across markets.

Small-Numbers Bargaining Problems

Bargaining problems will arise when there are only a few possible suppliers (or distributors). Small-number bargaining problems create another incentive for vertical integration. If a firm's suppliers have it "over a barrel," the most efficient thing for the firm to do may be to start producing inputs on its own. The same holds true for distribution.

As an example, consider Chapter 4's case study of corporate strategy in the hospital supply industry. In 1979, a group of 29 hospitals signed a contract establishing a single firm as the primary supplier for a wide variety of products. Before the contract was signed, the group had a wide range of possible suppliers (including other large firms and a network of smaller firms). After the contract was implemented, sunk investments were made by both parties, which had the effect of making it costly for the hospitals to switch suppliers.

Computer order-entry systems were installed, linking the hospitals directly with the supplier's warehouses. Hospital personnel were trained to use software

---

[29]The transactions cost approach is emphasized by Williamson; see Williamson, op. cit., for references.

[30]Simon, H. "Theories of Bounded Rationality," in Radner, C. B. and Radner, R., editors, *Decision and Organization*. Amsterdam: North Holland Publishing Company, 1972.

[31]See the discussion of capital markets in Chapter 8.

designed for this system. Any decision to change suppliers would bring with it the cost of retraining personnel and reworking the computerized order-entry system.

This example illustrates a general phenomenon. After one supplier has been in place for a time, the number of potential suppliers becomes much smaller than it was before the original choice was made. Bargaining power will shift over time from the purchaser to the supplier, and this will create an incentive for vertical integration.[32]

The key to small-numbers bargaining problems as a motive for vertical integration is *asset specificity*.[33] Whenever vertical relationships require investment in highly specific assets—the cost of which is sunk—a firm will eventually find itself dealing with suppliers who are to some extent immune to competition. This is because sunk costs raise barriers to potential entrants (Chapter 4). An asset specificity increases, vertical integration becomes more attractive.[34]

Small-numbers bargaining problems should be more serious, the more concentrated the vertically related supplying or distributing industries. Correspondingly, vertical integration should be greater, the more concentrated the vertically related industries.

Distortions in Input Choice

Firms may also integrate vertically to avoid the consequences of their own market power.[35] Suppose a firm has market power over a product that is used as an input in a downstream industry—an industry closer to the final consumer. By raising its price, the firm with market power creates an incentive for downstream firms to use less of its product, insofar as their technology allows them to do so. If the firm with market power integrates into the downstream industry, it can ensure that the product is used efficiently as an input by making input choices based on its cost of production. The firm can then exercise market power by raising the price of the final product.

---

[32]Recall from Chapter 4 that the hospital group did eventually license independent manufacturers to produce various hospital supplies under its own private label, a kind of vertical integration.

[33]Riordan, Michael H. and Williamson, Oliver E. "Asset Specificity and Economic Organization," *International Journal of Industrial Organization* Volume 3, Number 4, December 1985, pp. 365–378; Williamson, Oliver E. "Vertical Integration and Related Variations on Transaction-Cost Economics Theme," in Stiglitz, Joseph E. and Mathewson, G. Frank, editors, *New Developments in the Analysis of Market Structure*. Cambridge, Mass.: The M.I.T. Press, 1986, pp. 149–174.

[34]Kleindorfer, Paul and Knieps, Gunter, "Vertical Integration and Transaction-Specific Sunk Costs," *European Economic Review* Volume 19, Number 1, September 1982, pp. 71–87, discuss the use of long-term contracts as an alternative to vertical integration.

[35]See Vernon, John M. and Graham, Daniel A. "Profitability of Monopolization by Vertical Integration," *Journal of Political Economy* Volume 79, Number 5, September–October 1971, pp. 924–925; and Schmalensee, Richard. "A Note on the Theory of Vertical Integration," *Journal of Political Economy* Volume 81, Number 2, Part 1, March–April 1973, pp. 442–449.

Vertical integration should therefore be greater, the greater the market concentration. The greater the market concentration, the more likely are firms to have some market power, and the greater their incentive to integrate downstream and avoid distortions in demand. This effect should be most important in industries producing intermediate goods.

Strategic Motives for Integration

Firms may integrate vertically for strategic reasons: to raise rivals' input costs or to increase the absolute capital costs of entry, hence increasing the level to which the price can be raised without inducing entry.

A firm that controls high-quality supplies of an essential input will enjoy a cost advantage vis-à-vis less fortunate rivals. An integrated firm with market power over an essential input can exercise that power with respect to nonintegrated rivals, placing them at a cost disadvantage and, if necessary, disciplining rivals who become too rivalrous.[36] Such "price squeezes" were long alleged to be a feature of the U.S. steel industry.[37]

As noted in Chapter 8, vertical integration will increase entry costs if capital markets impose a risk premium on new firms or on small firms that seek to install substantial new capacity. Transaction costs in capital markets—impacted information and opportunism—mean that capital markets will do just that.

Firms in rapidly growing industries may find it necessary to integrate if the capacity of input-producing or output-using industries cannot keep pace. More than once in the early years of the American Industrial Revolution, dominant firms integrated forward into distribution because they grew so fast that their old distributors could not keep up with them.[38] Although this expansion may have been necessary from an efficiency point of view, it also had the effect of raising barriers to entry:[39]

> Except in the production of primary metals, a manufacturing enterprise rarely became and remained large until it had built its own extensive marketing organization. Its owners took this step when the maintenance of high-volume output required precise and detailed scheduling of the flows of finished products to mass markets or the maintenance of specialized distributing facilities and marketing services. The creation of distributing and marketing networks to provide such coordination, facilities, and services caused the mass producers

[36]For an argument that incomplete vertical integration may support strategic behavior, see Krattenmaker, Thomas G. and Salop, Steven C. "Competition and Cooperation in the Market for Exclusionary Rights," *American Economic Review* Volume 76, Number 2, May 1986, pp. 109–113. We pursue this topic in Chapter 17.

[37]Adams, Walter and Dirlam, Joel. "Steel Imports and Vertical Oligopoly Power," *American Economic Review* Volume 54, Number 5, September 1964, pp. 626–655.

[38]Chandler, op. cit.

[39]Ibid., p. 364.

to internalize several processes of production and distribution and the market transactions between them within a single enterprise. Such internalization permitted the visible hand of administrative coordination to make more intensive use of the resources invested in these processes of production and distribution than could the invisible hand of market coordination.

Such administrative coordination in turn created formidable barriers to entry. High-volume throughput and stock-turn reduced unit costs. Advertising and the provision of services maintained customer loyalty. Rival firms were rarely able to compete until they had built comparable marketing organizations of their own.

Thus vertical integration not only contributes to capital requirements barriers to entry, given bounded rationality and opportunism, but also creates product differentiation, which serves as an additional barrier to entry.[40]

Disincentives

Generally, vertical integration will occur in response to market characteristics that make it more economical to carry out transactions within the firm than across markets. There must be something that limits these economies. If there were not, the entire economy would consist of one gigantic firm.

Bounded rationality limits the scope of management control. As more and more stages of production are combined under a single management, production will become less and less efficient. There are, as we shall see, methods of internal organization designed to cope with such managerial diseconomies of large scale. Nonetheless, it ought to be expected that vertical integration will be reduced when firms are large: the management of a large firm will have enough on its hands without taking on vertically related activities.

Empirical Evidence on the Causes of Vertical Integration

The fundamental difficulty with empirical tests of the theory of vertical integration is the construction of a satisfactory measure of vertical integration.[41] Table 9-1 reports the results of studies that employed two different measures.

[40]See Hamilton, James L. and Lee, Soo Bock. "The Paradox of Vertical Integration," *Southern Economic Journal* Volume 53, Number 1, July 1986, pp. 110–126 for proof that if vertical integration raises entry barriers or facilitates collusion, it reduces social welfare.

[41]For an excellent discussion, see Caves, Richard E. and Bradburd, Ralph M. "The Empirical Determinants of Vertical Integration," manuscript, October 1986.

Table 9-1 Causes of Vertical Integration

Levy
VI1 $= -0.673^a - 0.151^a$ (Firm Size) $+ 0.070^b$ (Demand Growth) $+ 0.093^c$CR4   (1)

Caves and Bradburd
VI2 $= -4.99^a + 0.37^a$ (Buyer Conc) $+ 8.66^a$ (Importance) $+ 0.29$ CR4   (2)

Notes:
VA1 = value-added/sales ratio
Firm Size = industry sales/number of firms
Demand Growth = real growth rate in industry sales
VI2 = weighted average number of forward-integrated firms
Buyer Conc = estimated four-firm buying industry concentration ratio
Importance = average share of industry output in client industry purchases
For compactness, certain variables are suppressed from Equation (2).

a indicates statistical significance at the 1 per cent level; such an estimate would occur by chance only once in 100 times, on average.

b indicates statistical significance at the 5 per cent level; such an estimate would occur by chance only once in 20 times, on average.

c indicates statistical significance at the 10 per cent level; such an estimate would occur by chance only once in 10 times, on average.

Sources: Levy D. "Testing Stigler's Interpretation of 'The Division of Labor Is Limited by the Extent of the Market,' " *Journal of Industrial Economics* Volume 32, Number 3, March 1984, pp. 377–389; Caves, Richard E. and Bradburd, Ralph M. "The Empirical Determinants of Vertical Integration," manuscript, October 1986.

Levy[42]

The first study examines vertical integration in 38 industries, at roughly the three-digit Standard Industrial Classification level, for 3 successive years. The measure of vertical integration used in the first study (VI1) is the ratio of value-added to sales.

"Value-added" is a measure of the production that takes place within an industry. If the firms in an industry produced all the inputs they used, the ratio of value-added to sales would be 1. The more firms rely on firms in other industries for supplies, the more will sales reflect value-added in other industries and the smaller will be the ratio of value-added to sales. Greater ratios of value-added to sales therefore indicate greater vertical integration.[43]

[42]Levy, D. "Testing Stigler's Interpretation of 'The Division of Labor Is Limited by the Extent of the Market,' " *Journal of Industrial Economics* Volume 32, Number 3, March 1984, pp. 377–389.

[43]A major problem with the ratio of value-added to sales as a measure of vertical integration is that it is tends to be smaller, the closer an industry is to final consumer demand. See Adelman, Morris A. "Concept and Measurement of Vertical Integration," in National Bureau of Economic Research. *Business Concentration and Price Policy.* Princeton, N.J.: Princeton University Press, 1955, pp. 281–322.

The explanatory variables used in the first study were average firm size, the growth rate of industry demand, and the four-firm seller concentration ratio.[44]

The results of this study, reported in equation (1) of Table 9-1, indicate that vertical integration is greater in concentrated industries. This is to be expected if firms integrate vertically to avoid distortions in input use in downstream industries.

Vertical integration is greater in industries that face rapidly growing demand. This is to be expected if rapidly growing firms integrate to ensure supplies or adequate distribution.

Vertical integration is less in industries where average firm size is large. This is to be expected if bounded rationality limits the ability of managements to control large firms efficiently.

Caves and Bradburd

The second study discussed here uses the Input-Output Tables for the United States[45] to construct an alternative measure of vertical integration. In the second study, vertical integration is measured (VI2) as a weighted average fraction of the number of companies operating in both the base industry and the customer industry, with weights given by the fraction of base industry shipments to the customer industry.[46] This measure of vertical integration is therefore larger, the more firms in the industry are vertically integrated into the industry's important client industries.

Equation (2) of Table 9-1 reports coefficient estimates for three of the explanatory variables used in this second study. The variable "Buyer Conc" is actually the product of the weighted-average four-firm concentration ratio of customer industries and a Herfindahl index of dispersion of base industry sales across industries.[47] Buyer Conc should therefore be larger when the base in-

---

[44]Industry-average firm size was measured as industry sales divided by the number of firms in the industry; demand growth was the percentage growth in industry sales from one Census to the next, corrected for inflation. See Levy, op. cit., for further details.

[45]Input-Output Tables report the dollar value of shipments from each (roughly, four-digit Standard Industrial Classification) industry to each industry, along with a great deal of related information.

[46]Suppose industry 1 sells one third of its output to industry 2 and two thirds of its output to industry 3. If one fourth of industry 1's companies are integrated into industry 2 and one half of industry 1's firms are integrated into industry 3, the index of vertical integration for industry 1 is

$$(\tfrac{1}{3})(\tfrac{1}{4}) + (\tfrac{2}{3})(\tfrac{1}{2}) = \tfrac{5}{12}.$$

Note that the vertical integration index is bounded between 0 and 1. For the results reported in Table 9-1, the vertical integration index was subjected to a logarithmic transformation; the transformed variable is not bounded between 0 and 1. See Caves and Bradburd, op. cit., for further details.

[47]Like the Herfindahl index of market concentration, this dispersion index ranges from 0 to 1. It is near 0 for industries that sell to many client industries and near 1 for industries that sell to only a few client industries.

dustry sells its product to a few concentrated industries. If small-numbers bargaining problems are an incentive for vertical integration, high values of Buyer Conc should encourage vertical integration. The coefficient estimate in Table 9-1 confirms this expectation.

The variable labeled "Importance" is the weighted average share of the supplier industry's product in customer industries' input purchases, with weights given by the fraction of base industry shipments to the customer industry. Importance will be large when the base industry's product is a major input for client industries. Again, if small-numbers bargaining problems are an incentive for vertical integration, high values of Importance should encourage vertical integration. Again, the coefficient estimate in Table 9-1 confirms this expectation.

The coefficient of CR4 in equation (2) is positive, as expected. It is not, however, statistically significant.

Taken together, these studies provide considerable support for the transaction cost analysis of vertical integration. Vertical integration appears to be greater where small-numbers bargaining problems are likely to arise. There is modest support for the view that market concentration—treated here as a proxy for market power—induces vertical integration.

Conglomerate Integration

Motives for Conglomerate Mergers

The third U.S. merger wave took place in the late 1960s and early 1970s and consisted mainly of conglomerate mergers. Of the large mergers in U.S. manufacturing and mining over the period 1963 to 1972, 12.4 per cent were horizontal, 7.8 per cent were vertical, and the remaining 79.9 were conglomerate.[48] It seems likely that this predominance of conglomerate mergers reflects a very strict public policy toward horizontal and vertical mergers (to be reviewed in Chapter 10). But there are other reasons for conglomerate mergers.

Risk Spreading

Any market will be subject to fluctuations. Some years will be good, some years will be bad, and no firm or group of firms will be able to do much about it. A firm that operates in a single market will find that its sales and profits are tied to market conditions in a way that it can influence but not control. Some industries—for example, motor vehicles—are especially sensitive to macroeconomic fluctuations in the economy.

---

[48]Scherer, F. M. *Industrial Market Structure and Economic Performance,* 2nd ed. Chicago: Rand McNally College Publishing Company, 1980.

If firms in industries that are subject to cyclical fluctuations diversify into unrelated markets, they may be able to even out fluctuations in their income stream. If a firm operates in four truly unrelated industries, it is unlikely that all four of them will be in a downturn at the same time. If one market is down, at least one of the other three is likely to be up.

If a firm can succeed in stabilizing its income, it may improve its bond rating and reduce its cost of capital. This pecuniary benefit will reduce the firm's cost of operation and give it lower costs in all industries in which it operates. Society benefits when production becomes more efficient.

The Market for Management

The argument that takeovers are the market's way of replacing bad managements applies as much to conglomerate takeovers as it does to horizontal and vertical takeovers. Somewhat more generally, takeovers should occur whenever the market undervalues a firm, if there is someone with enough expertise to recognize that fact. This sort of undervaluation might occur at the start of periods of rapid technological change or demand growth.[49] The opportunity to take over inefficiently managed, undervalued firms is an additional incentive for conglomerate diversification.

We argued previously that impacted information and opportunism will limit the ability of capital markets to discipline managements that fail to maximize their profit. It will be difficult for outsiders to know if a firm's management is mishandling operations. It will be difficult for stockholders to know whether or not they should accept claims of mismanagement. Both sorts of transaction costs will be reduced in conglomerate firms.[50] It is less expensive for a corporate management to monitor the performance of a division than it is for outsiders to monitor the performance of the same division managed as an independent firm.

Corporate management, through internal audits, will be able to ascertain whether or not a division is being mismanaged. Because corporate management is able to reward employees for forthrightness (and punish them for deceit) in a way that capital markets cannot, opportunism ought to be less of a problem within the firm than across markets. In this way, the conglomerate firm acts as a "miniature capital market," operating on a smaller scale but better able to monitor performance than the external capital market because of superior access to information.[51]

---

[49]Gort, M. "An Economic Disturbance Theory of Mergers," *Quarterly Journal of Economics* Volume 83, Number 4, November 1969, pp. 624–642.

[50]Williamson, "Economics of Antitrust," p. 1482.

[51]Ibid.

Empire Building

Somewhat in conflict with this view is the belief that managers' desire for growth is a motive for conglomerate mergers, especially large ones.[52] It is large firms that have the most resources to devote to acquisitions and are least threatened by the possibility of a takeover. The larger the takeover target, the more resources are needed to effect a takeover and the greater the transaction costs. Combine the natural resistance of large firms to takeover attempts with the fact that antitrust laws impede the ability of large firms to diversify horizontally or vertically (Chapter 10), and there is a strong argument that large firms that seek growth will do so via conglomerate merger.

Effects of Conglomerate Mergers

On Profitability

Weston and Mansinghka[53] compared 63 conglomerate firms with a randomly selected group of Fortune 500 industrial firms. They found that in 1958 the ancestors of the conglomerate firms had profit rates below those of the industrial firms. The ratio of net income to net worth was 7.6 per cent for the conglomerate predecessors and 12.6 per cent for the industrials. After conglomeration, there was no significant difference in profitability for the two groups (13.3 per cent for conglomerates, 12.6 per cent for industrials).

Weston and Mansinghka argued that the 63 firms engaged in conglomerate mergers to stabilize firm profit and seek growth opportunities no longer available in their home industries. They interpreted the increase in profitability of the conglomerate firms as a result of efficiencies that flow from conglomeration.

Weston and Mansinghka also found that conglomerates had financed their growth by borrowing. Between 1958 and 1968, the debt-equity ratios of these firms increased from 95 to 169 per cent. Over the same period, the debt-equity ratios of the industrial firms went from 56 to 87 per cent.

This increase in debt-equity ratios raises the risk associated with investing in a conglomerate firm. The higher the debt-equity ratio, the greater the interest payments that must be made to service the firm's debt, and the greater the risk that a market downturn will throw it into bankruptcy. Capital markets will impose an increased cost of capital on firms that show an unusual increase in the debt-equity ratio. An increase in the cost of capital, to compensate for an increased debt-equity ratio, will tend to neutralize any benefit from reducing

[52]Mueller, Dennis C. "A Theory of Conglomerate Mergers," *Quarterly Journal of Economics* Volume 83, Number 4, November 1969, pp. 643–659.

[53]Weston, J. F. and Mansinghka, S. K. "Tests of the Efficiency Performance in Conglomerate Firms," *Journal of Finance* Volume 26, September 1971, pp. 919–936.

fluctuations in the firm's income stream that flow from conglomerate diversification.

Some evidence in support of this adverse capital market effect is presented by Reid,[54] who studied the performance of the Weston-Mansinghka conglomerates during the stock market slide of the late 1960s. He found that the average stock market price of these conglomerates fell 56 per cent from the end of 1968 to mid-1970. Over the same period, the stock market price of the Weston-Mansinghka control sample of industrial firms fell only 37 per cent.

Mueller[55] points out that if a less profitable firm merges with a more profitable firm, simple averaging suggests that the profit rate of the survivor firm will exceed that of the less profitable firm. Thus, to the extent that conglomerate firms acquire more profitable partners, one should expect the profit rate of the conglomerates to increase, even in the absence of efficiency effects. In a massive study of mergers over the period 1950 to 1972, Mueller finds support only for the averaging effect of mergers.[56]

Confirming evidence for the averaging effect of conglomerate mergers comes from a study of mergers in the food industry. Hall and Sweeney[57] analyzed food and nonfood mergers involving food industry firms over the period 1955 to 1980. Their conclusion was that operational efficiencies occurred only for mergers within the food industry. Conglomerate mergers resulted in increases in accounting measures of profit—which is consistent with the Mueller averaging argument—but not in shareholders' wealth.

These results, together with Reid's evidence on risk, undermine the Weston-Mansinghka argument that efficiency flows from conglomerate mergers.[58] The best explanation is given by Chandler:[59]

> The conglomerate had no staff offices for purchasing, traffic, research and development, sales, advertising, or production. The only staff not devoted to purely legal and financial matters was for corporate planning (that is, for the formulation of the strategy to be used in investment decisions). As a result,

[54]Reid, S. R. "A Reply to the Weston/Mansinghka Criticisms Dealing with Conglomerate Mergers," *Journal of Finance* Volume 26, September 1971, pp. 937–946.

[55]Ibid., p. 322.

[56]Mueller, Dennis C. *Profits in the Long Run.* Cambridge: Cambridge University Press, 1986, p. 181. The Mueller study includes mergers of all kinds, not just conglomerate mergers.

[57]Hall, Lana and Sweeney, Jan. "Profitability of Mergers in Food Manufacturing," *Applied Economics* Volume 18, Number 7, July 1986, pp. 709–727.

[58]A recent study of mergers among large industrial firms finds no support for the argument that acquired firms were less profitable, on average, than other firms in the same industry. This is additional evidence against the "market for management" explanation of mergers. See Ravenscraft, David J. and Scherer, F. M., "The Profitability of Mergers," manuscript, November 1986.

[59]Ibid., pp. 481–482.

the conglomerates could concentrate more single-mindedly on making investments in new industries and new markets and withdraw more easily from existing ones than could the older, large, diversified companies. On the other hand, the conglomerates were far less effective in monitoring and evaluating their divisions and in taking action to improve divisional operating performance. They had neither the manpower nor the skills to nurse sick divisions back to health.

The management of conglomerate firms specializes in the long-term allocation of resources, acting as a miniature capital market (see the previous discussion). The Achilles heel of the conglomerate is short-run resource allocation—the day-to-day operation of the firm's operations in many different industries, about some of which top management knows very little.

On Concentration

Because a conglomerate merger is a combination of firms operating in different markets, it will by definition have no direct effect on market concentration. There may nonetheless be an indirect effect on market concentration if divisions of conglomerate firms are more efficient than independent firms.

This question is addressed by Goldberg,[60] who studied the effect of conglomerate mergers on 211 industries. He found the effect on market concentration to be negligible.

Mueller[61] studied the impact of mergers on market share for firms among the 1,000 largest U.S. manufacturing firms in 1950. Studying mergers over a 23-year period, he found that firms acquired in either horizontal or conglomerate mergers suffered losses in market share thereafter. Mueller's work confirms that of Goldberg and further suggests an absence of efficiency effects from conglomerate organization.

When Mergers Don't Work

The mid-1980s have seen the fourth great merger wave in U.S. history, with roughly $125 billion worth of takeovers in each of 1984 and 1985. Table 9-2 lists acquisitions of $1 billion or more that took place in 1985.

Perhaps the most novel element in this recent wave of mergers is the number of divestitures it includes (four of these are listed in Table 9-2). Many of the large conglomerates that were put together in the 1960s and 1970s are taking themselves apart in the 1980s. Gulf & Western Industries sold 147 divisions for $1.78 billion (but also made 10 acquisitions) between March 1983 and

[60]Goldberg, L. G. "Conglomerate Mergers and Concentration Ratios," *Review of Economics and Statistics* Volume 56, Number 3, August 1974, pp. 303–309.

[61]Mueller, Dennis C. "Mergers and Market Share," *Review of Economics and Statistics* Volume 67, Number 2, May 1985, pp. 259–267.

Table 9-2 Billion-Dollar Acquisitions, 1985

Buyer	Seller	Value (Billions)
General Electric	RCA	$6.30
Kohlberg, Kravis, Roberts	Beatrice Company	6.20
Philip Morris	General Foods	5.75
Royal Dutch/Shell	Shell Oil	5.67
General Motors	Hughes Aircraft	5.20
Allied	Signal	5.00
R.J. Reynolds	Nabisco Brands	4.90
Baxter-Travenol	American Hospital Supply	3.80
U.S. Steel	Texas Oil and Gas	3.70
Capital Cities Communications	American Broadcasting	3.50
Nestle SA	Carnation	3.00
Monsanto	G.D. Searle	2.80
Coastal	American Natural Resources	2.46
InterNorth	Houston Natural Gas	2.26
Kohlberg, Kravis, Roberts	Storer Communications	1.90
HHF	Levi Strauss	1.85
Pantry Pride	Revlon	1.80
Olympia and York	Chevron (Gulf Canada)[D]	1.80
Kohlberg, Kravis, Roberts	Allied (50% of Union Texas Petroleum)[D]	1.80
Rockwell International	Allen-Bradley	1.65
Cooper Industries	McGraw Edison	1.50
Farley Metals	Northwest Industries	1.40
Textron	Avco	1.40
Chesebrough-Ponds	Stauffer Chemical	1.30
Cox Enterprises	Cox Communications	1.26
Procter & Gamble	Richardson-Vicks	1.24
MidCon	United Energy Resources	1.14
BASF AG	United Technologies (Inmont unit)[D]	1.00
Wickes	Gulf & Western (consumer and industrial products group)[D]	1.00

Superscript D indicates divestiture.

Sources: Wall Street Journal, January 2, 1986, page 6B; *New York Times,* December 9, 1985, Section 3, p. 1.

August 1985. At the same time, ITT was conducting a $1.7 billion divestiture program.

Many of the companies that engaged in conglomerate diversification in the merger wave of the 1960s and 1970s found themselves operating in markets far removed from their management's main areas of expertise. Even when companies in related markets merge, it can take years for the combination of hitherto competing enterprises to form a truly integrated operation. This casts further doubt on the hypothesis that conglomerate mergers generate efficiencies that improve market performance.

Case Study: Merger and Divestiture, and Bankruptcy

The LTV Corporation entered the steel industry by acquisition in 1968, when it purchased a controlling interest in the Jones & Laughlin (J&L) Steel Corporation for $426 million. This prompted an antitrust dispute with the Justice Department, but LTV acquired all of J&L in 1974.

In 1978, LTV acquired the Lykes Corporation and its subsidiary, Youngstown Sheet & Tube. Youngstown was failing, and by acquiring it, LTV took on a debt of $1.7 billion. But LTV turned things around. By 1981, LTV was the third largest steel firm in the United States and was making record profits.

In 1984, LTV acquired the Republic Steel Corporation for $714 million and became the second largest steel firm in the United States.

A host of problems surfaced after this acquisition. LTV had trouble making shipments on time because of problems with the order-entry system for the expanded steel division. There was also a good deal of excess capacity. LTV controlled 16 hot-rolled steel-bar mills after the Republic acquisition. It permanently closed five of those mills and mothballed another five.

After the Republic acquisition, LTV had operating losses of nearly $1 billion and saw its debt increase by $1 billion dollars (to $2.6 billion).

In an attempt to weather the crisis, LTV decided to raise $500 million through the sale of various divisions. Ironically, among these is its specialty steel division, one of the strongest in the company. After the Republic acquisition, the specialty steel division was one of the few parts of LTV that might have found a buyer.

But it was not to be. In July 1986, LTV filed for bankruptcy. A steel industry consultant indicated that "LTV's 21 major banks . . . would be ill-advised to agree to any reorganization plan that had LTV remaining in the steel business. 'That would be just throwing more money away. The company put together as LTV Steel was an ego trip. It is not a viable entity.'"

As an interesting sidelight, which casts some doubt on the hypothesis that firms are managed in the stockholders' interest, LTV paid its top executives nearly $1 million in bonuses for superior performance in 1986, a year in which the company lost $3.25 billion and filed for bankruptcy.

Sources: Cohen, Laurie P. and O'Boyle, Thomas F. "Ill-Fated Merger," *Wall Street Journal*, January 6, 1986, p. 1; Hayes, Thomas C. "An Uncertain Future for LTV," *New York Times*, July 19, 1986, p. 17; Mitchell, Cynthia F. "LTV Paid Performance-Tied Awards in 1986, After Bankruptcy-Law Filing," *Wall Street Journal*, April 13, 1987, p. 5.

One of the main arguments that conglomerate mergers would result in operating efficiencies relied on favorable capital market effects—a lower cost of

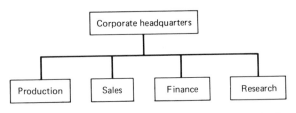

Figure 9-4 The unitary form of corporate organization.

capital following a reduction in fluctuations in income. But conglomeration did not always help a firm's financial rating. It appears that when a company operates in many unrelated markets, financial analysts have difficulty determining whether or not it is doing well.[62] Bounded rationality, impacted information, and opportunism can make it difficult for a conglomerate to raise funds even if its operations are basically healthy.

Internal Organization

Managerial loss of control in large corporations has prompted interest in the economics of internal organization.

The traditional unitary or U-form firm is organized along functional lines, as illustrated in Figure 9-4. One division of the firm handles sales, one manufacturing, one finance, and so on, in each case for the entire organization.

As a unitary firm expands, communication lines between operating levels and corporate headquarters become longer and longer. Information is lost, or at least garbled, in transmission. Central management finds itself dealing with both day-to-day matters and long-run strategy, and does a less than satisfactory job with both. Under a unitary form of internal organization, management loses control when the firm becomes too large.

In response to this managerial diseconomy of scale, du Pont and General Motors developed the multidivisional or M-form of internal organization.[63] Each division of a multidivisional firm is a replica, in miniature, of the U-form firm, as illustrated in Figure 9-5. Each division has its own sales operation, its own manufacturing operation, and so on:[64]

[62]See Brooks, Geraldine. "Some Concerns Find that the Push to Diversify was a Costly Mistake," *Wall Street Journal*, October 2, 1984, p. 33.

[63]Chandler, Alfred D., Jr., *Strategy and Structure: Chapters in the History of the Industrial Enterprise.* Cambridge Mass.: The M.I.T. Press, 1962.

[64]Ibid., p. 457.

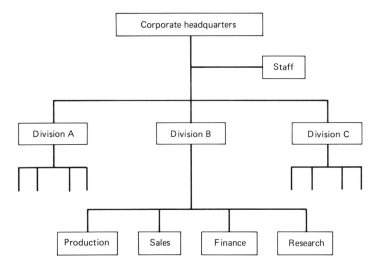

Figure 9-5   The multidivisional form of corporate organization.

In this type of structure, autonomous divisions continued to integrate production and distribution by coordinating flows from suppliers to consumers in different, clearly defined markets. The divisions, headed by middle managers, administered their functional activities through departments. . . . A general office of top managers, assisted by large financial and administrative staffs, supervised these multifunctional divisions. The general office monitored the divisions to be sure that their flows were tuned to fluctuations in demand and that they had comparable policies in personnel, research, purchasing, and other functional activities. The top managers also evaluated the financial and market performance of the divisions. Most important of all, they concentrated on planning and allocating resources.

Under the multidivisional form of internal organization, day-to-day operating decisions are made at the division level. Long-term strategic issues are settled at corporate headquarters. It is the corporate staff that allocates investment funds among the operating divisions. As noted previously, an internal capital market arises within the firm with funds generated by some divisions and transferred to whatever divisions promise the highest rate of return.

Williamson[65] emphasizes the superiority of the multidivisional form for mon-

[65]Williamson, Oliver E. *Corporate Control and Business Behavior*. Englewood Cliffs, N.J.: Prentice Hall, 1970; *Markets and Hierarchies: Analysis and Antitrust Implications*. New York: The Free Press, 1975. For a concise and critrical summary, see Hill, C. W. L. "Oliver Williamson and the M-Form Firm: A Critical Review," *Journal of Economic Issues* Volume 19, Number 3, September 1985, pp. 731–751.

itoring behavior and providing incentives to employees to implement corporate strategy. He would, in fact, replace the traditional microeconomic view of the firm as a production function with a view of the firm as a governance mechanism. Properly organized, a firm can use internal rewards and punishments to induce employees to provide accurate information, combatting the problems of impacted information and opportunism. Further, by allowing management to specialize at the division and corporate levels, the problem of bounded rationality is reduced.

Based on these arguments, Williamson predicts superior performance for firms organized on a multidivisional basis, compared with unitary firms. If multidivisional firms are more efficient than unitary firms, multidivisional firms should be more profitable than unitary firms, all else equal.

At the same time, however, the choice of management form can have strategic implications.[66] In particular, the multidivisional firm carries a greater burden of fixed and sunk costs than the unitary firm. By sinking assets in its markets, a multidivisional firm can demonstrate a commitment to its market and raise the cost of capital for potential entrants.[67] For strategic as well as efficiency reasons, therefore, multidivisional firms should be more profitable than unitary firms.

The hypothesis that multidivisional firms will be more profitable than other firms was tested by Teece.[68] In 20 industries, he identified the leading firm that first adopted the multidivisional internal organization and the largest similar firm that lagged behind. He then compared the rate of return on assets and the rate of return on stockholders' equity for the two firms, first when the multidivisional structure was employed by only one of the two firms and then when it was employed by both.

Teece's results showed that the multidivisional structure had a significant positive impact on profitability.[69] This finding supports the importance of internal organization as a determinant of profitability and shows that looking inside the black box of firm structure can improve our understanding of market performance.

---

[66]The discussion that follows paraphrases Boyer, Marcel and Jacquemin, Alexis. "Organizational Choices for Efficiency and Market Power," *Economics Letters* Volume 18, 1985, pp. 79–82.

[67]See Chapter 8's discussion of capital markets as a source of absolute cost advantages for incumbent firms.

[68]Teece, D. J. "Internal Organization and Economic Performance: An Empirical Analysis of Profitability of Principal Firms," *Journal of Industrial Economics* Volume 30, Number 2, December 1981, pp. 173–199.

[69]Generally supporting evidence is provided by Hill, C. W. L. "Internal Organization and Enterprise Performance: Some UK Evidence," *Managerial and Decision Economics* Volume 6, Number 4, December 1985, pp. 210–216.

Summary

The separation of ownership and control in the modern corporation means that firms may be managed to pursue the interests of managers rather than owners. This may involve sales maximization, growth maximization, or maximization of the compensation of management, instead of profit maximization. The threat of takeover will check this sort of behavior, although the management of large firms will have some discretion to pursue its own goals.

Firms may expand horizontally, vertically, or into unrelated markets.

Horizontal integration will increase market power, especially where there are expansion costs that prevent fringe firms from counteracting output restrictions. Horizontal integration may also allow cost-saving efficiencies, including run-length economies and the elimination of outmoded plants.

Vertical integration is a response to market imperfections, which create costs of transacting across markets. Vertical integration may also be pursued because it raises absolute cost and product differentiation barriers to entry.

Conglomerate mergers may be motivated by a desire to reduce the firm's risk and improve its standing in financial markets. There is some evidence to support this contention, but rather more to suggest that conglomerate mergers reflect managers' desire for growth, without resulting in much efficiency.

In every case, mergers have mixed effects: some to improve performance, some to increase market power and worsen performance. The net effect of mergers will have to be judged on a case-by-case basis. In general, Mueller's[70] verdict seems compelling:

> One cost of the pursuit of growth via external expansions . . . is that it is likely to come at the expense of more socially productive forms of growth. . . . Mergers compete directly with capital investment, R&D and other investment-type expenditures for cash flows and managerial decisionmaking capabilities. While a manager is perhaps indifferent between whether a given rate of expansion is achieved through internal or external growth, society is likely to be better off through the creation of additional assets.

Problems

9-1 (Mergers in quantity-setting markets) Suppose three firms supply a market in which the demand curve is

$$P = a - (q_1 + q_2 + q_3).$$

Each firm operates with a cost function

$$C(q) = cq.$$

[70]Mueller, Dennis C. "The Effects of Conglomerate Mergers: A Survey of the Empirical Evidence," *Journal of Banking and Finance* Volume 1, December 1977, p. 339.

a. What is the equation of the residual demand curve for firm 1? Use the fact that the residual marginal revenue curve has the same intercept as the residual demand curve but twice the slope to obtain the equation of firm 1's reaction curve (compare with Problem 5-2). In like manner, obtain the reaction curves of firms 2 and 3.

b. Set $q_1 = q_2 = q_i$ in the equations of the reaction curves and obtain the following:

Firms 1 and 2: $q_i = (\tfrac{1}{3})(q_c - q_3)$

Firm 3: $q_3 = (\tfrac{1}{2})q_c - q_i$,

where $q_c = a - c$ is competitive market output. Graph the reaction curves to obtain Figure 9-1. Solve for the Cournot triopoly outputs and price.

c. Use Equation (9.1) to obtain the postmerger reaction curve for firm 1/firm 2:

$$q_i = (\tfrac{1}{4})(q_c - q_3).$$

Graph the new reaction curve; solve for postmerger outputs and price.

9-2 (Mergers in price-setting markets) Use the cost function and demand curves of Problem 5-8 for an oligopoly of three firms.

a. Equate marginal revenue to marginal cost and show that the reaction curve of firm 3 is

$$p_3 - c = \frac{3\gamma}{2 + 3\gamma} \frac{q_c}{2} + \frac{1}{2 + 3\gamma}(p_i - c),$$

where p_3 is firm 3's price and p_i is the common price of firms 1 and 2.

b. Likewise, show that the premerger reaction functions for firms 1 and 2 are

$$p_i - c = \frac{\gamma}{1 + 2\gamma} q_c + \frac{1}{3(1 + 2\gamma)}(p_3 - c).$$

c. Using

$$MR = p_1 \Delta q_1 + p_2 \Delta q_2 + q_1 \Delta p_1$$

and

$$MC = c\Delta q_1 + c\Delta q_2$$

show that the reaction curve for divisions 1 and 2 after the merger is

$$p_i - c = \frac{3\gamma}{2(1 + 3\gamma)} q_c + \frac{1}{2(1 + 3\gamma)}(p_3 - c).$$

d. Graph the reaction curves, à la Figure 9-2.

Paper Topics

9-1 In 1980, Dart Industries and Kraft, Inc., were combined in a $2.5 billion merger. In June 1986, they announced plans to split into two separate companies, essentially reversing the original merger. Analyze this corporate marriage and divorce. What were the motives for the original merger? How, if at all, did the combination fall short of its goals? What were the reasons for the breakup? Discuss the impact of the merger and the breakup on structure and performance in relevant industries.

9-2 On July 2, 1986, p. 29 of the *New York Times* carried a column discussing the Federal Trade Commission's decision to challenge, under the antitrust laws, prospective mergers of the Coca-Cola Company and Dr. Pepper and of Pepsico, Inc., and Seven-Up. On page 28 of the same issue, the *Times* carried an article headlined ''Coke to Purchase Its Largest Bottler,'' which began, ''Taking the biggest step yet in expanding its role in the bottling business, the Coca-Cola Company said yesterday that it had signed a letter of intent to buy the largest Coke bottler in the country—the JTL Corporation—for about $1.4 billion.'' Analyze horizontal and vertical integration in the soft-drink industry. Discuss implications for structure and performance, and treatment under the antitrust laws.

9-3 In July 1986, U.S. Steel changed its name to the U.S.X. Corporation, reflecting a reorganization as a holding company of four divisions. At the time of the reorganization, the operations to be housed in the steel division accounted for 31 per cent of U.S.X.'s sales. Identify the major steps in U.S. Steel's diversification outside the steel industry. What were the motives for this diversification? What are the implications for structure and performance in the steel industry and in other industries in which U.S.X. operates?

10 Public Policy Toward Mergers

Crows are pardoned, but the pigeons are found guilty.

Juvenal, Satires, Hypocrisy and Vice

As we saw in Chapter 4, the earliest antitrust cases under Section 2 of the Sherman Act involved mergers. Cases that followed *Standard Oil* and *American Tobacco* established that mergers that achieved a very high market share and involved abusive practices toward competitors violated the Sherman Act's prohibition against monopolization.[1] But the 1920 decision in the *U.S. Steel* case signaled a reversal of this line of development of the Sherman Act. Until the *Alcoa* decision in 1945, dominant firms seemed beyond the reach of the Sherman Act. The 1953 *United Shoe Machinery* decision, also under Section 2, seemed to hark back to the earlier line of cases and the need to provide evidence of abusive practices before a violation could be found.

But by this time, as far as mergers were concerned, the circus had moved on. The original Section 7 of the Clayton Act was interpreted by the Supreme Court[2] as forbidding one firm to acquire shares in another "where the effect of such acquisition may be to substantially lessen competition." But the Court read Section 7 as permitting one firm to acquire the assets of another, even if the effect of this acquisition was to substantially lessen competition.[3]

With the Celler-Kefauver Act of 1950, Congress amended Section 7 of the Clayton Act so that it applied to mergers carried out by the transfer of assets as well as stock. Since the 1950 amendment, the main line of antitrust cases dealing with merger has proceeded under the amended Section 7 of the Clayton Act.

---

[1]See *United States v. E. I. duPont,* 188 F. 127 (C.C.D. Del 1911), and Elzinga, Kenneth G. "Predatory Pricing: The Case of the Gunpowder Trust," *Journal of Law and Economics* Volume 13, Number 1, April 1970, pp. 223–240.

[2]*Thatcher Manufacturing Company v. Federal Trade Commission,* 272 U.S. 554 (1926).

[3]See footnote 39, Chapter 3, and the accompanying text.

Horizontal, vertical, and conglomerate mergers raise somewhat different issues under the Clayton Act, and we treat each separately. We also examine the merger guidelines that have been issued by successive Justice Departments to explain to the business community the standards that will be applied to prospective mergers.

In 1956, the Brown Shoe Company merged with the G.R. Kinney Company. Brown Shoe was the fourth largest shoe manufacturer in the United States, and also owned 470 retail outlets.[4] Kinney, which had minor manufacturing interests, operated more than 400 retail shoe stores. The Brown Shoe–Kinney merger thus involved both horizontal (at the retail level) and vertical (manufacturer-distributor) combination. The Justice Department's challenge to this merger provided the Supreme Court with an opportunity to elucidate the application of the amended Clayton Act to both horizontal and vertical mergers.

Horizontal Mergers

The Interpretation of the Amended Section 7

Brown Shoe[5] was the Supreme Court's first interpretation of the amended Section 7 of the Clayton Act. The Court noted that the amendment was intended to further economic and noneconomic goals:[6,7]

> The dominant theme pervading congressional consideration of the 1950 amendments was a fear of what was considered to be a rising tide of economic concentration in the American economy. . . . Other considerations cited in support of the bill were the desirability of retaining "local control" over industry and the protection of small businesses. Throughout the recorded discussion may be found examples of Congress' fear not only of accelerated concentration of economic power on economic grounds, but also of the threat to other values a trend toward concentration was thought to pose.

[4]More than 760 independent retailers distributed only or primarily Brown shoes; Brown shoes were also distributed through other outlets.

[5]*Brown Shoe Co., Inc. v. United States*, 370 U.S. 294 (1962).

[6]370 U.S. 294, at 315–316; footnote omitted. As noted in Chapter 3, Congress' belief that concentration was increasing in the postwar period was incorrect.

[7]The court cited in a footnote, as we do here, a statement from Judge Hand's *Alcoa* decision that had been quoted in congressional debate (148 F. 2d 416, 429 (C.A. 2d Cir)): "Throughout the history of these [antitrust] statutes it has been constantly assumed that one of their purposes was to perpetuate and preserve, for its own sake and in spite of possible cost, an organization of industry in small units which can effectively compete with each other."

251

The Court used the *Brown Shoe* decision to give a concise statement of its reading of the policy toward mergers embodied in the new version of the law:[8]

1. Congress intended the law to cover both asset and stock mergers.
2. Congress intended the law to cover vertical and conglomerate mergers, as well as horizontal mergers, where the effect of the merger would be to lessen competition.
3. Congress sought to control incipient lessenings of competition.
4. Congress wished standards under Section 7 of the Clayton Act to be more severe toward mergers than standards under Section 2 of the Sherman Act.
5. Congress did not seek to prohibit procompetitive mergers.
6. Congress did not specify the method to be used to define the relevant market; it did not define the word *substantially*.
7. Congress intended mergers to be judged in the context of the industries in which they took place.
8. Congress was concerned with probable lessenings of competition; it did not limit Section 7 to certain lessenings of competition.

The Court followed the same steps as it applied Section 7 to the horizontal and vertical aspects of the *Brown Shoe* merger. It defined the relevant product markets and geographic markets, and evaluated the probable effect of the merger on competition.

Market Definition

Indicating that similar standards applied to product and geographic market definition,[9] the Court first promulgated a purely economic rule for defining product markets:[10]

> The outer boundaries of a product market are determined by the reasonable interchangeability of use or the cross-elasticity of demand between the product itself and substitutes for it.

The Court followed this statement, though, with a rather less pure extension:[11]

> However, within this broad market, well-defined submarkets may exist which, in themselves, constitute product markets for antitrust purposes. . . . The boundaries of such a submarket may be determined by examining such practical

---

[8]370 U.S. 294, at 316–323.

[9]Ibid., at 336.

[10]Ibid., at 325.

[11]Ibid.

indicia as industry or public recognition of the submarket as a separate entity, the product's peculiar characteristics and uses, unique production facilities, distinct customers, distinct prices, sensitivity to price changes, and specialized vendors.

The task of market definition in antitrust cases has tended to follow the second approach—practical indications of market boundaries—rather than the first—price elasticity of demand. Few economists who offer market definitions in antitrust cases do so based on numerical estimates of the cross-elasticity of demand between products or regions. The reason is simple: it is usually difficult to make numerical estimates of cross-elasticities of demand with any reliability. Instead, prospective market definitions are offered to courts based on judgments about the price elasticity of demand. Those judgments are based on the kinds of "practical indicia" previously mentioned.

Effect of the Merger

Having outlined the standards to be used to define the relevant market, the Court turned to the evaluation of the probable effect of the merger. It indicated four general standards, three of which seem unobjectionable.[12]

First, the Court highlighted the market share to be enjoyed by the mergered firm, and indicated that the effect of a given market share was to be evaluated in the context of market conditions:

> If a merger achieving 5% control were now approved, we might be required to approve future merger efforts by Brown's competitors seeking similar market shares.

Market share is, of course, one of the factors that, in theory, helps to determine market performance. The Court's focus on market share as an index of the likely effect of a merger is consistent with economic theory, but incomplete. Market share typically interacts with other factors, including entry conditions (competition from outside the market) and conjectural variations (competition from within the market), to determine market performance.

Second, the Court considered the ability of the mergered firm to engage in anticompetitive strategies toward rivals:

> Furthermore, in this fragmented industry, even if the combination controls but a small share of a particular market, the fact that this share is held by a large national chain can adversely affect competition. Testimony in the record . . . demonstrates that the large chains can set and alter styles in footwear to an extent that renders the independents unable to maintain competitive inventories.

---

[12]Ibid., at 343–345.

Encouraging product differentiation so that rivals need to maintain larger inventories, much of which will constitute a sunk investment,[13] is a way of increasing entry costs and discouraging entry. This is a specific example of strategic behavior that is profitable because it raises rivals' costs.

Third, the Court indicated that in applying Section 7, trial courts should consider "the history of tendency toward concentration in the industry." An emphasis on concentration is perfectly consistent with the oligopoly models of Chapters 5 and 6 and the evidence on structure–performance relationships reviewed in Chapter 7. Whatever the market share of the mergered firm, the impact of the merger on competition is likely to be more severe, the more concentrated the market within which the merger takes place.

The final standard set up by the Court for evaluating the probable effect of mergers goes to the heart of a fundamental and continuing controversy about the proper role of the antitrust laws. Should the antitrust laws advance economic goals alone—perhaps, among economic goals, efficiency alone?—or are other purposes proper? As previously noted, the Court recognized congressional concern over threats to noneconomic values posed by increasing concentration. With this in mind, the Court indicated that increased efficiency might, under Section 7, condemn a merger:[14]

> The retail outlets of the integrated companies, by eliminating wholesalers and by increasing the volume of purchases from the manufacturing division of the enterprise, can market their own brands at prices below those of competing independent retailers. Of course, some of the results of large integrated or chain operations are beneficial to consumers. Their expansion is not rendered unlawful by the mere fact that small independent stores may be adversely affected. It is competition, not competitors, which the Act protects. But we cannot fail to recognize Congress' desire to promote competition through the protection of viable, small, locally owned businesses. Congress appreciated that occasional higher costs and prices might result from the maintenance of fragmented industries and markets. It resolved these competing considerations in favor of decentralization.

Although the Court said explicitly that the purpose of the antitrust laws is to protect competition, and not competitors, it is hard to interpret an injury to competitors *through greater efficiency* as an injury to competition. It is, after all, in the nature of the competitive process that less efficient firms will be injured by a loss of profit and market share. That is the market's way of telling

---

[13]Out-of-style shoes could be sold only at a substantial markdown.

[14]370 U.S. 294, at 344. Although the cited efficiency stems from the vertical aspects of the merger, the Court included it in its discussion of the horizontal aspect of the merger, as we do.

them to improve their performance. This portion of the Court's ruling has generated severe criticism:[15]

> By and large, it is difficult to read the Court's opinion without concluding that its basic aim was to do what it could to protect small retailers from competition by the chains, which it believed were strengthened by mergers. . . . If this view is essentially right, then the antitrust laws were used to prevent competition on the ground that its prevention was the same thing as its protection.

In interpreting the antitrust laws, courts have repeatedly walked a fine line between protecting competition and protecting competitors. This is one of the areas of antitrust economics in which differences in policy positions are most sharply defined.

Economists working in the Chicago tradition generally insist that the purpose of the antitrust laws should be to promote efficiency, and that other goals are illegitimate. They maintain—and, as *Brown Shoe* shows, not entirely without reason—that any consideration given to competitors will be at the expense of competition.

Other economists,[16] without denying the desirability of promoting efficiency, view competition as a process. They argue that the competitive process, the invisible hand, will be best maintained by protecting opportunities for equally efficient competitors to compete, and that the competitive process will produce efficiency over the long run. In this view, economic and noneconomic goals of antitrust policy are broadly consistent.

Defenses

As the final part of its general interpretation of the application of Section 7 to horizontal mergers, the Court indicated two "mitigating factors" that a firm could present to defend a merger.[17] First, a merger could pass muster if one of the parties was on the verge of bankruptcy—if it was a "failing firm." Second, a merger could pass muster if it involved two small firms that, when combined, would be better able to compete with larger firms. Congress did not intend the amended Section 7 to prevent procompetitive mergers.

Brown Shoe—*Application of the Standards*

Product Market

For both the horizontal and vertical portions of the *Brown Shoe* case, the Supreme Court accepted the District Court's conclusion that the relevant prod-

---

[15]Peterman, John L. "The Brown Shoe Case," *Journal of Law and Economics* Volume 18, April 1975, p. 142.

[16]And, as the Court's description of congressional debate indicates, noneconomists as well.

[17]370 U.S. 294, at 346.

uct market included three separate "lines of commerce": men's, women's, and children's shoes. This conclusion was based on the practical indicia called for in the general standard for market definition:[18]

> These product lines are recognized by the public; each line is manufactured in separate plants; each has characteristics peculiar to itself rendering it generally noncompetitive with others; and each is, of course, directed toward a distinct class of customers.

An economist might express this position differently by saying that the cross-price elasticity of demand between, say, men's and children's shoes is low. Adult men will not start wearing children's shoes, no matter how high the price of the former and how low the price of the latter. The conclusion, from the point of view of market demand, seems correct.

A countervailing argument, however, comes from the supply side of the market. If the price of men's shoes goes up for some reason, manufacturers ought to be able to retool production lines from children's shoes to men's shoes. The cross-elasticity of supply between the three separate lines of commerce is probably fairly high. Nonetheless, courts have tended to define markets from the customer's point of view.[19]

Geographic Market

To analyze the effect of horizontal merger at the retail level on competition, the District Court took as separate geographic markets[20] "every city with a population exceeding 10,000 and its immediately contiguous surrounding territory in which both Brown and Kinney sold shoes at retail through stores they either owned or controlled."

Brown Shoe argued that in many areas a larger geographic market was appropriate: the standard metropolitan statistical area located around each central city. Such a market would have included shoe stores located in small towns ringing the main metropolitan area. The Supreme Court accepted the District Court's finding as reflecting "commercial realities" in the retail shoe market:[21]

> Such markets are large enough to include the downtown shopping centers in areas contiguous to the city, which are the important competitive factors, and yet small enough to exclude stores beyond the immediate environs of the city, which are of little competitive significance.

[18]Ibid., at 326.

[19]See *Tampa Electric Co. v. Nashville Coal Co. et al.,* 365 U.S. 320 (1960), at 327: "the area of effective competition in the known line of commerce must be charted by careful selection of the market area in which the seller operates, and to which the purchaser can practically turn for supplies."

[20]370 U.S. 294, at 337.

[21]Ibid., at 339.

Probable Effect of the Horizontal Merger

The Supreme Court first turned to an examination of the market shares of the combined firms in various cities:[22,23]

> during 1955 in 32 separate cities . . . the combined share of Brown and Kinney sales of women's shoes (by unit volume) exceeded 20%. In 31 cities . . . the combined share of children's shoe sales exceeded 20%; in 6 cities their share exceeded 40%. . . . In 118 separate cities the combined shares of the market of Brown and Kinney in the sale of one of the relevant lines of commerce exceeded 5%. In 47 cities, their share exceeded 5% in all three lines.

As noted previously, the Court indicated its willingness to condemn mergers that yielded market shares of as little as 5 per cent. It had no problem concluding that a merger that produced market shares as high as 40 per cent in some cities was likely to lessen competition substantially.

The Court considered some factors in addition to market share. It found evidence that a national chain could manipulate the inventory costs of rivals by promoting style changes that would increase inventory carrying costs. The Court also found evidence of a trend toward (horizontal and vertical) concentration in the industry and concluded that the Brown-Kinney merger would exacerbate this trend:[24]

> By the merger in this case, the largest single group of retail stores still independent of one of the large manufacturers was absorbed into an already substantial aggregation of more or less controlled retail outlets.

The Court recognized that the market shares involved in many geographic markets were small, but said:[25] "We cannot avoid the mandate of Congress that tendencies toward concentration in industry are to be curbed in their incipiency . . .".

By focusing on market share as the critical element in evaluating the effect of the merger, the Court made the process of market definition critical to the conclusion drawn. If either the product market or the geographic market had been defined more broadly, the combined Brown–Kinney market share would have fallen below 5 per cent in many markets. If the Court had considered market share along with other factors, such as entry conditions or conjectural variations, it might not have condemned a merger that yielded substantially higher market shares than those present in *Brown Shoe*.

---

[22]Ibid., at 342–343.

[23]Peterman, op. cit., argues that the market share figures used by the Court were incorrect, combining wholesale and retail sales.

[24]370 U.S. 294, at 345.

[25]Ibid., at 346.

257

Market Definition

Taking off from *Brown Shoe,* market definition in antitrust cases has proceeded in an ad hoc way. Lip service is always paid to the notion of cross-elasticity of demand, but the evidence judged consists of what is available.

Geographic Market

Elzinga and Hogarty[26] distinguish the following standards as having been used to define geographic markets in different antitrust cases:

1. Peculiar demand: a region is a market if it is characterized by an unusual demand for a product.
2. Little in from outside: a region is a market if most of the product consumed in the area is produced within the area.
3. Little out from inside: a region is a market if most of the product produced in the area is consumed within the area.
4. Transportation cost: a region is a market if transportation costs are high enough to trap consumers within the area or keep outside suppliers out.
5. Pricing: if prices are set on a regional basis and vary on a regional basis, the regions are distinct markets.
6. Industry recognition: a region is a market if businessmen generally so consider it.
7. Turnover: a region is a market if the market shares of the leading firms in the area are stable.

Elzinga and Hogarty themselves advocate an approach to geographic market definition using a combination of the "little in from outside" and "little out from inside" rules. Loosely, they begin with the largest plant involved in the merger; find an area including that plant such that 75 per cent of the product sold in the area is produced within the area; and then find the area that includes 75 per cent of the shipments of such plants. An area that satisfies the 75 per cent criterion in both directions is considered, under this approach, a market. For a more conservative standard, they substitute 90 per cent for 75 per cent.

Defining the market in terms of the areas to which and from which products are shipped is an approach that has the virtue of being clear-cut. So long as information about the origin and destination of shipments is available, it can actually be used in antitrust cases. It is not directly related, however, to the

---

[26]Elzinga, Kenneth G. and Hogarty, Thomas F. "The Problem of Geographic Market Delineation in Antimerger Suits," *Antitrust Bulletin* Volume 18, Number 1, Spring 1973, pp. 45–81; see also "The Problem of Geographic Market Delineation Revisited: The Case of Coal," *Antitrust Bulletin* Volume 23, Number 1, Spring 1978, pp. 1–18.

reason one defines a market in antitrust cases: to assess whether or not a firm or firms has, or is likely to develop, market power.

Product Market

Standards for product market definition have proceeded in a similarly ad hoc manner. As an example, consider the du Pont *Cellophane* case.[27]

The critical question in this case was whether or not cellophane was a product distinct from other kinds of flexible wrapping materials. The Supreme Court's standard was again the cross-elasticity of demand:[28]

> What is called for is an appraisal of the "cross-elasticity" of demand in the trade. . . . The varying circumstances of each case determine the result. In considering what is the relevant market for determining the control of price and competition, no more definite rule can be declared than that commodities reasonably interchangeable by consumers for the same purposes make up that "part of the trade or commerce," monopolization of which may be illegal.

This same standard of demand-side substitutability was later applied in *Brown Shoe*. Applying this standard, the majority of the Court found that cellophane was interchangeable in use with a wide variety of flexible wrapping materials, which for that reason constituted the relevant product market. In this market, du Pont's market share was only about 20 per cent, far short of that necessary for a finding of monopolization.

Applying the same standard of demand-side substitutability, three dissenting justices observed that the prices of other flexible wrapping materials had responded very little to substantial and persistent price cuts in cellophane. If all flexible wrapping materials were in the same market, the dissenting judges argued, the prices of other flexible wrapping materials would have fallen as the price of cellophane fell. The dissenting justices would have defined the product market as cellophane, within which du Pont had a market share of about 75 per cent. On this basis, they would have found a violation of Section 2 of the Sherman Act.

Two things are clear. First, the outcome of the *Cellophane* case depended on the definition of the market. Second, the difference in conclusions about the market was not due to a difference over the appropriate standard for market definition. Rather, it followed from a difference in judgment over the application of that standard.

---

[27]*United States v. E. I. duPont de Nemours and Company,* 351 U.S. 377 (1956); the issue here was monopolization, not merger.

[28]351 U.S. 377, at 394–395.

Cases that have hinged on supply-side substitutability are less common, but a Federal Trade Commission decision to allow a merger provides an example.[29] The Budd Company was a manufacturer of auto supplies and auto body parts. In 1968, Budd acquired the Gindy Manufacturing Corporation, a manufacturer of van trailers.

Van trailers were accepted as one product market in the case. A Federal Trade Commission administrative law judge defined two submarkets within this market: open-top and closed-top van trailers. In the closed-top van trailer submarket, Gindy's market share exceeded 10 per cent, and the administrative law judge found the merger to be in violation of Section 7 of the Clayton Act.

Budd appealed the decision to the Federal Trade Commission, which did not find the definition of the submarkets convincing:[30]

> Cross-elasticity of supply can also be an important consideration in defining markets. . . . The interchangeability of production and distribution facilities between two products is a strong indication that in measuring the relevant market and the degree of market power held by firms, the output of both products should be included since the manufacturer of one can shift readily to the production and sale of the other in response to profit opportunities. . . . Because the record establishes such a high degree of cross-elasticity of production, and identical marketing ease, among van trailers, we conclude that "open-top" and "closed-top" van trailers do not constitute separate submarkets.

Again, market definition determined the outcome of the case. Considerations of supply-side substitutability were used to justify a broad product-market definition. In this broad market, Gindy's market share was sufficiently small that the merger passed antitrust muster.

An Economic Approach to Market Definition

The various ad hoc approaches to market definition previously outlined represent practical attempts to deal with a difficult problem—market definition—with available data. What these approaches lack, however, is a unifying principle or theoretical foundation.

Consider, for example, the Elzinga and Hogarty 75 per cent shipment standard: an area is a geographic market if 75 per cent of the product produced in the area is sold in the area and if 75 per cent of the product sold in the area is produced in the area. Suppose in, say, the bituminous coal industry, we locate an area that satisfies these criteria. We find that a merger candidate

---

[29]*In the Matter of the Budd Company*, 86 F.T.C. 518 (1975).

[30]Ibid., at 572.

would have 75 per cent market share in this region. What can we say about the likelihood of injury to competition if the merger is permitted?

The answer is, "Not much." We know the area in which the product was sold before the merger. The important question, in terms of the exercise of market power, is whether the merged firm will be able to raise price without inducing entry into the region. Historical shipment patterns reveal very little about this issue. A distant firm that would not sell in a region at competitive prices might nonetheless be delighted to sell there if the price was raised enough to cover the cost of transportation to the region.[31]

Similar objections can be raised to geographic market definitions based on price patterns. Regional price differences may reflect differences in the cost of serving the regions. It will ordinarily be difficult to assess such cost differences. If suppliers can move easily from one region to another to earn a profit, they belong in the same market, even if prices across regions differed in the past.

An economic approach to market definition argues that the relevant market for assessing a firm's actual or potential market power should be defined to include all rivals that the firm would choose to have in a cartel, if it could:[32]

> The logic of the cartel criterion for forming an industry starts with the idea that a firm's industry should be considered to be composed of all sellers which a firm considers its competitors. A firm's competitors, in turn, are those sellers who would cause significant losses if that firm took independent action. A firm's industry should, then, be composed of those groups of sellers whose uncoordinated actions would affect the firm's profits most strongly.

Application of this standard does not eliminate the need to make judgments about hypothetical situations. But such judgments cannot be avoided in making assessments of future market power. What will happen if firms X and Y merge and raise the price of lutefish in the greater Lake Wobegon standard metropolitan statistical area? The "cartel" approach has the merit of directing judgments about hypothetical situations to the question that is of immediate concern in antitrust cases (will the merger create or sustain market power?) and away from questions that, although easier to answer, are not to the point (where was most of the product sold before the merger?).[33]

---

[31]Indeed, this is part of what was going on in *Addyston Pipe and Steel,* 175 U.S. 211 (1899): prices in the South and Midwest were raised sufficiently high that East Coast producers found it profitable to enter the regional market. This way lies the theory of limit pricing.

[32]Boyer, Kenneth D. "Is There a Principle for Defining Industries?", *Southern Economic Journal* Volume 50, Number 3, January 1984, p. 763. See also Boyer, Kenneth D. "Industry Boundaries," in Calvani, Terry and Siegfried, John, editors. *Economic Analysis and Antitrust.* Boston: Little Brown and Company, 1979.

[33]The "cartel" standard for market definition is included in the 1982 and 1984 Justice Department Merger Guidelines, which we will discuss.

The Effect of Horizontal Mergers on Competition

The *Philadelphia National Bank* case[34] involved a proposed merger between the number 2 and number 3 commercial banks in the Philadelphia area. The Supreme Court took advantage of this case to narrow the grounds upon which the effects of mergers on competition were to be judged under the Clayton Act. This portion of the Court's decision is worth quoting at length:[35]

> we come to the ultimate question under Section 7: whether the effect of the merger "may be substantially to lessen competition" in the relevant market. Clearly, this is not the kind of question which is susceptible of a ready and precise answer in most cases. It requires not merely an appraisal of the immediate impact of the merger upon competition, but a prediction of its impact upon competitive conditions in the future; this is what is meant when it is said that the amended Section 7 was intended to arrest anticompetitive tendencies in their "incipiency.". . . Such a prediction is sound only if it is based upon a firm understanding of the structure of the relevant market; yet the relevant economic data are both complex and elusive. . . . And unless businessmen can assess the legal consequences of a merger with some confidence, sound business planning is retarded. . . . So also, we must be alert to the danger of subverting congressional intent by permitting a too-broad economic investigation. . . . And so in any case in which it is possible, without doing violence to the congressional objective embodied in Section 7, to simplify the test of illegality, the courts ought to do so in the interest of sound and practical judicial administration. . . . This is such a case.
>
> We noted in *Brown Shoe* . . . that "[t]he dominant theme pervading congressional consideration of the 1950 amendments [to Section 7] was a fear of what was considered to be a rising tide of economic concentration in the American economy." This intense congressional concern with the trend toward concentration warrants dispensing, in certain cases, with elaborate proof of market structure, market behavior, or probable anticompetitive effects. Specifically, we think that a merger which produces a firm controlling an undue percentage share of the relevant market, and results in a significant increase in the concentration of firms in that market, is so inherently likely to lessen competition substantially that it must be enjoined in the absence of evidence clearly showing that the merger is not likely to have such anticompetitive effects.

The Court recognized the complexity involved in assessing the probable effect of a merger on competition, which involves judgments about hypothetical, counterfactual situations. A complete analysis of the likely effects of a merger will require a thorough review of structure–conduct–performance relationships. But such analyses are difficult, and (dare we say it?) different

---

[34]*United States v. Philadelphia National Bank et al.*, 374 U.S. 321 (1963).

[35]Ibid. at 362–363.

economists will sometimes reach different conclusions about the effect of a merger on performance.

But the Court also recognized that it is no service to the business community to set up a vague and unclear rule. "Your merger will be forbidden if it is found to harm competition, after a trial which will last three years in District Court, three years in appeals, and will cost you several million dollars plus the time of your top executives to defend." In the interests of clarity and ease of administration, the Court decided to evaluate the likely effects of a merger based mainly on the market shares involved.

As noted previously, one consequence of the focus on market share as the factor that determines the finding on market power is to give great importance to the market definition aspect of the analysis. If a market is broadly defined (in terms of products or areas), market shares will be low: no market power. If a market is narrowly defined, market shares will be high: market power. The mechanical nature of this approach, and cases that have seemed to hinge on unlikely market definitions have opened the "market share" approach to the assessment of market power to criticism.

Landes and Posner[36] have urged that courts should consider the market price elasticity of demand and the price elasticity of fringe supply, as well as a firm's market share, in making a judgment about market power.

Making a judgment about the price elasticity of demand can correct for an unrealistically narrow market definition. In Landes and Posner's example, a firm with a high market share in the production of widgets will not have much market power if gadgets, which are a very good substitute for widgets, are independently produced. If there is a good substitute available, the price elasticity of demand for widgets will be high, and the dominant widget producer will not have much power to raise the price.

Making a judgment about the price elasticity of fringe supply involves two separate issues. One is the rivalry to be expected from other producers—the conjectural variation, in terms of the oligopoly models of Chapter 5. The other is the ease with which new firms can come into the market—the entry conditions highlighted in Chapter 4.

Landes and Posner recognize that these factors are not new to the judicial assessment of market power, but argue that they deserve greater emphasis:[37]

> even when no quantitative measure of elasticity is available, our analysis is helpful in two ways: it points out common pitfalls in using market shares alone to estimate market power; and it suggests adjustments to simple market share calculations whereby those calculations can be made to yield a truer, though still rough, picture of the defendant's market power.

[36]Landes, William M. and Posner, Richard A. "Market Power in Antitrust Cases," *Harvard Law Review* Volume 94, Number 5, March 1981, pp. 937–996.

[37]Ibid., p. 983.

Areeda and Turner[38] likewise recognize that market share does not imply market power if entry barriers are low. But they reject the notion of making an evaluation of entry conditions part of judgments of market power. Like the Supreme Court in the *Philadelphia National Bank* case, Areeda and Turner emphasize the administrative difficulties that this practice would entail:[39]

> Determining the existence, "height," and effects of entry barriers is beset with some theoretical difficulties and with empirical problems of seemingly formidable proportions. Consequently, incorporating that factor into merger assessments would greatly increase the uncertainty, if not the indeterminacy, of most merger cases, at least unless the exception were limited to instances in which entry barriers were clearly negligible or nonexistent.

There is no easy answer to this problem. Courts and economists recognize that market share alone is an imperfect indicator of the presence or absence of market power. Whether one thinks that other factors should be considered, along with market share, depends on how well one thinks courts will do at economic analysis.

If you think courts will do well in analyzing structure–conduct–performance relationships, you will advocate full-blown structural analyses of merger cases. If you think courts are very good at law but do not have talent for economic analysis, you will advocate rules, even if those rules will sometimes lead to decisions that would be perceived as incorrect in a world of perfect information.

Vertical Mergers

Brown Shoe

The central doctrine in the legal treatment of vertical mergers under the Clayton Act was set down in *Brown Shoe:*[40]

> The primary vice of a vertical merger or other arrangement tying a customer to a supplier is that, by foreclosing the competitors of either party from a segment of the market otherwise open to them, the arrangement may act as a "clog on competition," . . . which "deprive[s] . . . rivals of a fair opportunity to compete."

---

[38]Areeda, Phillip and Turner, Donald F. *Antitrust Law,* Vol. IV. Boston: Little, Brown and Company, 1980.

[39]Ibid., p. 87.

[40]370 U.S. 294, at 323–324.

Having defined foreclosure as the vice of a vertical merger, the Supreme Court specified the factors to be examined in evaluating the probable effect of the merger. These included[41]

1. the share of the market foreclosed.
2. the nature and purpose of the agreement.
3. any trend toward vertical integration.

By these standards, the Court found that the merger of Brown's manufacturing operations with Kinney's retail outlets violated Section 7 of the Clayton Act.

Brown was the fourth largest U.S. shoe manufacturer;[42] Kinney operated the largest nonintegrated chain of shoe stores:[43]

> Thus, in this industry, no merger between a manufacturer and an independent retailer could involve a larger potential market foreclosure. Moreover, it is apparent both from past behavior of Brown and from the testimony of Brown's President, that Brown would use its ownership of Kinney to force Brown shoes into Kinney stores.

This statement goes to the first two of the standards previously outlined: the share of the market foreclosed and the nature and purpose of the agreement. As for the third standard, the Supreme Court accepted the District Court's finding that there was a trend toward vertical integration in the industry, and that manufacturers who acquired retail outlets tended to distribute through those outlets. The Court's further comments again go to its reading of congressional intent:[44]

> Brown argues, however, that the shoe industry is at present composed of a large number of manufacturers and retailers, and that the industry is dynamically competitive. But remaining vigor cannot immunize a merger if the trend in that industry is toward oligopoly. . . . It is the probable effect of the merger upon the future as well as the present which the Clayton Act commands the courts and the Commission to examine.
>
> Moreover, we have remarked above, not only must we consider the probable effects of the merger upon the economics of the particular markets affected *but also we must consider the probable effects upon the economic way of life sought to be preserved by Congress. Congress was desirous of preventing the formation of further oligopolies with their attendant adverse effects upon local*

[41]Ibid., at 328–334.

[42]Based on the number of shoes produced (370 U.S. 294, at 303).

[43]370 U.S. 294, at 332–333.

[44]Ibid., at 333.

control of industry and small business. Where an industry was composed of numerous independent units, Congress appeared anxious to preserve this structure (emphasis added).

The Court thus read the Clayton Act as embodying a congressional preference for small business, for reasons going beyond the economic effects of mergers. We have seen that the Congress that amended Section 7 of the Clayton Act was concerned with the political implications of economic concentration. Maintenance of opportunities for rivals to compete on the merits was seen as a way of securing economic efficiency *and* the social goal of diffusing discretionary private authority.

This severe policy toward mergers that might lead to the *development* of oligopoly should be contrasted with the treatment of oligopolistic behavior under Section 2 of the Sherman Act. As we saw in Chapter 5, courts will not condemn truly independent behavior by oligopolists, even if that behavior results in the exercise of market power. By the Clayton Act, Congress sought to impede the development of oligopoly. But if oligopoly develops through internal growth as a result of market forces (Chapter 8), it does not violate the antitrust laws.

Law and (vs.?) the Economics of Vertical Mergers

The reader will search the section of Chapter 9 that deals with vertical integration in vain. No mention of foreclosure as an incentive for vertical integration, either by merger or by internal expansion, will be found.

Foreclosure in Monopoly

Suppose Brown Shoe has a monopoly of shoe manufacture, and suppose further that there are entry barriers that prevent other firms from manufacturing shoes. What anticompetitive effects would flow from Brown's vertical integration into shoe retailing?

Vertical integration would allow the monopolist, Brown, to interfere with competition at the retail level. Brown could simply cut off independent shoe retailers. Alternatively, Brown could employ a price squeeze. It could raise the wholesale price at which it would sell shoes to independents and lower the retail price at its own outlets. Competition at the retail level would force the independents to match the lower retail price, compressing the distribution margin.

This strategy would certainly be injurious to competitors: the firms that were driven out of business or forced to operate on a lower margin would be injured. It is not clear, however, that it is an injury to competition, in the sense that the final consumer is made worse off as a result of Brown's vertical integration. Brown, by assumption a secure monopolist, was able to capture monopoly profit before vertical integration.[45] Competition in manufacturing could not be injured, because it was entirely absent.

If one purpose of the antitrust laws is to preserve competitive opportunities for equally efficient competitors, there is no need for a foreclosure theory of injury to competition. A price squeeze of the kind previously described would be an attempt to monopolize the market for the distribution of shoes. As such, it would be prohibited under the Sherman Act.

Foreclosure in Oligopoly

Now consider the same vertical integration in oligopoly. Brown is one of (say) 20 equal-sized shoe manufacturers, each with 5 per cent of the market.[46] It has distributed its 25 million pairs of shoes entirely through independent shoe stores, but it acquires a network of stores that will now distribute its product. What are the implications of this acquisition for market performance?

Several scenarios are possible. Suppose, first, that Brown simply acquires the firms, formerly independent, that had distributed its shoes. Then there is no foreclosure, simply a reorganization of previously existing vertical relationships. Other manufacturers will continue to distribute through their usual outlets.

On the other hand, Brown might acquire stores with which it had formerly had no relationship. Brown now cuts off its former distributors and distributes through its newly acquired retail outlets.

The independents who formerly distributed Brown's shoes are cut off from their customary source of supply. In addition, competing manufacturers who had distributed shoes through the stores acquired by Brown are cut off from their customer outlets. There will, in other words, be retailers in need of shoes to sell and manufacturers in need of outlets through which to sell shoes. Nothing about the Brown acquisition of a network of outlets prevents these two groups from finding each other. A disruption of customary channels of distribution is not the same thing as injury to competition.

Alternatively, Brown might distribute through its own outlets but continue to supply its old independent outlets as well.[47] In this case, total output at the retail level is increased by the amount of the increased output from Brown. This is likely to improve performance, not worsen it.

---

[45]We defer discussion of the possibility that vertical integration may allow profitable price discrimination to Chapter 15.

[46]Brown's market share in 1955 was actually 4 per cent; 370 U.S. 294, at 303.

[47]See Allen, Bruce T., "Vertical Integration and Market Foreclosure: The Case of Cement and Concrete," *Journal of Law and Economics* Volume 14, April 1971, pp. 251–274, for a demonstration that vertical integration (by merger or otherwise) does not automatically mean that a firm will cease to supply independents.

Economists generally do not see direct anticompetitive effects flowing from foreclosure via vertical merger. Foreclosure is not a convincing reason to condemn vertical mergers, especially in legislation that aims to halt the incipient development of market power. It is precisely where market power is incipient—in oligopoly—that foreclosure is unlikely to promote market power.[48] Policy concern with vertical foreclosure must rest on noneconomic grounds—the desire to preserve opportunities for equally efficient firms to compete.

Injury to Competition Through Vertical Merger

There are ways in which vertical mergers may injure competition. Because courts have focused on foreclosure, these more plausible effects have generally been ignored in antitrust cases.

Capital Requirements

As noted in Chapter 8, vertical integration can raise the absolute capital requirements for entry, which will make entry more difficult as long as capital markets operate on the basis of imperfect information:[49]

> To the extent that vertical integration inhibits entry at a single stage of production, a new entrant is compelled to begin operations at both stages. And this must necessarily raise the amount of capital required for entry. We should note that entry barriers heightened in this fashion result precisely from the joining of two stages of production, and thus, vertical integration may well contribute to the achievement of enhanced market power.

The entry-impeding effect of vertical integration will not arise if an entrant at one level can count on getting supplies from an independent at the other vertical level and at no cost disadvantage. These conditions highlight the importance of trends to vertical integration in an industry, which would dry up such independent sources of supply and put nonintegrated firms at an absolute cost disadvantage vis-à-vis integrated rivals.

Product Differentiation

Historically, as we saw in Chapter 9, the integration of manufacturing and distribution created "formidable barriers to entry."[50] This integration, although essential to the maintenance of a rapid turnover of output, had the additional

---

[48]See Hamilton, James L. and Lee, Soo Bock, "Vertical Merger, Market Foreclosure, and Economic Welfare," *Southern Economic Journal* Volume 52, Number 4, April 1986, pp. 948–961, for a recent formal treatment.

[49]Comanor, William S. "Vertical Mergers, Market Powers, and the Antitrust Laws," *American Economic Review* May 1967, p. 260.

[50]Chandler, *The Visible Hand,* p. 364.

effect of facilitating product differentiation.[51] An investment in product differentiation will often serve to raise rivals' costs.

Oligopolistic Coordination[52]

Suppose an oligopoly distributes a differentiated product through a competitive retail sector. Because the retail level is competitive, the retailers' margin over the price they pay the manufacturer[53] will reflect only a normal rate of return on capital.

If the oligopolists at the manufacturing level succeed in coordinating output restrictions, they will be able to exercise some market power. But these oligopolists will be under continual pressure from the retail level to lower prices. A retailer who distributes for manufacturer X can always complain about losing a sale to a distributor for manufacturer Y because of a slight shading of price. Sometimes the story may even be true; manufacturer X will never be entirely certain.

Competition at vertically related levels tends to work its way up or down the vertical chain and to interfere with the exercise of market power at the other horizontal levels.[54] Vertical integration will often, therefore, be a prerequisite to the successful exercise of market power under oligopoly.

Recall from Chapter 6 that vertical integration can also provide a discreet way for an oligopolist to shade the price. *All* oligopolists will have an incentive to integrate vertically, not only to prevent competition from filtering in but also to monitor the activities of their fellows. Like the effect of vertical integration on capital requirements, the role of vertical integration in furthering oligopolistic coordination suggests a concern with trends toward vertical integration in an industry.

Policy Implications

Antitrust treatment of vertical mergers is based on a slender reed: a foreclosure theory that is generally incorrect and tends to draw attention away from anticompetitive effects that are more likely to flow from vertical mergers.

Vertical mergers can make entry more difficult by increasing capital requirements and product differentiation. A vertically integrated oligopoly will be

[51]See the discussion of Chandler's *The Visible Hand* in Chapter 9. A similar view is expressed by Comanor, op. cit., p. 261.

[52]See Kaserman, David L. "Theories of Vertical Integration: Implications for Antitrust Policy," *Antitrust Bulletin* Volume 23, Number 3, Fall 1978, pp. 508–509.

[53]The logic of this argument does not change if there is a wholesale sector between the manufacturers and the retailers.

[54]Adams, Walter and Dirlam, Joel B., "Steel Imports and Vertical Oligopoly Power," *American Economic Review*, Volume 54, Number 5, September 1964, pp. 626–655, apply this analysis to the U.S. steel industry in the late 1950s and early 1960s.

insulated from competitive pressures that come from vertically related, competitive levels. This will make oligopolistic output coordination easier.

The Chicago school's view is that entry barriers are at most ephemeral, and that capital markets will supply funds to entrants on the same terms as to established firms. It is not surprising, therefore, that students of the Chicago school usually feel that vertical mergers should be presumed lawful under the antitrust laws.[55]

A more mainstream view, which is probably acceptable to most economists, is that of Areeda and Turner.[56] They argue that vertical mergers should be held illegal "only where both markets are (1) highly concentrated and (2) have substantial entry barriers." This recommendation reflects the belief that there are some circumstances under which vertical mergers will have anticompetitive effects, but that such circumstances are not as common as implied by the foreclosure theory of vertical mergers.

Conglomerate Mergers

Section 7 of the Clayton Act prohibits mergers "where in any line of commerce in any section of the country, the effect of such acquisition may be substantially to lessen competition. . ." As the Supreme Court made clear in *Brown Shoe,* this prohibition includes conglomerate mergers.

Courts have analyzed the anticompetitive effects of horizontal mergers in terms of the market shares of the firms to be merged. The anticompetitive effects of vertical mergers have been analyzed in terms of the shares of markets foreclosed by the vertical combination. In contrast, there is no single unifying theme that characterizes the anticompetitive effects courts have seen as flowing from conglomerate mergers. The treatment of conglomerate mergers under Section 7 of the Clayton Act is a hodgepodge, reflecting the different cases that have come before the courts.

Entry Barriers/Loss of A Potential Entrant

One such case is *Procter & Gamble.*[57] Procter & Gamble was (and remains) a large conglomerate marketing a variety of household cleaning products. These products were heavily advertised. Procter & Gamble was in fact the single largest advertiser in the country.

---

[55]Bork, Robert H. *The Antitrust Paradox.* New York: Basic Books, Inc., 1978, p. 245.

[56]Ibid., pp. 269–273.

[57]*Federal Trade Commission v. Procter & Gamble Co.,* 386 U.S. 568 (1967).

Procter & Gamble did not, however, sell liquid bleach. In 1957, it acquired the Clorox Chemical Company, which was the dominant firm in the liquid bleach industry. Clorox had a national market share of nearly 50 per cent and a larger market share in many regional markets.[58]

The Federal Trade Commission challenged the merger under Section 7 of the Clayton Act. Procter & Gamble appealed its decision to dissolve the merger to the Circuit Court of Appeals, which reversed the judgment. The Federal Trade Commission then appealed this reversal to the Supreme Court.

The Supreme Court endorsed the Federal Trade Commission's conclusion that the merger might substantially lessen competition:[59]

> The Commission found that the substitution of Procter with its huge assets and advertising advantages for the already dominant Clorox would dissuade new entrants and discourage active competition from the firms already in the industry due to fear of retaliation by Procter. . . . retailers might be induced to give Clorox preferred shelf space since it would be manufactured by Procter, which also produced a number of other products marketed by the retailers. . . . Further, the merger would seriously diminish potential competition by eliminating Procter as a potential entrant into the industry. Prior to the merger, the Commission found, Procter was the most likely prospective entrant, and absent the merger would have remained on the periphery, restraining Clorox from exercising its market power.

The Court agreed that the acquisition of Clorox by Procter & Gamble would raise product differentiation barriers to entry into the liquid bleach market. It also agreed that the merger would eliminate the most likely entrant into the market, which would injure competition. The Court affirmed the Federal Trade Commission's original condemnation of the merger.

In ratifying the Federal Trade Commission's action, the Court rejected one of the arguments that had been used to justify the merger:[60]

> Possible economies cannot be used as a defense to illegality. Congress was aware that some mergers which lessen competition may also result in economies but it struck the balance in favor of protecting competition.

Under this interpretation of the antitrust laws, competition is a process that ensures that the benefits of efficiency are passed along to consumers. Efficiencies that stem from or accompany the exercise of market power are not protected by the antitrust laws.

---

[58]Transportation costs limited the shipment of bleach to 300 miles from a plant. Geographic markets were thus regional.

[59]386 U.S. 568, at 575.

[60]386 U.S. 568, at 580.

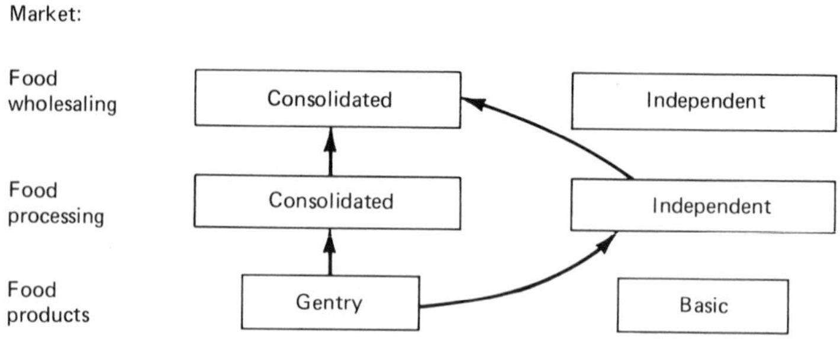

Market:

Figure 10-1 Reciprocity.

Reciprocity

When a firm operates in many industries, some of its divisions may buy products from independent companies, while others sell inputs to those same companies. The conglomerate may then attempt to use the patronage of its purchasing divisions to promote the sales of its supplying divisions, a practice known as *reciprocity* (Figure 10-1).

It is not surprising to learn that economists have been divided over the proper analysis of reciprocity. The structure-conduct-performance approach has been to treat reciprocity as interference with competition on the merits. The Chicago school has analyzed reciprocity as an efficient response to market failure.[61]

Stocking and Mueller[62] identify reciprocity as one technique that may be used by an oligopolist producing a differentiated product to shift the location of its demand curve. They acknowledge that reciprocity cannot be used in competitive markets. They expect it to be most useful for large, diversified firms that have some excess capacity.

In Chapter 4 we included interference with access to consumers as one of the strategies available to dominant firms seeking to maintain their position. Reciprocity will have this effect. Even if the firm practicing reciprocity gets business on an "all else equal" basis, entrants will have to come up with some inducement of their own to get a start in the market.

An example appeared in the 1965 *Federal Trade Commission v. Consolidated Foods Corporation* case.[63] In 1951 Consolidated acquired Gentry, Inc.

---

[61]Liebeler, Wesley J., "The Emperor's New Clothes: Why Is Reciprocity Anticompetitive?", *St. John's Law Review* Volume 44, 1970, p. 545 suggests that reciprocity is a vehicle for secret price cutting under oligopoly, and hence is procompetitive.

[62]Stocking, George W. and Mueller, Willard F. "Business Reciprocity and the Size of Firms," *Journal of Business* Volume 30, Number 2, April 1957, pp. 73–95.

[63]380 U.S. 592 (1965).

Consolidated was a food processor, and operated wholesale and retail food stores. Gentry manufactured dehydrated onion and garlic.

Gentry sold these products to food processors, who in turn sold their goods to Consolidated. Gentry, with a market share of 32 per cent in 1950, shared the market with Basic (58 per cent) and two smaller firms. Gentry's market share rose to 35 per cent by 1958, mostly at the expense of Basic.

The Federal Trade Commission challenged the merger on the ground that Consolidated could use its leverage as a purchaser from independent food processors to induce them to purchase from Gentry. Consolidated did in fact engage in such a reciprocal sales program, although it was eventually abandoned.

The Supreme Court agreed with the Federal Trade Commission that reciprocity was[64]

> one of the congeries of anticompetitive practices at which the antitrust laws are aimed. The practice results in "an irrelevant and alien factor," . . . intruding into the choice among competing products, creating at the least "a priority on the business at equal prices."

The Court condemned the merger on these grounds. This action affirms the purpose of the antitrust laws to preserve opportunities for equally efficient competitors.

Reciprocity is one of a number of practices[65] that the Chicago school has viewed as a response to the costs of transacting business across markets. In this view, reciprocity is a form of partial vertical integration, which responds to problems created by bounded rationality and opportunistic behavior.[66]

In Chapter 9, we reviewed the transaction cost analysis of vertical integration. Ordinarily, it is impossible to negotiate contracts between suppliers and consumers that allow for all possible eventualities (bounded rationality). But in some circumstances, one partner in a vertical arrangement will wish to renegotiate a contract to its own advantage (opportunism). After a supplier has been in place for some time, its bargaining position vis-à-vis a customer will be strengthened by the customer's commitment of sunk capital to the relationship.

Under reciprocity, however, both parties commit sunk capital to their mutual exchange relationship. A breakdown in the reciprocal arrangement—following bad-faith attempts to renegotiate a supplier–customer relationship—will cause the firm behaving opportunistically to lose its own sunk capital. Thus, under

---

[64]Ibid., at 594.

[65]We will meet others in Chapter 17.

[66]Walters, Stephen J. K. "Reciprocity Reexamined: The Consolidated Foods Case," *Journal of Law and Economics* Volume 29, Number 2, October 1986, pp. 423–438.

this analysis, reciprocity promotes efficiency by economizing on transaction costs.

The economic analysis of reciprocity, therefore, presents two possibilities. Reciprocity may either interfere with the market mechanism or it may be an efficient response to a failure of the market mechanism. Following the *Consolidated Foods* decision and the antitrust presumption that markets are the preferred mechanism for resource allocation, courts regard reciprocity as a factor that will bring a merger within the prohibition of Section 7.

Toehold Entry

The *Brown Shoe* decision makes it clear that the Clayton Act does not condemn mergers that promote competition. Antitrust authorities have generally allowed mergers that permit a firm that is established in one market to enter another.

The *Budd Company* case, which we have already discussed in connection with the role of market definition in antitrust cases, provides an example of what has come to be called *toehold entry*. In *Budd Company,* the Federal Trade Commission took the view that acquisition of a small firm—a toehold firm— by a large outsider could improve market performance by injecting competitive resources into the market. Since, under the commissioners' market definition, Gindy had a market share of less than 10 per cent, the Commission classified Gindy as a toehold firm and allowed the merger.

Summary

Section 7 of the Clayton Act condemns conglomerate mergers that may substantially lessen competition in relevant markets. Such a reduction in competition may result from raising entry barriers, removing potential entrants, or allowing anticompetitive practices such as reciprocity. But conglomerate mergers that improve competition do not run afoul of the law.

The Tradeoff Between Market Power and Productive Efficiency[67]

Horizontal, vertical, and conglomerate mergers may create efficiencies and result in real savings of resources. They may also create or preserve market power—the ability to control price. The analysis of mergers therefore confronts

---

[67]The discussion in this section and the following section mimics the literature and covers the tradeoff between market power and efficiency flowing from a merger. The issues raised, however, are relevant to all behavior covered by the antitrust laws.

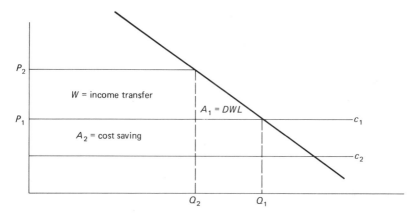

Figure 10-2 The market power–productive efficiency tradeoff.

one of the enduring conflicts of antitrust policy: what is the proper treatment of conduct that saves resources but makes consumers worse off? Should antitrust policy seek to minimize the deadweight welfare loss due to market power or to maximize consumer welfare?[68]

Consider a merger that reduces the cost of production but also creates (more generally, increases) market power, as illustrated in Figure 10-2.[69],[70] Before the merger, the average cost of production is c_1. To keep things as simple as possible, assume the absence of market power before the merger: $P_1 = c_1$.

Suppose the merger creates enough market power to allow a postmerger price increase to $P_2 > P_1$.[71] There is a transfer of income from consumers to the firm (area W) and a deadweight loss as output is restricted and resources that would ideally be used in this industry are transferred to the production of other goods (area A_1). This much is familiar from Figure 2-6.

[68]As noted in Chapter 3 (see footnote 10), the Chicago school uses the term *consumer welfare* to denote *consumer plus producer welfare*. A consumer welfare goal is taken here to mean maximization of consumers' surplus.

[69]This follows Williamson, Oliver E. "Economics as an Antitrust Defense: The Welfare Tradeoffs," *American Economic Review* Volume 58, March 1968, pp. 18–36; for other discussions, see Bork op. cit., chapter 5; Lande, Robert H. "Wealth Transfers as the Original and Primary Concern of Antitrust: The Efficiency Interpretation Challenged," *Hastings Law Journal* Volume 34, September 1982, pp. 142–150; and Williamson, Oliver E. "Economies as an Antitrust Defense Revisited," *University of Pennsylvania Law Review* Volume 125, Number 4, April 1977, pp. 706–713.

[70]It is by no means certain that most mergers yield cost savings; see Bok, Derek C. "Section 7 of the Clayton Act and the Merging of Law and Economics," *Harvard Law Review* Volume 74, December 1960, pp. 276, 318–321.

[71]As one can see by drawing the marginal revenue curve that corresponds to the demand curve, the postmerger firm is not maximizing its short-run profit. Firms that engage in limit pricing to discourage entry will hold the price below the short-run profit-maximizing level (Chapter 4).

275

But there is now an additional factor, due to the assumed reduction in costs. There is a saving of $c_1 - c_2$ on each of the Q_2 units sold. a saving of $(c_1 - c_2)Q_2$ in all. This is the area A_2.

The exact relation between areas A_1, A_2, and W will depend on the size of the postmerger price increase, the size of the unit cost decrease, and the price elasticity of demand. It is, however, evident from Figure 10-2 that the total savings due to the cost reduction are proportional to the postmerger output (Q_2), while deadweight loss is proportional to the reduction in output ($Q_1 - Q_2$). In most cases, postmerger output will be much greater than the output reduction (as in Figure 10-2, where $Q_2 > Q_1 - Q_2$). For this reason, a relatively modest reduction in unit cost (which determines the height of rectangle A_2) is likely to be enough to offset the deadweight welfare loss unless the demand is highly elastic.[72]

This is indeed the case. One can show formally that if deadweight loss is treated as the cost of market power, and if the price elasticity of demand is (for example) 2, a 1.1 per cent cost reduction will offset a 10 per cent increase in price.[73]

The situation is entirely different if income transfers are counted against market power. The income transfer (W), like the cost saving (A_2), is proportional to the postmerger output (Q_2). If income transfers are counted as a welfare loss flowing from market power, it is much less likely that the net welfare effect of a merger will be positive. There will be cases in which the income transfer plus the deadweight loss will exceed the cost saving, even though the cost saving alone exceeds the deadweight loss:[74]

$$A_1 + W > A_2 > A_1. \tag{10.1}$$

In all such cases, the decision not to count income transfers against the exercise of market power will determine the fate of a merger under the antitrust laws. A "consumer plus producer welfare" antitrust standard will be more generous toward mergers[75] than a consumer welfare standard. An antitrust policy that aims to minimize deadweight welfare loss counts monopoly profit as a social benefit, which offsets most of the loss in consumers' surplus following a price increase. The consumers' welfare standard counts the full loss of consumers' surplus against the exercise of market power.

[72]The more elastic the demand, the greater the deadweight loss that follows a given price increase; see the discussion of Figure 2-7.

[73]Williamson, "Economies . . . Revisited," Table 2.

[74]Deadweight loss will be a small fraction of the income transfer unless the price elasticity of demand is large. See Williamson, "Economies . . . Tradeoffs," p. 28.

[75]And, with appropriate changes in the analysis, to other behavior that creates, supports, or allows the exercise of market power, such as price discrimination, tying, or vertical restraints.

Public Policy Implications

Transaction costs rooted in opportunism and impacted information will make a quantitative cost-benefit analysis of welfare tradeoffs due to mergers difficult:[76]

> Although the government and the defendant have roughly equal access to market share statistics, and can present, interpret, and contest such data equally well, the same is not true with respect to a purported economies defense. Here, the data are distributed unevenly to the strategic advantage of the defendant; thus, an information impactedness condition exists. Not only can the defendant use its information advantage by disclosing the data in a selective way, but advocacy legitimizes such disclosure. Unless the government can demonstrate that the data are incomplete or significantly distorted, which may not be easy, the advocacy process is poorly suited for purposes of getting a balanced presentation of the evidence before the court.

Qualitative assessment of the market power–productive efficiency tradeoff will, however, be useful:[77]

> The courts may nevertheless find it instructive to permit arguments pertaining to technological and transactional economies to be brought before them. For one thing, permitting such arguments assures that economies will not be regarded perversely as anticompetitive. If the government argues that a merger has an anticompetitive purpose or effect, when, in fact, the evidence of either is extremely thin and speculative, permitting the defense to demonstrate that nontrivial economies exist presumably will make the court more reluctant to accept the government's contentions. On the other hand, when economies cannot be shown to exist or be negligible, courts will perceive little social loss in holding for the government.

A general approach to such a qualitative tradeoff can be suggested by analogy with a mainstream approach to vertical restraints.[78] Plaintiffs in a merger case[79]

---

[76]Williamson, Oliver E. "Economies . . . Revisited," p. 703. Williamson's remarks on opportunism and information impactedness seem particularly damaging to Bork's suggestion that "An argument could be made that where the agreement seems capable both of creating efficiency and leading to a restriction of output, the law ought not to interfere since there is no way of knowing whether its interference will have the net effect of aiding or injuring consumers" ("The Rule of Reason and the Per Se Concept: Price Fixing and Market Division," *Yale Law Journal* Volume 75, Number 3, January 1966, p. 390). Such a standard would give all benefit of the doubt to the party in a strategic position to release only information favorable to its own cause.

[77]Williamson, "Economies . . . Revisited," p. 728.

[78]See Chapter 17, footnote 116, and the accompanying text.

[79]Under Section 7 of the Clayton Act; the standard of proof to be met for other complaints would have to be consistent with the relevant statutes.

could be required to show that market structure is such that the merger may substantially lessen competition. If they do not satisfy this requirement, the merger would be permitted.

If plaintiffs demonstrate that the merger is likely to maintain or increase market power, the burden of proof would shift to defendants. Under a "dead-weight loss" standard for antitrust, defendants would have to show substantial[80] economies flowing from the merger. If defendants could not show such economies, the merger would be disallowed. Under a "consumer welfare" standard, defendants would have to show a substantial likelihood that prices would not rise after the merger. This procedure would place the burden of demonstrating economies on the parties with the information.[81]

Companies large enough to attract antitrust attention do not contemplate a merger[82] without engaging in substantial planning. This planning generates internal company documents that could be used to substantiate the economies sought from the merger. If economies were not the main motive for the merger, that would also be apparent.[83]

The idea of an efficiencies defense is sometimes criticized on the ground that efficiencies cannot be quantified.[84] In other words, courts cannot measure the various areas that appear in Figure 10-2. This is correct but beside the point. Even if efficiencies cannot be reduced to simple numerical terms, they can be described. Efficiencies can be characterized as large or small. Their existence can be proved or disproved to the satisfaction of a court.

It is, in fact, only in these terms that the probable effects of mergers (or other behavior) on market power can be described. If the effects of structure and conduct on market power and on productive efficiency can be described in the same general terms, those effects can be compared by courts.

---

[80]In both law and economics, the careful reader will beware of adjectives. *Substantial*, in this context, would have to be given meaning by legislation or by courts as case law developed. Areeda and Turner (op. cit., p. 168) would require cost savings to equal or exceed 5 per cent of the total cost before allowing an efficiency defense to a merger.

[81]Williamson, Oliver E. "Economies . . . Tradeoffs," p. 24: "But if efficiencies are to be a defense at all, it is clear that the companies—which are, presumably, sensitive to the relevant economies in proposing the merger in the first place—must be prepared to make the case for them in court. They have the data and these must be supplied."

[82]Or, for that matter, implement pricing schemes or vertical restraints, or enter into other behavior likely to attract antitrust attention.

[83]As Williamson notes ("Economies . . . Revisited," footnote 13), the rules that govern discovery in antitrust cases will limit the ability of defendants to hold back relevant information. This being the case, relevant information is sometimes buried in forests of irrelevant information. Resources devoted to cutting those forests down are truly a deadweight loss.

[84]Bork, op. cit., pp. 124–129; Posner, Richard A. *Antitrust Law: An Economic Perspective.* Chicago: The University of Chicago Press, 1976, p. 22.

Merger Guidelines[85]

The Justice Department periodically issues Merger Guidelines to inform the business community about public policy standards. Guidelines were issued in 1968 and 1982 and updated in 1984. Neither the law nor its interpretation by the courts has changed substantially in this period, but the standards embodied in the Guidelines have changed, reflecting the refinement of industrial economics and changing political attitudes toward the antitrust laws.

The 1968 Guidelines[86]

The 1968 Merger Guidelines closely followed the standards contained in the major antitrust cases under the Clayton Act. For example, standards for horizontal mergers were expressed in terms of market shares and concentration ratios.

Horizontal Mergers

Markets with four-firm seller concentration ratios of 75 per cent or more were termed "highly concentrated." In such markets, mergers in which the firms had the following market shares would be challenged:

Acquiring Firm	Acquired Firm
4%	4% or more
10%	2% or more
15%	1% or more

On the other hand, standards were more permissive if the leading four firms had less than 75 per cent of the market. In such markets, mergers in which the firms had the following market shares would be challenged:

Acquiring Firm	Acquired Firm
5%	5% or more
10%	4% or more
15%	3% or more
20%	2% or more

[85]For a recent discussion, see Williamson, Oliver E. "Transforming Merger Policy: The Pound of New Perspective," *American Economic Review* Volume 76, Number 2, May 1986, p. 114–119.

[86]Department of Justice, *Merger Guidelines,* May 30, 1968. See also *Journal of Reprints for Antitrust Law and Economics,* Summer 1969, pp. 181–200.

In line with the Clayton Act's emphasis on the prevention of incipient lessening of competition, the Justice Department announced that it would challenge mergers involving firms with more than 2 per cent market shares if concentration in the relevant market had been increasing.

The Justice Department included an exception for "failing firms" in the 1968 Merger Guidelines. If a merger permitted the survival of a firm that would otherwise go out of business, it would be allowed. This policy is consistent with the purpose of Section 7 of the Clayton Act to permit procompetitive mergers.

The Justice Department indicated that a showing of economies would not ordinarily preclude a challenge to a merger. This is consistent with the Supreme Court's reading of the law in (say) *Procter & Gamble*. Under Section 7 of the Clayton Act and under the 1968 Merger Guidelines, if there is a tradeoff between market power and efficiency, it is to be resolved against market power.

Vertical Mergers[87]

Similarly, the standards for vertical mergers were expressed in terms of the percentages of the market foreclosed. For example, the Justice Department would challenge a merger between a firm selling 10 per cent or more of a product and a firm buying 6 per cent or more of this product unless the merger raised no barriers to entry.

Conglomerate Mergers

The standards for conglomerate mergers expressed concern over the removal of potential entrants, the creation of advertising advantages, and reciprocity. These standards, of course, parallel Supreme Court decisions on conglomerate mergers.

The 1982 Guidelines

Market Definition

The 1982 Merger Guidelines give attention to one issue upon which the 1968 Guidelines were largely silent: market definition. For both product and geographic markets, the Justice Department will seek to include in the market products and firms that would have to be part of a cartel in order for the cartel to control the price successfully.

The 1982 Guidelines propose a 5 per cent rule to judge substitutability. If the price were raised 5 per cent, to whom would customers turn for supplies within a year? Those producers belong in the market. If the price were raised

---

[87]For discussion, see Scheffman, David T. and Spiller, Pablo T. "Geographic Market Definition under the U.S. Department of Justice Merger Guidelines," *Journal of Law and Economics* Volume 30, Number 1, April 1987, pp. 123–147.

5 per cent, what producers would begin to produce the product within a year? They too belong in the market.

But when the 1982 Guidelines explain what evidence will be used in applying the 5 per cent rule, it looks very much like the list of practical indicia from *Brown Shoe:* buyers' perceptions, sellers' perceptions, similarities in design, price movements, purchase patterns, and transportation costs. The 1982 Guidelines incorporate the notion of an *ideal cartel* rule as a principle for defining markets, but there is no way to get away from the application of judgment when markets are defined.

Horizontal Mergers

Standards for horizontal mergers are formulated in terms of changes in the Herfindahl index, the sum of squared market shares of firms in the industry (Chapter 5). Since the Guidelines express market shares in percentage terms, they measure the Herfindahl index from 0 to 10,000, not from 0 to 1.

The Justice Department defines industries with a Herfindahl index of 1,000 or less as unconcentrated. To interpret this definition, recall that the inverse of the Herfindahl index gives a numbers equivalent for the number of equal-sized firms that would produce a given Herfindahl index. If the Herfindahl index is 1,000 or less, that is equivalent to 10 or more equal-sized firms in the industry.

Industries with a Herfindahl index of 1,800 or more are termed "highly concentrated." Such a Herfindahl index corresponds to 5.5 or fewer equal-sized firms. Industries in the intermediate range—with Herfindahl indices between 1,000 and 1,800—are classified as moderately concentrated.

The Guidelines express standards for horizontal mergers in the terms of the Herfindahl index and the increase in the index caused by a merger. Suppose that two firms with market shares s_1 and s_2 merge. Before the merger, the contribution of these firms to the Herfindahl index was

$$(s_1)^2 + (s_2)^2. \tag{10.2}$$

After the merger, the contribution of the combined firm to the Herfindahl index is

$$(s_1 + s_2)^2 = (s_1)^2 + 2s_1s_2 + (s_2)^2. \tag{10.3}$$

Thus the increase in the Herfindahl index, as a result of the merger, is twice the product of the market shares of the merging firms ($2s_1s_2$).

This relationship helps us to interpret the 1982 Guidelines and compare them to the 1968 Guidelines. For example, in the 1982 Guidelines the Justice Department announces its intention to challenge mergers that increase the Herfindahl index by 100 points or more in highly concentrated industries ($H \geq 1,800$ after the merger). A merger between two firms with market shares of 7 per cent each, or between a firm with a 10 per cent market share and a firm with a 5 per cent market share, would cause increases in the Herfindahl index of about 100 points. But a merger between two firms with 6 per cent market shares would increase the Herfindahl index only 72 points and would not be challenged under the 1982 Guidelines. Such a merger would have been challenged under the 1968 Guidelines.

The 1982 Guidelines announce the policy of not challenging mergers in highly concentrated industries that raise the Herfindahl index less than 50 points. Thus a merger between two firms with 4 per cent market shares, increasing the Herfindahl index 32 points, would not ordinarily be challenged (again, in contrast to the 1968 Guidelines).

It is generally the case that the 1982 Guidelines embody a more lenient attitude toward horizontal mergers, in terms of market share, than the 1968 Guidelines.[88]

For mergers in highly concentrated industries that increase the Herfindahl index between 50 and 100 points, the Justice Department will base its decision on whether or not to challenge the merger on entry conditions and other factors, including firm conduct and market performance. The Justice Department thus moves beyond the Supreme Court's focus on market shares as the primary standard for evaluating mergers.[89]

The general policy of the 1982 Guidelines is to challenge mergers in moderately concentrated industries where the increase in the Herfindahl index is 100 points or more. Mergers in markets where the Herfindahl index after the merger is below 1,000 would not usually be challenged.

Nonhorizontal Mergers

The 1982 Guidelines combine vertical and conglomerate mergers under the general heading of "nonhorizontal" mergers:[90]

> By definition, non-horizontal mergers involve firms that do not operate in the same market. It necessarily follows that such mergers produce no immediate change in the level of concentration in any relevant market. . . . Although non-horizontal mergers are less likely than horizontal mergers to create competitive problems, they are not invariably innocuous.

The Guidelines indicate a willingness to challenge non-horizontal mergers that eliminate potential competitors, vertical mergers that raise barriers to entry

---

[88]For a graphic illustration, see Tollison, Robert D. "Antitrust in the Reagan Administration: A Report from the Belly of the Beast," *International Journal of Industrial Organization* Volume 1, Number 2, June 1983, pp. 211–221.

[89]It may well be that administrative agencies are better suited to make such judgments than trial courts.

[90]Department of Justice, 1982 Guidelines, p. 29.

(if one of the markets is highly concentrated), and vertical mergers that aid collusion.

Finally, the 1982 Guidelines admit the possibility of defending mergers either on "failing firm" or "efficiency" grounds, but indicate that such defenses will only rarely be successful.

The 1984 Guidelines

The 1984 Department of Justice Merger Guidelines are, for the most part, an extension and clarification of the 1982 Guidelines. For example, the general approach to market definition is the same in both Guidelines; the 1984 Guidelines emphasize that foreign suppliers will ordinarily be included in the market if the 5 per cent rule for market definition suggests that it is appropriate to do so.

With respect to horizontal mergers, the 1984 Guidelines emphasize that decisions on whether or not to challenge a particular merger involve more than a simple mathematical calculation based on the Herfindahl index. The mathematical expressions of the 1982 Guidelines remain, but the Justice Department indicates that it will also consider changes in market conditions, the financial condition of the firms in the market, the importance of foreign firms, entry conditions, and the ability of fringe firms to expand output.

There is one area in which the 1984 Guidelines clearly go beyond the 1982 Guidelines. That is with respect to efficiencies flowing from mergers:[91]

> The primary benefit of mergers to the economy is their efficiency-enhancing potential, which can increase the competitiveness of firms and result in lower prices to consumers. Because the antitrust laws, and thus the Guidelines, are designed to proscribe only mergers that present a significant danger to competition, they do not present an obstacle to most mergers. As a consequence, in the majority of cases, the Guidelines will allow firms to achieve available efficiencies through mergers without interference from the Department.
>
> Some mergers that the Department might otherwise challenge may be reasonably necessary to achieve significant net efficiencies. If the parties to the merger establish by clear and convincing evidence that a merger will achieve such efficiencies, the Department will consider those efficiencies in deciding whether to challenge the merger.
>
> Cognizable efficiencies include, but are not limited to, achieving economies of scale, better integration of production facilities, plant specialization, lower transportation costs, and similar efficiencies relating to specific manufacturing, servicing, or distribution operations of the merging firms. . . . the Department will reject claims of efficiencies if equivalent or comparable savings can reasonably be achieved by the parties through other means.

[91]Department of Justice, 1984 Guidelines, pp. 35–36.

The Justice Department will challenge only mergers that represent a "significant" danger to competition. In contrast, the Supreme Court has indicated that Congress intended the Clayton Act to be applied to probable incipient lessenings of competition. If there is uncertainty about the effect of a merger on competition, the mandate of Congress is to err on the side of preserving competition.

In many cases, the Court indicates that efficiencies will not save an otherwise illegal merger. Under the 1984 Guidelines, the Justice Department will consider efficiencies when it decides whether or not to challenge a merger. This is a change from the 1968 and 1982 Guidelines, which treated efficiencies as a defense, albeit an unlikely one, that firms could present once a decision to challenge has been made.

The 1987 Merger Guidelines

Although the emphasis on efficiency in the 1984 Department of Justice Merger Guidelines is consistent with the political position of the Chicago school—that the promotion of efficiency should be the sole aim of the antitrust laws—it is not a mainstream view of economists or policymakers. A quite different policy position is presented in the 1987 Horizontal Merger Guidelines of the National Association of Attorneys General.[92] These Guidelines, which are intended, among other things, to[93]

> inform the business community of the substantive standards used by the Attorneys General to review, and when appropriate, challenge specific mergers

unequivocally endorse the consumer welfare purpose of the antitrust laws:[94]

> The central purpose of the law is to prevent firms from attaining market or monopoly power, because firms possessing such power can raise prices to consumers above competitive levels, thereby effecting a transfer of wealth from consumers to such firms. . . .

The National Association of Attorneys General reject the notion that efficiency can, under the antitrust laws, exonerate mergers that harm consumers:[95]

> Goals such as productive efficiency, though subsidiary to the central goal of preventing wealth transfers from consumers to firms possessing market power,

[92]National Association of Attorneys General, *Horizontal Merger Guidelines of the National Association of Attorneys General,* Washington, D.C., March 10, 1987.

[93]Ibid., p. 2.

[94]Ibid., p. 3; footnotes omitted.

[95]Ibid., pp. 4–5, footnotes omitted.

are often consistent with this primary purpose. When the productive efficiency of a firm increases . . . the firm may pass on some of the savings'to consumers in the form of lower prices. However, there is little likelihood that a productively efficient firm with market power would pass along savings to consumers. To the extent that Congress was concerned with productive efficiency in enacting these laws, it prescribed the prevention of high levels of market concentration as the means to this end. Furthermore, the Supreme Court has clearly ruled that any conflict between the goal of preventing anticompetitive mergers and that of increasing efficiency must be resolved in favor of the former explicit and predominant concern of the Congress.

Summary

It is the policy of the antitrust laws, as embodied in Section 7 of the Clayton Act, to forbid mergers that are likely to lessen competition substantially. Section 7 does not require proof that a merger will substantially lessen competition. It does not indicate that mergers that are likely to lessen competition substantially will be permitted if they generate sufficient efficiency gains.

In the courts, horizontal mergers have been judged in terms of market shares. The Supreme Court has generally taken a hard line toward horizontal mergers, forbidding combinations that involve small market shares. In terms of the actual effect on competition, this strict standard may be too severe. Given congressional concern with incipient lessening of competition, a strict standard is probably on target. The most recent Justice Department Merger Guidelines, however, relax the market share standard that will lead to challenges of horizontal mergers.

Emphasis on market share as an index of market power has, in turn, given great importance to market definition as a factor that determines the outcome of antitrust cases. Market definition has traditionally proceeded on an ad hoc basis. The most recent Merger Guidelines contain a sensible theoretical approach to market definition—what producers in what areas would have to belong to a cartel to make it work? But as a practical matter, the information available to define markets in antitrust cases is not going to change, and judgments will end up being made on much the same basis as before.

Recent Merger Guidelines do show a willingness to consider such factors as entry conditions and the ability of the fringe to expand output, as well as market share, in making judgments about market power. Over the long run, this broadening may reduce the importance of market definition in antitrust enforcement.

Courts have evaluated the effects of vertical mergers in terms of an illfounded "foreclosure" theory. The 1982 and 1984 Department of Justice Merger Guidelines, although skeptical about the notion that anticompetitive effects can flow from vertical mergers, do identify legitimate channels through which such effects might arise. These include the raising of entry barriers, the elimination of potential competition, and the facilitation of oligopolistic coordination.

Conglomerate mergers are condemned under Section 7 for raising entry barriers, eliminating potential competition, and allowing reciprocity. Recent Department of Justice Merger Guidelines do not include reciprocity among the practices that will lead to challenge of a merger, reflecting doubts about its likelihood and its effects.

The 1982 and 1984 Merger Guidelines make much more explicit use of economic theory than did the 1968 Guidelines. They also give increasing weight to an "efficiency" justification for mergers that is not contained in the Clayton Act and is contrary to the decisions of the Supreme Court. This efficiency justification for anticompetitive mergers is rejected by the 1987 Horizontal Merger Guidelines of the National Association of Attorneys General, which interprets consumer welfare and the prevention of wealth transfers from consumers to producers as the primary goal of the antitrust laws.

Paper Topics

10-1 Consider *United States v. Aluminum Co. (Rome Cable)*, 377 U.S. 271 (1964); *United States v. Continental Can Co.*, 378 U.S. 441 (1964), and such other cases as you feel are necessary; analyze the role of market definition under the antitrust laws.

10-2 Read Landes, William M. and Posner, Richard A. "Market Power in Antitrust Cases," *Harvard Law Review* Volume 94, Number 5, March 1981, pp. 937–996. Read also the four comments published in *Harvard Law Review* Volume 95, Number 8, June 1982, pp. 1789–1874. Analyze the assessment of market power in antitrust cases.

10-3 Analyze Justice Harlan's concurring opinion in *Procter & Gamble*.

10-4 Analyze the place of *United States v. Falstaff Brewing Company*, 410 U.S. 526 (1973), in the development of conglomerate merger law under Section 7 of the Clayton Act.

10-5 Discuss the role of reciprocity in *United States v. General Dynamics Corporation*, 258 F. Supp. 36 (1966).

10-6 Compare and contrast the 1982 and 1984 Department of Justice Merger Guidelines with the 1968 Merger Guidelines and with the 1987 National Association of Attorneys General Horizontal Merger Guidelines.

10-7 Read Eckbo, B. Espen and Weir, Peggy, "Antimerger Policy Under the Hart-Scott-Rodino Act: A Reexamination of the Market Power Hypothesis," *Journal of Law and Economics* Volume 28, April 1985, pp. 119–149, and the references cited therein. Assess the goals and effects of the Hart-Scott-Rodino Act.

11

Sales Efforts

Song of the Open Road
I think that I shall never see
A billboard lovely as a tree.
Indeed, unless the billboards fall,
I'll never see a tree at all.

Ogden Nash

In Chapter 8, we examined (among other things) the impact of sales efforts on market structure. If there are economies of large scale in sales efforts, the minimum efficient scale of production *and* marketing will be greater than the minimum efficient scale of production alone. Economies of large scale can arise from advertising media rate schedules. They can also arise if advertising media are indivisible, so that advertising must be national to be effective.

Sales efforts can result in an absolute cost advantage to established firms over entrants if the incumbents benefit from brand loyalty cultivated by past advertising. New firms will then have to spend more than established firms on advertising, per dollar of sales, to achieve a given level of recognition among consumers. An absolute cost advantage for existing firms will also arise if advertising messages must be repeated to have their full effect. We will see that it is precisely through such repetition that advertising affects the sales of certain types of goods.

Existing firms will also have an absolute cost advantage if their sales efforts make those of new firms less effective (the noise effect). When such interference occurs, new firms have to advertise more than established firms because the latter are already advertising.

On the other hand, sales efforts do provide a way for the new firm to bring its product before the public. If sales efforts can be used to separate customers from their usual suppliers, they will make entry easier.

Here we examine sales efforts from another angle and study how they are affected by market structure. We begin with an analysis of the product and market characteristics associated with product differentiation. We then examine the methods by which sales efforts contribute to product differentiation. This is followed by a discussion of the relationship between distribution channels and sales efforts. Finally, we examine empirical studies of the effect of market structure on advertising and nonadvertising sales efforts.

The Basis of Product Differentiation[1]

In a competitive market, products are standardized. A firm will be able to sell all it wishes at the market price. It will not be able to sell anything above that price, no matter how much it advertises or promotes its product. In contrast, if products are differentiated, each variety will have its own demand curve. By engaging in sales efforts, a firm can change the location of the demand curve for its variety. It will generally be profitable to invest in shifting the location of the demand curve. But sales efforts will occur only in markets where there is some product differentiation, so that competition is to that extent already imperfect.

Since sales efforts arise in markets where products are differentiated, we begin with an analysis of the bases of product differentiation. In the section that follows, we concentrate on the contribution of sales efforts to product differentiation.

Product Attributes and Product Differentiation[2]

The products of modern industrial society are infinitely variable. Yet only a finite number of products can be produced, because there are sunk costs associated with redoing production lines to produce a variety that is a little longer, lighter, more durable, and so on.[3]

In a market with product differentiation, entry should occur as long as firms expect to make a profit. But as each new variety comes onto the market, the price falls. Eventually it falls sufficiently that entry is no longer profitable; new varieties would earn less than the normal rate of return. At this point, entry stops. It is this entry process that determines the number of varieties produced. The greater the sunk costs needed to produce a new variety, the smaller the (long-run) number of varieties.[4]

---

[1]This section follows Caves, Richard E. and Williamson, Peter J. "What Is Product Differentiation, Really?," *Journal of Industrial Economics* Volume 34, Number 2, December 1985, pp. 113–132.

[2]Lancaster, Kelvin. *Variety, Equity, and Efficiency: Product Variety in an Industrial Society.* New York: Columbia University Press, 1979.

[3]See Spence, Michael, "Product Differentiation and Welfare," *American Economic Review* Volume 66, Number 2, May 1976, pp. 407–414, and "Product Selection, Fixed Costs, and Monopolistic Competition," *Review of Economic Studies* Volume 43, June 1976, pp. 217–235.

[4]This explanation for the determination of the number of varieties is analytically identical to the treatment of the determination of market concentration in the absence of entry-deterring behavior in Chapter 8.

The number of varieties actually produced will usually be much less than the number of consumers. But individual consumers will generally have slightly different "most preferred" varieties, depending on the importance they attach to different product characteristics.

Since the number of varieties actually produced falls short of the number of consumers, most will have to settle for a variety that is second best, as far as they are concerned, compared with their ideal variety. Which variety a buyer actually chooses will depend on how close the available varieties come to the preferred product and on the prices of different varieties.

If a firm lowers the price of its variety, it will make its *price–attribute* combination more attractive to some consumers. A lower price will induce some consumers to switch brands. This action is enough to generate a downward-sloping demand curve for each variety.

One basis for product differentiation, therefore, is the fact that consumers have to chose among products that imperfectly satisfy their needs.

Caves and Williamson[5] assembled evidence on the bases of product differentiation for 36 Australian manufacturing industries.[6] They identified three broad types of product characteristics that contribute to product differentiation.[7]

Product differentiation based on product attributes is enhanced when products are tailored to individual purchasers. This occurs when products are made to order and when they are purchased infrequently.

Product differentiation is also enhanced when products have complex combinations of characteristics. This sort of differentiation is promoted by expenditures on research and development, and when a single purchase requires a major expenditure by the purchaser.

Finally, the need for postsales service is a source of attribute-based product differentiation. Giving different kinds of service to different consumers is a way of tailoring the product. Thus the first and third attribute-based sources of product differentiation overlap to some extent.[8]

[5]Op. cit.

[6]Caves and Williamson indicate that the Australian industries correspond roughly to three-digit industries in the U.S. Standard Industrial Classification.

[7]An explanation of the statistical technique that they employ, factor analysis, is beyond the scope of this book. They give an excellent nontechnical description of the technique, with references to the statistical literature.

[8]Resale price maintenance, by which producers guarantee a high margin to distributors, is a way for producers to encourage product-differentiating activity by dealers. We return to the topic of resale price maintenance in Chapter 17.

Incomplete Information and Product Differentiation[9]

It is costly for a consumer to acquire information, and bounded rationality[10] limits the amount of information a consumer can consider at any one time. Thus, it is optimal for the consumer to make decisions based on incomplete information.

A consumer will collect information from various sources until the marginal cost of collecting additional information equals the expected marginal benefit in terms of increased utility.

Consumers have various sources of information, including advice from friends, advertisements, sales personnel at the retail outlet, technical studies (*Consumer Reports*, for example), and their own previous experience. Some of these sources are more costly or more reliable than others. The buyer will typically take some information from several sources, but not so much information that decisions are made under the conditions of complete and perfect knowledge that are usually assumed for the classroom model of perfect competition.

If, then, a firm lowers its price, it will attract some additional sales from customers who are aware of its prices. But it will not capture the entire market. Because it is costly to acquire information, some consumers will remain ignorant of the lower price and will not switch suppliers. A price reduction will capture part of the market, but not all of it.[11] The result is a downward-sloping demand curve for the firm.

In their study of Australian manufacturing industries, Caves and Williamson found that promotional expenditures aimed at final consumers, including advertising and nonadvertising sales efforts, are a major source of product differentiation. Sales efforts directed to wholesaler and retail distributors are an independent source of product differentiation. These sales efforts differentiate the product because consumer decisions are made under conditions of imperfect information; sales efforts increase the number of consumers who know about the product.

Sales Efforts and Product Differentiation

Caves and Williamson showed that sales efforts controlled by the manufacturer contribute to product differentiation. This is what most studies have assumed. Thus, advertising is said to reduce the price elasticity of demand or to

---

[9]Porter, Michael E. *Interbrand Choice, Strategy, and Bilateral Market Power*. Cambridge, Mass.: Harvard University Press, 1976, chapter 5.

[10]See Chapter 9, especially the discussion of vertical integration.

[11]See Chapter 5 and the discussion of the basic Bertrand model of price-setting oligopoly.

create brand loyalty. But these studies are often vague regarding the mechanism by which this differentiation takes place. How precisely do sales efforts differentiate a firm's product?

Search Goods vs. Experience Goods

The way sales efforts affect demand depends on how consumers learn about a product's characteristics.[12] Product characteristics fall into two broad categories. *Search characteristics* can be described explicitly. A consumer can learn about them before a purchase is made (or not made). *Experience characteristics,* in contrast, can be appreciated only by using the product.

Most goods have both types of characteristics. Nonetheless, it usually makes sense to talk about *search goods* and *experience goods,* with predominantly one or the other kind of characteristic.

For example, a personal computer is best thought of as a search good. It can be described in terms that allow a consumer to compare alternative products without actually using them. A personal computer is IBM compatible or it is not. It has so many disk drives; it has a memory of a given size. It has so many ports, and it can be expanded in specific ways. It is true that one important facet of a personal computer is its keyboard, which is an experience characteristic. But the keyboard makes only a relatively minor contribution to the overall package of characteristics. A personal computer is for the most part a search good.

On the other hand, software is an experience good. It is no doubt true that one can write a description of a word processing package. A particular word processing program is compatible with certain types of computers and printers. A word processor can handle documents of up to a certain length. It treats footnotes in a certain way. But very few people who have ever used a word processing program will believe that it can be judged without hands-on contact. There are cases in which measurement and description fall short of experience.[13]

Advertising and the Differentiation of Search Goods

The difference in the ways consumers acquire information about search goods and experience goods dictates a difference in the way these goods are

---

[12]Nelson, Phillip. "Advertising as Information," *Journal of Political Economy* Volume 82, Number 4, July–August 1974, pp. 729–754.

[13]It is all well and good to be told that water freezes at 0°C, and that if the air is below this temperature, precipitation will fall as a crystalline solid. If you have lived your entire life at the equator, you will not, by this description, understand snow.

Table 11-1 Ratio of Television
Network to Magazine
Advertising by Goods, 1966

Goods	Ratio
Experience	
Automobiles	1.93
Foods	2.35
Toiletries	2.46
Tobacco	2.61
Drugs	2.58
Search	
Apparel	1.59
Household furniture	0.84

Source: Nelson, Philip. "Advertising as Information," *Journal of Political Economy*
Volume 82, Number 4, July–August 1974,
p. 746.

advertised. In order to influence the sale of search goods, advertising must provide the information that the consumer needs before the decision is made.[14]

Advertisements in newspapers and magazines can contain a good deal of information. In addition, a consumer can reread such advertisements. In comparing search goods and experience goods, therefore, one would expect search goods to be advertised more in newspapers and magazines and less on television and radio. Table 11-1, which reports the ratio of spending on television network advertising to spending on magazine advertising for several products, suggests that this is the case.

Advertising and the Differentiation of Experience Goods

For experience goods, on the other hand, detailed information is of little use. Such products must be tried before they can be judged. Advertising influences the demand for experience goods because consumers believe that goods that are advertised are better buys. Advertising promotes the demand for such goods simply by informing the consumer that the good is advertised.[15]

Why should consumers believe that experience goods that are advertised are better buys? To facilitate the comparison of differentiated goods, think of price and cost as being measured in dollars per unit of utility. Firms with a lower cost per unit of utility will earn a greater profit, per unit sold, than other firms. For this reason, such firms will have a greater incentive to promote sales than

[14]Nelson, op. cit.

[15]Ibid.

higher-cost firms. Since advertising increases sales, these firms will have a greater incentive to advertise. They will spend more per dollar of sales on advertising, all else equal, than other firms.[16]

At the same time, the lower the cost per unit of utility, the lower the profit-maximizing price.[17] By lowering its price, a firm will sell more and increase its total profit (even though the profit per unit falls somewhat as the price is reduced).

Thus experience goods that are least costly, per unit of utility, will be most heavily advertised and will have the lowest price per unit of utility. Experience goods that are advertised will be better buys than experience goods that are not advertised. The fact that a product is heavily advertised indicates that the good is likely to have a low price per unit of utility.[18]

In addition, advertising makes consumers more familiar with a variety's brand name. Familiarity makes it more likely that a brand will be tried. Familiarity also makes repeat purchases more likely if a brand has been tried and found satisfactory. Thus:[19]

> Advertising makes the public "brand-conscious"; it is not so much a question of making the consumer buy things which he would not have bought otherwise, but of crystallising his routine habits, of making him conscious that keeping to a certain routine in consumption means not only buying the same commodities in a vague sort of way, but sticking to the same brands.

A single advertisement in a newspaper can contain most of the information needed to describe a search good fully. On the other hand, experience goods are often advertised repeatedly—on successive pages of a magazine or several times on a single television show. This difference in promotional technique makes sense if one of the functions of advertising, for experience goods, is simply to make the consumer familiar with the brand name.[20]

---

[16]This follows from the Dorfman-Steiner condition described in Chapter 8.

[17]This is easily seen for the case of monopoly; see Figure 7-2 and the accompanying text.

[18]Here opportunism and impacted information enter the picture. If advertising conveys the information that a good is likely to have a low price per unit of utility, producers of inferior goods will have an incentive to advertise. Consumers will be unable to distinguish plausible and implausible advertising claims before purchase. All advertising claims will therefore be discounted to some extent. If you don't believe this, perhaps we should discuss some mountain land in Florida that you might wish to invest in.

[19]Kaldor, Nicholas. "The Economic Aspects of Advertising," *Review of Economic Studies* Volume 18, 1950–1951, p. 18.

[20]Compare advertisements for personal computers in, say, the daily *New York Times* with advertisements for perfume in the Sunday *New York Times Magazine*. The former may have a two-page ad containing detailed information about one or two dozen computers and accessories. The latter will often have similar ads, consisting simply of a photograph and the product's name, repeated throughout the magazine.

One implication[21] is that experience goods will be advertised more, per dollar of sales, than search goods. A study by Nelson showed that this was the case for 12 search and 28 experience good industries in 1957. The average advertising–sales ratio for the 12 search goods was 1.395 per cent. For 10 durable experience goods, it was 2.177 per cent. For 18 nondurable experience goods, it was 4.085 per cent.[22]

Sales Efforts and Distribution Channels

In the modern mass production and consumption society, products will often pass through two or more levels of distribution on their way from the manufacturer to the final consumer. Wholesalers buy in bulk from the manufacturer and resell to retailers in smaller, more convenient lots. Wholesalers maintain local inventories of the product to guard against interruptions in supply. They often provide credit to retailers. When necessary, wholesalers provide specialized storage facilities (for example, refrigeration). Wholesalers' sales personnel promote the product to retailers.

Retailers, on the other hand, market the product to the final consumer. They also maintain local inventories to guard against interruptions in supply. Retailers provide credit to customers and service the product after the sale. They often advertise the product, especially in local media or via in-store displays.

Manufacturers, wholesalers, and retailers all contribute to a variety's differentiation from other brands. Thus, a full understanding of the impact of sales efforts on demand requires consideration of the interaction between them. This interaction largely determines the division of sales efforts between media advertising and other promotional activities.

Production and Distribution[23]

In the United States, wholesale distributors were among the first firms to operate on a national basis, soon after the Civil War. Wholesalers preceded retailers and manufacturers into the national market soon after the railroad and the telegraph linked together what had been independent regional markets.[24]

[21]See Nelson, op. cit., pp. 735–738, for a formal demonstration.

[22]The average for all experience goods was 3.427 per cent. See Nelson, op. cit., p. 739.

[23]It may be useful for you to review the discussion of vertical integration in Chapter 9.

[24]Chandler, Alfred D., Jr. *The Visible Hand: The Managerial Revolution in American Business.* Cambridge, Mass.: The Belknap Press, 1977.

These early wholesalers maintained large purchasing organizations, which kept contact with producers and sought to obtain the best available buys. At the same time, wholesalers' sales forces traveled from town to town, finding retail outlets for the goods acquired by the purchasing organization.

The wholesaler occupied a middle position on a circuit in which goods flowed from manufacturer to retailer to the final consumer, while money flowed from the final consumer back to the manufacturer.

Parts of the wholesale function were mechanical—buying in large lots and reselling in small lots, holding inventories, and providing credit. But *information* as well as funds flowed from the final consumer through the wholesaler to the manufacturer.[25] The wholesaler transmitted information from the retail level to the manufacturing level. The independent wholesaler assumed a central role in the differentiation of products based on product attributes:[26]

> The specification of the things that the manufacturers were to produce was made out (in general), not by the manufacturers themselves, nor by the consumers, from whom the demand proceeded, but by the wholesale merchants. The manufacturer made things to the orders received from the wholesalers; the retailer selected his own orders from the choice of things offered by the wholesalers, and repeated the orders according to the strength of consumers' demand for the individual products. It devolved, therefore, on the wholesalers to determine what should be produced and made available to the market. . . .

National wholesalers were able to displace local wholesalers partly because they had better access to information (operating, as they did, over a larger area) and partly because their rapid turnover of products allowed national wholesalers to reduce their average cost substantially.

But these very factors led to the erosion of the mass wholesaler's position. Mass retailers arrived on the American scene less than 20 years after the mass wholesalers. They were able to displace mass wholesalers for exactly the same reasons that mass wholesalers had been able to displace local wholesalers.

Department stores and chain stores, which dealt directly with the final consumer, were better able than wholesalers to anticipate the products that would satisfy final consumer demand. Where retailers controlled distribution, they conveyed information from the final consumer to the producer; they controlled product differentiation.

To operate nationally, the mass retailer had to develop a nationwide purchasing organization comparable to that of the mass wholesaler. But one set of transactions—the sale from the wholesaler to the retailer—was internalized

[25]Kaldor, op. cit., pp. 16–17.

[26]Ibid.

when the retailer integrated backward to perform the wholesale function. This allowed mass retailers to reduce costs in a way that mass wholesalers could not.

Mass retailers enjoyed two other advantages over mass wholesalers.[27] First, they were better able to add new product lines (wholesalers' personnel were trained to handle a specific line of products). Second, they were better able to add outlets to their existing organization.

The position of wholesalers in the distribution chain was soon under attack from the other direction, and again for reasons that were related to product differentiation. Shortly after the arrival of mass retailers on the national scene, mass producers developed in industries where the technology allowed the use of capital- and energy-intensive techniques to increase greatly the rate of output.[28] The first mass producers to integrate forward into distribution did so because the distributors either could not handle the increased volume of output or would not provide special services that the products required.[29]

The provision of marketing services to the final consumer is one of the elements of product differentiation.[30] So is the provision of service after the sale. The need to differentiate the product and maintain demand was an important motive for vertical integration from manufacturing into distribution where the technology allowed rapid rates of output. It is not profitable to produce rapidly if the product stacks up in warehouses.

The result, especially for consumer-good industries, is that the early pattern of wholesaler dominance has been replaced by either producer or retailer dominance.[31] Producers tend to dominate distribution where production is capital- and energy-intensive, allowing production at rapid rates and requiring a distribution network that can move the product quickly to the final consumer. The petroleum industry is an example.

Retailers tend to dominate distribution where the technology is less conducive to mass production.[32] Food industries are an example. Independent wholesalers maintain a role in distribution mainly for producer goods and where the *breaking bulk* aspect of the wholesale function is important—that is, where deliveries to the retailer are in small lots.

---

[27]Chandler, pp. 236–237.

[28]Chandler, op. cit.

[29]Recall that in Chapter 9 we indicated that the inability of distributors to handle a firm's output is an incentive for producers to integrate forward into distribution.

[30]Caves and Williamson, op. cit.

[31]The terms are from Kaldor, op. cit.

[32]Chandler, op. cit., p. 372.

Distribution and Sales Efforts

Retailers contribute to product differentiation in two ways.[33] The quality of the retail outlet and the services provided by the retailer after the sale are attributes of the product. This is clear to anyone who has ever purchased a product with a warranty requiring service only at an authorized dealer (automobiles and personal computers are examples).

At the same time, sales personnel in the retail store provide information to the potential consumer. If the retailer is an independent agent, consumers may well regard these salespeople as a more reliable source of information than the manufacturer. Even if the retailer is not entirely independent (as, for example, an exclusive dealership), sales personnel in the store can tailor information to the needs of individual consumers in a way that general advertising by the manufacturer cannot. Thus the retail outlet affects both of the basic sources of product differentiation identified by Caves and Williamson: product attributes and consumer information.

We can classify retail outlets into two groups according to the nature of the retailer's influence on product differentiation:[34]

Convenience Outlets: Retail outlets where little or no sales assistance in the form of salesperson interaction is provided with the sale and the locational density of outlets is high.

Non-convenience Outlets: Retail outlets where sales assistance is provided with the sale and outlets are selectively rather than densely located.

Supermarkets are a good example of convenience outlets. Vendors of personal computers are a good example of nonconvenience outlets.

In convenience outlets, the retailer provides minimal assistance to the consumer. The manufacturer can, in effect, force the retailer to carry his variety by developing a positive brand image with the final consumer. If consumers ask for a specific brand, the retailer will either stock that brand or lose sales. For this reason, the optimal way for the manufacturer to promote sales of convenience goods is to advertise over the head of the distributor to the final consumer. This promotes product differentiation and increases the bargaining power of the manufacturer vis-à-vis the distributor.[35] It explains the importance

---

[33]Porter, Michael E. "Consumer Behavior, Retailer Power, and Market Performance in Consumer Good Industries," *Review of Economics and Statistics* Volume 56, Number 4, November 1974, pp. 419–436; see also *Interbrand Choice.*

[34]Porter, Michael E. "Consumer Behavior," p. 422.

[35]For a case study in the food industry, see Adelman, M. A. *A&P: A Study in Price-Cost Behavior and Public Policy.* Cambridge, Mass.: Harvard University Press, 1959.

297

of branding by manufacturers in food industries and explains why food retailers try to develop "store brands" to bolster their own bargaining position relative to manufacturers.

The strategy of branding through advertising to the final consumer will not work for goods sold through nonconvenience outlets. In nonconvenience outlets the retailer takes an active role in helping consumers to make up their minds. The retailer provides information before the initial purchase and service after the sale, which affects the odds of a repeat purchase. Advertising from the manufacturer to the final consumer may get a consumer inside the retailer's door, but from that point on, the retailer will be able to guide the consumer to any of several alternative brands.

For nonconvenience goods, the manufacturer will have to devote sales efforts to the retailer. Only by convincing the retailer to promote the product will the manufacturer be able to differentiate it in the eyes of the final consumer.[36]

An extreme example occurs in medicine. The "retailer"—the physician—exercises almost complete control[37] over the choice made by the "final consumer"—the patient. Pharmaceutical and medical supply firms, as a result, spend massive amounts of money to promote their products to physicians. Drugs that can be sold without a prescription, on the other hand, are advertised to the final consumer. For nonprescription drugs, such advertising limits the power of the drug store relative to the manufacturer.

Empirical Evidence

Market Structure and Sales Efforts

Price-Cost Margins

We begin with the Dorfman-Steiner condition (Chapter 8), which indicates that the optimal advertising-sales ratio for a firm will be the product of the price-cost margin and the elasticity of demand with respect to advertising:

$$\frac{p^A A}{PQ} = \frac{P - c}{P} \epsilon_{QA} \tag{11.1}$$

Because more profitable firms have more to gain by increasing their sales, we expect them to spend more, per dollar of sales, than less profitable firms.

---

[36]One would therefore expect manufacturers to be more likely to integrate forward into retail distribution for nonconvenience goods. This turns out to be the case.

[37]The spread of generic substitutes for name-brand prescription drugs has changed this situation. It is not surprising that when patents expire and generic substitutes become available, prices and profits on the formerly patented brands fall sharply. But I digress.

The Dorfman-Steiner condition also suggests that if any other elements of market structure affect advertising intensity, it will be because they affect the elasticity of demand with respect to advertising (ϵ_{QA}). We therefore examine the impact of market concentration and other elements of market structure on the advertising elasticity of demand.

Market Concentration[38]

We expect sales efforts to occur only where competition is imperfect. As concentration rises from low levels, individual producers will become aware of their mutual interdependence and conscious of the fact that they operate, to some extent, on individual demand curves. As concentration increases, the advertising elasticity of demand will also rise. Increases in concentration from low levels, therefore, should be accompanied by increases in advertising per dollar of sales.

At intermediate levels of concentration—oligopoly—advertising may well exceed the joint-profit–maximizing level. In the absence of collusion, each oligopolist will decide how much to advertise by considering the effect of his own advertising on the demand for his own variety. Any negative effect on the demands for rivals' varieties will be ignored. If there are noise effects, each oligopolist will have to advertise more, all else equal, simply to neutralize the advertising of others. The result will be greater advertising under oligopoly than under monopoly, all else equal.

There may be tacit or overt collusion with respect to sales efforts in the same way that there may be tacit or overt collusion on price. All the difficulties of collusion, discussed in Chapter 6, become relevant here. But it is likely to be even harder to coordinate sales efforts than pricing.

A factor that discourages independent pricing under oligopoly is the certainty of retaliation upon detection. Retaliation is certain, because rivals can always match price cuts (they may not like it, but they can do it). It is harder for rivals to match a successful promotional campaign than a price cut. If a promotional campaign catches the public's fancy,[39] rivals may be unable to imitate it. The incentive of the individual firm to try to differentiate its product under oligopoly is greater than its incentive to cut its price; the payoff from a successful ad-

---

[38]Greer, Douglas F. "Advertising and Market Concentration," *Southern Economic Journal* Volume 38, Number 1, July 1971, pp. 19–32; Cable, John. "Market Structure, Advertising Policy, and Intermarket Differences in Advertising Intensity," in Cowling, Keith, editor. *Market Structure and Corporate Behavior: Theory and Empirical Analysis of the Firm*. London: Gray-Mills Publishing Ltd., 1972, pp. 105–124; Sutton, C. J. "Advertising, Concentration and Competition," *Economic Journal* March 1974, pp. 56–69. See also Comanor, William S. and Wilson, Thomas A. *Advertising and Market Power*. Cambridge, Mass.: Harvard University Press, 1974, pp. 144–150.

[39]At this point, an image of two old geezers sitting on porch steps and talking about wine coolers comes to mind. Note that wine coolers are an experience good and that the purpose of such an ad, repeated many times, is to inform the consumer that the product is advertised and, by repetition, to establish a brand name. But I degress.

vertising campaign is potentially much greater than the payoff from cutting the oligopoly price.

At very high concentration levels, however, firms will become aware of the impact their advertising has on the sales of rivals. The external (to the firm) effects of advertising will be internalized as concentration increases. When concentration reaches its upper limit, the industry will be monopolized and all effects of advertising on demand will be internal to the single supplier.

We should thus expect that as concentration increases from intermediate to very high levels, sales efforts per dollar of sales will fall. If this analysis is correct, the relation between concentration and advertising should have the kind of inverted-U shape shown in Figure 11-1. All else equal, advertising intensity should rise as concentration reaches intermediate levels, and then should fall as concentration approaches 100 per cent.

The level of concentration at which advertising intensity turns down shows the concentration level at which recognition of interdependence starts to influence advertising under oligopoly. For the sample of British industries illustrated

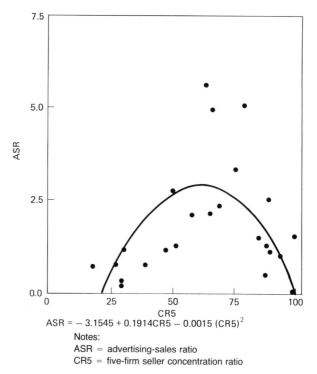

$$ASR = -3.1545 + 0.1914CR5 - 0.0015\,(CR5)^2$$

Notes:
ASR = advertising-sales ratio
CR5 = five-firm seller concentration ratio

Figure 11-1 The advertising-concentration relationship for 25 British industries in 1963, the maximum advertising-sales ratio of 2.95 per cent estimated to occur at a five firm seller concentration ratio of 63.8 per cent. Source: Sutton, C. J. "Advertising, Concentration and Competition," *Economic Journal* March 1974, Volume 84, pp. 56–69.

in Figure 11-1, maximum advertising intensity occurs, on average, when the largest five firms in the industry share 63.8 per cent of market sales. We will later present additional evidence on this point.

Demand Characteristics

Products sold mainly to final consumers should be more susceptible to differentiation than products sold mainly as intermediate goods to other producers. The elasticity of demand with respect to advertising should be greater, the grater the fraction of sales to final consumers.

Industrial customers are much more likely than individual consumers to make decisions based on an informed comparison of alternative varieties. Industrial consumers are much less likely than individuals to make decisions based on brand names.[40] The greater the fraction of sales to final consumers, the more likely are the products to be subject to branding and sold through convenience outlets, and the greater, all else equal, should be advertising per dollar of sales.

Growth

If market demand is stable, sales efforts can increase the demand facing one firm only at the expense of its fellows. In a growing industry, advertising will have the additional effect of claiming some of the new customers coming to market. For this reason, the elasticity of demand with respect to sales efforts should be greater, the more rapid the growth of industry demand.

A Test

Strickland and Weiss[41] estimated the average relationship between the advertising-sales ratio and the variables discussed previously, for a sample of 408 four-digit Standard Industrial Classification Industries, for the year 1963.[42] Their results are shown in Table 11-2.

As predicted by the Dorfman-Steiner condition, advertising-sales ratios are greater, on average, the greater is profitability. Industry growth of demand and sales to final consumers also have the predicted effects on advertising intensity (positive, in both cases).

Strickland and Weiss tested for an inverted-U effect of market concentration on advertising by including a linear and a quadratic concentration term as

[40]An exception to this argument is noted by Porter, *Interbrand Choice*, p. 109. Industrial purchasers will treat major inputs as search goods, but they are likely to make minor purchases in much the same way that individuals purchase convenience goods. This explains the common finding that in producer-good industries, profitability rises with advertising intensity. Although such products are sold as intermediate goods, they have the character of sales to individuals.

[41]Strickland, Allyn D. and Weiss, Leonard W. "Advertising, Concentration, and Price-Cost Margins," *Journal of Political Economy* Volume 84, Number 5, October 1976, pp. 1109–1121. Similar results are obtained by Martin, Stephen. "Advertising, Concentration, and Profitability: The Simultaneity Problem," *Bell Journal of Economics* Volume 10, Number 2, Autumn 1979, pp. 639–647.

[42]The estimates are obtained by two-stage least squares.

Table 11-2 Market Structure and Advertising

$$ASR = -0.0245^a + 0.0544^bPCM + 0.0737^aCR4 - 0.0643^aCR4^2 + 0.0539^bGR + 0.0269^aCDS$$

Notes
ASR = advertising-sales ratio
PCM = price-cost margin
CR4 = four-firm seller concentration ratio
GR = average annual growth rate of industry sales, 1954 to 1963
CDS = fraction of industry sales going to final consumers

a indicates statistical significance at the 1 per cent level; such an estimate would occur by chance only once in 100 times, on average.

b indicates statistical significance at the 5 per cent level; such an estimate would occur by chance only once in 20 times, on average.

Source: Strickland, Allyn D. and Weiss, Leonard W. "Advertising, Concentration, and Price-Cost Margins," *Journal of Political Economy* Volume 84, Number 5, October 1976, p. 1117; for compactness one explanatory variable is omitted from the results reported here.

explanatory variables. Both terms have statistically significant coefficients. At low levels of concentration, the positive effect of the linear term dominates the concentration–advertising relationship and advertising intensity rises with concentration. As concentration increases, the negative impact of the concentration-squared term takes over, and further increases in concentration cause advertising intensity to fall. The turning point in the concentration–advertising relationship—the top of the inverted U—occurs when the four-firm seller concentration ratio is 57 per cent.

Distribution Channels and Sales Efforts

The preceding analysis of retail distribution channels and product differentiation suggests that advertising to the final consumer will effectively differentiate the product only for goods sold through convenience outlets. For goods sold through nonconvenience outlets, retail sales personnel will contribute greatly to product differentiation, and sales efforts will have to be directed by the manufacturer to the retailer.

These predictions are borne out by empirical results, some of which are shown in Table 11-3. Porter estimates a market structure–performance equation in the tradition of the studies reported in Chapter 7 (see, for example, Table 7-2). Aside from the fact that he finds a negative and significant impact of concentration on profitability,[43] his results for consumer goods sold through

[43]In an extension, not reported here, Porter showed that this negative coefficient is due to an interaction between high concentration and rapid growth. In growing industries, firms have an incentive to compete in order to maintain their market position. Profitability is thus lower, all else equal, in concentrated and growing industries.

Table 11-3 Type of Retail Outlet and the Advertising–Profitability Relationship

Convenience Goods

$(P - T)/SE = 61.37^b - 0.58308^bCR8 + 0.01057^cMES + 0.60016^aASR$
$+ 0.02364^bGR + 0.00198^aACR \quad R^2 = 0.871$

Nonconvenience Goods

$(P - T)/SE = 77.38^b + 0.15305\ CR8 - 0.00132\ MES + 0.22419\ ASR$
$+ 0.00889GR + 0.00511\ ACR \quad R^2 = 0.347$

Notes: For samples of 19 convenience-good and 23 nonconvenience-good industries.

$(P - T)/SE$	= profit minus taxes as a percentage of stockholders' equity
CR8	= eight-firm seller concentration ratio
MES	= minimum efficient scale plant output as a percentage of industry output
ASR	= advertising-sales ratio
GR	= growth rate of industry sales
ACR	= absolute capital requirements for entry at minimum efficient scale

a indicates statistical significance at the 1 per cent level; such an estimate would occur by chance only once in 100 times, on average.

b indicates statistical significance at the 5 per cent level; such an estimate would occur by chance only once in 20 times, on average.

c indicates statistical significance at the 10 per cent level; such an estimate would occur by chance only once in 10 times, on average.

Source: Porter, Michael E. "Consumer Behavior, Retailer Power, and Market Performance in Consumer Good Industries," *Review of Economics and Statistics* Volume 56, Number 4, November 1974, p. 429.

convenience outlets are exactly as predicted by the traditional structure-conduct-performance model.

Technical factors that impede entry—minimum efficient scale and absolute capital requirements—have the expected positive effect on profitability. In addition, profitability is larger, the more rapid the growth of industry sales.

Advertising, as expected for convenience goods, has a positive and statistically significant coefficient. This is consistent with the hypothesis that for goods sold through convenience outlets, advertising to the final consumer differentiates the product and strengthens the manufacturer's position vis-a-vis the retailer.

In contrast, the standard model performs very poorly for consumer goods sold through nonconvenience outlets. Concentration, advertising, and absolute capital requirements have coefficients of the expected sign, but they are not estimated with any precision. The coefficient of minimum efficient scale, similarly insignificant, has a negative sign.

In extensions that are not reported here, Porter shows that advertising per firm (rather than advertising per dollar of sales) has a significant positive effect on the profitability of consumer goods sold through nonconvenience outlets. This is what one would expect if entrants need to advertise in proportion to the

303

size of the market, rather than in proportion to their own sales. This kind of indivisibility in advertising will raise the cost of entry.

Porter's results confirm the importance of retail outlets for market performance and for the nature of structure–conduct–performance relationships generally. For consumer goods sold through convenience outlets, market structure influences performance very much as indicated by the standard structure–conduct–performance model. Advertising to final consumers raises raises entry barriers and profitability, all else equal. For consumer goods sold through nonconvenience outlets, however, the effect of advertising on performance is captured by advertising per firm rather than advertising per dollar of sales. For these industries, the standard model does not satisfactorily explain performance.

Informative vs. Goodwill Advertising

Boyer[44] reports evidence that is relevant to Nelson's analysis of the advertising of search and experience goods.

It is expected that sales of experience goods will be promoted mainly by branding, and that advertising of experience goods will be repetitive and will aim to remind the consumer of the product's name and purpose. Advertising of experience goods aims to cultivate goodwill. Boyer expects this sort of advertising to be typically carried out by manufacturers[45] and to have the effect of increasing their profits.

On the other hand, Boyer argues that advertising by retailers is mainly informative. He supports this conclusion partly by citing statistics indicating that retailers advertise mainly in newspapers, as opposed to radio and television. Nelson, as indicated previously, expected search goods to be advertised mainly in newspapers, because newspapers are an ideal medium for informative advertising. If advertising by retailers is informative, it should improve market performance. If advertising by retailers is informative, retailer profitability should be less, all else equal, the greater the advertising by retailers.

If this distinction between goodwill (manufacturing) and informative (retailing) advertising is correct, the effect of advertising on profitability should be positive for manufacturing industries but negative for retailing industries.[46] Boyer tested this hypothesis by estimating the average impact of market concentration and advertising on profitability separately for samples of manufac-

---

[44]Boyer, Kenneth D. ''Informative and Goodwill Advertising,'' *Review of Economics and Statistics* Volume 56, Number 4, November 1974, pp. 541–548.

[45]Of course, this is also a prediction Porter would make for manufacturers of consumer goods sold through convenience outlets.

[46]A similar prediction is made by Hicks, John R. ''Economic Theory and the Evaluation of Consumer Wants,'' *Journal of Business* Volume 35, July 1962, p. 258.

Table 11-4 Goodwill and Informative Advertising

Manufacturing
$P/A = 0.073^a - 0.00011\ CR4 + 1.096^a ASR \quad R^2 = 0.625$

Retailing
$P/A = 0.054^a + 0.00044^c CR4 - 0.377^c ASR \quad R^2 = 0.254$

Notes: For samples of 41 consumer-good industries at the manufacturing level and 21 consumer-good/service industries at the retail level.

P/A = profit as a fraction of industry assets
$CR4$ = four-firm seller concentration ratio
ASR = advertising-sales ratio

a indicates statistical significance at the 1 per cent level; such an estimate would occur by chance only once in 100 times, on average.
c indicates statistical significance at the 10 per cent level; such an estimate would occur by chance only once in 10 times, on average.

Source: Boyer, Kenneth D. "Informative and Goodwill Advertising," *Review of Economics and Statistics* Volume 56, Number 4, November 1974, p. 545.

turing and retailing industries. The results, shown in Table 11-4, confirm the distinction between informative and goodwill advertising. It is goodwill advertising that has the effect of raising barriers to entry. Informative advertising, as Nelson would have predicted, improves performance.

Advertising and Other Sales Efforts

The empirical tests previously reported refer only to expenditures on media advertising. It is only recently that economists have obtained access to data describing differences across industries in nonadvertising sales efforts, which include salespeople, coupons, displays, and samples. That these other sales efforts are important, in terms of size, is shown by Table 11-5, which gives the breakdown of advertising and other sales efforts, as a percentage of industry sales, for the 10 industries[47] with the largest level of combined (advertising plus nonadvertising) sales efforts per dollar of sales.

A recent study[48] estimates the average effect of market structure variables—percentage of sales to final consumers and market concentration—on advertis-

[47]The original data source is the Federal Trade Commission's *1975 Annual Line of Business Report.* These industries are roughly at the four-digit Standard Industrial Classification Level.

[48]Weiss, Leonard W., Pascoe, George, and Martin, Stephen. "The Size of Selling Costs," *Review of Economics and Statistics* Volume 65, Number 4, November 1983, pp. 668–672.

Table 11-5 Advertising and Other Sales Efforts

Industry	ASR (%)	OSR (%)
Proprietary drugs	20.1	15.0
Toiletries	13.8	14.8
Bread, cake, etc.	2.0	26.3
Cutlery (including razors)	12.8	12.8
Chewing gum	12.3	13.1
Distilled liquors	11.9	13.4
Household vacuum cleaners	3.0	22.2
Typewriters	1.2	22.5
Hosiery	9.4	14.1
Calculating, accounting machines	2.8	19.3

Source: Weiss, Leonard W., Pascoe, George, and Martin, Stephen. "The Size of Selling Costs," *Review of Economics and Statistics* Volume 65, Number 4, November 1983, p. 669.

Table 11-6 Market Structure and Sales Efforts

Media Advertising

$$ASR = -0.054 + 0.040^c CDS + 0.229^a CR4 - 0.205^b CR4^2 \qquad R^2 = 0.0856$$

Other Sales Efforts

$$OSR = -0.022 + 0.061^b CDS + 0.372^a CR4 - 0.372^a CR4^2 \qquad R^2 = 0.555$$

Notes: For a sample of 92 consumer-good industries. Certain explanatory variables have been suppressed for compactness.

ASR = advertising-sales ratio
OSR = ratio of spending on other sales efforts to sales
CR4 = four-firm seller concentration ratio
CDS = fraction of industry sales going to final consumers

a indicates statistical significance at the 1 per cent level; such an estimate would occur by chance only once in 100 times, on average.

b indicates statistical significance at the 5 per cent level; such an estimate would occur by chance only once in 20 times, on average.

c indicates statistical significance at the 10 per cent level; such an estimate would occur by chance only once in 10 times, on average.

Source: Weiss, Leonard W., Pascoe, George, and Martin, Stephen. "The Size of Selling Costs," *Review of Economics and Statistics* Volume 65, Number 4, November 1983, p. 671.

[49]The study reported estimates of similar equations for a sample of 182 producer-good industries. The main results of significance were that expenditures on both types of sales efforts rose with the percentage of sales going to final consumers and with the average distance the product was shipped (a measure of market size). Concentration had no significant effect on sales efforts for producer-good industries.

ing and other sales efforts. The results for a sample of 92 consumer-good industries are reported in Table 11-6.[49] They confirm the inverted-U hypothesis concerning the impact of market concentration on sales efforts. Advertising per dollar of sales rises until the four-firm seller concentration ratio reaches 56 per cent; then it falls. Spending on other kinds of sales efforts per dollar of sales rises until the four-firm seller concentration ratio reaches 50 per cent; then it falls. Both types of sales efforts rise with sales to final consumers.[50]

Summary

The degree of differentiation in a market reflects variations in product characteristics and sales efforts by manufacturers. Sales efforts can create or reinforce product differentiation. However, they are not uniform in composition or effect.

Advertising affects the demand for search goods by providing information to consumers. Such advertising, especially by retailers, is likely to improve market performance.

Advertising affects the demand for experience goods by informing consumers that a good is advertised. The fact that a product is advertised carries the message that the product is likely to be a better buy. Advertising of experience goods does not convey information but seeks to establish, by repetition, a brand identity. Such advertising raises barriers to entry and is likely to worsen market performance.

Manufacturers advertise convenience goods directly to the final consumer. For such products, retailers will have relatively little influence on product differentiation.

Retailers assume a central role in the differentiation of nonconvenience products. Manufacturers in such markets will direct their sales efforts toward the retailer.

Advertising and nonadvertising sales efforts are influenced by market structure. More profitable products tend to be advertised more intensely, as predicted by the Dorfman-Steiner model. Sales efforts are greater, per dollar of sales, the more sales are made to final consumers. Empirical studies support the existence of an inverted-U relationship between concentration and sales efforts. Advertising and nonadvertising sales efforts appear to rise with concentration until the four-firm concentration ratio reaches about 50 per cent, and to fall as concentration rises thereafter.

[50]For another study of advertising and nonadvertising sales efforts, see Caves, Richard E. "Information Structures of Product Markets," Harvard Institute of Economic Research Discussion Paper No. 1002, August 1983. Uri, Noel D., "A Re-Examination of the Advertising and Industrial Concentration Relationship," *Applied Economics* Volume 19, Number 4, April 1987, pp. 427–435, finds a quadratic impact of concentration on advertising, using Federal Trade Commission Line of business advertising data.

12 Research and Development[1]

> *A shallow courtier present, impatient of the honours paid to Columbus, and meanly jealous of him as a foreigner, abruptly asked him whether he thought that, in case he had not discovered the Indias, there were not other men in Spain, who would have been capable of the enterprize? To this Columbus made no immediate reply, but, taking an egg, invited the company to make it stand on one end. Every one attempted it, but in vain; whereupon he struck it upon the table so as to break the end, and left it standing on the broken part; illustrating in this simple manner, that when he had once shown the way to the new world, nothing was easier than to follow it.*
>
> **Washington Irving, The Life and Voyages of Christopher Columbus.** *Boston: Twayne Publishers, 1981, p. 165.*

It ought to be unnecessary to emphasize the importance of technological progress to anyone who has ever asked, "Will we need a calculator for the exam?" But the pace of academic generations being what it is, let us remark that instruction in the use of something called a *slide rule* was once a standard element of the college preparatory program in American high schools. The slide rule dealt not with proper conduct on the playground but was in fact a primitive calculator, able to provide approximate solutions to nontrivial arithmetic, trigonometric, and logarithmic calculations. It has been rendered totally obsolete by the pocket calculator, which is able to provide much more accurate answers, much more rapidly, and to much more complicated problems.

The issues raised by R&D for public policy may be succinctly illustrated, using pocket calculators as an example. Few will dispute that society is better off with calculators than with slide rules—even those who purchased calculators at the dawn of the calculator era, when relatively few firms produced very simple calculators and sold them for 10 or more times the price of what currently passes for a top-of-the-line model. Few also will dispute that society is even better off with many firms competing to supply a wide variety of pocket calculators to consumers at markedly lower prices.

Yet if society is better served by quasi-monopolistic provision of pocket calculators than by competitive provision of slide rules, what is one to make of the argument that society is best served by markets supplied by many firms, each so small that it cannot influence the market price? Why worry about

---

[1]For a recent survey of the literature covered in this chapter, see Baldwin, William L. and Scott, John T. *Market Structure and Technological Change.* London: Harwood Academic Publishers, 1987. See also Kamien, Morton I. and Schwartz, Nancy L. *Market Structure and Innovation.* Cambridge: Cambridge University Press, 1982.

competition in the provision of existing products if competition between new products and old will bring quantum leaps in performance? Why condemn monopoly in the provision of calculators if it dominates competition in the provision of slide rules? Why condemn monopoly in the provision of calculators if it is the lure of monopoly profit that leads to the development of commercially successful pocket calculators? Yet if monopolistic provision of new products dominates competitive provision of existing products, what is one to do with the unavoidable observation that competition in the provision of pocket calculators better serves society than monopoly in the provision of pocket calculators? Is there a way for society to evoke technological innovation while avoiding permanent market power?

These questions were highlighted by Joseph Schumpeter, one of the great economists and students of economic thought of the twentieth century. Schumpeter disdained the textbook version of perfect competition as largely irrelevant to the performance of modern industrial economies:[2]

> But in capitalist reality as distinguished from its textbook picture, it is not that kind of competition which counts, but the competition from the new commodity, the new technology, the new source of supply, the new type of organization . . .—competition which strikes not at the margins of the profits and the outputs of the existing firms but at their foundations and their very lives.

He argued that large firms and monopoly power might very well promote technological progress, and that markets populated by large firms might best serve society over the long run:[3]

> As soon as we go into details and inquire into the individual items in which progress was most conspicuous, the trail leads not to the doors of those firms that work under conditions of completely free competition but precisely to the doors of the large concerns. . . .

In addition:[4]

> A system—any system, economic or other—that at *every* given point in time fully utilizes its possibilities to the best advantage may yet in the long run be inferior to a system that does so at *no* given point in time, because the latter's failure to do so may be a condition for the level or speed of long-run performance.

---

[2]Schumpeter, Joseph A. *Capitalism, Socialism, and Democracy.* New York: Harper & Row, Colophon ed., 1975, p. 84.

[3]Ibid., p. 83.

[4]Ibid., p. 84.

In this chapter, we examine theory and evidence on Schumpeterian propositions concerning the relationships between market power, firm size, and technological progressiveness. We also review other structural characteristics that seem likely to affect the rate of technical advance in an industry and discuss policy questions raised by the patent system and by research joint ventures.

Structure, Conduct, and Technological Performance

Market Power

We begin by considering the impact of product market structure on the incentive to innovate.[5] To obtain the sharpest contrast, we use Figure 12-1 to compare the profits available to a successful innovator under competitive and monopolistic organization of production.

Figure 12-1(a) (which may be compared with Figure 7-2) shows the effect of a cost-reducing innovation on the output decision of a profit-maximizing monopolist. For simplicity, the average cost per unit is assumed to be constant before and after the innovation, and the demand curve is assumed to be linear.[6]

A profit-maximizing monopolist will select an output that makes its marginal revenue equal to its marginal cost. The monopoly profit when average cost is c_1 is therefore $(P_1 - c_1)Q_1$, and the monopoly profit after innovation is $(P_2 - c_2)Q_2$. The gross increase in monopoly profit due to innovation is

$$(P_2 - c_2)Q_2 - (P_1 - c_1)Q_1, \qquad (12.1)$$

and this measures the incentive to innovate under product market monopoly.[7] With a little algebraic sleight-of-hand, the expression (12.1) can be rewritten as

$$P_2 \, \Delta Q + Q_1 \, \Delta P - c_2 \, \Delta Q - Q_1 \, \Delta c. \qquad (12.2)$$

---

[5]The seminal analysis is Arrow, Kenneth J. "Economic Welfare and the Allocation of Resources for Invention," in *The Rate and Direction of Inventive Activity: Economic and Social Factors*. Princeton, N.J.: Princeton University Press, 1962, pp. 609–625. An important comment, to be discussed, is Demsetz, Harold. "Information and Efficiency: Another Viewpoint," *Journal of Law and Economics* Volume 12, Number 1, April 1969, pp. 1–22.

[6]As a result, the marginal revenue curve has the same intercept as the demand curve but a slope that is twice the magnitude of the demand curve. We return to this point in the following section.

[7]The net profit from innovation is Equation (12.1) less the cost of discovering and implementing the innovation. If this cost is the same under competition and monopoly, a comparison of the gross profits from innovation will give a reliable reading of the relative incentive to innovate.

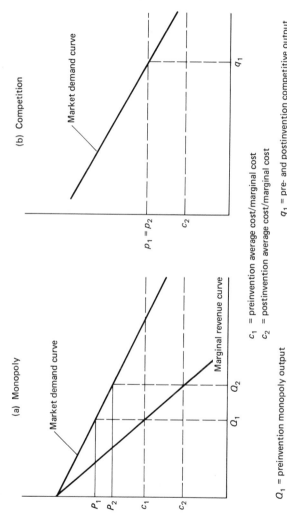

(a) Monopoly

(b) Competition

Q_1 = preinvention monopoly output
Q_2 = postinvention monopoly output
Gain from innovation:

$$(P_2 - c_2)Q_2 - (P_1 - c_1)Q_1$$

c_1 = preinvention average cost/marginal cost
c_2 = postinvention average cost/marginal cost

q_1 = pre- and postinvention competitive output
$c_1 - c_2$ = postinvention profit per unit

$$(c_1 - c_2)q_1$$

Figure 12-1 The incentive to innovate under monopoly and under competition.

311

The first two terms in (12.2) are the marginal revenue from the sale of $\Delta Q = Q_2 - Q_1 > 0$ units of output. The third term in (12.2) is the postinnovation cost of producing ΔQ additional units. The final term is the cost saving ($\Delta c = c_2 - c_1 < 0$) on the Q_1 units of output that had been produced before the innovation. Thus the increase in profit due to innovation, for a monopolist, is marginal revenue, less marginal cost, plus cost savings due to innovation.

Suppose that the same innovation takes place in the same market but that the initial structure of the industry is competitive. Before innovation, price $p_1 = c_1$, the average and marginal cost of production.

A single firm discovers the new technology and is able to produce at an average cost of c_2 rather than c_1. If the innovative firm attempts to set a monopoly price, P_2, it would be undersold by firms employing the old technology.[8] If the innovative firm acts as a monopolist, it must therefore limit the price and supply the market at price $p_1 = p_2 = c_1$.[9] The innovator's gross gain from innovation when the initial structure of the market is competitive is the postinnovation profit,

$$(c_1 - c_2)q_1 = (-\Delta c)q_1 > 0. \tag{12.3}$$

The proof that the profit to be gained from innovation is greater if the initial structure of the industry is competitive depends on the fact that

$$c_1 \Delta Q > P_2 \Delta Q + Q_1 \Delta P. \tag{12.4}$$

The proof of inequality (12.4) is essentially geometric and is illustrated in Figure 12-2. Substituting inequality (12.4) into (12.2), we obtain the following relationship:

$$P_2 \Delta Q + Q_1 \Delta P - c_2 \Delta Q - Q_1 \Delta c < c_1 \Delta Q - c_2 \Delta Q - Q_1 \Delta c \tag{12.5}$$
$$= (-\Delta c)Q_2 < (-\Delta c)q_1.$$

The first expression in (12.5) is the gain from innovation under monopoly. The final expression in (12.5) is the gain from innovation under competition. Thus successful innovation brings a greater reward to a competitive producer than it would to a monopolist facing the same initial cost and demand conditions.

---

[8]The case of a drastic innovation, in which the postinnovation monopoly price is less than $p_1 = c_1$, is left for Problem 12-2.

[9]Alternatively, under a patent system, the innovative firm might license its new process to other firms at a royalty of $c_1 - c_2$ per unit sold. The end result is the same: post-innovation output of q_1, sold at price p_1 per unit.

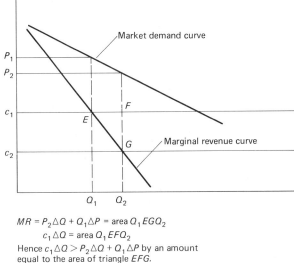

$$MR = P_2 \triangle Q + Q_1 \triangle P = \text{area } Q_1 EGQ_2$$
$$c_1 \triangle Q = \text{area } Q_1 EFQ_2$$

Hence $c_1 \triangle Q > P_2 \triangle Q + Q_1 \triangle P$ by an amount
equal to the area of triangle EFG.

Figure 12-2 Derivation of Inequality (12-4).

Leaving the details of the model aside, the economic rationale for this result is straightforward. A competitive firm starts with zero economic profit; all of the profit that flows from innovation is a gain. But a monopolist earns economic profit in the preinnovation period. To a monopolist, the additional profit that flows from innovation is only the increase in profit in the postinnovation period, not all of the postinnovation profit. Further, because the monopolist restricts output in order to raise the price in the postinnovation market, the cost-saving innovation is applied to fewer units of output under monopoly than under competition.[10] The result is that the reward from successful innovation is greater for a competitive firm than for a monopolist, if they operate with the same cost functions and in markets with identical demand curves.

Market Size (and How to Measure It)

An analysis due to Demsetz[11] confirms that the monopolist's preinnovation restriction of output is essential to the result that the incentive to innovate is greater under a competitive market structure than under monopoly.

Suppose we retain all the assumptions of the previous section but compare a competitive market with a monopoly market that is twice as large in the sense

[10]This reflects no special virtue of the innovative firm in the competitive market and no special vice of the monopoly innovator. The presence of competitors with access to the old technology compels the competitive innovator to limit the price to c_1.

[11]Op. cit.

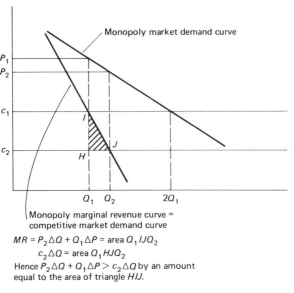

Monopoly market demand curve

Monopoly marginal revenue curve = competitive market demand curve

$MR = P_2 \Delta Q + Q_1 \Delta P = $ area $Q_1 IJQ_2$

$c_2 \Delta Q = $ area $Q_1 HJQ_2$

Hence $P_2 \Delta Q + Q_1 \Delta P > c_2 \Delta Q$ by an amount equal to the area of triangle HIJ.

Figure 12-3 The incentive to innovate with accordion-like demand.

that at any price, twice as much output would be demanded in the monopoly market as in the competitive market. Because of a convenient property of linear demand curves, it is straightforward to compare two such markets on a single graph, as in Figure 12-3.

We know from Chapter 2[12] that the marginal revenue curve associated with a linear demand curve has the same price-axis intercept as the demand curve but a slope that is twice that of the demand curve. Because a linear marginal revenue curve falls twice as rapidly as the associated linear demand curve, a given price will cross a linear demand curve at precisely twice the output at which it crosses the corresponding marginal revenue curve. Thus, in Figure 12-3, the price line c_1 crosses the marginal revenue curve at the output Q_1 and the monopoly demand curve at the output $2Q_1$. It follows that in Figure 12-1, competitive industry output $q_1 = 2Q_1$.[13]

Interpret Figure 12-3, therefore, as depicting two markets: a monopolized market and a competitive market that is exactly half the size of the monopolized market in the sense that, at any price, exactly half as much is demanded in the competitive market as in the monopolized market. Alternatively, one might imagine the demand curve contracting, accordion-like, in a single market as one passes from monopoly to competition. Under either interpretation, the

[12]Footnote 6 and Problem 2-1.

[13]See Problems 2-1 and 12-1.

demand curve for the competitive market coincides with the marginal revenue curve under monopoly. Preinnovation output is the same under either regime: Q_1.

The monopolist's incentive to invent—the gross increase in economic profit due to innovation before subtracting the cost of innovation—is the same as in the previous section:

$$(P_2 - c_2)Q_2 - (P_1 - c_1)Q_1 = P_2\Delta Q + Q_1\Delta P - c_2\Delta Q - Q_1\Delta c. \quad (12.6)$$

With the accordion-like compression of demand in the competitive market, however, the incentive to invent under competition is cut in half, compared with the model in which competition and monopoly operate on identical demand curves. A successful innovator under competition will limit the price to c_1 (to avoid competition with firms able to use the old technology) and earn an economic profit of $c_1 - c_2$ on each of the Q_1 units sold in the shrunken market at price c_1. When the preinnovation structure of the product market is competitive, the successful innovator gains

$$(c_1 - c_2)Q_1 = (-\Delta c)Q_1 \quad (12.7)$$

(before allowing for the cost of innovation). Because $Q_1 = (\frac{1}{2})q_1$, this is just half the incentive to invent under competition when monopoly is compared with competition under a single demand curve [compare expressions (12.7) and (12.3)].

With this accordion-like compression of demand, the innovator under competition gains a profit equal to the cost saving on the initial monopoly output. The monopolist enjoys this saving, but in addition expands output and earns a net profit on the additional output ($\Delta Q = Q_2 - Q_1$). It follows that the incentive to invent under monopoly in the larger market is larger than the incentive to invent under competition in the smaller market.[14]

This argument demonstrates that the incentive to innovate is less when the product market is monopolized before innovation because output is less under monopoly. A cost-saving innovation is applied to fewer units of output under

[14]Subtracting (12.7) from (12.6), the difference between the incentive to invent under monopoly in the larger market and the incentive to invent under competition in the smaller market is

$$P_2\Delta Q + Q_1\Delta P - c_2\Delta Q > 0.$$

The first two terms on the left are the change in total revenue as output rises from Q_1 to Q_2 (the area under the marginal revenue curve over the output range Q_1 to Q_2, area Q_1IJQ_2 in Figure 12-3). The third term on the left is the change in total cost, using the new technology, as output rises from Q_1 to Q_2 (the area Q_1HJQ_2 in Figure 12-3). Thus the incentive to invent under monopoly in the larger market exceeds the incentive to invent under competition in the smaller market by the monopolist's increase in profit as output expands from Q_1 to Q_2 (area HIJ in Figure 12-3).

315

monopoly than under competition, cost and demand being equal, because a monopolist will restrict output.

The policy conclusion that Demsetz draws from this analysis is that if the analysis of the incentive to innovate under competition and monopoly with the same demand curve suggests[15]

> that there are special adverse effects of monopoly on the incentive to invention, a framer of public policy would deduce that antitrust should be pursued more diligently than is dictated by considerations of output restriction only. But he would be wrong. If it is thought desirable to encourage invention by granting monopoly power through the patent or through secrecy, the above analysis suggests that antitrust should be pursued less diligently than is dictated by considerations of output restrictions only, for, at least in the linear model of two industries of equal output size, the more monopolistic will give the greatest encouragement to invention.

This conclusion seems too strong, however. Economists use demand curves as a conceptual device to describe the relationship between price and the quantity demanded in a single market. There is no reason to think that the quantity demanded at any price would double, accordion-like, if a market were monopolized. There is no particular reason to assume such an expansion in demand if what one wishes to examine is the relative performance of competition and monopoly as ways of organizing a given market. The demonstration that monopoly gives a greater incentive to innovate than competition if the demand curve is shifted so that output is the same under both regimes does not translate into a conclusion that monopoly gives a greater incentive to innovate than competition *in a single market.*[16]

---

[15]Op. cit., pp. 18–19.

[16]Comparing consumers' surplus under competition with consumers' surplus plus monopoly profit under monopoly in markets of the kind compared by Demsetz shows that the monopolized market yields greater social welfare (consumers' surplus plus monopoly profit) than the competitive market (see Problem 12-1). This is not a particularly compelling argument in favor of monopoly. Perhaps the most deadly comment on Demsetz is by Ng, Y. K., "Competition, Monopoly, and the Incentive to Invent," *Australian Economic Papers* Volume 10, Number 16, June 1971, pp. 45–49, who shows that if one shifts demand curves so that postinnovation output (rather than preinnovation output) is equalized, Arrow's result (greater incentive to innovate under competition than under monopoly) is restored. As noted by Kamien and Schwartz, op. cit., p. 43, Ng therefore shows that in Demsetz's paper "the scale effect is not eliminated but is merely shifted in favor of the monopolist." For other comments on Demsetz, see Kamien, Morton I. and Schwartz, Nancy L. "Market Structure, Elasticity of Demand and Incentive to Innovate," *Journal of Law and Economics* Volume 13, Number 1, April 1970, pp. 241–252; Yamey, B. S. "Monopoly, Competition, and the Incentive to Invent: A Comment," *Journal of Law and Economics* Volume 16, Number 1, April 1973, pp. 169–177; Bowman, Ward. "The Incentive to Invent in Competitive as Contrasted to Monopolistic Industries," *Journal of Law and Economics* Volume 20, Number 1, April 1977, pp. 227–228; and Lunn, John. "Market Structure and the Incentive to Invent," *Eastern Economic Journal* Volume 9, Number 4, October–December 1983, pp. 333–336.

A large literature[17] investigates the relationship between the number of patents granted to firms in an industry and the size of industries in which the patent might be used.[18] These studies confirm the importance of demand as a determinant of innovative activity, particularly when account is taken of differences across industries in the extent to which the underlying technology favors innovation.

Oligopoly

The analysis of the two previous sections suggests that firms without market power will have the greatest incentive to innovate.[19] If we are to progress, however, we must move from the tidiness of competition and monopoly to the messiness of oligopoly.

This shift in focus is entirely consistent with Schumpeter's original analysis. Schumpeter pictured capitalism as a process within which the lure of profit repeatedly summons up new innovators to supplant the old. The "perennial gale of creative destruction"[20] replaces the old fief of monopoly power with a new one that is expected to prove just as temporary. In this spirit, a large literature explores the proposition[21]

> that industries where "competitive oligopoly" prevails are likely to progress most rapidly. . . . The basic point is that progress is likely to be rapid (1) when firms are large enough or few enough to afford and benefit from research and (2) when they are under competitive pressure to innovate—utilize the results of research.

The analysis of oligopolistic rivalry in R&D has investigated the impact of market structure on technological performance. Within this general framework, specific topics have been the timing of innovation under oligopoly, the impact of uncertainty on innovation, the impact of imperfect appropriability (inability

[17]Schmookler, Jacob. *Invention and Economic Growth.* Cambridge, Mass.: Harvard University Press, 1966; Rosenberg, Nathan. "Science, Invention, and Economic Growth," *Economic Journal* Volume 84, Number 333, March 1974, pp. 90–108; Stoneman, P. "Patenting Activity: A Re-evaluation of the Influence of Demand Pressures," *Journal of Industrial Economics* Volume 27, Number 4, June 1979, pp. 385–401; and Scherer, F. M. "Demand-Pull and Technological Invention: Schmookler Revisited," *Journal of Industrial Economics* Volume 30, Number 3, March 1982, pp. 225–237.

[18]Size is measured in various ways: by capital-good investment in using industries for capital-good inventions, using industry material purchases for inventions used as inputs; and also by sales of the innovating industry. See Scherer, op. cit.

[19]The ubiquitous "all else" being equal (which, of course, it never is).

[20]Schumpeter, op. cit., p. 84.

[21]Villard, Henry H. "Competition, Oligopoly, and Research," *Journal of Political Economy* Volume 66, Number 6, December 1958, p. 491.

to control the use of the results of successful R&D), and the possibility of strategic use of R&D programs. It is to this literature that we now turn.

Timing

Like all investment projects, R&D involves time in an essential way. A firm seeking to develop a new technique or product must sink its funds into the project for some time before it profits from lower costs or revenues from the sale of a new product. There are good reasons for thinking that there are *increasing returns to time* in R&D in the sense that the present discounted value of the cost of research projects is likely to fall as the research project is spread over a longer and longer time:[22]

1. The acquisition of knowledge is a cumulative process in which "Each sequential step provides knowledge useful in the next step. Time can be saved by overlapping steps, but then one takes actions . . . without all the knowledge prior steps have furnished. As more and more actions are based on a given amount of prior knowledge, more and more costly mistakes are made."

2. At the start of a development project, there will typically be several approaches that seem equally promising. "Alternative technical approaches . . . can be explored in series until a success emerges, but this takes time. Expected time to successful solution can be reduced by running technical approaches concurrently, but this increases the expected value of project cost because more approaches which will ultimately prove unnecessary will be" tried.[23]

3. "Development time can be compressed by allocating more and more technical personnel to each task, but" the usual decreasing returns to scale set in as more and more labor crowds a fixed capital stock.

Leaving oligopoly aside for the moment, the economic decision involved in scheduling R&D therefore involves balancing the present discounted value of the marginal profit from developing a product or technique a bit earlier with

[22]Scherer, F. M. "Research and Development Resource Allocation Under Rivalry," *Quarterly Journal of Economics* Volume 81, Number 3, August 1967, pp. 360–361.

[23]Exploring multiple approaches can avoid premature selection of a technology that may ultimately turn out to be unsatisfactory. See Nelson, Richard R. "Uncertainty, Learning, and the Economics of Parallel Research and Development Efforts," *Review of Economics and Statistics* Volume 43, Number 4, November 1961, pp. 351–364. There is some reason to think that U.S. development of nuclear-generated electric power focused too quickly on a single design; see Adams, Walter and Martin, Stephen. "Public Support of Innovative Activity: Lessons from U.S. Industrial Policy," in de Jong, H. W. and Shepherd, W. G. editors, *Mainstreams in Industrial Organization*. Dordrecht: Martinus Nijhoff Publishers, 1986, pp. 413–439.

the present discounted value[24] of the marginal cost of the speedup.[25] The first projects to be developed will be those that promise the greatest payoff and are least subject to increasing costs of speedup.

Now return to the problem of oligopolistic rivalry in R&D. A firm that develops a new variety of a product or a less costly way to produce an existing variety will profit *because it takes customers away from its rivals.* It follows that smaller firms will have a greater incentive to innovate *because they have the most to gain from successful innovation.* Smaller firms will aim for earlier development, and will react more immediately to rivals' innovations, than larger firms.[26] Up to this point, we are entitled to conclude that oligopolistic industries that are not highly concentrated (perhaps those that have a fringe of smaller firms) will be most progressive.[27]

A qualification is in order, however. The gain in market share that follows successful innovation is likely to be strongest until rivals successfully imitate the new product or technique. After imitation, the original innovator will gain market share less rapidly and may see its gains vanish entirely. If imitators can regain market share from an innovator very quickly, the most profitable strategy for a firm may be to come in second in the race to advance product design and production techniques.

Coming in second is most likely to be the preferred strategy if it is less costly to imitate a successful innovation. This will often be so. Even if copying is not possible (perhaps prohibited by patent laws), information about a successful innovation is likely to reveal that certain lines of research are not as promising as they appear to be. Imitators can confine their efforts to projects that are more likely to succeed.

---

[24]See footnote 15, Chapter 4.

[25]Scherer, "Research," p. 363.

[26]See Scherer, op. cit., for separate models of oligopolistic introduction of new products and techniques. Like all models, Scherer's are limited by their assumptions. Perhaps the most important is that the technology of innovation is deterministic in the sense that a firm can pick the time of development by altering the funds it devotes to innovation. In a world of uncertainty, this will be true only in an expected-value sense. Kamien, Morton I. and Schwartz, Nancy L., "The Degree of Rivalry for Maximum Innovative Activity," *Quarterly Journal of Economics* Volume 90, Number 2, May 1976, pp. 245–260, present a model that takes explicit account of uncertainty regarding the time of rivals' successful innovations and yields results similar to those of Scherer. We take up the topic of uncertainty later.

[27]This raises the possibility that competitive oligopoly may lead firms to invest too much in innovation, seeking to introduce innovations quickly when the socially optimal strategy would be to delay innovation and conserve on costs. See Barzel, Yoram, "Optimal Timing of Innovations," *Review of Economics and Statistics* Volume 50, Number 3, August 1968, pp. 348–355, and Kamien, Morton I. and Schwartz Nancy L., "Timing of Innovations Under Rivalry," *Econometrica* Volume 40, Number 1, January 1972, pp. 43–60.

In markets for which the advantage of the leading innovator is short and followers gain a substantial cost advantage, all firms may prefer to be imitators. But if all firms prefer to be imitators, the rate of technological advance under oligopoly may well be less than under either competition or monopoly.[28] Recognition that innovation is an inherently uncertain process somewhat weakens this possibility. When there is a possibility that rivals will be unsuccessful in their research projects, passively waiting for a chance to take a "free ride" on their work is not the best strategy. There is always a residual incentive for each firm to undertake its own R&D program.[29] This tends to confirm the notion that competitive oligopoly will be the industrial structure most conducive to technological advance. It also emphasizes the importance of uncertainty as a characteristic of R&D.

Uncertainty, Patenting, and Strategic Innovation[30]

Imperfect predictability is in fact an essential characteristic of R&D. It is an essential element of the Schumpeterian process of creative destruction as well.

Suppose an incumbent firm and a potential entrant compete to develop a new, cost-saving production technique. The technology of innovation is uncertain. By spending more, a firm will reduce its *expected* development time, but actual development time will depend on the luck of the draw.

The first firm to develop the new cost-reducing technology receives a patent that gives it a legal monopoly of the use of the new technique. If the incumbent firm patents the technology, it remains a monopolist. This possibility means that the incumbent firm will pursue R&D as a strategic device to preserve its position.

---

[28]Baldwin, William L. and Childs, Gerald L. "The Fast Second and Rivalry in Research and Development," *Southern Economic Journal* Volume 36, Number 1, July 1969, pp. 18–24. Baldwin and Childs suggest the U.S. steel industry as a possible example of slow innovation induced by ease of imitation. For a simulation study that suggests that imitators may be better off than innovators, see Nelson, Richard R. and Winter, Sidney G. "The Schumpeterian Tradeoff Revisited," *American Economic Review* Volume 72, Number 1, March 1982, pp. 114–132.

[29]Reinganum, Jennifer F. "A Dynamic Game of R and D: Patent Protection and Competitive Behavior," *Econometrica* Volume 50, Number 3, May 1982, pp. 671–688.

[30]This discussion follows Reinganum, Jennifer F., "Uncertain Innovation and the Persistence of Monopoly," *American Economic Review* Volume 73, Number 4, September 1983, pp. 741–748, and "Uncertain Innovation and the Persistence of Monopoly: Reply," *American Economic Review* Volume 74, Number 1, March 1984, pp. 243–246. See also Gilbert, Richard J. and Newbery, David M. G., "Preemptive Patenting and the Persistence of Monopoly," *American Economic Review* Volume 72, Number 3, June 1982, pp. 514–526, and "Uncertain Innovation and the Persistence of Monopoly: Comment," *American Economic Review* Volume 74, Number 1, March 1984, pp. 238–242; and Dasgupta, Partha and Stiglitz, Joseph. "Uncertainty, industrial structure, and the speed of R&D," *Bell Journal of Economics* Volume 11, Number 1, Spring 1980, pp. 1–28.

If a potential entrant receives the patent, it comes into the market and shares oligopoly profits with the incumbent, the former monopolist. For the moment, suppose that the cost saving is sufficiently modest that innovation by the rival would not drive the incumbent out of the market.[31]

Consider the relative incentives to invent of an incumbent monopolist and a potential entrant. We know from Chapter 5's discussion of oligopoly that oligopolists will ordinarily fail to maximize their joint profit. Although oligopolists will usually succeed in exercising some monopoly power, they will generally extract less profit from a market than would a monopolist.[32] It follows that an incumbent monopolist will have more to gain from prior innovation of a modestly cost-saving technique than a potential entrant.

Suppose, for example, that the present discounted value of monopoly profit from the innovation is $1,000,000. Let the present discounted value of oligopoly profit be nearly as great, $900,000, and suppose that the majority of that amount ($500,000) goes to the entrant. It follows that the entrant will be willing to invest up to $500,000 in the R&D program that will serve as its ticket into the oligopoly. But the incumbent firm is willing to pay up to $1,000,000 − $400,000 = $600,000 to preserve its monopoly position and keep the entrant out.[33]

So long as the two firms share the postinnovation market, the incumbent always has an incentive to invest more on R&D than the potential entrant, since the incumbent has the lure of the difference between monopoly and oligopoly profits to strive for. Successful innovation will bring the entrant only a fraction of oligopoly profits, and profit under oligopoly is less than profit under monopoly.

Suppose, on the other hand, that the cost-saving innovation is so great that the first firm to obtain the patent will be a monopolist in the postinnovation market.[34] The gross benefit to successful innovation is then the same for both firms: the postinnovation monopoly profit. But the net benefit from successful innovation is less, for the incumbent, than the gross benefit. The incumbent firm will receive its current stream of monopoly profit until innovation occurs.

[31]See Chapter 5 and Problems 5-3–5-5 for a discussion of oligopoly in which firms have different costs. For an argument that such cost differences may emerge as a by-product of technical advance, see Flaherty, M. Therese. "Industry Structure and Cost-Reducing Investment," *Econometrica* Volume 48, Number 5, July 1980, pp. 1187–1209.

[32]In quantity-setting Cournot models, oligopolists fail to maximize their joint profit unless conjectural variations equal 1, indicating perfect matching of output restrictions. See (5-5)–(5-8) and the accompanying text.

[33]This argument can be reformulated in terms of marginal costs and benefits; see Reinganum, "Uncertain Innovation," pp. 745–746.

[34]This requires that the postinnovation monopoly price be less than the minimum value of average cost available under the old technology.

It follows that for drastic cost-saving innovations, incumbent firms with market power will have a smaller incentive to innovate than entrants or firms without market power. By spending less on innovation, an incumbent firm with market power can delay the introduction of the new technology and extend the period over which it can expect to enjoy its current stream of monopoly profit. In a world of uncertainty, drastic cost-saving innovations may come from firms with or without market power. But firms without market power have a greater incentive to seek drastic innovations in the hope of acquiring a position at the top of the heap.

When innovation is uncertain, marginal improvements in existing technology can be expected to come from incumbent firms. But the drastic improvements—the ones that generate the gale of creative destruction—should come, on average, from new firms.[35]

Appropriability

From a social point of view, efficiency in a market system requires that goods and services be distributed at prices equal to their marginal cost. The marginal cost of knowledge, once produced, is almost zero.[36] This suggests that information, once produced, should be priced at its cost of transmission.

But this is incompatible with the private production of information in a market system. Profit-seeking firms will not commit resources—which, after all, have an opportunity cost—to R&D without the expectation of an eventual return. Without the prospect of a profit from successful innovation, the market will not generate technological progress. Hence[37]

> there appears to be an unpleasant tradeoff between incentives on the one hand and the efficiency with which the industry achieves the levels of cost reduction it actually does achieve, on the other.

---

[35]This discussion abstracts from the possibility of patent licensing and from the related possibility that an incumbent firm might find it possible to buy out a rival that had successfully innovated. See Salant, Stephen W. "Preemptive Patenting and the Persistence of Monopoly: Comment," *American Economic Review* Volume 74, Number 1, March 1984, pp. 247–250; Gilbert, Richard J. and Newbery, David M. G. "Preemptive Patenting and the Persistence of Monopoly: Reply," *American Economic Review* Volume 74, Number 1, March 1984, pp. 251–253; and Gallini, Nancy T. and Winter, Ralph A. "Licensing in the Theory of Innovation," *Rand Journal of Economics* Volume 16, Number 2, Summer 1985, pp. 237–252.

[36]There are certainly costs of transmitting information. But the cost of transmitting existing information is typically much less than the cost of producing it in the first place.

[37]Spence, Michael. "Cost Reduction, Competition, and Industry Performance," *Econometrica* Volume 52, Number 1, January 1984, p. 102.

The patent system, which grants a legal monopoly for 17 years[38] in return for disclosure of a description of the patented product or process, may be thought of as a "rough and ready" approach to resolving this tradeoff. A 17-year monopoly provides the necessary prospect of a private return to successful innovation but ensures that the use of the new knowledge will eventually become available to all.

The real-world workings of the patent system are considerably more complex than this simple description suggests. Patents are at most an imperfect guarantee of appropriability.[39]

One study[40] of innovations and imitation in four major industries (chemicals, drugs, electronics, and machinery) indicates that imitators can bring out a competing product in about two thirds of the time and at about two thirds of the cost of the original innovator. About 70 per cent of the innovations in this study were patented. Sixty per cent of the patented innovations in this study had been imitated within 4 years of their introduction, although patenting appeared to increase the cost of imitation by about 11 per cent.

Another study,[41] involving 100 firms in 13 manufacturing industries, suggests rapid spillovers of information about R&D programs among firms in an industry. For these firms[42] "information concerning development decisions . . . is generally in the hands of at least some of their rivals within about 12 to 18 months, on the average, after the decision is made. . .". There is no lack of ways for such information to be transmitted:[43]

> In some industries there is considerable movement of personnel from one firm to another, and there are informal communications networks among engineers and scientists working at various firms, as well as professional meetings at which information is exchanged. In other industries, input suppliers and customers are important channels (since they pass on a great deal of information), patent applications are scrutinized very carefully, and reverse engineering is carried out.

[38]The Drug Price Competition and Patent Term Restoration Act of 1984 extends the patent protection period for new drugs in order to compensate for the time during which such drugs undergo clinical tests but also makes it easier to market generic substitutes once patent protection expires. See Grabowski, Henry and Vernon, John. "Longer Patents for Lower Imitation Barriers: The 1984 Drug Act," *American Economic Review* Volume 76, Number 2, May 1986, pp. 195–202.

[39]See Levin, Richard C. "A New Look at the Patent System," *American Economic Review* Volume 76, Number 2, May 1986, pp. 199–202.

[40]Mansfield, Edwin, Schwartz, Mark, and Wagner, Samuel. "Imitation Costs and Patents: An Empirical Study," *Economic Journal* Volume 91, Number 364, December 1981, pp. 907–918.

[41]Mansfield, Edwin. "How Rapidly Does New Industrial Technology Leak Out?," *Journal of Industrial Economics* Volume 34, Number 2, December 1985, pp. 217–223.

[42]Ibid., p. 219.

[43]Ibid., p. 221.

Such spillovers are all to the good, from one point of view. The leakage of information from one firm to another reduces the cost of innovation, and this cost reduction represents a real saving of resources for society.[44] There is, on the other hand, an adverse effect on incentives.

Firms in some industries may be able to protect their innovations without a truly effective patent system. The familiar entry barriers discussed in Chapter 8 may discourage rivals who would otherwise imitate an innovation from coming into a market.[45]

There may also be private gains to innovation that encourage innovation.[46] For example, a firm that successfully developed a technique that would make it profitable to pump oil from hitherto high-cost fields could predict that the price of such fields would rise sharply after its new technique came into use. By using its private, advance information, the innovating firm could realize tremendous capital gains by buying up high-cost fields at a low price before releasing information about its new process. The resulting capital gains, a private return to innovation, would not be a social benefit. But the lure of such gains would be a substantial private incentive to innovate.

It follows that even in the absence of perfect appropriability, the private rewards for innovation may exceed the social benefits. Even if this is the case, however, we should expect the incentive to innovate to be greater, the greater the ability of the innovator to appropriate the resulting profit.

Economies of Scale

The Schumpeterian hypothesis is that it is desirable to organize production in large firms because such a system is conducive to technological advance. Large firms are more likely to have market power, all else equal. But it may well be that larger firms produce more rapid technological advance even if they lack market power.[47]

There may be economies of large scale in R&D in the sense that the output of an R&D program rises more than proportionately with its size. In the end, this is a question about the production function for knowledge. Large R&D

[44]Spence, op. cit., p. 103.

[45]Mansfield et al., op. cit., p. 910; Lunn, John. "The Roles of Property Rights and Market Power in Appropriating Innovative Output," *Journal of Legal Studies* Volume 14, Number 2, June 1985, p. 426.

[46]Hirschleifer, Jack. "The Private and Social Value of Information and the Reward to Inventive Activity," *American Economic Review* Volume 61, Number 4, September 1971, pp. 561–574.

[47]See Nelson and Winter, op. cit. For a formal treatment, see Kohn, Meir and Scott, John T. "Scale Economies in Research and Development," *Journal of Industrial Economics* Volume 30, Number 3, March 1982, pp. 239–249; and Fisher, F. M. and Temin, Peter. "Returns to Scale in Research and Development: What Does the Schumpeterian Hypothesis Imply?" *Journal of Political Economy* Volume 81, Number 1, January-February 1973, pp. 56–70.

operations may be able to employ substantially more sophisticated equipment than smaller operations. Large research teams, composed of experts in many disciplines, may benefit from intellectual cross-fertilization in a way that is unavailable to small research teams. A larger research operation will be able to spread the risk of failure across multiple research projects. The odds that all projects will fail is much less than the odds that any one project will fail.[48]

Alternatively, it may be that an R&D program of a given size produces a more valuable output, the larger the firm of which it is a part. The larger the output of the firm that develops a cost-saving innovation, for example, the greater the volume of output to which the innovation will be applied. In addition, research programs may produce potentially useful but unexpected results. The larger and more diversified a firm, the more likely it is to be in a position to exploit discoveries with commercial possibilities.[49]

Product Differentiation

An important reason to develop new products is to realize the benefits of product differentiation, which can insulate a firm from the competition of existing rivals and raise the costs of entry for new rivals:[50]

> research resembles other market strategies which are designed to promote product differentiation in that it affects not only the rivalry which exists among established firms but also the barriers faced by new firms wishing to enter an industry. Where research is a major competitive factor, new entrants are forced to recognize that the cost and risk of research is an important component of the cost of entry.

Firms should therefore spend more on new product R&D, all else equal, in markets where products are differentiable. Some studies suggest that this includes industries producing durable consumer goods and industries producing investment goods.[51]

The benefit from raising entry costs will be less if it is already costly to enter. The incentive to invest in barriers to entry will therefore be less where

---

[48]This argument is conceptually similar to the argument that a conglomerate firm will be less risky because it operates in unrelated industries: not all of its markets are likely to be in a downturn simultaneously. See Chapter 9.

[49]See Nelson, Richard R. "The Simple Economics of Basic Scientific Research," *Journal of Political Economy* Volume 67, June 1959, pp. 297–306. For confirming empirical evidence, see Link, Albert N. "An Analysis of the Composition of R&D Spending," *Southern Economic Journal* Volume 49, Number 2, October 1982, pp. 342–349.

[50]Comanor, William S. "Market Structure, Product Differentiation, and Industrial Research," *Quarterly Journal of Economics* Volume 81, Number 4, November 1967, pp. 639–657.

[51]Ibid., p. 648.

entry is already impeded either by the need to achieve large scale for efficient operation or by large absolute capital requirements for entry at efficient scale. High technical barriers to entry should discourage new product R&D, all else equal.

Empirical Evidence

There is a large literature on the relationship between various elements of market structure and R&D inputs or outputs. Here we review three recent studies.[52]

Scott

The view that *competitive oligopoly* is most conducive to technological advance suggests that the relationship between market concentration and research and development may exhibit the inverted-U relationship that is often found between market concentration and spending on advertising (Chapter 11). This hypothesis is tested by Scott,[53] and a portion of his results are reported in Table 12-1.

These basic results support the notion of an inverted-U relationship between market concentration and spending on R&D per dollar of sales. The latter is estimated to rise with concentration until CR4 = 64 per cent and to fall as concentration increases beyond this level.

In more complicated tests, which are not reported here, Scott examines the average relationship between market concentration and spending on R&D after

[52]As one might expect, industry studies are an important element of this literature. For examples, see Mansfield, Edwin. "Size of Firm, Market Structure, and Innovation," *Journal of Political Economy* Volume 71, Number 6, December 1963, pp. 556–576 (and Williamson, Oliver E. "Innovation and Market Structure," *Journal of Political Economy* Volume 73, Number 1, February 1965, pp. 67–73) and "Industrial Research and Development Expenditures," *Journal of Political Economy* Volume 72, Number 4, August 1964, pp. 319–340; Comanor, William S. "Research and Technical Change in the Pharmaceutical Industry," *Review of Economics and Statistics* Volume 47, Number 2, May 1965, pp. 182–190; Grabowski, Henry G. "The Determinants of Industrial Research and Development: A Study of the Chemical, Drug, and Petroleum Industries," *Journal of Political Economy* Volume 76, Number 2, March/April 1968, pp. 292–306; and Link, Albert N. "Firm Size and Efficient Entrepreneurial Activity: A Reformulation of the Schumpeterian Hypothesis," *Journal of Political Economy* Volume 88, Number 4, August 1980, pp. 771–782.

[53]Using a sample of 3,388 divisions of 437 firms operating in some 260 roughly four-digit Standard Industrial Classification manufacturing industries for 1974. The source for the data is the Federal Trade Commission's Line of Business Program. For further details, see Scott, John T. "Firm versus Industry Variability in R&D Intensity," in Griliches, Zvi, editor. *R&D, Patents, and Productivity*. Chicago: The University of Chicago Press, 1984, pp. 233–252.

Table 12-1 Empirical Tests of Structure–R&D Relationships

Scott
RDS $= 0.00094 + 0.00049^a$CR4 $- 0.0000038^a$CR4^2 (1)

Lunn and Martin

(low-tech) RDS $= 1.1706^a - 0.0110^a$PCM $+ 2.2818^a$MS $+ 0.0075^a$CR4
                                      $+ 0.1328^a$ (Asset Size)   (2)
 (high-tech) RDS $= 12.9048^a - 0.1447^a$PCM $- 0.6671$ MS $- 0.0098$ CR4
                                      $+ 0.4183^a$ (Asset Size)   (3)

Lunn

Process $= -245.36 + 0.509^b$CR4 $+ 21.630^a$/1 if high-tech   (4)
                               \0 if low-tech
 Product $= -283.79 + 0.427$ CR4 $- 2.302^b$ASR $+ 94.618$/1 if high-tech   (5)
                                     \0 if low-tech

Notes:

RDS = spending on R&D per dollar of sales, for divisions of firms, classified by industry

CR4 = industry four-firm seller concentration ratio

MS = market share

PCM = price-cost margin

Asset Size = logarithm of division assets invested in the industry

"low-tech" indicates an industry low in technological opportunity

"high-tech" indicates an industry high in technological opportunity

Process = number of process patents awarded to firms in the industry

Product = number of product patents awarded to firms in the industry

ASR = industry-average spending on advertising and other sales efforts per dollar of sales

Certain variables have been omitted from the results reported by Lunn and Martin and Lunn.

a indicates statistical significance at the 1 per cent level; such an estimate would occur by chance only once in 100 times, on average.

b indicates statistical significance at the 5 per cent level; such an estimate would occur by chance only once in 20 times, on average.

Sources:

Scott, John T. "Firm versus Industry Variability in R&D Intensity," in Griliches, Zvi, editor. *R&D, Patents, and Productivity.* Chicago: The University of Chicago Press, 1984, pp. 233–252.

Lunn, John and Martin, Stephen. "Market Structure, Firm Structure, and Research and Development," *Quarterly Review of Economics and Business* Volume 26, Number 1, Spring 1986, pp. 31–44.

Lunn, John. "An Empirical Analysis of Process and Product Patenting: A Simultaneous Equation Framework," *Journal of Industrial Economics* Volume 34, Number 3, March 1986, pp. 319–330.

controlling for differences across industries in demand conditions and technological opportunity (and differences across firms in R&D spending). When these additional factors are considered, the inverted-U relationship between concentration and spending on R&D disappears. These results highlight the importance of demand conditions and technological opportunity as determinants of technological advance.

Lunn and Martin

In a study using a similar sample,[54] Lunn and Martin examine the impact of various elements of market and firm structure on R&D spending. Industries low and high in technological opportunity were studied separately.[55]

In both high- and low-technological opportunity industries, high-profit (as measured by the price-cost margin) operations spend *less* on R&D, all else equal. This indicates the importance of competition as a stimulus to innovation. Firms in competitive markets invest in R&D in search of profit.

The Schumpeterian hypothesis is that the organization of production in large firms favors technological advance. As we noted previously, this may reflect advantages of market power or of large size. For industries low in technological opportunity, the results of Lunn and Martin [Equation (2)] support both of these possibilities. In low-technological opportunity industries, operations with larger market shares and operations in concentrated industries spend more on R&D per dollar of sales, all else equal. It is fair to interpret these results as evidence that market power encouraged investment in innovation in low-technology industries. But it also appears that larger operations—with greater assets—in low-technological opportunity industries spend more on R&D even after differences in market share and market concentration are taken into account.

The results for high-technological opportunity industries are different. Neither market share nor market concentration has a statistically significant impact on research spending [Equation (3)]. On the other hand, large firms in high-technological opportunity industries spend more per dollar of sales, all else equal, on R&D.

Lunn

Other insights are provided by Lunn[56], who examines the impact of various elements of market structure on the number of patents granted to firms in an industry.[57] Lunn studies new process patents and new product patents separately.

[54]A total of 2,297 divisions of 424 firms, operating in 218 roughly four-digit Standard Industrial Classification industries for 1975, also derived from the Federal Trade Commission's Line of Business Program. See Lunn, John and Martin, Stephen. "Market Structure, Firm Structure, and Research and Development," *Quarterly Review of Economics and Business* Volume 26, Number 1, Spring 1986, pp. 31–44.

[55]The chemical, electrical, electronic, and metallurgical industries were classified as high in technological opportunity.

[56]Lunn, John. "An Empirical Analysis of Process and Product Patenting: A Simultaneous Equation Framework," *Journal of Industrial Economics* Volume 34, Number 3, March 1986, pp. 319–330.

[57]The data set combines information from the Federal Trade Commission's Line of Business Program with information on 15,112 patents issued between June 1976 and 1977, and is due to Scherer. See Scherer, F. M. "The Propensity to Patent," *International Journal of Industrial Organization* Volume 1, Number 1, March 1983, pp. 107–128.

Process patents are positively related to market concentration, which is consistent with the Schumpeterian hypothesis. There are also more process patents in industries that are high in technological opportunity.

New product patents, in contrast, are not affected (in a statistically significant way) by market concentration or technological opportunity. But there is less patenting of new products in industries in which average spending on advertising per dollar of sales is high. This confirms the importance of product differentiation as an incentive for new product innovation. If products are already differentiated by advertising and other sales efforts, firms produce fewer new products than would otherwise be the case.

Patents and Antitrust Policy

The patent system, which grants a legal monopoly for a limited period, conflicts with antitrust laws, which promote competition. At a fundamental level, however, this conflict vanishes. The patent system grants a temporary legal monopoly as a way of promoting dynamic efficiency—efficiency in the production of technological advance. Antitrust laws promote competition as a way of obtaining static efficiency—efficiency in the production and allocation of resources using existing technology. Both policies aim to improve market performance.[58]

It has nonetheless been necessary for courts to define the limits that antitrust policy places on the legal monopoly granted by patent policy to the innovator. The relationship between patent and antitrust law has developed along lines broadly consistent with Sections 1 and 2 of the Sherman Act. A patent holder may exploit the legal monopoly granted by the patent, but cannot use a patent as an element of conspiracy or to interfere with the ability of other firms to compete.[59] Two antitrust decisions illustrate these themes.

Two distinct issues arose in *United States v. General Electric Company,*[60] which involved three patents related to electric light bulbs. The patents were held by General Electric and gave it effective control of the market for electric light bulbs. General Electric's market share in 1921 was 69 per cent; another 24 per cent of the market was supplied by manufacturers licensed by General Electric to use its patents.

The first antitrust question in the case involved General Electric's network for the distribution of light bulbs. Some light bulbs were distributed directly

[58]Bowman, Ward S. *Patent and Antitrust Law: A Legal and Economic Appraisal.* Chicago: The University of Chicago Press, 1973, p. 1.

[59]In particular, a patent holder cannot tie the sale of the patented product to the sale of some other unpatented good. See *International Salt Co., Inc., v. United States*, 332 U.S. 392 (1947). We take up the topic of tying in Chapter 15.

[60]272 U.S. 476 (1926).

by General Electric and others by some 400 large distributors who serviced contracts negotiated by General Electric. General Electric also maintained a network of some 21,000 smaller distributors. The light bulbs were marketed on an *agency basis*. General Electric retained ownership. Dealers did not pay General Electric for the bulbs until they were sold. The bulbs were sold at prices set by General Electric, subject to restrictions on the kinds of consumers to whom sales could be made.[61] Did this complex distribution network constitute a restraint of trade?:[62]

> it is said that the system of distribution is so complicated and involves such a very large number of agents, distributed throughout the entire country, that the very size and comprehensiveness of the scheme brings it within the Antitrust law. We do not question that in a suit under the Anti-trust Act the circumstance that the combination effected secures domination of so large a part of the business as to control prices is usually most important in proof of a monopoly violating the act. But under the patent law the patentee is given by statute a monopoly of the making, using and selling the patented article. The extent of his monopoly . . . is not limited in the grant of his patent, and the comprehensiveness of his control of the business in the sale of the patented article is not necessarily an indication of illegality. . . . As long as he makes no effort to fasten upon ownership of the articles he sells control of the prices at which his purchaser shall sell, it makes no difference how widespread his monopoly. It is only when he adopts a combination with others by which he steps out of the scope of his patent rights and seeks to control and restrain those to whom he has sold his patented articles in their subsequent disposition of what is theirs that he comes within the operation of the Anti-trust Act.

It is the premise of the antitrust laws that markets best allocate resources and set prices. If society grants a legal monopoly via a patent, the patent holder is entitled to set the price at which he sells. As long as the patent holder does not combine with others or restrain the terms of resale after the property is sold, the antitrust laws will not interfere with the use of the monopoly granted by patent law.[63]

The second antitrust question present in the *General Electric* case involved the terms by which General Electric licensed other firms—primarily Westing-

---

[61]In the *General Electric* case, this raises issues of resale price maintenance and nonprice vertical restraints, which we treat in Chapter 17. It is instructive to compare Chief Justice Taft's remarks on agency sales in *General Electric* with Justice Fortas' much maligned opinion in *Schwinn*.

[62]272 U.S. 476, at 485.

[63]See *United States v. General Electric Company*, 358 F. Supp. 731 (1973), which found the agency system in violation of the Sherman Act after the expiration of the relevant patents.

house—to produce light bulbs. Under the terms of the license, Westinghouse was obligated to sell the light bulbs it manufactured at the same prices as General Electric light bulbs.[64] Would the antitrust laws limit this use of a legal monopoly?:[65]

> It is well settled . . . that where a patentee makes the patented article and sells it, he can exercise no future control over what the purchaser may wish to do with the article after his purchase. It has passed beyond the scope of the patentee's rights. . . . But the question is a different one which arises when we consider what a patentee who grants a license to one to make and vend the patented article may do in limiting the licensee in the exercise of the right to sell. The patentee may make and grant a license to another to make and use the patented articles but without his right to sell them. . . . If the patentee goes further and licenses the selling of the articles, may he limit the selling by limiting the method of sale and the price? We think he may do so provided the conditions of sale are normally and reasonably adapted to secure pecuniary reward for the patentee's monopoly. One of the valuable elements of the exclusive right of a patentee is to acquire profit by the price at which the article is sold. . . . When the patentee licenses another to make and vend and retains the right to continue to make and vend on his own account, the price at which his licensee will sell will necessarily affect the price at which he can sell his own patented goods. It would seem entirely reasonable that he should say to the licensee, "Yes, you may make and sell articles under my patent but not so as to destroy the profit that I wish to obtain by making them and selling them myself."

So long as a patent holder acts alone, licenses that allow the patent holder to realize a profit from the monopoly granted under the patent do not violate the antitrust laws.

It is otherwise if the patent holder acts in concert with others, as indicated by the opinion in *Hartford-Empire Co. et al., v. United States.*[66] Hartford-Empire, Owens-Illinois Glass Company, Corning Glass Works, Hazel-Atlas Glass Company, and other companies owned and cross-licensed among themselves more than 800 patents concerning machinery for the manufacture of glass containers. Their control of the industry was effective: in 1938, 94 per cent of the glass containers manufactured in the United States were made on machines subject to the patent pool.

The Supreme Court, quoting an earlier decision, made it clear that the use

---

[64]And apparently, although this may have been an informal understanding, to distribute Westinghouse's light bulbs in a way similar to that of General Electric.

[65]272 U.S. 476, at 489–490.

[66]323 U.S. 386 (1945).

of patents to further conspiracy in restraint of trade is contrary to the antitrust laws:[67]

> "Rights conferred by patents are indeed very definite and extensive, but they do not give any more than other rights a universal license against positive prohibitions. The Sherman law is a limitation of rights, rights which may be pushed to evil consequences and therefore restrained."
> . . . It is clear that, by cooperative arrangements and binding agreements, the appellant corporations, over a period of years, regulated and suppressed competition in the use of glassmaking machinery and employed their joint patent position to allocate fields of manufacture and to maintain prices of unpatented glassware.

Section 2 of the Sherman Act, which permits monopoly gained through competition on the merits, also permits the exercise of the lawful monopoly granted by a patent. But a patent does not grant the right to combine with others in restraint of trade, which is a violation of Section 1 of the Sherman Act.

Research Joint Ventures

A research joint venture is a cooperative effort to develop a new product or technology. Under such an arrangement, the cost and risk of the development process are shared by the parent firms. If a new product or process is developed, it will be made available to all of the parent firms.

A research joint venture may promote efficiency in a number of ways. It may be able to reach a size that would be unavailable to any single parent firm. It has the effect of alleviating some of the appropriability problems raised by the spillover of knowledge within an industry. A research joint venture will not eliminate the possibility that other firms will be able to take a free ride on the knowledge produced by a research activity. But it does determine, at least with respect to partner firms, how valuable assets produced by the joint venture will be utilized. By making knowledge a common asset, a research joint venture helps disseminate information, once acquired, throughout the economy.

But research joint ventures may have undesirable effects as well. Such a project is likely to preclude competitive research among member firms. The number of approaches used to attack a research problem will be reduced, which may turn out to be inefficient from a social point of view.[68]

---

[67]323 U.S. 386, at 406–407, quoting *Standard Sanitary Manufacturing Co. v. United States*, 226 U.S. 20, at 49.

[68]See Nelson, Richard R. "Uncertainty."

The exchange of information among parent firms that is essential in managing research joint ventures may contribute to the tacit collusion that tips market performance under oligopoly toward monopoly.[69] A joint venture may serve as a device to punish an overly rivalrous partner[70] "by withholding the continuing cooperation essential for joint venture success." A research joint venture, which is a common asset of the member firms, may encourage the strategic use of R&D to raise entry costs. Entry barriers are also a common asset that will benefit all parent firms.[71]

For antitrust purposes, research joint ventures are judged under a rule of reason. There has been little policy concern with joint ventures for basic research. In contrast, joint ventures for applied research, formed by leading firms in the same industry and involving restraints on the use of results that seem unrelated to the purpose of the venture, have attracted the attention of antitrust authorities.[72] Joint ventures that are a cover for collusion are, of course, illegal per se under Section 1 of the Sherman Act.

The National Cooperative Research Act of 1984 is designed to improve productivity by encouraging R&D:[73]

> The framers and supporters of the law hoped . . . that the promotion of cooperation would increase net social benefit of R&D investment by improving appropriability, lowering costs, lowering risks, decreasing wasteful overbidding (in the sense of too many trials), and reducing actual duplication . . .

The National Cooperative Research Act mandates the use of the rule of reason in antitrust cases involving research joint ventures. It permits firms to notify the Federal Trade Commission and the Justice Department of a joint

---

[69]As noted by Katz, Michael L., "An Analysis of Cooperative Research and Development," *Rand Journal of Economics* Volume 17, Number 4, Winter 1986, p. 541, "a cooperative R&D arrangement might serve as a 'chance for the guys to get together' to discuss means of colluding in the product market (possibly having the effect of raising [the conjectural variations parameter])." This view is emphasized by Pfeffer, Jeffrey and Nowak, Phillip, "Patterns of Joint Venture Activity," *Antitrust Bulletin* Volume 21, Number 2, Spring 1976, pp. 315–339 (a study that covers all types of joint ventures), and contested by Berg, Sanford V. and Friedman, Philip, "Causes and Effects of Joint Venture Activity: Knowledge Acquisition vs. Parent Horizontality," *Antitrust Bulletin* Volume 25, Number 1, Spring 1980, pp. 143–168.

[70]Brodley, Joseph F. "Joint Ventures and Antitrust Policy," *Harvard Law Review* Volume 95, Number 7, May 1982, pp. 1530–1531.

[71]Vickers, John. "Pre-emptive Patenting, Joint Ventures, and the Persistence of Oligopoly," *International Journal of Industrial Organization* Volume 3, Number 3, September 1985, pp. 262–263.

[72]*Antitrust Guide Concerning Research Joint Ventures.* Washington, D.C.: U.S. Department of Justice, Antitrust Division, November 1980.

[73]Scott, John T. "Diversification versus Cooperation in R&D Investment," Dartmouth College Working Paper 86-10, November 1986, revised 1987, p. 27.

venture, after which member firms are liable for actual damages, rather than treble damages, for any antitrust violations stemming from the project.

A study of joint research projects registered during the first 18 months after the enactment of the National Cooperative Research Act finds that [74]

> [t]he cooperative R&D protected by the NCRA has occurred in industries that were, during the 1970s, concentrated, high productivity, and having R&D activities purposively combined by diversified firms with R&D in other industries. . . . the act does not appear to be fostering R&D where competing firms dared not invest because of appropriability problems.

This raises the possibility that the National Cooperative Research Act actually makes society worse off[75]

> because from society's standpoint, the gains from increases in appropriability may be outweighed by the losses from decreases in competitive races . . . for the innovative rewards. That is because the joint ventures appear to be taking place where R&D activity and productivity have been relatively robust.

At present, however, our experience with the National Cooperative Research Act is too limited to allow us to draw final conclusions.

Summary

R&D is a complex phenomenon and raises complex issues for public policy. There is some reason to think that large firm size—and, in some cases, market power—favor innovation. Intense price competition stimulates innovation as firms seek to escape the forces of competitive markets. But demand conditions and technological opportunity are equally important. Particularly for new product innovation, R&D is an alternative to advertising and other sales efforts as a device to differentiate products and raise the cost of entry for rivals.

Public policy toward innovative activity requires a delicate balance. Overly strict enforcement of the antitrust laws with respect to patent holders frustrates the goal of encouraging innovation. Overly relaxed enforcement may allow strategic behavior that would frustrate competition on the merits.

This tradeoff has been resolved by treating patent holders the same way as any other holder of a legally acquired monopoly. A patent holder may exercise his monopoly, but may not combine with others to acquire a greater monopoly or to use the patent to impede competition in other markets.

[74]Ibid., p. 35.

[75]Ibid., p. 39.

Public policy toward research joint ventures balances the beneficial effect of increased appropriability of research output—a private benefit that should encourage research activity—with the adverse effect of cooperative research on competitive research. Policy in this area has favored cooperative research, perhaps excessively so.

Problems

12-1 Compare monopoly profit plus consumers' surplus in a monopolized market with demand curve

$$P = a - bQ$$

with consumers' surplus in a competitive market with demand curve

$$P = a - 2bQ,$$

when the cost per unit is a constant, c, in either case.

12-2 Consider the models illustrated in Figures 12-1 through 12-3. Suppose the cost reduction allowed by innovation is so great that $P_2 < c_1$. Analyze the incentive to invent under competition and monopoly (for specificity, use the demand curve $P = a - bQ$ for the case where both markets have the same demand curve).

Paper Topics

12-1 Explore the legal and economic implications of the rules that apply to the patenting of the output of biotechnological R&D.

12-2 Discuss the development and marketing of the cotton gin by Eli Whitney.

12-3 Study the relationship between department size and research output at your college or university. You will have to confront the following issues: How do you measure research output (working papers, published articles, books)? How do you correct for differences across specialties in rates of research output? How do you treat differences in teaching obligations? Are individual faculty members in larger departments more productive than those in smaller departments, all else equal?

12-4 Examine the record of the U.S. steel industry in terms of technological progressiveness (for starters, see Adams, Walter, "Big Steel, Invention, and Innovation," *Quarterly Journal of Economics* Volume 80, Number 2, May 1966, pp. 167–189, a comment and reply in the same journal the following year, and Oster, Sharon, "The Diffusion of Innovation Among Steel Firms: The Basic Oxygen Furnace," *Bell Journal of Economics* Volume 13, Number 1, Spring 1982, pp. 45–56). You may wish to focus on the development of steel "minimills"; in this case, see Miller, Jack Robert. "Steel Minimills," *Scientific American* Volume 250, Number 5, May 1984, pp. 32–39 and Szekely, Julian. "Can Advanced Technology Save the U.S. Steel Industry?" *Scientific American* Volume 257, Number 1, July 1987, pp. 34–41.

12-5 Discuss the legal and economic implications of *SCM Corporation v. Xerox Corporation,* 463 F. Supp. 983 (1978), which concerns patent and antitrust law.

12-6 Contrast the views of the patent/antitrust law overlap in Turner, Donald F., "Patents, Antitrust, and Innovation," *University of Pittsburgh Law Review* Volume 28, Number 2, December 1966, pp. 151–160, and Bowman, Ward S., *Patent and Antitrust Law: A Legal and Economic Appraisal.* Chicago: The University of Chicago Press, 1973.

13

Industrial Economics and International Trade

> *Merchants have no country. The mere spot they stand on does not constitute so strong an attachment as that from which they draw their gains.*
>
> **Thomas Jefferson**

Industrial economists have long recognized the importance of foreign competition for domestic market performance. In contrast, international economists have traditionally taken an aggregate, general equilibrium approach to the analysis of trade flows. This analysis has focused on differences across countries in endowments of factors of production—land, labor, capital, and natural resources—to explain international trade.

More recently, economists who study international trade have supplemented their traditional approach to the analysis of trade flows by using industry-level models to explore the impact of market structure on imports and exports. This approach emphasizes elements of market structure—scale economies, product differentiation, and transaction costs—as factors motivating trade flows.

As might be expected, this new analysis of trade flows draws heavily on the economics of market and firm structure. Here we review what industrial economics has to say about trade flows and their impact on domestic market performance.

Determinants of Trade Flows/Foreign Direct Investment

Explanations Drawn from International Economics

According to the Heckscher-Ohlin *theory of comparative advantage,* differences in factor endowments across countries are the engine of international trade. Countries that are relatively rich in capital equipment will specialize in the production of goods that require a relatively large amount of capital. Countries that are relatively rich in labor will specialize in the production of goods that require a relatively large amount of labor. Capital-rich countries will trade capital-intensive products for the labor-intensive products of labor-rich countries.[1]

Humblingly enough, attempts to verify this theory in its basic form for the United States have generally been unsuccessful. Examinations of U.S. trade with all other foreign nations typically show that the United States, on balance, exports labor-intensive goods and imports capital-intensive goods, contrary to the predictions of the factor proportions theory of trade flows.[2] The stubborn rejection of the theory by the facts has motivated various extensions of the *factor proportions theory* of trade flows.

One extension focuses on the fact that what economists taking a macro view of the economy call *labor* is in fact quite heterogeneous. Labor includes blue-collar workers on the assembly line, highly trained researchers who develop new products or processes, and engineers who put them to use. The prediction that countries with a highly skilled work force will, all else equal, tend to export goods produced with skilled labor is a natural extension of the basic factor proportions theory of trade flows.

A similar extension creates a *product life cycle* or *technology gap* theory of foreign trade. A country that invests heavily in R&D will place new products on world markets or produce familiar products at a lower cost. R&D-intensive countries will enjoy a momentary comparative advantage in the production of such goods. But as knowledge of the new products and technologies spreads, that comparative advantage will vanish. R&D-intensive countries will continually reinvent their comparative advantage; other countries will specialize in the production and export of familiar goods produced with mature technologies.

Market Structure, Firm Structure, and Foreign Trade[3]

The focus of international trade has traditionally been at the macro, national level. Explanations are sought for a country's aggregate trade flows, imports

---

[1]The factor proportions theory of international trade is traced from the early-nineteenth-century work of David Ricardo. For an analysis at the industry level, see Williams, James R. "Commodity Trade and the Factor Proportions Theorem," *Canadian Journal of Economics* Volume 10, Number 2, May 1977, pp. 282–288.

[2]Leontief, Wassily. "Domestic Production and Foreign Trade; The American Capital Position Re-Examined," *Proceedings of the American Philosophical Society* Volume 97, September 1953, pp. 332–349, and "Factor Proportions and the Structure of American Trade: Further Theoretical and Empirical Analysis," *Review of Economics and Statistics* Volume 38, November 1956, pp. 386–407. For discussion, see Hufbauer, G. C. "The Impact of National Characteristics & Technology on the Commodity Composition of Trade in Manufactured Goods," in Vernon, Raymond, editor, *The Technology Factor in International Trade*. New York: National Bureau of Economic Research, 1970, pp. 145–231, especially pp. 167–172.

[3]For a recent survey, see Caves, Richard E. *Multinational Enterprise and Economic Analysis*. Cambridge: Cambridge University Press, 1982.

and exports of all commodities and often to all other countries. However, drawing on their own traditions, industrial economists' analyses of trade flows have more often been at the micro, industry level.

Horizontal Relationships Across National Boundaries

Three strategies are available to firms that sell a product in more than one country. A firm may produce in its home market and export to a foreign market. A firm may produce in its home market for sale in its home market, but open a plant abroad for sale in a foreign market. Or a firm may arrange a contract with a foreign firm—a license—and have the product produced by an independent firm in the foreign market.

For the moment, we focus on the first two alternatives: export and foreign direct investment. Figure 13-1(a) describes the decision of a firm that chooses to export to a foreign market.

We suppose that the firm's markets can be described by demand curves, one for the home (domestic) market and one for the export (foreign) market.[4] We recognize two types of fixed cost.[5] The first, F_{corp}, is the cost of fixed assets that benefit all divisions of a firm. It would include the costs of corporate management, of a corporate R&D program, and of promotional activity to develop a corporate brand name.

The second element of fixed cost is associated with plant rather than corporate operations. F_{dp} is the fixed cost of operating a plant in the domestic market.[6]

Suppose now that there are constant marginal costs, c, per unit of output in domestic or foreign plants. A firm that produces at home and exports to foreign markets will operate one plant, bearing only one load of fixed plant costs, but it will have to pay shipping costs (s per unit) and any tariffs (t per unit) to market its product in the foreign market.

A profit-maximizing firm will market, in each country, a quantity that makes

---

[4]If the product being produced is standardized, these are residual demand curves, and their location will depend on how the firm expects rivals to react. If the product being produced is differentiated, these are demand curves for the particular variety produced by the firm.

[5]See Caves, op. cit., chapter 1; Helpman, Elhanan. "A Simple Theory of International Trade with Multinational Corporations," *Journal of Political Economy* Volume 92, Number 3, June 1984, pp. 451–471; Smith, Alasdair. "Strategic Investment, Multinational Corporations and Trade Policy," *European Economic Review* Volume 31, Numbers 1–2, February–March 1987, pp. 89–96.

[6]In a more realistic model, we would have a firm face a menu of options for plant size, each size having its own fixed cost and, perhaps, marginal cost. This consideration is not essential to understanding the export/foreign direct investment choice, and we abstract from it here.

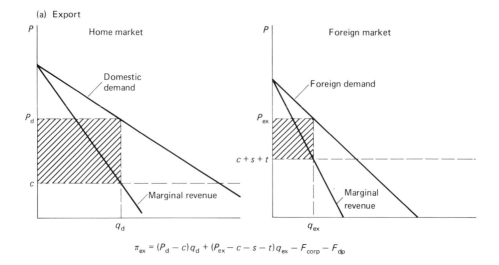

(a) Export

$$\pi_{ex} = (P_d - c)\,q_d + (P_{ex} - c - s - t)\,q_{ex} - F_{corp} - F_{dp}$$

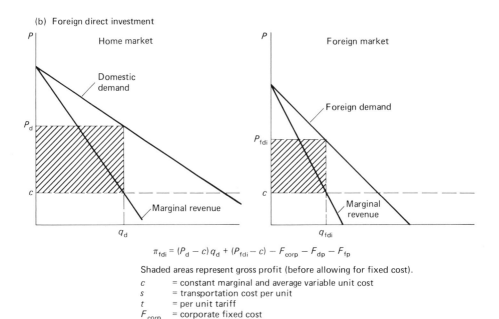

(b) Foreign direct investment

$$\pi_{fdi} = (P_d - c)\,q_d + (P_{fdi} - c) - F_{corp} - F_{dp} - F_{fp}$$

Shaded areas represent gross profit (before allowing for fixed cost).

c	= constant marginal and average variable unit cost
s	= transportation cost per unit
t	= per unit tariff
F_{corp}	= corporate fixed cost
F_{dp}	= fixed cost per domestic plant
F_{fp}	= fixed cost per foreign plant

Figure 13-1   The export vs. foreign direct investment decision.

its marginal revenue in that country its equal to marginal cost.[7] These sales levels are illustrated in Figure 13-1(a). The firm's profit is

$$\pi_{ex} = (P_d - c)q_d + (P_{ex} - c - s - t)q_{ex} - F_{corp} - F_{dp}. \quad (13.1)$$

Figure 13-1(a) also shows, as the shaded areas, the firm's gross profit (revenue minus variable costs), which does not allow for fixed costs.

A few conclusions are evident from Figure 13-1(a). The greater the unit shipping or tariff costs, the greater the firm's marginal cost of supplying the foreign market and the smaller its profit-maximizing level of sales in that market if it chooses an export strategy. Tariffs and shipping costs discourage export sales. Indeed, if $s + t$ is sufficiently large, the profit-maximizing level of export sales is zero.

Compared with export sales, one advantage and one disadvantage attend the opening of a foreign plant. The advantage is that by opening a plant abroad, the firm will avoid shipping and tariff charges. By engaging in foreign direct investment, a firm reduces its marginal cost of supplying the foreign market.

The disadvantage of foreign direct investment is that opening an additional plant means that the corporation must cover an additional element of plant-level fixed costs. Further, the fixed cost of operating a foreign plant, F_{fp}, can be expected to be greater than that of operating a domestic plant. For a firm moving into alien territory is a stranger in a strange land, and entry will involve fixed costs that do not arise on the home market: the cost of acquiring information about the way business is done in the foreign market.[8]

Taking account of the lower marginal cost but greater fixed cost of foreign direct investment, a firm that chooses to open a plant abroad will earn the following profit:

$$\pi_{fdi} = (P_d - c)q_d + (P_{fdi} - c)q_{fdi} - F_{corp} - F_{dp} - F_{fp}. \quad (13.2)$$

A profit-maximizing firm will select outputs that equate marginal revenue with marginal cost, market by market. Since the marginal cost in the foreign market is lower under foreign direct investment than under an export regime, sales in the foreign market should be greater under foreign direct investment (all else equal).

Whether a firm will prefer export or foreign direct investment depends on

[7]By assuming a constant marginal cost, we abstract from an important factor: the possibility that increasing total output, through sales in foreign markets, may lower the marginal cost or perhaps (through learning by doing) the entire average variable cost curve. Such cost savings are a benefit of trade that we ignore for ease of exposition.

[8]Caves, op. cit., p. 13.

which marketing strategy yields the greater profit. If tariffs and shipping costs are low in relation to price, export is likely to be the more profitable option. It follows that bulky products, which sell at a low price per unit, are less likely to be exported. High tariffs per unit will discourage export and encourage foreign direct investment.[9]

If the fixed cost of operating a foreign plant is small, foreign direct investment is more advantageous. It follows that a firm is more likely to invest in a country where business practices are similar to those of the home country. American firms should be more likely to open plants in English-speaking Canada than Japan, for example, all else equal.[10]

A firm that is already operating in a home market has a fixed cost advantage over a new firm contemplating entry into a foreign market. The operating firm has already committed the assets underlying the corporate fixed costs, F_{corp}. When a home-based firm enters a foreign market, its marginal commitment of fixed assets bears costs F_{fp}, the fixed costs associated with operating a plant in a foreign country. For a new enterprise starting up with a base in a foreign market, the marginal commitment of fixed assets bears costs $F_{corp} + F_{dp}$— plant costs in a home market but also corporate overhead costs.

Where corporate overhead costs are large, firms that are already established abroad are the most likely entrants into horizontally related markets. Such corporate overhead costs may reflect a management superstructure, a research program, a distribution network, or a program of product differentiation. These intangible assets encourage diversification across national boundaries.[11] Foreign direct investment is more likely to occur where such assets are important. It is not by coincidence that automobile companies operate on a world basis.

Licensing[12]

Foreign direct investment is not the only option open to a firm that rejects an export strategy. It may grant a license to a firm based in the foreign market, allow the foreign firm to produce and sell in that market and collect a royalty on the sales.

From the point of view of the firm granting the license, the unique advantage of licensing is that it avoids the fixed cost of acquiring information about the way business is conducted in the foreign market. The foreign firm, the licensee, already has this information: more than anything else, information about the foreign market is what the foreign-based firm brings to the bargain. Licensing is therefore more likely to occur when information costs are large relative to

---

[9]The same is true for nontariff trade barriers, such as quotas.

[10]Caves, op. cit., pp. 14–15.

[11]Ibid., pp. 3–7.

[12]Ibid., pp. 204–207. Chapter 12's discussion of patents touched briefly on licenses of technology.

the profit to be made. In very small and very foreign markets, a firm that rejects exporting may sensibly decide to license a local firm to produce its product.

Licensing, however, involves all of the transactions costs that plague inter-firm-contractual relationships (Chapter 9). A firm exploring the possibility of granting a license will have limited information about the target market. It will most likely have a range of possible licensees, all of which will represent themselves as best qualified. Accurate information about their qualifications will be impacted in the target market, and the license-granting firm will not be able to rely on the representations of the potential licensees (guile). Once a particular firm is chosen, the licensor is likely to commit specific sunk assets to the relationship, and over time, bargaining power will shift to the licensee. Transaction costs, in short, militate against licensing as a strategy for serving foreign markets.

Market Structure and the Export/Foreign Direct Investment Decision[13]

Economies of Scale

We have seen that economies of scale at the corporate level—which will arise when F_{corp} is large—favor foreign direct investment. At the same time, however, economies of scale at the plant level favor export.

The more important are economies of scale at the plant level, the more profitable it will be to consolidate production in a single plant. Such consolidation will allow the firm to benefit from the low average cost attained at high output levels.

Economies of scale are likely to be especially important in encouraging firms in small countries to export. It is only by exporting that such firms will be able to attain the economies of large-scale production.[14] When minimum efficient plant scale is large in relation to the home market, export is favored over foreign direct investment.

Scale Economies and Product Differentiation[15]

The combination of economies of scale and product differentiation has emerged as the core of the new industrial economics' analysis of international trade.

[13]The seminal discussion is Hymer, Stephen H. *The International Operations of National Firms: A Study of Direct Foreign Investment.* Cambridge, Mass.: MIT Press, 1976 (reprint of the 1960 dissertation). See papers by John H. Dunning and Alan M. Rugman, David J. Teece, and Donald J. Lecraw in *American Economic Review,* Volume 75, Number 2, May 1985.

[14]Glejser, Herbert, Jacquemin, Alexis, and Petit, Jean. "Exports in an Imperfect Competition Framework: An Analysis of 1,446 Exporters," *Quarterly Journal of Economics* Volume 94, Number 3, May 1980, pp. 507–524, Proposition 1.

[15]See Ethier, Wilfred J. "National and International Returns to Scale in the Modern Theory of International Trade," *American Economic Review* Volume 72, Number 3, June 1982, pp. 389–405; Krugman, Paul. "New Theories of Trade Among Industrial Countries," *American Economic Review* Volume 73, Number 2, May 1983, pp. 343–347; and for a comprehensive treatment, Helpman, Elhanan and Krugman, Paul R. *Market Structure and Foreign Trade.* Cambridge, Mass.: MIT Press, 1985.

The orthodox theory of international trade emphasizes differences in factor endowments as the engine of trade. In this view, countries that are relatively rich in capital will have a comparative advantage in the production of capital-intensive goods—goods that require relatively more capital than labor to be produced. Such countries will, in this view, produce capital-intensive goods and export them to other countries that are labor- or land-rich and that, therefore, specialize in the production of labor- and land-intensive goods, respectively.

This elegant and logically compelling factor proportions theory of international trade has had mixed success, at best, in explaining trade flows.[16] It is particularly unsatisfactory in explaining a major element of post–World War II trade: trade among industrialized countries, with similar factor endowments, in different varieties of the same broad product class.

The combination of economies of scale and product differentiation can explain this intraindustry trade. Product differentiation encourages the production of multiple varieties of a product, but economies of scale encourage the consolidation of production of a single variety in one country. Firms in different countries specialize in production and trade one variety for another. The combination of product differentiation and economies of scale encourages international trade and discourages foreign direct investment.

Oligopoly[17]

Figure 13-1 pictures the firm as a monopolist on its own demand curve. We can use Chapter 5's reaction curve analysis of quantity-setting oligopoly to examine the impact of oligopolistic interactions on the export/foreign direct investment decision.[18]

Figure 13-2 shows reaction curves for a foreign market in which a single domestic firm competes with a single foreign firm. Two reaction curves are shown for the domestic firm. The first is the domestic firm's reaction curve under an export strategy when its marginal cost includes the cost of production, shipping, and tariffs $(c + s + t)$. The second is the domestic firm's reaction curve under a foreign direct investment strategy when its marginal cost is the cost of production (c). Recall from Chapter 5 that when oligopolists behave independently, in a Cournot model a firm with lower marginal cost enjoys a larger market share. A firm that serves a foreign market by export places itself at a marginal cost disadvantage: it must pay shipping and tariff charges on every unit sold. If this firm opens a foreign plant, it must cover the associated fixed plant costs, as previously discussed. But it will benefit in one way that our earlier analysis did not indicate. By operating a plant in the foreign market,

---

[16]Leontief, op. cit.

[17]This section follows Smith, op. cit.

[18]See Figures 5-6 and 5-7 and the accompanying text.

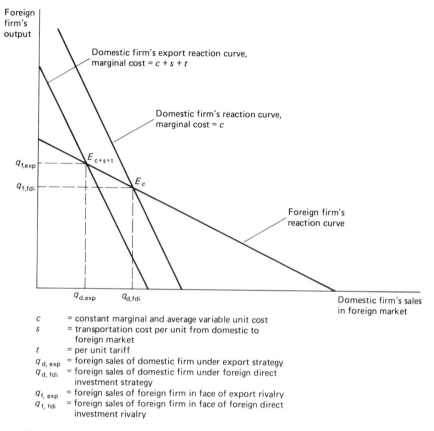

c = constant marginal and average variable unit cost
s = transportation cost per unit from domestic to foreign market
t = per unit tariff
$q_{d,\,exp}$ = foreign sales of domestic firm under export strategy
$q_{d,\,fdi}$ = foreign sales of domestic firm under foreign direct investment strategy
$q_{f,\,exp}$ = foreign sales of foreign firm in face of export rivalry
$q_{f,\,fdi}$ = foreign sales of foreign firm in face of foreign direct investment rivalry

Figure 13-2 Foreign-market reaction curves under export/foreign direct investment.

its marginal cost will fall and its reaction curve will shift away from the origin. In the new oligopoly equilibrium, the domestic firm's output will be larger, and the foreign firm's output smaller, than under an export strategy. Oligopolistic interactions in Cournot quantity-setting markets favor foreign direct investment.

Concentration[19]

In this section, we assume that firms are better able to exercise market power in concentrated markets. Does market power favor exports or foreign direct

---

[19]White, Lawrence J. "Industrial Organization and International Trade," *American Economic Review* Volume 64, Number 6, December 1974, pp. 1013–1020. See also Glejser et al., op. cit.

investment? The answer depends on whether or not trade policy permits dumping.

We know from Chapter 2 (and Chapter 5) that the degree of market power depends on the price elasticity of demand. If the quantity demanded falls rapidly in response to modest price increase, a profit-maximizing firm or group of firms that exercises market power will prefer to set a price near cost rather than give up sales.

It follows—and we will see formally in Chapter 15—that if a firm exercising market power serves markets with different elasticities, it will profit by setting a lower price in markets with higher price elasticities of demand.

It seems reasonable to suppose that a firm or group of firms protected from rivalry in its home market will face a more elastic demand in foreign markets. In foreign markets, such a firm will encounter competition from foreign suppliers that it does not face in its home market. Firms with market power in their home market will typically prefer to set a lower price in foreign markets than at home.

With a lower price abroad, firms exercising market power will export more than a competitive industry with the same marginal cost structure.[20] Thus market power at home favors export sales.

But this conclusion depends critically on the assumption that firms are permitted to charge a lower price abroad than at home. Such dumping will be resisted by competitors in foreign markets, who will seek to have their governments compel a single price in all markets. If dumping is forbidden, firms may be able to tailor prices to markets by opening plants in foreign markets. This is particularly likely to occur if the product supplied by foreign plants can be differentiated in some low-cost way from the product of home-market plants. Such differentiation will facilitate the charging of different prices in different markets. When dumping is forbidden, domestic market power encourages foreign direct investment.

The theory of limit pricing yields a more conclusive prediction about the impact of domestic market power on the role of foreign suppliers. Firms with market power will hold price above marginal cost. The higher the domestic price, the greater the profit to be gained by entry. The more concentrated are sales in the hands of domestic producers, the greater domestic producers' control of home market price and the more likely that they will set a price that induces entry by foreign suppliers.[21] Whether this entry takes the form of

---

[20]White, op. cit., Figure 1.

[21]Particularly in concentrated markets, domestic firms may behave strategically to discourage foreign entry. But the costs of foreign suppliers will be known imperfectly at best. Even if firms that exercise market power limit the price, they are more likely to invite entry inadvertently than a competitive industry.

imports or of investment by foreign producers in the home market depends on a balancing of fixed and marginal costs, as pictured in Figure 13-1.

Vertical Relationships Across National Boundaries[22]

The transaction cost approach to vertical integration (Chapter 9) can be applied to vertical integration across as well as within national boundaries. The transaction costs that favor vertical integration over markets as a way of organizing production include bounded rationality, opportunism, and small-numbers bargaining problems.

A firm is likely to be even less able to anticipate possible problems in foreign markets—with which it is unfamiliar—than in its home market. For the same reason—limited information—a foreign firm will be vulnerable to opportunistic misrepresentation (putting the best foot forward) by its international partner.

When a firm sinks assets in a foreign economy, it is virtually certain that at some point it will face small-numbers bargaining problems. Possession is nine-tenths of the law, especially in a foreign court. If operation in a foreign market involves investment in an extensive distribution network or in product-differentiating marketing efforts tailored to that market, vertical integration is encouraged.

When international sales involve product-differentiating R&D, problems of appropriability will similarly encourage vertical integration abroad. Otherwise, nasty disputes involving the ownership of the new product varieties are likely to arise.

Conglomerate Relationships Across National Boundaries

We have seen (Chapter 9) that the desire to even out fluctuations in the corporate income stream is a major motive for conglomerate diversification. A nationwide recession, however, will affect all national industries to some extent. If it is profitable to reduce fluctuations in the firm's income stream, a firm will be encouraged to supply foreign markets, whose macroeconomies are independent of that of the home market. In principle, such foreign markets could be supplied either by export or by direct foreign investment. The desire to reduce risk by spreading the firms' operations over many markets will encourage international operations, but the choice between exporting, foreign direct investment, and licensing will depend on the production and transaction cost considerations previously outlined.

---

[22]Caves, op. cit., pp. 15–24.

Table 13-1 Determinants of Trade Flows/Foreign Direct Investment

EXSR $= -0.262 + 0.023^a$Schooling $+ 0.588^a$Technical $- 0.567^b$ASR $R^2 = 0.487$	(1)
FDI $= -2.431 + 0.396^a$Technical $+ 0.294^a$ASR $- 0.776^a$MES $+ 0.450^a$ACR	
$+ 0.778^a$CR4 $R^2 = 0.653$	(2)

Notes:
EXSR = share of exports in shipments of domestic output
FDI = logarithm of share of foreign profits in total profits
ASR = advertising-sales ratio
MES = output of a minimum efficient scale plant as a fraction of industry output
ACR = absolute capital requirements of a minimum efficient scale plant
Schooling = median number of years of education of the work force
Technical = proportion of scientists and engineers in work force
For a sample of 72 roughly three-digit Standard Industrial Classification industries.

a indicates statistical significance at the 1 per cent level; such an estimate would occur by chance only once in 100 times, on average.

b indicates statistical significance at the 5 per cent level; such an estimate would occur by chance only once in 20 times, on average.

Sources: Pugel, Thomas A. *International Market Linkages and U.S. Manufacturing: Prices, Profits, and Patterns.* Cambridge, Mass.: Ballinger Publishing Company, 1978, and "The Determinants of Foreign Direct Investment: An Analysis of U.S. Manufacturing Industries," *Managerial and Decision Economics* Volume 2, Number 4, December 1981, pp. 220–228. Certain variables have been omitted from the results reported here.

Empirical Evidence[23]

Exports/Foreign Direct Investment

Table 13-1 presents a portion of the results of a study of exports and foreign direct investment for a single sample of U.S. industries.

The share of exports in the output of domestic producers is greater, the more highly qualified the work force. The number of years of education of the work force and the proportion of scientists and engineers are measures of *human capital*. As predicted by the theory of international trade, the United States, which has an abundance of skilled workers, is more likely to export products that require the labor of skilled workers.

Export share is smaller, however, when advertising per dollar of sales is large. Advertising, interpreted here as an index of product differentiation, reflects the existence of the kind of corporate overhead asset that is thought likely to favor foreign direct investment over export as a strategy for serving foreign markets.

[23]Perhaps the most ambitious study is Caves, Richard E., Porter, Michael E., and Spence, A. Michael. *Competition in the Open Economy.* Cambridge, Mass.: Harvard University Press, 1980. See also Marvel, Howard P. "Foreign Trade and Domestic Competition," *Economic Inquiry* Volume 18, Number 1, January 1980, pp. 103–122; and Grubaugh, Stephen G. "Determinants of Direct Foreign Investment," *Review of Economics and Statistics* Volume 69, Number 1, February 1987, pp. 149–152.

This is confirmed by equation (2), which shows that foreign direct investment is on average larger, the greater is advertising per dollar of sales. Equation (2) also shows that the larger is minimum efficient scale, the smaller is foreign direct investment. This provides indirect support for the hypothesis that economies of scale encourage the consolidation of production in fewer large plants. Equation (2) also suggests that home market concentration favors foreign direct investment.

Bilateral Trade Flows

A recent study[24] applies the international-industrial economics analysis of trade flows to the U.S.–Japanese trade balance. The results are much more congenial to the factor proportions theory of trade flows than might be expected, since studies of U.S. trade with all countries tend to find that U.S. exports tend to be labor intensive.

Results from the study are reproduced in Table 13-2. The analysis shows the average impact of product and industry characteristics on net exports at the industry level.

If X is the value of U.S. exports to Japan and M is the value of U.S. imports from Japan, the variable studied in Table 13-2 is

$$\text{TB} = \frac{X - M}{X + M}, \tag{13.3}$$

which is net exports as a fraction of total trade flows. TB will be positive if the U.S. industry sells more in Japan than the U.S. buys from the corresponding Japanese industry. TB will be small in magnitude when net exports are a small fraction of total trade flows.

According to the results reported in Table 13-2, U.S. industries that are capital intensive (KLR), highly differentiated (ASR), R&D intensive (R&D), and protected by nontariff barriers are more likely to have positive trade balances.

The finding that the capital-rich United States is more likely to have a positive trade balance in capital-intensive products is the prediction of the factor proportions theory. The finding that R&D favors exports tends to confirm product life cycle explanations of trade flows.

When an industry produces products that are heavily advertised, consumer tastes may be highly culture specific. It will be harder for foreign suppliers to market such products successfully, all else equal, and imports of such products should therefore be less than would otherwise be the case.

---

[24]Audretsch, David B. and Yamawaki, Hideki. "The Determinants of U.S.–Japanese Bilateral Trade." Berlin: International Institute of Management, May 1987.

Table 13-2 The U.S.–Japan Trade Balance

$TB = 0.1487 + 0.0106^aKLR - 0.1683^aSKILL - 0.0055^aCR4 + 55.6310^cASR$
$\qquad\qquad + 0.0258TARIFF + 0.0674^aNONTARIFF + 0.0787^aR\&D \qquad R^2 = 0.160$

Notes:

TB	= U.S. exports to Japan, less U.S. imports from Japan, as a fraction of total trade between the United States and Japan
KLR	= industry capital-labor ratio
SKILL	= difference between average annual industry wage per employee and average annual wage of an individual with less than 8 years of education
CR4	= 1977 four-firm concentration ratio
ASR	= advertising-sales ratio for convenience-good industries[25]
TARIFF	= ratio of U.S. tariff rate to average tariff rate of other industrialized countries
NONTARIFF	= index of nontariff trade barriers into the United States
R&D	= percentage of total employment accounted for by scientists and engineers engaged in research and development

For a sample of 230 four-digit Standard Industrial Classification industries, 1977.

a indicates statistical significance at the 1 per cent level; such an estimate would occur by chance only once in 100 times, on average.

b indicates statistical significance at the 5 per cent level; such an estimate would occur by chance only once in 20 times, on average.

c indicates statistical significance at the 10 per cent level; such an estimate would occur by chance only once in 10 times, on average.

Source: Audretsch, David B. and Yamawaki, Hideki. "The Determinants of U.S.–Japanese Bilateral Trade." Berlin: International Institute of Management, May 1987.

Nontariff trade barriers include quotas and other less rigid impediments to trade: minimum quality or safety regulations, for example. Industries that benefit from such barriers to foreign competition are more likely to have positive trade balances. Tariffs that protect U.S. markets have no significant effect on trade flows, perhaps because U.S. tariffs differ little from those that protect other countries.

For U.S. trade with Japan, the industry-level trade balance is more likely to be negative in industries that use skilled labor and in concentrated industries. The first result points out a difference between U.S. trade with Japan and U.S. trade overall. U.S. exports generally are favored by the use of skilled labor. The second result—imports larger than exports for products produced in concentrated industries—is consistent with the market power explanation of concentration and trade flows previously given. Firms in concentrated industries are more likely to hold price above marginal cost. All else equal, this is more

---

[25]Convenience goods are marketed through outlets in which assistance by sales personnel is of little importance in choosing among brands; sales assistance dominates producer advertising efforts for goods marketed through nonconvenience outlets. See Chapter 11.

Table 13-3 Imports and Price-Cost Margins

Belgium	$PCM = 14.54^a + 0.040\ CR4 - 0.254^a IMSR$	$R^2 = 0.27$	(1)
France	$PCM = 16.13^a + 0.238^a CR4 - 0.547^b IMSR$	$R^2 = 0.42$	(2)
Netherlands	$PCM = 51.19^a - 0.127\ CR4 - 0.459^c IMSR$	$R^2 = 0.27$	(3)

Notes:

PCM = price-cost margin
CR4 = four-firm seller concentration ratio
IMSR = imports as a fraction of domestic value of shipments

a indicates statistical significance at the 1 per cent level; such an estimate would occur by chance only once in 100 times, on average.

b indicates statistical significance at the 5 per cent level; such an estimate would occur by chance only once in 20 times, on average.

c indicates statistical significance at the 10 per cent level; such an estimate would occur by chance only once in 10 times, on average.

Source: Pagoulatos, Emilio and Sorenson Robert. "Foreign Trade, Concentration, and Profitability in Open Economies," *European Economic Review* Volume 8, 1976, pp. 255–267. Certain variables are omitted from the results reported here.

likely to create an opportunity for foreign suppliers to enter the domestic market.

Foreign Trade and Domestic Market Performance

Market Power

Structure-conduct-performance analysis suggests that the ability of domestic firms to exercise market power will be less in the presence of competition by foreign suppliers.

This is the prediction of the theory of limit pricing. The presence of fringe producers, who are able to expand output rapidly if it is profitable to do so, will limit the ability of dominant firms to hold price above marginal cost. Foreign suppliers, who will be able to shift output from other markets, will constitute a formidable fringe.

The same prediction is yielded by the theory of oligopolistic collusion. Recall from Chapter 6 the twin problems of oligopolists: agreement and adherence. Differences, we argued, create disagreements, and impede oligopolistic coordination. Foreign producers are likely to bring a perspective to the market that is very different from that of the home firms. Successful oligopolistic collusion, tacit or otherwise, is less likely when foreign producers have a large fraction of the market.

This expectation is confirmed by most empirical tests. Typical results are reported in Table 13-3, which indicates that price-cost margins are typically lower in three Common Market countries, the greater are imports relative to the shipments of domestic producers.[26]

Summary

The decision to export or engage in foreign direct investment responds to the same economic forces that determine firm structure within a national market. Overhead corporate assets—management superstructure, product differentiation, an innovative research team—encourage horizontal foreign direct investment. Transaction costs that encourage vertical integration within a market also promote it across national boundaries. Scale economies combined with product differentiation encourage intraindustry trade among industrialized countries.

The classical factor proportions theory of international trade flows is not confirmed for overall U.S. trade flows, although it does appear to provide a satisfactory explanation of the U.S. balance of trade with a major trading partner, Japan. Imports are more likely to occur, all else equal, into concentrated markets (which are more likely than unconcentrated markets to allow the exercise of market power by domestic firms). R&D, an investment in new products and more efficient production techniques, favors a positive trade balance.

At the same time, domestic market performance responds to international trade flows. Foreign competition is a significant factor limiting the ability of domestic firms to exercise market power.

Paper Topics

13-1 Evaluate the Foreign Trade Antitrust Improvements Act of 1982 and the U.S. Department of Justice Antitrust Division's March 1, 1977 Antitrust Guide for International Operations.

13-2 Two elements of antitrust proposals submitted by the Reagan administration to Congress in February 1986 involve international trade: the Foreign Trade Antitrust Improvements Act of 1986 and the Promoting Competition in Distressed Areas Act of 1986. Explain their motivation and their likely effect, if implemented.

---

[26]Neither concentration nor import share had a significant effect on Italian price-cost margins. See also Esposito, Louis and Esposito, Frances Ferguson. "Foreign Competition and Domestic Industry Profitability," *Review of Economics and Statistics* Volume 53, November 1971, pp. 343–353; Pugel, Thomas A. "Foreign Trade and US Market Performance," *Journal of Industrial Economics* Volume 29, Number 2, December 1980, pp. 119–129; Turner, Philip P. "Import Competition and the Profitability of United Kingdom Manufacturing Industry," *Journal of Industrial Economics* Volume 29, Number 2, December 1980, pp. 155–166; Marvel, op. cit.; and Koo, Anthony Y. C. and Martin, Stephen. "Market Structure and U.S. Trade Flows," *International Journal of Industrial Organization* Volume 2, Number 3, September 1984, pp. 173–198.

14

Industrial Economics and Macroeconomics

What man has made, man can change.

Frederick Moore Vinson

In the nether regions between industrial economics and macroeconomics, there is a vast literature concerning the influence—or lack of it—of market power on inflation and the aggregate output level. Like the Keynesian approach, which is central to modern macroeconomics, the roots of this literature lie in the Great Depression of 1929.

If price does not fall when demand falls, output will fall even more than it would with flexible prices. If output falls, the eventual result is unemployment and reduced income, which will induce further reductions in demand. Thus price rigidity at the micro level—if widespread—can prolong recession and depression at the macro level. If market power contributes to price rigidity, it follows that market power increases the susceptibility of the economy to recession and unemployment.[1]

Debates over the influence of market power on macroeconomic performance have been marked by both acrimony and ambiguity. It has been a long-standing position of the Chicago school that market power can have no influence on macroeconomic performance, and it is generally accepted that this is the case if the economy is in full employment equilibrium. But the idea that, in other circumstances, market power will induce price rigidity and worsen macroeconomic performance, like the Cheshire cat, vanishes quite slowly.

---

[1]See, generally, Hall, Robert E. "Market Structure and Macroeconomic Fluctuations," *Brookings Papers on Economic Activity* Number 2, 1986, pp. 285–322. Hall's innovative empirical tests are, unfortuantely, carried out at the two-digit industry level.

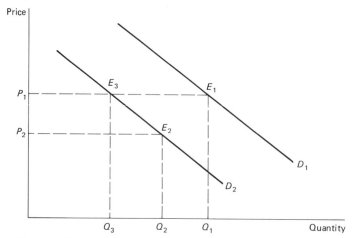

Notes: the demand curve shifts downward from D_1 to D_2. If price is flexible downward, price falls along the industry supply curve to P_2, and output falls to Q_2. If price is inflexible and remains at P_1, the entire burden of adjustment to the demand shift is on quantity, which falls to Q_3.

Figure 14-1   Price rigidity and output under demand fluctuations.

Administered Pricing[2]

Despite earlier contributions,[3] policy and academic concern with price flexibility and the implications, if any, of market structure for price flexibility crystallized in the aftermath of the Great Depression of 1929. A study by Gardiner Means of wholesale prices collected by the Bureau of Labor Statistics (BLS) revealed substantial inflexibility:[4]

> Means tabulated the frequency of change of some 677 monthly prices and found that a large number changed very infrequently. Indeed, in the eight-year period, 1926 through 1933, fourteen prices did not change a single time and seventy-seven changed only one to four times.

The implications of price inflexibility for output (and, indirectly, employment) are illustrated in Figure 14-1. Suppose demand shifts downward in a particular market, perhaps as a result of an economy-wide recession. In a

[2]For references, see Beals, Ralph E. ''Concentrated Industries, Administered Prices, and Inflation: A Survey of Recent Empirical Research.'' Council on Wage and Price Stability, 1975; and Gordon, Robert J. ''Output Fluctuations and Gradual Price Adjustment,'' *Journal of Economic Literature* Volume 19, Number 2, June 1981, pp. 493–530.

[3]Mills, Frederick C. *The Behavior of Prices.* New York: National Bureau of Economic Research, 1927.

[4]Stigler, George J. and Kindahl, James K. *The Behavior of Industrial Prices.* New York: National Bureau of Economic Research, 1970, p. 12.

354

competitive market, the price will decline along the short-run industry supply curve.[5] The result is a decline in output from Q_1 to Q_2 and a decline in price from P_1 to P_2.

If, on the other hand, price is inflexible and remains at P_1, the reduction in demand induces a larger reduction in output, from Q_1 to Q_3. Since employment reduction will eventually follow output reduction—firms will not indefinitely maintain the workforce appropriate for the higher output level—declines in demand will lead to greater increases in unemployment when prices are rigid than when prices are flexible.

As unemployment rises, however, disposable income will fall, consumption demand throughout the economy will fall, and the initial downward shift in demand will be reinforced. It follows that widespread price rigidity in individual markets can exacerbate cyclical macroeconomic fluctuations.

Based on his study of BLS prices, Means made a distinction between *market prices* "made in a market as a result of the interaction of buyers and sellers" and *administered prices* "set by administrative action and held constant for a period of time."[6] Inflexible administered prices were held to have contributed to the severity and persistence of the Depression.

Means presented the administration of prices as a relatively new phenomenon characteristic of industrial society.[7] It was soon pointed out[8] that the same BLS data analyzed by Means for the period 1926–1933 showed no substantial change in price flexibility over the period 1890–1936. Thus the Depression of 1929 could not be attributed to *increasing* inflexibility of prices.

Means' work spawned an immense literature, but the notion of an administered price as a price set by a seller is so vague as to be, for all practical purposes, without content. Outside of classrooms and auction markets, all prices are set by the seller.[9] Prices of canned goods at the corner grocery store are set by the seller and held constant for a period of time—until they are changed. This does not mean that the grocery manager can change price any less frequently than a competitive market would require. From an analytical and policy-making point of view, the pertinent question involves the circumstances, if any, under which sellers' discretion to set price leads to patterns of price changes that differ from those that would hold under competition.

[5]See Figure 2-1 and the accompanying text.

[6]*Industrial Prices and Their Relative Inflexibility.* Senate Document 13, 74th Congress, 1st Session, January 17, 1935, p. 1.

[7]Ibid., p. 9.

[8]See Mason, Edward S. "Price Inflexibility," *Review of Economics and Statistics* Volume 20, Number 2, May 1938, pp. 53–64, discussing Mills, op. cit.

[9]For discussion, see Adelman, M. A., "Steel, Administered Prices, and Inflation," *Quarterly Journal of Economics* Volume 75, Number 1, February 1961, pp. 16–40, and "What Is 'Administered Pricing'?," in *Anthology of Studies of Industrial Concentration by the Conference Board: 1958–1972.* New York: The Conference Board, March 1973, Section XI, pp. 19–26.

For this reason, the administered pricing literature soon focused on the pricing behavior of firms with market power. Although Means in 1935 explicitly distinguished administered pricing and monopoly,[10] by 1939 he had come to identify market concentration as essential to the administration of prices:[11]

> the dominant factor making for depression insensitivity of prices is the administrative control over prices which results from the relatively small number of concerns dominating certain markets.

By the postwar[12] period, the focus of the market structure–macroeconomic performance debate had shifted from price setting to price changing— inflation:[13]

> In the beginning of a demand inflation, market dominated prices tend to rise more rapidly while administration-dominated prices lag well behind. Then in a period of readjustment, market dominated prices fall back while administration-dominated prices continue to rise until the two groups are more nearly in balance. . . . Thus, administration-dominated prices help to slow up the classical inflation rather than initiate it. Only in the later stages of this demand inflation did administered prices catch up with the general rise.

In a world of inflationary price increases, therefore, the predicted effect of market concentration (identified as a source of administered prices) is to prolong the period of adjustment. In the first stage of a boom, price increases in concentrated industries will lag behind those in the rest of the economy. This will slow down aggregate price inflation. But after prices in competitive sectors have adjusted to the new higher price level, those in the administered sector will continue to rise, and catch up with the rest of the economy.

One part of the Chicago school's response to this argument—which denies that market power at the microeconomic level has any implications for macroeconomic phenomena—relies on the theory of profit-maximizing monopoly behavior:[14]

[10]Means, op. cit.: "Administered prices should not be confused with monopoly. The presence of administered prices does not indicate the presence of monopoly."

[11]National Resources Committee, *The Structure of the American Economy*, Part I, 1939, p. 143.

[12]Keeping in mind the pace of academic generations, what is meant here is the post–World War II period.

[13]Means, Gardiner. *Administrative Inflation and Public Policy*. Washington, D.C.: Anderson Kramer Associates, 1959.

[14]Stigler, George J. "Administered Prices and Oligopolistic Inflation," *Journal of Business*, Volume 35, Number 1, January 1962, pp. 1–13, p. 8; reprinted in *The Organization of Industry*. Homewood, Ill.: Richard D. Irwin, Inc., pp. 235–251, p. 244.

The traditional economic theory argues that oligopoly and monopoly prices have no special relevance to inflation. A monopolist (to take the simpler case) sets a profit-maximizing price for given demand-and-cost conditions. If inflation leads to a rise in either demand or costs, a new and usually higher price will be set. The price will usually be above the competitive level at any given time, but its pattern over time will not be other than passively responsive to monetary conditions.

The argument was soon made, however, that pricing under oligopoly could be expected to be very different from pricing under monopoly, and that the differences justified interest in price rigidity under oligopoly.[15] This argument developed into the principal and persuasive theoretical argument for price inflexibility under oligopoly.

The Kinked Demand Curve and Full-Cost Pricing

The Kinked Demand Curve

If Means founded one literature, Sweezy founded another.[16] His remarkable contribution was to provide a simple exposition of the argument that the fragility of oligopolistic collusion would induce price rigidity. Combined with a related argument drawing on business practices—the principle of full cost or target rate of return pricing—the kinked demand curve analysis of oligopoly pricing has had remarkable staying power.[17]

Sweezy's argument—illustrated in Figure 4-2—is based on the[18] "obvious fact that rivals react differently according to whether a price change is upward or downward."

Suppose that through tacit or overt collusion under oligopoly a firm finds itself selling a quantity q_K at the oligopoly price P_K. How will the firm perceive the demand for its own product?[19]

---

[15]Galbraith, John Kenneth. "Monopoly Power and Price Rigidities," *Quarterly Journal of Economics* Volume 50, May 1936, pp. 466–468.

[16]Sweezy, Paul M. "Demand Under Conditions of Oligopoly," *Journal of Political Economy* Volume 47, Number 4, August 1939, pp. 568–573; and Hall, R. L. and Hitch, C. J. "Price Theory and Business Behavior," *Oxford Economic Papers* Volume 2, May 1939, pp. 12–45. For a critical review, see Stigler, George J. "The Literature of Economics: The Case of the Kinked Oligopoly Demand Curve," *Economic Inquiry* Volume 16, Number 2, April 1978, pp. 185–204.

[17]In a reversal of the usual strategies, persistent empirical attacks on the existence of administered pricing (by students working in the Chicago tradition) have run aground on the shoals of the theoretical plausibility of price inflexibility under oligopoly—a plausibility based as much as anything else on Sweezy's five-page article.

[18]Sweezy, op. cit., p. 568.

[19]Some product differentiation is presumed here, an assumption that does not seriously distort reality.

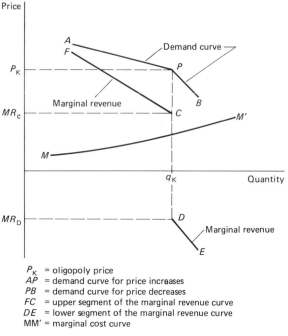

Figure 14-2   The kinked demand curve.

Price decreases will most likely be matched by rivals, upon discovery, as they seek to avoid losses of market share. In this event, the demand curve will be fairly steep for prices below P_K.[20] Lowering the price will bring only modest increases in sales, as the price reductions are matched by rivals. On the other hand, rivals will often be generous enough not to match price increases. Imperfect cooperation being what it is, rivals will be glad to take customers away from a firm indiscreet enough to administer a price above the oligopoly price P_K. Price increases will bring sharp reductions in sales, and the demand curve will be relatively flat for prices above P_K.

When the demand curve changes sharply in slope, the result is a gap in the marginal revenue curve.[21] The gap occurs at the output level corresponding to firm sales (q_K) at the oligopoly price.

To go from a gap in the marginal revenue curve to price inflexibility under oligopoly, we need to discuss the implications of the gap for the output choice of a profit-maximizing firm.

[20]This much, at least, the theory of the kinked demand curve has in common with Stigler's theory of oligopoly. See Stigler, George J., "A Theory of Oligopoly," *Journal of Political Economy* Volume 72, Number 1, February 1964, pp. 44–61, and footnote 19, Chapter 6, and the accompanying text.

[21]See footnote 9, Chapter 2, and the accompanying text.

We know that when a firm with a smooth (nonkinked) demand curve maximizes its profit, it selects an output that makes marginal revenue equal to marginal cost. If marginal revenue were greater than marginal cost, it would always pay the firm—in terms of increased profit—to expand output.

Suppose the firm is selling output q_K at price P_K, and the marginal cost curve falls between the upper and lower limits of the marginal revenue gap:

$$MR_C \geq MC \geq MR_D. \tag{14.1}$$

It would not pay the firm to increase its output above q_K because the marginal cost of producing additional output would exceed the marginal revenue (MR_D) from an additional sale. Nor would it pay the firm to reduce its output by one unit: the loss of revenue (MR_C) would exceed the cost saving.

When the demand curve exhibits discontinuous changes in slope, the profit maximization equality (marginal revenue = marginal cost) is replaced by an inequality (marginal cost between the upper and lower limits of marginal revenue). The result is that fluctuations in cost within the marginal revenue gap will not result in price fluctuations. Similarly, prices under oligopoly will be stable in the face of demand fluctuations:[22]

> Each firm cannot detect the changes in other firms' demand curves. They cannot discriminate between cases when rivals lower their price to cheat on collusive arrangements, and when rivals lower their price in response to a problem in their demand. The gains from being able to enforce collusive behavior outweigh the losses from failing to adapt price to shifts in the demand curve.

The fragility of oligopolistic coordination will induce a price stability, in response to demand changes and cost changes, that is unknown in competitive markets.

---

[22]Stiglitz, Joseph E. "Price Rigidities and Market Structure," *American Economic Review* Volume 74, Number 2, May 1984, p. 354. For a similar summary (by a critic), see Stigler, George J. "The Kinky Oligopoly Demand Curve and Rigid Prices," *Journal of Political Economy* Volume 55, Number 5, October 1947, reprinted in *The Organization of Industry*. Homewood, Ill. Richard D. Irwin, Inc., pp. 208–234, p. 216. For a critique of this argument, see Weston, J. Fred. "Pricing Behavior of Large Firms," *Western Economic Journal* Volume 10, Number 1, March 1972, p. 12: "The rationalization sometimes offered is that firms in concentrated industries find it easier to maintain their tenuous and imperfect collusion if price changes are not required too often. But this rationale ignores their reaction to other dynamic variables that would be more destructive to the tenuous collusion than adjusting to price changes." It is no doubt correct that factors other than cost and demand shifts will disturb oligopolistic understanding, but it does not follow that the desire to avoid such instability will be absent. If it is costly to oligipolists to disturb oligopolistic understanding, the kinked demand curve argument goes through.

Full Cost/Markup Pricing

Up to this point, as Sweezy acknowledged, the kinked demand curve is a theory of oligopolistic price stability, but only half a theory of oligopoly price:[23]

> the analysis suggested here runs in terms of movements in price from a currently existing situation. No attempt is made to explain how the current price and output situation came about except as it may be explained by reference to a previously existing situation.

The kinked demand analysis explains the reluctance of firms to alter price under oligopoly; it does not explain the level of price under oligopoly.

Although any standard oligopoly model[24] can be paired with the kinked demand curve to explain the level and stability of oligopoly price, the model of price setting that came to be associated with administered pricing arose out a survey of pricing practices in British business.[25] The survey found that many firms explained their pricing decisions in terms of a markup over cost, not in terms of setting the price equal to marginal cost.

In one version, full-cost pricing, the price is determined by adding a markup factor m to average labor (ULC) and materials (UMC) costs at a standard output level:[26]

$$P_f = (1 + m)(ULC + UMC). \qquad (14.2)$$

In an alternative but closely related formula the price is set to allow a target rate of return on capital, r_T, at the standard output level. If UKC is the unit capital input at the standard output level, the price would be set as

$$P_T = r_T UKC + ULC + UMC. \qquad (14.3)$$

First, observe that these two approaches to price setting are equivalent: any price set under Equation (14.2) can be reached under Equation (14.3) by picking the appropriate target rate of return.[27]

---

[23]Sweezy, op. cit., p. 572.

[24]See Chapter 5 and the references cited therein.

[25]Hall and Hitch, op. cit. See also A. D. H. Kaplan, Joel B. Dirlam, and Robert F. Dirlam. *Pricing in Big Business*. Washington, D.C., Brookings Institution, 1958.

[26]For similar formulations, see Eckstein, Otto and Fromm, Gary. "The Price Equation," *American Economic Review* Volume 58, Number 5, Part 1, December 1968, pp. 1159–1183.

[27]That is, pick r_T so that $r_T UKC = m(ULC + UMC)$.

Second, observe that Equation (14.3) (and therefore Equation (14.2) can be perfectly consistent with either competition or monopoly or oligopoly—in long-run equilibrium.[28]

Consider the most common case—constant average costs.[29] If a firm is in long-run equilibrium, output will be at the level that is taken to be standard for pricing purposes. Standard unit labor, material, and capital costs will then be actual unit labor, material, and capital costs. If r_T is taken to be the normal rate of return on investment—the opportunity cost of capital—Equation (14.3) will yield the long-run competitive equilibrium price. If r_T is taken to be the rate of return on investment that would be earned by a monopolist, Equation (14.3) will yield the monopoly price. Intermediate values of r_T—reached for values of the Herfindahl index less than 1 and conjectural variations between 0 and 1[30]—correspond to oligopoly outcomes.

There is, then, no conflict between these versions of rule-of-thumb pricing and profit maximization in long-run equilibrium. The situation is different when some shock disturbs the market equilibrium. Leaving kinks and rule-of-thumb pricing aside, a firm that maximizes its profit by picking an output that equates marginal revenue and marginal cost will ordinarily reduce its output if a change in the market shifts the firm's perceived demand curve (and therefore the marginal revenue curve) back. Reduced output will typically result in a reduced price.

Under the kind of rule-of-thumb pricing described in Equation (14.2) and (14.3), output fluctuations will not result in price changes. Output reductions may increase unit costs, but prices are based on standard unit costs—the average cost at the projected output level. Under such rules, prices will be inflexible and output fluctuations will exceed those that would occur under marginal cost pricing.[31]

Viewed most charitably, full-cost and target rate-of-return pricing are forms of behavior that converge with profit maximization in equilibrium but differ from it otherwise. In this view, the markup or target rate of return will be determined by the interaction of market structure and firm conduct, as in standard oligopoly models.[32]

---

[28]See Pappas, James L. and Hirschey, Mark. *Fundamentals of Managerial Economics,* 2nd ed. Chicago: The Dryden Press, 1985, pp. 359–361.

[29]See Figure 2-2 and the accompanying text.

[30]See equation (5.8) and the accompanying text.

[31]For further discussion, see Blair, John M. "Market Power and Inflation: A Short-Run Target Rate of Return Model," *Journal of Economic Issues,* Volume 8, June 1974, pp. 453–478.

[32]Recall from Chapter 6 that simple rules for price setting may facilitate collusion.

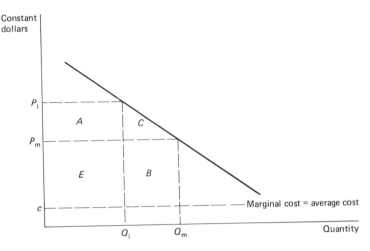

Notes:
P_m = real (constant dollar) monopoly price
P_i = real price set in incorrect expectation of inflation
$(P_i - c)Q_i$ = $A + E$ = real profit at price P_i
$(P_m - c)Q_m$ = $B + E$ = real profit at price P_m
$B - A$ = increase in profit if the price is lowered from P_i to P_m
$B + C$ = increase in producers' plus consumers' welfare if the price is lowered from P_i to P_m

Figure 14-3 Transaction costs and price rigidity.

Transaction Costs and Price Rigidity

Transaction costs may induce price rigidity even in the absence of the kind of oligopolistic interactions previously considered. The argument is illustrated in Figure 14-3.[33]

Figure 14-3 shows a firm's demand curve, where the price is measured in constant dollars—corrected for inflation. Real marginal and average cost are constant at c per unit. For simplicity, assume that there are no fixed costs.

Let P_m be the real monopoly price. At this price, the firm would earn a profit $(P_m - c)Q_m$—the area $E + B$ in Figure 14-3.

Suppose that in expectation of, say, 20 per cent inflation, the firm increases its nominal price by 20 per cent. To change the price, the firm incurs transaction

[33]Figure 14-3 is adapted from Mankiw, N. Gregory. "Small Menu Costs and Large Business Cycles: A Macroeconomic Model of Monopoly," *Quarterly Journal of Economics* Volume 100, Issue 2, May 1985, pp. 529–537. Compare Figure 10-2 and the accompanying text. For a model that uses transaction costs and uncertainty to explain the simultaneous existence in a market of sales on long-term contracts at one price and spot-market sales at another price, see Carlton, Dennis W. "Contracts, Price Rigidity, and Market Equilibrium," *Journal of Political Economy* Volume 87, Number 5, Part 1, October 1979, pp. 1034–1062. Klein, Benjamin, "Contract Costs and Administered Prices: An Economic Theory of Rigid Wages," *American Economic Review* Volume 74, Number 2, May 1984, pp. 332–338, explores some of the same issues in the context of labor markets.

or "menu" costs T. This cost will reflect the expense of printing new price lists, distributing them to customers, and having salespeople inform customers of the new price.

If the expected inflation does not materialize—perhaps because of an unexpected macroeconomic contraction—the firm's real price will exceed the profit-maximizing level. At the inflation-based price P_i, the firm will earn the profit $(P_i - c)Q_i$—the area $A + E$ in Figure 14-3.

It follows that by lowering its price to P_m, the firm will increase its profit by the area $B - A$ (and $B - A$ must be positive, since P_m is the profit-maximizing price: profit at P_i *must* be less than profit at P_m). In a world without transaction costs, the firm will indeed lower its price to P_m.

But if the firm must pay transaction costs T to change its price, it will lower the price only if $B - A > T$. Unless lost profits due to incorrect pricing are sufficiently large to cover transaction costs, the firm will hold the price rigid in the face of an unexpected demand shift.

If the price is lowered from P_i to P_m, the net gain in producers' plus consumers' welfare is $B + C$.[34] It follows that from a social point of view, the price should be lowered only if the welfare gain exceeds the cost of changing the price: if $B + C > T$.

Private self-interest cannot be counted on to accomplish the socially desirable result. If

$$B + C > T > B - A, \qquad (14.4)$$

a firm maximizing its own profit will hold the price rigid, even though a price change is desirable from a social point of view.[35]

Econometric Evidence[36]

Predictions of price rigidity under oligopoly come from the analysis of oligopolistic reactions to shifts in cost and demand, and from the analysis of the impact of transaction costs on price changes. We now turn to the evidence economists have assembled on the market structure–price change relationship.

---

[34]Consumers' surplus increases by $A + C$; profit increases by $B - A$. The net increase in consumers' plus producers' welfare is $A + C + B - A = B + C$.

[35]Mankiw, op. cit., Proposition 2.

[36]Studies of market structure and wage change are not discussed here; see Hamermesh, Daniel S. "Market Power and Wage Inflation," *Southern Economic Journal* Volume 10, Number 2, October 1972, pp. 204–212; Greer, Douglas F. "Market Power and Wage Inflation: A Further Analysis," *Southern Economic Journal* Volume 41, Number 3, January 1975, pp. 466–479; and for a theoretical approach, Ross, Stephen A. and Wachter, Michael L. "Wage Determination, Inflation, and Industrial Structure," *American Economic Review* Volume 63, Number 4, September 1973, pp. 675–692.

Price/Price Change Equations

What might be called the classic form of statistical analysis of price change involves testing for a residual effect of market concentration on industry price change after controlling for changes in cost and demand.

Typical econometric tests of the impact of market concentration on price change can be motivated with reference to the markup price formula Equation (14.2).[37] If the price is determined as a markup on unit labor and unit material costs, the change in price can be analyzed as a function of the change in these costs. By including a measure of the growth rate of industry sales, one can control for demand fluctuations.[38] Given explanatory variables of this kind, tests for any residual effect of market concentration on price change can be used as a test for administering pricing.

Examples of results from this sort of study are given in Table 14-1.[39] Equation (1) shows more rapid price change, all else equal, in more concentrated industries over the period 1953 to 1959. This can be interpreted as a delayed inflation in concentrated industries, which on the kinked demand theory would have extended the post–World War II inflation into the 1950s.[40]

Equation (2) shows a negative impact of concentration on price increases from 1967 to 1968 (and equations not reported here suggest that this negative effect persisted through 1969). Concentration thus appeared to dampen the inflation of the late 1960s.

There are many studies of the kind reported in Table 14-1. The results appear to be sensitive to the time period over which inflation is measured—just when a period of inflation is taken to begin or end. The results are also sensitive to details of specification: how demand change is measured, whether cost change variables are weighted by the shares of different factors in cost, and so on. The

[37]For a compact and lucid derivation, see Aaronovitch, S. and Sawyer, Malcolm C. "Price Change and Oligopoly," *Journal of Industrial Economics* Volume 30, Number 2, December 1981, pp. 137–147.

[38]See Lustgarten, Steven, "Administered Inflation: A Reappraisal," *Economic Inquiry* Volume 13, Number 2, June 1975, pp. 191–206, for an alternative measure of demand based on input-output tables.

[39]Equation (1) extends dePodwin, Horace J. and Selden, Richard T. "Business Pricing Policies and Inflation," *Journal of Political Economy* Volume 71, Number 2, April 1963, pp. 116–127. Weiss' work is in turn extended by Dalton, James A., "Administered Inflation and Business Pricing: Another Look," *Review of Economics and Statistics* Volume 55, Number 4, November 1973, pp. 516–519, who weights cost changes according to shares in total cost. For Canadian evidence, see Sellekaerts, Willy and LeSage, Richard. "A Reformulation and Empirical Verification of the Administered Price Inflation Hypothesis: The Canadian Case," *Southern Economic Journal* Volume 39, Number 3, January 1973, pp. 345–350 (who give a lucid literature review); and Jones, J. C. H. and Laudadio, L. "Concentration, Relative Price Flexibility and 'Administered Prices': Some Canadian Experience," *Antitrust Bulletin* Volume 22, Number 4, Winter 1977, pp. 775–799.

[40]Weiss, Leonard W. "Business Pricing Policies and Inflation Reconsidered," *Journal of Political Economy* Volume 74, April 1966, pp. 177–187.

Table 14-1 Market Concentration
and Price Change

$P59/P53 = 73.80^a + 0.1375^a CR4$	(1)
$P68/P67 = 92.65 - 0.037^a CR4$	(2)

Pt = industry price index in year t
$CR4$ = industry four-firm seller concentration ratio

a indicates statistical significance at the 1 per cent level; such an estimate would occur by chance only once in 100 times, on average.

Sources: Weiss, Leonard W., "Business Pricing Policies and Inflation Reconsidered," *Journal of Political Economy* Volume 74, April 1966, pp. 177–187, and "The Role of Concentration in Recent Inflationary Price Movements: A Statistical Analysis," *Antitrust Law and Economics Review* Volume 4, Spring 1971, pp. 109–121. For compactness, coefficients of cost and demand change variables are not reported; coefficients in Equation (2) have been rescaled for comparability.

complete literature contains evidence that supports the administered pricing hypothesis and other evidence that does not support it. On balance, this type of test has yielded equivocal results.

Of particular interest is the argument[41] that price inflexibility should be found only at intermediate ranges of market concentration. The argument that price flexibility will result from the fragility of oligopolistic coordination has no relevance when concentration is low; oligopolistic coordination is then absent. Nor does this argument have much relevance when concentration is high; this is near monopoly, and firms will probably know each other well enough so that kinks in firm demand curves smooth out. The conclusion is that price inflexibility will be most pronounced at intermediate concentration levels. The concentration–inflation relationship will be either U-shaped (early in periods of inflation) or ∩-shaped (during later catchup periods).[42]

Buyers' Prices vs. Sellers' Prices

We now discuss a remarkable episode in the scholarship of industrial economics, one involving a research project that has come to lead a life of its own.

[41]Qualls, P. David. "Market Structure and Price Behavior in U.S. Manufacturing, 1967–1972," *Quarterly Review of Economics and Business* Volume 18, Winter 1978, pp. 35–58. Qualls finds evidence of a U-shaped impact of concentration on inflation over 1968–1969, and weaker evidence of a ∩-shaped impact for the 1969 contraction.

[42]For a similar argument in the context of sales efforts, see the text accompanying Figure 11-1.

Means advanced the theory of administered price based on an analysis of BLS wholesale prices for various commodities. A fundamental criticism of his work focused on the nature of these price series.

The most serious criticism involved the fact that the prices reported to the BLS are list prices, not transaction prices.[43] It is well known that in certain industries—steel is a traditional example, the world oil market is another—breakdowns in oligopolistic price control take the form of selective surreptitious shadings of price below the published price. Early studies[44] suggested that BLS sellers' price indices differed importantly from—and were less flexible than—buyers' or transaction prices.

If transaction prices in concentrated industries are flexible, the fact that paper prices are inflexible is of little interest. Critics of the administered pricing literature have therefore maintained that prices are not in fact inflexible in concentrated industries. Administered pricing, in this view, is "A Theory in Search of A Phenomenon,"[45] so dazzled by the appearance of price rigidity that the reality of price flexibility is missed.

For a study published by the National Bureau of Economic Research (NB), Stigler and Kindahl collected a sample of buyers' prices for commodities thought likely to fall in the "administered" category.[46] Prices were collected for the period 1957 through 1966; the number of prices collected varied from year to year. Buyers sampled included government agencies, large industrial firms, and a few hospitals (sampled for pharmaceutical drug prices). About half of the transactions sampled took place under long-term contracts (but were sometimes subject to price renegotiation during the contract period).[47] In contrast, the BLS price indices cover mainly short-run spot prices.

Stigler and Kindahl found a persistent tendency for BLS sellers' prices to be inflexible downward, compared with NB buyers' prices:[48]

---

[43]Another criticism concerned the effect of the number of firms surveyed by the BLS on calculations of the frequency of price change. This criticism appears to have been based on a misunderstanding of Means' techniques. See Means, Gardiner C. "The Administered-Price Thesis Reconfirmed," *American Economic Review* Volume 62, Number 3, June 1972, footnote 8, pp. 293–294.

[44]McAllister, Harry E., Staff Paper No. 8 and Flueck, John, Staff Paper No. 9. *Government Price Statistics*. Washington, D.C.: U.S. Government Printing Office, January 21, 1961. Both are discussed by Stigler, op. cit.

[45]Blair, John M. "Administered Prices: A Phenomenon in Search of a Theory," *American Economic Review* Volume 49, May 1959, pp. 431–450; and Bailey, Martin J. "Discussion," *American Economic Review* Volume 49, May 1959, pp. 459–461.

[46]Stigler and Kindahl, *Industrial Prices*, p. 23. Stigler and Kindahl also concentrated on commodities that had not been subject to substantial quality change.

[47]Ibid., p. 36.

[48]Ibid., p. 7.

Table 14-2 Changes in Buyers'/Sellers' Prices

	Contractions		Expansions	
Price change	BLS	NB	BLS	NB
Decreases	23	40	14	19
No change	19	10	20	14
Increases	26	18	36	37

Notes:

"Contractions" covers the periods July 1957–April 1958 and May 1960–February 1961; "Expansions" covers the periods February 1961–October 1964 and November 1964–November 1966.

"No change" indicates that the price index rises or falls less than 1/20th of 1 per cent per month.

Source: Stigler, George J. and Kindahl, James K. *The Behavior of Industrial Prices.* New York: National Bureau of Economic Research, 1970, pp. 8–9.

Price quotations are not revised downward immediately when market conditions, and transaction prices, change: both the costs of changing prices and the desire to confirm the persistence of the price change dictate some delay.

A comparison of movements of the two series is reported in Table 14-2, which describes changes of 68 commodities in two contractionary periods and price changes of 70 commodities in two expansionary periods.

There is (as Stigler and Kindahl note) no reason to expect all prices to change in the same direction at different times in a business cycle. Prices in each market will be influenced by local market conditions, as well as by general macroeconomic trends. With this qualification in mind, the general expectation is that prices will fall in periods of macroeconomic contraction and rise in periods of macroeconomic expansion.

The BLS series shows 26 of 68 price indices rising in contractions (38 per cent), while the NB series reports only 18 increases (26 per cent). Only 23 of the BLS sellers' prices fell during the contractionary periods, while 40 NB buyers' prices—nearly 60 per cent—declined.

Now examine price changes during the two expansionary periods, in which price increases ought to be expected. The two sets of price indices show virtually the same number of increases—36 for the BLS sellers' price indices, 37 for the NB buyers' price indices. The NB series show somewhat greater countercyclical movement than the BLS series: 19 of the NB buyers' price indices fell during the expansionary periods, compared with only 14 of the BLS sellers' price indices.

Stigler and Kindahl conclude:[49]

> As a summary figure, in the four cycles we find prices moving in the same
> direction as business 56 per cent of the time; remaining constant 17 per cent
> of the time; and moving perversely 27 per cent of the time. Since there is no
> reason on earth or in space why all prices should move in the same direction,
> especially during relatively mild expansions and contractions, we find no evi-
> dence here to suggest that price rigidity or "administration" is a significant
> phenomenon.

In defense of this conclusion, it should be emphasized that Stigler and Kindahl deliberately collected price indices for commodities thought likely to be
subject to administered price rigidity. The finding that 59 per cent of such
prices fall during recessions and 52 per cent rise during expansions may indeed
be evidence that oligopolistic price rigidity is less widespread than some had
alleged.

Nonetheless, the conclusion that the tabulations of price change contain "no
evidence . . . to suggest that price rigidity or 'administration' is a significant
phenomenon" seems too strong. After all, 41 per cent of the NB buyers' prices
did not fall during contractions and 48 per cent of these prices did not rise
during expansions. These changes seem consistent with a belief in oligopolistic
price rigidity.

Means and others soon asserted that the buyers' price series in fact supported
the existence of administered price inflexibility.[50] This dialogue is marked by
the usual bickering over the time periods used to delineate expansion and
contraction.

A more useful discussion can also be motivated by considering Table 14-2.
The two sets of price series described there move differently, but not startlingly
so. This is especially evident for the two expansionary periods, when 36 of the
70 BLS prices increased, as opposed to 37 of the 70 NB prices.

Statistical comparisons[51] of BLS and NB prices indeed suggest that the two

---

[49]Ibid., p. 9; footnote omitted. The figures are arrived at as follows: 40 NB decreases during
contractions plus 37 NB increases during expansions implies 77 price changes in the direction of
business, 56 per cent of 138 price changes; 18 NB increases during contractions plus 19 NB decreases
during expansions gives 37 price movements against the direction of business, 27 per cent of 138 price
movements.

[50]Means, "The Administered-Price Thesis Reconfirmed," pp. 292–306; but see Stigler, George
J. and Kindahl, James K. "Industrial Prices, as Administered by Dr. Means," *American Economic
Review* Volume 63, Number 4, September 1973, pp. 717–721. For an argument supporting Means, see
Moore, Milton. "Stigler on Inflexible Prices," *Canadian Journal of Economics* Volume 5, Number 4,
November 1972, pp. 486–493.

[51]Weiss, Leonard W. "Stigler, Kindahl, and Means on Administered Prices," *American Economic
Review* Volume 67, Number 4, September 1977, pp. 610–619; Ross, Howard N. and Krausz, Joshua.
"Buyers' and Sellers' Prices and Administered Behavior," *The Review of Economics and Statistics*
Volume 68, Number 3, August 1986, pp. 369–378.

sets of price series do not differ in important ways. Both series contain evidence that prices from unconcentrated markets are more flexible than prices from concentrated markets:[52]

> Buyers' and sellers' prices may diverge in ways, but they are in perfect agreement that oligopolies can exert their market power to affect the rate of change in prices over time.

New Directions in an Old Debate

The traditional argument of administered price theory is that firms will delay price adjustments in oligopoly:[53]

> Over time economic developments occur that render the existing price structure more and more out of keeping with industry demand and supply conditions. A firm, in deciding whether or not to adjust to the new developments, is forced to balance the loss in profits due to the inappropriate price structure against the potential profit loss if an attempt to alter prices should lead to a breakdown in the level of oligopoly cooperation.

More recently, an argument that concentration will speed up price adjustment has been made. Where concentration is high, cooperation may be more effective:[54]

> As regards the influence of industrial structure, this is based on the hypothesis that in highly concentrated, oligopolistic sectors which are characterised by low costs of search and communication among sellers, price changes can be effectively coordinated and thus the process of adjustment to equilibrium can be speeded up.

These arguments are not necessarily inconsistent. Imperfect cooperation may impede price change at low levels of concentration, but oligopolistic coordination may improve as concentration rises.[55]

[52]Ross and Krausz, op. cit., p. 378.

[53]Ross, Stephen A. and Wachter, Michael L. "Pricing and Timing Decisions in Oligopoly Industries," *Quarterly Journal of Economics* Volume 89, Number 1, February 1975, p. 118.

[54]Domberger, Simon. "Price Dynamics and Industrial Structure in the U.K.: An Input-Output Analysis," *The Manchester School of Economic and Social Studies* Volume 48, Number 3, September 1980, p. 285.

[55]See Qualls, op. cit., A supporting argument is provided by Dixon, R., "Industry Structure and the Speed of Price Adjustment," *Journal of Industrial Economics* Volume 32, Number 1, September 1983, p. 29, who interprets Stigler's theory of oligopoly as implying "faster (and more orderly)" price adjustments "in industries which have fewer firms. . .".

A new empirical approach has been to estimate the speed of price adjustment directly and to examine directly the impact of market concentration on the speed of adjustment.[56] The point of departure is what economists call the *partial adjustment model,* which supposes actual price change from one period to the next to be proportional to the difference between the actual and the desired price:

$$P_t - P_{t-1} = a(P_t^* - P_{t-1}), \ 0 \le a \le 1, \qquad (14.5)$$

where P_t^* is the desired price in period t, P_t is the actual price in period t, and a measures the speed of adjustment. Combining terms in P_{t-1}, Equation (14.5) becomes

$$P_t = aP_t^* + (1 - a)P_{t-1}. \qquad (14.6)$$

When the price is adjusted partially in each period to a desired level, it is a weighted average of the desired price and the previous period's price. If a is small, most of the weight in this average goes to the previous period's price. Adjustment to the desired price then proceeds slowly. If a is large, most of the weight in the average that determines the current price goes to the desired price, and adjustment is rapid.

Domberger[57] estimated values of the speed-of-adjustment parameter for 21 British industries over the period 1963 to 1974. He then estimated the following equation to explain differences in the speed of adjustment parameter in terms of differences in industry concentration:[58]

$$a = 0.3141 + 0.0066 CR. \qquad (14.7)$$

Domberger's research suggests that market concentration accelerates, rather than delays, price adjustments. Such evidence as is available from the United

---

[56]Domberger, op. cit., and "Price Adjustment and Market Structure," *Economic Journal* Volume 89, March 1979, pp. 96–108; see also Winters, L. A. "Price Adjustment and Market Structure: A Comment," *Economic Journal* Volume 91, December 1981, pp. 1026–1030; Domberger, Simon. "Price Adjustment and Market Structure: A Reply," *Economic Journal* Volume 91, December 1981, pp. 1031–1035; and Dixon, op. cit.

[57]Domberger, "Price Adjustment and Market Structure."

[58]Ibid., p. 104. The intercept coefficient is significant at the 5 per cent level, and the coefficient of concentration is significant at the 1 per cent level. A dummy variable for engineering industries is omitted from the text; its coefficient was -0.3549 and was statistically significant at the 1 per cent level. The estimate of the speed of adjustment parameter (a) can be transformed into an estimate of the mean adjustment period $[(1 - a)/a]$. Equation (14.7) implies that increases in concentration reduce the mean adjustment period, in contrast to Carlton's results.

States, however, points in exactly the opposite direction. Carlton, using the Stigler-Kindahl sample, finds that the relationship between the average length of a period of price rigidity and the four-firm seller concentration ratio is[59]

$$\text{Average duration} = 4.97 + 16.12\text{CR4}. \qquad \textbf{(14.8)}$$

Exploring the basis for the difference in results offers a topic for future research.

What concerns would a positive impact of concentration on the speed of adjustment raise for macroeconomic policy makers?[60]

> although faster rates of price adjustment imply higher rates of inflation in response to exogenous shocks, it could be argued that greater concentration improves matters by shortening the period of disequilibrium in product markets. However, . . . the central issue is that of economic stability. It will be influenced by the market structure–price adjustment relationship in two important ways. First, a low rate of inflation is tolerable, even desirable given that it allows the economy to sustain claims on real resources which are irreconcilable in the short run. Reducing the lag of price adjustment eliminates some of the "slack" in the system thereby exposing the incompatibility of claims and thrusting the distributional issues to the fore. Secondly, shorter lags of price adjustment raise the likelihood of inflationary expectations playing a major role in the generation of inflation. A sharp rise in the rate of inflation will be noticed sufficiently to generate a wage response, even if it is of short duration, whereas a "prolonged" creeping inflation will not.

In the long run, labor and management cannot both claim larger shares of national income. Inconsistent demands on national income can be accommodated, in the short run, by increasing price. But as inflation erodes the real value of nominal increases in wages or dividends, the underlying inconsistency will reassert itself. Labor will have to accept lower real wages, or stockholders will have to accept lower real dividends. If concentration speeds the adjustment of prices to cost shocks, the issue of the distribution of income among various classes of recipients will have to be confronted that much sooner.

Further, rapid price inflation over the short run may generate demands for wage increases to "correct" or "compensate" for the price increases. Such wage increases will become cost increases and in turn induce subsequent price markups to cover costs. Shifts in inflationary expectations cannot affect inflation

---

[59]"The Rigidity of Prices," *American Economic Review* Volume 76, Number 4, September 1986, p. 655, footnote 23. There are 27 observations, each a product at the five-digit Standard Industrial Classification level. Concentration is for 1963 at the four-digit level. Both coefficients are significant at the 1 per cent level.

[60]Domberger, "Price Dynamics," p. 301.

in the long run, but they can induce business cycles and periods of stagflation in the short run.[61]

Summary

Microeconomic price rigidity is a concern because it can contribute to poor macroeconomic performance, extending macroeconomic disequilibrium at low levels of output and employment.

Oligopolists who have worked out a comfortable industry equilibrium will be reluctant to disturb that equilibrium by changing the price in response to minor shifts in demand and costs. The argument that prices are likely to be rigid in the presence of market power is reinforced if there are transaction costs associated with changing price. If it is costly to change price, the benefits of doing so will have to exceed a threshold level before price-making firms begin to move.

These arguments suggest that at intermediate levels of concentration, prices will be more rigid in the face of changing market conditions than under very low or very high levels of market concentration.

Considerable empirical evidence supports this view, although it is by no means unambiguous. The estimation of price-change equations appears sensitive to the timing of the periods over which price change is measured. There may be systematic differences between the behavior of indices of sellers' prices (which are available at least cost) and indices of buyers' prices. Buyers' and sellers' price indices both appear to support the existence of administered, inflexible prices, although this remains the topic of lively debate. Direct estimates of the impact of market concentration on the speed of price adjustment have produced conflicting results, and conclusions based on this line of research must await additional evidence.

[61]See, for example, Dornbusch, Rudiger and Fischer, Stanley. *Macroeconomics,* 4th ed. New York: McGraw-Hill Book Company, 1987, chapter 14.

15

Price Discrimination/ Exclusionary Practices

Blest be the tie that binds.

As we have seen in Chapter 4, a firm with market power—the power to control price—does not by that fact monopolize within the meaning of Section 2 of the Sherman Act. Monopolization requires not only that a firm have market power but also that it engage in some extraordinary conduct, "not normal industrial development," showing "an intent and purpose to exclude others."

Price discrimination and contracts alleged to have the effect of interfering with competitive rivalry are among the practices that courts have found sufficient to justify findings of monopolization under Section 2. In an early landmark Section 2 case, one of the charges against the Standard Oil Company was that it had benefited from differentially low railroad rates—a form of price discrimination.[1] In a later Section 2 decision, the United Shoe Machinery Corporation was condemned for monopolization in part because it marketed its product under leases thought to be exclusionary and anticompetitive.[2]

Price discrimination and exclusionary practices have thus been linked in antitrust law through the interpretation of Section 2 of the Sherman Act. In the antitrust area, further links have been forged by the Clayton Act, which in various sections condemns what is called price discrimination and contracts thought to be restrictive—tying, exclusive dealing, and requirements contracts. But economic theory also links these forms of business conduct. As we will see, one of the motives for tying together the sale of separate products is to accomplish price discrimination.

---

[1]*Standard Oil Company v. United States,* 221 U.S. 1 (1911). See discussions in Chapters 4 and 16.

[2]*United States v. United Shoe Machinery Corporation,* 110 F. Supp. 295 (1953).

Price Discrimination

Economics of Price Discrimination

Price discrimination is[3] "The act of selling the same article, produced under a single control, at different prices to different buyers. . .". The qualification that the different prices must be charged for "the same article" is critical. Physically identical units of a good are different articles, in an economic sense, if they are sold in different markets. If there are persistent cost differences in marketing the product on different markets, under competitive conditions physically identical units of a product will be sold in different markets at persistently different prices.

Hence price differences for different sales of a product do not constitute price discrimination unless the sales are made under identical cost conditions. At the same time, price discrimination in an economic sense occurs if physically identical units of a product are sold at a common price in markets that are served at different costs per unit.

Sales by a producer to wholesale and retail distributors provide an example. If a manufacturer sells to both wholesalers and retailers under competitive conditions, the wholesaler will typically pay a lower price. It costs a manufacturer less to supply a wholesaler than a retailer, because the wholesaler performs storage, shipping, and distribution functions that the manufacturer must perform for direct sales to retailers. The reduced cost of supply, in a competitive market, will be passed on to the wholesaler in terms of lower prices. Such price differences are not price discrimination because the different units of the product, although physically identical, are different goods in an economic sense. They are not the same article.

Sporadic price discrimination is characteristic of the adjustment of competitive markets toward equilibrium. Producers will know most about what market conditions have been for prices close to the current price. They will not automatically know if market conditions have changed or how the market will react to a radically different price. Experimentation with different prices will generate the kind of information producers need to make the price and output decisions that will move the market from an old equilibrium to a new one.[4]

What we are concerned with, then, is not sporadic price discrimination or persistent price differences in competitive markets. Our immediate concern is the economic analysis of *systematic* price discrimination by firms with market

[3]Robinson, Joan. *The Economics of Imperfect Competition,* 2nd ed. London: Macmillan & Co., Ltd., and St Martin's Press, 1969, p. 179.

[4]Posner, Richard A. *The Robinson-Patman Act.* Washington, D.C.: American Enterprise Institute for Public Policy Research, 1976, pp. 12–13; Bork, Robert H. *The Antitrust Paradox.* New York: Basic Books, 1978, p. 388. See also Chapter 17's discussion of resale price maintenance by Levi Strauss in the marketing of jeans.

power. The classic economic analysis of this phenomenon distinguishes three types of price discrimination:[5]

1. First-degree price discrimination—the supplier sells each unit of output for the highest price that buyers are willing to pay for that unit of output.
2. Second-degree price discrimination—the supplier divides output into successive batches and sells each batch for the highest price that buyers are willing to pay for that batch of output.
3. Third-degree price discrimination—the supplier divides customers into distinct groups and charges a profit-maximizing price for sales to each group.

If the batches of output that are priced separately under second-degree price discrimination are made smaller and smaller, until each batch contains only one unit, this reduces to first-degree price discrimination. First-degree price discrimination is therefore a limiting or extreme version of second-degree price discrimination. For this reason, we confine our discussion to first- and third-degree price discrimination. Second-degree price discrimination is considered in Problem 15-1.

First-Degree Price Discrimination[6]

Figure 15-1 allows us to contrast first-degree price discrimination with single-price monopoly. Let a monopolist supply a market with the demand curve shown in Figure 15-1. If the monopolist must sell all output at a single price, it will maximize its profit by selecting the output that makes its marginal revenue equal to its marginal cost; the single monopoly price is then determined by going up to the demand curve. Under monopoly, output is restricted (compared with competition). This restriction of output produces the income transfer and deadweight loss effects discussed in Chapter 2.

Suppose, however, that this product is sold at a flea market. By haggling, the producer is able to infer the maximum price that would willingly be paid for each successive unit of output. The monopolist then charges the *reservation price* P_1 for the first unit of output, a somewhat lower price P_2 (not shown on the graph, but found by going up to the demand curve from $Q = 2$ units of output) for the second unit of output, and so on.

We pause to note a general requirement for price discrimination. If the monopolist is to sell at a higher price to some customers than to others, there must be something that prevents the customers who benefit from the low price from reselling to those less favored by the monopolist. If such resale is possible,

[5]Pigou, A. C. *The Economics of Welfare,* 4th ed. London: Macmillan & Co., Ltd, 1963, chapter XVII.

[6]Figure 15-1 and the accompanying text follow Williamson, Oliver E. "The Economics of Antitrust: Transaction Cost Considerations," *University of Pennsylvania Law Review* Volume 122, Number 6, June 1974, pp. 1447–1449.

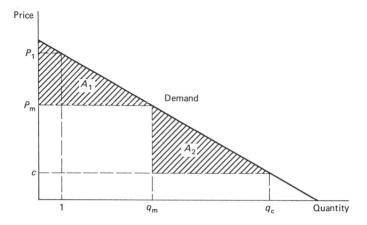

A_1 = consumers' surplus under single-price monopoly
A_2 = deadweight welfare loss under single-price monopoly
$A_1 + A_2$ = increase in monopolist's profit under first-degree
price discrimination, before allowing for transaction
costs
A_2 = increase in social welfare under first-degree price
discrimination, before allowing for transaction costs

Figure 15-1 First-degree price discrimination.

arbitrage between low-price and high-price customers will eventually break
down the discriminatory scheme. For this reason, price discrimination often
occurs for services (for example, medical care) or goods (for example, electric
power) that cannot be stored.[7]

Assuming that such arbitrage is impossible, the monopolist is able to capture
all of the consumer surplus in the market by selling each unit of output for the
maximum price. By capturing all consumer surplus for itself, the monopolist
earns a greater profit than it would by charging a single price. The increase in
profit consists of consumers' surplus under monopoly (the area in Figure 15-1
below the demand curve and above the monopoly price) and the deadweight
loss under monopoly.

First-degree price discrimination eliminates the deadweight welfare loss associated with single-price monopoly. Recall that deadweight welfare loss is the
consumer surplus lost on output that is not produced under single-price monopoly—output that is not produced because the single-price monopolist restricts output and moves back up the demand curve. Under first-degree price

---

[7]Learning cannot be resold (some of my colleagues insist that it cannot even be given away); thus
public universities are able to charge different prices (in-state and out-of-state tuition) for a single
product. Scholarships given by a university to its own students are, in effect, a way for the university
to lower the price of learning for some "consumers."

discrimination, however, there is no output restriction. The monopolist charges each consumer the maximum price that that consumer will pay for each unit of output, but the monopolist sells to anyone willing to pay the marginal cost of production. Since there is no restriction of output under first-degree price discrimination, there is no deadweight welfare loss.

It follows that if the goal of antitrust policy is the minimization of deadweight welfare loss, first-degree price discrimination is clearly a good thing from a policy point of view. It eliminates the deadweight welfare loss associated with single-price monopoly.

Two qualifications must be made to this optimistic conclusion. The first relates to the transaction costs involved in implementing a discriminatory scheme, and the second relates to the costs of monopolization.

In practice, there are costs associated with determining the reservation prices of different consumers and with policing the market to prevent resale. The monopolist will engage in price discrimination if the increase in profit (consumers' surplus plus deadweight welfare loss under single-price monopoly) exceeds the associated transaction costs. In terms of Figure 15-1, the monopolist will engage in price discrimination if $A_1 + A_2 > T$, where T is the transaction costs of implementing the discriminatory scheme.

But under a minimization of deadweight loss welfare standard, the social gain from price discrimination is only the deadweight welfare loss under single-price monopoly (A_2 in Figure 15-1).[8] From a social point of view, price discrimination is beneficial only if $A_2 > T$. If (as is entirely possible)

$$A_1 + A_2 > T > A_2, \tag{15.1}$$

the monopolist will find it privately profitable to engage in price discrimination even though price discrimination is harmful from a social point of view. Even if the goal of public policy is to minimize deadweight welfare loss, society cannot count on the self-interest of firms with market power to induce socially desirable behavior.

Further, this analysis may fail to capture all of the social costs of price-discriminating monopoly. In Chapter 2 we noted the possibility that costs of monopolization may consume the revenue that appears as monopoly profit in the standard monopoly model. Costs of monopolization reflect a socially wasteful allocation of resources as firms compete to acquire or maintain a position of market power. First-degree price discrimination will generate greater eco-

---

[8]The difference between the increase in the monopolist's profit under price discrimination and the increase in social welfare due to price discrimination is the consumers' surplus under single-price monopoly (A_1 in Figure 15-1). Under single-price monopoly, this surplus is retained by consumers; under price discrimination, it is transferred to the monopolist. But it is part of social welfare under either regime.

nomic profit; this may simply lead to greater investment of resources to acquire or protect the power to discriminate in price.[9] This is not a social gain.

The Chicago School's response[10] to this argument is that if monopoly is acquired due to superior efficiency, the expenditure of the resources that produces that efficiency cannot be condemned as socially wasteful. However, the expenditure of resources invested to acquire or maintain monopoly in ways that the antitrust laws disapproves would be condemned under the antitrust laws.

This is essentially the approach of Section 2 of the Sherman Act toward monopolization. The crux here, of course, is to specify which private firm actions are disapproved of under the antitrust laws and which are not. The Chicago approach would condemn cartels, but little else.

First-degree price discrimination fares even less well if public policy condemns income transfers that result from the exercise of market power. Under such a policy, the resulting increase in monopoly profit is counted against the practice of price discrimination. In the absence of transaction costs, the incremental profit under discrimination is areas $A_1 + A_2$ in Figure 15-1. If the elimination of deadweight welfare loss, A_2, is credited as a social benefit of a discriminatory scheme, the net loss from price discrimination under an antitrust policy that condemns income transfers from consumers to producers is A_1: the loss of consumers' surplus by consumers who would have purchased at the monopoly price.

In summary, first-degree price discrimination will eliminate the deadweight welfare loss associated with single-price monopoly. Whether or not this represents a social gain depends on the transaction costs of implementing the discriminatory scheme, the extent to which monopoly profit is invested in socially undesirable ways, and the extent to which society condemns income transfers from consumers to producers that depend on the exercise of market power.

Third-Degree Price Discrimination[11]

It is useful to analyze first-degree price discrimination as a way of placing in perspective the costs and benefits of discrimination. But it is third-degree discrimination—the charging of separate profit-maximizing prices in separate markets—that we encounter in the real world.

Figure 15-2 illustrates a situation in which a monopolist can segment its

---

[9]Posner, Richard A. *Antitrust Law: An Economic Perspective.* Chicago: The University of Chicago Press, 1976, pp. 62–64, 242–243.

[10]Due to Bork, op. cit., p. 396.

[11]Figure 15-2 and the accompanying text follow Schmalensee, Richard. "Output and Welfare Implications of Monopolistic Third-Degree Price Discrimination," *American Economic Review* Volume 71, Number 1, March 1981, pp. 242–247. See also Yamey, Basil. "Monopolistic Price Discrimination and Economic Welfare," *Journal of Law and Economics* Volume 17, Number 2, October 1974, pp. 377–380.

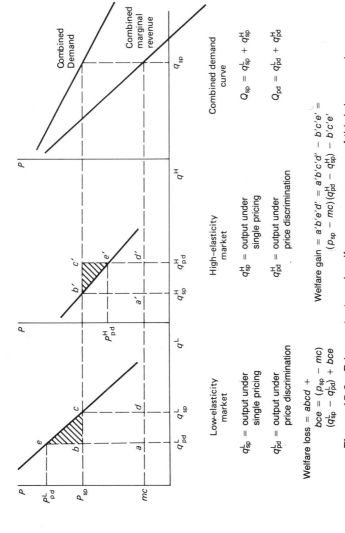

Figure 15-2 Price, output, and welfare consequences of third-degree price discrimination.

Low-elasticity market

q_{sp}^L = output under single pricing

q_{pd}^L = output under price discrimination

High-elasticity market

q_{sp}^H = output under single pricing

q_{pd}^H = output under price discrimination

Combined demand curve

$Q_{sp} = q_{sp}^L + q_{sp}^H$

$Q_{pd} = q_{pd}^L + q_{pd}^H$

Welfare loss = $abcd$ +

$\quad bce = (p_{sp} - mc)$

$\quad (q_{sp}^L - q_{pd}^L) + bce$

Welfare gain = $a'b'e'd' = a'b'c'd' - b'c'e' =$

$\quad (p_{sp} - mc)(q_{pd}^H - q_{sp}^H) - b'c'e'$

market into two parts, one with a higher price elasticity of demand than the other.[12] In such a case, a profit-maximizing firm will reduce sales and increase the price in the low-elasticity market but expand sales and reduce the price in the high-elasticity market.

When output is reduced in the low-elasticity market, welfare falls. The welfare loss has two components: the profit the monopolist would have earned by selling additional output at the single-price monopoly level and the consumers' surplus lost when output is reduced. In the notation of Figure 15-2, the welfare loss in the low elasticity market is

$$(p_{sp} - mc)(q_{sp}^L - q_{pd}^L) + bce, \tag{15.2}$$

where mc is marginal cost (assumed, for simplicity, to be constant).

When output is increased in the high-elasticity market, welfare increases. The increase in welfare is the profit plus consumers' surplus on the additional output sold. In the notation of Figure 15-2, this is[13]

$$(p_{sp} - mc)(q_{pd}^H - q_{sp}^H) - b'c'e'. \tag{15.3}$$

Adding (15.2) and (15.3), the net welfare change is

$$(p_{sp} - mc)(Q_{sp} - Q_{pd}) - (b'c'e' + bce), \tag{15.4}$$

which breaks down into two parts. The first component, $(p_{sp} - c)(Q_{sp} - Q_{pd})$, is the net welfare change due to the change in output under price discrimination when output is valued at the single-price monopoly price. Since the second term in (15.4) is subtracted, it follows immediately that if output falls after the move to price discrimination, social welfare falls because of price discrimination.[14]

Whether or not output falls under price discrimination depends on the cur-

---

[12]The markets may be separated geographically, as for example with the sale of Japanese television sets in Japan and the United States. The discussion that follows assumes that the position of the demand curves is such that both markets are served under the single-price regime. It is possible that price discrimination will make it profitable for markets to be served that would not be served under a single-price regime. If this is the case, the net welfare effect of third-degree price discrimination is more likely to be positive, all else equal. See, for example, Robinson, op. cit., chapters 15 and 16, and Schmalensee, op. cit., p. 245.

[13]The monopolist loses profit on units that had been sold at price p_{sp}, $(p_{sp} - p_{pd}^H)q_{sp}^H$, when the price is lowered in the high-elasticity market. But this is not a social loss: it is transferred to consumers as consumers' surplus.

[14]Of course, the reduction in welfare will be so much the worse if there are transaction costs associated with administering the price discrimination scheme or if the increased profit of the monopolist under price discrimination is counted as a social bad.

vature of the demand curves, in the neighborhood of p_{sp}, in the separate markets. If the demand curves are linear, total output is unchanged by the move from single-price to discriminatory monopoly. Thus, if the demand curves are linear, the first term in (15.4) is zero and price discrimination causes a net welfare loss.[15]

The second term in (15.4), $- (b'c'e' + bce)$, reflects what Robinson[16] calls "the maldistribution of resources as between different uses." Under price discrimination, the price in the low-elasticity market, p_{pd}^L, is greater than the price in the high-elasticity market, p_{pd}^H. There are some consumers in the low-elasticity market who would take the product if they could get it for p_{pd}^H; there are some consumers in the high-elasticity market who would give up the product if they had to pay p_{pd}^L for it. It is this aspect of price discrimination—depriving some consumers of the product even though they value it more than others who are able to obtain it—that creates the second term in (15.4), and this term is unambiguously negative. An efficient allocation of resources among consumers requires that all consumers place the same value on the marginal unit of output; price discrimination prevents this equal valuation.

In the end, however, the welfare effect of price discrimination is ambiguous. If output increases enough under price discrimination, the first term in Equation (15.4) will counterbalance the second term, and the overall effect of price discrimination on welfare will be positive. The possibility that price discrimination will increase welfare is even more likely if price discrimination allows markets to be served that would not be served under single-price monopoly. But if price discrimination does not affect total output, or reduces total output, it reduces social welfare.

Case Study: Third-Degree Price Discrimination

In the early 1970s, the United Brands Company and its European affiliate marketed Chiquita bananas to the European Economic Community. The bananas were sold to local ripeners and wholesalers for distribution in national markets. United enjoyed a large market share—45 per cent—but competed against other large firms [Castle and Cole (Dole brand) and Del Monte].

United Brands' bananas were all of the same variety and entered Europe through either Rotterdam or Bremerhaven. Unloading costs at the two ports differed by only a few cents per 20-kilogram box.

---

[15]There are few general results if demand curves are nonlinear; see Schmalensee, op. cit., p. 245.

[16]Op. cit., p. 206.

Yet prices to distributors differed sharply from country to country within the Common Market. The average difference in weekly prices per 20-kilogram box ranged from 11.3 to 17.6 per cent over 1971–1974, and some differences were much larger. Prices to Denmark reached 2.38 times the price to Ireland (both markets being served from Bremerhaven).

The antitrust law of the European Economic Community (Articles 85 and 86 of the Treaty of Rome) forbids the abuse of a dominant market position, and United Brands' pricing practices (among other things) eventually landed it in front of the European Court of Justice. Among other defenses, United Brands explained the price differences as reflecting local market conditions. The European Economic Community countered that the effect of the price differences was to impose obstacles to the movement of goods within the community—barriers to competition across national boundaries.

In a landmark decision on February 14, 1978, the Court of Justice ruled that a dominant firm could not charge what the market would bear except while respecting the laws of the market imposed by the Treaty of Rome. Since it was ripeners and distributors who bore the risks of the marketplace, it was they, and not United Brands, who should determine local prices. United Brands' policy of price discrimination was found to be an abuse of a dominant market position under Common Market antitrust law.

See *United Brands Company et United Brands Continental BV contre Commission des Communautes europeennes.* Luxembourg: Recueil de la Jurisprudence de la Cour, Cour de Justice des Communautes Europeennes, 1978, pp. 207–351.

The Robinson-Patman Act[17]

Section 2 of the Clayton Act, as amended by the Robinson-Patman Act, states:

> It shall be unlawful for any person engaged in commerce . . . to discriminate in price between different purchasers of commodities of like grade and quality . . . where the effect of such discrimination may be substantially to lessen competition or tend to create a monopoly in any line of commerce. . . . *Provided,* That nothing herein contained shall prevent differentials which made only due allowance for differences in the cost of manufacture, sale or delivery resulting from the differing methods or quantities in which such commodities are . . . sold or delivered. . . . *And provided further,* That nothing contained herein shall prevent price changes from time to time where in response to changing conditions affecting the market. . . .

[17]For excellent discussions of the Robinson-Patman Act, see symposia on the occasion of the act's 50th anniversary in the Fall 1986 issue of *The Antitrust Bulletin* and the April 1986 issue of the *Antitrust Law Journal.*

If these words were given the meaning a layperson would most likely give them, there would appear to be little conflict between the economic analysis of systematic price discrimination and the treatment of what is called price discrimination under the antitrust laws. Under the language of the Robinson-Patman Act, price differences may reflect either cost differences or changes in market conditions. In language omitted in the preceding extract, the Robinson-Patman Act permits price differences if the lower price is intended to meet competition—''the equally low price of a competitor.'' In addition, price discrimination is prohibited only ''where the effect . . . may be substantially to lessen competition.''

From an economic point of view, none of these provisions seem objectionable. But the words of the Robinson-Patman Act have been given a rather different reading by the courts and the Federal Trade Commission, with the result that the act is almost universally condemned by economists. To understand why, we need to explore the background and interpretation of federal law against price discrimination.

Background of the Robinson-Patman Act[18]

The first specific legal assault on price discrimination, the original Section 2 of the Clayton Act, can be traced ultimately to claims that Standard Oil employed price wars to maintain its dominant position and benefited from discriminatorily low rail rates.[19] Allegations of predatory pricing and secret rail rebates played an important role in public agitation against Standard Oil in particular and trusts in general, but the legality of such practices under the Sherman Act remained unclear after the 1911 *Standard Oil* decision.[20] An important purpose of the 1914 Clayton Act and the Federal Trade Commission Act was to clarify antitrust policy in light of this decision.

The original Section 2 forbade price discrimination, but contained a qualifying clause that exempted price differences due to ''differences in the grade, quality, or quantity of commodity sold.'' Courts held that under this language, even modest quantity differences could be used to justify unlimited price differences.[21] This loophole effectively neutralized the prohibition against price

---

[18]For accounts of the genesis of the Robinson-Patman Act, see Rowe, Frederick M. *Price Discrimination Under the Robinson-Patman Act*. Boston: Little, Brown and Company, 1962, chapter 1; Posner, *The Robinson-Patman Act;* American Bar Association, Section of Antitrust Law, Monograph Number 4, *The Robinson-Patman Act: Policy and Law* Volume 1 (1980); and Ross, Thomas W. ''Winners and Losers Under the Robinson-Patman Act,'' *Journal of Law and Economics* Volume 27, Number 2, October 1984, pp. 243–271.

[19]Price discrimination that injures the competition in the market inhabited by the discriminating firm has come to be called *primary line discrimination*. Price discrimination that injures competition among the customers of the discriminating firm is called *secondary line discrimination*.

[20]Posner, *The Robinson-Patman Act,* pp. 22–23.

[21]*Goodyear Tire and Rubber Co. v. Federal Trade Commission,* 101 F.2d 620 (6th Cir. 1939).

discrimination. The 1936 Robinson-Patman Act amendments to Section 2 closed the "quantity discount" loophole, replacing the "grade, quality, or quantity" exemption with the "differences in cost" provision quoted in the preceding extract. Under the amended Section 2 of the Clayton Act, the burden of showing that cost differences justify price differences falls on the firm accused of price discrimination.

The passage of the 1936 amendments to the Clayton Act is connected with A&P—the Great Atlantic and Pacific Tea Company—and the rise of chain stores in distribution, in the same way that the passage of the Sherman Act is connected with Standard Oil and the rise of trusts in manufacturing.[22]

The rise of mass distribution in the early years of the twentieth century included the development of mass wholesalers, but the place of the wholesale sector was soon challenged as mass producers integrated forward into distribution and mass retailers integrated backward into production. Mass wholesaler enterprises that integrated forward into retailing survived,[23] but small wholesalers saw their place—at least their place as independent enterprises—contract steadily as the nature of the economy changed.

Nothing typified this evolution more than the rise of the chain store. Chain stores' share of retail sales was 9 per cent in 1926 but 25 per cent in 1933.[24] The earliest growth of chains was in the distribution of food, but by 1929 chain stores had an important place in pharmaceuticals (Walgreen), clothing (J.C. Penney), and department stores (F.W. Woolworth, Montgomery Ward).[25] But A&P, which rose from one store in 1858 to more than 15,000 in 1929,[26] typified the chain store phenomenon in the public consciousness.

Chain stores evoked considerable public hostility. Twenty-three states passed taxes on chain stores; typically, the fee per store rose as the number of stores per chain increased.[27] However, the fee-per-store tax did little to limit the increasing volume of sales passing through each store.[28]

A persistent criticism of chain stores was that they benefited from a variety

[22]For an accessible account of these transformations, see Chandler, Alfred D., Jr. *The Visible Hand: The Managerial Revolution in American Business.* Cambridge, Mass.: The Belknap Press of Harvard University Press, 1977.

[23]Marshall Field is an example; Chandler, op. cit., p. 225.

[24]Palamountain, Joseph Cornwall, Jr. *The Politics of Distribution.* Cambridge, Mass.: Harvard University Press, 1955, p. 7.

[25]Ross, op. cit., p. 246.

[26]With sales of over $1 billion but only 11.3 per cent of national grocery sales in 1929; Ross, op. cit. The classic discussion remains that of Adelman, M. A. *A&P: A Study of Price-Cost Behavior and Public Policy.* Cambridge, Mass.: Harvard University Press, 1959.

[27]Ross, op. cit., p. 247.

[28]Rowe, op. cit., p. 9.

of unfailr purchasing practices, which was alleged to give them an unfair competitive advantage. This claim is worth examining. Suppose, as seems likely, that chain stores are able to bargain with suppliers and get lower prices for the products they retail. What happens next?[29] One of two things. Possibly, the chain stores pocket the difference (a form of limit pricing). This is good for the chain stores and for their stockholders. It does not benefit consumers or disadvantage competitors.

On the other hand, the chain stores may pass on their lower cost to consumers and undersell rivals. This is bad for rivals but good for consumers and, in some sense, the essence of the competitive process. Would a market share of 11.3 per cent (A&P's share of the national grocery market in 1929) carry with it the power to control price or exclude competitors?[30] Most economists think not.

In December 1934 the Federal Trade Commission issued a report on the operations of chain stores.[31] The report, which was based on a 7-year study, concluded that, at most, 20 per cent of the pricing advantages of chain stores could be traced to lower input prices. The remainder was due to lower costs and more efficient operations.[32] The resentment of displaced competitors toward chains was natural enough, but the belief in competitive advantages due to massive purchasing power was apparently misplaced.

The National Industrial Recovery Act of 1933, basically an attempt to find a way out of the Great Depression, authorized agreements among competitors as a way of raising prices and, hopefully, income. The act turned into a preliminary skirmish in the attack on chains:[33]

> The Codes of Fair Competition authorized by the National Industrial Recovery Act . . . in many cases expressed the objectives of the numerically dominant independent merchants who sought to freeze the orthodox pattern of distribution into law. In some codes, producers were barred from distributing outside the conventional wholesaler-retailer channel. Other codes ensured that chain

[29]In the words of Kermit the Frog. There is a deeper question: if chain stores can bargain for lower prices, this implies that the firms supplying the chain stores operate in markets that are imperfectly competitive. If the supplying markets were perfectly competitive, no customer could bargain their prices down because (over the long run) they would be selling at average cost, and supplying firms would not sell at less than average cost.

[30]A follow-up question is, what was the market share in local markets? Chapter 4 suggests that power to control price will depend as much on conjectural variations as on market share, and conjectural variations in local markets may be influenced as much by absolute size as by national or local market share. Thus the case against the existence of market power in local markets might not be as weak as a national market share of 11.3 per cent, taken alone, suggests.

[31]Federal Trade Commission. *Chain Stores: Final Report on the Chain-Store Investigation.* Senate Document Number 4, 74th Congress, 1st Session (1935).

[32]American Bar Association, op. cit., p. 10.

[33]Rowe, op. cit., p. 10.

distributors and mail-order houses, notwithstanding their performance of typical "wholesaling" functions such as bulk storage and delivery, were classified as "retailers" entitled to receive only the prevailing retailer's functional discount. Food industry codes limited the quantity discounts chain buyers could secure, and many prohibited "brokerage" commissions to buyers whose direct purchasing techniques saved the seller fees otherwise paid to independent brokers.

The National Industrial Recovery Act was declared unconstitutional in 1935, and hostility toward chains sought another outlet. The result was the Robinson-Patman Act of 1936.

The original version of the Robinson-Patman Act was drafted by H. B. Teegarden, counsel for the United States Wholesale Grocers Association. It was introduced in the House of Representatives 15 days after the Supreme Court found the National Industrial Recovery Act to be unconstitutional.[34]

As one discussant of the legislative history of the Robinson-Patman Act observes,[35] "logic is not always the strong point of the legislative process." The legislative history of the Robinson-Patman Act weaves together two distinct and inconsistent threads, the first frankly protectionist toward small business and the second concerned with preserving opportunities for equally efficient firms to compete.

Typical of the first approach are the remarks of Representative Wright Patman:[36]

> the day of the independent merchant is gone unless something is done and done quickly. He cannot possibly survive under that system. So we have reached the crossroads; we must either turn the food and grocery business of this country . . . over to a few corporate chains, or we have got to pass laws that will give the people, who built this country in time of peace and who saved it in time of war, an opportunity to exist. . . .

Committee reports, in contrast, emphasized efficiency as a condition of protection. The Senate Judiciary Committee sought[37]

> the preservation of equal opportunity to all usefully employed in the service of distribution comportably with their ability and equipment to serve the producing and consuming public with real efficiency, and the preservation to that public of its freedom from the threat of monopoly or oppression in obtaining its needs and disposing of its products.

[34]American Bar Association, op. cit., pp. 14–15.

[35]Posner, *The Robinson-Patman Act,* p. 28.

[36]Hearings Before the House Committee on the Judiciary on Bills to Amend the Clayton Act, 74th Congress, 1st Session 5–6 (1935); quoted in Rowe, op. cit., p. 13.

[37]Senate Report Number 1502, 74th Congress, Second Session 3 (1936); quoted in Rowe, op. cit., p. 20.

Similarly, the House Judiciary Committee held that[38]

[t]he purpose of this proposed legislation is to restore, so far as possible, equality of opportunity in business by strengthening antitrust laws and by protecting trade and commerce against unfair trade practices and unlawful price discrimination, and also against restraint and monopoly for the better protection of consumers, workers, and independent producers, manufacturers, merchants, and other businessmen. . . .

Further:[39]

. . . There is nothing in it to penalize, shackle, or discourage efficiency, or to reward inefficiency. There is nothing in it to fix prices, or enable the fixation of prices; nor to limit the freedom of price movements in response to changing market conditions.

The committee reports seem consistent with the general intent of the antitrust laws: to promote consumer welfare[40] by condemning artificial impediments to the competitive process.

The debates, in contrast, have a protectionist flavor that is alien to antitrust policy. It seems clear that this protectionist strain was part of congressional intent with respect to the Robinson-Patman Act. The Senate Judiciary Committee felt that the original requirement of a probable substantial lessening of competition flowing from a price discrimination was[41]

too restrictive . . . whereas the more immediately important concern is in injury to the competitor victimized by the discrimination. Only through such injuries, in fact, can the larger general injury result. . . .

For this reason, the Senate Judiciary Committee added an "injury to competitors" clause to the "injury to competition" clause. Price discriminations would be illegal[42]

where the effect of such discrimination may be substantially to lessen competition or tend to create a monopoly in any line of commerce, *or to injure,*

[38]House Report Number 2287, 74th Congress, Second Session, 3 (1936); quoted in Rowe, op. cit., p. 20.

[39]House Report Number 2287, 74th Congress, Second Session, 17 (1936); quoted in Rowe, op. cit., p. 20.

[40]See footnote 10 of Chapter 3; as used in this text, *consumer welfare* does not mean *consumer plus producer welfare.*

[41]Senate Report Number 1502, 74th Congress, Second Session 4 (1936); quoted in Rowe, op. cit., p. 15.

[42]This language is part of the act; also quoted by Rowe, op. cit., p. 14.

> *destroy, or prevent competition with any person who either grants or knowingly*
> *receives the benefit of such discrimination, or with customers of either of them*
> *. . . (emphasis added).*

Thus the Robinson-Patman Act aims at preventing injury to competition *and* injury to competitors. This mingled measure[43] was passed by both houses of Congress and signed by the President in June 1936.

Enforcement of the Robinson-Patman Act

As with the Clayton Act and (after 1914) the Sherman Act, there are three avenues through which the Robinson-Patman Act may be enforced: by the Department of Justice, by the Federal Trade Commission, and by private suits in which individuals seek to recover (treble) damages for actions in violation of the law.

In practice, only two of these avenues have been traveled, and one of these two seems (at this writing) to be closed. The Department of Justice has never actively enforced the Robinson-Patman Act.[44] Historically, the Federal Trade Commission has been the major enforcer.[45] From 1936 to 1963, the Commission filed more than 1,300 Robinson-Patman Act complaints, 200 in 1963 alone.[46] But the Commission's enforcement of the Robinson-Patman Act fell off sharply after that year. It filed six Robinson-Patman Act complaints over fiscal years 1975–1982 and none at all in 1983, 1984, and 1985.[47] Private Robinson-Patman suits, on the other hand, continue to seek enforcement of the law.[48]

The Definition of Price Discrimination Under the Robinson-Patman Act

The Robinson-Patman Act makes it unlawful ''to discriminate in price between purchasers of commodities of like grade and quality,'' subject to qualifications to be discussed below.[49] The immediate questions are these: (1) When

[43]Apologies to Samuel Taylor Coleridge.

[44]Posner, *The Robinson-Patman Act,* p. 29; Whiting, Richard A. ''R-P: May It Rest in Peace,'' *Antitrust Bulletin* Volume 31, Number 3, Fall 1986, p. 711.

[45]For a critical analysis of the Federal Trade Commission's enforcement of the Robinson-Patman Act, see Amacher, Ryan, Higgins, Richard, Shughart, William II and Tollison, Robert. ''The Behavior of Regulatory Activity Over the Business Cycle: An Empirical Test,'' *Economic Inquiry* Volume 23, Number 1, January 1985, pp. 7–19.

[46]Whiting, op. cit.

[47]And at least one complaint in 1986. Whiting, op. cit.

[48]Posner, *The Robinson-Patman Act,* p. 29, reports 19 decisions in private Robinson-Patman cases in 1975 but notes that many private cases are settled before a decision is rendered.

[49]Since the Robinson-Patman Act applies to *commodities,* it does not prohibit price discrimination with respect to services. From an economic point of view, of course, there is no distinction between services and commodities; they are both products sold across markets. So it goes.

are goods of like grade and quality? (2) For goods of like grade and quality, what sort of pricing constitutes price discrimination within the meaning of the Robinson-Patman Act?

When are goods of like grade and quality? An important question is whether grade and quality are to be determined by examination of the physical characteristics of the commodity or by market perceptions of differences. In *Federal Trade Commission v. Borden Company*,[50] the Supreme Court interpreted the Robinson-Patman Act as defining grade and quality in terms of physical properties.

This *Borden* case involved the sale of evaporated milk. Borden produced evaporated milk and marketed it under its own nationally advertised brand name. Borden also produced evaporated milk that was physically identical to its branded product but marketed it on a private label basis for distribution by local chains or stores under their own brand name. Borden sold its branded evaporated milk at a higher price than the private label variety. The Federal Trade Commission took exception to this practice, and Borden appealed to a Circuit Court of Appeals, arguing that branded and private label evaporated milk were not of like grade and quality, since they were regarded as different products by the public. The Circuit Court of Appeals accepted Borden's argument, and the Federal Trade Commission appealed to the Supreme Court.

The Supreme Court sided with the Commission. If different brand names justified different prices, every price difference would be accompanied by a different brand name. The result would be to gut the Robinson-Patman Act, and this the Court was unwilling to do.

Suppose goods are physically identical. What pricing systems are discriminatory under the antitrust laws? The Supreme Court settled this question in *Federal Trade Commission v. Anheuser-Busch, Inc.*[51] In the early 1950s, Anheuser-Busch faced competition in the St. Louis, Missouri area from three regional brewers, and as a result charged a lower price in the St. Louis market than in other regional markets.[52] The Federal Trade Commission thought this practice to be a violation of the Robinson-Patman Act. Anheuser-Busch argued before the Circuit Court of Appeals that price discrimination in the sense of the Robinson-Patman Act required that the lower price be "below cost or unreasonably low for the purpose or design to eliminate competition and thereby obtain a monopoly."[53] The Circuit Court of Appeals, acting on this and other

---

[50]383 U.S. 637 (1966).

[51]363 U.S. 536 (1960).

[52]Consideration of Figure 15-2 will explain such a price pattern. The demand curve facing Anheuser-Busch in the St. Louis market would be more elastic, because customers could turn to the regional suppliers. Thus the St. Louis market could be represented as the center graph in Figure 15-2, with other markets, with less elastic demand, as a graph on the left.

[53]363 U.S. 536, at 546.

arguments, reversed the Federal Trade Commission, which then took the issue to the Supreme Court. The Court ruled that "there are no overtones of business buccaneering in the Section 2 phrase 'discriminate in price.' Rather, a price discrimination within the meaning of that provision is merely a price difference."

It appears, then, that price discrimination in the sense of the Robinson-Patman Act occurs if physically identical goods are sold at different prices. Where physically identical goods bear different brand names, the distributor of the unbranded version will bear marketing and promotional costs that the producer bears for the branded version. But the Robinson-Patman Act requires the producer to charge the same price to a distributor who purchases a less valuable, unbranded variety than the distributor who purchases a more valuable, branded variety. By selling both versions of the product at the same price, but bearing lower costs for the unbranded version, the producer will earn a greater rate of return on sales of the unbranded variety. In other words, by requiring identical prices on physically identical goods, the Robinson-Patman Act requires producers to discriminate, in an economic sense, against purchasers of unbranded varieties.[54]

Cost Justification

In principle, price differences may be excused under the Robinson-Patman Act if the seller can show that the price differences reflect cost differences. As a practical matter, however, two different problems have eliminated the cost-justification defense.

The first problem involves showing a connection between a cost difference and a price difference. Sellers bear the burden of showing this connection. It is often impossible to allocate overhead costs among various products in any sensible way. Allowance for a normal rate of return on investment—an element of economic cost—and for differences in investment to serve different markets is not permitted. Yet the Federal Trade Commission has set a severe standard of proof, disallowing claims of cost justification unless the connection between cost difference and price difference is clear-cut and precise.[55]

There is an even more fundamental objection. Profit-maximizing firms do not make output and price decisions on the basis of cost considerations alone. Cost reflects the supply side of the pricing equation, but the price will be determined by the interaction of demand and supply. To ignore the influence

---

[54]Rowe, Frederick M. "Price Differentials and Product Differentiation: The Issues Under the Robinson-Patman Act," *Yale Law Journal* Volume 66, Number 1, November 1956, pp. 27–30.

[55]See Adelman, op. cit., pp. 163–172; Rowe, Frederick M. *Price Discrimination*, pp. 273–312; Bork, op. cit., pp. 391–394; Schwartz, Marius. "The Perverse Effects of the Robinson-Patman Act," *Antitrust Bulletin* Volume 31, Number 3, Fall 1986, pp. 737–738.

of differences on the demand side of the market is to condemn the workings of the competitive process.[56]

The Good Faith Defense

A price difference that would otherwise be condemned as discriminatory under the Robinson-Patman Act will also be allowed if the seller can show that the lower price was offered "in good faith to meet an equally low price of a competitor."

In *Standard Oil Co. v. Federal Trade Commission,*[57] the Federal Trade Commission argued that the good faith defense would not apply if the price discrimination so allowed would injure competition. The Supreme Court apparently had some difficulty in understanding how this could happen,[58] but in any event ruled that[59] "it is a complete defense to a charge of price discrimination for the seller to show that its price differential has been made in good faith to meet a lawful and equally low price of a competitor." In so doing, the Court sought to place the Robinson-Patman Act firmly in the tradition of other antitrust laws:[60]

> In the Sherman Act and the Clayton Acts, as well as the Robinson-Patman Act, "Congress was dealing with competition, which it sought to protect, and monopoly, which it sought to prevent." . . . We need not now reconcile, in its entirety, the economic theory which underlies the Robinson-Patman Act either to abolish competition or so radically to curtail it that a seller would have no substantial right of self-defense against a price raid by a competitor.

Injury to Competition Under the Robinson-Patman Act

The *Standard Oil of Indiana* case serves to introduce another topic under the Robinson-Patman Act. Some injury to competition must be shown to flow from a price discrimination before it can be condemned under Section 2.[61]

---

[56]It seems likely that this is what was going on in the *Anheuser-Busch* case. See footnote 52. See also the subsequent discussion of *Utah Pie* and Chapter 16.

[57]340 U.S. 231 (1951).

[58]340 U.S. 231, at 242: "the actual core of the defense . . . still consists of the provision that wherever a lawful lower price of a competitor threatens to deprive a seller of a customer, the seller, to retain that customer, may in good faith meet the lower price. Actual competition, at least in this elemental form, is thus preserved."

[59]340 U.S. 231, at 246.

[60]340 U.S. 231, 248–249. Citation omitted. In a footnote that is omitted here, the Court acknowledges the contention that the Robinson-Patman Act is inconsistent with other antitrust laws.

[61]No such requirement attaches to Sections 2(c), (d), or (e) of the Robinson-Patman Act, which deal with brokerage payments and advertising allowances.

Two principal types of injury have been distinguished. Primary-line injury falls to firms competing with the firm that grants the discriminatorily low price. Secondary-line injury falls to firms competing with the firm that receives the discriminatorily low price.[62]

Primary-Line Injury

Primary-line injury to competition was the issue in *Utah Pie Co. v. Continental Baking Co. et al.*,[63] a case that has the distinction of having produced what is probably the most severely criticized antitrust decision of all time.[64] In that case, the Supreme Court found an injury to competition in the fact that prices had fallen in a regional market after the entry of new producers.[65]

Falling prices, of course, are exactly what economic theory predicts after the entry of new suppliers into a competitive market. Falling prices alone do not demonstrate an injury to competition.

The issue of primary-line injury to competition under the Robinson-Patman Act is intimately related to the treatment of predatory pricing under the Sherman Act. We resume consideration of that topic in Chapter 16.

Secondary-Line Injury

Secondary-line injury—injury to competition between firms favored by a differentially low price—is recognized as the main target of the Robinson-Patman Act.[66] The leading case in determining injury to competition among the customers of a discriminating firm is *Federal Trade Commission v. Morton*

---

[62]*The Standard Oil of Indiana* case involves allegations of third-line injury to competition, that is, injury to firms competing with the customers of the firm that receives the discriminatorily low price. *Perkins v. Standard Oil Company*, 395 U.S. 642 (1969), deals with fourth-line injury to competition. There is an infinite sequence here somewhere.

[63]386 U.S. 685 (1967).

[64]See, for example, Bowman, Ward S. "Restraint of Trade by the Supreme Court," *Yale Law Journal* Volume 77, Number 1, November 1967, pp. 70–85; and Elzinga, Kenneth G. and Hogarty, Thomas F. "*Utah Pie* and the Consequences of Robinson-Patman," *Journal of Law and Economics* Volume 21, Number 2, October 1978, pp. 427–434.

[65]It was the misfortune of these producers that they operated in other markets, where they charged higher prices for the product in question (frozen fruit pies). This brought them into conflict with the Robinson-Patman Act.

[66]See *Federal Trade Commission v. Anheuser-Busch, Inc.*, 363 U.S. 536, at 543–544: "It is, of course, quite true–and too well known to require extensive exposition—that the 1936 Robinson-Patman amendments to the Clayton Act were motivated principally by congressional concern over the impact upon secondary-line competition of the burgeoning of mammoth purchasers, notably chain stores."

Salt Company.[67]

Morton sold its salt to retailers under a discount schedule that made the price per case dependent on the total quantity purchased:[68]

	Price Per Case
Less-than-carload purchases	$1.60
Carload purchases	1.50
5,000 cases in 12 consecutive months	1.40
50,000 cases in 12 consecutive months	1.35

Only five firms had ever qualified for the lowest price. These firms operated chains of grocery stores.[69] Before the Supreme Court, Morton argued in vain that the Federal Trade Commission had failed to show an injury to competition. The Court's reaction was that the law did not require the Commission to show an actual injury to competition:[70]

> "the statute does not require that the discriminations must in fact have harmed competition, but only that there is a reasonable possibility that they 'may' have such an effect." Here the Commission found what would appear to be obvious, that the competitive opportunities of certain merchants were injured when they had to pay [Morton] substantially more for their goods than their competitors had to pay.

Further:[71]

> That [Morton's] quantity discounts did result in price differentials between competing purchasers sufficient in amount to influence their resale price of salt was shown by evidence. This showing in itself is adequate to support the Commission's appropriate findings that the effect of such price discriminations "may be substantially to lessen competition . . . and to injure, destroy and prevent competition."

This finding is consistent with economic theory: a difference in input prices can create exactly the kind of limit price differential that will allow the firm

[67]334 U.S. 37 (1948).

[68]334 U.S. 37, at 41.

[69]Ibid.; the chains included A&P, Safeway, and Kroger.

[70]334 U.S. 37, at 46–47; the Court quotes its decision in *Corn Products Refining Company v. Federal Trade Commission,* 324 U.S. 726, at 742.

[71]334 U.S. 37, at 47.

with the lower price to exercise some degree of market power over the long run:[72]

> Price discrimination impairs efficiency in the market in which the purchasers from the discriminating seller sell, by creating competitive cost disparities unrelated to differences in the relative efficiency of the competitors. The purchaser to whom the discriminating seller sells at a lower price may be no more efficient than the competing seller who is charged a higher price.

Thus it is reasonably clear that *price discrimination*—in the economic sense of price differences not proportional to cost differences—can injure secondary-line competition. But as we have seen, the Robinson-Patman Act, as interpreted, does not condemn price discrimination but rather *price differences*. Forcing a vertically integrated firm to pay the same price for supplies as a nonintegrated retailer that performs no distribution functions results in price discrimination in an economic sense and places the integrated firm at a competitive disadvantage. But such price discrimination is compelled by the Robinson-Patman Act, not condemned by it.

A later decision suggests that price discrimination must be systematic, rather than sporadic, to be prohibited by the Robinson-Patman Act.[73] Subject to this qualification, the rule of *Morton Salt* is that secondary-line injury to competition may be inferred from the existence of a price difference large enough to influence resale prices. No examination of the likely effect of the price differential on market performance is required. On this reading, persistent price differences for physically identical products are, for all practical purposes, illegal per se under the Robinson-Patman Act.

Policy Debate

The Robinson-Patman Act is almost universally condemned by economists. The charges laid against it are serious. It is alleged that the Robinson-Patman Act:[74]

1. *contributes to price rigidity:* A multimarket firm will hesitate to set different prices in different markets unless it believes it can meet the substantial and expensive burden of showing a cost justification that will satisfy the Federal Trade Commission;

---

[72]Posner, Richard A. *Antitrust Law,* footnote 14.

[73]*American Oil Company v. Federal Trade Commission,* 325 F. 2d 101 (7th Cir. 1963). See Posner, *The Robinson-Patman Act,* pp. 39–40.

[74]American Bar Association, op. cit., pp. 27–37.

2. *contributes to oligopolistic price discipline:* secret price cuts are the Achilles' heel of tacit or overt collusion, and we know from Chapter 6 that individual oligopolists always have an incentive—in the short run—to cut their price and profit at their colleagues' expense; public policy that discourages selective price cuts serves to reinforce oligopolistic price discipline;

3. *discourages entry by firms established in other markets:* we know from Chapter 5 that among the most likely potential entrants to a market will be firms producing the same product in other geographic markets; a new firm will often need to start with a low price in order to attract customers; public policy that discourages the charging of different prices in different markets will force an entrant to stay out unless it is willing to lower price in all of its markets;

4. *induces inefficient product differentiation:* the Robinson-Patman Act condemns price differences for physically identical products. It follows that by introducing minor physical changes, different varieties of an underlying product can be sold at different prices without coming under the purview of the act; it also follows that the act induces more product differentiation than the market would otherwise sustain;

5. *imposes an undue regulatory burden:* The burden consists not only of expenses that must be met by business (and therefore, ultimately, the consumer) to justify price differences to the government, but also inefficiently high distribution costs that must be borne by business (and therefore, ultimately, the consumer) when business opts for inefficient methods of distribution because of the cost of justifying the offering of different prices to different types of distributors.

Against these charges, the benefits attributed to the Robinson-Patman Act are frankly noneconomic.[75] Regardless of the economic effects of price discrimination,[76] a public policy against price discrimination is often justified on grounds of fairness. In this view, price differences to rivals ought to be based on cost differences; otherwise, those paying the higher price are placed at an unfair cost disadvantage.

---

[75]Ibid., pp. 22–27; Kintner, Earl W. and Bauer, Joseph P. "The Robinson-Patman Act: A Look Backwards, a View Forward," *Antitrust Bulletin* Volume 31, Number 3, Fall 1986, pp. 586–591; Silcox, Clark R. and MacIntyre, A. Everette. "The Robinson-Patman Act and Competitive Fairness; Balancing the Economic and Social Dimensions of Antitrust," *Antitrust Bulletin* Volume 31, Number 3, Fall 1986, pp. 647–661.

[76]As we have seen, deadweight loss measures of the welfare consequences of price discrimination are generally ambiguous.

It is not for the economist to agree or disagree with this position, because it is not the economist's job to explain to society what the social welfare function should be. It is the economist's job to explain the cost of alternative rules. Most economists—even those who agree that fairness is an appropriate goal for public policy, even those who think that maintaining opportunity for equally efficient rivals to compete is an efficient way to attain desirable market performance—would prefer to see the Robinson-Patman Act abolished. Although its words condemn price discrimination, it often seems to compel price discrimination, in a way that protects inefficient modes of distribution and imposes substantial costs on society.

Tying

Economic Analysis of Tying

Tying contracts create an artificial connection between the availability of two distinct products. Product A (the tying product) is made available only if the purchaser agrees to take product B (the tied product) as well.[77] Economists delineate three effects that may result from tying contracts. Tying contracts may serve to strategically deter or impede entry by raising entry costs. They may allow a firm that has market power to increase the profit it reaps by allowing price discrimination. Tying contracts may make production more efficient by allowing a firm to control the quality of products used in combination with its own product.

Tying as Strategic Behavior

We know from Chapter 4 that a dominant firm that can raise the entry costs of rivals can deter or delay entry while continuing to exercise market power. One explanation of tying contracts is that it reinforces market power by raising entry costs. If rivals must enter two markets to compete effectively, they will face the prospect of making a greater capital investment than would otherwise be necessary. This will increase interest costs if (as is usually the case) the cost of financial capital rises with the amount borrowed or if (as is usually the case)

---

[77]Tying is closely related to *full line forcing,* under which a manufacturer requires "acceptance of a full line of goods or services as a condition of purchase or lease of some part of it." (Hilton, George W. "Tying Sales and Full-Line Forcing," *Weltwirtschaftliches Archiv* Volume 81, 1958, p. 265), and to *commodity bundling,* in which goods that can be sold separately are sold as components of a package (see Paper Topic 15-4).

entry into two markets is perceived as increasing the risk that entry will be unsuccessful. Thus:[78]

> The tying clause creates a barrier to entry. In most cases, it will increase the capital investment needed by a potential entrant, as he may have to produce a substitute for the tying product in order to enter the market for the tied product. At worst, if the tying product is protected by a strong patent and the only use for the tied product is in conjunction with the tying product, the tying arrangement will result in a complete barrier to entry until the patient expires.

Case Study: Tying to Affect Entry Conditions

The Motion Picture Patents Company had a legal monopoly over certain essential components of motion picture projectors. It formed a cartel with producers and distributors of films and sold projectors on the condition that they be used only to show films that were produced by members of the collusive group. By tying together motion picture projectors and the exhibition of motion pictures, a legal monopoly over movie projectors was extended to the market for motion pictures:*

> The success of the "Motion Picture Trust" . . . was phenomenal. It started as a combination of owners of the key patents in the motion picture field, including the patents covering projectors and film. The ten American manufacturers of motion pictures were then added to the combination as

*Spivack, Gordon B. "The Chicago School Approach to Single Firm Exercises of Monopoly Power: A Response," *Antitrust Law Journal* Volume 53, Issue 3, September 1983, p. 664, footnote 69.

[78]Baldwin, W. L. and McFarland, David. "Tying Arrangements in Law and Economics," *Antitrust Bulletin* Volume 8, Numbers 5–6, September–December 1963, p. 773. Compare the remarks of Telser, Lester G., "Abusive Trade Practices: An Economic Analysis," *Law and Contemporary Problems,* Volume 30, Number 3, Summer 1965, p. 492, on full-line forcing: "Some may wish to argue that full-line forcing represents the manufacturer's effort to impede entry if a rival cannot secure dealers without offering them an equally full line. This might have the effect of limiting access to the retail market. In addition, if it requires a larger capital to provide a wider range of products and if the firm faces a rising cost of capital in financial markets, full-line forcing might allow fewer firms to enter the industry. Even if larger capital requirements are not an insurmountable barrier and merely delay entry without entirely preventing it, the firm able to impose its entire line on its dealers may thereby slow the erosion of its monopoly profits." It is easy to show formally that this effect can occur by modifying the model of Gaskins, Darius W., Jr., "Dynamic Limit Pricing: Optimal Limit Pricing Under Threat of Entry," *Journal of Economic Theory* Volume 3, September 1971, pp. 306–322, so that the rate of fringe expansion falls as (say) the absolute size of minimum efficient scale investment rises.

licensees. For a time, the group's films were distributed by over a hundred independent distributors. The group then decided, however, to handle its own distribution, and the General Film Company was established for that purpose. Within two years, all but one of the independent distributors had been driven out of business.

For further information, see *Motion Picture Patents Company v. Universal Film Manufacturing Company et al.*, 243 U.S. 502 (1917).

Even the classic Chicago school rejection of the possibility that tying can be used to extend or "lever" market power from one market to another includes an admission that if tying raises rivals' costs, it will therefore be a profitable strategy:[79]

> Firms which have some monopoly power over prices and output can impose coercive restrictions on suppliers and customers. In the normal case, however, they will lose revenue if they do impose such restrictions, and this casts some doubt on how prevalent or continued the practice would be. Such firms would lose revenue because they cannot both obtain the advantage of the original power and impose additional restrictions so as to increase their monopoly power. The coercive restrictions on customers are possible only if the price which would be charged without the restriction is reduced. . . . even a firm with complete monopoly power over prices and output cannot both get the advantage of such power and impose additional coercive restrictions on suppliers and customers. At most such a firm, and of course one with only some monopoly power, can decide to impose additional costs upon itself for the sake of a restriction. *Such a restriction might be valuable if the effect of it would be to impose greater costs on possible competitors*. But except for this special case, there is clearly no apparent advantage to a firm with monopoly power as against one without such power (emphasis added).

Tying to Increase and Return from Existing Monopoly Power

Interrelated Demand[80]

Tying frequently joins goods that are used together. One explanation for such tying can be found in Chapter 9's discussion of horizontal integration [see equation (9.1) and the accompanying text].

[79]Director, Aaron and Levi, Edward H. "Law and the Future: Trade Regulation," *Northwestern University Law Review* Volume 51, Number 2, May–June 1956, p. 290.

[80]Bowman, Ward S., Jr. "Tying Arrangements and the Leverage Problem," *Yale Law Journal* Volume 67, Number 1, November 1957, p. 25, footnote 18; Baldwin and McFarland, op. cit., pp. 769–770. See also Blair, Roger D. and Kaserman, David L. "Vertical Integration, Tying, and Antitrust Policy," *American Economic Review* Volume 68, Number 3, June 1978, pp. 397–402. See also Burstein, M. L. "The Economics of Tie-In Sales," *Review of Economics and Statistics* Volume 42, Number 1, February 1960, pp. 68–73.

A single-product monopolist, maximizing its own profit in its own market, will adversely affect the demand for all complementary products. Raising the price of personal computers, for example, will adversely affect the demand for compatible disk drives and software. A firm with the power to set price for complementary products will take marginal losses of revenue in all related markets into account when it sets output in each market. For this reason, a firm with market power over complementary products will restrict the output of each product somewhat less than would single-product monopolists, and will earn more monopoly profit than would a group of single-product monopolists. Tying allows a firm with market power over the tying good to set its own best prices for complementary goods and thereby increase its profit.

Tying as a Metering Device[81]

We have seen that a firm with market power can increase its profit above the single-price monopoly level if it is able to discriminate in price, charging a higher price to consumers willing to pay more for the product. The tricks here are to learn what consumers are willing to pay and to prevent consumers who get lower prices from reselling to those who suffer higher prices.

Case Study: Tying for Price Discrimination*

A machine was invented for stapling buttons to high-button shoes, an operation formerly done by hand at a higher cost. The patentee had a number of prospective customers for his machine, some of whom made a great many shoes, others only a few. The invention saved each user a fixed amount on each button attached. Thus the machine was worth more to the more intensive users. If the patentee attempted to sell it at different prices to the different users, however, he would have encountered two problems. To determine in advance how intensively each buyer would use the machine would have been difficult; to prevent those who paid a low price from reselling to those who paid a high price might have proved impossible. A tie-in would resolve these difficulties. The machine might be sold at cost, on condition that the unpatented staples used in the

*Bowman, op. cit., pp. 23–24, discussing *Heaton-Peninsular Button-Fasterner Co. v. Eureka Specialty Co.*, 65 Fed. 619 (C.C.W.D. Mich. 1895).

[81]A mainstay of the Chicago school analysis of tying and one of the rare instances in which the oral tradition of Aaron Director managed to wend its way into print. Director and Levi, op. cit., pp. 291, 294; Bowman, op. cit., pp. 23–24; Bork, op. cit., pp. 376–378; Posner, pp. 173–178.

machine be bought from the patentee. Through staple sales, the patentee could obtain a device for measuring the intensity with which his customers used the machines. Hence by charging a higher than competitive price for the staples, the patentee could receive the equivalent of a royalty from his patented machines.

If there is a product that is used in conjunction with the monopolized product, and if consumers use more of this other product, the greater the value they place on the monopolized product, tying can be used to accomplish price discrimination. Lease or sell the monopolized product at a modest price to all consumers. Require that the tied product be used with the monopolized product, and charge a price above cost for the tied product. Those who use the monopolized product more intensively will use more of the tied product and pay more for the package.[82]

If the purpose of the tying firm is to discriminate in price, other alternatives are available. The firm can lease the product over which it has market power and attach a meter to measure the intensity of use.[83] This might involve greater policing costs than a tying scheme. This kind of metering is commonly used with photocopying machines.

Price discrimination will allow the discriminating firm to increase its profit. It is possible that some of this additional monopoly profit will be spent to protect the ability to discriminate; to that extent, price discrimination via tying will involve a welfare loss. In any event (as we have seen), the welfare effect of price discrimination in the market for the tying product is ambiguous. It follows that the welfare effects of tying to accomplish price discrimination are also ambiguous.

In the market for the tied product, equally efficient suppliers—perhaps even more efficient suppliers[84]—will be foreclosed from competing for the business of consumers taking the tying product unless the independent suppliers can market a substitute for the tying good along with the tied product. Tying means that performance in the market for the tied good is not determined by competition on the merits.

There is a feedback loop from the market for the tied good to the market for the tying good. Tying will reduce the market share of independent suppliers in the market for the tied good. This makes it more likely that an entrant into

---

[82]Bork, op. cit., pp. 377–378, suggests that price discrimination explains tying of punch cards to tabulating machines [*International Business Machines Corp. v. United States,* 298 U.S. 131 (1936)] and block booking of motion pictures [(*United States v. Loew's Inc.,* 371 U.S. 38 (1962)].

[83]Bowman, op. cit., p. 24.

[84]Spivack, op. cit., p. 664.

the market for the tying good will have to enter the market for the tied product as well. The need to enter two markets raises the cost of entering the market for the tying product and should (all else equal) deter entry into the market for the tying product. This is a version of the strategic explanation for tying.

Tying for Quality Control

A frequent justification for tying is that it maintains the quality of complementary inputs and protects the goodwill of the firm imposing the tie.[85] Parent firms of a franchise operation, for example, often argue that they must require franchisees to purchase supplies from them. A bad reputation based on the use of substandard inputs at one franchise will, it is argued, harm the whole operation long after the delinquent firm is gone.

A franchise is based on a contractual relationship, and there is an alternative to tying that will allow quality control. The franchisor can include in its contract specifications for supplies to be used by the franchisee. The franchisee can then purchase from any supplier that meets these specifications. Tying will be the preferred method of quality control when it is less expensive for the parent firm to police the agreement by tying.[86]

Case Study: Systems Sales and Quality Control

The Jerrold Electronics Corporation was among the first firms in the United States to sell community television antenna systems (the early market for which was consumers in outlying geographic areas afflicted with the curse of weak television reception). Because its product was new, independent workmen were often not qualified to install or maintain it. Yet when the product did not live up to its advance billing, it was Jerrold's reputation that was tarnished.

After unfortunate experience with independent distributors, Jerrold instituted the policy of selling its product only on a complete system basis—all components sold as a package—and only with post-sales service tied to the sale. This policy was designed to protect Jerrold's image during a period when the survival of the industry (not to mention, that of Jerrold itself) was uncertain.

In due course, the government challenged these tie-ins under Section 1 of the Sherman Act and Section 3 of the Clayton Act. In an intriguing ruling, the

---

[85]This justification was offered in *International Business Machines Corp. v. United States*, 298 U.S. 131 (1936), *International Salt Co., Inc., v. United States*, 332 U.S. 392 (1947), and *Siegel v. Chicken Delight, Inc.* 448 F. 2d 43 (9th Cir. 1971).

[86]See, generally, Klein, Benjamin and Saft, Lester F. "The Law and Economics of Tying Contracts," *Journal of Law and Economics* Volume 28, Number 2, May 1985, pp. 345–361.

District Court for the Eastern District of Pennsylvania found that the restraints had been lawful to begin with when justified by the firm's need to protect the reputation of its new product in a new industry. But the court also found that the restraints violated the antitrust laws by the end of the period in question, when the firm's reputation was established and its survival was no longer an issue. A policy question raised by this ruling is how a firm is to determine when its reputation is solid enough so that restrictive contracts are no longer legal.

For additional information, see *U.S. v. Jerrold Electronics Corporation*, 187 F. Supp. 545 (E.D. Pa. 1960).

Public Policy Toward Tying

Tying of commodities is prohibited under Section 3 of the Clayton Act when the effect of the tie may be to substantially lessen competition. Tying involving services may be condemned as a restraint of trade under Section 1 of the Sherman Act.

Many of the early tying cases, which found tying in violation of one or another of the antitrust laws, involved a patented product as the tying product. The *Northern Pacific* case gave the Supreme Court a chance to summarize the law for the general situation when patients were not involved:[87]

> a tying arrangement may be defined as an agreement by a party to sell one product but only on the condition that the buyer also purchases a different (or tied) product. . . . Where such conditions are successfully exacted competition on the merits with respect to the tied product is inevitably curbed. Indeed "tying agreements serve hardly any purpose beyond the suppression of competition.". . . They deny competitors free access to the market for the tied product, not because the party imposing the tying requirements has a better product or a lower price but because of his power or leverage in another market. At the same time buyers are forced to forego their free choice between competing products. For these reasons "tying agreements fare harshly under the laws forbidding restraints of trade.". . . They are unreasonable in and of themselves whenever a party has sufficient economic power with respect to the tying product to appreciably restrain free competition in the market for the tied product and a "not insubstantial" amount of interstate commerce is affected.

When the tying good is not patented, the result is a conditional per se rule that closely resembles the rule of reason. If the firm imposing the tie is able[88]

[87]*Northern Pacific Railway Co. v. United States*, 356 U.S. 1 (1957), at 5–6; citations omitted.

[88]*Jefferson Parish Hospital District No. 2 v. Hyde*, 104 S. Ct. 1551 (1984), at 1559.

"to force a purchaser to do something that he would not do in a competitive market," the tie is illegal per se. But the inquiry to determine whether this condition is met will end up resembling tests for market power under the rule of reason.

Our review of the various explanations of tying shows that the Supreme Court's often quoted conclusion that "tying agreements serve hardly any purpose beyond the suppression of competition" is incorrect. Tying may serve the legitimate goal of protecting product quality. The *Jerrold* decision suggests that the "rule of reason" portion of the conditional per se rule that attaches to tying is broad enough to permit tying for legitimate purposes.[89] But when tying shows force and little else, it will be condemned.

When the tying good is patented, the situation is less complicated. The fact that the government has granted a patent on the tying good is taken to show that the tying firm has enough market power to force the tie on consumers.[90]

Policy Debate

If tying is employed strategically, it raises barriers to entry and so worsens the performance of the market for the tying good. Whatever its purpose, tying means that performance in the market for the tied good is not determined by competition on the merits.

When tying is a device used to carry out price discrimination, it increases the income transfer from consumers to the discriminating firm.

The Chicago school rejects concern with each of these effects of tying contracts. In its view, income transfer effects are not a proper subject for policy concern; it is only deadweight loss that merits attention.[91] The conclusion that income transfer effects are not a concern of antitrust policy is a political judgment about the goals of public policy (which cannot be proved or disproved on economic grounds). It is based on the conclusion that Congress did not intend the antitrust laws to mitigate income transfers stemming from market power. This conclusion is not generally accepted, although it is a tenet of the Chicago school's approach to antitrust policy.[92]

---

[89]*United States v. Jerrold Electronics Corporation,* 187 F. Supp. 545 (E.D. Pa. 1960).

[90]*Jefferson Parish Hospital District No. 2 v. Hyde,* 104 S. Ct. 1551 (1984), at 1560.

[91]Bork, op. cit., p. 375, specifically addressing the tying issue. There remain hints that complete understanding of the subtleties of the Chicago definition of consumer welfare escapes the bench; thus tying "can increase the social costs of market power by facilitating price discrimination, thereby increasing monopoly profits over what they would be absent the tie. . ." *Jefferson Parish Hospital District No. 2 v. Hyde,* 104 S. Ct. 1551 (1984), at 1559.

[92]See Chapter 3.

As far as exclusion of competitors is concerned, a position in the Chicago tradition is that[93]

> the exclusion of competitors that is objectionable from an antitrust standpoint is exclusion that results in an increase in market price above the competitive level. A tie-in imposed as a means of price discrimination is neither intended nor likely to increase the price level in the market for the tied product at all, the purpose of the tie-in being, rather, to enable the monopolist to extract higher profits from his monopoly in a separate market. Only in the rare case where the sale of the product represents a substantial share of all sales of the tied product might preventing the independent producers of the tied product from selling it to consumers of the tying product substantially affect competition in the market from the tied product.

The view that exclusion of competitors offends the antitrust laws only if it results in an increase in price above the competitive level is untenable.[94] It ignores substantial evidence that Congress intended to encourage competitive performance by maintaining opportunities for equally efficient rivals to compete, and that courts have so interpreted the antitrust laws over the years.[95]

The possibility that tying might adversely affect competition in the market for the *tying* good is, in the Chicago view, undercut by the Chicago conclusion that capital markets are not a source of impediments to entry. Where capital markets are not afflicted by bounded rationality and opportunism, if it is profitable to enter tied markets, capital markets will fund the entrant's investment.

---

[93]Posner, pp. 174–175. In the paragraph that follows, Posner argues that since the tying firm has no incentive to drive independent producers of the metering product out of business, the tying firm *will* buy the metering product from independents if they are equally efficient. This conclusion fails if there are circumstances under which a firm with market power would profit by driving independent producers of the tying product out of business. If there were no independent producers of the metering product, any firm contemplating entry into the market for the tying product would have to enter the market for the metering product as well. This would raise the cost of entry and hence would benefit the firm with market power over the tied good.

[94]Thus, see Adelman, M. A. "The Antitrust Laws: An Assessment of Their Role in the United States Economy," *Antitrust Law Journal* Volume 46, Issue 3, August 1977, pp. 806–814 reprinted in Fox, Eleanor M. and Halverson, James T. editors. *Industrial Concentration and the Market System*, Section of Antitrust Law. American Bar Association, 1979, pp. 70–78, p. 71:

> Legislators have never shown much interest in consumer welfare. Their chief concern has always been to protect some business firms against others, especially larger ones, and to prevent businessmen from being shut out of any particular market. The basic legal concept is not competition or monopoly, but *exclusion*.

[95]Spivack, op. cit., pp. 664–665.

The possibility that imperfect and impacted information in capital markets might support a strategic motive for tying is not admitted.[96]
   In short:[97]

> The tie-in or leverage area is one in which Chicago School theory comes into clear conflict with some of the principal non-economic goals of antitrust— preserving a deconcentrated industrial structure, dispersing economic power, and providing free access to markets.

Problem

15-1 Let the market demand curve be

$$P = 1000 - (\tfrac{1}{10})Q$$

and let the market be supplied by a monopolist who produces according to the cost function

$$C(Q) = 100Q.$$

a. If the monopolist charges a single profit-maximizing price for his product, what is that price? How much output is produced? What is the deadweight welfare loss, and what is the income transfer (monopoly profit) from consumers to the monopolist? Illustrate graphically.

b. (First-degree price discrimination) If the monopolist is able to charge a separate price for each unit of output sold, how much will be produced? What is consumers' surplus? What is the income transfer from consumers to the monopolist? Illustrate graphically.

c. (Second-degree price discrimination) Suppose the monopolist is able to divide output into batches of 3,000 units each, charging $700 per unit for the first 3,000 units, $400 per unit for the second 3,000 units, and $100 per unit for the final 3,000 units. What is consumers' surplus? What is the income transfer from consumers to the monopolist? Illustrate graphically.

d. (Third-degree price discrimination) Suppose the monopolist is able to divide his market into three groups of consumers with the following demand curves:

$$P_1 = 1,000 - (\tfrac{1}{2})Q_1$$
$$P_2 = 1,000 - (\tfrac{1}{3})Q_2$$
$$P_3 = 1,000 - (\tfrac{1}{5})Q_3.$$

---

[96]See Chapter 8 and the discussion of capital requirements as an impediment to entry. French, John D., "A Lawyer's Response," *Antitrust Law Journal* Volume 52, Issue 3, September 1983, p. 647, comments: "And it is rewarding to see the smile that comes over the faces of the members of the jury when an economist explains how the bank on the corner cannot wait to extend loans to a new entrant who is about to challenge an entrenched monopolist charging a supracompetitive price."

[97]Spivack, op. cit., pp. 663–664.

What is consumers' surplus? What is the deadweight welfare loss? What is the income transfer from consumers to the monopolist? How does total output in this case compare with output in the one-price monopoly case?

Paper Topics

15-1 Analyze the good faith defense to price discrimination contained in the Robinson-Patman Act [see *United States v. United States Gypsum Co. et al.*, 438 U.S. 422 (1978); *Exxon Corp. v. Governor of Maryland*, 437 U.S. 117 (1978); and *Great Atlantic and Pacific Tea Co. v. Federal Trade Commission*, 440 U.S. 69 (1979)].

15-2 Discuss the interpretation and effects of Section 2(c) of the Robinson-Patman Act and its prohibition of brokerage payments to retail firms that perform wholesale functions.

15-3 Discuss the evolution of the treatment of damages in private actions under the Robinson-Patman Act; see *Brunswick Corp. v. Pueblo Bowl-O-Mat, Inc.*, 429 U.S. 477 (1977), and *J. Truett Payne Co. v. Chrysler Motors Corp.*, 451 U.S. 557 (1981).

15-4 Consult Stigler, George J. "United States v. Loew's Inc.: A Note on Block Booking," *Supreme Court Review* 1963, pp. 152–157; Adams, William James and Yellen, Janet L. "Commodity Bundling and the Burden of Monopoly," *Quarterly Journal of Economics* Volume 90, Number 3, August 1976, pp. 475–498; and Schmalensee, Richard L. "Commodity Bundling by Single Product Monopolies," *Journal of Law and Economics* Volume 25, Number 1, April 1982, pp. 67–71 and the references cited therein. Discuss the law and economics of commodity bundling.

15-5 See *Northern Pacific Railway Co. et al. v. United States*, 356 U.S. 1 (1957); and *Jefferson Parish Hospital District No. 2 v. Hyde*, 466 U.S. 2 (1984) and the references cited therein. Discuss the evolution of the market power requirement in tying cases.

15-6 Analyze the law and economics of exclusive dealing. See Bok, Derek C. "The Tampa Electric Case and the Problem of Exclusive Arrangements Under the Clayton Act," *Supreme Court Review* 1961, pp. 267–322; and Marvel, Howard P. "Exclusive Dealing," *Journal of Law and Economics* Volume 25, Number 1, April 1982, pp. 1–25.

15-7 Explore the details of the Chiquita banana case. What elements other than price discrimination were involved? For background, see also *United States v. United Fruit Company*, 1958 CCH Trade Cases Paragraph 68, 941.

16

Predation

Kill an admiral from time to time to encourage the others.

Voltaire, **Candide**

We begin with a concise explanation of the concept of *predatory pricing* and the role some suppose predatory pricing to have played in an early landmark antitrust case:[1]

> According to most accounts, the Standard Oil Co. of New Jersey established an oil refining monopoly in the United States, in large part through the systematic use of predatory price discrimination. Standard struck down its competitors, in one market at a time, until it enjoyed a monopoly position everywhere. Similarly, it preserved its monopoly by cutting prices selectively wherever competitors dared enter. Price discrimination, so the story goes, was both the technique by which it earned its dominance and the device with which it maintained it.

Predation was thus at the heart of the development of basic antitrust law on monopolization under Section 2 of the Sherman Act. Section 2 of the Clayton Act (1914), which prohibits anticompetitive price discrimination, demonstrates continued congressional concern with predatory pricing. Antitrust cases involving predatory pricing continue to turn up regularly on court dockets.

Recent antitrust cases have alleged new methods of predation. IBM, for example, has been accused of changing product designs for the purpose of injuring rivals.[2] Eastman Kodak has been accused of designing cameras and film cartridges for the same reason.[3]

---

[1] McGee, John S. "Predatory Pricing: The Standard Oil (N.J.) Case," *Journal of Law and Economics* Volume 1, October 1958, p. 138.

[2] *California Computer Products, Inc., et al. v. International Business Machines Corp.* 613 F. 2d 727 (9th Cir. 1979).

[3] *Berkey Photo, Inc., v. Eastman Kodak Company*, 603 F. 2d 263 (2d Cir. 1979).

There are at least two other reasons why predation deserves our attention. First, in perhaps no other area of industrial economics has academic research been so fundamentally motivated by the need to satisfy policy requirements. Economists have studied market power and the conditions that sustain it (if any) for its own sake. The same is true of advertising, R&D, and other elements of the structure-conduct-performance framework. But the study of predation by economists consists largely of the formulation or criticism of rules offered to courts for use in deciding antitrust cases. For this reason, the predation literature touches on fundamental issues of antitrust policy, issues that go far beyond the economics of predation as such. What should be the role of antitrust policy? How much competence about economic matters should society expect from a legal system populated by noneconomists? How should the cost of administering antitrust rules affect the choice of antitrust rules? These are issues that affect all of antitrust economics. Here we meet them, for the first time, in the specific context of public policy toward predation. We deal with them in a general context in Chapter 18.

Second, the analysis of predation is one of the areas in which the lines between Chicago and non-Chicago positions are most sharply drawn. In perhaps no other area has the Chicago influence on methodology been so great but the acceptance of Chicago positions so small. Understanding why the most extreme Chicago results on predation are not accepted by most economists and policy-makers illuminates the continuing dialogue over methodological approaches to the study of industrial economics.

In this chapter, we first discuss economic models of predatory pricing. With this background, we move on to consider the rules that have been used by courts, and have been proposed for their use, in cases involving predatory pricing. Finally, we discuss the related topic of predatory innovation.

Predatory Pricing: Economics

It seems sensible to work through a stylized version of the Standard Oil story. There are two questions to keep in mind. First, what kind of market structure is required for predatory pricing to be profitable at all, so that it is a strategy that a dominant firm would consider? Second, in which circumstances is predatory pricing the most profitable strategy for maintaining dominance, so that it would be the strategy actually chosen by a dominant firm?

Standard Oil

The stylized Standard Oil story: a dominant firm operates in many local markets. In some of those markets, it enjoys market power. In others, it does not. In one market where its actions are constrained by a fringe of small competitors, it sets a price below cost. By so doing, it loses money in that market. But the dominant firm is sustained by its operations in other markets. Fringe firms, lacking such resources, suffer losses in the short run and exit in the long run. With the rabble gone, the dominant firm inherits a monopoly. It then restricts output, pushes up price, and earns economic profits.

Two preliminary remarks are in order. First, this story is told about a firm that operates in many local geographic markets. This firm competes with many rivals, each of which operates in one local market. The logic of this story would be much the same for a dominant firm that produced many brands of a differentiated product, competing with many rivals that each produced one competing brand.

Second, note that we have not said that "the large firm raises price in other markets when it cuts price in the target market." This argument is sometimes called the *recoupment fallacy*.[4] If the dominant firm is already maximizing its profit, price increases in other markets would reduce its profit in those markets. A large firm could not raise price elsewhere to recoup losses that stemmed from predatory pricing unless for some reason it was not maximizing its profit in other markets.

But it is not necessary for a firm to be able to raise prices to engage in predatory pricing. It is only necessary for the firm to hold price above cost in some market or markets. In other words, one prerequisite for the use of predatory pricing as a strategy toward rivals is that the predatory firm has market power in some market.[5] If a firm has such market power and is using it to hold price above marginal cost, the firm will have economic profits that could be used to cover losses in a local market. If a firm operates in many competitive local markets, it will not be able to subsidize losses in one of them even if it wishes to do so.

It is clear that predatory pricing involves time in a fundamental way.[6] A dominant firm cuts price below cost, losing money in the short run but driving rivals out of business and increasing its power to control price. This accomplished, the dominant firm raises price and earns so much additional economic profit that it more than makes up for its short-run losses.

There is no way to avoid the time element: the losses come now, the profits come later. Predatory pricing is an investment in market power, and like all investments, it is inherently dynamic. Nonetheless, for ease of exposition, static models are usually used to analyze predatory pricing. Dynamic considerations

---

[4] Bork, Robert H. *The Antitrust Paradox: A Policy at War with Itself.* New York: Basic Books, Inc., 1978, p. 5.

[5] This point is made by McGee, op. cit., p. 139.

[6] In this aspect, the analysis of predatory pricing is akin to the dynamic analysis of cartel stability (Chapter 6).

are usually brought into the argument in elaborations of the static models. This is the approach we take here.[7]

When Will Predation Be Profitable?

Figure 16-1 illustrates the first stage of the predation process. To keep things simple, suppose that the predator is always able to put supplies on the market at long-run average cost. This will be the case, for example, if the predator can produce in other markets to supply the target market, and if transportation costs are small relative to price.

The victim, which by assumption operates in only a single market, will not be able to bring supplies in from other markets. The victim will operate on a parabolic short-run average cost curve of the kind shown in Figure 16-1.

We need to know something about the situation before predation so that we can specify the opportunity cost to the predator of undertaking a predatory campaign. For this purpose, suppose that before the predatory campaign, price equals the long-run average cost. Before predation begins, the status quo is long-run competitive equilibrium. This is not critical to the course of the argument that follows.[8]

We also need to make some assumption about the way the target firm behaves. The simplest assumption is that the target firm is a price taker. It maximizes its profit, given the price set by the predator. If the target firm is a price taker, its supply curve is its (short-run) marginal cost curve, above the *shutdown point* that is the minimum point on the average variable cost curve.[9]

Stage 1—Losses

During the first stage of predation, the predator lowers price below long-run average cost. The victim, acting as a profit-maximizing price taker, reduces output from q_c to q_{pred}, moving down its marginal cost curve. Losses per unit sold, for the victim, are given by the distance *JM*—the difference between the short-run average cost at output q_{pred} and the predatory price. Since the victim sells $AJ = LM$ units, total losses for the victim are given by the area *ALMJ*.

---

[7] See, however, McGee, John S. "Predatory Pricing Revisited," *Journal of Law and Economics* Volume 23, Number 2, October 1980, p. 307:

> Thirty-odd years ago, Fritz Machlup told his theory seminar about a technique some economists used in criticizing others' work. If they didn't like an argument, they denounced it as "static" rather than "dynamic," as of course it "should" be. All too often, a "static" model simply meant whatever the other fellow happened to be using.

So much for reasoned scholarly analysis.

[8] You should be able to work through the changes if price (through some sort of oligopolistic understanding) were being held above long-run average cost before predation began.

[9] See the discussion of Figure 2-1(a). The variable cost curve is not drawn in Figure 16-1, but the marginal cost curve stops at the shutdown point.

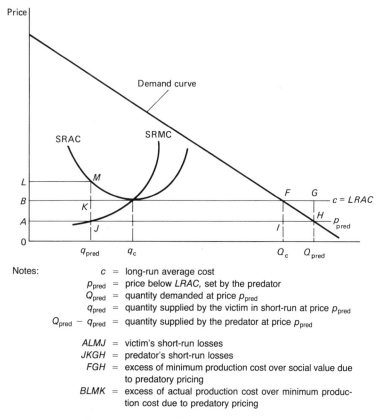

Notes:
$$c = \text{long-run average cost}$$
$$p_{pred} = \text{price below } LRAC, \text{ set by the predator}$$
$$Q_{pred} = \text{quantity demanded at price } p_{pred}$$
$$q_{pred} = \text{quantity supplied by the victim in short-run at price } p_{pred}$$
$$Q_{pred} - q_{pred} = \text{quantity supplied by the predator at price } p_{pred}$$

$$ALMJ = \text{victim's short-run losses}$$
$$JKGH = \text{predator's short-run losses}$$
$$FGH = \text{excess of minimum production cost over social value due to predatory pricing}$$
$$BLMK = \text{excess of actual production cost over minimum production cost due to predatory pricing}$$

Figure 16-1 Predatory pricing: stage 1.

Since Figure 16-1 describes the firms' operations for a single period, the victim will lose this much, per period, as long as it continues to operate.[10]

Now consider the position of the predator. When price is lowered to p_{pred}, the quantity demanded increases by $Q_{pred} - Q_c$. At the same time, the quantity supplied by the victim falls from q_c to q_{pred}. This means that the quantity the predator must supply in order to maintain the low predatory price increases from $Q_c - q_c$ to $Q_{pred} - q_{pred}$.

The predator is losing $c - p_{pred}$ on every unit sold (the distance $AB = JK = IF = HG$) and is selling $Q_{pred} - q_{pred}$ units (the distance $JH = KG$). The

---

[10] Nothing much is changed if the predator lowers price to the victim's shutdown point. In this case, the victim would simply shut down and lose its fixed costs, per period, as long as it maintains its fixed assets in the market.

predator's losses, per period, are given by the area *JKGH*. Call this per-period loss $-\pi_{\text{pred}}$. By comparing the predator's losses (*JKGH*) and the victim's losses (*ALMJ*), it is evident that the predator loses substantially more, per period, than the victim.

What are the welfare consequences of the predatory campaign? There is an increase in consumers' surplus, but both firms incur economic losses. The result is a net welfare loss due to predation.

The area *ABFH* is the increase in consumers' surplus[11] under the predatory campaign. This increase has two components.

The rectangle *ABFI* represents an increase in consumers' surplus to consumers who were in the market before the predatory campaign began. The area of the rectangle ABFI measures the savings enjoyed under predation by those who would have purchased Q_c units at the higher price c.

The area *IFH* represents the consumers' surplus enjoyed by those consumers who come into the market to take advantage of the predatorily low price. The extra sales ($Q_{\text{pred}} - Q_c$, the distance *IH*) made when price is lowered from c to p_{pred} are made to consumers who would be willing to pay more than p_{pred} for what they purchase.[12] The area IFH gives the consumers' surplus that these incremental consumers enjoy by having the right to buy at price p_{pred}.

Against this increase in consumers' surplus must be set the losses of the two firms. The predator sells $Q_{\text{pred}} - q_{\text{pred}}$ units at a loss of $c - p_{\text{pred}}$ each. The predator's total losses are represented by the area *JKGH*. The victim sells q_{pred} units at losses $AL = JM$ each. The victim's total losses are represented by the area *AMLJ*.[13]

The gain in consumers' surplus is given by the area *ABFH*. The firms' losses are given by the area *ALMKGH*. Firms' losses exceed the gain in consumers' surplus by the areas *BLMK* and *FGH*. The sum of these two areas is the net welfare loss from predation.

Stage 2—Profit

We now turn to the second stage of the predation process, depicted in Figure 16-2. The victim has folded its tent and gone in the night; the dominant firm remains in solitary splendor as a monopolist in the local market. As a proper profit-maximizing monopolist, the predator produces the output that makes its marginal revenue equal to its marginal cost, Q_m. The price at which Q_m units will be willingly demanded is P_m, which is found by going up the demand curve from the output level Q_m. Monopoly profit is given by the area *BNRS*

---

[11] See Figure 2-5 and the accompanying text.

[12] The maximum amount that would be paid for each unit of output is given by the height of the demand curve at that output level. See Chapter 15's discussion of price discrimination.

[13] The area *BLMK* reflects increased unit costs in the victim's plant due to lower output under predation.

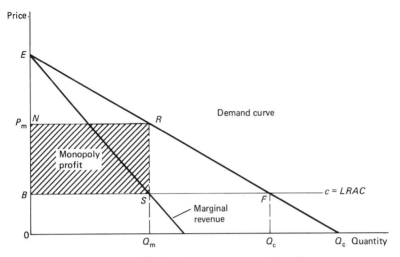

Figure 16-2   Predatory pricing—stage 2.

in Figure 16-2. The area *SRF* measures the deadweight welfare loss under monopoly.

The Return from Predation

At the start of the predatory campaign, what is the present discounted value[14] of the income stream expected by the predator? The predator suffers losses $(-\pi_{\text{pred}}$ per period) during stage 1. Afterward, it earns profits (π_{m} per period). Taking an interest rate r^* as representing the opportunity cost of capital, the present discounted value of the dominant firm's income stream is

$$
\begin{aligned}
PDV_{\text{pred}} = & -\pi_{\text{pred}} - \frac{1}{1 + r^*}\,\pi_{\text{pred}} - \cdots - \frac{1}{(1 + r^*)^T}\,\pi_{\text{pred}} \\
& + \frac{1}{(1 + r^*)^{T+1}}\,\pi_{\text{m}} + \frac{1}{(1 + r^*)^{T+2}}\,\pi_{\text{m}} + \cdots
\end{aligned}
\qquad \textbf{(16.1)}
$$

if it takes T periods to drive the fringe from the market.[15]

A dominant firm will consider predatory pricing as a strategy toward rivals only if the present discounted value is positive. If the present discounted value is negative, predation would not be profitable.

---

[14] See Chapter 4's treatment of dynamic limit pricing for a discussion of present discounted value.

[15] The successful predator will produce less in stage 2 than in stage 1. This will lead to a reduction in capital investment (unless excess capacity is maintained strategically to discourage reentry). If capital assets are sunk, a portion of the value of scrapped capital assets capital assets will be a loss for the firm, a loss that would have to be subtracted from PDV_{pred}.

The present discounted value of the income stream resulting from predation depends on the predatory price (p_{pred}) chosen by the dominant firm. The guiding factor here is a tradeoff between losses per period (during stage 1) and the number of periods it takes to drive the victim from the market. The lower the price set by the predator, the more rapidly the victim will depart. The lower is p_{pred}, the greater will be the losses per period (for both the predator and the target firm), but the shorter will be stage 1 and the more rapidly will stage 2, with its monopoly profits, arrive. In what follows, suppose that the predator resolves this tradeoff and picks p_{pred} to make Equation (16.1) as large as possible.

Then, whether or not Equation (16.1) is positive will depend on three things: the discount rate, the predator's losses in stage 1, and the payoff in stage 2.

Discount Rate

If the discount rate is very high, a predatory firm gives great weight to the short-run losses entailed by a campaign of predatory pricing and little weight to the monopoly profit received after the victim is driven from the market. On the other hand, if the discount rate is very low, the predator values long-term monopoly profits, dollar per dollar, almost as much as earlier short-term losses. The lower the discount rate, all else equal, the more likely is predation to occur.

Losses in Stage 1

The payoff from predation will depend on how long the predation period lasts and how great the losses are during that period. Particularly important here is the extent to which the victim's capital assets are sunk—their value unrecoverable upon exit.[16]

For example, suppose a firm operates a franchise from a fast-food pizza chain near the campus of Leviathan State University. To this end, the firm erects a building, for use as a retail outlet, in a mall near student housing. The rental cost[17] of the building is a fixed cost, since it will be the same no matter how many pizzas the firm sells per time period. For the most part, however, the firm's investment in the building is not a sunk cost. If the franchisee finds the retail market for pizza unprofitable, it will be able to rent or sell the building to some other retail operation (hamburgers; clothing; even, although this may seem unlikely at Leviathan State, a bookstore) and recover most of its investment. This is because retail outlets are relatively nonspecific assets. The same building could, with a modest additional investment, be used in a number of different industries.

---

[16] See Chapter 4 for a discussion of sunk costs.

[17] What is meant here is the opportunity cost of funds committed to the construction of the building. See the discussion of rental costs of capital services in Chapter 2.

the other hand, the firm's investment in pizza ovens is pretty much sunk. is not much one can do with a pizza oven except bake pizza, and such is are sufficiently bulky that transporting them to another market for use resale would involve a substantial expense relative to the probable resale alue.[18] If the franchisee exits the Leviathan State pizza market, it is likely to take a large capital loss on its pizza ovens.

One can infer from this analysis that if the assets employed in an industry are sunk, the price war upon which successful predation depends will be of long duration. The more are assets sunk, the greater is the cost to the victim of leaving the market and the longer a price war will have to be to succeed.

If assets are truly sunk, they may well remain in the market even after the target firm goes into bankruptcy. Under bankruptcy, the assets of the firm would be sold. These assets would most likely pass to a new management, at bargain prices, and continue to produce pizzas in competition with the predator.

It is possible that if the target firm decides to sell out, the predator firm would be interested in purchasing its assets. This raises a possible additional motive for predatory pricing: to drive down the purchase price of the assets of the target firm before acquisition by the predator. We will return to this topic.

Payoff in Stage 2

Finally, the payoff from predation will depend on how great the monopoly profits are once the victim is driven from the scene. But here we find ourselves in the situation contemplated in Chapter 4, in which a dominant firm attempts to exercise market power and preserve its position.

Suppose, first, that there are no entry costs. In this case, since the victim has access to the same long-run average cost curve as the predator, the victim can return to the market as soon as the predator raises the price. If the victim does not return to the market during stage 2, new firms can enter. If entry can take place rapidly and with no sunk expense, the force of potential competition alone will prevent the exercise of market power.

In other words, if markets are contestable—if there are no significant entry costs—predatory pricing will not be a profitable strategy. A firm will have no reason to endure a period of substantial losses with no expectation of being able to raise the price at the end of that period.

As noted previously, sunk costs make it harder to drive a target firm out of the market. If capital assets are embedded in a market, they will remain even if a particular management goes bankrupt. Sunk costs thus stretch out period 1, although they make period 2 profitable. There must be some costs of entry, or predation will not take place. No firm will ever monopolize the fast-food market near Leviathan State University, by predation or any other means.

[18] If the pizza market around Leviathan State is so bad that the firm wants to leave, it presumably would have to take a low price if it sold its pizza ovens to another firm in the same geographic market.

Suppose there are some costs of entry. Then the dominant-firm models of Chapter 4 indicate that the present discounted value of profits in stage 2 will be greater, the larger the entry costs.[19]

If there are costs of entry, the successful predator will be faced, in stage 2, with the choices outlined in Chapter 4. The dominant firm may limit price, and preserve its position over time, at the expense of some short-run profit. In this case, the dominant firm will earn the same profit in each stage 2 period, as implied by Equation (16.1). From Chapter 4, we know that the dominant firm will make more profit under this strategy, the greater are entry costs.

Alternatively, the successful predator may set a high price and slowly give up market share. We know from Chapter 4 that this dynamic limit pricing strategy will produce a greater present discounted value income stream for the predator, the greater the monopoly profit before entry and the slower the rate at which market share is given up to the fringe once entry begins. Under dynamic limit pricing, the dominant firm will earn a larger economic profit early in stage 2 and less later in stage 2 (as entry erodes market share) than under static limit pricing.

In any event, if there are costs of entry, there will be some payoff once the target firm is driven from the market. If entry costs are great enough, the profit to be gained in stage 2 will be sufficient to make the present discounted value of a predatory campaign positive. If entry is sufficiently costly, profit-maximizing firms will rationally consider predation as a strategy.

Predation Ever Successful?

The Chicago school has offered two main arguments to attack the proposition that predatory pricing can *ever* drive an equally efficient rival from a market. The first stage of predation, in this view can never be successful. If predation can never drive rivals from the market, the nature of the payoff in stage 2 (which will never be reached) loses interest.

The first argument that predation can never be successful raises the possibility of financial support for the target firm from capital markets. The second argument raises the possibility of financial support for the target firm from customers.

Capital Markets?

If predation is successful, the predator will earn economic profits in stage 2, when prices are increased. This means that it will be profitable for the target

---

[19] Ordover, Janusz A. and Willig, Robert D., "An Economic Definition of Predation: Pricing and Product Innovation," *Yale Law Journal* Volume 91, Number 1, November 1981, p. 12, point out that it may be less expensive for a target firm, with its experience in the market, to reenter than it would be for an inexperienced firm to enter. For predation to be successful, a market will have to be surrounded by barriers to reentry as well as barriers to entry.

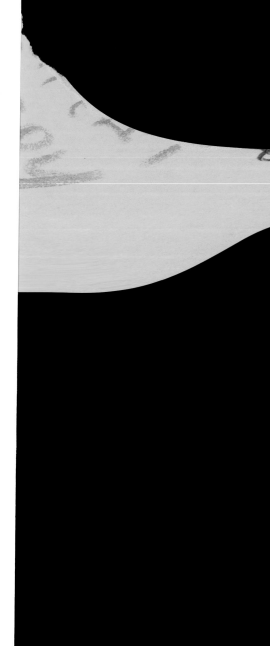

firm to be around in stage 2. But if it is profitable for the target firm to be around in stage 2, it will (it is argued) be able to find backers to provide the financial resources—loans or equity—needed to sustain the target firm's existence through the price war. But if the target firm can obtain such fin~~~~ assistance, it cannot be driven from the market. A dominant firm ~~~~ this and conclude that predatory pricing is doomed to fail. ~~~~ pricing is doomed to fail, it will never be tried. A cl~~~

> If the potential victim would find resistance to predation a pr~~
> his liquid assets, a lender should find it equally profitable to lend u.
> capital. In fact, in any case in which the predator must use a techniq~
> inflicts proportionally equal or greater losses upon himself, the victim wo~
> merely have to show the predator his new line of credit to dissuade the predator
> from attacking.

The argument that funding from the capital market will prevent successful predation is usually accompanied by a supporting argument that capital markets would have to be irrational to refuse to supply funds to targets of predation:[21]

> If resisting predation is a profitable activity, the imperfection theorist would
> have to explain why capital will not flow to profitable users, not just because
> of occasional mistakes in appraisal, but by a systematic refusal to invest in
> profitable resistance to predation. Nobody has troubled to explain that form of
> irrationality in capital suppliers, and we are justified in believing that it does
> not exist.

The flaw in the claim that capital markets would have to be irrational to refuse aid to targets of predation is that there *are* sound reasons to think that real-world capital markets will systematically refuse to fund target firms, or at least that such firms will be able to acquire funds only at differentially high interest rates.

Recall Chapter 8's discussion of the role of capital costs as a determinant of entry conditions and market structure. Suppliers of financial capital will have only limited information about the target firm's ability to survive a period of predatory pricing. There will be uncertainty about the target firm's resources and the quality of its management. There will be uncertainty about the predator's resources and the determination of its management to pursue a predatory strategy to the bitter end.

The target firm has some of this information (information impacted on one side of the financial market), but suppliers of capital will know that the target

---

[20] Bork, op. cit., pp. 147–148.

[21] *Ibid.*, p. 147. Essentially the same argument is made by McGee, "Predatory Pricing Revisited," p. 297, and Easterbrook, Frank H. "Predatory Strategies and Counterstrategies," *University of Chicago Law Review* Volume 48, Number 2, Spring 1981, pp. 269–270.

firm has an incentive to convey a misleadingly optimistic impression of its ability to survive (opportunism). The predator has the rest of the information that financial markets need, but also has an incentive to convey a misleadingly convincing impression of its determination to drive the target firm from the market. Given this combination of incomplete and impacted information with opportunism, financial markets will not provide capital to a target firm, except at a risk premium that pushes the costs of the target firm above those of the predator. This cost differential will allow the predator to profit at prices that mean losses for the target firm.

It is worth emphasizing, as we did in Chapter 8, that this behavior does not represent capital market imperfection. It represents efficient operation under conditions of imperfect and impacted information. Under these circumstances, efficient capital markets create an opportunity for predation. When capital markets operate under conditions of differentially imperfect information, the extreme Chicago position that predatory pricing can never be tried fails.

Consumer Coalitions?

The second Chicago school argument that attacks the possibility of predatory pricing depends on the plausibility of the notion that consumers will come to the aid of target firms. Thus:[22]

> Suppose, however, that capital markets are closed to the victim. . . . The intended victim has still another resource. It can turn to its customers for assistance. Because customers are the ultimate victims of the predator's future monopoly prices, they should be willing to help the intended immediate victim. The easiest way is to continue to buy at the old price, spurning the predator's low-price offer. This initially seems implausible, because any one customer would be too small to ensure the survival of the victim; each customer thus would buy the predator's low-priced goods, attempting to take a free ride on those who supported the victim. But the victim can solve the free-riding problem by offering long-term contracts at the competitive price, which would be less than the price the predator would charge if it obtained a monopoly. Once the victim has assured its continuity through long-term contracts, the predator should cease offering the predatory price. (If it continues, it is simply squandering its wealth.) Thus each customer signing the contract makes itself better off by precluding future monopoly pricing. . . .
>
> If any customer is worried that it will have to forego low prices while the victim is setting up a network of contracts, thus giving its competitors an advantage, the victim can make the effectiveness of the contract contingent on obtaining enough commitments to support use of its entire production capacity. Once that has been accomplished, and the intended victim's survival assured, the contracts would go into effect and the predation end nearly simultaneously. . . .

---

[22] Easterbrook, op. cit., pp. 270–271; McGee, "Predatory Pricing Revisited," pp. 310–311, refers to consumer contracts.

It is instructive to think about how a scheme of consumer aid via long-term contingency contracts might have been applied in a historical instance of predatory pricing. To this end, consider the facts of the *Mogul Steamship* case.[23]

The Mogul Steamship Company was (as you may have suspected) a shipping company, formed in 1883 and operating mainly in Australia. Mogul sought to operate in China when business was slow in Australia.

A shipowner's conference—a cartel—regulated freight rates for the China trade. In 1885 Mogul was denied admission to the conference. The conference implemented a program to exclude independent shippers from the market:[24]

> In 1885 the conference decided "that if any non-Conference steamer should proceed to Hankow to load independently any necessary number of Conference steamers should be sent at the same time to Hankow, in order to underbid the freight which the independent shippers might offer, without regard to whether the freight they should bid would be remunerative or not." Three independent ships were sent to Hankow, two of them being Mogul ships; and the agents for the conference lines responded by sending such ships as they thought necessary. Freight rates fell dramatically. It was accepted in the Court of Appeal and in the House of Lords that they fell to a level unremunerative alike to the independent and the conference shipowners. . . . Apparently in the event the losses of the conference were larger than those of the outsiders, since some conference ships sailed empty from Hankow, while all the outsiders' vessels were able to load up with some cargo and did not have to sail in ballast.
>
> It is reasonably clear that the intentions of the conference were those of predatory pricing, that the conference contemplated pricing below cost, and that in the event its members did cut prices below their costs (in the sense that the voyages were unremunerative at the prices changed).

It appears that the efforts to exclude Mogul Steamship from the market were successful.[25] Mogul's suit resulted in a finding that the actions of the shipping conference were not an unlawful restraint of trade under British law.

The *Mogul Steamship* case provides a context for discussing the customer coalition argument against the feasibility of predatory pricing. How would consumer coalitions have worked in the Mogul Steamship case?

Freight services of the kind involved in *Mogul Steamship*[26] "are broadly

---

[23] *Mogul Steamship Co. v. McGregor, Gow & Co. et al.*, 54 L.J.Q.B. 540 (1884/1885); 57 L.J.K.B. 541 (1887/1888); 23 Q.B.D. 598 (C.A.) (1889); [1892] A.C. 25. The text follows Yamey, B. S. "Predatory Pricing: Notes and Comments," *Journal of Law and Economics* Volume 15, Number 1, April 1972, pp. 129–142. McGee, John S., "Ocean Freight Rate Conferences and the American Merchant Marine," *University of Chicago Law Review* Volume 27, Number 2, Winter 1966, p. 278, interprets the sort of price cutting described by Yamey as a rational response to sporadic entry.

[24] Yamey, op. cit., pp. 139–140. Citations omitted.

[25] Ibid., p. 141.

[26] McGee, "Ocean Freight Rate Conferences," p. 205.

characterized by the scheduled carriage of heterogeneous cargoes that typically are originated by many shippers and several ports and destined for many consignees at several ports." Mogul Steamship would have had to approach shippers in many different ports and offer each of them the following arrangement: "Here are my books; you can see what my costs are. I will sign a contract promising to ship your goods for the foreseeable future at cost plus a normal profit. But the contract goes into effect only when I have enough contracts to fill all of my ships, in all ports in which they regularly call, for the foreseeable future. Of course, the rates I offer you are higher than those the shipping conference is offering just now, and they have empty ships in the harbour, but if my customers don't sign these contracts, I will leave the China trade and the conference rates will go back up. I will check back with you next week after I have lined up all of the other contracts."

Mogul Steamship would have to cover enormous transaction costs in negotiating such contracts. Mogul's attorneys would have to contact customers shipping many different commodities from many different ports. No customer would have complete information about the shipping market; information about market conditions would be both imperfect and impacted. Further, it would be apparent to customers that Mogul Steamship had an interest in presenting an optimistic picture of the scenario. Conference representatives would, of course, deny the possibility that shipping rates would rise if Mogul left the market. The notion of a contingency contract would no doubt strike many of the shippers as unusual. How could they interpret the information about costs contained in Mogul's books, except with considerable investment of their own resources? How would Mogul Steamship and its customers agree on what a normal profit for Mogul would be?

To pose these questions, of course, is to answer them. Coalitions of customers will not rescue the targets of predation because the transaction costs associated with the negotiation of long-term contingency contracts are prohibitive:[27,28]

> The dominant firm can be expected to contest pre-entry sales just as it contests post-entry sales. Also, prospective customers would be reluctant to jeopardize a known source of supply before the entrant has irreversibly committed himself by incurring fixed costs. Finally, long-term contracts are both costly and hazardous.

[27] Williamson, Oliver E. "Predatory Pricing: A Strategic and Welfare Analysis," *Yale Law Journal* Volume 87, Number 2, December 1977, p. 295, footnote 37.

[28] It should also be pointed out that if the target of an allegedly predatory pricing campaign reached agreements with customers to hold price above the allegedly predatory level, and if this took place in the United States, the target firm and its customers would be involved in a conspiracy in restraint of trade that could be challenged under Section 1 of the Sherman Act. This will no doubt be taken, in some circles, as yet another argument for the repeal or revision of the antitrust laws.

The common theme of both Chicago school arguments that predation will not be able to drive target firms from the market is that if there is a profit to be made by staying in the market, resources will be provided (by customers or by capital markets) to fund resistance to predation. However, this is correct only in a world without transaction costs or opportunistic behavior.

In the real world, potential financial backers are less well informed than those in need. They cannot trust borrowers to provide accurate information. Nor can they acquire accurate information on their own without incurring considerable transaction costs. The result is that while a target firm might be able to acquire additional funds, it can do so only at a cost of capital greater than that available to the predator firm. This cost differential will make predation a feasible strategy.

A related point that should be made deals with the circumstances under which a dominant firm will find predatory pricing profitable. By engaging in an occasional episode of predatory pricing, a dominant firm can make it risky—as far as capital markets are concerned—to provide funds to potential entrants or fringe firms. A dominant firm can therefore use predatory pricing to raise the cost of capital to actual or potential rivals. Even if predatory pricing is a losing proposition when attention is confined to the market in which it takes place, it may be profitable from a global point of view. The *demonstration effect* of predatory pricing will insulate the dominant firm from competition in all of the markets in which it operates.

When Will Predation Be Chosen?

The fact that predatory pricing can be profitable does not mean that a firm will engage in predatory pricing. Predatory pricing will be employed only if it is the *most* profitable strategy available.

A mainstay of the original Chicago attack on predatory pricing as a real-world phenomenon was the argument that in any circumstances in which predatory pricing is profitable, there is *always* another, more profitable, alternative. The classic statement of this argument, by McGee, refers to Standard Oil:[29]

> Assume that Standard has an absolute monopoly in some important markets, and was earning substantial profits there. Assume that in another market there are several competitors, all of whom Standard wants to get out of the way. Standard cuts price below cost. Everyone suffers losses. Standard would, of course, suffer losses even though it has other profitable markets: it could have been earning at least competitive returns and it is not. The war could go on until average variable costs are not covered and are not expected to be covered; and the competitors drop out. If, instead of fighting, the would-be monopolist bought out his competitors directly, he could afford to pay them up to the

---

[29] McGee, "Predatory Pricing," pp. 139–140.

discounted present value of the expected monopoly profits to be gotten as a result of their extinction. Anything above the competitive value of their firms should be enough to buy them. In the purchase case, monopoly profits could begin at once; in the predatory case, large losses would first have to be incurred. . . .

Since the revenues to be gotten during the predatory price war will always be less than those that could be gotten immediately through purchase, and will not be higher after the war is concluded, present worth will be higher in the purchase case.

McGee presents a detailed review of the instances of alleged predatory pricing that are reported in the record of the *Standard Oil* case. He shows that the record does not support the charges of predatory pricing. The most convincing reading of the record is that Standard Oil repeatedly bought out smaller rivals to maintain its position in the oil refining market. Thus McGee's argument about the relative merits of merger and predatory pricing as techniques for maintaining dominance seems correct, as far as his specified topic—the original *Standard Oil* case—is concerned.

A counterargument, however, is that McGee's logic is[30] "irrelevant to present-day circumstances, since acquiring a major competitor is clearly and unconcealably unlawful whereas predatory pricing may be difficult to detect."

In other words, Section 2 of the Sherman Act and Section 7 of the Clayton Act forbid mergers as a strategy for monopolization. Under current antitrust policy, purchase is not an option that dominates predation everywhere and always as a rivalrous strategy. McGee responds[31] that the illegality of mergers for monopolization weakens another of the supposed incentives to engage in predatory pricing.

If merger by dominant firms is legal, a predator may instigate a price war to drive down the purchase price of a rival. If merger by dominant firms is illegal, a predator would have to carry a price war to the bitter end—exit of the rival, tail between its legs.

McGee's response seems correct, but it does not refute the original argument. Under current interpretations of U.S. antitrust law, merger is not an option that dominates predatory pricing everywhere and always as a strategic option. Under some circumstances, predatory pricing will be the most profitable strategy for a dominant firm.

Recapitulation

Alarm over allegations of predatory pricing was an important factor in early popular support for the antitrust laws. The hard-core Chicago analysis of preda-

---

[30] Posner, Richard A. "The Chicago School of Antitrust Analysis," *University of Chicago Law Review* Volume 27, Number 4, p. 939.

[31] McGee, "Predatory Pricing Revisited," p. 298.

tory pricing, based on elementary price theory, is that predatory pricing cannot occur.

As is almost always the case, the Chicago analysis is correct on its own assumptions. The particular assumptions that are critical to this analysis are two. First, it is assumed that the cost of obtaining information is so low that financial markets or coalitions of customers will provide financial support to firms that are targets of predatory campaigns. Second, it is assumed that entry is always so free and easy that there can be no payoff to a successful predatory campaign. If these assumptions hold, predatory pricing will not be profitable and predatory pricing will not occur.

The Chicago methodology—the insistence on using elementary price theory for the analysis of predatory pricing—has had great influence on the way economists think about predatory pricing. Largely as a result of the Chicago analysis, economists recognize that predatory pricing will not occur in markets without barriers to entry or reentry. But the extreme Chicago analysis has not been accepted either by courts or by mainstream economists. Courts continue to hear cases on predation, and economists continue to propose rules for courts to use in those cases.

The Chicago position has failed in policy circles because it is based on extreme and unreal assumptions. There *are* transaction costs that interfere with the flow of information in capital markets. An occasional episode of predatory pricing *will* raise the cost of capital to potential entrants and therefore will be profitable for firms with market power. For these reasons, most economists are not willing to rule out predatory pricing on a priori grounds. Even writers who clearly use the Chicago approach to most policy questions[32] recognize that predatory behavior can, under some circumstances, be a sensible strategy for a profit-maximizing firm.

Predation may be used in the real world. If it occurs, it is a technique for monopolization that violates Section 2 of the Sherman Act. How, then, should predation be treated by courts? What standards should courts use to decide if predation has taken place? It is to these questions that we now turn.

Rules for the Legal Treatment of Predatory Pricing

From the point of view of antitrust policy, the problem posed by predation generally and predatory pricing in particular is that it usually has to be dealt with in what is alleged to be stage 1, when prices have supposedly been lowered to drive rivals out of the market. This presents a problem for courts because there are many reasons why prices might fall, and most of them reflect increased competition rather than predation.

---

[32] Posner, op. cit., p. 940.

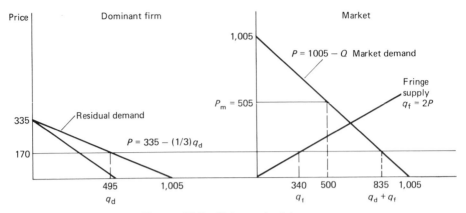

Figure 16-3 Entry and pricing.

An Example

For concreteness, consider the following example (see Figure 16-3). A dominant firm operates in many markets, in some of which it has market power. In one such market, it is a monopolist and produces with the cost function

$$C(q_d) = 5q_d, \tag{16.2}$$

where q_d is the quantity supplied by the dominant firm.

The market demand function is[33]

$$P = 1,005 - Q \quad \text{or} \quad Q = 1,005 - P, \tag{16.3}$$

where Q is the total quantity. As a proper profit maximizer, the monopolist selects the output that makes marginal revenue equal to marginal cost. The monopolist therefore produces the output $q_d = 500$, which it sells (see the equation of the demand curve) at a price of $505.

Now a firm with a marginal cost function

$$MC = (\tfrac{1}{2})q_f \tag{16.4}$$

(where q_f is the quantity supplied by the fringe firm) enters the market. The fringe firm acts as a price taker and maximizes its profit by picking an output

---

[33] Recall from Chapter 2 that the marginal revenue curve for a linear demand curve has the same price-axis intercept as the demand curve and a slope exactly twice the slope of the demand curve. See footnote 9, Chapter 2, and Problem 2-1.

which makes marginal cost equal to price.[34] The fringe firm's supply function is therefore

$$P = (\tfrac{1}{2})q_f \quad \text{or} \quad q_f = 2P. \tag{16.5}$$

The residual demand curve faced by the former monopolist is found by subtracting the fringe supply function from the market demand function:

$$q_d = Q - q_f = 1{,}005 - P - 2P = 1{,}005 - 3P,$$
$$\text{or} \quad P = 335 - (\tfrac{1}{3})q_d. \tag{16.6}$$

The former monopolist, now acting as a dominant firm, will maximize its profit by selecting the output that makes the marginal revenue from this residual demand curve equal to its marginal cost. Thus the dominant firm sets

$$MR = 335 - (\tfrac{2}{3})q_d = 5, \quad \text{so} \quad q_d = 495. \tag{16.7}$$

We obtain the price from the residual demand curve:

$$P = 335 - (\tfrac{1}{3})(495) = 335 - 165 = 170. \tag{16.8}$$

At a price of $170, the fringe firm supplies (see the fringe supply function Equation 16.5)

$$q_f = 2(170) = 340. \tag{16.9}$$

The quantity supplied to the market is then

$$q_d + q_f = 495 + 340 = 835. \tag{16.10}$$

The quantity demanded when the price is $170 (from the market demand function, Equation 16.3) is

$$Q = 1{,}005 - 170 = 835. \tag{16.11}$$

The market is in equilibrium at a price of $170 per unit: the quantity demanded equals the quantity supplied. The price has fallen from $505 before

[34] See Chapter 2's discussion of the behavior of the competitive firm.

entry to $170 after entry, and output has increased from 500 to 815 units. Entry has lowered price, increased output, and improved market performance.

Now comes the entrant into Federal District Court with an antitrust suit. The price has been cut with the purpose of driving it from the market! The dominant firm is able to sustain its losses because of its profit in other markets. The entrant has no such support. This is (gasp!) predatory pricing, a violation of Section 2 of the Sherman Act. The entrant has lost an additional profit of $335 per unit (the difference between the preentry price, $505, and the postentry price, $170) on each of the 340 units it has put on the market. That adds up to a lost profit of $113,900 (per time period). Would the court please award the entrant treble damages and issue an injunction requiring the dominant firm to raise its price back up to $505?

What standards should a court apply in hearing such a claim? Keep in mind that all the court will *know* is that the price has gone down. It will not know the costs of either firm. The court will have to decide if the price reduction is the result of competitive forces (which, in the preceding example, is the case) or simply the first stage of a predatory scheme.

Marginal Cost/Short-Run Average Cost

A 1975 paper by Areeda and Turner[35] spawned the modern literature on predatory pricing. They recognize that the difficult problem in predation policy is to specify a standard that will detect predatory pricing without making it too easy for a rival being buffeted by competition on the merits to bring a private antitrust suit for the purpose of frustrating competition.

Areeda and Turner use conventional profit maximization analysis to identify predatory situations. They rely on the fact that if a firm is engaged in predatory pricing, it must be giving up profit in the short-run in the expectation of future profit.

A competitive firm maximizes its profit by picking an output that makes marginal cost equal to price. A firm with some market power will pick an output that makes its marginal cost equal to its marginal revenue. Since marginal revenue is less than price,[36] price will always exceed marginal cost for a firm that is exercising market power (i.e., $P > MR = MC$). In no case will a profit-maximizing firm set a price less than its marginal cost. Areeda and Turner

---

[35] Areeda, Phillip and Turner, Donald F. ''Predatory Prices and Related Practices Under Section 2 of the Sherman Act,'' *Harvard Law Review* Volume 88, Number 4, February 1975, pp. 697–733; see also Areeda, Phillip and Turner, Donald F. *Antitrust Law*, Vol. III, Boston: Little, Brown and Company, 1978, pp. 150ff.

[36] See Figure 2-3 and the accompanying text.

therefore hold a price to be predatory if it is less than the firm's reasonably anticipated short-run marginal cost.

It is worthwhile to summarize the factors that Areeda and Turner decided not to include in their proposed rule for predatory pricing. They conclude that it is inappropriate to condemn limit pricing as predatory, even though it will exclude less efficient rivals from the market. They would permit a limit price as long as that price is above the firm's short-run marginal cost.[37] Areeda and Turner treat a price above short-run marginal cost as competition on the merits,[38] and for that reason they would not condemn such a price under Section 2 of the Sherman Act.

Areeda and Turner recognize the problems created for the legal treatment of predatory pricing by temporary price reductions:[39]

> Where entry is easy and relatively costless, the monopolist would have to maintain the lower price to forestall renewed entry. But where a new entrant must make a large investment in facilities, personnel training, distribution development, or product promotion, he will not enter the market without the prospect of survival for a period sufficiently long to recover at least those initial costs. The potential entrant will not, therefore, enter when he thinks that the monopolist will adopt that lower price in response to entry. *If the monopolist reduces his price once or twice, he will discourage future entry.* In such circumstances, monopoly may be maintained without a permanent price reduction, and thus consumers will not receive the long-term benefit of the higher output at lower price by which rivalry was destroyed or prevented. This result is certainly not a happy one (emphasis added).

Despite this analysis, Areeda and Turner would not classify temporary price reductions as predatory, as long as the price remains above short-run marginal cost. They base this conclusion on the administrative difficulties courts would face in dealing with temporary price reductions.

Areeda and Turner suggest three ways in which courts might deal with temporary price reductions. First, they might simply forbid monopoly pricing. Under such a rule, courts would be transformed into regulatory agencies, required continually to monitor prices and costs of industries and firms under

---

[37] As noted by Hay, George A., "A Confused Lawyer's Guide to the Predatory Pricing Literature," in Salop, Steven C., editor, *Strategy, Predation, and Antitrust Analysis*. Washington, D.C.: Bureau of Competition, Federal Trade Commission, September 1981, pp. 162–164, there is a welfare loss under limit pricing. It is less than the welfare loss under monopoly without the threat of entry.

[38] Areeda and Turner, "Predatory Prices," p. 706.

[39] Ibid.

their jurisdiction. This, Areeda and Turner argue, is a burden that courts are ill-equipped to assume.

Second, courts might hold it illegal for a dominant firm to lower price in response to entry or expansion by a rival. Such a rule would have the effect of holding a protective umbrella over entrants and would sometimes prevent a dominant firm from competing on the merits. A rule against price lowering in the face of entry would, for example, condemn the dominant firm of Figure 16-3 and prevent the improvement in market performance that followed entry. To enforce a rule against price lowering, courts would have to decide whether price changes reflected changes in product design or were merely attempts to evade the rule. This too would involve a heavy administrative burden.

Third, courts might allow price reductions but insist that if a dominant firm reduces price in the face of entry, it cannot reverse the price cut. A "no price-cut reversal" policy would encourage a dominant firm to engage in the kind of dynamic limit pricing strategy reviewed in Chapter 4: setting a high price and giving up market share to entrants as slowly as possible. The performance of the U.S. steel industry after the formation of U.S. Steel suggests that this is not the kind of market performance one wishes to encourage. Areeda and Turner also observe that a rule prohibiting the reversal of post-entry price cuts would have to allow exceptions for changes in cost or demand. Dealing with claims of special circumstances would again involve the detailed administrative work that Areeda and Turner would have courts avoid.

After going through these arguments, Areeda and Turner conclude that prices above marginal cost should not be treated as predatory. They then acknowledge that it will ordinarily be difficult to extract information about marginal cost from business records. Areeda and Turner therefore fall back on a proxy rule that would hold that prices above reasonably anticipated short-run average variable cost are nonpredatory.[40]

The Areeda-Turner analysis has served as a starting point for economic arguments in a number of antitrust decisions.[41] It has also been criticized by economists working in both the structure-conduct-performance and the Chicago traditions. The former find Areeda and Turner too permissive on the ground that their approach ignores strategic behavior. The latter group finds Areeda and Turner too strict on the ground that their rule would invite private lawsuits designed to stifle competition.

---

[40] Areeda and Turner make several qualifications to this basic rule. They would allow $AVC > P > MC$ in periods of weak demand or excess capacity. They would allow $MC > P > AC$. They would allow promotional pricing below AVC to be used by firms without monopoly power.

[41] For example, *International Air Industries, Inc., et al. v. American Excelsior Company*, 517 F. 2d 714 (5th Cir. 1975) and *California Computer Products, Inc. (Calcomp) v. International Business Machines Corp.*, 613 F. 2d 727 (9th Cir. 1979).

A Rule of Reason Approach

Scherer[42] expresses concern that Areeda and Turner's "no price less than short-run average variable cost" rule would permit "preemptive entry deterrence":[43]

> At the first sign of attempted entry, the monopolist must increase its output . . . cut its price . . . and make clear to the would-be entrant that it will not back off. If the entrant then adds its . . . output . . . the price will fall . . . and both the entrant and the monopolist will lose money. The expectation of such losses will act to discourage the would-be entrant from proceeding with its entry, which normally takes time and an accumulating investment.

It is clear from our earlier discussion that Areeda and Turner recognize the possibility of strategic entry-deterring behavior. Their disagreement with Scherer is not about economics but about the way courts work and can be expected to work. Scherer advocates what amounts to a rule of reason standard for the treatment of alleged predation:[44]

> Key variables . . . include the relative cost positions of the monopolist and the fringe firms, the scale of entry required to secure minimum costs, whether fringe firms are driven out entirely or merely suppressed, whether the monopolist expands its output to replace the output of excluded rivals or restricts supply again when the rivals withdraw. . . . I do not know how these variables can be assessed properly without a thorough examination of the factual circumstances accompanying the monopolist's alleged predatory behavior, how the monopolist's officials perceived the probable effects of its behavior (i.e., intent), and the structural consequences actually flowing from the behavior.

What administrative costs are involved in trying rule of reason cases? An extreme example is provided by *Zenith Radio Corporation v. Matsushita Electric Industrial Co., Ltd., et al.*,[45] which involved (among other things) allegations of predatory pricing in the U.S. market for television sets. Although

---

[42] Scherer, F. M. "Predatory Pricing and the Sherman Act: A Comment," *Harvard Law Review* Volume 89, Number 5, March 1976, pp. 869–890; "Some Last Words on Predatory Pricing," *Harvard Law Review* Volume 89, Number 5, March 1976, pp. 901–903; see also Areeda, Phillip and Turner, Donald F. "Scherer on Predatory Pricing: A Reply," *Harvard Law Review* Volume 89, Number 5, March 1976, pp. 891–900.

[43] Scherer, "Predatory Pricing and the Sherman Act," p. 871.

[44] Ibid., p. 890.

[45] 513 F. Supp. 1100 (1981); see also *Matsushita Electric Industrial Co., Ltd., et al. v. Zenith Radio Corp. et al.*, 46 CCH S. Ct. Bull. P.

this is one of the largest and most complicated cases of its kind, it demonstrates the costs involved in enforcing the antitrust laws under a rule of reason.

The earliest portion of the case was filed in 1970. A District Court opinion, dismissing the suit, was handed down in 1981. A Federal Appeals Court reversed the dismissal and ordered a trial. In a 1986 decision, the Supreme Court confirmed the original decision of the District Court, and accepted Matsushita's argument that the structure of the relevant market was not one in which predatory pricing could be expected to be profitable.

This case, in other words, spent 16 years wandering around the federal courts. Consider the following description of the record generated at the District Court:[46]

> We have observed that this case is before us on what may be the most ample record for summary judgment purposes ever before a court. The keystone of this record is plaintiff's roughly 11,500 page F[inal]P[roposed]S[ettlement], with its roughly 6000-page appendix, which cross-references approximately 250,000 pages of documents.

Defendants also filed their own Final Proposed Settlement. The amount of material generated by this case is, admittedly, extreme. But it is not unusual for an antitrust case to last for 3 to 5 years, to generate over 100,000 pages of documentary evidence, to employ multiple law firms on both sides, and to involve economists, accountants, and industry consultants as expert witnesses. No one who has ever been involved in such a proceeding will treat lightly the argument that simple rules of law are desirable because they simplify proceedings.

Intent

Posner defines as predatory[47] "pricing at a level calculated to exclude from the market an equally or more efficient competitor." Under this definition, Posner would condemn either pricing below short-run marginal cost or pricing[48] "below long-run marginal cost with the intent to exclude a competitor."

Posner acknowledges that these would be difficult standards to apply. All of the problems of inferring economic costs from business records that would arise under the Areeda-Turner rule would also arise under the Posner rule. To deal with the measurement of costs, Posner suggests that a practical substitute for long-run marginal cost would be what he calls *average balance-sheet cost,*

---

[46] *Zenith Radio Corporation v. Matsushita Electric Industrial Co., Ltd., et al.*, 513 F. Supp. 1100 (1981), at 1130.

[47] Posner, Richard A. *Antitrust Law: An Economic Perspective.* Chicago: The University of Chicago Press, 1976, p. 188.

[48] Ibid., p. 189.

namely,[49] "the company's total costs as stated on its books divided by the number of units of output produced." This suggestion is in the spirit of the idea of Areeda and Turner that average variable cost be used as a proxy for marginal cost. As long as an adjustment were made for a normal rate of return on capital, and as long as costs were not subject to substantial short-run changes, Posner's average balance-sheet cost would be a feasible approach to the measurement of cost in predatory pricing cases.

It would also be difficult to measure intent:[50]

> What juries (and many judges) do not understand is that the availability of evidence of improper intent is often a function of luck and of the defendant's legal sophistication, not of the underlying reality. A firm with executives sensitized to antitrust problems will not leave any documentary trail of improper intent; one whose executives lack this sensitivity will often create rich evidence of such intent simply by the clumsy choice of words to describe innocent behavior. Especially misleading here is the inveterate tendency of sales executives to brag to their superiors about their competitive prowess, often using metaphors of coercion that are compelling evidence of intent to the naive.

Posner is aware of the danger that competitors will try to use rules against predatory pricing to prevent price reductions by rivals. In a suggestion that anticipates later work, Posner[51] recommends that plaintiffs in private antitrust cases be required to show that the market involved has structural characteristics that would make predatory pricing profitable. Posner would have plaintiffs show that the alleged predator possessed market power and that the market was surrounded by barriers to entry and reentry. Only then would the case proceed to the consideration of facts involving the allegedly predatory behavior.

No Postentry Output Increase

Like Scherer, Williamson[52] emphasizes the strategic aspects of predatory behavior:

> If by responding aggressively to a current threat of entry a dominant firm can give a "signal" that it intends to react vigorously to entry in later time periods or different geographical regions, discounted future gains may more than offset sacrifices of current profit. Signaling, whether intertemporal or interspatial, is plainly strategic behavior. Areeda and Turner nevertheless model the predatory pricing issue mainly in static terms.

[49] Ibid., p. 190.

[50] Ibid., pp. 189–190.

[51] Ibid., p. 191.

[52] Williamson, op. cit., p. 287. McGee's parable about the use of the terms *static* and *dynamic*, quoted in footnote 7, is directed to Williamson's remarks.

Williamson proposes an "output restriction rule" to combat strategic behavior, in contrast to Scherer's rule of reason approach.[53] Williamson would forbid a dominant firm to increase output in response to entry. The firm would have to increase output to enforce a lower price during stage 1 of the predation process (see Figure 16-1). If a dominant firm is forbidden to increase output, it cannot predate. Williamson would impose the rule of no increase in output for 12 to 18 months following entry.

Williamson advances three considerations in defense of his proposed rule.[54] He would favor:

1. Rules that encourage greater preentry output.
2. Rules that encourage a lower cost of postentry supply.
3. Rules that require entrants to know less or to bear less uncertainty.

Williamson is able to show that the rule of no increase in output following entry outperforms both a rule requiring a price greater than short-run marginal cost and a rule requiring a price greater than the short-run average variable cost, at least in the context of the particular model he uses to illustrate his argument. Williamson also suggests that an output rule would be easier to enforce than any cost rule, because it will be easier to measure output than to translate accounting cost records into measures of economic cost.

How would an output rule affect dominant firm behavior? The rule would remove temporary price reduction as a strategic option for a firm with market power. Under the no increase in output rule, a dominant firm could set a high price and encourage entry, as under dynamic limit pricing. It could also expand output before entry, knowing that it would not be able to expand output after entry. But this is simply static limit pricing: keep the price low enough so that potential entrants do not find it profitable to become actual entrants.

Of these two options—static or dynamic limit pricing—we would expect a dominant firm to select the one that yields the greatest present discounted value income stream.

Drawing on Chapter 4's treatment of dominant firm behavior, we conclude that a dominant firm will set a high price if it has a high discount rate (preference for short-run profits) and if there are significant costs of entry (loss of market share comes slowly). If a dominant firm has a low discount rate and if entry is easy, it will opt for static limit pricing.

In a comment on Williamson's output proposal, Areeda and Turner give four reasons for preferring a cost-based rule to an output-based rule:[55]

---

[53] Like all the authors discussed here, Williamson appends a number of qualifications to his proposed rule, qualifications that are designed to deal with special cases. We confine our discussion to the main rule proposed by each author.

[54] Op. cit., p. 293.

[55] Areeda, Phillip and Turner, Donald F. "Williamson on Predatory Pricing," *Yale Law Journal* Volume 87, Number 7, June 1978, p. 1339.

First, predatory pricing rules must take into account the proclivity of competitors to challenge a rival's price cuts. . . . The threat of litigation may therefore deter legitimate competitive pricing. Second, pricing at SRMC [Short Run Marginal Cost] is the result in competitive markets. . . . Third, rules requiring price floors higher than SRMC will tend to preserve inefficient rivals or attract inefficient entry. Fourth, elimination or exclusion of rivals may . . . cause long-run welfare losses that exceed the short-run gains from fuller use of capacity, but such long-run consequences cannot feasibly be incorporated into legal rules because they are intrinsically speculative and indeterminate.

Areeda and Turner's first and third objections to the output-based rule involve the incentives it creates for entrants. An equally efficient entrant can use the threat of a predatory pricing suit to discourage hard competition by a dominant firm. This seems to be a valid complaint, but it is not unique to the output rule. Any legal standard that provides a way for firms that *are* victims of predation to seek relief will be open to abuse by firms that would like to portray themselves as victims of predation.

If a dominant firm that is forbidden to increase output decides to set a high price and let its market share slowly melt away, the high price will permit high-cost fringe firms to operate. This is Areeda and Turner's third objection to an output-based rule: it would protect inefficient firms. The same objection will apply to any rule that has the effect, direct or indirect, of supporting the dominant firm's price.

Areeda and Turner also object to a rule penalizing a firm that, after entry, acts as predicted by the competitive model (lowering price to short-run marginal cost). Finally, they argue against rules that require courts to make judgments about complex tradeoffs.

Areeda and Turner also question Williamson's claim that a output-based rule would be easier to enforce that a cost-based rule. Williamson would allow a dominant firm to increase output if industry demand were growing. Areeda and Turner point out that this exception would require courts to evaluate forecasts of future demand, forecasts that are just as difficult to make as cost estimates.

No Postexit Price Increase

Baumol[56] favors one of the alternatives rejected by Areeda and Turner as a policy for predatory pricing. Like Williamson, Baumol is concerned with the intertemporal and strategic aspects of predatory pricing, which he feels are missed by the static Areeda-Turner approach. Baumol would allow an established firm to cut price in response to entry, but he would forbid the firm to raise price if at some later date the entrant moves on to happier hunting grounds.

[56] Baumol, William J. "Quasi-Permanence of Price Reductions: A Policy for Prevention of Predatory Pricing," *Yale Law Journal* Volume 89, Number 1, November 1979, pp. 1–26.

Under a rule of no price increase after exit, a dominant firm would not be forced to hold a price umbrella over rivals. The rule aims directly at temporary price reductions, which are the indirect target of Williamson's output rule. Where the output rule encourages firms to increase output before entry (hence, to lower price), the price rule requires the dominant firm to live with any postentry price reductions. An inference is that the output rule would give maximum force to potential competition, while the price rule would rely on actual competition to obtain desirable market performance.[57]

Baumol defends his price rule as being relatively easy to enforce, although he acknowledges that some allowance would have to be made for the possibility of inflation. The problems that inflation would raise in deciding whether or not a price increase reflected successful predation would certainly be no worse than the administrative problems created by cost-based or output-based rules, but perhaps not much better.

A Two-Stage Approach

Joskow and Klevorick[58] present a very careful treatment of the kinds of effects one must look for in evaluating proposed rules on predatory pricing. They are concerned with three types of costs: costs that result from condemning competitive pricing as predatory; costs that result from allowing predatory pricing to escape condemnation; and enforcement costs.

Joskow and Klevorick distinguish four categories of enforcement costs, which they define in a broad sense. The first enforcement cost is the cost of the resources employed in the judicial system. The second enforcement cost includes whatever welfare losses result from strategies chosen by dominant firms in response to the rule. They suggest, for example, that Williamson's output rule might induce dominant firms to impede entry in other ways, such as excessive cultivation of brand preference via advertising or other sales efforts. The cost of such sales efforts would be due to the legal rule against an output response to entry.

The third enforcement cost is the cost of private litigation aimed at preventing competition. Not only will such lawsuits congest the courts, they will discourage competition on the merits.

Finally, Joskow and Klevorick count the cost of the uncertainty introduced into firms' decision making when legal standards are unclear. This is one of the standard arguments for the use of per se rules. Per se rules may sometimes punish the innocent, but at least everyone knows what the rules are. If the rules

---

[57] There is a certain irony here, since Baumol's important work on contestable markets emphasizes potential competition as a determinant of market performance. But I digress.

[58] Joskow, Paul L. and Klevorick, Alvin K. "A Framework for Analyzing Predatory Pricing Policy," *Yale Law Journal* Volume 89, Number 2, December 1979, pp. 213–270.

are unclear, firms will make less efficient decisions. Inefficient business decisions are a cost of unclear rules.

Joskow and Klevorick argue that markets are different enough so that no single rule will be appropriate for all cases. Trying to force a uniform approach on the entire economy will inevitably lead to bad decisions in particular cases. To avoid this problem, Joskow and Klevorick propose a two-step treatment of predatory pricing.

In the first stage, they would require an examination of market structure and of the market power of the alleged predator.[59] Entry conditions, as usually defined in the structure-conduct-performance framework, would have to be such that a firm that obtained a dominant position by predation could expect to enjoy monopoly power without inducing immediate entry or reentry. The predator would have to possess enough market power to have the potential to carry out a predatory campaign.

The purpose of the first-stage analysis would be to eliminate cases where concern over predatory pricing is plainly unwarranted:[60]

> Unless a reasonable case could be made that there was a serious monopoly problem in the industry, no detailed investigation of the alleged predator's intent or behavior, nor speculation about the long-run consequences of its pricing policy, would be undertaken. . . . a claim that predatory pricing had taken place could be pursued only if the plaintiff could show that the market context in which the behavior was taking place was in fact conducive to predatory pricing.

This is a fairly severe standard. Placing the burden of proof on the plaintiff will discourage "harassment" suits.

For cases that reached the second stage of the inquiry, Joskow and Klevorick would draw on the rules proposed by other analysts. They would condemn a dominant firm that set a price between average cost and average variable cost, unless the firm could show that this was a profit-maximizing (actually, a loss-minimizing) strategy. They would condemn a price reduction, even if the price remained above average cost, if the price reduction were reversed within 2 years. Thus, for the second stage of their rule, Joskow and Klevorick would follow Areeda and Turner and Baumol.

Rival Exit Necessary for Profitability (I)

Ordover and Willig[61] give a general definition of predatory behavior that includes predatory pricing but is not limited to pricing policy. A business

---

[59] As noted previously, this suggestion was anticipated by Posner.

[60] Op. cit., p. 244.

[61] Ordover, and Willig, "An Economic Definition of Predation: pp. 8–53.

strategy is predatory, they argue, if it is profitable only on the condition that rivals are driven from the market.

In this view, if a firm cuts price and would make a profit even if all of its rivals remain active, that price is not predatory. If some rivals do leave the market, and the firm that initiated the price cut makes a greater profit on that account, that is its good fortune but it is *not* predation. If a firm cuts price and will not make money unless some rivals leave the market, that *is* predation.

Ordover and Willig accept the argument that only certain types of markets will support predatory pricing. In their view, a market must be concentrated before predatory pricing could make sense. If the market is not concentrated, competition from remaining firms will enforce competitive performance, even if some rivals are driven from the market. The market also has to be surrounded by entry barriers (sunk entry costs) and reentry barriers.

If an allegation of predatory pricing passes this preliminary test—if the market structure *can* support a predatory pricing strategy—Ordover and Willig would apply an *incremental cost* test that is a generalization of the price-cost tests proposed by Areeda and Turner.[62]

Ordover and Willig would compare the revenue generated by an output increase with the incremental cost of the increase. Incremental cost would be measured to avoid fixed expenses that the firm would have had to pay no matter what its output. If the incremental revenue exceeds the incremental cost, the output increase is profitable to the firm, and Ordover and Willig would not condemn the output increase as predatory.

Consumer Recovery

A very different approach is taken by Easterbrook.[63] He accepts the Chicago arguments that predation is unlikely ever to be profitable. He criticizes the proposals that we have reviewed and tartly observes,[64] "Every proponent of a predation test argues that the tests proposed by other scholars are impractical. I think they are all correct."

If predation is to remain an offense under the antitrust laws, Easterbrook would prefer to minimize the possibility of abusive use of the antitrust laws to frustrate competition. He would deny rivals the right to initiate private suits over alleged predatory pricing. Instead, he would allow *consumers* to sue to recover damages based on the overcharges resulting from successful predation.[65]

---

[62] Ordover and Willig show that specific versions of their general test reduce to Areeda and Turner's average variable cost and marginal cost tests; op. cit., pp. 16–17.

[63] Easterbrook, op. cit., pp. 263–337.

[64] Ibid., p. 313.

[65] Ibid., p. 331.

Easterbrook expects consumers to realize that predatory pricing is taking place when rivals approach them to discuss possible long-term contracts, by which the consumers will aid targets of predation.[66] Those who think that there are substantial transaction costs involved in the negotiation of long-term contracts will not regard this as a realistic possibility.

Easterbrook emphasizes both the complexity of predatory pricing cases and the possibility that any rule against predatory pricing will be twisted to repress competition, not preserve it. He advocates a rule of per se legality for predatory pricing.[67]

Recapitulation

It will occur to the reader that writing about predatory pricing seems to have become a cottage industry among economists. We have seen the following treatments advocated:

1. Condemn prices that fall below average variable cost.
2. Apply a full-fledged structure-conduct-performance analysis to evaluate the intent and effect of the challenged conduct.
3. Force a dominant firm to maintain output if entry occurs, so that there is room for the entrant.
4. Allow a dominant firm to expand output and lower price in the face of entry, but force it to maintain the lower price even if the entrant withdraws.
5. Use a quick-and-dirty structural test to eliminate most predation cases; to the few remaining cases, apply tests of the kind previously advocated.
6. Declare predatory pricing to be legal, since it is unlikely to be an important problem in any event.

Whoever said "If you laid all the economists in the world end to end, they would not reach a conclusion" would find some satisfaction in this list. Since we are unlikely to settle the controversy over rules for the legal treatment of predatory pricing here, we settle for a less ambitious goal: to understand the reasons for it.

Joskow and Klevorick[68] identify six reasons why economists take different positions toward predatory pricing:

1. Economists employ different models—some static, some dynamic.
2. Economists make different assumptions about market characteristics: some believe predatory pricing to be rare, others common; some believe that dominant firms maintain excess capacity, others do not.

---

[66] See the previous discussion of *Mogul Steamship*.

[67] Op. cit., pp. 333–337.

[68] Op. cit., pp. 214–217.

3. Economists have different views on the cost of administering legal controls over prices and outputs.
4. Economists have different views about the ability of courts to administer economic rules.
5. Economists have different views on the relative desirability of the per se and rule of reason approaches.
6. Economists have different views on the likelihood that firms will resort to litigation.

No single rule for predatory pricing can be shown to be right or best on economic grounds. Each proposed rule has costs and benefits. Which rule one prefers depends on the importance one attaches to different costs and benefits *and* on one's political preferences concerning the role of antitrust policy.

A choice among rules has important implications for government regulation of business conduct. Under the rule of reason approach, courts will take a relatively active role in industries that are the subject of predation suits. But this approach would mean the enforcement of relatively few big cases. In a world of limited resources, a rule of reason approach to predation means comprehensive enforcement of a limited number of cases.

The average cost-based approach and the two-stage approach (a preliminary structural analysis followed by a rule-of-reason analysis for cases that pass the first stage) to predation represent a compromise between the full-fledged rule of reason treatment and the simpler per se rules. They would economize on enforcement costs, while minimizing the odds of condemning competitive behavior as predation.

The various per se rules (no output increase after entry, no price increase after exit) would minimize enforcement costs and give maximum coverage to prohibitions against predatory behavior. They would also condemn a good deal of behavior that, to an omniscient observer, would appear to be competitive.

A predation rule that denied rivals the right to recover damages but allowed consumers to sue in order to recover stage 2 overcharges would as a practical matter, make predatory behavior legal per se. Transactions costs would prevent consumers from seeking redress under such a rule.

A decision on which rule to implement is an exercise in political economy, not economics. If someone tries to tell you otherwise, hold on to your wallet.

Predatory Innovation

Perhaps the most lively controversy in recent discussions of predatory behavior involves the claim that in some circumstances, the development of new products can be exclusionary and reduce social welfare.

Consider the following parable. Red Cedar Computers, Inc., introduces the Winesap home computer. With the Winesap, they introduce a variety of accessories designed to hook into the central unit. The accessories include a printer, a modem, memory boards, disk drives, and a range of monitors. The Winesap is a tremendous commercial success. Eighteen months after it is introduced, independent producers are marketing their own versions of accessories for the Winesap, which compete with the Red Cedar products.

Three years after the introduction of the Winesap, Red Cedar introduces the new, improved Winesap II. It has more memory and is faster, at least for some tasks, than the Winesap I. The accessories that independent producers had marketed for use with the Winesap I are incompatible with the Winesap II. After inventories of the Winesap I are exhausted, Red Cedar discontinues it and concentrates its production and marketing efforts on the Winesap II. Have the independent producers fallen prey to a strategy designed to exclude them from the accessories market? Or are they simply victims of the relentless march of progress?

This parable is not entirely fanciful; the issues it raises are similar to those of the *Calcomp* case.[69] Although the context is different, the issues are much the same as those raised by predatory pricing. Lower prices are usually regarded as a good thing, but the predatory pricing literature (outside of Chicago) would condemn predatory pricing. Similarly, the introduction of new, improved products is usually regarded as a good thing. Should the introduction of new products for strategic purposes, to exclude rivals, be condemned as predatory?

Rival Exit Necessary for Profitability (II)

Ordover and Willig[70] would apply their general test for predation to innovation as well as to pricing. They argue that if a new product would be profitable without the exit of rivals, its introduction should not be treated as predatory. But if an innovation would be profitable only on the condition that rivals are driven from the market, Ordover and Willig would condemn it as predatory.

As with price predation, Ordover and Willig would make a preliminary examination of market structure. If the innovator does not have market power, and there are no barriers to entry or reentry, an innovation could not be predatory: the innovator could not raise price after the exclusionary innovation came on the market because of the entry or reentry that a price increase would induce.[71]

At the second stage of the predation test, Ordover and Willig would compare the incremental revenue from the innovation, given the survival of the rival, with the incremental cost, where incremental cost includes revenues lost on the

---

[69] *California Computer Products, Inc., et al. v. International Business Machines Corp.,* 613 F. 2d 727 (9th Cir. 1979).

[70] Op. cit.

[71] Ibid., p. 26.

sale of competing products.[72] Where the innovation involves systems of products, as in the Winesap story, Ordover and Willig would condemn innovators who refused to make compatible components (Winesap I) available to the market at compensatory prices. They would also condemn innovation if it could be shown that the project was undertaken to acquire market power by driving the rival from the market. They suggest that this would be difficult to prove, since it requires a conclusion about the innovator's intent.

Ordover and Willig are sensitive to the possibility that litigation alleging predatory innovation might be used in attempts to throttle competition. For this reason, they would place the burden of proving predatory innovation on the firm making the claim. In particular, the plaintiff would have to show that the structure of the market was such that predation would be a rational strategy.[73]

Debunking Predatory Innovation[74]

Sidak takes vigorous exception to the arguments of Ordover and Willig on two main grounds. The first objection to the treatment of innovation as predatory views system sales as a back-door device to tie together the sales of different products. The second objection asserts that such a rule would discourage socially desirable innovation.

We know from Chapter 15 that tying together the sale of different goods will (in extreme cases) allow a monopolist to extract all of the consumers' surplus in a market as monopoly profit. This eliminates the deadweight welfare loss from monopoly but maximizes the income transfer from consumers to the monopolist.

Sidak shows that in some circumstances—the main requirement is that the central unit and accessories be used in variable proportions—a technological tie across system components can have the same effects as a contractual tie linking one product to another.

The example Sidak uses[75] involves cameras and film. Suppose a firm manufactures cameras and film cartridges that are technologically tied. The cameras can only be used with cartridges in the form supplied by the manufacturer, and the manufacturer's film cartridges can only be used in the cameras it produces.

By selling the camera below cost—to get it into the hands of consumers—and selling the film above cost, the manufacturer can extract more profit from individuals who take more pictures (since they will purchase more film). Con-

---

[72] Ibid., p. 30. In the story told previously, revenue lost on the sales of Winesap I after the introduction of the Winesap II are an opportunity cost to the firm of introducing the Winesap II.

[73] Ibid., pp. 50–51.

[74] Sidak, Joseph Gregory. "Debunking Predatory Innovation," *Columbia Law Review* Volume 83, Number 5, June 1983, pp. 1121–1149.

[75] Ibid., pp. 1130–1131.

ceivably, the monopolist could produce the same film/camera output as would a competitive market but extract the maximum possible economic profit from the market.

If no social weight is attached to the redistribution of income from the consumer to the monopolist, technological tie-ins that allow the monopolist to meter the intensity with which consumers use the product are an improvement over single-price monopoly. But such metering schemes will work only in the absence of independent suppliers of the metering product.

If independent producers market film that they sell competitively at marginal cost, the camera monopolist can no longer discriminate in price via a technological tie. The monopolist can sell cameras at a price below marginal cost, but competition in the market for film will prevent the camera monopolist from charging a price greater than marginal cost for film.

If entry into the production of cameras is blockaded, the monopolist may set a monopoly price for cameras. Output of cameras will be restricted, which will result in a deadweight welfare loss. At the same time, under single-price monopoly, less income will be transferred from the public to the monopolist than under price discrimination.

If entry into the market for cameras is not blockaded and the monopolist raises the price of cameras, that will create an incentive for rivals to come into the camera market. At this point, the analysis runs into the dominant-firm scenarios of Chapter 4. If a camera monopolist raises price in the camera market and attracts rivals, its ability to exercise control over price will eventually be eroded. If the monopolist limits price to preclude entry, price will be lower and output greater on that account. In either case, breaking the technological tie will make it harder for the monopolist to exercise market power over the long run.

The monopolist can avoid this dismal prospect by periodically bringing out new, improved cameras that use new, improved film dispensed in new, improved cartridges that happen to be shaped differently from those produced by independent film suppliers. The independents will imitate the new cartridges in due course, but their investment in the old film product will be lost. By demonstrating a commitment to periodic design changes, the monopolist can deter entry.

The question, then, is whether the new, improved cameras represent genuine improvements or are aimed simply at excluding rivals. On this issue, Sidak would give the benefit of the doubt to the innovator. His second criticism of the Ordover-Willig analysis of predatory innovation is the chilling effect it would have on innovation.[76] Sidak emphasizes the importance of appropriability (Chapter 12) as an inducement for investment in R&D. Firms will have little incentive to engage in uncertain R&D if they do not think they will be able to keep the profits that flow from successful innovation. Sidak argues that

[76] Ibid., pp. 1140–1143.

441

administration of the Ordover-Willig rules would lead to complex, unmanageable litigation, the very prospect of which would discourage R&D.

Sidak sees the cost of a technological tie-in as the increased cost of competition in the auxiliary market (film, in the example). Independents in the auxiliary market must enter the main market (cameras) or match the periodic design changes of the firm in the main market. It will be costly to match design changes. But independents will be able to do so. All they have to do is buy one of the monopolist's redesigned products and take it apart. Imitation will be swift.

In Sidak's view, the increased cost in the auxiliary market is a small price to pay for the inducement that the prospect of economic profit gives to innovation. Sidak rejects any sort of rule-of-reason test on the ground that it will lead to complex and unmanageable litigation. He proposes that innovation be treated as legal per se.

In a reply defending the Ordover-Willig approach,[77] Ordover, Sykes, and Willig dispute particularly the claim that their test would be difficult to administer. They point out that the first part of the test—showing that the predator has market power and that the market is surrounded by entry and reentry barriers—involves concepts that are familiar to courts from monopolization and merger cases. If a plaintiff were successful in passing this first-stage test, the firm accused of predatory innovation could provide (at relatively little expense) the cost data needed to show that the innovation was compensatory. The alternative approach in the second stage—showing that the innovation was undertaken with predatory intent—is not likely to be used by a plaintiff unless there is a "smoking gun" that reveals intent in unambiguous terms.

Since relatively few plaintiffs are expected to meet these strict requirements, Ordover, Sykes, and Willig argue that few spurious predatory innovation suits would be brought. If few predatory innovation suits are without merit, there would not, they argue, be a chilling effect on innovation.

Summary

The treatment of what is alleged to be predatory behavior raises difficult questions. If it occurs, predation will be similar to behavior that is usually encouraged under the antitrust laws—lower prices, new products. For this reason, economists' views on predation cover a wide spectrum. Four main positions can be distinguished.

The Chicago school's position is that predation will not occur, except perhaps by mistake or miscalculation. Because there are no long-run impediments

---

[77] Ordover, Janusz A., Sykes, Alan O., and Willig, Robert D. "Predatory Systems Rivalry: A Reply," *Columbia Law Review* Volume 83, Number 5, June 1983, pp. 1150–1166.

to entry, and because capital markets work pretty much as they should under complete and perfect innovation, no predator could gain monopoly power by driving rivals from the market. Since firms will not invest resources without the prospect of a return, firms will not engage in predatory behavior.

The minimal structure-conduct-performance position, characterized by the Areeda-Turner short-run average cost rule, accepts the possibility that predatory pricing could occur and proposes to deal with it by using tests that focus on its static consequences. If a price is below average cost, it is treated as predatory. This rule will not catch all cases of strategic behavior, but it will economize on administrative costs.

Akin to the short-run average cost rule are two-stage tests, which would make a plaintiff prove that the market structure would sustain a predatory strategy before allowing a rule of reason inquiry. Placing the burden of proof on plaintiffs in the first stage would discourage nuisance suits.

The central structure-conduct-performance position proposes rules designed to deal with strategic behavior—that is, preventing output increases or forbidding the reversal of price decreases. Such rules would be easy to enforce but might chill competitive behavior.

The maximal structure-conduct-performance position advocates a full-fledged rule of reason analysis of predatory behavior. Such treatment is unlikely to mistakenly condemn competitive behavior as predatory. Under this approach to predation, however, enforcement will be limited to big cases, and much strategic behavior will escape notice.

Any rule that condemns lower prices and new products may, under some circumstances, have a chilling effect on competition. Rules that make it difficult to prove predation will make it more likely that firms will engage in predation. Rule of reason treatments are perhaps less likely to make mistakes of either kind but will involve substantial litigation costs.

Paper Topic

16-1 Discuss the evolution of antitrust analysis of predation in *California Computer Products v. International Business Machines*, 613 F. 2d 727 (9th Cir. 1979); *William Inglis & Sons Baking Co. v. ITT Continental Baking Co.*, 668 F. 2d 1014 (9th Cir. 1981); and *Transamerica Computer Co. v. International Business Machines*, 698 F. 2d 1377 (9th Cir. 1983).

17

Vertical Restraints

Selling the Sizzle Instead of the Steak

The focus of antitrust policy is the exercise of horizontal market power—the power to control price in a market. Nonetheless, vertical relationships—between a supplier and a producer or between a producer and a distributor—are a concern of antitrust policy when they have implications for horizonal market structure, conduct, and performance.

At first glance, a sale by a manufacturer to a distributor seems no different from any other transaction among firms. The USX Corporation sells sheet steel to General Motors, which combines it with other inputs to manufacture a new product, an automobile at the plant gate. General Motors sells the automobile at the plant gate to a dealer, who combines it with other inputs to produce a new product, an automobile plus presales information, dealer preparation, and postsales service on the dealer's lot. In each case, products produced by firms further away from the consumer are combined with other goods and services to produce a new product closer to the final consumer. That the first example involves a physical transformation of the inputs, while the second involves mainly the addition of services (including a change of location) to a physical input, does not alter the fact that a new product results in each case.

In a market system, transactions among independent producers are usually conducted on an arm's-length basis. Once the USX Corporation sells sheet steel to General Motors, it takes no further interest in the fate of its product. This is often the case for sales by a producer to a distributor. But in many cases, manufacturer–distributor sales involve one or more *vertical restrictions,* which limit the conduct of the distributor as a condition of the transaction.

Such restrictions take a variety of forms, including the following:

1. Resale price maintenance: the manufacturer specifies a minimum price below which the dealer may not sell the product (occasionally, RPM in-

444

volves the specification of a maximum price above which the dealer may not sell the product).

2. Territorial restrictions
   a. Territorial confinement: the manufacturer specifies a geographic area within which the dealer may sell.
   b. Exclusive dealership: the dealer agrees not to purchase from any other supplier.[1]
   c. Primary responsibility: the dealer agrees to spend a specified amount promoting the product in a certain area; with this condition met, the dealer may operate in other areas.
   d. Location clause: the manufacturer places no restrictions on the area in which the dealer sells, but the dealer agrees to operate only from a specified location.
   e. Profit-passover: one dealer may sell in an area assigned to another dealer; a portion of the profit from the sale goes to the dealer in the "invaded" territory.

3. Customer restrictions
   a. The dealer agrees to sell only certain types of customers.
   b. The dealer agrees not to sell to certain types of customers (two cases are common: the dealer agrees not to sell to other dealers who specialize in discount sales; certain classes of customers are reserved for the manufacturer, who assumes the dual role of manufacturer/distributor).

These restraints all involve some degree of vertical control: restrictions imposed by the producer on the conduct of independent firms in a vertically related industry.

Our topics in this chapter are the economic analysis and public policy treatment of vertical restraints. Why do producers impose vertical restraints? What are the effects of vertical restraints on market performance? What is the current public policy position toward vertical restraints? What is the appropriate public policy position toward vertical restraints?

Economic Analysis of Vertical Restraints

Resale price maintenance is the strongest form of vertical control (short of vertical integration between the manufacturer and the distributor) because resale price maintenance directly affects price. *Minimum* resale price maintenance is much more common than maximum resale price maintenance. Nonprice vertical restraints, which limit competition among dealers of a single brand, allow

---

[1]Sometimes combined with an exclusive territory, in which the manufacturer agrees not to supply other dealers in the dealer's territory.

retailers to charge higher retail prices than would otherwise be possible. Non-price vertical restraints therefore have effects similar to those of minimum resale price maintenance but represent less complete forms of control because their effect on price is indirect.

A producer's profit per unit sold depends on the wholesale price, the price charged by the producer to the dealer.[2] If the wholesale price is held constant, fixing a minimum retail price increases the *retailer's* profit on every unit sold but does not directly benefit the producer. Indeed, if the wholesale price is held constant, the producer is made worse off if resale price maintenance increases the retail price. As the retail price increases along a fixed demand curve, the quantity demanded will fall, reducing the total profit earned by the producer. The same is true for any vertical restraint that protects a dealer from competition by other dealers in the same brand—that reduces *intrabrand* competition.

The direct benefit of resale price maintenance, holding the wholesale price and the location of the demand curve constant, is to the retailer. This suggests one possible explanation for vertical controls. Vertical controls may be an exercise of market power by retailers. Retailers with market power may use producers to facilitate retailer oligopolistic coordination.

A manufacturer can benefit from vertical restraints only if[3] (1) vertical restraints somehow allow a higher wholesale price, holding the quantity demanded constant, or (2) vertical restraints increase the quantity demanded of a manufacturer's product, holding the wholesale price constant (or some combination of the two). In the first case, a vertical restraint is an instrument for the direct exercise of market power. In the second case, it is a device for dealing with a particular type of market failure: the failure of the market for distribution services to provide product-differentiating activity desired by a manufacturer in the presence of a competitive retail product market.

Market Power Explanations of Vertical Restraints

Dealer Market Power

The dealer market power explanation for vertical restraints suggests that dealers use a manufacturer to impose and police minimum resale prices (or

---

[2]There may be independent wholesalers who operate between the manufacturer and the retailer. For simplicity, we suppose here that the manufacturer performs the wholesaling function; this does not affect the results of the analysis. Bowman, Ward S., Jr., "The Prerequisites and Effects of Resale Price Maintenance," *University of Chicago Law Review*, Volume 22, Number 4, Summer 1955, pp. 825–873, discusses historical instances of wholesale price maintenance. Yamey, B. S., *The Economics of Resale Price Maintenance*, London: Sir Isaac Pitman 1954, points out that wholesalers have favored resale price maintenance; resale price maintenance favors smaller retailers at the expense of larger ones. Larger retailers are more likely to integrate backward and perform the wholesale function themselves.

[3]This formulation is due to Porter, Michael E. *Interbrand Choice, Strategy, and Bilateral Market Power*. Cambridge, Mass.: Harvard University Press, 1976, p. 64

other restraints that have the effect of holding up retail prices) as a way of furthering dealers' collusive behavior.

Recall our discussion (Chapter 6) of the problems of oligopolistic coordination. The two problems that beset any oligopoly—including one at the retail level—are agreement and adherence. If oligopolists are to exercise control over price, they must secure agreement on a common pattern of behavior. Once such agreement is obtained, the oligopoly must be able to enforce adherence, overcoming the incentive of each member firm to increase output and increase its own profits. We also saw that a generally accepted pricing rule can greatly facilitate tacit collusion (the basing point system is an example). Resale price maintenance, by serving as such a rule, can make successful collusion (tacit or overt) at the retail level easier.

The manufacturer informs individual retailers about the details of the resale price maintenance program. This eliminates the need for continuous direct communication among retailers. Further, the manufacturer can discipline retailers who fail to hold to the cartel price by cutting off their supplies. Vertical restraints imposed by the manufacturer thus make it easier to secure agreement and provide a way of ensuring adherence.

The impact of such vertical restraints on market performance will depend on the breadth of their coverage. If only a single manufacturer is affected, the restraints will limit *intrabrand* competition—competition among the dealers in that brand. If all manufacturers agree to similar vertical restraints, *interbrand* competition—competition among dealers of different brands—will also be restricted.

For what kinds of markets will dealer-sponsored vertical restraints be plausible? Several conditions must be met. First, unless resale price maintenance covers all manufacturers, the target manufacturers must have some market power. If consumers make no distinction between the product affected by resale price maintenance (or other restraints) and other products, retailers will be unable to enforce a higher retail price on a single product. If retailers tried to raise the retail price of a single brand, consumers would simply switch to another brand without an artificially enhanced price. The requirement that target manufacturers have some market power raises a problem for dealer sponsorship of vertical restraints. It is precisely the brands with market power that will be in the strongest position to resist pressure from dealers.[4]

It follows that retailer market power as well as manufacturer market power is one prerequisite for dealer-sponsored resale price maintenance. If retailers do not possess some market power, they cannot persuade the manufacturer to

[4]Marvel, Howard P. "How Fair Is Fair Trade?," *Contemporary Policy Issues* Volume 111, Number 3, Part I, Spring 1985, p. 26. As a related point, another prerequisite for resale price maintenance as an instrument of dealer market power is that the manufacturer must be unwilling or unable to integrate forward into distribution in the face of dealer exercise of market power. Manufacturers with market power will be in the strongest position to integrate forward, all else equal.

447

impose a higher retail price, a price that would reduce sales and the manufacturer's profit.

For retailers to persuade the manufacturer to do their bidding, it would appear useful for them to provide important services to the manufacturer. Recalling our discussion of sales efforts (Chapter 11), retailers provide important services for products marketed through nonconvenience outlets. Such products are distributed through selected retail outlets, and the assistance of sales personnel is an important factor in the purchase decision of the final consumer.

Industry studies suggest that retailer-sponsored resale price maintenance occurred in the (pharmaceutical) drug trade in the United States, Britain, and France.[5] Dealer-sponsored resale price maintenance is also believed to have taken place in the cosmetics and liquor industries in the United States.[6] These are all industries that have had active dealer trade organizations. In these cases, dealers' motivation seemed to involve not only higher prices but also protection from mass-marketing, discounting retail outlets.

The Chicago school has generally regarded the possibility of dealer-sponsored vertical restraints as remote. Their major arguments are as follows:[7]

1. Retail cartels are unlikely to be successful because of the large number of rivals in retail markets.
2. Retail cartels are improbable because of the large number of potential entrants at the retail level.
3. Since a successful retail cartel would reduce manufacturers' profits, manufacturers will have an incentive to disrupt it.
4. Differentiation (which can mean differentiation among retailers, as well as among the products of different manufacturers), which is a precondition for the use of vertical restraints, will make successful oligopolistic coordination less likely.

Taking these arguments in reverse order, the fourth point is a standard part of the economic analysis of oligopolistic coordination (Chapter 6). Product differentiation interferes with successful oligopolistic coordination. If some dealers benefit from favorable locations or favorable images, they will therefore have less incentive to cooperate with other dealers.

If differentiation exists at the manufacturing level, manufacturers with a strong brand image may be able to resist dealers' demands. This in fact becomes the third point raised by the Chicago school: if manufacturers have enough

[5]Yamey, op. cit.; Bowman. op. cit.

[6]Bowman, op. cit.

[7]This formulation follows Ornstein, Stanley I. "Resale Price Maintenance and Cartels," *Antitrust Bulletin*, Volume 30, Number 2, Summer 1985, pp. 412–413.

bargaining power to resist vertical restraints, a complete account of vertical restraints will have to explain why manufacturers cooperate in imposing them. It is possible[8] that retailers could "buy" manufacturers' cooperation by sharing cartel profits with the retailers. In this view, manufacturers and dealers cooperate in an arrangement to exercise market power jointly.

The first two objections to the possibility of dealer cartels depend on the structure of retail markets. The usual assumptions of the Chicago school are that retail markets are competitive, with many small firms in the market and with free and easy entry and exit. If these assumptions are correct, successful retailer cartels will indeed be unlikely.

But these assumptions are not universally accepted. Porter[9] describes retail markets as highly concentrated oligopolies:

> Retailers never sell a consumer good in a national market. Because the consumer must travel to the retail establishment it must be in reasonable proximity to him. Hence the relevant market for consumer goods may be as large as a city or small region, but certainly no larger and in many cases much smaller. For some goods where convenience is important to the consumer, the relevant retail market may encompass that group of consumers within a five-minute drive of the retail establishment. . . . the concentration of retail establishments in the relevant retail market is often high. Two to five retail establishments commonly make up such a market.

If Porter is correct, the first Chicago school objection to the plausibility of dealer cartels fails. If small-numbers oligopoly is the common type of retail market structure, recognition of oligopolistic interdependence is likely.

We know from Chapter 4 that entry conditions affect the extent to which incumbent firms can exercise market power. It may well be that there are a large number of potential entrants for some types of retail markets. But this will not be the case[10] if incumbent retailers invest in highly specific sunk assets. For retail outlets, physical-asset and human-asset specificity seem likely to be important.

Physical-asset specificity arises when the retailer invests in capital goods suited for the particular product or type of product of a given manufacturer. Pharmacists, for example, may need to invest in refrigerated storage space with elaborate temperature controls in order to maintain the quality of certain medications. Such equipment will be difficult to transport and of little use for

---

[8]As Ornstein acknowledges.

[9]Porter, op. cit., p. 13; footnote omitted.

[10]Williamson, Oliver E. "Vertical Integration and Related Variations on a Transaction-Cost Economics Theme," in Stiglitz, Joseph E. and Mathewson, G. Frank, editors, *New Developments in the Analysis of Market Structure*. Cambridge, Mass.: The MIT Press, 1986, pp. 149–174.

retailing other products. Their cost is therefore sunk, and the need to invest sunk assets constitutes a barrier to the entry of other firms (Chapter 4).[11]

Human-asset specificity arises when employees of retail firms possess special skills that are not easily replicated or transferred. Sales personnel in nonconvenience outlets are likely to have such skills, which they acquire by experience in demonstrating the manufacturer's product to consumers.[12] A new entrant might hire away experienced sales personnel from established firms. In such a case, an entrant must expect to pay a higher wage to the personnel with the desirable human assets in order to induce them to change jobs (changing jobs involves costs, and the employees will insist on some compensation to cover expenses). This will translate into differentially higher wage costs for the entrant than for established retailers.

Where distribution is through nonconvenience retail outlets, retailers are likely to have enough bargaining power to induce manufacturers to cooperate in vertically imposed oligopolistic behavior. This conclusion that retailers can be a source of resale price maintenance is supported by Sharp,[13] based on experience at the Federal Trade Commission. He indicates that the most common type of resale price maintenance is that induced by dealers. Sharp points out that retailers are heterogeneous and that manufacturers will be susceptible to pressure for resale price maintenance from one or a few critical dealers. This may, he suggests, lead manufacturers to adopt resale price maintenance in the absence of a formal dealer cartel. Resale price maintenance again appears as an instrument of tacit collusion. Excluding resale price maintenance cases that arise in response to dealer pressure, he indicates, excludes[14] "more than 80 percent of RPM cases."

Manufacturer Market Power

How will resale price maintenance support collusion among manufacturers?[15]

---

[11]Since physicians invest in specialized storage equipment as part of their business, they are not discouraged on that account from entry into the dispensing of prescription drugs.

[12]Examples include stereo equipment and home computers.

[13]Sharp, Benjamin S. "Comments on Marvel: How Fair Is Fair Trade?," *Contemporary Policy Issues* Volume 111, Number 3, Part I, Spring 1985, pp. 37–42.

[14]Ibid., p. 39.

[15]Pitofsky, Robert. " The *Sylvania* Case: Antitrust Analysis of Non-Price Vertical Restrictions," *Columbia Law Review* Volume 78, Number 1, January 1978, pp. 15–16; footnotes omitted. A similar argument is made by Williamson, Oliver E. "Assessing Vertical Market Restrictions: Antitrust Ramifications of the Transaction Cost Approach," *University of Pennsylvania Law Review* Volume 127, Number 4, April 1979, pp. 967–968.

Assume a supplier cartel with dealers free to set price as they see fit. If suppliers choose to shave the cartel price in order to increase volume, they can offer open or secret discounts to dealers with some expectation that the discounts can be passed along to consumers. Industry-wide resale price maintenance would make open dealer price-cutting impossible, and would thus diminish the incentive for supplier price-cutting and thereby assist in stabilizing the cartel. More importantly, resale price maintenance eliminates, or at least reduces, pressure from dealers on suppliers to depart from an agreed cartel price. When dealers are free to price as they see fit, the more efficient or aggressive dealers cut into distributor markups and often take volume away from other dealers. Dealers losing out in the competitive battle then turn to their suppliers for assistance—either by requesting that the supplier cut off the price-cutter or by demanding that the supplier give them a lower wholesale price in order to make an adequate profit on the supplier's brand. If the dealer is an exclusive outlet, it threatens to shift to another supplier; if the dealer is a common outlet for a number of brands, it threatens to deny the supplier shelf space or adequate representation. And when suppliers give in to this sort of dealer pressure, the horizontal supplier cartel begins to crumble. In this respect, vertical price-fixing stabilizes inter-brand supplier cartels.

This argument follows directly from Stigler's theory of oligopoly (Chapter 6), which suggests that a cartel will be more stable, the easier it is to detect cheating. Resale price maintenance facilitates manufacturer collusion because it makes it more difficult for manufacturers to shade an oligopolistic price secretly and makes it easier for manufacturers to resist competitive pressure from the retail level.

The reaction of the Chicago school to this explanation for vertical restraints has generally been to accept it as a theoretical possibility but to argue that it is of limited real-world significance.[16] For example, Posner writes:[17]

this collusion-enhancing effect of resale price maintenance depends on each retailer's handling only one manufacturer's brand of the product in question, which is the exceptional rather than the normal resale price maintenance situ-

[16]An exception is Popofsky, M. Laurence, "Resale Price Maintenance Revisited," *Antitrust Law Journal* Volume 49, Issue 1, Summer 1980, p. 115, who describes the use of resale price maintenance to stabilize a manufacturer cartel as "mere hypothesis . . . indeed an hypothesis without empirical data to support it." The criticism of an argument on the grounds that it is a hypothesis seems strange in view of the predilection of the Chicago school for strictly theoretical arguments. The assertion that the supplier cartel argument is without empirical support is incorrect, as the light bulb example discussed by Telser shows. For references to other examples, see Overstreet, Thomas R., Jr. *Resale Price Maintenance: Economic Theories and Empirical Evidence.* Washington, D.C.: Bureau of Economics Staff Report to the Federal Trade Commission, November 1983, p. 22, footnote 2; and Ornstein, op. cit.

[17]Posner, Richard A. "The Rule of Reason and the Economic Approach: Reflections on the *Sylvania* Decision," *University of Chicago Law Review* Volume 45, Number 1, Fall 1977, p. 7.

ation. The retailer who handles the brands of several manufacturers will increase his purchases of, and his sales efforts for, the brand of the manufacturer who offers him the lowest wholesale price—the cartelist who is cheating. The presence of resale price maintenance will not make this type of cheating any easier to detect.[18]

This conclusion is seconded by Bork,[19] who points out that manufacturers would not need resale price maintenance to detect cheating if retailers did not operate on an "exclusive dealership" basis. If retailers handle the brands of more than one manufacturer, they will peddle news of a price cut by any one manufacturer in hopes of eliciting matching cuts from others. News of price cutting travels quickly along a network of nonexclusive retailers.

Telser[20] presents an example of manufacturer-inspired resale price maintenance in the manufacture of light bulbs. General Electric, Westinghouse, and other companies used a form of resale price maintenance as part of a cartel agreement based on licensing of patent rights. As the Posner-Bork argument predicts, under the terms of the program, retail dealers were exclusive agents.

Bork[21] points out that even under resale price maintenance, manufacturers could offer secret price cuts to dealers. The increased dealer margin would allow dealers to engage in increased *nonprice competition* (advertising, other sales efforts), increasing the market share of the firm cutting the cartel price. In a similar vein, Bowman[22] finds the manufacturers' cartel explanation of resale price maintenance unconvincing because "An extremely tenuous arrangement or understanding among manufacturers is assumed, one which is likely to collapse at the slightest provocation." The point of both of these comments is that resale price maintenance will not cure all problems of oligopolistic coordination at the manufacturing level, and this seems correct. It remains possible that resale price maintenance will make such coordination easier than would otherwise be the case.

---

[18]Posner continues:

> Furthermore, exclusive territories or other nonprice restrictions on dealer competition are also potential methods of shoring up a manufacturers' cartel. They prevent a cheater from arguing that any increase in his market share above the quota assigned him by the cartel was due not to his price cutting but to competition among his dealers. To be sure, nonprice restrictions would be effective in shoring up cartels only in exclusive dealing situations. . . .

[19]Bork, Robert H. "The Rule of Reason and the Per Se Concept: Price Fixing and Market Division," *Yale Law Journal*, Volume 75, Number 3, January 1966, p. 411.

[20]Telser, Lester G. "Why Should Manufacturers Want Fair Trade?," *Journal of Law and Economics* Volume 3, Number 1, October 1960, pp. 86–105.

[21]Op. cit., pp. 412–413. The same argument is made by Ornstein, op. cit., pp. 407–408. This is consistent with Posner's comments, quoted in footnote 18.

[22]Bowman, op. cit., p. 839.

Bilateral Monopoly

The dealer cartel theory of vertical restraints seems limited to cases in which dealers provide important services to the manufacturer, in which dealers can impose similar restraints on all manufacturers, and in which branding is sufficiently weak that manufacturers cannot resist pressure from dealers.

The manufacturer cartel theory is most plausible if each dealer represents a single manufacturer. Even when this is the case, nonprice competition at the retail level will present problems for manufacturing cooperation.

In each case, it is in the interest of firms at one vertical level to oppose the exercise of market power at the other level. The bilateral monopoly theory of vertical restraints, which is in some sense a compromise between the dealer cartel and manufacturer cartel theories, asserts that this conflict of interest will not always arise.

The bilateral monopoly theory of resale price maintenance originated with the Chicago school as a demonstration of anticompetitive effects of vertical restraints at a time when fair trade laws (to be discussed) allowed states to legalize resale price maintenance. The bilateral monopoly theory has since been abandoned by the Chicago school but adopted as an element of the structure-conduct-performance analysis of vertical restraints.

Bowman[23] proposes that in many cases resale price maintenance is jointly sponsored by manufacturers and retailers as a way of reinforcing partial market power at each vertical level. In this basic story,[24] manufacturers offer resale price maintenance to dealers, who agree not to patronize other manufacturers.

This raises the cost of entry at the manufacturing level. Potential entrants must either bear the expense of entry on two levels or distribute through retailers who remain outside the agreement. The increased cost of entry at the manufacturing level allows a greater wholesale price. Manufacturers and retailers reinforce each other's market power and split the resulting economic profits. Manufacturers *and* dealers earn more with resale price maintenance than they would without it.

Bowman presents several examples that seem consistent with this story, including book publishing and distribution, wallpaper, whiskey, fashion patterns, and others. He concludes that a specific kind of market structure is most conducive to jointly sponsored resale price maintenance:[25]

> when there are relatively few manufacturers and relatively large-scale operation
> is required for efficient production; for then, foreclosing all but a small pro-

[23]Bowman, Ward S., Jr. ''Resale Price Maintenance—A Monopoly Problem,'' *Journal of Business* Volume 25, July 1952, pp. 141–155.

[24]Bowman, ''Prerequisites and Effects,'' pp. 844–848.

[25]Op. cit., p. 847.

portion of dealer outlets makes it more difficult for outside manufacturers to reach efficient size.

In addition:[26]

> if the co-operating manufacturers make trade-marked or branded products which have high consumer acceptance, which is maintained in part by the organized dealers, the entry of competing manufacturers will be more difficult.

Bowman remarks that if dealers are foreclosed, a potential entrant will still have the option of entering on both levels. Bowman cites the standard Chicago position[27] that capital markets will provide funds for entry if firms in the market are making an economic profit. However, the argument that capital markets will not impede entry fails if transaction costs rooted in impacted information and opportunism translate into higher interest rates for entrants.

Although Bowman indicates doubts about the possibility that capital markets could be a source of impediments to entry, he points out that vertical agreements may nonetheless raise the risk of successful entry:[28]

> When the range and diversity of product sales required for successful operation on one level (reselling) is much broader than the other (manufacturing), it is possible that combining the proper proportions for successful operation on each level is a complicated, risky, time-consuming process. Securing dealer customers is not costless, as the makers of the Kaiser automobile knew or learned.

This reasoning is perfectly consistent with the general hypothesis that vertical integration can have consequences for horizontal market power (a hypothesis rejected by the Chicago school).

Porter[29] extends Bowman's analysis by explaining the source of retailer influence over manufacturers. Porter suggests that the retailer's bargaining chip in the manufacturer–distributor relationship is the retailer's contribution to product differentiation:[30]

---

[26]Ibid.

[27]See our discussion of capital requirements as a determinant of entry conditions in Chapter 8, especially the argument by Bork cited in footnote 35, which is the reference cited by Bowman.

[28]Bowman, ''Prerequisites and Effects,'' pp. 847–848.

[29]Op. cit., pp. 64–68.

[30]Ibid., p. 65. Porter's argument is anticipated by Comanor, William S. ''Vertical Territorial and Customer Restrictions: White Motor and Its Aftermath,'' *Harvard Law Review* Volume 81, Number 7, May 1968, p. 1425.

> RPM is likely to occur where the retailer can add significantly to the promotion of a product, or where the retailer's contribution to product differentiation is relatively high. . . . the retailer's contribution to product differentiation is the primary . . . source of his market power.

Thus resale price maintenance, increased product differentiation, and economic profit for producers and distributors go together.

Market Failure Explanations for Vertical Restraints

An alternative view of vertical restraints is that they are a manufacturer's response to imperfections in the market for distribution services. This position is most prominently associated with the work of Telser[31] and has become the orthodox Chicago school explanation for vertical restraints.

A prerequisite for the market failure theory is that demand for the manufacturer's product depends on services provided by the retailer. These services must be specific to the manufacturer's product, and there must be something about them that prevents the retailer from charging for them separately. For example, postsales service does not qualify because it can usually be charged for separately from the manufacturer's product.

Perhaps the most important example of such services is presale demonstration of the product, which has an important effect on the demand for products sold through nonconvenience outlets. A manufacturer may wish to induce dealers in his product to increase their presale services in order to increase demand for his product. Dealers cannot charge a separate price for presale demonstrations. But the manufacturer can lower the wholesale price, giving retailers a larger margin, some of which can be used to finance a greater investment in presale services.

It is here that the market failure element comes into play. Suppose the manufacturer lowers his price to all dealers. Some dealers react as the manufacturer expects, providing the desired special services. But other dealers do not. Their costs are lower, so they are able to undersell dealers who provide the special services. Consumers who do not want the special services will buy from the low-price dealers. Consumers who do want the special services can visit the dealers who provide them, "consume" the special services, and then purchase the product from a low-price dealer. The dealers who provide the special services are not compensated, and eventually the services will no longer be offered.

---

[31]Op. cit. Essentially the same argument appears in Bowman, "Prerequisites and Effects," p. 843; Bork, op. cit., p. 414 (footnote 80); and Yamey, op. cit.

455

Case Study: Free Riding and (?) Market Failure

As part of its marketing arrangements, the General Motors Corporation imposed a *location clause* on its dealers. They could sell automobiles anywhere in the world, but only from dealerships authorized by General Motors in a franchise agreement.

In the late 1950s and the early 1960s, some Chevrolet dealers in the Los Angeles area began to cooperate with discount houses. These discount houses maintained minimal displays, sometimes working from catalogues. When a customer placed an order with a discount house, a franchised dealer would supply the vehicle at a very small markup over General Motors' price to the dealer. By 1960, 12 of 85 Chevrolet dealers in the Los Angeles area were cooperating with discount houses. Sales through discounters accounted for 2 per cent of 1960 Chevrolet sales in this area.

Chevrolet dealers who eschewed the use of discounters enlisted General Motors' assistance and were able to cut discounters off from their sources of supply.

In a landmark case, these actions were held to be a conspiracy—between some franchised dealers and General Motors—in restraint of trade. The defense that discounters were cut off as a way of enforcing the (presumably legal) location clause was held to be irrelevant in view of the Sherman Act's per se prohibition of conspiracy in restraint of trade.

Implicit in this episode are many of the policy questions raised by manufacturer–distributor relationships. Did sales through discounters represent a failure in the market for distribution—General Motors unable to purchase the product-differentiating services it wanted in the market for retail services? Would sales near cost for 2 per cent of the market prevent General Motors from marketing high-price, high-sales-effort services to customers who preferred such a combination? Or did sales through discounters represent competition in the retail market for automobiles, providing vehicles near cost to customers who, for whatever reason, did not want the high-price, high-service combination offered through franchised dealers?

See *United States v. General Motors Corporation et al.*, 384 U.S. 127 (1966).

This is a situation of market failure in the market for dealer services. The manufacturer cannot "buy" the distribution services he wants because low-price dealers get a free ride on the services provided by other dealers and, ultimately, make it unprofitable for such dealers to provide the desired services. Thus the manufacturer is unable to maximize his profit.

But it is not at all clear that free riding represents failure in the product market, which involves retailers and final consumers rather than manufacturers and retailers. Some customers—especially those already knowledgeable about the product—will prefer a low-price, low-service combination to a high-price, high-service package. Retailers, who are closer than the manufacturer to the final consumer, will often be in a better position to take the pulse of the marketplace. It may well be that what is considered market failure in the market for distribution services is simply market working in the market for distribution of the product:[32]

> In the distribution sector, vertical restraints will lead directly to higher markups than would otherwise exist. Although these markups may result in higher distributor profits, they will generally be associated with inflated dealer costs. . . . more dealer services are provided than would be demanded by consumers in unrestricted markets. . . . market restrictions lead directly to an inefficient use of society's resources at the distribution stage.

By imposing minimum resale prices, the manufacturer prevents free riding. With resale price maintenance, dealers who skimp on special services cannot undersell other dealers. Without a price advantage, dealers who do not provide special services would lose sales to dealers who do provide the special services. Under retail price maintenance, all dealers are induced to provide the services the manufacturer desires.

By preventing intrabrand price competition, the manufacturer channels rivalry at the retail level into nonprice competition. The higher the maintained retail price, the more resources will retailers devote to providing special services. By adjusting the retail price, the manufacturer can obtain the level of special services that will maximize his profit.

---

[32]Comanor, op. cit., pp. 136–137; For similar views, see Pitofsky, op. cit., pp. 1–38; and *Hearings on S. 2549 Before the Subcommittee on Antitrust and Monopoly of the Senate Judiciary Committee*, 89th Congress, 2d Session, 1966, p. 1088 (Statement of Donald F. Turner). In this connection, it is instructive to consider the argument of Posner, Richard A. *Antitrust Law: An Economic Perspective.* Chicago: The University of Chicago Press, 1976, pp. 11–12:

> Suppose . . . that a cartel fixes prices somewhere above the competitive level . . . , and the entry of new firms . . . is for some reason impeded. Each member of the cartel will have an incentive, by expending resources on making his output more valuable to consumers than the output of the other members of the cartel, to increase his sales relative to the other cartelists. . . . The process of increasing nonprice competition (higher quality, better service, etc.) will continue until, at the margin, the costs of the cartel members have risen to the cartel price level. The higher costs are a cost of monopoly, although there is a partially offsetting benefit since the additional nonprice competition has some value, though less than its cost, to the consumer.

In an accompanying footnote, Posner continues: "If consumers valued the additional services (or whatever) generated by this competition above its cost, presumably the services would have been produced in a price-competitive market as well."

In an apparent inconsistency, Posner later (pp. 149–50) accepts the free riding argument.

Any vertical restraint that prevents one dealer from "poaching" on the customers of another will alleviate the free rider problem. This is true of territory and customer restraints as well as of resale price maintenance.

The free rider explanation of vertical restraints seems especially plausible for new entrants at the manufacturing level. In this case, the manufacturer guarantees a high retail price to induce "missionary work"[33] by dealers on behalf of a new brand (perhaps even a new product). In the same vein, it is sometimes[34] suggested that resale price maintenance will allow a manufacturer to induce a greater number of outlets to carry his product.

Free riding arises in markets for the distribution of goods marketed through nonconvenience outlets. It is precisely for such goods that dealers influence demand through prepurchase sales efforts. These are, of course, the dealers identified by Porter as likely to have bargaining power vis-à-vis producers.

This suggests that bilateral monopoly and special services are complementary explanations of vertical restraints. The market power and market failure explanations are not mutually exclusive. The bilateral monopoly analysis suggests that vertically related firms with some market power in their home markets will have an incentive to cooperate and invest in product differentiation as a way of reinforcing their market positions. The free rider analysis suggests that this cooperation will not work unless there is some way to prevent uncooperative dealers from spoiling the market.[35]

Free riding does not explain resale price maintenance of goods that require no special dealer services. An example (to be discussed subsequently in another context) is the resale price maintenance program of Levi Strauss for blue jeans during the 1970s. To explain resale price maintenance in such circumstances, recent generalizations of the free rider effect have focused on the retailer's influence on the perceived quality of the product. Even if retailers provide no specific presale services, nonetheless the demand for a manufacturer's product may be favorably affected if the product is marketed through high-quality retail outlets. In such situations, the quality of the outlet "certifies" the quality of the product.[36]

---

[33]Steiner, Robert L. "The Nature of Vertical Restraints," *Antitrust Bulletin* Volume 30, Number 1, Spring 1985, pp. 143–197.

[34]Gould, J. R. and Preston, L. E. "Resale Price Maintenance and Retail Outlet," *Economica* N.S. Volume 32, No. 127, August 1965, pp. 302–312. See also Mathewson, G. F. and Winter, R. A. "Vertical Integration by Contractual Restraints in Spatial Markets," *Journal of Business* Volume 56, Number 4, October 1983, pp. 497–517.

[35]Thus, Telser, op. cit., p. 97, footnote 10, indicates that exclusive dealing *and* resale price maintenance are needed for effective collusion among manufacturers, although he criticizes Yamey and Bowman for interpreting this as a cooperative arrangement with retailers.

[36]Marvel, H. P. and McCafferty, S. "Resale Price Maintenance and Quality Certification," *Rand Journal of Economics* Volume 5, Number 3, Autumn 1984, pp. 346–359.

Telser acknowledges both the special service and the producers' cartel explanations for manufacturer's support of resale price maintenance (and, by implication, vertical restraints generally):

> First, a single manufacturer producing a differentiated product over which he possesses some degree of monopoly power may find it advantageous to establish minimum retail prices in order to induce those retailers who handle his product to offer special services jointly with it thereby increasing total sales. Second, a group of manufacturers may couple resale price maintenance with a kind of exclusive dealing as part of their broad scheme to create a producers' cartel.

This explains why manufacturers might be interested in vertical restraints. It does not address the welfare effects of such restraints.

Welfare Consequences of Vertical Restraints

Static Welfare Effects

The Chicago analysis of the welfare effect of vertical restraints is straightforward. Their basic welfare test is derived by analogy with monopoly.[37] A firm with monopoly power imposes welfare losses on society by restricting output. Hence, if a vertical restraint results in an output restriction, it reduces welfare. If it results in an output expansion, it increases welfare.

But, the Chicago analysis goes, a manufacturer would never impose vertical restraints with the purpose of restricting output. A manufacturer with some market power can set a profit-maximizing wholesale price and reap whatever monopoly profit is available to him. Having set the profit-maximizing wholesale price, the manufacturer will want to keep the distribution margin as small as possible. If the manufacturer were to impose vertical restraints that allowed retailers to restrict output *further,* he would only reduce his own profit below the maximum level.[38] It follows that we can trust the manufacturer's pursuit of his own self-interest to prevent the imposition of vertical restraints that would reduce social welfare.

Implicit in this argument is the belief that vertical relationships cannot alter horizontal market structure. In other words, vertical integration—either complete, through merger, or incomplete, through contractual restrictions—does not raise capital requirements barriers to entry or impose a higher cost of capital on entrants. The structure of retailing is competitive, and product-differentiating activity by retailers cannot contribute to manufacturers' market power. If any of these propositions fail, manufacturers have an incentive to increase retailers' margins because retailers' activities can reinforce manufacturers' market power.

---

[37]Bork Robert H. "The Rule of Reason and the Per Se Concept: Price Fixing and Market Division," *Yale Law Journal* Volume 75, Number 3, January, 1966, p. 375.

[38]Ibid., p. 403.

The output restriction welfare test is based on a faulty analogy. Economists define output restriction as the welfare vice of monopoly because a monopolist restricts output along a fixed demand curve. A manufacturer imposes vertical restraints (and this is true under either the bilateral monopoly or free rider theories of vertical restraints) with the purpose of inducing a shift in the demand curve for his product. The welfare analysis of vertical restraints has more in common with the welfare analysis of advertising, which acts to shift the demand curve, than with the welfare analysis of monopoly over an undifferentiated product. Just as advertising by firms with market power will generally exceed the socially optimal level,[39] so it is possible for a single manufacturer to find vertical restraints profitable even though they impose welfare losses on society.

The Chicago school analysis of the welfare effects of vertical restraints fails to confront a critical tradeoff between the welfare of marginal consumers—who will not buy the product without special services—and of inframarginal consumers—who would purchase the product without the services and who would prefer not to pay for services they do not want.

Vertical restraints are attractive to producers because of the special services they evoke from retailers, who they protect from free riders. Manufacturers will have an incentive to increase such special services as long as there are consumers willing to pay for them in the form of a higher price. For these marginal consumers, the services are worth as much as or more than the cost of providing them. Sales to these consumers increase social welfare.

But not all consumers will place equal value on the special services supported by vertical restraints. Some, perhaps most, consumers might prefer to have the product at a lower price without the services.[40] Under vertical restraints, these inframarginal consumers will suffer a welfare loss because they have to pay more for the special services (via a price increase for the final product) than they feel the services are worth.[41] If there are enough customers who prefer

---

[39]See the discussion of Dixit and Norman's analysis in Chapter 8.

[40]For example, some manufacturers of construction equipment have found it profitable to impose customer restraints on their dealers, with specific reference to prepurchase sales efforts promoted by such sales. Yet many purchasers of construction equipment are experienced builders who have used similar equipment in the past and have no need of presales information.

[41]See Telser, op. cit., p. 116; Williamson, Oliver E. "Assessing Vertical Market Restrictions: Antitrust Ramifications of the Transaction Cost Approach," *University of Pennsylvania Law Review* Volume 127, Number 4, April 1979, p. 966; Scherer, F. M. "The Economics of Vertical Restraints," *Antitrust Law Journal* Volume 52, Number 3, September 1983, pp. 687–718; Comanor, William S. "Vertical Price Fixing and Market Restrictions in the New Antitrust Policy," *Harvard Law Review* Volume 98, March 1985, pp. 983–1102; Comanor, William S. and Kirkwood, John B. "Resale Price Maintenance and Antitrust Policy," *Contemporary Policy Issues* Volume 111, Number 3, Part I, Spring 1985, pp. 9–16; and White, Lawrence J. "Resale Price Maintenance and the Problem of Marginal and Inframarginal Customers," *Contemporary Policy Issues* Volume 111, Number 3, Part I, Spring 1985, pp. 17–22.

not to pay for special services, the inability of manufacturers to buy such services from distributors is not so much a failure in the market for distribution services as the invisible hand efficiently allocating resources in the retail product market.

The net welfare effect of vertical restraints involves a tradeoff between marginal and inframarginal customers. Manufacturers will find vertical restraints profitable if they support special services that draw new customers into the market. Manufacturers will not take into account the welfare losses imposed on consumers who do not value the special services. The argument that vertical restraints must be socially beneficial—because if they were not, manufacturers would not seek to impose them—is incorrect.

Dynamic Welfare Effects

New Entry

As noted previously, restraints that protect dealer margins may make it easier for a new firm, or a firm marketing a new protect, to attract dealers willing to do missionary work. This may be thought of as an extension of the marginal vs. inframarginal customer analysis. If a product is new, *all* consumers are marginal and benefit from the presales service. There is a further presumption that market performance will improve as the number of competitors increases. In such circumstances, restraints are likely to improve welfare.

These arguments, however, do not justify restraints forever. As consumers acquire information about the product, the net effect of restraints might become negative because inframarginal consumers come to place less value on special services.

Mistakes/Inertia

Economists favor the price system as a method of resource allocation, in part, because they believe the price system will induce firms to seek efficient (least-cost) means of production. There is some evidence that vertical restraints interfere with the information-transmitting properties of markets, which are essential to cost minimization.

In 1976, the Federal Trade Commission filed a complaint against Levi Strauss, alleging the use of a minimum resale price maintenance program.[42] As we will see, such a program would be a per se violation of the Sherman Act's prohibition of restraint of trade.

The Federal Trade Commission's action forced Levi Strauss to alter its familiar distribution pattern. Levi jeans had been distributed through two sorts

---

[42]See Overstreet, op. cit.; Steiner, op. cit.; Oster, Sharon, "The FTC v. Levi Strauss: An Analysis of the Economic Issues," in Lafferty, R. N., Lande, R. H., and Kirkwood, J., editors. *Impact Evaluations of F.T.C. Vertical Restraints Cases*, Washington, D.C.: Bureau of Competition, Bureau of Economics, Federal Trade Commission, August 1984, pp. 47–87.

of outlets: traditional outlets, such as department stores, and chains of jeans stores. Resale price maintenance prevented intrabrand competition between the two types of outlets. As a result of the Commission's action, Levi Strauss abandoned its price maintenance program (although it did continue customer restraints designed to keep its jeans out of discount outlets).

When resale price maintenance was abandoned, it was the jeans stores that cut prices. Department stores followed these price cuts. Prices on other brands of jeans soon fell as well.

Retail prices fell, but Levi prospered. Levi's sales and profits in the third quarter of 1977 were roughly 30 per cent greater than those in the same period in 1976. Sales rose 60 per cent from 1976 to 1980, and the price of Levi Strauss stock rose 400 per cent.[43]

The fall in retail prices meant a gain in consumers' surplus, for Levi's jeans alone, estimated at about $75 million per year. The gain in consumers' surplus for all jeans (pressured by competition to follow Levi and lower prices) has been estimated to be about $250 million per year.[44]

Once Levi Strauss abandoned resale price maintenance, chains of jeans stores were free to experiment with lower prices. They did so because they believed that demand was very elastic and that increased sales would more than compensate for a lower price on each sale. If the jeans stores had been wrong, they would have been able to raise the price. This kind of price experimentation generates information about market demand. Resale price maintenance (and, to a lesser extent, other vertical restraints) prevents dealers from developing this kind of information.

Interference with the information-generating functions of the market, in turn, produces inertia in decision making. Some dealers may argue to the producer that price competition will be profitable for all concerned. But they will have no evidence (information will be impacted on the dealer side of the market). Other dealers (in the Levi Strauss case, the traditional outlets) will argue for the status quo. Change will be risky, and often will not be made when it would be with the kind of information that would be supplied in the absence of vertical restraints.

The argument here is not that vertical restraints cause welfare losses because businesspeople misunderstand their own best interests and "persist in foolish and expensive behavior."[45] The argument is that vertical restraints, by inter-

---

[43]Steiner, op. cit., pp. 179–180.

[44]Ibid., p. 180, footnote 68.

[45]Bork, op. cit., p. 391, footnote 41.

fering with price competition, artificially reduce the flow of information to businesspeople and prevent the market from revealing profitable alternatives.[46]

There is evidence that established dealers have sought price maintenance as a way of slowing the development of more efficient forms of distribution. This appears to have been one motive for dealer sponsorship of resale price maintenance in the pharmaceutical drug trade in the United States, England, and France at the time of the rise of mass merchandising drug stores.[47] By preventing mass merchandisers from dealing in major brands, traditional outlets can make it harder for more efficient outlets to gain consumer acceptance (that is, traditional outlets can raise barriers to entry in distribution).

As noted previously, a manufacturer may wish to impose vertical restraints to protect high-class outlets that will certify the quality of the manufacturer's product. But traditional outlets may favor resale price maintenance as a way of denying low-cost outlets the brand names that would certify *outlet quality* in the eyes of the public.[48]

Empirical Evidence

Empirical studies of resale price maintenance fall into two categories: studies that analyze the effect of resale price maintenance on prices and case studies. Overstreet[49] provides a summary of empirical evidence on the effects of resale price maintenance up to 1983.

Price studies typically compare prices before and after the imposition of resale price maintenance, or prices for similar products in areas with and without maintenance. As might be expected, these studies generally show that resale

---

[46]Bork, *The Antitrust Paradox: A Policy At War With Itself.* New York; Basic Books, Inc., 1978, p. 388, has argued that price discrimination should be permitted *because* it allows experimentation with prices:

> Sellers' inability to raise or lower prices selectively, to feel for the balance of market forces, makes prices more rigid and markets less sensitive to changing demands and costs. The ability to make transitory discriminations is thus a valuable element in the continuing process of adjustment, and it is unfortunate that the law should interfere with such discriminations.

The inability of retail sellers—who, after all, are closer to the final consumer—to lower prices selectively under resale price maintenance will also make prices more rigid and less sensitive to changing demands and costs than would otherwise be the case.

[47]Telser, op. cit.; Yamey, op. cit.

[48]Steiner, op. cit., p. 173, footnote 53. See also Blake, Harlan M. and Jones, William K. "Towards a Three-Dimensional Antitrust Policy," *Columbia Law Review* Volume 65, Number 3, March 1965, p. 442, footnote 73.

[49]Op. cit., Section VI.

price maintenance results in an increase in prices (although the estimates are crude and vary greatly in magnitude).

The problem with these studies, as Overstreet notes, is that they do not distinguish between the main alternative explanations of vertical restraints. If resale price maintenance is used to promote market power, it should result in higher prices. If it is used by manufacturers to eliminate free riding at the retail level, it should result in higher prices. The observation that resale price maintenance generally results in higher prices does not help us understand what is going on.

Case studies are, at least potentially, more useful. Overstreet summarizes studies of resale price maintenance[50]

1. used by Magnavox to support marketing efforts by the distributors of its televisions.
2. used by Levi Strauss to attract high-quality dealers, but apparently continued when it had ceased to be socially or privately beneficial.
3. used by Florsheim shoes, most likely to prevent free riding on services provided by high-quality stores.
4. instituted by manufacturers of audio components in the industry's infancy to attract dealer support and prevent free riding on special services provided by dealers, but continued after the industry matured and provision of such services was no longer efficient.
5. used by Adolph Coors to support quality-control efforts by dealers in Coors' beer.
6. used to support a manufacturers' cartel among bakers of bread.

These studies (and other evidence discussed by Overstreet) provide support for all of the theories of vertical restraints previously discussed. Resale price maintenance is apparently sometimes used to support entry by new firms, to combat free riding, and to increase or maintain market power.[51]

Conclusion

By and large, economists agree on the effects of vertical restraints on distribution. Both the bilateral monopoly and market failure analyses recognize that sales efforts by dealers will increase the quantity demanded of a manufacturer's product, holding price constant. Economists differ sharply, however,

---

[50]These capsule summaries cannot, of course, do justice to the studies, which contain a number of qualifications; see Overstreet, op. cit., and the sources cited there for more complete descriptions.

[51]For supporting econometric evidence, see Gilligan, Thomas W. "The Competitive Effects of Resale Price Maintenance," *Rand Journal of Economics* Volume 17, Number 4, Winter 1986, pp. 544–556.

on whether or not this effect is an interference with or a consequence of competition.

At one extreme, distribution is regarded as little different from any other product: it is produced, it is sold, and in the absence of market power, competition can ordinarily be trusted to regulate the allocation of resources to distribution. In this view, the excess product differentiation that results from enhanced dealer margins represents a misallocation of resources.

At the other extreme, the view that competition can be trusted to allocate resources in distribution (and perhaps elsewhere in the economy) is rejected. The generalized free rider problem is seen as explaining vertical and other restraints on competition.[52] Even if market failure prevents optimal resource allocation *within* markets, rivalry will yield optimal resource allocation by producing an optimal set of *restrictions* on competition:[53]

> the market automatically trades off intrabrand and interbrand competition and yields the combination of the two that maximizes social wealth.

In this view, the product differentiation that results from enhanced retail margins improves product market performance by correcting distribution market failure. The fact that a restriction regulates transactions among firms is enough to show that it is efficient. If the restriction were not efficient, it would not appear.

Most economists hold views between these two extremes. It is generally accepted that *some* efficiencies can flow from vertical restraints (especially for new products or new entrants). But unless there is *product* market failure, vertical restraints that correct so-called "failure" in the market for distribution allow the exercise of market power and worsen market performance:[54]

> A survey of economists probably would show that they think fair trade reduces distributional efficiency.

---

[52]Popofsky, M. Laurence and Bomse, Stephen V. "From *Sylvania* to *Monsanto*: No Longer a 'Free Ride'," *Antitrust Bulletin*, Volume 30, Number 1, Spring 1985, Section II, pp. 87–98.

[53]Posner, Richard A. "The Next Step in the Antitrust Treatment of Restricted Distribution: Per Se Legality," *University of Chicago Law Review* Volume 48, Number 1, Winter 1981, p. 19. For similar views, see Demsetz, Harold. "The Trust Behind Antitrust," in Fox, Eleanor M. and Halverson, James T., editors, *Industrial Concentration and the Market System*. Section of Antitrust Law. American Bar Association, 1979, pp. 45–52; Bock, Betty. "An Economist Appraises Vertical Restraints," *Antitrust Bulletin*, Volume 30, Number 1, Spring 1985, p. 135; Phillips, Almarin and Mahoney, Joseph. "Unreasonable Rules and Rules of Reason: Economic Aspects of Vertical Price-Fixing," *Antitrust Bulletin*, Volume 30, Number 1, Spring 1985, p. 107. (It may be unfair to cite Phillips and Mahoney in this context. They qualify their comment by indicating that optimal transaction forms will arise only with free entry.)

[54]Marvel, op. cit., p. 25.

Public Policy Toward Vertical Restraints

Legislative treatment of vertical restraints has varied from one extreme to the other. Judicial treatment of resale price maintenance has been consistently hostile, while judicial treatment of nonprice vertical restraints has varied from hostility to hospitality. In the mid-1980s, the Reagan administration urged courts to permit all vertical restraints, and, in the view of some[55] acted "in a manner which literally encouraged companies to act contrary to clear interpretations of the Sherman Act." Congressional and other support for antitrust restrictions on vertical restraints remains strong.

Laws[56]

If courts find that vertical restraints restrain trade, they will be prohibited under the Sherman Act. In a 1911 decision to be discussed presently, the Supreme Court found resale price maintenance to be a per se violation of the Sherman Act. Later decisions applied the Sherman Act to other vertical restraints. But resale price maintenance was subject to special legal treatment.

Through the 1930s, various states passed *fair trade laws,* which allowed resale price maintenance. These laws were often supported by retailers' trade associations, apparently as a way of impeding the growth of low-cost mass merchandisers. In their strongest form, these fair trade laws included *nonsigner clauses.* Under such a clause, manufacturers who had resale price maintenance agreements with *any* dealers in a state could force *all* dealers to maintain prices (including dealers who were not parties to the resale price maintenance agreement).

By 1937, 42 states had passed fair trade laws. Federal law dominates state law with respect to interstate commerce, which was therefore exempt from state fair trade laws. But in 1937, Congress passed the Miller-Tydings Act, which made resale price maintenance legal under the Sherman Act where it was legal under state law. The Miller-Tydings Act reversed the per se illegality of resale price maintenance.

The effect of the Miller-Tydings Act was considerably weakened in 1951, when the Supreme Court found that it did not legitimize nonsigner clauses. But Congress legislatively reversed the Court's decision the following year with an amendment (the McGuire Act) to the Federal Trade Commission Act.

From 1952 to 1975, resale price maintenance was legal under federal law where it was legal under state law. In 1975, Congress repealed both the Miller-Tydings Act and the McGuire Act. At this point, the original per se prohibition

[55]Brett, Barry J. "*Monsanto*: Great Expectations Unfulfilled," *Antitrust Bulletin* Volume 30, Number 1, Spring 1985, p. 52.

[56]This section is based on Overstreet, op. cit., pp. 3–7.

of resale price maintenance resumed its full force. Legislative treatment of resale price maintenance had come full circle in 64 years.

Case Study: Fair Trade Law

One recent Sunday night, Pawhuska [Oklahoma] pharmacist Alan E. Irby quit fixing a faucet in his house to open his store for an old customer. While he filled the man's prescription, he says, "we talked about his wife Pansy and the Shriners and the Blue and Gold Cub Scout Banquet." He adds, "You know, there's a certain amount of charm about living in a small town."

But the charm fades fast when customers start comparing local prices with the prices at the Wal-Mart down the highway. With more than 1,000 stores, Wal-Mart is able to buy large quantities of items at a discount and then sell them for less. The strategy has made Sam M. Walton, Wal-Mart's founder and chairman, a billionaire, but it hurts retailers like Harry's Super Foods in Ringling [Oklahoma], where a box of 32 large diapers sells for a dollar more than Wal-Mart.

"It makes you look like you're profiteering," says owner Harry Goodman.

At the Pawhuska Wal-Mart, maintenance drugs like insulin, blood-pressure medicine and ulcer remedies are priced as much as $10 below the prices at local stores, and initially Wal-Mart advertised its lower prices heavily. "Some of my better customers were coming in here and waving the ad in my face," says John E. Snider, a druggist in Hominy, south of Pawhuska. "It hurt me professionally. It hurt my image."

Mr. Snider was angry enough to hire a lawyer in Tulsa and round up four other pharmacists to join him in the suit against Wal-Mart. They say the discounter is breaking a little-known state law that requires a merchant to sell products at least $6\frac{3}{4}\%$ above cost, unless the store is having a sale or matching a competitor's price.

After more than two years of legal wrangling, a Tulsa federal judge recently ruled that Oklahoma's law was constitutional and set a trial for late [1987].

Source: Blumenthal, Karen. "Arrival of Discounter Tears the Civic Fabric of Small-Town Life," *Wall Street Journal*, April 14, 1987, p. 1.

Their Interpretation

The legal treatment of nonprice vertical restraints has also varied, as successive Supreme Courts have refined and reversed the interpretation of the antitrust laws as they apply to vertical restraints. We discuss the high points (if that is the appropriate term) of this evolution.

Dr. Miles

Dr. Miles Medical Company v. John D. Park & Sons Company[57] dealt with a minimum resale price maintenance scheme employed by a producer of patent medicines. In this case, the Dr. Miles Medical Company unsuccessfully challenged a wholesale dealer who refused to adhere to the program.

To justify its resale price maintenance program, Dr. Miles argued that[58]

> most of its sales were made through retail druggists and that the demand for its remedies largely depended upon their good will and commendation, and their ability to realize a fair profit; that certain retail establishments, particularly those known as department stores, had inaugurated a "cut-rate" or "cut-price" system which had caused "much confusion, trouble and damage" to [Dr. Mile's] business and "injuriously affected the reputation" and "depleted the sales" of its remedies; that this injury resulted "from the fact that the majority of retail druggists as a rule cannot, or believe they cannot realize sufficient profits" by the sale of medicines "at the cut-prices announced by the cut-rate and department stores," and therefore are "unwilling to, and do not keep" the medicines "in stock" or "if kept in stock, do not urge or favor sales thereof, but endeavor to foist off some similar remedy or substitute, and from the fact that in the public mind an article advertised or announced at 'cut' or 'reduced' price from the established price suffers loss of reputation and becomes of inferior value and demand."

This argument encapsulates several of the market failure arguments for vertical restraints. It is in the producer's interest to guarantee a high margin to his dealers in order to induce them to push his product. It is in the producer's interest to maintain a high retail price in order to protect the quality image of his product. Dealers cannot provide the services and image that the manufacturer wants if they face competition from low-price, low-service outlets.

The majority of the Supreme Court would have none of this. The Court endorsed a lower court condemnation of a similar scheme in another case:[59]

> Thus all room for competition between retailers, who supply the public, is made impossible. If these contracts leave any room at any point of the line for the usual play of competition between the dealers in the product marketed by the complainant, it is not discoverable. Thus a combination between the manufacturer, the wholesalers and the retailers to maintain prices and stifle competition has been brought about.

[57]220 U.S. 373 (1911).

[58]Ibid., pp. 374–375.

[59]Ibid., p. 400, quoting *John D. Park & Sons Company v. Samuel B. Hartman*, 153 Fed. Rep. 24, p. 42.

468

The Court concluded,[60] "That these agreements restrain trade is obvious."

The Supreme Court interpreted an elimination of intrabrand competition through vertical agreement to control price as a restraint of retail trade. This is not, under the rule of reason,[61] enough to violate the Sherman Act: the rule of reason prohibits only unreasonable restraints of trade. The Court then considered and rejected two arguments that the restraint on trade imposed by resale price maintenance was reasonable.

Dr. Miles' first argument was that the restraints were reasonable because the products were produced according to a secret formula. The Court insisted that this did not grant a right to restrain trade among independent distributors:[62]

> this argument rests on monopoly of production and not on the secrecy of the process or the particular fact that may confer that monopoly. It implies that, if for any reason monopoly of production exists, it carries with it the right to control the entire trade of the produced article and to prevent any competition that otherwise might arise between wholesale and retail dealers. . . . But, because there is monopoly of production, it certainly cannot be said that there is no public interest in maintaining freedom of trade with respect to future sales after the article has been placed on the market and the producer parted with his title.

The Court's logic is based on the fundamental premise of the antitrust laws: markets are the preferred mechanism to allocate resources. Competition among distributors will allocate the appropriate amount of resources to dealer services; thus "it certainly cannot be said that there is no public interest in maintaining freedom of trade with respect to future sales after the article has been placed on the market and the producer parted with his title." This emphasis on freedom of trade once goods have passed across markets recurs, as we will see, in later cases involving vertical restraints.

Dr. Miles' second argument for the reasonableness of the restraint was simply that[63] "a manufacturer is entitled to control the prices on all sales of his own products."

The Court made clear that it would judge this objection according to the rule of reason:[64]

> The public have an interest in every person's carrying on his trade freely: so has the individual. All interference with individual liberty of action in trading,

---

[60]Ibid.

[61]Set forth in another 1911 case, *Standard Oil*, 221 U.S. 1 (1911). See Chapter 3.

[62]220 U.S. 373, p. 403.

[63]Ibid., p. 400.

[64]Ibid., pp. 406–407, quoting *Nordenfelt v. Maxim-Nordenfelt & Co.*, 1904, A.C., p. 565.

and all restraints of trade themselves, if there is nothing more, are contrary to public policy, and therefore void. That is the general rule. But there are exceptions: restraints of trade and interference with individual liberty of action may be justified by the special circumstances of a particular case. It is a sufficient justification, and indeed it is the only justification, if the restriction is reasonable—reasonable, that is, in reference to the interests of the parties concerned and reasonable in reference to the interests of the public. . . .

Was the interest of Dr. Miles in maintaining a high retail price reasonable in terms of the public interest? The Court thought not:[65]

The bill asserts the importance of a standard retail price and alleges generally that confusion and damage have resulted from sales at less than the prices fixed. But the advantage of established retail prices primarily concerns the dealers. The enlarged profits which would result from adherence to the established rates would go to them and not to [Dr. Miles]. It is through the inability of the favored dealers to realize these profits, on account of the described competition, that [Dr. Miles] works out its alleged injury. If there be an advantage to a manfuacturer in the maintenance of fixed retail prices, the question remains whether it is one which he is entitled to secure by agreements restricting the freedom of trade on the part of dealers who own what they sell. As to this, [Dr. Miles] can fare no better with its plan of identical contracts than could the dealers themselves if they formed a combination and endeavored to establish the same restrictions, and thus to achieve the same result, by agreement with each other. If the immediate advantage they would thus obtain would not be sufficient to sustain such a direct agreement, the asserted ulterior benefit to [Dr. Miles] cannot be regarded as sufficient to support its system.

In its bill of complaint, Dr. Miles asserted that the motive of its resale price maintenance program was to attract dealer support and maintain an image of quality. This is, however, an indirect benefit: the higher margin goes in the first instance to dealers, who spend some of it in ways desired by Dr. Miles. The Court then observed that such a program would be condemned, under the antitrust laws, if it were the product of a dealer cartel. The Court concluded that if the direct benefit to dealers of fixing prices is not enough to make an agreement reasonable, the indirect benefit to Dr. Miles is not enough to make the fixing of prices reasonable.

Students working in the Chicago tradition have interpreted the Court's decision as reflecting (1) a failure to analyze manufacturers' motives for engaging in resale price maintenance and (2) a simplistic comparison of horizontal and vertical restraints. This reading of the decision seems incorrect.

[65]Ibid., pp. 407–408.

Posner[66] quotes precisely the portion of the Court's decision just given and writes:

> The Court begins by saying that the profits generated by the minimum retail price inure to the dealers rather than to Dr. Miles. This should have made the Court wonder why Dr. Miles was in court defending the agreements.

Bork[67] quotes a portion of the same section and remarks:

> Aside from its equation of horizontal and vertical price fixing, this passage is interesting because it failed to ask whether the manufacturer's interest in eliminating price competition between its distributors could be related to a valid purpose capable of legitimating the contracts.

But it seems clear, from the fact that the Court referred to the bill of complaint (quoted earlier, both here and in the decision), that the Court knew why Dr. Miles was in court defending its program. Dr. Miles asserted that its interest was to attract dealer support and to maintain an image of quality before the public. Contrary to Posner's reading, the Court understood why Dr. Miles supported the resale price maintenance program. Contrary to Bork's reading, the Court considered this argument and concluded that this interest did not make a restraint of trade reasonable.

It may be—and this is the usual Chicago school interpretation of the case—that the Court failed to understand the purposes behind a manufacturer's use of resale price maintenance, and that the Court condemned Dr. Miles by drawing a false analogy between horizontal and vertical price fixing. But it is at least as plausible that the Court considered the versions of the efficiency argument that were put before it and rejected them:[68]

> the decision in *Dr. Miles* may have been based as much on the premise that resale price maintenance unreasonably limits "the freedom of trade on the part of dealers who own what they sell" as on its more frequently noted holding that the effects are the same as those of a horizontal agreement among the same set of dealers.

[66]Posner, Richard A. "Antitrust Policy and the Supreme Court: An Analysis of the Restricted Distribution, Horizontal Merger and Potential Competition Decisions," *Columbia Law Review* Volume 75, Number 2, March 1975, p. 286.

[67]Bork, Robert H. "The Rule of Reason, and the Per Se Concept: Price Fixing and Market Division," *Yale Law Journal* Volume 74, Number 5, April 1965, pp. 810–811.

[68]As suggested by Phillips and Mahoney, op. cit., p. 102. Footnote omitted. The quotation is from the Supreme Court decision, 220 U.S. 373, pp. 407–408.

Colgate

We know from our discussion of public policy toward dominant firms (Chapter 4) that antitrust laws do not prohibit monopoly in and of itself. Firms that acquire market power as a result of the normal process of competitive rivalry are not subject to antitrust attack. On the other hand, firms that acquire or maintain market power through methods that are not normal industrial development violate the antitrust laws. The decision in *United States v. Colgate & Company*[69] is consistent with this reading of the antitrust laws.

Colgate engaged in a program to support resale prices of soap and related products. To achieve this end, Colgate promoted the program with dealers, announced that it would refuse to supply dealers who sold below suggested prices, and in fact cut off dealers who did so. But there was no evidence of a contract or conspiracy between Colgate and its dealers. The Court declined to find a violation of the Sherman Act:[70]

> The purpose of the Sherman Act is to prohibit monopolies, contracts and combinations which probably would unduly interfere with the free exercise of their rights by those engaged, or who wish to engage, in trade and commerce—in a word to preserve the freedom to trade. In the absence of any purpose to create or maintain a monopoly, the act does not restrict the long recognized right of trader or manufacturer engaged in an entirely private business, freely to exercise his own independent discretion as to parties with whom he will deal. And, of course, he may announce in advance the circumstances under which he will refuse to sell.

As in *Dr. Miles*, the Court found the central purpose of the Sherman Act to be the preservation of freedom to trade. Truly independent action is not prohibited by the antitrust laws.

Later decisions have limited the scope of *Colgate*. Communications between a manufacturer and dealers might be enough to establish collective action and to establish a violation of the antitrust laws. So might threats by the manufacturer or any actions that go beyond the announcement of a price policy and the intention to terminate dealers who fail to cooperate. But the recent *Monsanto* decision (as we shall see) has breathed new life into the Colgate doctrine.

White Motor

The case of *The White Motor Company v. United States*[71] dealt with territorial and customer restrictions rather than direct restraints on price.

White Motor manufactured trucks and parts. Some of its products were distributed through independent dealers. These dealers were confined to specific

[69]250 U.S. 300 (1919).

[70]Ibid., p. 307.

[71]372 U.S. 253 (1963).

territories. Further, White Motor reserved certain classes of customers[72] to itself and required dealers to agree not to sell to them.

A lower court found these provisions of White's marketing system to be per se violations of the Sherman Act. White appealed this decision, and the Supreme Court indicated that, at least provisionally, a rule of reason standard should be applied:[73]

> Horizontal territorial limitations . . . are naked restraints of trade with no purpose except stifling of competition. A vertical territorial limitation may or may not have that effect. We do not know enough of the economic or business stuff out of which these arrangements emerge to be certain. They may be too dangerous to sanction or they may be allowable protections against aggressive competitors or the only practicable means a small company has for breaking into or staying in business. . . . We need to know more than we do about the actual impact of these arrangements on competition to decide whether they have such a "pernicious effect on competition and lack . . . any redeeming virtue" . . . and therefore should be classified as per se violations of the Sherman Act.

To gather more information, the Supreme Court returned the case to the lower court for trial. But the case was settled by a consent decree in the lower court, and there were no opportunities for further Supreme Court rulings.

The Court's treatment of *nonprice* restraints in this case has been widely criticized as inconsistent with its treatment of *price* restraints in *Dr. Miles*.[74] Price, territorial, and customer restraints all act to restrict intrabrand competition. If a manufacturer's interest in indirectly promoting the sales of his product will not save *price* restrictions (as in *Dr. Miles*), it is difficult to see why it should save *nonprice* restrictions. If, on the other hand, a rule of reason approach is called for to balance out the affirmative and negative effects of nonprice restraints, it is hard to see why this approach should not be used for price restraints.

Schwinn

Four years after *White Motor*, *United States v. Arnold Schwinn & Co.*[75] gave the Supreme Court another chance to address the issues raised by nonprice vertical restraints.

---

[72]Principally, state and federal governments.

[73]372 U.S. 253, p. 263; citations omitted.

[74]Posner, "Antitrust Policy and the Supreme Court," p. 292; Bork, "The Rule of Reason and the Per Se Concept: Price Fixing and Market Division," *Yale Law Journal*, Volume 74, Number 5, April 1965, pp. 717–779. See also Justice Clark's dissent.

[75]388 U.S. 365 (1966).

Schwinn had been the leading U.S. manufacturer of bicycles in 1951, with a market share of 22.5 per cent. By 1961, its market share had fallen to 12.8 per cent (although its absolute sales had increased; Schwinn had simply failed to keep pace with the market).

Schwinn distributed its bicycles through 22 wholesale distributors. These dealers were confined to exclusive territories and were permitted to sell only to franchised retailers. Certain shipments to retailers were made on a consignment basis: Schwinn retained ownership of the bicycles. Over half of the bicycles were shipped directly to retailers, with wholesalers receiving a commission for handling the paperwork. Retail dealers were subject to customer restrictions: they were not permitted to sell to other dealers (specifically, discount houses), but only to final consumers.

Schwinn contended that the purpose of its program was to make it more competitive,[76] and this was accepted by the trial court. For the Supreme Court, however, it was not enough:

> But this argument, appealing as it is, is not enough to avoid the Sherman Act proscription; because, in a sense, every restrictive practice is designed to augment the profit and competitive position of its participants. . . . The antitrust outcome does not turn merely on the presence of sound business reason or motive. . . . Our inquiry is whether, assuming nonpredatory motives and business purposes and the incentive of profit and volume considerations, the effect upon competition in the marketplace is substantially adverse.

Few economists would argue with this approach as a general standard.[77] But the Court's application of this standard evoked widespread criticism. The Court found the restraints on distribution to be in violation of the Sherman Act when Schwinn sold the bicycles to dealers, but not in violation when the bicycles were shipped to dealers on consignment. This focus on the legal form of the transactions is consistent with the holding in *Dr. Miles* that the public has an interest[78] "in maintaining freedom of trade with respect to future sales after the article has been placed on the market and the producer parted with his title." But it does not reflect any difference in the effect (whatever that effect is) of the restrictions on the marketplace. Price will depend on the quantity

---

[76]For economic analysis that supports this contention, see Williamson, Oliver E. "Assessing Vertical Market Restrictions," pp. 975–985.

[77]See, however, Bork, Robert H. "The Rule of Reason and the Per Se Concept: Price Fixing and the Rule of Reason," *Yale Law Journal* Volume 75, Number 3, January 1966, p. 390: "An argument could be made that where the agreement seems capable both of creating efficiency and leading to a restriction of ouput, the law ought not to interfere since there is no way of knowing whether its interference will have the net effect of aiding or injuring consumers."

[78]220 U.S. 373, p. 403.

supplied and on sales efforts, whether the quantity supplied is sold to dealers or marketed through dealers on a consignment basis.

The general view of this decision was that it could not be reconciled with the standard it allegedly applied. Those who felt that the effects of vertical restraints were anticompetitive urged that almost all such restraints be declared per se violations of the Sherman Act, regardless of their legal form.[79] Those who felt that vertical restraints were efficiency enhancing urged that almost all such restraints be viewed as legal.[80] So it goes.[81]

Sylvania

Ten years after *Schwinn*, the Supreme Court issued a decision in the case of *Continental T.V., Inc., v. GTE Sylvania*.[82] The issues in the two cases were much the same. Sylvania produced and marketed television sets. In the early 1960s, in response to a decline in market share, Sylvania reorganized its distribution network around retailers who were subject to location clauses. The distributors could sell to whomever they wished, but they could sell only from locations authorized by Sylvania.

Continental, based in San Francisco, was one of Sylvania's most successful dealerships. Sylvania appointed a new dealer not too far from one of Continental's outlets, while denying Continental permission to open a new outlet in Sacramento. Continental did so anyway, and was terminated by Sylvania. The result was a private antitrust suit by Continental, alleging that location clauses were a restraint of trade in violation of Section 1 of the Sherman Act.

In District Court, the instructions to the jury followed those of *Schwinn*. The jury was told that if Sylvania had, by contract, combination, or conspiracy, controlled the terms of sale of merchandise after sale to the dealer, it had violated the Sherman Act. Not surprisingly, the jury found Sylvania to be in violation of the antitrust law.

Sylvania (facing damages of 3 times $591,505 = $1,774,515) appealed this decision to the Circuit Court of Appeals. A divided panel reversed the District Court. The majority of the Court of Appeals accepted the view that the restrictions in *Sylvania*—location clauses—were less likely to harm competition than the customer restrictions in *Schwinn*. This being the case, the per se rule of *Schwinn* did not apply. Under a rule of reason, the Court of Appeals exonerated Sylvania.

---

[79]Comanor, op. cit., pp. 1419–1438.

[80]Bork, Robert H. *The Antitrust Paradox: A Policy At War With Itself.* New York: Basic Books, 1978.

[81]Apologies to Kurt Vonnegut and Linda Ellerbee.

[82]433 U.S. 36 (1977).

But two members of the appeals panel dissented. They argued that the restrictions in *Schwinn* and *Sylvania* could not be distinguished and that the *Schwinn* rule should be applied.

Thus the question reached the Supreme Court. Are customer restrictions and territory restrictions equivalent as far as the antitrust laws are concerned? If not, are location clauses reasonable because they enhance efficiency? If so, are location clauses reasonable because they enhance efficiency? Stay tuned—news at 11!

The majority opinion in *Sylvania* is 21.5 pages long; 16 of those pages are devoted to a discussion of *Schwinn*. In those 16 pages, the majority

1. indicated that it could find no distinction between the restrictions in *Schwinn* and *Sylvania*.
2. indicated that *Schwinn*[83] "was an abrupt and largely unexplained departure from *White Motor Co. . . .*".
3. overruled the per se rule of *Schwinn*.
4. affirmed the ruling of the Circuit Court of Appeals—Sylvania's location clauses did not violate the antitrust laws.

The interesting part of the story concerns item 3, which was preceded by a detailed discussion of the market impact of nonprice vertical restraints. The impact of nonprice vertical restraints on market performance was characterized as a tradeoff between intrabrand and interbrand competition. In its analysis of possible procompetitive effects of vertical restraints on interbrand competition, the Court referred to efficiencies that depend on market failure for their validity:[84]

> new manufacturers . . . can use the restrictions in order to induce competent and aggressive retailers to make the kind of investment of capital and labor that is often required in the distribution of products unknown to the consumer. Established manufacturers can use them to induce retailers to engage in promotional activities or to provide service and repair facilities. . . . Because of market imperfections such as the so-called "free rider" effect, these services might not be provided by retailers in a purely competitive situation. . . .

Since the per se rule applies to practices that have a "pernicious effect on competition and lack . . . any redeeming virtues," [85] a rule of reason treatment of nonprice vertical restraints was called for.

---

[83]Ibid., p. 47.

[84]Ibid., p. 55.

[85]*Northern Pacific Railroad Co. v. United States*, 356 U.S. 1, p. 5; see Chapter 5.

In a footnote, the majority of the Court explained its view that price and nonprice vertical restraints did not merit identical treatment:[86]

1. [U]nlike nonprice restrictions, "[r]esale price maintenance is not only designed to, but almost invariably does in fact, reduce price competition not only *among* sellers of the affected product, but quite as much *between* that product and competing brands."[87]
2. "[I]ndustry-wide resale price maintenance might facilitate cartelizing".[88]
3. Congress recently has expressed its approval of a per se analysis of vertical price restrictions by repealing those provisions of the Miller-Tydings and McGuire Acts allowing fair-trade pricing at the options of the individual states. . . . No similar expression of congressional intent exists for nonprice restrictions.

In a concurring opinion, Justice White indicated that he was willing to exonerate Sylvania but found it unnecessary to overrule *Schwinn*. The customer restrictions employed by Schwinn, in Justice White's view, had more serious anticompetitive effects than the territory restraints of Sylvania. Under customer restraints, dealers were forbidden to sell to discounters, a direct restraint on price competition. Under territory restraints, dealers could sell to whomever they wished, as long as they did it from the approved location.[89]

Two of Justice White's comments on the majority opinion anticipated major themes of the debate that has followed *Sylvania*. First, Justice White argues that the majority had misunderstood the *Schwinn* rationale for distinguishing between sale and agency transactions, which was [90] "the notion in many of our cases involving vertical restraints that independent businessmen should have the freedom to dispose of the goods they own as they see fit." *Schwinn*, he argued, was planted firmly in the antitrust tradition:[91]

> But while according some weight to the businessman's interest in controlling the terms on which he trades in his own goods may be anathema to those who view the Sherman Act as directed solely toward economic efficiency, this principle is without question more deeply embedded in our cases than the

[86]433 U.S. 36, p. 51, footnote 18.

[87]Quoting Justice Brennan in *White Motor,* 372 U.S., p. 268.

[88]Quoting (perhaps disingenuously) Posner, "Antitrust Policy and the Supreme Court," p. 294.

[89]Justice White also outlined a market structure analysis that suggested that Sylvania was in less of a position than Schwinn to injure market performance. 433 U.S. 36, pp. 63–64.

[90]Ibid., pp. 66–67.

[91]Ibid; footnotes and citations omitted.

notions of "free rider" effects and distributional efficiencies borrowed by the majority from the "new economics of vertical relationships." . . . Perhaps the Court is right in partially abandoning this principle and in judging . . . nonprice vertical restraints solely by their "relevant economic impact"; but the precedents which reflect this principle should not be so lightly rejected by the Court. The rationale of *Schwinn* is no doubt difficult to discern from the opinion, and it may be wrong; it is not, however, the aberration the majority makes it out to be here.

Justice White's comment reflects what has been a fundamental premise of antitrust policy: the market mechanism is an efficient vehicle for resource allocation. Competition by independent businesspeople, each pursing his or her own self-interest, will over the long run maximize social welfare. Contractual restraints that limit the ability of independent businesspeople to make their own decisions about the terms on which they will sell their products worsen market performance.

The premise implicit in the free rider argument is quite different. In this view, competitive product markets cannot be trusted to allocate resources effectively. But competition one stage before the product market—in the market for interfirm relationships—will produce an efficient set of contractual restraints on product market competition. In the absence of barriers to entry, if restraints on product market competition were not efficient, they would not survive. And in the view of the Chicago school, there are no persistent private barriers to entry:[92] "The only important source of long-lasting monopoly is the government."

In another prescient comment, Justice White pointed out that the distinction that the majority sought to establish between price and nonprice restrictions was difficult to make. He suggested that [93] "The effect, if not the intention, of the Court's opinion is necessarily to call into question the firmly established *per se* rule against price restraints." This proved to be correct.

Monsanto[94]

Seven years after *Sylvania*, the issue of price vs. nonprice vertical restraints appeared to be on its way to the Supreme Court. This turned out not to be the case, but important principles from *Colgate* were revived.

From 1957 to 1968, the Spray-Rite Service Corporation was a wholesale distributor of agricultural herbicides for the Monsanto Company. Monsanto was a large but by no means dominant firm in this market. Monsanto's market

[92]Demsetz, op. cit., p. 51.

[93]433 U.S. 36, p. 70.

[94]For an extended mulling over of the implications of *Monsanto*, see the symposium in the Spring 1985 issue of the *Antitrust Bulletin*.

share in corn herbicides was 15 per cent in 1968; its market share in soybean herbicides was 3 percent.

In 1967, Monsanto reorganized its distribution system. It appointed distributors for 1-year terms and indicated that it would base renewal decisions on various criteria related to the quality and intensity of their sales efforts, especially in the dealer's geographic "area of primary responsibility." Monsanto suggested resale prices to distributors.

Spray-Rite was Monsanto's 10th largest dealer (out of roughly 100) in 1968. It was a known price cutter, "buying in large quantities and selling at a low margin."[95] In 1968, Monsanto declined to renew Spray Rite's distributorship.

Monsanto's distribution policies were effective: in 1972, it had a 28 percent share of the corn herbicide market and a 19 per cent share of the soybean herbicide market. Spray-Rite, unable to obtain Monsanto products, [96] went out of business in 1972.

Spray-Rite sued Monsanto, alleging a conspiracy between Monsanto and its distributors in restraint of trade. In the District Court, the jury was instructed that nonprice restraints were illegal per se if they were part of a scheme to fix prices. The jury found for Spray-Rite, awarding $3.5 million in damages (trebled to $10.5 million). The Court of Appeals affirmed this decision, and Monsanto appealed to the Supreme Court.

The main issue raised by Monsanto before the Supreme Court concerned the nature of evidence needed to prove a conspiracy. The Court of Appeals had relied on evidence showing complaints by other dealers to Monsanto about Spray-Rite's price cutting. This was enough, the Court of Appeals held, to establish a conspiracy between Monsanto and the complaining dealers.

The Supreme Court did not agree. Harking back to *Colgate*, the court emphasized[97] "the basic distinction between concerted and independent action . . .". The Court accepted Monsanto's argument that complaints by some dealers about others would naturally arise in the course of enforcing nonprice restraints, and indicated that stronger proof of joint action was required:[98]

> something more than evidence of complaints is needed. There must be evidence that tends to exclude the possibility that the manufacturer and nonterminated distributors were acting independently. . . . the antitrust plaintiff should present direct or circumstantial evidence that reasonably tends to prove that the manufacturer and others "had a conscious commitment to a common scheme designed to achieve an unlawful objective."

[95]*Monsanto Co. v. Spray-Rite Service Corp.*, 104 S.Ct. 1464 (1984), p. 1467.

[96]Spray-Rite distributed other brands of herbicides. In 1968, 16 per cent of its sales were of Monsanto products.

[97]104 S.Ct. 1464, p. 1469.

[98]Ibid., p. 1471; citations omitted.

Round 1 for Monsanto: evidence of complaints from dealers is not enough to prove a conspiracy. Was there additional evidence on the record?

Sadly for Monsanto, there was. After Spray-Rite had been terminated, Monsanto pressured other price-cutting dealers to maintain resale prices, and evidence indicated that they did so. Statements in a distributor's newsletter to his dealers suggested a common scheme to get the "market place in order." On this record, the Supreme Court held that there was a basis for the jury's decision even under the more stringent standard for proof of conspiracy. Round 2 (and the match, as far as Monsanto was concerned) to Spray-Rite.

But the most interesting parts of the decision may be the ones that are not there. The Department of Justice filed an *amicus curiae* brief, urging the Supreme Court to reconsider the *Dr. Miles* rule making retail price maintenance unlawful per se. The Justice Department would have done more than file a brief, but Congress passed a rider to the appropriation bill for the Department of Justice, forbidding it to present oral arguments for the reversal of *Dr. Miles*.

The Department's brief offered the Court an opportunity to face directly the issue raised in Justice White's *Sylvania* opinion and to resolve perceived inconsistencies between price and nonprice vertical restraints. The Court declined the opportunity. It noted the government's brief in a footnote,[99] observed that it was not necessary to resolve the issue in order to decide the case, and moved on. Round 3 for *Dr. Miles*.

The State of the Law

Precedent

The application of the Sherman Act to vertical restraints has undergone an evolution not unlike the treatment of conscious parallelism. It is illegal per se to conspire to maintain resale prices. No demonstration of an unreasonable effect is required. But a manufacturer acting independently may announce a policy of retail price maintenance and terminate dealers who do not follow it. Normal business practices involved in such a policy will not be taken to show conspiracy.

Nonprice vertical restraints are judged under a rule of reason. They are judged according to their effect on the market, which (at least) will require a weighing of effects on intrabrand and interbrand competition.

Vertical Restraint Guidelines

Department of Justice

In January 1985, the Department of Justice issued Vertical Restraint Guidelines "to explain the enforcement policy of the U.S. Department of Justice

[99]Ibid., pp. 1469–1470, footnote 7.

480

. . . concerning nonprice vertical restraints.''[100] A major goal was to ''reduce the uncertainty associated with enforcement of the antitrust laws in this area.''[101] As we shall see, there remains little doubt about the Justice Department's enforcement policy in this area.

The Justice Department adopts an efficiency view of vertical restraints:[102]

> The competitive consequences of restraints that affect interbrand competition are different from those that only affect intrabrand competition. Restraints on interbrand competition may have a significant negative impact on economic welfare. By contrast, vertical restraints that only affect intrabrand competition generally represent little anticompetitive threat and involve some form of economic integration between different levels of production or distribution that tend to create efficiencies.

In the view of the Justice Department, the efficiencies of vertical restraints are so great that it is appropriate to treat as vertical restraints that have every appearance of being horizontal:[103]

> If a single manufacturer complies with a request of its dealers, the resulting restraint would be properly characterized as a vertical restraint imposed by the manufacturer.

Indeed,[104]

> the fact that a supplier also engages in distribution does not make a restraint ''horizontal.''

The first position, read literally, indicates that a dealer's cartel restricting competition in the distribution of the differentiated product of a major brand through the manufacturer will be viewed as not imposing a horizontal restraint on competition. The second indicates that a distributor may restrain distribution of its product if it is also a manufacturer.

---

[100]U.S. Department of Justice, Antitrust Division, *Vertical Restraints Guidelines*, January 23, 1985, p. 1. Henceforth cited as Guidelines.

[101]Ibid.

[102]Ibid., pp. 6–7.

[103]Ibid., pp. 7–8.

[104]Ibid., pp. 9–10.

Although the Guidelines deal with nonprice restraints, there are circumstances in which their reach is somewhat broader:[105]

> if a supplier adopts a bona fide distribution program embodying both nonprice and price restrictions, the Department will analyze the entire program under the rule of reason if the nonprice restraints are plausibly designed to create efficiencies and if the price restraint is merely ancillary to the nonprice restraints.

This rule of reason approach is adopted despite the fact that the Supreme Court in *Monsanto* explicitly distinguished price from nonprice vertical restraints and declined to reverse the *per se* rule against vertical price-fixing.[106]

The Justice Department Guidelines list the efficiencies which may flow from vertical restraints, including the following:[107]

1. Taking advantage of economies of scale in distribution by limiting the number of retail outlets.
2. Facilitating the entry of a new producer.
3. Ensuring provision of presale services.
4. Through exclusive dealerships, preventing dealers from using the investment of one supplier in advertising to sell goods of other suppliers.
5. Reducing transaction costs by allocating risk between producer and distributor and perhaps in other ways.

Although the Justice Department Guidelines indicate that[108] "vertical restraints generally have a procompetitive or competitively neutral effect," they also list possible anticompetitive effects of vertical restraints. These include collusion among dealers, collusion among suppliers, and bilateral collusion.[109] These possibilities are said to be unlikely unless concentration is high, firms in the other market affected by the restraint account for a large portion of the market, and entry into the market that is the source of the restraint is difficult.[110]

The possibility of anticompetitive exclusion is also mentioned, but it is subject to similar limitations of concentration and entry.[111] The Guidelines do not acknowledge the possibility that a single firm might use vertical restraints

[105]Ibid., p. 11

[106]104 S.Ct. 1494, p. 1469.

[107]Guidelines, pp. 14–15.

[108]Ibid., p. 16.

[109]Ibid.

[110]Ibid., p. 18.

[111]Ibid., pp. 18–21.

to cultivate product differentiation in a way that would restrict competition and worsen market performance.

The Guidelines describe a two-stage process for evaluating vertical restraints. First, the Department of Justice will apply a simple test of market structure to eliminate cases where anticompetitive effects are not possible. Vertical restraints used by firms with less than 10 per cent of the relevant market[112] will not be challenged; nor will vertical restraints that cover less than 60 per cent of the firms in the relevant vertical markets.[113]

In the event that a vertical restraint fails this first-stage test, the Department will conduct a rule of reason analysis to evaluate the effect of the restraint on competition. Particular attention will be given to entry conditions (as determined by the necessity to invest in sunk assets, good will, or human capital), but other factors will also be considered. These might include, among other things:

1. the actual effect of the practice, if there is any information available.
2. whether or not the market is susceptible to collusion.
3. whether and to what extent the restraint is exclusionary.
4. whether the restraints are used by small firms or new entrants.
5. whether or not the firms involved can identify procompetitive efficiencies that stem from the restraint.

National Association of Attorneys General

The proof of the pudding is in the eating, and the real content of the Department of Justice's Vertical Restraint Guidelines will be revealed by the enforcement pattern that emerges under them. During the first five years of the Reagan administration, the Department filed no vertical restraint cases. By the second term of the Reagan administration, the Federal Trade Commission had similarly gone out of the vertical restraints business.

In December 1985, the National Association of Attorneys General (NAAG) issued its own Vertical Restraints Guidelines. In doing so, the NAAG criticized the Department of Justice for its failure to enforce the law:[114]

> The Justice Department has not filed an enforcement action against vertical restraints in five years, and their recently adopted enforcement policy is in fact a policy of no enforcement. The Department has ignored clear and unequivocal legal precedents established by the U.S. Supreme Court in permitting illegal practices to go unpunished.

[112]Market definition procedures follow the 1982 and 1984 Merger Guidelines; see Chapter 10.

[113]Guidelines, pp. 23–29. The Guidelines here embody a measure of concentration that is similar to the Herfindahl index.

[114]Attorney General Robert Abrams of New York, as quoted in an NAAG press release dated December 6, 1985, p. 2.

There are many differences between the Department of Justice's Guidelines and those of the NAAG.

The NAAG Guidelines would treat resale price maintenance as illegal per se, even if used in conjunction with nonprice restraints. They also treat horizontal conspiracy among the dealers of a single brand as illegal per se; they would not use the argument that such conspiracies have the same effect as vertical agreements to place them under a rule of reason. The NAAG Guidelines, following *Sylvania*, suggest a rule of reason for nonprice restraints that balances the effects of the restraint on intrabrand and interbrand competition; the rule of reason test proposed in the Department of Justice Guidelines do not weigh the adverse effect of the restraint on intrabrand competition.

The NAAG Guidelines were presented

> as a statement of the general enforcement policy of the state attorneys general to be supplemented in each state according to variations in state law, federal circuit law and individual prosecutorial prerogatives.

As such, the effect of these guidelines will be determined by their implementation on a state-by-state basis. They do make it clear that the efficiency interpretation of vertical restraints is no more universally accepted among law enforcement officials than it is among economists.

Conclusion

The positions in the debate over public policy toward vertical restraints are clearly drawn. At one extreme, the Chicago approach (which under the Reagan administration is accepted by the Justice Department and the Federal Trade Commission) is that vertical restraints should be legal per se.[115]

Recognizing that this position is unlikely to be adopted by courts in the immediate future, these scholars advocate (as a fallback position) the use of structural tests that would eliminate most vertical restraint cases and the treatment of surviving cases under a rule of reason.

On paper, this position is not far from that of some scholars who use the structure-conduct-performance approach. A common proposal[116] would require the plaintiff in a vertical restraints case to establish some degree of market power on the part of firms imposing the restraints. After this, a rule of reason would apply, perhaps with the burden of proof shifting to defendants to show

---

[115]Bork, Robert H. "The Rule of Reason and the Per Se Concept," *Yale Law Journal* Volume 75, Number 3, January 1966, p. 475; Posner, Richard A. "The Next Step in the Antitrust Treatment of Restricted Distribution: Per Se Legality," *University of Chicago Law Review* Volume 48, Number 1, Winter 1981, pp. 6–26.

[116]Posner, "Next Step," p. 25; Steiner, op. cit., p. 146.

that the restraints, on balance, improve performance. This agreement is more apparent than real, however. In contrast to the structuralist approach, the Chicago school position does not accept the possibility that product differentiation is a source of market power.

Still others in the structuralist tradition would have courts continue to treat some types of vertical restraints as illegal per se. These restraints (for example, minimum price restrictions and restraints that contribute to the maintenance of minimum prices, such as airtight territorial and customer restrictions and supplier restraints imposed as a result of a dealer cartel), on the structuralist analysis, are said to be almost always restrictive of product market competition.[117] The Chicago school does not accept these propositions: since, in their view of the world, entry is almost always free and easy (unless blocked by the government), the market in interfirm relationships will not allow socially harmful restraints to survive.

Paper Topics

17-1 Analyze the experience of Kaiser Enterprises in the American automobile industry.

17-2 Analyze *United States v. General Electric Co.*, 272 U.S. 476 (1926).

17-3 Review Victor P. Goldberg. "Resale Price Maintenance and the FTC: The Magnavox Investigation," *William and Mary Law Review* Volume 23, Spring 1982, pp. 439–500. Discuss the impact of resale price maintenance on market performance in this case.

17-4 Read C. W. Guillebaud. "The Marshall MacMillan Correspondence Over the Net Book System," *Economic Journal*, Volume 75, Number 299, September 1965, pp. 518–538. Report on the use of resale price maintenance in book publishing in the United Kingdom.

17-5 Analyze the following, with respect to the "*Colgate* doctrine": *United States v. A. Schrader's Son, Inc.*, 252 U.S. 85 (1919); *Frey & Son, Inc., v. Cudahy Packing Co.*, 256 U.S. 85 (1919); *United States v. Parke, Davis & Co.*, 362 U.S. 29 (1960); and *Russell Stover Candies, Inc., v. Federal Trade Commission,* 718 F.2d 256 (8th Cir. 1983).

17-6 Analyze *Albrecht v. Herald Co.* Why might a manufacturer wish to impose *maximum* resale prices? What are the effects of such restraints on market performance?

[117]Pitofsky, op. cit., p. 28.

18

Public Policy Toward Private Enterprise

It displays many of the signs of a secular religion, and one of these is the emergence of a band of celebrants who fiercely resist any intellectual challenge to their mystery.

Robert H. Bork[1]

Antitrust as It Has Been

Description

Public vs. Private Litigation

Table 18-1 reveals a fairly steady post–World War II growth in the number of government antitrust cases.[2] Once a government case establishes an antitrust violation, private plaintiffs can come forward to claim treble damages. It should therefore be expected that the number of private antitrust cases will exceed the number of public cases. Table 18-1 reveals that this is indeed the case. The ratio of private to public cases increases sharply after 1966.

This increase reflects, in part, learning by doing. The late 1950s saw government antitrust action against conspiracy in the electrical equipment industries (Chapter 6). These cases were followed by a 1-year peak in private antitrust activity in 1962.[3] The publicity generated by these events undoubtedly increased businessmen's awareness of their rights under the antitrust laws.

The early years of the Reagan administration have seen a relative decline in

---

[1]"Contrasts in Antitrust Theory: I," *Columbia Law Review* Volume 65, Number 3, March 1965, p. 401.

[2]The jump in government cases for the period 1961–1965 appears to reflect a large number of Federal Trade Commission complaints under the Robinson-Patman Act. See Posner, Richard A. "A Statistical Study of Antitrust Enforcement," *Journal of Law and Economics* Volume 13, Number 2, October 1970, p. 370, footnote 9.

[3]The number of private antitrust cases was 378 in 1961, 2,005 in 1962, and 380 in 1963. Source: Salop, Steven C. and White, Lawrence J. "Economic Analysis of Private Antitrust Litigation," *Georgetown Law Journal* Volume 74, Number 4, April 1986, pp. 1001–1064.

Table 18-1 Antitrust Cases Filed, 1941–1984

Fiscal Year	U.S. Government Cases	Private Cases	Private / Govt.
1941–1945	181	297	1.64
1946–1950	256	529	2.07
1951–1955	197	1,045	5.30
1956–1960	317	1,163	3.67
1961–1965	663	3,220	4.86
1966–1970	275	3,591	13.06
1971–1975	392	6,501	16.58
1976–1980	376	7,241	19.26
1981–1984	449	4,621	10.29

Column four shows the ratio of private to government cases.

Source: Salop, Steven C. and White, Lawrence J. "Economic Analysis of Private Antitrust Litigation," *Georgetown Law Journal* Volume 74, Number 4, April 1986, Table 1 p. 1002.

the number of private antitrust cases, although the ratio of private to public cases is still twice as large as it was in the 1950s. It is too soon to say if this represents either a permanent reduction in the level of private antitrust activity or a trend toward even lower levels of private enforcement. The reduction in private cases is undoubtedly related to evolving legal standards that have made it more difficult for private plaintiffs to prevail. The use of Areeda-Turner–like rules in predatory pricing cases is an example (Chapter 16). Rule of reason treatment for nonprice vertical restraints is another example (Chapter 17). Private plaintiffs are now less likely to succeed than they were in (say) the 1970s, and the number of private cases has fallen since that period.[4]

Administration

The Georgetown Project on Private Antitrust Litigation has collected information on some 2,350 antitrust cases filed between 1973 and 1983. For these cases, the average single-district private antitrust suit filed before 1980 lasted a little less than 2.5 years. Half of these cases lasted for 1.5 years or less. The average therefore includes a "tail" of very long cases, which pulls the average above the median. This is confirmed by considering multidistrict cases, which averaged 5.7 years in length.[5]

Private cases appear not to differ greatly from government cases in terms of length. Posner[6] reports the average length of Department of Justice antitrust

[4]Ibid., p. 1043.

[5]Ibid, p. 1009.

[6]Posner, op. cit., p. 377, Table 7.

cases from 1890 to 1964 as varying from 29 to 45 months, without any obvious trend; cases that reached the Supreme Court averaged from 29 to 80 months. Federal Trade Commission restraint-of-trade cases follow a similar pattern, although they tend to be longer than Department of Justice cases.[7]

In comparison, the median length of 769 civil cases which ended in five district courts in 1978 was about 10 months.[8] Antitrust cases tend to be longer than other federal court cases.

Outcomes

The federal government has an excellent track record as far as antitrust cases are concerned. Over the period 1890–1967, the Department of Justice's won-loss record never fell below 64 per cent, staying above 78 per cent after 1940.[9] In the postwar period, Federal Trade Commission decisions, if appealed to the courts, have usually been won by the Commission. But the Commission itself is cautious, dismissing 20 to 30 per cent of the complaints brought by its staff.

Of 1,959 single-district cases covered by the Georgetown project, results were known for 1,628. The remaining cases were either still awaiting trial, being appealed, transferred to state court, or combined with some other case.[10]

Of these 1,628 cases, 88 per cent were settled by the parties before the court reached a judgment. This compares with a settlement rate of 72 per cent in federal court civil cases generally.[11] Of the cases that were not settled (192 cases), at least some plaintiffs prevailed in 55 cases—28.6 per cent. Plaintiffs' success rate in federal cases generally is estimated at more than 50 per cent.[12]

Penalties

The Department of Justice relies on injunctive relief in civil cases. In some cases, such injunctions simply direct that the offending behavior (such as price fixing) cease. In other cases, relief involves divestiture or some other structural

[7]Ibid., p. 379, Table 9.

[8]Grossman, Joel B. et al., "Measuring the Pace of Civil Litigation in Federal and State Trial Courts," *Judicature,* Volume 65, August 1981, pp. 86–113, as reported by Salop and White, op. cit., p. 1009.

[9]Based on 5-year averages; Posner, op. cit., p. 381, Table 11.

[10]Outcomes were simply unknown for 68 cases.

[11]For a sample of 770 civil cases terminating in 1978 in five district courts; Grossman, Joel B. et al., op. cit., p. 106 as reported by Salop and White, op. cit., p. 1011.

[12]For 819 cases decided in U.S. District Court in Cook Country, Illinois, 1959–1979; Preist, George L. and Klein, Benjamin, "The Selection of Disputes for Litigation," *Journal of Legal Studies* Volume 13, January 1984, pp. 1–55, as reported in Salop and White, op. cit., p. 1011.

change intended to eliminate the offense. In yet other cases, the court will maintain a regulatory role vis-à-vis the convicted firm to ensure good behavior. This may involve courts in industry regulation for a decade or more.[13]

Criminal offenses under the antitrust laws may bring with them fines and jail terms. Maximum fines were raised in 1974 from $50,000 to $100,000 for individuals and $1,000,000 for corporations. Maximum imprisonment was raised in 1974 from 1 to 3 years. Fines administered have been negligible, especially for corporations, and jail terms have been a rarity.[14]

The average award to plaintiffs in 36 single-district cases covered the Georgetown Project was $456,000; the median award was $194,000. The average does not include one extremely large award ($276 million in *Litton v. A.T.&T*). For 12 multidistrict private antitrust cases, awards to plaintiffs ranged from $250,000 to $218 million, averaging $44.5 million. The average award in these cases is much larger than the average award for single-district cases, but the multidistrict cases combined 337 underlying cases.[15]

Legal costs appear to average between 10 and 20 per cent of plaintiffs' monetary awards. Salop and White estimate the legal fees per case, for plaintiffs and defendants, at $200,000 to $250,000 1984 dollars. The typical length and cost of cases appeared to be roughly constant over the period 1973–1982. An implied estimate of the cost of private antitrust litigation is $250 million per year.[16]

Effects of Antitrust

On Market Structure

There is evidence, mostly indirect, that the antitrust laws, especially the Celler-Kefauver Act of 1950, have held down industrial concentration. The effect of the Celler-Kefauver Act has been to reduce sharply the importance of horizontal mergers in overall mergers, as suggested by Table 18-2.[17]

---

[13]Posner, op. cit., pp. 385–389.

[14]Ibid., pp. 391–393, Tables 19, 20, 21.

[15]In 1984 dollars. Data from the Georgetown Project on Private Antitrust Litigation, as described by Salop and White, op. cit., p. 1012.

[16]Ibid., pp. 1016. Reich, Robert B., "The Antitrust Industry," *Georgetown Law Journal* Volume 66, Number 5, June 1980, pp. 1068–1069, estimates total expenditures related to antitrust at $2.5 billion in 1979: "This estimate includes $2.1 billion for private attorneys and their overhead, $81 million for government attorneys and their overhead, $17 million for judges and their overhead, $30 million for economists and other consultants, and $290 million for reams of paper to be duplicated, endless telephone calls, and ubiquitous travel and hotel accommodations" (footnotes omitted). Reich's estimate, which includes private defense against government actions, is for antitrust in a much broader sense than the estimate of Salop and White.

[17]See also Chapter 9, footnote 48, and the accompanying text.

Table 18-2 Types of Large Mergers, U.S. Manufacturing and Mining

Type	1948–1953		1954–1959		1960–1964	
	Number	**%**	**Number**	**%**	**Number**	**%**
Horizontal	18	31.0	78	24.8	42	12.0
Vertical	6	10.3	43	13.7	59	17.0
Conglomerate	34	58.7	193	61.5	247	71.0

Source: Stigler, George J. "The Economic Effects of the Antitrust Laws", *Journal of Law and Economics* Volume 9, October 1966, p. 232, Table 2.

It can be argued[18] that in the absence of the antitrust laws, the typical industrial structure in U.S. manufacturing would involve a dominant firm with a competitive fringe rather than oligopoly. I suspect that most economists would accept this judgment. Whether the predominance of oligopoly will survive the merger wave of the 1980s remains to be seen.

On Market Performance

The impact of antitrust laws on market performance is expected to occur through deterrence. Firms act to maximize their profit, and this will occasionally lead them to pursue strategies that violate the antitrust laws. The more rigorously the antitrust laws are enforced, the more likely is it that illegal behavior will be detected, with the resulting expense of defending a long trial and eventual fines. Rigorous enforcement of the antitrust laws will make it unprofitable to engage in strategies that violate the antitrust laws, because it will make the expected profit of such strategies less than that of available alternatives.

This deterrent effect will be strongest for firms actually affected by antitrust actions. It should also be strong for other firms in industries where some firms have been targets of enforcement activity. The knowlege that antitrust authorities pay attention to a market increases the likelihood that illegal activity will come to light.

To test this hypothesis, Feinberg estimates a structural market power equation, similar to those presented in Chapter 7, that tests the average impact of antitrust enforcement on price-cost margins for 288 firms in 89 industries. His results are as follows:[19]

[18]Dewey, Donald J. "The New Learning: One Man's View," in Goldschmid, Harvey J., Mann, H. Michael, and Weston, J. Fred, editors, *Industrial Concentration: The New Learning.* Boston: Little, Brown and Company, p. 3.

[19]Feinberg, Robert M. "Antitrust Activity and Subsequent Price Behavior," *Review of Economics and Statistics* Volume 62, Number 4, November 1980, pp. 609–612. For compactness, certain coefficients are suppressed from the results reported. Superscript b indicates statistical significance at the 5 per cent level (the estimated coefficient would occur by chance once in 20 times); superscript c indicates statistical significance at the 10 per cent level (the estimated coefficient would occur by chance once in 10 times).

$$PCM = 4.57 - 2.38^b \begin{Bmatrix} 1 \text{ if this firm} \\ \text{had antitrust} \\ \text{charge, } 0 \\ \text{otherwise.} \end{Bmatrix} - 0.74 \begin{Bmatrix} 1 \text{ if other firms} \\ \text{in the industry had an} \\ \text{antitrust charge and} \\ \text{this firm did not;} \\ 0 \text{ otherwise.} \end{Bmatrix}$$

$$+ 0.038^c \text{ CR4} + 0.034^b \text{ (CR4)} \begin{Bmatrix} 1 \text{ if the industry has} \\ \text{very high barriers to} \\ \text{entry; } 0 \text{ otherwise.} \end{Bmatrix}$$

(18.1)

PCM is a price-cost margin that has subtracted from it an estimate of the normal rate of return on capital; the equation is thus an estimate of the determinants of an empirical version of the Lerner index of market power (Chapter 2). *PCM* is measured for June–September 1971, while the antitrust prosecution variables refer to the period 1955–1970. The equation therefore estimates the effects of past antitrust enforcement on the exercise of market power.

Feinberg finds a statistically significant negative effect—a reduction of 2.38 percentage points—of antitrust enforcement on the market power of the firm charged. There is a negative effect of antitrust enforcement against other firms—a reduction of 0.74 percentage points—but this effect is not statistically significant. As we would expect from the empirical studies reported in Chapter 7, market concentration and high entry barriers tend to increase the exercise of market power. Similar results are reported by Block, Nold, and Sidak[20] in a study of the white bread market in 20 cities over the period 1964–1976.[21] They find the citywide average change in the price markup over the average cost of white bread to be lower, the greater the increases in the budget of the Antitrust Division of the Justice Department, to be lower if the Antitrust Division had pursued antitrust actions against white bread bakers in neighboring cities, and to be lower if the Antitrust Division had pursued an antitrust action in the home city. These results are consistent with those of Feinberg: antitrust actions appear to temper the exercise of market power. These results also suggest a spillover effect of antitrust enforcement across geographic markets.[22]

---

[20]Block, Michael Kent, Nold, Frederick Carl, and Sidak, Joseph Gregory. "The Deterrent Effect of Antitrust Enforcement," *Journal of Political Economy,* Volume 89, Number 3, June 1981, pp. 429–445.

[21]Not all cities were included for all years; see Block et al., op. cit., p. 434, footnote 13.

[22]Additional evidence for such a spillover effect is reported by Block, Michael K. and Feinstein, Jonathan S., "The Spillover Effect of Antitrust Enforcement," *Review of Economics and Statistics* Volume 68, Number 1, February 1986, pp. 122–131, in a study of antitrust action against bid rigging in the highway construction industry.

Antitrust as It Should Be: Administration

In antitrust, as elsewhere, form and substance overlap. In this section, we treat the enforcement and administration of the antitrust laws. As we shall see, proposals for change in enforcement, penalties, and procedures are often a substitute for substantive change in antitrust standards.

Enforcement

Private Enforcement

U.S. antitrust laws are subject to dual enforcement, by the federal government and by individuals who have been injured by activity that violates these laws. The wisdom of private enforcement of the antitrust laws has been questioned on three main grounds.[23]

Perverse Incentives

It is in society's interest that consumers who are victims of market power minimize their injury by seeking the best available substitutes for products sold at a price above marginal cost. If purchasers of monopolized goods believe that they will be able to recover overcharges in court, they will have less incentive to avoid injury (and this effect will be stronger if injured parties can recover treble damages).

Guile

Under a system of private enforcement, individuals will have an incentive to claim antitrust injury where none exists. The opportunity cost of a false claim to the perverse plaintiff is at most the cost of mounting the suit, and this cost will be assumed by the defendant if the plaintiff succeeds at trial. The cost to the innocent defendant is at least the cost of mounting a defense, as well as potentially treble damages plus the plaintiff's legal fees in the event of a miscarriage of justice.

The risk of treble damages will often induce an innocent defendant to settle, even if the defendant is certain of the merits of its case. The most obvious social costs of this sort of nuisance suit are the value of the legal resources devoted to the suit. But such suits may discourage efficient firms from competing vigorously, lest they become the target of spurious antitrust suits.[24] This induced inefficiency is also a social cost.

Under current procedures, the unsuccessful plaintiff in a private antitrust suit pays only his own legal costs. The incentive to bring nuisance suits would be

[23]Breit, William and Elzinga, Kenneth G. "Antitrust Enforcement and Economic Efficiency: The Uneasy Case for Treble Damages," *Journal of Law and Economics* Volume 17, Number 2, October 1972, pp. 329–356.

[24]Baumol, William J. and Ordover, Janusz A. "Use of Antitrust to Subvert Competition," *Journal of Law and Economics* Volume 28, Number 2, May 1985, pp. 247–265.

much reduced if an unsuccessful plaintiff were required to pay the costs of the defendant's defense. On the other hand, such a change would also discourage meritorious private suits.

Reparations Costs

Under a system of private antitrust enforcement, real resources are devoted to establishing the amount of damages. The resources consist of the services of expert witnesses on both sides of the case, who dispute both the existence and the amount of damage for the benefit of the court, as well as the services of the law clerk(s) and judge(s) involved in setting the amount of damages.

Such "reparations" costs also arise under the current system of public enforcement. Public enforcement of the antitrust laws provides for fines less than or equal to a maximum amount, rather than damages. Real resources are devoted to setting the amount of the fine under a system of public enforcement.

Public Enforcement

The most important shortcomings that have been laid at the feet of public enforcement of the antitrust laws involve the ability and the incentive of public enforcers to bring antitrust actions.

Ability

Private parties will often have superior access to information about violations of the law. If a merger will interfere with competition on the merits, competitors will recognize anticompetitive effects more surely than civil servants. A customer—especially an industrial customer—will often recognize that it is subject to monopoly overcharges. It may, of course, pass the information along to a public enforcement agency.[25] But the ability of public enforcement agencies—the Department of Justice and the Federal Trade Commission—to pursue violations is limited by the budget constraint imposed by Congress.

Far be it from an economist to argue against the consequences of a budget constraint. In a society of limited resources, enforcement agencies should be subject to such a constraint. A budget constraint will, in principle, force an enforcement agency to sift through potential cases and focus on the violations that are most costly to society. But a system of solely public enforcement of the antitrust laws will inevitably miss some offenses that would be prosecuted under a mixed public and private system.

Incentives

Guile—the pursuit of self-interest—will on occasion induce private enforcers to use the antitrust laws in ways that impose costs on society. But public enforcers can also be expected to pursue their own self-interest.[26] The self-

---

[25]This was a factor in the electrical equipment cases discussed in Chapter 6.

[26]McChesney, Fred S. "On the Economics of Antitrust Enforcement," *Georgetown Law Journal* Volume 66, Number 5, June 1980, pp. 1103–1111.

interest of public enforcers will not always coincide with the dictates of public policy:[27]

> The Antitrust Division is made up of several hundred trial lawyers (many of them engaged at any given time in investigation and other activities preparatory or incidental to trial), under a tiny staff of supervisors. The supervisors exercise little in the way of supervision, review, control, or direction. . . .
>
> The initiative in the division lies with the trial lawyers—along with the execution, the theorizing, the design of remedies, and virtually every other aspect of the enforcement process. Trial lawyers tend to be combative rather than reflective, and the division's trial lawyers, because they are relatively poorly paid, tend to be young or mediocre, or to be zealots. They are not the right people to be the custodians of the government's antitrust policy, but that is what they are.

Zealousness can cut two ways. The target of the preceding argument is excessive enforcement of the antitrust laws under a system of public enforcement. Zealousness based on youth or inexperience or ideology could certainly lead public enforcers to bring cases of doubtful merit in terms of the social welfare function implicit in the antitrust laws. But zealousness based on the same factors can lead to inadequate public enforcement of the antitrust laws.

Suppose, for example, that Congress intends the antitrust laws to prohibit resale price maintenance on the ground that it interferes with competition in the market for distributive services.[28] This is an expression of a social welfare function, and it indicates that resale price maintenance is a social bad. If public enforcement of the antitrust laws falls to officials who decline to enforce the social welfare function expressed by Congress, there is a social loss. This is so even if resale price maintenance causes no losses in terms of the welfare function advanced by those entrusted with the responsibility of enforcing the law.[29,30]

[27]Posner, Richard A. *Antitrust Law: An Economic Perspective*. Chicago: The University of Chicago Press, 1976, pp. 230–231. Footnote omitted.

[28]Or any other ground that Congress thinks appropriate.

[29][Federal Trade] "Commissioner Bailey characterized the Commission as having undertaken an administrative sit-in during which it will refuse to enforce the law as interpreted. Chairman Miller described his role as analogous to the civil rights advocates who engaged in civil disobedience until the Supreme Court rejected the "separate but equal doctrine." Brett, Barry J. *"Monsanto:* Great Expectations Unfulfilled," *Antitrust Bulletin* Volume 30, Number 1, Spring 1985, p. 49, footnote 51. Citations omitted.

[30]This is a specific example of subgoal pursuit, a problem associated with managerial loss of control in hierarchical organizations. How are policymakers to ensure that subordinates implement the policy of the organization rather than pursue private goals? See, generally, Williamson, Oliver E. *Markets and Hierarchies* New York: The Free Press, 1975.

We have no good theory of the incentives that motivate public prosecutors.[31] Economists are more cautious about the merits of private enforcement of the antitrust laws than was once the case.[32] It is fair to say, however, that most economists continue to favor a dual system of enforcement. In this way,[33]

> public enforcement, which is inevitably selective and least likely to concern itself with local, episodic, or less than flagrant violations, is supplemented by private enforcement, which increases the likelihood that a violator will be found out, greatly enlarges his penalties, and thereby helps discourage illegal conduct.

Deterrence and the Case for Multiple Damages[34]

Effective deterrence requires that the expected profit from violating the law be negative (or at least, not positive). If a firm's best estimate is that it will lose money by violating the law, it will decide, in its own self-interest, not to violate the law.

To understand what deterrence in this sense requires, assume for the moment that all violations of the antitrust laws are detected, and set aside problems of measuring the economic effects of such violations. How should damages to be set to deter (say) the formation of cartels?

The private gain to firms that form a cartel is the economic profit garnered by the cartel. Offending conduct will be deterred if the penalty for violation is set equal to the monopoly overcharge.

How does this conclusion change if only half of all cartels are detected? To deter violations in this case, the fine imposed on the unlucky few must be twice the monopoly overcharge. The *expected* fine for offending the antitrust laws would then be $2 \times (\frac{1}{2}) \times$ (monopoly profit), sufficient to drive the expected profit earned by violating the law to zero.

By the same reasoning, if only one out of three cartels are detected, damages should be set equal to three times monopoly profit. There is, in other words, an economic rationale for multiple damages under the antitrust laws.

[31]Schwartz, Warren F, "An Overview of the Economics of Law Enforcement," *Georgetown Law Journal* Volume 66, Number 5, June 1980, p. 1093; Dorman, Roderick G. "The Case for Compensation: Why Compensatory Components Are Required for Efficient Antitrust Enforcement," *Georgetown Law Journal* Volume 66, Number 5, June 1980, p. 1115.

[32]Breit, William and Elzinga, Kenneth G. "Private Antitrust Enforcement: The New Learning," *Journal of Law and Economics* Volume 28, Number 2, May 1985, p. 413.

[33]Areeda, Phillip and Turner, Donald F, *Antitrust Law*. Boston: Little, Brown and Company, Volume II, 1948, p. 33.

[34]See Posner, *Antitrust Law*, pp. 221–225; Page, William H. "Antitrust Damages and Economic Efficiency: An Approach to Antitrust Injury," *University of Chicago Law Review* Volume 47, Number 3, Spring 1980, pp. 467–504; Landes, William M. "Optimal Sanctions for Antitrust Violations," *University of Chicago Law Review* Volume 50, Number 2, Spring 1983, pp. 652–678; Easterbrook, Frank H. "Detrebling Antitrust Damages," *Journal of Law and Economics* Volume 28, Number 2, May 1985, pp. 445–467.

This rationale does not legitimize the notion of *treble* damages. The appropriate multiple used to convert private gain to penalty depends on the ease of detection of the offense. Cartels, especially those maintained by tacit cooperation, may be relatively difficult to detect, justifying multiple damages. But other conduct (predatory pricing, resale price maintenance) is relatively difficult to conceal. Multiple damages are not appropriate for offenses that are easy to detect.

Proposals for Change

The main inefficiencies associated with private antitrust enforcement reflect the perverse incentives that multiple damages create for private plaintiffs. At the same time, models of deterrence support the use of multiple damages for concealable offenses.

One might, at least, use different multipliers to calculate damages for different offenses or for different categories of plaintiffs. One suggestion is to allow treble damages for suits by customers or suppliers, but not by competitors.[35] This would limit the incentive of competitors to make strategic use of the antitrust laws to shackle more efficient rivals. Another suggestion[36] would limit treble damages to cases tried under the rule of reason. Such cases are more complex than those tried under per se rules. Without the prospect of treble damages, private plaintiffs might be reluctant to undertake the desirable level of private enforcement.

Yet another approach[37] would drive a wedge between the damages paid by the guilty defendant and the damages received by the injured plaintiff. Let the defendant, if convicted, pay treble damages. This will deter violations. Let the victim receive (say) single damages. This will compensate the plaintiff for the harm done but reduce the incentive for strategic misuse of the antitrust laws. The difference could be turned over to the Department of the Treasury.

The Politics of Antitrust Enforcement

The setting of penalties for violating the antitrust laws is inextricably intertwined with the standards imposed by the antitrust laws:[38] "anything that is done to make it harder for plaintiffs to use our antitrust institutions anticompetitively also makes it easier for others to get away with acts of monopolization." The result is that proposals for changes in antitrust penalties are some-

---

[35]Posner, *Antitrust Law*, p. 231. A form of this proposal was included in amendments to the antitrust laws suggested by the Reagan administration in legislation proposed in January 1986.

[36]Salop and White, op. cit., pp. 42, 1035–1036.

[37]Baumol and Ordover, op. cit., pp. 263–264; Salop and White, op. cit., p. 1034.

[38]Baumol and Ordover, op. cit., p. 263.

times put forward by those who would like to make, indirectly, substantive changes in the antitrust laws:[39]

> There is widespread disagreement across much of the legal profession (and some of the economics profession) about the wisdom of the legal lines that have been drawn in many areas of antitrust law. There are few dissenters to the propositions that . . . horizontal price-fixing is anti-competitive . . . and should carry heavy penalties to deter it or that mergers in highly concentrated industries with high barriers to entry should be discouraged. Beyond those points, however, agreement dissolves. Partly the disagreements involve the efficiency consequences of certain practices—tying, exclusive dealing, full-line forcing, vertical price and non-price restraints, price discrimination, and predatory pricing—and their ability to create or enhance market power. Partly the disagreements involve the size of markets, ease of substitutability in supply and demand, and ease of entry (. . .). The disagreements also involve the noneconomic questions of whether upstream entities simply should or should not be able to dictate terms of sale to downstream entities. It is no accident that those who believe that judicial interpretation of the Sherman and Clayton Acts in these areas are inhibiting efficient business practices are also those most concerned about the inhibiting effects of the treble damage remedy.

Procedures

Economic Analysis in Adversary Proceedings

As we have seen, roughly 88 per cent of antitrust cases are settled before trial. The verdicts in cases that go to trial invariably depend in a critical way on economic issues. What is the relevant market? What are the market shares of the firms in the market? Do firms cooperate, tacitly or otherwise?[40] Yet the methods of the adversary process are uniquely ill-suited to economic analysis:[41]

> First, the plaintiff puts in his evidence, much of it merely the raw data of his case and all of it subject to cross-examination designed to undermine the trier's confidence in the plaintiff and his witness; then there is plaintiff's redirect examination designed to restore that confidence; then defendant does the same, subject of course to cross-examination and redirect and recross, etc.; and finally the plaintiff puts on his rebuttal case, again subject to cross-examination, re-

[39]Salop and White, op. cit., footnote, p. 1051, footnote 154.

[40]Although the question is not likely to be put in these terms in court, are conjectural variations near 1 or near -1?

[41]Posner, *Antitrust Law*, pp. 232–233.

direct, and recross. As a result of this sequencing, the evidence bearing on a particular issue is not presented all at once. Weeks or even months may elapse between the presentation of the plaintiff's version of an event . . . and the defendant's version . . . and weeks later there may be still more evidence on the same issue, presented in the plaintiff's rebuttal. Not only does evidence . . . get introduced piecemeal, at different stages of the trial, but much of the trial is taken up with evidence not addressed to any issue in dispute but introduced simply in order to create a favorable atmosphere. And there are constant interruptions in the presentation of evidence, for cross-examination, objections, and procedural motions.

Economists generally agree that something should be done to improve this aspect of antitrust procedure. One proposal[42] to sanitize the presentation of economic evidence in antitrust cases would have the plaintiff and defendant agree before trial, as much as possible, on matters of fact relevant to the case. A written summary of such facts would be submitted to the court and become part of the trial record. Testimony would concern only matters in dispute.

Alternatively,[43] economists acting as expert witnesses for each side could submit written reports to a neutral economist employed by the court. This economist would make a written report to the court. As a safeguard for due process, the report of the neutral economist could be criticized in writing by experts for the parties to the case.

There is, in any event, much to be said for having economists' testimony embodied in written form. This would at least make explicit the assumptions that underlie the analysis. It would put the economic aspects of the case before the court in an organized, and one would hope coherent, form. In addition, seeing a draft of a particularly far-fetched argument in print—with the knowledge that other economists might also see it in print—might cause the argument to be withdrawn before presentation.[44]

---

[42]Posner, *Antitrust Law,* p. 233; endorsed by Scherer, F. M. "The Posnerian Harvest: Separating Wheat from Chaff," *Yale Law Journal* Volume 86, Number 5, April 1977, pp. 1001–1002.

[43]Areeda and Turner, op. cit., Volume II, pp. 84–85.

[44]Or perhaps not. Scherer, op. cit., p. 983: "The trouble is, economic analysis is an elastic instrument and, I am sorry to report, some economists' consciences are also elastic, so one can find economists who with apparent conviction will explain away any pattern of behavior, however bizarre, as the consequence of special but highly competitive industry circumstances." See also Fisher, Franklin M. "Multiple Regression in Legal Proceedings," *Columbia Law Review* Volume 80, Number 4, May 1980, pp. 702–735, and "Statisticians, Econometricians, and Adversary Proceedings," *Journal of the American Statistical Association* Volume 81, Number 394, June 1986, pp. 277–286; and Meier, Paul. "Damned Liars and Expert Witnesses," *Journal of the American Statistical Association,* Volume 81, Number 394, pp. 269–276.

Case Study: Antitrust Procedures

Escondido, California, May 6, 1983

The day after the judge announced an out-of-court settlement in a 21-month-old antitrust trial, Tom Black, a juror, got on his bicycle and rode from his home in Clairemont to San Diego and back, 50 miles, hard and fast, until he could ride no more.

"It was either that or punch somebody out," he said later.

On Monday, Mr. Black, 33 years old, an assistant planner for the city of Escondido, was sitting in a jury box in San Diego County Superior Court when Judge Norbert Ehrenfreund announced the agreement.

Twenty-three owners of Fotomat franchises, who had sued the giant film processing concern for $20 million more than six years ago, had finally agreed to settle, the judge said.

After 299 trial days, 115 witnesses, 3,000 exhibits, 38,000 pages of testimony and an estimated cost to country taxpayers of $2 million, the suit was dropped.

The judge turned to the 12 jurors and two alternates. They had been exemplary, dedicated, committed, diligent citizens, he said. He thanked them for the year and nine months they had given the court; he said he would make sure that for the rest of their lives, they would never have to serve on another jury.

A few jurors wept. Mr. Black arose with mixed emotions, relief and fury, and asked that he be allowed to make a statement to the court.

"I said I would like to believe everything that the judge had said," he recalled, "but that it was very obvious that we had all been used as pawns and that the outcome had nothing to do with justice.

"I just had to say something. I was outraged. I think it's pretty obvious that the only people who got anything out of this whole proceeding were the lawyers. I feel that the jury was essentially used as a bargaining chip."

The Fotomat store owners contended in their suit that in 1969 the film processor embarked on a plan to eliminate the franchises so it could take over the stores itself.

It took the plaintiffs 14 months to present their case and the defendants 8 more months to present theirs.

"It was beyond boring," Mr. Black said. "It wasn't like a criminal case, where you have a smoking gun. There was nothing interesting to look at."

After a few months one juror had to be replaced because he could not stay awake.

The settlement, which called for Fotomat to pay the franchise holders $10 million, was announced the day the plaintiffs' attorneys were to begin closing arguments.

499

Mr. Black said he could not believe that after all that time there would be no need for the jury. "I really feel that my time was wasted," he said. "I basically had to put my life on hold for two years."

He suggested strict time limits for civil jury trials and that opposing parties not be allowed to settle out of court once they bring the case to trial.

Source: Associated Press, reported in the *New York Times,* May 7, 1983, p. 9.

Antitrust as It Should Be:
The Per Se Rule vs. the Rule of Reason

The dominant standard of the Sherman Act is the rule of reason. As laid down in *Standard Oil*,[45] the rule of reason requires trial courts to evaluate the effect of the challenged behavior on competition. What is often regarded as the classic statement of the rule of reason appears in the *Chicago Board of Trade* decision:[46]

> the legality of an agreement or regulation cannot be determined by so simple a test, as whether it restrains competition. Every agreement concerning trade, restrains. To bind, to restrain, is of their very essence. The true test of legality is whether the restraint imposed is such as merely regulates and perhaps thereby promotes competition or whether it is such as may suppress or even destroy competition. To determine that question the court must ordinarily consider the facts peculiar to the business to which the restraint is applied; its condition before and after the restraint was imposed; the nature of the restraint and its effect, actual or probable. The history of the restraint, the evil believed to exist, the reason for adopting the particular remedy, the purpose or end sought to be attained, are all relevant facts. This is not because a good intention will save an otherwise objectionable regulation or the reverse; but because knowlege of intent may help the court to interpret facts and predict consequences.

It is clear—if only from our discussion of merger policy in Chapter 10— that evaluating the effect of various practices on competition will lead to big cases involving what amounts to a full-blown economic analysis of relevant

---

[45]221 U.S. 1 (1911); see Chapter 3.

[46]*Chicago Board of Trade v. United States,* 246 U.S. 231 (1918), at 238.

markets. The need to define markets and measure market shares is enough to guarantee big cases under the rule of reason.

Because the effects of some practices appear to be uniformly adverse to competition, the Supreme Court held them to be illegal *per se:* without any specific showing of anticompetitive effect.[47] Use of the *per se* rule, when the challenged practice is clearly anticompetitive, has been justified primarily on the grounds of administrative convenience and predictability. If the expense of a full-blown trial can be avoided with very little chance that an incorrect decision will result, society is better off. At the same time, the business community is well served if the rules that govern competition are clear-cut.

The original *per se* cases involved cartels. The reach of the *per se* rule was broadened in later cases[48] to cover practices whose efficiency and market power effects remain the subject of vigorous controversy. It may well be that some practices condemned as illegal *per se* are in some cases pro-competitive. But there is no confusion over the nature of the law and a saving of judicial resources.

The result of the broadening of the scope of the *per se* rule has been a continuing, if low-level, debate over the proper scope of the *per se* rule. There are signs that this debate will become more intense in the future.

The fundamental entry in this debate, as in so many others in antitrust economics, is by Bork.[49] As we noted in Chapter 6, the *per se* rule can be traced to Judge Taft's Circuit Court decision in *Addyston Pipe and Steel*.[50] In that opinion, later endorsed by the Supreme Court, Taft argued that the reasonableness of prices imposed by a combination was not a question that the law needed to address. A combination that chose to set reasonable prices could, if it wished, set unreasonable prices. It is the theory of the antitrust laws that the public interest is served when prices are set by market forces.

It is this theme that has become an integral part of the antitrust laws. But Bork finds in the decision another theme, so far undeveloped: the notion of ancillary restraints or reasonable restraints of trade.

---

[47]See Chapter 6's discussion of *Addyston Pipe & Steel* and *Trenton Potteries.*

[48]For example, *Dr. Miles Medical,* 220 U.S. 373 (1911), discussed in Chapter 17. See also *United States v. Socony-Vacuum Oil Company,* 310 U.S. 150 (1940).

[49]Bork, Robert H. "The Rule of Reason and the Per Se Concept: Price Fixing and Market Division," *Yale Law Journal* Volume 74, Number 5, April 1965, pp. 775–847, and Volume 75, Number 3, January 1966, pp. 373–475. The comments by J. R. Gould and B. S. Yamey (*Yale Law Journal* Volume 76, 1967, pp. 722–730, and Volume 77, 1968, pp. 936–949) and replies by Bork (*Yale Law Journal* Volume 76, 1967, pp. 731–743 and Volume 77, 1968. pp. 950–964) highlighted the portions of the original articles that dealt with resale price maintenance, drawing attention from broader themes.

[50]*United States v. Addyston Pipe & Steel Company,* 85 Fed 271 (6th Cir. 1898).

As interpreted by Taft:[51]

> the common law held void agreements in restraint of trade whose sole purpose
> was merely to restrain competition but upheld those which were merely sub-
> ordinate to the accomplishment of another purpose.

In this vein, Bork argues that the Sherman Act should permit restraints of
trade that create efficiency without supporting market power. To determine
which restraints should be permitted, Bork would rely on the kind of market
share rule that he suggested elsewhere for mergers:[52]

> It may be stated as a general rule . . . that where there is some integration of
> activities, and when market share is too small to make restriction of output
> profitable, the purpose of an agreement eliminating competition must be the
> creation of efficiency. It would theoretically be possible, therefore, to decide
> the legality of all horizontal price-fixing and market-division agreements which
> protect integrations of activities by the aggregate market power of the parties.

Bork would condemn price-fixing and market division agreements that are
not associated with any integration of activity among the parties to the agreement.[53] If such parties maintain independent operations but divide up a market,
the only purpose of the agreement can be to control price. Bork would also
condemn "agreements not to compete which are incapable of adding to the
efficiency of the integration which they seemingly accompany."[54] Bork would
have the Sherman Act allow all other restraints of trade:[55]

> These two categories define the proper scope of the per se rule: agreements
> eliminating competition which have no efficiency-creating potential. Following
> the common law terminology, agreements in the per se category may be termed
> "naked" to distinguish them from "ancillary" restraints.

If this standard were adopted, the effect would be to abolish the *per se*
rule.[56] As soon as it became apparent that the presence of ancillary restraints

---

[51]Bork, Robert H. "The Rule of Reason and the Per Se Concept: Price Fixing and Market Division," *Yale Law Journal* Volume 74, Number 5, April 1965, p. 797. For legal scholars in the crowd,
it may be worth noting that Bork suggests that Taft's references to the common law were a diplomatic
way for a circuit court judge to correct earlier decisions of the Supreme Court.

[52]Bork, Robert H. "The Rule of Reason and the Per Se Concept: Price Fixing and Market Division," *Yale Law Journal* Volume 75, Number 3, January 1966, p. 381.

[53]Ibid., p. 383.

[54]Ibid.

[55]Ibid., p. 384.

[56]Comment, "Fixing the Price Fixing Confusion: A Rule of Reason Approach," *Yale Law Journal*
Volume 92, Number 4, March 1983, pp. 727–728.

would lift a price-fixing or market division agreement out of the *per se* category, *every* cartel would be formulated to appear as an ancillary restraint, incidental to the creation of some efficiency or other.

The result would be a twofold rule of reason inquiry. First, an inquiry would determine whether or not a restraint actually carried with it "efficiency-creating potential." If a court found that the restraint was indeed ancillary to some efficiency-creating integration of economic activity, a second inquiry would examine whether or not the market shares of the firms committed to the restraint were "too small to make restriction of output profitable." The outcome of this inquiry would depend critically on market definition and the measurement of market share. Our discussion of merger policy[57] suggests that this is not a way to streamline antitrust proceedings or economize on enforcement costs.[58]

The Politics of Antitrust Rules—The Shape of Things to Come?

It has recently been suggested[59] that the incorporation of the free rider concept in Supreme Court decisions[60] is the harbinger of a general willingness to judge the lawfulness of restraints of trade in terms of their efficiency effects:[61]

> Viewed more broadly, *Sylvania's* economic standard of antitrust analysis and its specific recognition of the free-rider concept also are playing an increasingly significant part in horizontal cases which, as a consequence, are more like to be subject to a rule of reason analysis. This is because the free-rider concept . . . is only a subset of broader market imperfection or market failure analysis. . . . "atomistic competition" is not always the most efficient marketplace solution viewed from the perspective of [consumer plus producer welfare].[62]

There is some reason to doubt that courts (and jurors) can render effective decisions based on efficiency analysis of market restraints:[63]

> evaluation of the efficiency of practices such as franchise input tie-ins and resale price maintenance requires complex theoretical analysis to reach ambig-

---

[57]See Chapter 10.

[58]It might, on the other hand, increase the real income of economists specializing in industrial economics. But I digress.

[59]Popofsky, M. Laurence and Bomse, Stephen V. "From *Sylvania* to *Monsanto:* No Longer a 'Free Ride,' " *Antitrust Bulletin* Volume 30, Number 1, Spring 1985, pp. 67–98.

[60]Such as *Sylvania* and *Monsanto;* see Chapter 17.

[61]Popofsky and Bomse, op. cit., pp. 95–96; footnotes omitted.

[62]See Chapter 3, footnote 10.

[63]Leffler, Keith. "Toward a Reasonable Rule of Reason: Comments," *Journal of Law and Economics* Volume 28, Number 2, May 1985, p. 381.

uous conclusions. Given these results, . . . the efficiency analysis of these practices provides no guide to policy. The exercise provides no useful conclusion; indeed, the requisite theoretical complications and empirical detail are likely to be beyond the abilities of those who debate and decide in courtrooms. . . . a simple examination of the direct competitive effects in the product markets concerned provides a workable, reasonably efficient antitrust guide to presumptive legality or illegality.

The decision as to the proper scope of the per se rule is political, not economic. Narrowing the scope of the *per se* rule would raise the cost of antitrust enforcement. It would also make it harder for plaintiffs, public or private, to prove violations of the antitrust laws.

Whether this would be good or bad depends on the tradeoffs between the elements of the cost of antitrust enforcement. If society is strongly averse to condemning efficient behavior, the scope of the rule of reason should be large. Antitrust cases will then be long and expensive, and some anticompetitive behavior will escape condemnation.

If society prefers to conserve enforcement expenses when the effect of behavior on competition seems almost always adverse, the scope of the per se rule should be large. This will condemn some efficient behavior but economize on legal, judicial, and expert resources.

Antitrust as It Should Be: General Goals

In Chapter 3, we reviewed congressional intent behind the antitrust laws. There is, of course, no reason why the 100th Congress, or the country that elects it, should be bound by the intentions of the 50th Congress. Indeed, the debate over congressional intent is of interest mainly as an element of a larger debate: whatever the original goals of the antitrust laws, what should the goals of the antitrust laws be?

Resource Misallocation vs. Consumer Welfare

Using the discussion of congressional intent in Chapter 3 as a base, we can succinctly characterize one part of the debate over the goals of public policy toward private enterprise. Should antitrust policy seek to minimize the resource misallocation effects of market power—deadweight loss—

$$G_1 = \text{minimize DWL} \qquad (18.2)$$

or should it seek to minimize consumer injury from the exercise of market power—deadweight loss plus the transfer of income from consumers to producers:

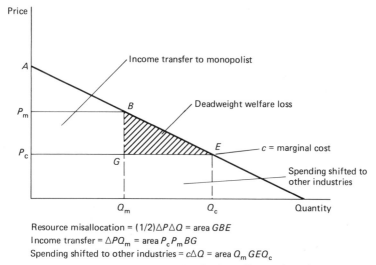

Resource misallocation = $(1/2)\Delta P\Delta Q$ = area GBE
Income transfer = ΔPQ_m = area $P_c P_m BG$
Spending shifted to other industries = $c\Delta Q$ = area $Q_m GEQ_c$

Figure 18-1 Allocative and redistributive effects of market power.

$$G_2 = \text{minimize (DWL} + \pi), \tag{18.3}$$

where π is economic profit due to market power?

Common Ground

There are certain underlying consistencies between these alternative goals. They both refer to strictly economic consequences of market power, rather than political or social consequences. They both seek to achieve the same ultimate result: elimination of output restriction due to market power.

Note in Figure 18-1 (which replicates Figure 2-6) that if deadweight loss equals zero, economic profit also equals zero. Thus, if G_1 is achieved (no deadweight welfare loss due to output restriction), G_2 is also achieved (no income transfers from consumers to producers). The reverse is also true: if $DWL + \pi = 0$ in a market, $DWL = 0$ in that market. If no firm exercises market power, in long-run equilibrium, there is neither resource misallocation nor income transfer from consumers to producers.

There is a further convergence between the two standards to the extent that monopoly profits are transformed into social costs as firms compete for market power.[64] Such competition might take the form of advertising, sales efforts

[64]Tullock, Gordon. "The Welfare Costs of Tariffs, Monopolies, and Theft," *Western Economic Journal* Volume 5, June 1967, pp. 224–232; Posner, Richard A. "The Social Costs of Monopoly and Regulation," *Journal of Political Economy* Volume 83, Number 4, August 1975, pp. 807–827; see Chapter 3.

coaxed from dealers through vertical restraints, excess capacity, or expenditures to influence regulatory agencies. The extent to which this transformation occurs will differ from industry to industry. In general, market power will result in resource misallocation due to output restriction, resource misallocation as firms compete to acquire or maintain market power, and income transfers from consumers to producers.

Differences

Although the two standards converge when all exercise of market power is eliminated, they differ otherwise. The resource misallocation standard treats the economic profit of producers as a social welfare gain and uses it to offset the income loss consumers suffer due to market power. The consumer welfare standard does not treat monopoly profit as a social welfare gain, with the result that the entire income loss of consumers is treated as a social welfare loss.

As we have seen in our discussion of public policy toward mergers (Chapter 10), the choice of deadweight loss or loss of consumer welfare as the injury flowing from market power determines the severity of public policy toward mergers. Under a public policy that aims to minimize deadweight welfare loss, mergers that generate productive efficiencies are likely to be approved even if the resulting cost savings are not passed on to consumers. Under a consumer welfare standard, mergers that increase prices to consumers are more likely to be condemned.

Economics and Political Choices

The choice of a policy goal for antitrust policy is fundamentally political rather than economic. As noted in Chapter 3, economists have traditionally refrained from camouflaging political positions as economic conclusions:[65]

> any program or project that is subjected to applied welfare-economic analysis is likely to have characteristics upon which the economist as such is not professionally qualified to pronounce, and about which one economist is not professionally qualified to check the opinion of another. These caveats—which surely include the income-distributional and national defense aspects of any project or program, and probably its natural-beauty aspects as well—may be exceedingly important, perhaps even the dominant factors governing any policy decision, but they are not a part of that package of expertise that distinguishes the professional economist from the rest of humanity.

The choice of minimization of deadweight loss as the goal of antitrust policy implies the political judgment that the transfer of income from consumers to

[65]Harberger, Arnold C. "Three Basic Postulates for Applied Welfare Economics: An Interpretive Essay," *Journal of Economic Literature* Volume 9, Number 3, September 1971, p. 785. See footnote 16, Chapter 2, and the accompanying text.

producers that goes with market power is socially acceptable. The choice of maximization of consumer welfare implies the political judgment that this transfer of income is not acceptable.

Economists have often opted for a deadweight loss measure of social welfare on the ground of neutrality. If the decision to treat producers and consumers differently is to be made, in this view, it should not be made by economists.[66]

Others have argued that antitrust policy should be neutral with respect to transfers of income from consumers to producers because the antitrust laws are not an effective tool for dealing with problems of income distribution:[67]

> an "imaginary" neutrality assumption might be supported by the argument that antitrust is poorly suited to advance redistributional objectives. Macroeconomic policy instruments (taxes, transfers, expenditures) with which to correct distributional conditions are not only available but superior to the use of antitrust for this purpose. Typically these instruments involve the promotion of regional development, subsidizing a group that is involved in a transitional adjustment, alleviating conditions of poverty, etc., and are applied on a broad scale. Antitrust, by contrast, is concerned with industry conditions of a much more local variety.

If the income redistribution goals involve the transfer of income to particular groups,[68] antitrust policy is a clumsy tool.[69] But the income distribution goal imputed to antitrust policy has not usually had specific segments of the population as targets. Rather, it has been the prevention of income transfers due to the exercise of market power from consumers—whether rich or poor, deserving or not—to producers—whether rich or poor, deserving or not. These transfers depend on local market conditions—specifically, the presence or absence of market power. Antitrust will be more efficient than macroeconomic policy as a way of mitigating income transfers that flow from the exercise of market power.

---

[66]This is the position of Harberger, op. cit. See also Bork, Robert H. *The Antitrust Paradox: A Policy at War with Itself.* New York: Basic Books, 1978, p. 111.

[67]Williamson, Oliver E. "Allocative Efficiency and the Limits of Antitrust," *American Economic Review* Volume 59, Number 2, May 1969, p. 108; see also Williamson, Oliver E. "Economies as an Antitrust Defense: The Welfare Tradeoffs," *American Economic Review* Volume 58, Number 1, March 1968, p. 28.

[68]To pick two examples that are likely to meet general approval among the users of this book: (1) transfer income to college students so that they can pursue their studies; (2) transfer income to college professors so that they can pursue their research.

[69]For the examples of footnote 68, scholarships and research grants are superior to antitrust policy as a way of aiding these clearly deserving target groups.

The Chicago school view is that the sole goal of the antitrust laws should be the minimization of resource misallocation due to market power: G_1.[70,71] The position that income transfers stemming from market power should be a concern of antitrust policy is rejected on the ground that producers are consumers too:[72]

> Those who continue to buy after a monopoly is formed pay more for the same output, and that shifts income from them to the monopoly and its owners, who are also consumers. This is not dead-weight loss due to the restriction of output but merely a shift in income between two classes of consumers.

This argument ignores a fundamental difference between monopoly profit and other categories of income. The usual categories of income are wages, rent, interest, and economic profit. Wages, rent, and interest[73] are determined in factor markets as the owners of factors of production[74] offer their services for sale. Consumers, *as consumers,* receive no income at all. Income is received by individuals who own the services of factors of production.

Economic profit is determined in markets for output, not markets for input services. The fact that monopoly profits are eventually distributed to individuals who dispose of the income as consumers does not place economic profit on the same functional basis as factor incomes. The argument that there is no economic basis for distinguishing income transfers due to market power from other income flows is incorrect.[75]

The fact that the functional basis for income due to market power is different from that of other income flows does not dictate the condemnation of monopoly income on economic grounds. That decision remains political rather than economic.

[70]Bork, Robert H. and Bowman, Ward S. "The Crisis in Antitrust," *Columbia Law Review* Volume 65, Number 3, March 1965, pp. 363–376; Bork, "Contrasts in Antitrust Theory: I"; "Rule of Reason"; "Legislative Intent and the Policy of the Sherman Act," *Journal of Law and Economics* Volume 9, October 1966, pp. 7–48; "The Goals of Antitrust Policy," *American Economic Review* May 1967, pp. 242–253; *The Antitrust Paradox.*

[71]Recall (see footnote 10 of Chapter 3) that Bork labels his preferred goal *consumer welfare,* although this is inconsistent with the meaning usually given to these words.

[72]Bork, *The Antitrust Paradox,* p. 110.

[73]For a discussion of the relationship between the interest rate and the rental cost of capital services, see Chapter 2, footnote 3.

[74]Land, labor, and capital.

[75]The difference in the functional basis of economic profit and other categories of income can be illustrated with the familiar circular flow diagram.

The argument that antitrust policy should concern itself with the income distribution consequences of market power must confront what might be called the "We have met the enemy and he is us" objection:[76]

> a general case that user interests greatly outweigh seller interests is not easy to make and possibly reflects a failure to appreciate that profits ramify through the system in ways—such as taxes, dividends, and retained earnings—that greatly attenuate the notion that monolithic producer interests exist and are favored.

This suggests that the original *political* basis for antitrust concern over income distribution has been eroded by changes in the ownership of firms with market power. Economic profit, in the form of dividends, is now widely distributed throughout the economy. If we attack monopolists' income, we are no longer on the trail of J. P. Morgan: we are on the trail of ourselves.

This objection depends on a matter of fact: how widely distributed among the general public is the ownership of firms with market power? It may be correct for some industries and not for others.[77] It may provide a basis for the political decision not to direct antitrust policy toward the elimination of monopolistic income transfers. It should nonetheless be recognized that this decision, if taken, would be taken on political and not economic grounds.

Dual Economic/Political Goals

The Competitive Process

A persistent element in the debate over the purposes of the antitrust laws focuses on competition in the sense of rivalry among firms as a goal of the antitrust laws. Competition as rivalry is defended as a political goal of antitrust and as a way of attaining economic goals (G_1 or G_2) with a minimum of direct public control of private enterprise. Closely related to this goal—perhaps simply another way of expressing the same idea—is the goal sometimes imputed to the Clayton Act: the maintenance of economic opportunity and freedom of action for independent firms.[78]

---

[76]Due to Williamson, Oliver E. "Economies as an Antitrust Defense Revisited," *University of Pennsylvania Law Review* Volume 125, Number 4, April 1977, p. 711.

[77]It would fail if market power were exercised by a family-owned firm. This suggests a case-by-case approach.

[78]Fox, Eleanor M. "The Modernization of Antitrust: A New Equilibrium," *Cornell Law Review* Volume 66, Number 6, August 1981, p. 1149.

A mainstream defense of the competitive process as a goal of antitrust policy is as follows:[79]

> Competitive markets are fundamental to the American system not simply because they encourage economic efficiency and material progress, but also because they advance extremely important political objectives. The great virtue of the competitive process is that it makes possible the attainment of a viable economy with a minimum of political interference. It largely polices itself.

Competition as a process is said to be desirable because it minimizes political control of the economy. This is not an economic goal. But competitive rivalry is also thought to bring about "economic efficiency and material progress." These are economic goals. Those who advance competitive rivalry as an object of the antitrust laws generally do so in the belief that rivalry and efficiency are compatible—in fact, that rivalry is an effective way to attain the benefits of efficiency.

This position is consistent with the structure-conduct-performance approach to industrial economics, which suggests that lowering barriers to entry and increasing the number of competitors in a market will improve market performance.[80]

Scholars working in the Chicago tradition have rejected the propriety of any goals other than allocative and productive efficiency for public policy:[81]

> "Competition" may be read as a process of rivalry. This is a natural mode of speech, because rivalry is the means by which a competitively structured industry creates and confers its benefits, and because the event that triggers the

---

[79]Blake, Harlan M. and Jones, William K. "In Defense of Antitrust," *Columbia Law Review,* Volume 65, Number 3, March 1965, pp. 382–383. For similar views, see Fox, op. cit., who defends the "competition process" as a goal of antitrust policy, and Pitofsky, Robert, "The Political Content of Antitrust," *University of Pennsylvania Law Review* Volume 127, Number 4, April 1979, p. 1059: "After decades of agonizing interpretation, a sort of working compromise has been reached, so that the goal of antitrust is to preserve a competitive process even at the cost at times of the disappearance of less efficient small business."

[80]Baumol, William J., Panzar, John C., and Willig, Robert D. "On the Theory of Perfectly Contestable Markets," in Stiglitz, Joseph E. and Mathewson, G. Frank, editors, *New Developments in the Analysis of Market Structure.* Cambridge, Mass.: MIT Press, 1986, pp. 339–365, point out that the theory of contestable markets is broadly consistent with the theory of entry barriers going back to Bain. This suggests, in turn, that the antitrust goal of maintaining the competitive process is consistent with the economic theory of contestable markets.

[81]Bork, *The Antitrust Paradox,* pp. 58–59.

application of law is often the elimination of rivalry by merger or cartel agreement. Yet it is a loose usage and invites the further, wholly erroneous conclusion that the elimination of rivalry must always be illegal. . . .

But this identification of competition with rivalry will not do for antitrust purposes. It makes rivalry an end in and of itself, no matter how many or how large the benefits flowing from the elimination of rivalry. And it is clear what those benefits are. Our society is founded upon the elimination of rivalry, since that is necessary to every integration or coordination of productive economic efforts and to the specialization of effort. No firm, no partnership, no corporation, no economic unit containing more than a single person could exist without the elimination of some kinds of rivalry between persons.

The conclusion is that antitrust aimed at maintaining rivalry would be[82]

a prescription for the complete atomization of society. That policy is unthinkable, since it would call not only for general abject poverty but for the death by starvation of millions of people.

The consequences of directing antitrust toward maintaining freedom of action are viewed, from Chicago, as similarly dire:[83]

"Competition" may be read as the absence of restraint over one person's or firm's economic activities by any other person or firm. . . . This is not a useful definition, however, for the preservation of competition would then require the destruction of all commercial contracts and obligations.

What we have here is a failure to communicate. It will be generally conceded that the atomization of society, the destruction of all commercial contracts, and the death by starvation of millions of people are not desirable as goals of antitrust or any other policy. But these are not exactly (or even remotely) the aims of those who have advocated the maintenance of competitive rivalry and freedom of action/opportunity under the antitrust laws.

Antitrust policy embodies a number of rules that aim to maintain competitive rivalry, freedom of decision of independent firms, and opportunity to compete.[84] One may argue that these policies are undesirable. But the fact that they

[82]Ibid., p. 59.

[83]Ibid.

[84]The per se prohibition of resale price maintenance and the treatment of tying contracts and exclusive dealing contracts are examples.

exist shows that antitrust can further competitive rivalry without pulverizing business and destroying all commercial contracts.[85]

Strictly Noneconomic Goals

Second Best Critique of Economic Goals[86]

The analysis employed in this textbook, like the vast majority of analyses in the field of industrial economics, is partial equilibrium. We have examined the impact of market power within a single market. It is in this context that economists argue that restriction of output is bad from a social point of view. Partial equilibrium analysis does not easily transfer to a general equilibrium context, in which one considers all markets simultaneously.

Suppose all markets in an economy are competitive and in long-run equilibrium. If one market is suddenly monopolized, the monopoly producer will restrict output and raise price. Some consumers will leave the monopolized market and transfer their spending to other markets. These other goods yield less utility per dollar of cost than the monopolized product (otherwise, consumers would have purchased them in the premonopoly situation). Society is made worse off by the exercise of market power—there is a deadweight loss—because monopoly prices drive a wedge between private and social cost.

This argument depends critically on the assumption that all markets are, to begin with, competitive.

Suppose one market is monopolized to begin with, and a second market becomes monopolized. Under monopoly, output is restricted and resources are shifted of the second market. If we take a general equilibrium view and consider all markets together, can we assert that the monopolization of the second market will make society worse off?

We cannot. To begin with, there is too little output, from a social point of view, in the first market. Society will be better off if output in the first market increases. When the second market is monopolized, resources are shifted from the second market to other markets throughout the economy. If any of these

---

[85]Schwartz, Warren F., "An Overview of the Economics of Antitrust Enforcement," *Georgetown Law Journal* Volume 66, Number 5, June 1980, pp. 1085–1086, suggests that "it is not sufficient to postulate goals like increasing individual freedom of choice or reducing undue social or political power as relevant. Value must be placed on various degrees of accomplishment of these ends so that their achievement can be traded off against the sacrifice of other ends and the incurring of enforcement costs." The fact that antitrust policy currently embodies tradeoffs, without such valuations, raises doubts about the correctness of Schwartz's conclusion. One could also take the position that it is not sufficient to postulate a goal like efficiency for antitrust policy without placing a value of various degrees of achieving efficiency. Then the achievement of efficiency could be traded off against other goals of antitrust and enforcement costs.

[86]Lipsey, R. G. and Lancaster, Kelvin. "The General Theory of the Second Best," *Review of Economic Studies* Volume 24, Number 63, October 1956, pp. 11–32.

resources end up, because of the changing pattern of demand, in the first market, output will increase in the first market. Monopolization of the second market will create a welfare gain in the first market. If a sufficient output increase occurs in the first market, the welfare gain in this market may more than offset the deadweight loss in the second market, leaving society better off after monopolization of the second market. It follows that an antitrust policy that eliminates monopoly in the second market would make society worse off.

This is the world of second best, in which the most that policymakers can hope to do is eliminate some but not all market power in the economy. It is the world for which policymakers must make policy. We don't even try to eliminate all market power in the economy; market power acquired through competition on the merits does not offend the antitrust laws. It follows that we will never be sure whether or not the general equilibrium consequences of attacking market power on a market-by-market basis leave society better off.

For this reason, some students of antitrust[87] deny that economic theory can guide antitrust policy or that antitrust policy improves allocative efficiency. This, it is argued, limits the usefulness of economics as a guide for antitrust,[88] opening the way for guidelines based on the concerns of history and sociology.

It will not surprise you to learn that most economists dispute the rejection of partial equilibrium analysis. The theory of second best only raises the possibility that enforcing competition in some but not all markets will make society worse off. It does not show that society will actually be made worse off by a market-by-market procompetitive policy.[89] To the extent that monopoly profits are converted into social costs, as firms compete to acquire or maintain positions of market power, the saving from eliminating market power in a single market will be greater than deadweight loss alone, and the likelihood that enforcing competition would make society worse off is so much the less.[90] The likelihood that enforcing competition would make society worse off is less, in any event, if income redistribution is treated as a welfare cost of market power.

Implications of the Second-Best Critique for Antitrust Policy

Almost all economists agree that the theory of the second best does not limit the usefulness of partial equilibrium analysis as a source of instruction for antitrust policy. Agreement stops there.

---

[87]Sullivan, Lawrence A. "Book Review," *Columbia Law Review* Volume 75, Number 5, June 1975, pp. 1214–1229.

[88]Ibid., p. 1221: "To impeach allocative efficiency as a policy guide is not to reject the techniques of economic analysis out of hand; it is merely to view the strengths and limits of that mode of analysis from a better perspective."

[89]Bork, op. cit., p. 113; Areeda and Turner, op. cit., Volume II, p. 309.

[90]Posner, *Antitrust Law*, pp. 13–14.

A conclusion in the Chicago school tradition is as follows:[91]

> An occasional antitrust scholar has taken the possibility of second best as destroying the rationality of the [consumer plus producer welfare][92] basis of the law (which it does not) and therefore freeing the courts to evolve new rules based on other social and political values. The suggestion is little short of preposterous. Aside from the political-jurisprudential and constitutional objections to any such unconfined role for the courts . . . it would be utterly improper for the courts to decide that Congress had made a policy error in choosing to promote competition and deciding, for that reason, to take the statutes as authority to enforce different values of their own choosing.

The Chicago school rejects the second-best criticism of an economic basis for antitrust policy, and uses that rejection as another opportunity to reject any purpose for antitrust policy other than the promotion of allocative and productive efficiency. This rejection of noneconomic goals for antitrust policy depends on the peculiarly Chicagoish reading of congressional intent (Chapter 3), which holds that Congress passed the antitrust laws to further strictly economic goals, and, among economic goals, only economic efficiency.

In contrast, a structure-conduct-performance view uses the broad consistency of noneconomic and economic goals as one defense of economic guidelines for antitrust:[93]

> competitive policy is still supported by considerations of power dispersion, broadened entrepreneurial opportunities, impersonal market forces, and "fair" income distribution. The encouragement of feasible competition would also seem to be the premise of antitrust statutes.

In the spirit of this latter conclusion, various noneconomic goals continue to be suggested for antitrust. Most often, these suggestions are made on an "all else equal" basis.

Typical is the argument that introducing the noneconomic goal of power dispersion into merger policy will cost little in terms of efficiency. Beginning

---

[91]Bork, *The Antitrust Paradox*, p. 114. For an apparently contradictory view, see Bork, "The Goals of Antitrust Policy," p. 246: "In my view, the desideratum of judicial responsibility is so crucial that even if Congress had written statutes which explicitly ordered the federal courts to balance consumer and small business interests in each case, which it did not, I think the courts should flatly refuse to accept the delegation."

[92]The words that appear in the original are *consumer welfare,* used to include monopoly profit. See footnote 10, Chapter 3.

[93]Areeda and Turner, op. cit., Volume II, p. 310. Areeda and Turner give economic goals priority (Volume I, p. 13):"populist goals should be given little or no independent weight in formulating antitrust rules and presumptions. They are substantially served by a pro-competitive policy framed in economic terms." See the subsequent discussion of consistency among antitrust objectives.

from the proposition[94] that "most mergers at a scale large enough to attract antitrust attention yield inappreciable efficiency benefits," one can reason that[95]

> mergers contribute little in general either to efficiency or monopoly. They are a deadly serious but preponderantly sterile game that diverts managerial attention from running existing operations well.
>
> To the extent that such a low-level balance of monopoly costs and efficiency benefits prevails, the injection into federal merger policy of noneconomic goals, such as the desire for maximum decentralization of power, seems . . . entirely appropriate.

This combines two different types of arguments. The judgment that the costs and benefits of mergers balance out at a very low level is the professional opinion of an economist. It should be treated—and disputed—as such.[96] The judgment that maximum decentralization of power is an appropriate goal for antitrust policy is, of course, political. When an economist expresses a political preference, it deserves only as much[97] consideration as the opinion of any other citizen. For our purposes, however, the point is that the noneconomic goal of dispersal of power is often advanced by economists in the belief that it is broadly consistent with the principal economic goals of antitrust.

Even consideration for the small businessman is most often presented as a goal that is desirable only when consistent with economic goals:[98]

> To be sure, it was not the purpose of the antitrust laws to create havens for inefficient small businessmen. . . . But it *was* the purpose of the antitrust laws to expand the range of consumer choice and entrepreneurial opportunity by encouraging the formation of markets of numerous buyers and sellers, assuring ease of entry to such markets, and protecting participants—particularly small businessmen—against exclusionary practices.

[94]Scherer, "The Posnerian Harvest," pp. 987–988. On the correctness or incorrectness of this proposition, see Chapters 9 and 10.

[95]Ibid., p. 988.

[96]The Chicago school position is that it is impossible to measure the efficiencies that flow from mergers and inappropriate to require firms to explain efficiencies to economists. See Scherer, F. M., "Economies of Scale and Industrial Concentration," and McGee, John S., "Efficiency and Economies of Size," in Goldschmid, Harvey J., Mann, H. Michael, and Weston, J. Fred, editors, *Industrial Concentration: The New Learning*. Boston: Little Brown and Company, 1974, pp. 16–55 and 56–97, respectively.

[97]Or, democracy being what it is, as little.

[98]Blake and Jones, "In Defense of Antitrust," p. 384; footnote omitted. Courts have not always been so careful; see Chapter 10's discussion of *Brown Shoe*.

Underlying Consistency?

The discussion of the previous section introduces yet another basic difference in the positions of the Chicago and the structure-conduct-performance schools of industrial economics. Both generally agree that economic considerations deserve priority in shaping the antitrust laws. The structure-conduct-performance position, however, is that economic, mixed, and noneconomic goals are broadly compatible:[99]

> Populist values are served, to a very considerable extent, by the antitrust policies that promote economic efficiency and progressiveness. The competitive market is one in which power is not unduly concentrated in the hands of one or a few firms. They are sufficiently numerous to offer real alternatives to their suppliers and customers, whose fate is thus determined by impersonal market forces rather than by the arbitrary fiat of another. And the several firms that share that market will necessarily have less individual economic or political significance than would be had by a single firm, or by substantially fewer firms, controlling that market. Accordingly, the goals of dispersed power and wider business opportunities are served by an antitrust policy which eliminates monopoly not attributable to economies of scale or superior skill, and which prevent those mergers, agreements, or practices which obstruct efficient competition. Populist goals and efficiency goals are consistent over a wide range.

The Chicago view is quite different:[100]

> the introduction of goals other than [consumer plus producer welfare][101] into antitrust is destructive of antitrust as law. Confining antitrust to [consumer plus producer welfare], on the other hand, permits courts to employ the teachings of economic analysis to estimate whether the net effect of a particular structure, act, or agreement is likely to be an increase or a decrease in output. The judgment must often prove rough and may change over time as economic understanding progresses. But these kinds of uncertainty we must always live with in a legal system. . . . The kind of uncertainty which a legal system ought not to tolerate . . . is that which arises because judges are making case-by-case and ex-post-facto the political choices.

---

[99]Areeda and Turner, op. cit., Volume I, p. 23.

[100]Bork, "The Goals of Antitrust Policy," p. 253.

[101]The words that appear in the original are *consumer welfare,* used to include monopoly profit. See footnote 10, Chapter 3.

Antitrust as It Should Be: Public Policy Alternatives

Output Restriction Standard

Beginning with the position that the sole concern of antitrust should be consumer plus producer welfare,[102] the Chicago school recommendation is that[103] "The task of antitrust is to identify and prohibit those forms of behavior whose net effect is output restricting and hence detrimental." In other words, if a merger or a business practice does not restrict output, it cannot create a welfare loss due to resource misallocation. It should not, therefore, be a subject of antitrust concern.

The logic behind this argument is correct if there is no product differentiation and no opportunity for strategic behavior. In such a market, the only way firms can raise the price is by restricting output and moving back up along the demand curve.

If products are differentiated, a firm will be able to shift the location of the demand curve for its brand by engaging in advertising and sales efforts. A firm will be able to increase both price and output, moving outward from one demand curve to another. In this way, output can increase even as the exercise of market power imposes resources misallocation costs on society.[104]

If incumbent firms can engage in strategic behavior, they can raise the costs of rival firms. This will reduce the profit-maximizing output of such firms. In the limit, the output of rival firms will be driven to zero: they will be excluded from the market. Such strategies have the effect of reducing market output below the competitive level even if the output of the incumbent firm increases.

From the Chicago viewpoint, antitrust should concern itself with little beyond cartels, horizontal mergers creating large market shares, and predation from antitrust attention.[105]

---

[102]Bork, *The Antitrust Paradox,* p. 109.

[103]Ibid., p. 122. See also Demsetz, Harold, "The Trust Behind Antitrust," in Fox, Eleanor M. and Halverson, James T., editors, *Industrial Concentration and the Market System,* Section of Antitrust Law. American Bar Association, 1979 p. 50: "In general, those marketing practices most often attacked in antitrust cases, such as tie-ins, allow . . . control over price to be exercised in a way that results in large rates of output and lower prices (at least for some customers) than would be profitable for such firms should these marketing practices be made illegal. These practices allow expansion of output by enabling firms to lower price to those customers who value the product less."

[104]Elsewhere ("The Rule of Reason and the Per Se Concept: Price Fixing and Market Division," *Yale Law Journal* Volume 75, Number 3, January 1966, pp. 421–2) Bork denies that product differentiation should be a basis for antitrust concern: "Entry into the field of differentiation would tend to return the profitability of that activity to the competitive level. . . . If product differentiation succeeds, it is because consumers like and respond to it." For a contrasting view, see the discussion of Dixit and Norman's work in Chapter 8.

[105]Bork, *The Antitrust Paradox,* p. 406. See Demsetz, op. cit., pp. 50–51, for a similar view.

Consumer Welfare Standard

Lande, who argues that consumer welfare (G_2) is the standard Congress intended the antitrust laws to follow, suggests[106] a price increase rather than an output restriction approach. Such a rule would condemn (for example) mergers thought likely to result in a higher price to consumers even if they generated cost savings retained by producers.

Recall from the discussion of predatory pricing in Chapter 16 that Baumol would allow established firms to cut price in response to entry, but would forbid them to raise price if the offending entrant departed from the market. The idea of a price-raising standard for mergers under the antitrust laws is similar to Baumol's proposal for predatory pricing.

A price-raising standard for antitrust would treat as beneficial any cost savings passed along to consumers in the form of lower prices. Such a standard would not treat cost savings as beneficial if they were retained by the firm as monopoly profits. Mergers (or other practices) that created market power but produced cost savings so great that prices fell would not be condemned under a price-raising standard.[107] The effect of this standard would be to deny an efficiency defense to the use of market power.

A Middle Ground

An alternative approach, based on the view that antitrust serves political as well as economic purposes, would deny an efficiency defense for price fixing and market division but allow it for other offenses, as a limiting principle to protect consumer interests:[108]

> In cases of hard-core violations, such as horizontal price-fixing and market divisions, the limiting principle would not come into play. Freedom to decide what and how much to produce, and where, to whom, and at what price to sell, is central to the nervous system of markets and therefore to long-run consumers' interests. No defense of efficiency would be allowed. So, too, there would be no change in the established per se rule against classic group boycotts, which protects economic opportunity and freedom to compete on the merits, because enforcement of the rule causes no harm to consumers.
>
> Other per se principles could be candidates for challenge as inconsistent with consumer interests. These include rules of law that prohibit maximum

[106]Lande, Robert H. "Wealth Transfers as the Original and Primary Concern of Antitrust: The Efficiency Interpretation Challenged," *Hastings Law Journal* Volume 34, September 1982, pp. 145–146.

[107]Recall from the discussion in Chapter 7 of the Demsetz efficiency hypothesis that as the costs of a firm with market power fall, the firm's profit-maximizing price falls.

[108]Fox, "The Modernization of Antitrust," pp. 1183–1184; footnote omitted.

vertical price-fixing, minimum vertical price-fixing, especially in fragmented markets by producers without market power, and tying arrangements in which the tie does not endanger the price or quality of the goods in the market for the tied product. A successful challenger would be required to demonstrate that application to the per se rule harms long-run consumer interests viewed from a perspective harmonious with . . . competition process.

The "challenger" portion of this proposal would place the burden of proving that application of an established per se principle would harm consumers on the firm seeking to set aside this rule. This is efficient from the point of view of transaction costs. It would place the burden of proof on the party in the best position to produce information about the effect or likely effect of the practice in question.

By placing the burden of proof on the firm seeking to avoid a per se rule, this proposal would give priority to the established per se rules of antitrust law. Those rules (against tying or resale price maintenance, for example) reflect the traditional antitrust concern with the preservation of opportunities to compete— the competitive process. The Chicago school (as we have seen) would sharply limit the scope of the per se rule.

What Makes Economists' Differences, and What Difference Does It Make?

Why Industrial Economists Differ

One of the great Chicago economists has singled out two fundamental premises of antitrust policy:[109]

1. Open competition is the only process by which a nation committed to freedom and to containment of government can organize its economic affairs efficiently.
2. Open competition is not only desirable, not only feasible, but naturally robust.

The first premise is a political statement, and the second is a statement about market economies. I believe that most economists, at least most economists schooled in the workings of market systems, would accept these premises.

The implications drawn from these premises by students of the Chicago school reflect a belief that, although competition may sometimes result in mar-

---

[109]Demsetz, op. cit., pp. 45–46.

ket failure, competition in the development of institutional arrangements for transactions will guarantee efficiency:[110]

1. The detailed operations of the market are best left to businessmen, consumers, and their competitive behavior.
2. Long-lasting characteristics of the largely *unregulated* business world almost certainly reflect underlying efficiencies.
3. The only important source of *long-lasting* monopoly is the government.

Thus, product market competition may prevent manufacturers from buying the kinds of distribution services they want (the free rider problem). If such services are efficient, markets will develop institutional forms—resale price maintenance, for example—that correct for failure in the market for distribution services. But such restrictions are efficient only if they are able to survive under competition without government support. Identical restraints, permitted by the government under fair trade laws, are presumed to be inefficient. If they were not inefficient, they would not need government protection to survive.

The conclusions drawn from the same two premises by students of the structure-conduct-performance school are rather different. Open market competition is widely believed to be robust, and the invisible hand of competition can be trusted to allocate resources within markets. But institutional arrangements are thought to evolve in a "market for competition" that is not itself competitive, and such arrangements are vulnerable to manipulation for strategic purposes.[111]

In this view, institutional arrangements (such as tying or resale price maintenance) that allow one firm to constrain the decisions of other firms are suspect because they interfere with otherwise robust open market competition. The role of antitrust is to sustain the institutions within which open market competition can take place.

It would be pleasant to report a convergence of views in this area. Scholarship precludes this possibility.

A century ago, in language that sounds only slightly archaic, the argument was made that potential competition would prevent concentrated industries from exercising market power:[112]

[110]Ibid., pp. 47–51.

[111]Krattenmaker, Thomas G. and Salop, Steven C. "Competition and Cooperation in the Market for Exclusionary Rights," *American Economic Review* Volume 76, Number 2, May 1986, argue that the market for competition will consistently fail to yield an efficient outcome because competition is a public good. The consumers who would benefit from competition are not in a position to ensure that rivals overcome strategically imposed barriers to competition. It is instructive to contrast this argument with Easterbrook's analysis of predatory behavior (Chapter 16).

[112]Giddings, Franklin H. "The Persistence of Competition," *Political Science Quarterly* Volume 2, Number 1, March 1887, p. 76.

Other things being equal, new capital will hesitate longest about entering into competition with established producers in those industries in which each producer must have a plant that is costly in proportion to the value of the total product of all producers. But the combination that would reap advantage of this hesitancy must face the fact that it is precisely this expensiveness of plant that entails heavy fixed charges . . . and impels competition to a ruinous extreme if more capital is tempted into business than the normal social need requires. . . .

Hence, as combinations learn their unalterable limitations in "the nature of things," they must adjust prices and production, by a conscious policy, to the normal basis that otherwise would be reached in a more wasteful way.

A contemporary observer conceded the logical force of this argument:[113]

There is a sense in which much of the orthodox system of political economy is eternally true. Conclusions reached by valid reasoning are always as true as the hypotheses from which they are deduced. If we admit the fact of unlimited competition, we concede in advance many doctrines which current opinion is now disposed to reject. This refuge will always be open to the latter-day defenders of the faith, as they are confronted by greater and greater discrepancies between their system and the facts of life. . . .

but rejected its application to the nineteenth-century world:[114]

A startling recent development is the system of combinations by which producers of particular articles have attempted arbitrarily to control the supply and the market value of their respective products. . . . While we slept, as it were, and dreamed of the regulation of values by the automatic flow of capital to points of highest profit, the principle apparently ceased to operate within very extensive fields.

Why Does It Make a Difference?

Economists differ fundamentally over the way in which competition is robust. What is in this century called the Chicago school believes that potential competition and competition in the market for competition are robust, and that this robustness will compel efficient performance. What is in this century called the structure-conduct-performance school believes that actual market competition is robust, given a suitable environment, and that government can and should act to provide that environment. These differences existed a century

[113]Clark, John B. "The Limits of Competition," *Political Science Quarterly* Volume 2, Number 1, March 1887, p. 45.

[114]Ibid., p. 54.

ago, and they are likely to exist a century from now (names may be changed to protect the innocent).

But economists agree, to a large extent, on why it is important to ensure that markets work. Thus (from the Chicago school):[115]

> The regime of capitalism brings with it not merely unexampled economic performance and a social and cultural atmosphere that stresses the worth of the individual, but, because of the bourgeois class it creates, trains, and raises to power, the possibility of stable, liberal, and democratic government. Antitrust goes to the heart of capitalist ideology, and since the law's fate will have much to do with the fate of that ideology, one may be forgiven for thinking that the outcome of the debate is of more than legal interest.

and (from the other side of the stage):[116]

> The primary purpose of antitrust is to perpetuate and preserve, in spite of possible cost, a *system of governance* for a competitive, free enterprise economy. It is a system of governance in which power is decentralized; in which newcomers with new products and new techniques have a genuine opportunity to introduce themselves and their ideas; in which the "unseen hand" of competition instead of the heavy hand of the state performs the basic regulatory function on behalf of society.

Antitrust policy is important because the maintenance of a competitive system is essential to the preservation of democratic institutions in a market economy. Public satisfaction with democratic institutions will not long survive either widespread government support for inefficient and ineffective firms or widespread exercise of market power throughout the economy. Limited government intervention in the marketplace is, paradoxically, necessary to ensure the survival of limited government.

Paper Topics

18-1 How does the concept of *antitrust injury* affect private enforcement of the antitrust laws? See Page, William H. "Antitrust Damages and Economic Efficiency: An Approach to Antitrust Injury," *University of Chicago Law Review* Volume 47, Number 3, Spring 1980, pp. 467–504.

18-2 Consult Breit, William and Elzinga, Kenneth G., "Private Antitrust Enforcement: The New Learning," *Journal of Law and Economics* Volume

---

[115]Bork, *The Antitrust Paradox*, p. 425.

[116]Adams, Walter. "Public Policy in a Free Enterprise Economy," in Adams, Walter, editor, *The Structure of American Industry,* 7th ed. New York: The Macmillan Company, 1986, p. 405.

28, Number 2, May 1985, pp. 405–443, for references to the literature on efficient antitrust offenses. How does the optimal fine depend on the social welfare function? Consider three alternative social welfare functions: (1) the harm from market power is deadweight loss less cost savings; (2) the harm from market power is deadweight loss plus income transfers less cost savings; (3) the harm from market power is deadweight loss plus income transfers. What is the optimal fine, in each case, for the merger shown in Figure 10-1? What are the implications of the notion of the *efficient offense* for antitrust enforcement?

18-3 Contrast the recommendations that Bork and Posner make for antitrust policy. Explain the differences. Consult Bork, Robert H., *The Antitrust Paradox: A Policy at War with Itself.* New York: Basic Books, 1978, and Posner, Richard A., *Antitrust Law: An Economic Perspective.* Chicago: The University of Chicago Press, 1976.

Case Index

Name Index

528

Subject Index